the
WARRIOR GENERALS

Also by Thomas B. Buell

The Quiet Warrior: A Biography
of Admiral Raymond A. Spruance

Master of Sea Power: A Biography
of Fleet Admiral Ernest J. King

The Second World War: Europe
and the Mediterranean (with others)

War and Diplomacy Across
the Pacific, 1919–1952 (with others)

the
WARRIOR
GENERALS

COMBAT LEADERSHIP
in the
CIVIL WAR

THOMAS B. BUELL

THREE RIVERS PRESS   NEW YORK

Title page: *Prisoners from the Front* by Winslow Homer. A relative
of Francis C. Barlow, Homer was a combat artist during the war and often
accompanied Barlow during his early campaigns. This painting, made shortly
after the war, established Homer's reputation as a major artist. The young
Federal general is Barlow. (Metropolitan Museum of Art)

Published by Three Rivers Press, a division of Crown Publishers, Inc.,
201 East 50th Street, New York, New York 10022.
Member of the Crown Publishing Group.

Random House, Inc. New York, Toronto, London, Sydney, Auckland
www.randomhouse.com

THREE RIVERS PRESS and colophon are trademarks of Crown Publishers, Inc.

Originally published in hardcover by Crown Publishers, Inc., in 1997.

Printed in the United States of America

Text maps by Charles Apple

Design by Lenny Henderson

Library of Congress Cataloging-in-Publication Data
Buell, Thomas B.
The warrior generals: combat leadership in the Civil War / by
Thomas B. Buell
p.   cm.
1. Generals—United States—History—19th century.   2. Generals—
Confederate States of America.   3. United States—History—Civil
War, 1861–1865—Campaigns.   4. Command of Troops—History—19th
century.   5. Military art and science—United States—History—19th
century.   I. Title.
E467.B93   1997
973.7'13—dc20   96-32959
                                                          CIP

ISBN 0-609-80173-2

10 9 8 7 6 5 4 3 2 1

First Paperback Edition

To the soldiers who followed the generals,
for better for worse

CONTENTS

Part IV: Eastern Theater, 1863

Part V: Western Theater, 1863

Part VI: Eastern Theater, 1864

Part VII: Western Theater, 1864

Part VIII: Finis

Appendices

MAPS, APPENDICES, AND NOTES

Four maps are used to clarify and supplement the text: (1) a composite of the states of the Union and of the Confederacy; (2) the western theater, centered on Tennessee and Kentucky; (3) the eastern theater, centered on Virginia; and (4) western Mississippi and the Vicksburg Campaign. These maps display the principal place names contained in the text and important terrain features like mountains and rivers. Railroads, vital both to North and South, are shown as well. Roads are not indicated as they were largely primitive, their location is often guesswork, and they clutter the maps. In addition, the Vicksburg map (pp. 236–37) provides a graphic overview of the maneuvers and locations of opposing military organizations. The principal reference for these maps is *The West Point Atlas of American Wars,* which has a reputation for accuracy.

The appendices include chronologies for the six protagonists who are the subject of this book (see Appendix A). The chronologies are followed by three sets of tables that may be found useful. One or more of the six protagonists fought in nearly every major battle or campaign of the Civil War. The "Engagement Summary" table (see Appendix B) correlates who fought where and when, the dates, and the corresponding chapter, an overview which should help the reader's perspective. The two tables that follow (see Appendices C and D) provide data as to strengths and casualties for selected battles. With a few exceptions, I have chosen not to burden the text with these numbers, which are so often unreliable in any event. Most of the figures are extracted from *Numbers & Losses in the Civil War in America: 1861–65,* by Thomas L. Livermore, the standard reference for many historians. Finally, I have clarified the sometimes confusing administrative structure of the Confederate armed forces (see Appendix E).

Because I believe that annotated footnotes would unnecessarily distract from smooth and uninterrupted reading, I have inserted no more than an occasional supplementary footnote. Each chapter, however, is accompanied by a bibliographic essay that identifies and discusses the chapter's principal sources. The bibliography itself contains the fullest and most comprehensive expression of the research material that comprises this book's fabric and foundation.

LIST OF ILLUSTRATIONS

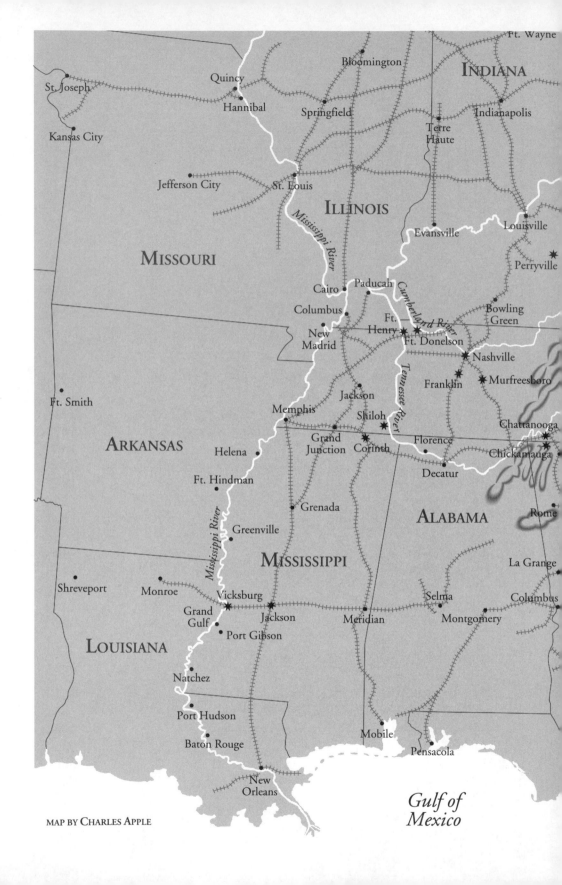

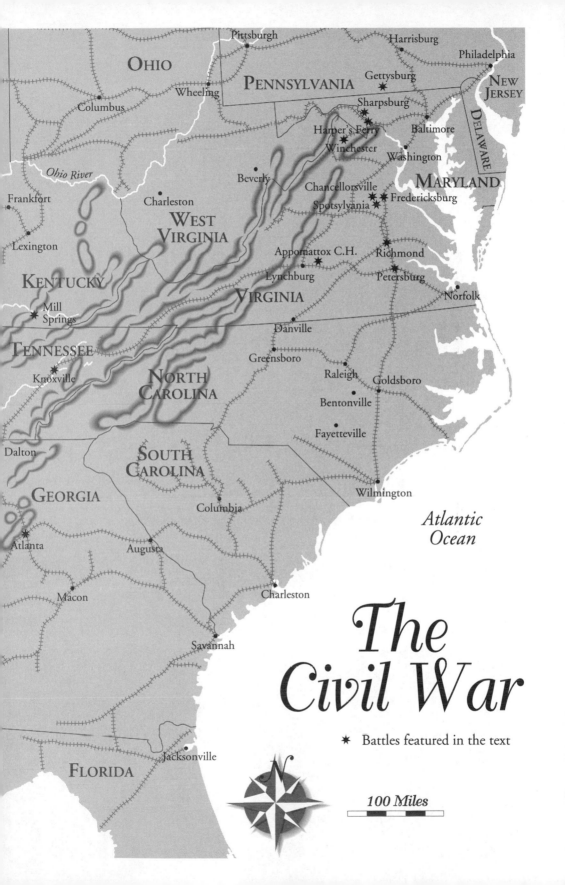

The
Civil War

* Battles featured in the text

100 Miles

The Western Theater

St. Louis

ILLINOIS

Ohio River

Evansville

KENTUCKY

MISSOURI

Smithland

Cairo

Paducah

Columbus

Tennessee River

Cumberland River

Belmont

Ft. Henry

Clarksville

Ft. Donelson

Union
City

Danville

Duck River

Franklin

ARKANSAS

Mississippi River

Humbolt

Spring
Hill

Columbia

Jackson

Mount
Pleasant

Memphis

Pittsburg
Landing

Savannah

Pulaski

Shiloh

Grand
Junction

Corinth

Florence

Iuka

N

MISSISSIPPI

Tuscumbia

Decatur

30 Miles

ALABAMA

Tupelo

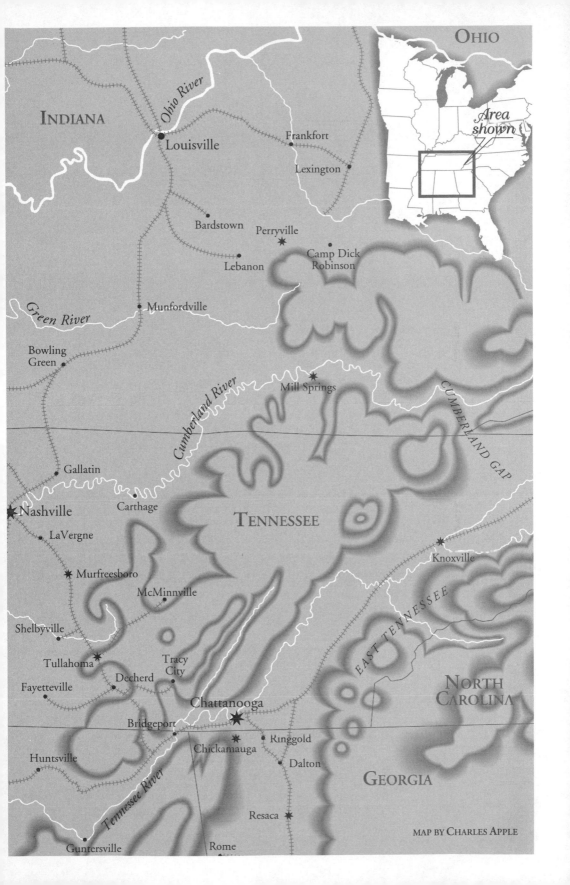

OHIO

INDIANA

Area shown

Ohio River

Louisville

Frankfort

Lexington

Bardstown

Perryville

Lebanon

Camp Dick
Robinson

Green River

Munfordville

Bowling
Green

Cumberland River

Mill Springs

CUMBERLAND GAP

Gallatin

Carthage

TENNESSEE

Nashville

LaVergne

Knoxville

Murfreesboro

McMinnville

EAST TENNESSEE

Shelbyville

NORTH
CAROLINA

Tullahoma

Tracy
City

Decherd

Fayetteville

Chattanooga

Bridgeport

Ringgold

Huntsville

Chickamauga

Dalton

GEORGIA

Tennessee River

Resaca

MAP BY CHARLES APPLE

Guntersville

Rome

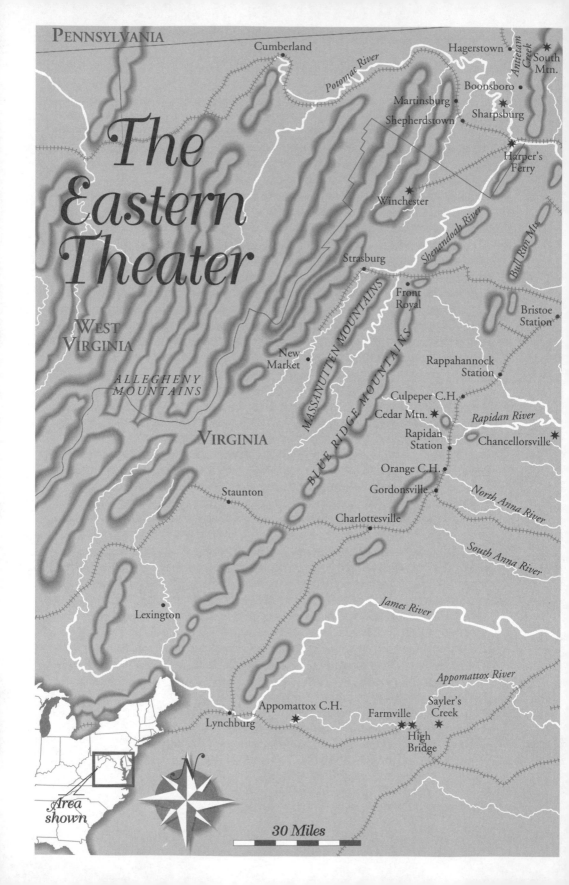

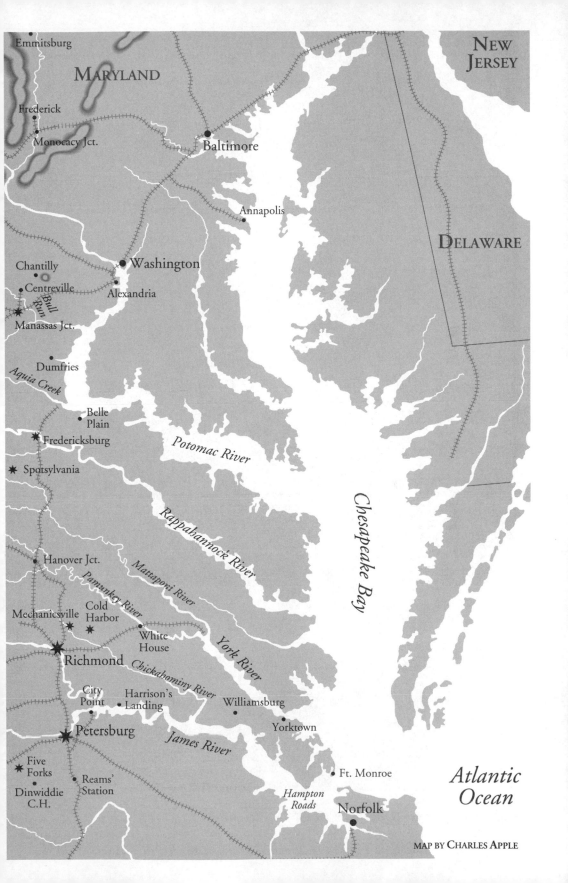

Emmitsburg

MARYLAND

Frederick

Monocacy Jct.

Baltimore

NEW JERSEY

Annapolis

DELAWARE

Chantilly
Centreville
Bull Run
Manassas Jct.

Washington
Alexandria

Dumfries

Aquia Creek

Belle Plain

Fredericksburg

Spotsylvania

Potomac River

Chesapeake Bay

Rappahannock River

Hanover Jct.

Mattaponi River

Pamunkey River

Mechanicsville
Cold Harbor

White House

York River

Richmond

Chickahominy River

City Point
Harrison's Landing

Williamsburg

Petersburg

James River

Yorktown

Five Forks

Reams' Station

Dinwiddie C.H.

Ft. Monroe

Hampton Roads

Norfolk

Atlantic Ocean

MAP BY CHARLES APPLE

The Yeoman: Ulysses S. Grant (Library of Congress)

The Aristocrat: Robert E. Lee (Library of Congress)

The Knight-Errant: John B. Hood (Museum of the Confederacy)

The Roman: George H. Thomas (Library of Congress)

The Cavalier: John B. Gordon (Library of Congress)

The Puritan: Francis C. Barlow (National Archives)

INTRODUCTION

Americans watching the news in January 1996 saw United States Army engineers struggling in brutal winter weather to construct a pontoon bridge across a flooding Bosnian river. The force of the current had swept away the bridge's anchors; until it was spanned, the river prevented American forces from reaching the region where they would establish their base camp. The commanding general explained in an interview that, because the primitive roads were impassable, he had moved his troops and equipment by railroad. His men, he went on to say, had to live in tents, as there were no buildings available for shelter.

These could well have been scenes of the Civil War, of Federal army engineers striving to build a pontoon bridge across the raging Duck River in Tennessee in December 1864. Lashed by the sleet and rain of a winter storm, they had to span the river to continue their pursuit of the retreating Confederate army commanded by General John B. Hood. Throughout the western theater, Major General George H. Thomas, commanding the Federal Army of the Cumberland, had used railroads to move troops and supplies because his vehicles could not negotiate the rude Tennessee roads. His soldiers, too, lived in tents.

Had Thomas emerged from the past and stood alongside the American general in Bosnia, the two men would have spoken a common language, for the exercise of military leadership is timeless. Thomas would instantly have recognized the circumstances, especially when weather and terrain reduce warfare to its brutal fundamentals. Sophisticated weapons then become impotent, and military operations are reduced to weary, sodden soldiers slogging through the mud, rifles slung over their shoulders.

The obligations of general officers in twentieth-century armies have changed little from those in the Civil War: the intelligent employment of the army's combat power; the discipline, morale, and well-being of the troops; transportation and supply; rapid and secure communications; the gathering of intelligence; the need for accurate maps; interaction with irregular forces and hostile civilians; relations with politicians, the public, and the media. Indeed, all of these have confronted American generals for more than two centuries. They are among the measures by which we assess their leadership qualities.

Yet the Civil War tested the American capacity for leadership under conditions unimaginable today, accustomed as we are to a standing army whose officers undergo years of training and maturing as a requisite to high command. The Civil War began with no equivalent core of experience; the United States Army of 1860 had four elderly general officers. At war's end five years later, over a thousand men of every conceivable background and level of competence had worn the general's insignia. Some were professional soldiers like Ulysses S. Grant and Robert E. Lee, who rose to the very highest level of army command. Others were civilian volunteers like Francis C. Barlow and John B. Gordon, men in their twenties and thirties who successfully commanded entire divisions (the age of company and battalion commanders in today's army). These thousand generals, leaders of all stripes, alone determined by force of arms whether there would be one American nation, or two, or perhaps even more.

We cannot contain our amazement when we try to envision how, almost overnight, these freshly minted generals mobilized massive armies on a scale that dwarfed the minuscule prewar army, then took them to war on battlefields that spanned half the continent. Terrible mistakes were made that prolonged the war at a dreadful cost in lives and treasure, but the successful generals learned how to adapt and improve. By war's end the most enlightened of them had developed strategies, tactics, and technologies that became doctrine for the American army of the twentieth century. Among these developments were the employment of mobile, combined arms; the art of logistics and science of engineering; the structure of armies, corps, and divisions; the firepower of advanced ordnance; and the staff system for planning and operations.

One of the greatest difficulties in understanding how Civil War generals functioned is that much of the war's history is biased and distorted. Upon scholarly inquiry, truisms about popular historical events and personalities are often discovered to be entirely misleading or wrong. It was something that Samuel Johnson knew about. "Many things which are false," he once said, "are transmitted from book to book, and gain credit in the world."

So it has been with much of Civil War history. The misconceptions are pervasive and widespread, even among those who are in a position to know better. A few years ago I accompanied a party of Army War College students on a staff ride across Virginia Civil War battlefields. These senior army officers, steeped in the principles of their profession, expressed the view that the Confederacy's generals were the superior leaders in terms of competency and experience; the Federal generals ultimately prevailed, they asserted, not because of their leadership skills, but rather the abundance of Northern manpower and matériel. This prevailing but mistaken view of the Civil War generals is considered common knowledge from grammar school to the senior service colleges. While it does not bear up to scrutiny, rarely is it challenged.

The importance of the western and eastern theaters is similarly distorted. Ken Burns's popular PBS Civil War documentary, like most works on the war, emphasized the eastern campaigns. Gettysburg received nearly an entire episode, Franklin and Nashville but a few moments of passing commentary, yet the Tennessee campaign was the more decisive on the outcome of the war.

Under these circumstances, Civil War history and the roles of its generals cry out for clarification and revision. In researching this book, I relied as much as possible on primary sources. As I did so, facts came to light that have cleared away layers of mythology and folklore. What follows on these pages is a fresh assessment of what happened and why.

In order to analyze comprehensively the qualities of combat leadership, North and South, I selected representatives from the body of generals that most dominated military operations. I chose three opposing pairs: Grant and Lee; Thomas and Hood; Barlow and Gordon—Federal and Confederate generals, respectively. Each was among the war's most influential leaders, albeit each was limited to varying extents by his own human flaws. Together with having equivalent scopes of responsibility and common backgrounds (West Point or volunteer), each pair commanded forces that met on fields of battle. These pairings also allowed both theaters (western and eastern) to receive comparable attention.

THE YEOMAN

Ulysses Simpson Grant was the embodiment of the traditional yeoman—a sturdy, solid, middle-class countryman, who in time of war entered the service of his nation as a rugged and dependable soldier. He came from the provinces to lead great armies of citizens against other citizen armies representing a political system fighting fanatically for survival. Ultimately he ascended to head of state on cunning and the strength of his wartime reputation. We shall see, however, that the Yeoman stumbled often in his execution. In his earliest campaigns his careless planning and want of foresight could have been disastrous at Fort Donelson and Shiloh. Nor were instances of his bad judgment confined to the field of battle, for he caroused with Confederate officers under flags of truce, tolerated corruption in matters of procurement and supply, and staffed his headquarters with riffraff. Nonetheless, he rose from regimental commander to general in chief of the Federal armies.

Reservoirs of energy tempered with self-control were Grant's salvation. Like a sweating yeoman confronting obstacles of great proportion, Grant squared his shoulders, pressed on, and with club swinging extracted himself from self-inflicted crises. Averse to thinking things through, Grant made decisions impulsively. "In war," Grant once remarked to a staff officer, "anything is better than indecision. We must decide. If I am wrong, we shall soon find it out, and can do the other thing. But not to decide wastes both time and money, and may ruin everything."

While at first he attempted to pacify civilians by respecting their property, Grant ultimately resorted to the torch and the requisition. Loath to divide his forces, only once did Grant attempt to turn the tactical flank of an engaged enemy, entrusting the failed maneuver to William Tecumseh Sherman at Chattanooga. His attempts at strategic envelopments against Lee were similarly unsuccessful. Consequently Grant hammered his enemy with heavy blows in campaigns of attrition, a way of war to which generals resort in the absence of original thought. Yet he was perceptive to Lincoln's wishes and political nuances, and he conditioned his plans in ways that he knew would please the president and Congress.

THE ARISTOCRAT

Legend and nostalgia have obscured beyond recognition the essential nature of Robert Edward Lee. His ascent to glory began with Douglas Southall Freeman, who wrote in his Pulitzer Prize–winning hagiography that Lee "was one of the small company of great men in whom there is no inconsistency to be explained, no enigma to be solved. What he seemed, he was—a wholly human gentleman, the essential elements of whose positive character were two and only two, simplicity and spirituality." In other words, Freeman portrayed Lee as saintlike and above criticism, a rarely disputed theme that most later writers have uncritically recited and embellished.

The phenomenon of his reputation is that a general could lose so many campaigns, suffer casualties of such staggering proportions, and yet still be admired as both folk hero and military genius. The fact is that Lee is both a social symbol of Southern heritage and a political icon. Retrospective adherents to the aims of the Confederacy genuflect before his portrait. Any suggestion that Lee falls short of his elevated status is disregarded or resented. In such circumstances his actual military record is often irrelevant.

Lee's military record has indeed become increasingly blurred, because his personal traits are the crux of his aristocratic image. (Freeman listed thirty-five in his index, all laudatory.) Historians and public alike have turned a blind eye to even the very worst in Lee's military leadership. Lee's invasion of Maryland in the fall of 1862 stands as one example, the decision itself predicated on fallacious thinking—Lee was convinced that the people of Maryland would welcome him and his army as liberators. Instead they spurned him. When cornered at Sharpsburg, Lee bungled the deployment of the Confederate divisions during the Battle of Antietam by failing to send them when and where they were needed, but in Freeman's analysis, "[T]he larger tactical direction of the action had fallen to Lee and he had discharged it flawlessly."

During the subsequent retreat into Virginia, the remnants of Lee's army degenerated into a mob that robbed and terrorized its own people, but authors sidestep this tragedy. Even authoritative twentieth-century references are silent. *The Wartime Papers of R. E. Lee,* edited by Clifford Dowdey and Louis H. Manarin (Boston, 1961), for example, has excluded Lee's correspondence during the period from September 19 to November 6, 1862, the time of disintegration within the Army of Northern Virginia. Not until I consulted *War of the Rebellion: A Compilation of the Official Records of the Union and Confederate Armies,* published in the late nineteenth century by the War Department, did the extent of the Maryland disaster become evident.

What, then, are we to make of Lee? He was committed to preserving the status quo, his vision was locked firmly in the past, and he sacrificed his army to protect the privileges of the oligarchy to which he belonged. Lee's fundamental strategy was fighting for the sake of fighting, surrender was never an option if the war could still be prolonged, and in the end he destroyed his state trying to save it.

THE ROMAN

Thousands of monuments cover the Gettysburg countryside, commemorating the soldiers and regiments of the July 1863 battle that popular history considers the turning point of the Civil War. Eight hundred miles to the west, parking lots, malls, and suburban homes blanket the battlefield at Nashville, where in December 1864 the Federal army of George Henry Thomas destroyed the Confederate Army of Tennessee, commanded by John B. Hood. Gettysburg, while dramatic in character and scope, did not materially shorten the war, for the Confederate armies long afterward remained potent and dangerous. Not until the battle at Nashville, seventeen months later, did Confederate military power finally collapse, and the end of the war become a matter of time.

The role of the western theater, that area between the Appalachian Mountains and the Mississippi River, is largely neglected in Civil War literature. There are more books solely on Gettysburg than on the entire war in Tennessee, yet the state rivaled Virginia in its impact and influence. George Thomas and Tennessee are synonymous in the history of the war in the west, which we shall discover in the chapters that follow.

Like the generals who created the Roman Empire's professional armies, Thomas made the Army of the Cumberland the most modern and lethal armed force of its day. He was a rarity, a Southerner who both remained loyal to the Federal government and became a distinguished general officer. Without the political sponsorship considered necessary for promotion and choice assignments, he rose to the highest ranks on merit alone and refused prestigious commands if their antecedents conflicted with his principles.

A progressive thinker in an army in which thought had become stultified from decades of stagnation, Thomas exploited the technology that offered enormous potential for advancing weapons and resources, mastered the art of logistics, and understood and employed combined arms—infantry, artillery, and cavalry—as no other general on either side. In matters of command and control, transportation, communications, intelligence, and cartography, Thomas's imprint on military doctrine would carry well into the twentieth century. In time of combat, Thomas's mind functioned with clarity and precision, it never succumbed to fluster or fear, and he became known as the indomitable Rock of Chickamauga.

Grant considered Thomas a rival, and he often disparaged Thomas's exacting preparations for battle. Yet it was Thomas's superb army sweeping Missionary Ridge at Chattanooga that allowed Grant to gain credit for the victory and ultimate promotion to general in chief of the Federal armies. Later, sending threats and unwise preemptive orders to attack from Washington, Grant shamefully interfered with Thomas's life-and-death struggle against Hood at Nashville. In the end, Nashville would become Thomas's finest hour.

THE KNIGHT-ERRANT

The Knight-Errant of the Middle Ages is a familiar figure in literature, a chivalrous soldier searching for adventure, seeking opportunities to exhibit his military skills, and behaving with gallantry, courage, and honor. Southerners easily equated knighthood with the valor and values of Confederate officers, and few equaled John Bell Hood in romantic stature.

"When he came," wrote Richmond diarist Mary Chesnut, "with his sad Quixote face, the face of an old crusader who believed in his cause, his cross, his crown—we were not prepared for that type exactly as a beau idéal of wild Texans. Tall—thin—shy. Blue eyes and light hair, tawny beard and a vast amount of it covering the lower part of his face—an appearance of awkward strength. Someone said that great reserve of manner he carried only into ladies' society. Mr. Venable added he had often heard of the 'light of battle' shining in a man's eyes. He had seen it once. He carried him orders from General Lee and found [him] in the hottest of the fight. 'The man was transfigured. The fierce light of his eyes—I can never forget.' "

An opportunist who sought to elevate his status with the sword, Hood was splendid as a brigade and division commander. His Texas Brigade was swaggering, aggressive, skillful, and proud, among the best in the Army of Northern Virginia. His reputation grew as the Gallant Hood, his rise in the Confederate army was meteoric, and he became its youngest general of full rank. Sent to the western theater in 1863, Hood lost a leg at Chickamauga. Because of Hood's aggressiveness, in 1864 Jefferson Davis chose him to save Atlanta by stopping Sherman. In the end the fight was between Hood and Thomas at Nashville, while Sherman marched unopposed to the sea.

Arrayed in full armor and adorned with trappings, the mounted Knight-Errant of the Middle Ages became obsolete against the longbow and the pike. In much the same way, Hood's stylized fighting could not match the deadly weapons and advanced maneuvers of the Army of the Cumberland. The ardor of the Army of Tennessee could not compensate for its shortcomings in tactics, technology, and matériel. The Battle of Nashville was the paradigm of the Civil War, for it pitted the army of the future against the army of the past.

THE PURITAN AND THE CAVALIER

Francis Channing Barlow and John Brown Gordon embodied the irreconcilable ideals that led to the Civil War. Barlow was by nature a puritan, not as a matter of religious faith, but rather as a system of values, one expressed by George Santayana when he described his fictional protagonist in *The Last Puritan:* "His puritanism had never been mere timidity or fanaticism or calculated hardness: it was a deep and speculative thing: hatred of all shams, scorn of all mummeries, a bitter merciless pleasure in the hard facts." Like the religious Puritans who had populated New England, Barlow sought perfection. He found shades of gray in people and institutions intolerable, and corruption—especially in government—had to be swept away and society purified.

Historically, the Cavalier attempted to preserve things as they were. Gordon personified this figure as it evolved into the Southern equivalent: courtly gentleman, horseman and gallant, who clung to custom and tradition—and above all to the preservation of slavery. While Barlow sought purity, Gordon tolerated imperfections and foibles within his own sphere with a smile and a shrug, and his practices were shaped by accommodation.

Yet Barlow and Gordon became superb combat commanders, the very best of those civilian volunteers who quickly mastered the art of war. Indifferent to pain as they recovered from grievous wounds and debilitating diseases, their steel and stamina sustained them as they served from start to finish. Circumstances brought the regiments, brigades, and divisions they commanded into repeated contact, including the Seven Days and Antietam in 1862, Gettysburg in 1863, Spotsylvania in 1864, and Appomattox in 1865. Both were fearless, their leadership so compelling that their men were drawn into the center of the storm in every battle. No two generals could have been more equally matched, and neither yielded in their fierce and costly battles. The saga of the Puritan and the Cavalier on the fields of battle is one of the most striking stories of the Civil War.

Some of these men are immediately recognized. Others have been in the shadows and will now be brought into full view. Taken together, their stories encompass almost the whole Civil War. Through them we shall encounter a host of others: generals who were brothers in arms both able and inept; political authorities who could either help or harass them and often did both; and the rank and file who followed these six men into battle, for better for worse. The canvas is broad, and the picture that emerges will reveal how the elements of combat leadership—fighting spirit, courage, intelligence, stamina, and good fortune—combine, in incalculable ways, to achieve victory.

PART I

IN THE

BEGINNING

1

ORIGINS OF THE WARRIORS

————◆·◆·◆————

The two Harvard sophomores huddled in their unheated room in the Yard. One shivered beneath his blanket; the other, Francis Barlow, who took insouciant delight in disdaining hardships, dismissed the cold. Barlow was slender—some mistakenly thought him delicate—and the flickering candlelight illuminated the smooth olive skin of his chin and jaw. His voice was reedy, but among the faculty and student body, Barlow spoke with bite and assurance and unassailable poise.

"[H]e talked for a great part of the night about Napoleon," his classmate remembered. The discourse began with Napoleon's campaigns and his system of rewarding his best soldiers with marshals' batons and decorations, and then moved on to such leaders as Alexander the Great, Julius Caesar, Hannibal, Wellington, Marlborough, and Frederick the Great. "The Corsican was the hero who beyond all others had fascinated him," recalled the classmate, "whose career he would especially love to emulate. We were a pair of boys in a peaceful college, living in a time which apparently would afford no opportunity for a soldier's career. I have often thought of that talk."

Like George Santayana's last puritan, Barlow was in the world but not of it. "Barlow had been a sad puzzle to the faculty," remembered the classmate, "[who were] often perplexed to know what to do with him or what would become of him." "Barlow always perceived existing facts and relations with singular precision and quickness," wrote another classmate in memoriam. "He prided himself in college upon having no illusions, and was resolved to see things as they really were. He then, and ever afterwards, spoke his thoughts without restraint, and with a singular and almost contemptuous disregard of consequence.... He acted and spoke without paying any regard to what man could do, or say, or think about him."

The society that claimed Francis Channing Barlow was proud of its enlightenment, its idealism and ideas, its literary laureates like George

Ticknor and Henry Wadsworth Longfellow, and its prophets of transcen-
dentalism like Ralph Waldo Emerson and William Ellery Channing. His
father, David Hatch Barlow, went from Vermont to Harvard, where he shone
as a bravura poet and first scholar of his class of 1824. Upon graduation
from divinity school in 1829, he was ordained a Unitarian minister and a
year later married Almira Penniman of Brookline, Massachusetts. The
Boston elite considered them the handsomest of couples: a beautiful, intelligent woman and an able, cultured, graceful minister, a promising match of
brains and breeding. But in a matter of years a failed and broken Barlow
abandoned his family and disappeared into obscurity, leaving Almira broke
and the sole parent of their three boys.

George Ripley, first scholar at Harvard a year before David Barlow, had
left his Unitarian pulpit in 1840 to found Brook Farm, the celebrated
utopian community outside Boston. The congenial "farmers" were largely
Brahmins and intellectuals who labored in the morning, read the classics
after lunch, and made music in the evenings. Their children learned Greek,
Latin, and mathematics in the tiny schoolhouse and romped in the pastures.
Almira gratefully accepted Ripley's invitation to board in the so-called Hive,
the communal farmhouse. Voluptuous, good-natured, and kindhearted, she
became a conspicuous anomaly, her hands uncalloused, a romantic presence
enrapturing the men and enraging the women. Nathaniel Hawthorne sat
dreamily on a sofa, listening and watching. A decade later he wrote *The
Blithedale Romance,* a tale about Zenobia, a passionate beauty in conflict
with a community of utopians.

Almira's flirting and indolence got her evicted. Never to remarry, she wandered gypsylike among charitable families. The precarious life so bonded
mother and sons that Francis Barlow's love for his mother and brothers
endured forever pure and intense. His mother became a regular in the
Peabody bookshop seminars, organized by her close friend Margaret Fuller,
the "Queen of Cambridge," who urged her women disciples to grow intel-
lectually and spiritually. An inspired Almira tutored her son for Harvard.
"Barlow came admirably fitted," recalled a classmate, "and this good preparation, standing back of great quickness and power of mind, made it easy for
him almost without study to take a leading place."

"Poor and struggling under peculiar burdens," Barlow would graduate as
first scholar in the summer of 1855. As he sat at the feet of the Harvard masters, he beheld with pitiless eyes an imperfect world ripe for redemption.
Two imperfections nonetheless lurked beneath his cloak of puritan principles: a fierce eagerness for acclamation, and a blinding contempt for people
and institutions that failed to measure up.

Boston could not retain him. "My dear Frank," wrote Emerson, "I am
resigned to your going to New York where so many high prizes glitter for
your ambition but I am sorry you do not decide for Massachusetts, humbler
but finer. Perhaps you will after looking at Broadway." In New York he was
first a tutor, then a reporter for Horace Greeley on the *New York Tribune.*
But it was the profession of law, he discovered, that appealed to his sense of

order and logic. He was admitted to the bar in May 1858 and remained committed to its practice for the remainder of his life.

What kind of woman would attract the cynical puritan? Perhaps someone like his mother, whom he so admired. He found such a person in Arabella Wharton Griffith, ten years his senior, a feisty intellectual who moved easily and independently in New York society. George Templeton Strong wrote in his diary that she was "certainly the most brilliant, cultivated, easy, graceful, effective talker of womankind, and has read, thought, and observed much and well." A raconteur who mimicked dialects like a skilled actor, Arabella enchanted her listeners, yet she had remained single as she entered her thirties. "Men generally don't respond to her a great deal," wrote Strong. "They say she talks conversation and isn't natural."

Arabella Griffith had found her man. They announced their engagement.

The Southern institutions that John Brown Gordon cherished afforded him the quintessential life of the privileged. His lithe, graceful body was at home with the horse and the hunt and with the wind in his face; he moved as easily in the drawing room, inherently exercising every nuance of etiquette expected of a cavalier. Women involuntarily tingled when he spoke with rapturing voice, but his eyes betrayed a dreamy restlessness, for Gordon was his father's son.

Gordon's Scottish and English ancestors were among those who had changed the Deep South from a wilderness to a region of plantations and county seats. A fifth-generation American himself, his family line included veterans of the Revolutionary War, patriots, planters, preachers, and politicians. His entrepreneurial father, Zachariah Herndon Gordon, was a Baptist preacher and a go-getter in civil affairs and business, who by 1850 had the largest estate in the county. Gordon's mother, Malinda Cox Gordon, bore a dozen children. Gordon was the fourth, born on the family plantation in Upson County, Georgia.

Tutors and a private school groomed young Gordon easily to pass the entrance examinations at Franklin College at Milledgeville (later the University of Georgia at Athens), and he enrolled as a sophomore. Though one of the boys, he was a scholar too, taking a gold medal in debating. He entered his senior year in August 1852, expecting to graduate with top honors. Suddenly and without explanation, he withdrew that October. He never returned. Nor did he ever reveal why he had left.

Gordon's path became uncertain. He was first a lawyer, then a newspaper correspondent, and finally a partner in his father's coal mine. When Gordon went to Atlanta to read for the law in early 1854, he was dazzled by the sister-in-law of his senior partner. Fanny Rebecca Haralson, a beautiful girl of sixteen, came from a prominent family with deep Georgia roots. Her father, Hugh Anderson Haralson, once a powerful congressman, still practiced law.

After a brief, intense courtship, they planned an elaborate church wedding on her seventeenth birthday. When her father fell ill, John Gordon and Fanny

Fanny Rebecca Haralson was seventeen when she married John Gordon, seven years before the Civil War began, and he called her his "girl-wife." She accompanied him on nearly every campaign and bravely tried to rally retreating Confederate soldiers in the Shenandoah Valley. While Southern women were discouraged from serving as nurses, Fanny helped her husband recover from near fatal wounds so that he could return to the war. They were inseparable through almost fifty years of marriage. (National Archives)

Arabella Wharton Griffith was thirty-seven when she married the twenty-six-year-old Francis Barlow the day after he had enlisted in the Federal army following Fort Sumter. Going into combat with her husband, she served as a frontline nurse and went through enemy lines looking for him when he was wounded at Gettysburg. She died in an army hospital of typhoid in 1864. Winslow Homer made this sketch of Arabella when she accompanied Barlow and the Army of the Potomac in the 1862 Peninsular Campaign. (Cooper-Hewitt Museum)

(his "girl-wife") were married instead at her father's deathbed. They would be inseparable through almost fifty years of marriage. Gordon gave her the gift of a poem on their thirty-seventh wedding anniversary, her fifty-fourth birthday.

> *The day of days I now remember,*
> *The sweetest far was in September,*
> *When woods and fields and star-lit skies,*
> *And mellow suns and Autumn's sighs,*
>
> *Made earth so fair and life so sweet;*
> *As Heaven bowed this world to greet,*
> *And threw its sheen o'er nature's face*
> *And clasped all things in Love's embrace—*
>
> *'Twas natal day to fair young bride;*
> *'Twas natal day to new-borne pride*
> *In him, whose life and hope and care,*
> *This fair young bride henceforth must share.*
>
> *So young she was, so winsome, coy,*
> *So lithe her form, so pure her joy,*
> *So rare her grace, so e'er discreet,*
> *So trusting, true, so fair and sweet;*
>
> *That happy man ne'er won for wife,*
> *To lift his aims and brighten life,*
> *More helpful hand or mind, I ween*
> *Than this sweet girl of seventeen.*
>
> *Though birthdays come and years pass by,*
> *Though clouds may dim September's sky,*
> *Though threads of gray may streak thy hair,*
> *And roses fade from cheeks so fair;*
>
> *Still Beauty's seal is on thy brow,*
> *No brighter, nobler, then as now.*
> *My love's still warm as 'twas when you*
> *Were seventeen, I twenty-two.*

The cadet from Kentucky had been a target of ridicule in his early years at West Point. His provincial accent, slow thinking, and large, lank frame accentuated his awkwardness. It was not what John Bell Hood had expected, for he had come to the Military Academy dreaming of becoming an army officer, a knightly profession in which he could both experience adventure and by military merit earn honors and titles and entrée into the better classes.

The initiation had proven baffling. New cadets were like novitiates in a monastic order—the list of forbidden pleasures filled pages of rules that were enforced with martial authority. Theoretically conditioned by discipline and punishment, boys presumably matured into cadets and then officers who conformed to the army way. Yet obstreperous cadets so schemed to beat the system by smuggling women and liquor onto the post or sneaking off post, that regulations became a mockery.

Marching off demerits largely occupied Hood's free time. When Hood became a senior, the new superintendent, Captain Robert E. Lee, declared a crackdown, expecting that his cadet officers would support his reforms. Hood did not get the message. Appointed a cadet lieutenant, a position of honor and authority within the corps, Hood skipped out for an evening at Benny Haven's. Lee publicly excoriated Hood and busted him to cadet private. Had he committed another infraction between Christmas and the June graduation, Hood would have been expelled. While others more gifted went under, he survived the ordeal with grit and perseverance.

He had come to the academy from a singular childhood. His father, John W. Hood, was a quack who hawked trusses and supporters that he claimed would position the organs where they belonged and so restore health. Although Hood's practice was a sham, he made money, and the inheritance of his wife, Theodosia French, added to his wealth. Altogether he accumulated property, slaves, a home, and a family.

The third of three sons, young Hood saw little of his father, who was away on business. Theodosia was indulgent, and Hood became a hellion. Family tradition describes him as tall and virile, unrestrained in appetite and behavior. A congressman uncle got Hood an appointment to West Point, where he reported on July 1, 1849.

The academy lay fifty miles up the Hudson River from New York City, on a bluff overlooking the river's spectacular scenery. Established in 1802 to produce engineers for public works, its technical curriculum was brutal for boys from the backwoods. (In contrast, tactical training was rudimentary and was largely confined to parade ground drills.) To avoid riling the politicians who appointed the ill prepared, the entrance exams were elementary and acceptance pro forma. The academy itself, however, was so rigorous that attrition usually eliminated the unfit.

Branch assignment upon graduation was by class standing. The cream went into the corps of engineers, the bottom dwellers into the infantry, and the remainder into the artillery or cavalry. Ranked forty-fourth in his class of fifty-five, Hood tried by special pleading through his congressman uncle to get into the cavalry, but instead he was sent to the Fourth Infantry Regiment, stationed in California. Content in the service, he did not leave to search for gold as others did but remained in uniform, among the remote army posts, for the next two years.

Assigned to the newly established Second Cavalry Regiment in 1855, he began his first commissioned service with Lee and George Thomas.

Southampton County is a remote rural region in southeastern Virginia, just across the border from North Carolina and inland from the Dismal Swamp and the coastline. The terrain is mostly marsh and bog, a backwater of the

Nottoway River flowing south into Albemarle Sound. Even today the passing traveler feels an air of brooding darkness. Farms are scattered wherever
the land is high and dry enough for cultivation.

The county was a place of horror and carnage in the late summer of 1831.
Nat Turner, together with seven companions, murdered his master and his
family and went into the countryside recruiting others. Numbering perhaps
seventy, Turner's band swept from one isolated dwelling to another, killing
indiscriminately, until about sixty whites were dead. One farm boy and his
terrified family fled by carriage and then by foot through the swamps to the
village of Jerusalem (now Courtland).

When he got into the town, the boy, George Henry Thomas, found panicked women and shouting men swarming in the streets. The fifteen-year-old
Thomas remained calm, as he always would in times of crisis, but he was
bewildered. Why had Turner killed his master, who had treated him
humanely? Harmony and respect between slave and master, and the slave's
acquiescence to the status quo, were articles of faith now shattered. The
Southern soul shuddered. With ruthless retribution, militia and volunteers
captured and killed blacks both culpable and innocent. Thomas had known
many of the condemned now twisting on the gibbets, and their victims as
well. Repercussions spread throughout the South, as jittery whites imposed
repressive measures on their slaves to prevent a recurrence.

Thomas longed to escape the oppressiveness of Southampton County, to
leave the family farm where his father, John Thomas, had first brought his
mother, Elizabeth Rochelle. Their marriage had prospered: the three-room
house had been enlarged to accommodate the children, three girls and
three boys, and the farm grew to something over eight hundred acres
worked by slaves. John Thomas had died mysteriously in 1829, when he
was forty-five and the boy was thirteen. Elizabeth had kept family and
farm intact.

After attending a private academy, Thomas went into town to work as
deputy county clerk. John Y. Mason, the district congressman, nominated
him for an appointment to West Point. "He is Seventeen or Eighteen years
of age [Thomas was nearly twenty], of fine size, and of excellent talents
with a good preparatory education." He entered the academy on July 1,
1836.

"I still recollect," Thomas wrote his brother John fifteen years later, "a
piece of advice you gave me on my way to West Point. . . . 'Having done
what you conscientiously believe to be right, you may regret, but should
never be annoyed, by a want of approbation on the part of others.' " In so
many words Thomas had expressed the values that guided him from cadet
to general. Having freely chosen the career of a professional soldier, he was
obligated to obey orders and institutional regulations that in many
instances offended his sense of propriety and justice. Exercising the nicest
sense of loyalty and discretion, Thomas found ways to comply with such
imperatives, however foolish or ill founded, and then got on with those
issues he considered vital to the good of the army. But when beliefs held

dear in his soul were at stake, Thomas was indomitable, as the Civil War would prove.

There are no stories about Thomas as a cadet, even in the memoirs of his roommate, William T. Sherman. According to the record, Thomas stayed out of trouble, was a cadet officer, and stood in the upper third of his class. Of seventy-six new cadets, forty-two graduated in July 1840, and Thomas was twelfth in class standing. Future Civil War leaders, too numerous to name, were among his classmates.

In one of his rare surviving letters, he told his brother about a visit to the academy shortly after graduation. "I took a trip up to West Point the other day," he wrote, "to see the old Place, the *fellows,* as we call each other, and to strut before the officers, my former oppressors. . . . I don't know of any trip which has given me more real pleasure than this, there was not the least change in any one at the academy, but in the officers, every one of whom offered his hand when he met me, and they all seemed glad to see as an officer one whom they had never spoken to as a cadet.

"I had made it a rule while in the academy never to speak to an officer but of business, and I believe it had the good effect of making them respect me after I graduated. I was very much flattered with the reception the cadets gave me not a man among them but what seemed happy to see me, and I had a crowd around me . . . from the time I arrived thru to the time I came away."

While many academy graduates were ambivalent about their plans (some resigned at graduation), Thomas knew with certainty that the army would be his life. He began his commissioned career as a second lieutenant of artillery in the fruitless Seminole Wars in Florida. Because cannon were useless in the Florida swamps, artillery officers functioned as infantry and threatened to resign, which would open promotion vacancies. "[I]f that should be the case," Thomas wrote John shortly after graduation, "I shall not be so much displeased as I shall be a little higher in the army list, and as I shall have to depend on my sword for a living for some time at least if not always I shall not grumble a great deal."

Because an ambitious officer sought to distinguish himself in action, Thomas was frustrated. "My duties at this post are so many that my whole time is taken up," he wrote a friend a year after graduation. "I have to do the duty of commissary, quartermaster, ordnance officer, and adjutant; and if I find time to eat my meals, I think myself most infernal fortunate." The post commander, he reported, had pushed off on an expedition "to oust Sam Jones [a Seminole chief who would not submit to life on a reservation] from his cornfields. . . . I have been left behind to take care of this infernal place in consequence of being commissary, etc. This will be the only opportunity I shall have of distinguishing myself, and not to be able to avail myself of it is too bad."

A new commander took over, and Thomas accompanied the next patrol. The soldiers outwitted the Seminoles and returned with sixty captives—men, women, and children—from the depths of the Everglades. It was such a rare triumph that Thomas received mention in dispatches and a brevet promotion to first lieutenant.*

Like most army officers, Thomas's other early assignments were east coast garrisons, some pleasant, others onerous. He lived simply, saved and invested his pay, and sent money home to help settle family debts. Army life on the whole was agreeable.

Deep rooted in an exclusive aristocratic society, the Lee family of Virginia contained members both famous and flawed, as if the inbreeding of generations of cousins had produced men often erratic and self-destructive, and women genteel and sickly. Henry Lee was one such man, both hero and scoundrel. Popularly known as Light Horse Harry in the Revolutionary War, he won acclaim as a military leader and became one of George Washington's most trusted lieutenants. After the war he went adrift. He married a cousin, Matilda Lee, and took control of her inheritance, an estate on the Potomac called Stratford. He squandered her assets, and Matilda died young.

Ann Hill Carter, whose family was the wealthiest in the state, became Lee's second wife while still a girl, seventeen years his junior. His mania for speculation resumed. Twice Lee was confined in debtors' prison. Pursued by creditors, he fled to the Caribbean, abandoning his wife and five small children, among them Robert Edward, born in the decaying Stratford. They never again saw their husband and father, who died on a remote Georgia island when Robert was eleven.

Mother and children moved to Alexandria, across the Potomac from Washington. Impoverished and disgraced by her husband, Ann Carter Lee became an invalid. She and her son were inseparable. Lee became his mother's nurse, her companion, and her accountant, a mannerly boy with splendid good looks and an excellent mind, a mother's dream. She hoped for redemption through him, in whom she exhorted perfection, and she nearly got it. Whenever he fell short of his mother's expectations, Lee suffered depression and guilt.

Lee always would have to contend not only with fragile women, but also with scandalous male relatives. The hereditary passions that had wrecked the father bedeviled the son, and he wore a girdle of restraint and self-discipline. His pursuit of impeccable behavior dominated his life, particularly his fervor for prudence and accountability. Every ledger had to be exact. He once was mistakenly overpaid, and he was ashamed when he discovered the error. "It has caused me more mortification," he wrote in a mea culpa to the adjutant

---

* A word about "brevet promotions," as they often will be referred to in this book. The army did not award decorations—medals—as we know them today. As a consequence, the brevet was the equivalent of a decoration that honored and recognized outstanding performance of duty. The brevet rank that was conferred was ambiguous. It was not a permanent promotion, it did not convey increased seniority, there might or might not be an increase in pay, and whether the insignia of the temporary rank could be worn was a matter of interpretation. During the Civil War, brevet promotions became so numerous and indiscriminate as to render them meaningless.

general, "than any other act in my life, to find that I have been culpably negligent where the strictest accuracy is both necessary and required."

The wealthier Alexandria families established private academies, and they allowed Lee to attend with his cousins. There was hope that he would be different from other Lee men. Without an inheritance and owning nothing, he seemed willing to work for a living. The military was a possibility, given his father's association with George Washington. People in Alexandria spoke of Washington with a comfortable familiarity. Here he had dined, and there he had worshiped, and in this place he had strolled. Lee felt his presence.

The Military Academy seemed therefore logical. The competition for nominations was intense, so Lee and his mother pulled strings. Advocates, including eight congressmen, wrote to Secretary of War John Calhoun, some suggesting that the country was obligated to Light Horse Harry and owed his son an appointment. Lee got it.

Lee was in a class by himself at West Point. His conduct was impeccable, and while still a cadet he taught mathematics as an assistant professor. Leadership positions came naturally; in his senior year he was appointed corps adjutant, the ranking cadet. In his zeal to be first in academic standing, he relinquished his adjutant position to cram for the final exams. Lee just missed, graduating second in June 1829. As expected, he chose the corps of engineers.

Ann Carter Lee died a month after her son's commissioning. Lee mourned and then courted a childhood friend, Mary Anne Randolph Custis, whose home was Arlington, a mansion overlooking the capital from a bluff on the west bank of the Potomac. Mary was an only child, somewhat younger than Lee. George Washington Parke Custis was the lord of the manor, the adopted son of George Washington, more interested in embellishing his legacy than attending to his estate. Arlington was the repository for Washington's silver and china and such paraphernalia as his field tent, beneath which Custis ostentatiously entertained. After a summer's courting Lee left to build coastal fortifications in Savannah.

Family honor seemed irredeemable when Lee's half brother Henry was denounced as an adulterer on the floor of the U.S. Senate. Robert Lee's own courtship was imperiled; the Lee practice of marrying into wealth had been disastrous for the women, and Custis wanted to protect his daughter from a recurrence. But Lee was irresistible. Mary wanted to trust him, regardless. The father relented. Robert Lee and Mary Custis were married with great ceremony at Arlington on June 30, 1831. The parties and celebrations lasted for weeks.

Rough army posts and rude quarters replaced the glitter and gaiety. Accustomed to luxury, Mary often remained at Arlington while Lee supervised distant public works projects, a father in absentia to their seven children. The marriage became an impasse. Mary would not follow him around the country; Lee would not leave the army. Occasionally he pushed papers at Washington headquarters and lived at Arlington. In time Mary became an invalid and Lee became her caregiver, as he had with his mother.

Why, then, did Lee languish at lonely hardship posts, persisting in a sacrificial life with few pleasures? Perhaps it was his way of redeeming the family name disgraced by father and brother, and of honoring the expectations of his mother. Then, too, there was a close association with George Washington, both through his father and wife. As the noble Washington had suffered indignities yet had persevered on behalf of his country, so too would Lee. Fatalistically, stoically, Lee accommodated the tedium of peacetime service. Whatever his reasons, the army always came first.

"My family is American, and has been for generations," wrote Ulysses Simpson Grant in the opening sentence of his memoirs. The eighth generation of a family line that began in Connecticut in 1630, Grant was the first child of Hannah Simpson and Jesse R. Grant. His people had hewed wood and drawn water in laying the foundations of their country. Ambitious and successful, Jesse Grant carried on the tradition as both tanner and farmer, earning respect and exerting influence within his community of Georgetown, just across the Ohio River from Kentucky. He expected much of his son, who would forever stumble and miss the mark in desperate struggles to gratify his father.

Sent to boarding school at sixteen, Grant came home for Christmas to discover a letter from his senator announcing his appointment to the Military Academy. Only then did Jesse Grant reveal that he had applied for the appointment without his son's knowledge. Ulysses had no choice but to obey his father's will, even though he was apprehensive of the consequences should he wash out as a cadet.

(Grant's name subsequently underwent several transformations. To his family he was always Ulysses. As a new cadet he signed his name "Ulysses H. Grant." On the rolls it became Ulysses S. Grant, the name used on his commission, and so he accepted it as his own. After graduation he asked his fiancée, Julia Dent, to select a name for him that started with S. He did not, he wrote her, know what the letter stood for. It became Simpson, from his mother's family. His nickname in the army would be Sam.)

Equipped with neither ambition nor martial talent, Cadet Grant worked just enough to graduate and so avoid disgrace. Jesse Grant asked the army for progress reports and scowled when he read them, an early instance of his lasting practice of clumsy intercession on behalf of his son. Only in the studio of the drawing master did Grant find a place. There cadets painted and sketched to give them an eye for the details of a fortification and the features of a terrain. Grant's landscapes and portraits were beautifully rendered. Artist first and leader last, Grant wore no chevrons to grace his uniform, and on parade he brought up the rear as a file closer even in his senior year.

A splendid horseman, Grant asked for the cavalry at graduation but got the infantry, because of his mediocre record. Now a fledgling officer, he ordered a uniform fitted with gold buttons and epaulets and striped trousers, but its delivery was delayed. "This was a time of great suspense," wrote Grant. "I was impatient to get on my uniform and see how it looked, and probably wanted my old school-mates, particularly the girls, to see me in it."

His uniform came while he was on graduation leave, and Grant went to Cincinnati to promenade. A guttersnipe taunted him, and he returned home in humiliation. And there a stableman mimicked his uniform, and his neighbors laughed. "The conceit was knocked out of me," he wrote, "which gave me a distaste for military uniform that I never recovered from." Like many of Grant's remembrances, this was not entirely true, for Grant would wear a gaudy uniform once again as a newly promoted Civil War general, but thereafter rumpled field dress became his trademark.

Grant's first posting was to an infantry regiment at Jefferson Barracks near St. Louis. His academy roommate, Frederick T. Dent, invited Grant to the family estate nearby. Late that winter he met Dent's sister Julia, home from school, a robust woman of seventeen. The visits to the Dent home became frequent, and the couple walked and rode at every opportunity.

Orders unexpectedly dispatched Grant's regiment to Texas in May 1844, as a prelude to the Mexican War. Grant hired a horse and set off in a rainstorm to see Julia. A swollen, raging river seemed impossible to cross. "I looked at it a moment to consider what to do," he wrote in his memoirs. "One of my superstitions had always been when I started to go any where, or to do anything, not to turn back, or stop until the thing intended was accomplished."

(Let it be noted that this apologia is yet another instance of Grant using his memoirs to shape his image for the benefit of history. In the fall of 1862, when he attempted to seize Vicksburg by overland rail, Confederate raiders forced him to return to Memphis in humiliation. His memoirs must always be taken carefully.)

Soaked and disheveled, the river crossed, Grant sat with Julia, his hands trembling with both cold and anxiety. With awkward phrases they agreed to a secret engagement and exchanged love tokens—she a lock of her hair, he his ring. "Parting with that ring Julia," he later wrote to her, "was the strongest evidence I could have given you . . . of the depth and sincerity of my love for you."

Four years of separation, punctuated with a brief leave, would pass until they married. Nothing was said to her parents. Her father knew the army, he wanted none of it for Julia, and he would do all in his power to shield her from the miseries and degradation of life as an army wife. So opposed was he that Grant wrote surreptitiously to Julia through a third party. Her letters in reply were so infrequent that Grant suffered agonies and imagined the worst. Yet his love letters flowed without interruption, pleading with her for assurance of her faithfulness and commitment. She set his worries to rest during his leave; she gave him her ring, inscribed with her name, and it became his most precious possession.

The ring gave him hope as he returned to Mexico. "In going away now," he wrote to Julia, "I feel as if I had some one else than myself to live and strive to do well for."

2

MEXICO: LEARNING THE PROFESSION

―――・◆・―――

American diplomatic policy in the Western Hemisphere in the mid–nineteenth century was predicated upon the principle of manifest destiny, a belief held by many Americans that by use of force the United States was destined to expand across the continent, including the vast southwestern and western territories under the tenuous governance of Mexico. If Mexico would not cede California and the territories north of the Rio Grande and the Colorado River, argued the expansionists, then the mandate of manifest destiny would justify a war to expropriate them.

Events leading to the Mexican War, which would involve Grant, Thomas, and Lee, began in eastern Texas in 1836. American settlers declared their independence from Mexico in a brutal insurrection, the Alamo being the best-remembered battle. For almost a decade the area was the de facto Republic of Texas, but it repeatedly applied for admission as a slave state. Its annexation seemed inevitable, despite the furor of abolitionist opposition. Congress voted to annex Texas in March 1845, and it was admitted as a slave state in December. These developments precipitated the southward movement of army forces, Grant's regiment among them.

With the Texas annexation a fait accompli, President James K. Polk and his Democratic administration tried to persuade Mexico to concede its legitimate claims to the territory, undertaking a series of initiatives that were both supported and opposed with uncommon fervor in Congress and in the press. The State Department tried diplomacy and negotiation, but Mexico rejected the American purchase offers. The administration convinced itself that military force was the sole alternative and sought to fabricate a pretense for war that would not shamelessly violate international law. Polk needed just the right kind of general in command, militarily capable but without political ambition. Zachary Taylor, considered a competent soldier but not a political threat, got the assignment over the howls of General in Chief Winfield Scott, who wanted the command for himself but who was a Whig with known presidential ambitions.

Taylor's first objective was to occupy the Republic of Texas territory with American forces in September 1845. "We were sent to provoke a fight," Grant wrote, "but it was essential that Mexico should commence it." Mexico, however, did not oppose the provocative movement of American troops to Corpus Christi. In light of the Mexican inertia, Grant felt war to be so unlikely that the army surely would return to the states, allowing him to marry Julia. These uncertainties, coupled with his father's pestering him to resign, inclined Grant seriously to weigh leaving the army.

A letter from Julia kept him in. "You beg of me not to resign," he wrote back in January 1846 from Corpus Christi. "[I]t shall be as you say Julia for to confess the truth it was on your account that I thought of doing so, although all the letters I get from my father are filled with persuasion for me to resign. For my own part I am contented with army life, all that I now want, to be happy is for Julia to become mine, and how much I would sacrifize if her parents would give now their willing concent."

As the war in Mexico progressed, Julia's letters became increasingly ardent. She would come to Mexico to share his tent, she wrote, or even his prison cell if he ever were captured.

"Mexico showing no willingness to come to the Nueces to drive the invaders from her soil," wrote Grant in his memoirs, "it became necessary for the 'invaders' to approach to within a convenient distance to be struck." Taylor pushed his three thousand men 120 miles south to the Rio Grande, the boundary between the Republic of Texas and Mexico, in early March 1846. "It was necessary to occupy a position near the largest centre of population possible to reach," wrote Grant, "without absolutely invading territory to which we set up no claim whatsoever."

George Thomas had joined Taylor's army as a first lieutenant in an artillery company commanded by Braxton Bragg (in the Civil War they would command opposing armies). The fagged-out troops arrived on the north bank of the Rio Grande on March 29, opposite the Mexican town of Matamoros. Assuming that Mexico would fight, Taylor's men erected a fort on the north side of the river. Thomas wheeled his cannon into position and sited them to the south, where the Mexicans were constructing their own earthworks and fortifications.

Logistics determined strategy. Fifteen miles of swamps and forest isolated Taylor from his supply base at Point Isabel, where the Rio Grande entered the Gulf of Mexico. With the fortifications nearing completion, Taylor marched the bulk of his army to Point Isabel to unload his supplies from ships at anchor, leaving Thomas and a corporal's guard to hold the fort. Sensing that the reduced garrison was vulnerable, the Mexicans fired across the river. Thomas and his mates answered.

The Mexicans and Thomas's artillery exchanged fire for a week. The garrison rejected a demand for surrender and waited for Taylor to rejoin them.

When Taylor had completed unloading his supply ships, he returned upriver to relieve the garrison. At a place called Palo Alto, the larger Mexican army confronted Taylor's relief force. Taylor ordered an attack.

Grant was a quartermaster in charge of supplies in the rear, but he went to the front to see the action. He watched a cannonball decapitate a soldier and shear the jaw of another. The small arms were flintlock muskets firing balls and buckshot. "At a distance of a few hundred yards," wrote Grant, "a man might fire at you all day without your finding it out." At closer range the killing started. "There is no great sport in having bullets flying about one in evry direction," he wrote Julia, "but I find they have less horror when among them than when in anticipation. . . . You want to know what my feelings were on the field of battle! I do not know that I felt any peculiar sensation. War seems much less horrible to persons engaged in it than to those who read of the battles."

The Mexicans withdrew, and Taylor got his first victory. When a few days later the Mexicans took a stand behind ponds called Resaca de la Palma, Grant led an infantry company through the undergrowth and into a clearing. He found only dead and wounded. "The ground had been charged over before," he wrote. "My exploit was equal to that of the soldier who boasted that he had cut off the leg of the enemy. When asked why he did not cut off his head, he replied: 'Some one had done that before.' "

Taylor had his second victory and lifted the siege. He received word from Washington that Congress had declared a state of war because Mexico had fired upon American forces. Free to act, he crossed the river into sovereign Mexican territory and captured Matamoros. "We then became the 'Army of Occupation,' " wrote Grant.

Between battles the war was leisurely. After lingering for the summer in Matamoros, Taylor set off for his next objective, Monterrey, a junction of roads to the major Mexican cities. The city of Camargo, a hundred miles up the Rio Grande, would be used as an intermediate staging point. Riverboats transported the supplies and the bulk of the troops. Thomas and the artillery, escorted by Grant's infantry brigade, went by foot along the riverbank, marching at night to escape the August heat. While Thomas struggled and sweated with teams and caissons, Grant supervised the supply wagons, resorting to Mexican teamsters and pack mules (a hellish combination) in the mountains. (Grant hated the job of quartermaster, but the army would consistently refuse his requests for transfer to the infantry. He remained a disgruntled quartermaster for the duration of his pre–Civil War service.)

Camargo became pestilent as troops and supplies accumulated. Tormented by swarms of poisonous creatures, soldiers sweltered, drank contaminated water, and died from disease. Thomas, however, was by then a veteran at improvisation. When Major Philip N. Barbour stepped off the boat in early August, he found that Thomas and the advance party had commandeered the plaza and were cool in its shade. "Dined with Thomas and fared well," he recorded. "They had a most excellent dish that I never saw before, though it was an exceedingly simple one, viz.: fried peaches. Thomas told me there were plenty of fine peaches in town just ripening." Eating well and sleeping comfortably, Thomas would always be stout.

With his army festering and Washington fuming, Taylor broke camp in September and hauled another hundred miles westward to Monterrey, the final leg of America's northern intrusion into the heart of Mexico. The march was deliberate and measured, the countryside lush with corn and fruit, fresh water and flowers, and framed with spectacular views of distant mountains. Mexican cavalry cantered nervously ahead.

After a two-week march the invaders saw the cathedral spires of Monterrey. A huge fortress called the Citadel, together with fortifications of stone and adobe, protected the city. Closer in they heard church bells. Puffs of smoke came from the Citadel, and cannonballs bounced across the ground. Sharpshooters hunkered on the rooftops. As the Mexicans intended to defend their city from within, the Americans would have to dig them out. When the infantry engaged in house-to-house fighting, Thomas took his artillery in with them. The Mexicans ambushed Thomas in a narrow street; his horses went down screaming in a thrashing, bloody heap. Thomas untangled the harnesses, wheeled his cannon about, and fired canister to support the infantry. Fresh horses withdrew his guns and caissons to the rear.

Thomas repeated his potent artillery tactics for the next two days. Block by block, house by house, the artillery fought alongside the infantry, its canister sweeping alleys and solid shot pounding walls. Grant could have been a noncombatant—he was expected to stay in camp with the supplies—but he voluntarily went forward and joined the troops of his regiment. The Americans owned the city within four days, and an armistice on September 26, 1846, allowed the Mexicans to evacuate the city with dignity.

It was an exhilarating time for Thomas. Again he had excelled in combat. And again his superiors mentioned him in dispatches. His reward was a second brevet promotion, to captain. Grant's performance was unnoticed.

Whigs rejoiced and Democrats groaned at the news of Taylor's third consecutive triumph. The war had to be won with the Democrats getting the credit, but Taylor's successes had generated a boom to nominate him as the Whig candidate for president. Further, Taylor seemed willing. To nullify Taylor, Polk sent rival Winfield Scott to Mexico with duplicitous assurances of support. Pulling rank as the supreme commander, Scott planned to land the bulk of the army (including Grant and his regiment) at Veracruz and then march 260 miles overland to seize Mexico City.

Taylor retained 4,500 volunteers and a few hundred regular soldiers, Thomas and the light artillery batteries among them. Miffed and resentful, Taylor sought battle indiscriminately in an aimless expedition south of Monterrey in late February 1847. He blundered into a massive army commanded by the notorious general/presidente Antonio López de Santa Anna. The Americans dug in among rugged ravines near the hacienda of Buena Vista and awaited the assault.

The day of fighting was ferocious. The Mexicans concentrated on Thomas's end of the line, which began to buckle under the weight of numbers. Thomas held his ground, directing the fire of his cannoneers from the hinge of the American flank. Reinforcements came just in time—Colonel Jefferson Davis* with his Mississippi regiment, and Captain Braxton Bragg with more artillery. By the end of the day the Battle of Buena Vista was over.

The Mexicans melted into the hills, leaving a battlefield of bodies. The weary surviving Americans took roll call. When the numbers came in, the casualties were horrendous, some 15 percent of Taylor's force. Taylor estimated that the Mexicans had lost perhaps twice that number, but no one wanted to count the corpses.

Taylor had confounded the Washington Democrats. In the view of the Polk administration, the worst had happened, for Taylor's victory had assured his nomination as the Whig presidential candidate. He would win the election of 1848.

Orders came to Lee three months after Congress had declared war against Mexico. He first reported to Brigadier General John E. Wool, one of Taylor's field commanders, in San Antonio. This elderly veteran of the War of 1812 was assembling troops to seek action in central Mexico. Nothing happened in four months. No shots were fired. Lee fixed roads, laid out trench lines, and volunteered to scout for the Mexicans who never materialized. Ultimately he went to Scott's staff, one among many of the regulars stripped from Taylor.

Like Lee, engineer officers were for the first time in combat in a foreign land. Accustomed to independent assignments, they rarely had served on large staffs. The chief engineer of the army, Colonel Joseph G. Totten, changed that policy by packing the general staffs with his best officers. The cream went to Scott.

Scott was ponderous and ostentatious, a nineteenth-century conquistador who intended to subdue Mexico by seizing its capital, through intimidation if he could, otherwise by fighting. The campaign began when Scott's flotilla arrived off Veracruz in early March 1847 and went ashore unopposed. Pageantry and rewards worked at first. The Americans were a bonanza to the Mexicans, buying supplies and hiring laborers. The ragtag Mexican army was large and mobile, its soldiers brave but poorly led and equipped. The expanses allowed it to avoid the lumbering Americans.

Lee was quickly involved in combat. At Veracruz he sited the batteries that battered the city into submission in three days, an easy first victory for Scott, the principal casualties being Mexican civilians. The Mexican army disappeared, and Scott went inland toward Mexico City. With the army in transit, Lee planned march routes and improved and improvised roads and river crossings. Scouts discovered Santa Anna's army entrenched in hills

---

* The future president of the Confederacy.

known as Cerro Gordo. Before he could commit to battle, Scott needed to
know the strength and location of the enemy, the nature of the terrain, and
the avenues of approach. Lee volunteered to get the information.

Guided by compass and stars, Lee glided stealthily toward the campfires
flickering in the distance, his ears attuned to sounds in the night, his eyes to
silhouettes of man and rifle on picket. Nearer to the enemy camps, he heard
the murmur of Spanish tongues and smelled horses and cooking food. With
pounding heart he crept even closer until he saw huddled forms and stacked
arms.

When he returned, Lee awakened Scott and under lantern glow revealed
with calm precision what lay before the general's army. Then Lee cleared his
throat. Permit me to suggest, said Lee deferentially, that the general in chief
consider sending General Twiggs's division behind the Mexican lines over a
path I have found. Scott was impressed with the wisdom of Lee's recommendation, and the old general gazed at his young engineer with quiet admiration. "Do it, Twiggs," said Scott.

Lee was in the thick of battle for the next two days, guiding troops into
position to envelop and rout the Mexican army, advising Twiggs on developments, and siting artillery. When the Cerro Gordo battle was over, Lee
received lavish praise and a brevet to major.

The Americans went on to Mexico City, a fortress with a moat of
swamps, its roads few and well defended. Fields of jagged lava offered possible flanking routes, but they were formidable to bodies of troops and
artillery. Lee again was everywhere—reconnoitering, reporting, advising,
and guiding. Even though only a captain, he became a regular member of
Scott's war council, and generals sought his advice. After a month of fighting, Lee became so exhausted for want of sleep that once he fainted. Yielding to the pressure, Santa Anna evacuated the city, and Scott took possession
on September 15, 1847.

Combat service for Lee and Grant ended in Mexico City. How did their
Mexican experiences govern their later thinking and practices in the Civil
War? Any answer is largely speculation. Much would be forgotten, and the
things remembered would become irrelevant and overtaken by events. Lee's
case is especially puzzling, for when he fought in the Civil War, he inexplicably failed to practice things that had worked well for him in Mexico. Consider these examples:

• His feats of reconnaissance made victories possible in Mexico. Yet Lee
often failed to reconnoiter in the Civil War, either personally or through his
staff. Time and again he ordered attacks into areas sight unseen, as if dis-
missing his Mexican experiences.

• While engineers had been heroic and indispensable in Mexico, Lee
hardly used them in Virginia in such tasks as mapmaking or building roads
and bridges. He even forbade engineering companies in the Army of Northern Virginia.

• Lee's commander in Mexico, Scott, assigned skilled officers to his staffs and delegated freely. By contrast, Lee's staffs in Virginia were small and error prone, and he often did for himself what other general officers would consign to subordinates.

Grant's regiment had fought for some sixteen months, and Grant had seen as much combat as any officer in Mexico. But his tasks had been to feed and equip the line companies—an obscure, unrewarding role, however vital. Unlike Lee, Grant wrote about what he had seen and learned. His memoirs, written in retirement, in many cases put on a good face for history. Nonetheless, several features are worth repeating:

• Grant shrewdly realized that the actions of general officers in the field were often as politically motivated as were those in Washington. As the Civil War would again prove, campaigns and strategy could never be predicated solely upon military considerations.

• The ponderous, pompous Scott was always in full regalia, his retinue of staff and hangers-on prancing in his wake. His appearances before the troops were always flamboyant, and he expected to receive honors. On the other hand, "General Taylor never wore uniform, but dressed himself entirely for comfort," wrote Grant. His solitary presence was slouching and casual, his staff much like their chief. Grant would later emulate Taylor.

• Grant's prose was flawed in spelling and grammar, and sometimes clarity, but he wanted to be remembered as a good writer. Thus when Grant described Taylor, he was perhaps describing the way he thought of himself. "Taylor was not a conversationalist," wrote Grant, "but on paper he could put his meaning so plainly that there could be no mistaking it. He knew how to express what he wanted to say in the fewest well-chosen words, but would not sacrifice meaning to the construction of high-sounding sentences."

For George Thomas things were quiet after the Battle of Buena Vista. The fighting was over, the volunteers went home, and the regulars returned to garrison duty. The artillery had been magnificent. The army awarded Thomas a brevet promotion to major, something of a record, his third since graduation six years before. His old neighbors in Southampton County commissioned an elaborate ceremonial sword for their local hero and a resolution of praise. Thomas sent them a gracious letter of acceptance and was dismayed when he learned that more was expected. "I hope they will not enact the absurd ceremony of presenting me with the sword," he wrote his brother John. "If I could get off with a dinner only I should have great cause to congratulate myself."

By then a bachelor in his thirties, Thomas expressed ambivalence as to whether he wanted a wife and family. "I am sorry," he wrote to John on October 1848, "you are not successful in your selection of a fair lady to share her fortunes with me, as I should prefer one from the Old State to any other, and as I am now so much of a stranger there I am afraid I should not know where to look for one." Five years later he would marry a woman from New York.

Lee, Grant, and Thomas had fought where they had been sent, they had survived, and stoically they returned to their stateside posts to resume a dreary, peacetime way of life. The war had tested their courage in combat. Each had proven himself a brave and resourceful warrior well suited to the profession of arms; each had accepted the horrors of war and hardships of campaigning with unflinching equanimity.

The war they had helped to win had been fought for squalid reasons. Pettiness and selfishness tainted whatever remnants of glory remained from a war that had smelled so badly from the beginning. The generals promptly disgraced themselves and the army by bickering publicly for credit for the victory at Mexico City. Charges and countercharges intensified, politicians and journalists joined in the uproar, and courts of inquiry followed at which Lee, among others, testified.

"The Southern rebellion was largely the outgrowth of the Mexican war," Grant wrote in his memoirs, for like many others he believed that it had unleashed unrestrained regional passions. The South had gained another slave state and envisioned further expansion in the Caribbean, in Central America, and on the continent. The North was determined that the United States would never again go to war for the benefit of slavery, nor would it ever again acquiesce to another slave state entering the Union. Beyond that, however, Grant was mortified that his country had so ruthlessly trampled a weaker neighbor. "Nations, like individuals, are punished for their transgressions. We got our punishment in the most sanguinary and expensive war of modern times."

3

INTERLUDE: BETWEEN WARS

———◆———

The Mexican War became history, and Congress demobilized the army. Regular officers in large numbers resigned to seek civilian careers. Those who remained were part of a shrunken army absent a mission. The light artillery batteries were dismounted, as they were unnecessary for fighting Indians. Guns and caissons were consigned to storage in the armories, the horses went to pasture, and the artillery officers were reassigned.

The Military Academy carried on despite efforts to close it. George Thomas reported there in the spring of 1851 as head of cavalry and artillery instruction. He found a mess. The horses were nags, their obsolete "dragoon" saddles torture to ride. Thomas pulled strings to get both replaced, without success. A year later reform-minded Robert E. Lee came aboard as superintendent, and together the two Virginians brought horses and equipment up to snuff.

The roster of staff and students at the academy was a roll call of future Civil War leaders, beginning with the superintendent through such youngsters as J. E. B. Stuart, Philip H. Sheridan, and John Hood. The irreverent corps, accustomed to ridiculing the academy officers, respected Thomas as a soldier of stature who taught from experience. Under his tutelage cadets were graded in artillery and cavalry tactics for the first time.

A widow from Troy, New York, customarily took residence at the West Point hotel with her two daughters, with the obvious intent of inviting suitors for them from the staff and faculty. One of the daughters, Frances Lucretia Kellogg, was thirty-one years old, already a spinster by the standards of the day. She was pleased when Thomas came to tea on the veranda and shyly edged toward her, and when he spoke to her she sensed that he was a good man, unpretentious and solid, perhaps lonely like herself. They met more frequently, sometimes strolling across the Plain, or sitting on a bench overlooking the river valley. In time they spoke of marriage, something they both wanted, but they would have to enter into it clear-eyed. He intended to remain a career army officer, Thomas cautioned, going where the service sent him, and she would often be alone. Frances assured him that she would readily accept such a life, regardless of the hardships.

They were married at an Episcopal church in Troy in November 1852. Thomas's disappointed family in Southampton County felt him slipping away from his Virginia roots; they would see even less of him on his infrequent leaves, his Northern wife not at all. Virginians would later speculate that she had induced the Roman to remain loyal to the United States when the Civil War began.

The Thomases remained at West Point until his orders came in May 1854 to command an artillery battalion that the army had been trying to transfer to Fort Yuma, Arizona Territory, one of the hardest of the hardship posts. Thomas would be separated from Frances for two years. Moving the battalion from New York City had been a series of disasters. A ship had sunk and troops had drowned on the first try. A second voyage, before Thomas's arrival, had also been aborted.

Thomas found a seaworthy ship and promptly got underway, led his command across the Isthmus of Panama, and sailed from there to California. From San Diego the troops hiked through the summer inferno to Fort Yuma, 150 miles eastward across the desert. It was a near disaster—heat prostration would have killed his men had Thomas not conserved their strength. Afterward he berated the army command for its madness in ordering the march at that time of year.

The army had established the garrison two years before on the site of a Spanish mission at the confluence of the Colorado and Gila Rivers, a congested crossing for prospectors, pioneers, and livestock going to California. The garrison was expected to impose order upon the frontier anarchy and to prevent Indian raids. The parching heat was insufferable. "Whenever the subject of climate or temperature was brought up in Thomas' hearing," wrote Francis F. McKinney, "he was liable to repeat the story about one of his men who had died in Yuma. His ghost came back to the fort's guardroom looking for the dead man's blankets, as he had found it too cold for comfort in hell." *

The sun and boredom stupefied most of the officers and men. Thomas was an exception, since by disposition he was a self-taught linguist and natural scientist. The desert laboratory stimulated his intellect, and he shrugged off physical hardships. Scientists had asked officers on remote posts to collect new species of plant and animals, and Thomas contributed with enthusiasm. Resuming studies he had begun in Florida, he found a rare species of bat that he sent to Washington. Authorities in the fields of both botany and

---

* Francis F. McKinney wrote the most authoritative biography of Thomas, *Education in Violence,* and I will often refer to it. See the bibliography for a more extensive discussion of McKinney's work.

zoology knew and respected his name. While most soldiers disdained the indigenous Indians as primitive savages, Thomas studied their language and produced a rudimentary dictionary entitled "Vocabulary of the Kuchan Dialect of the Yuma Linguistic Family." Modern scholars consider his manuscript as a primary resource in the study of Native American ethnology.

Across the continent, Secretary of War Jefferson Davis petitioned Congress to increase the army by four regiments to combat Indian revolts in the southwest. In selecting the best leaders for these prized new regiments, Davis conferred both with ranking officers and with politicians who would want officers assigned from their states in return for their support of Davis's plans. The generals remembered Thomas's record in Mexico, and the Virginia delegation included him on its shortlist. He was among those chosen.

Davis promoted Thomas to major and ordered him to duty with the newborn Second Cavalry Regiment. Thomas had been a captain but sixteen months, a stunning advancement in an institution in which officers waited a lifetime for such rewards. When he reported to Jefferson Barracks, Missouri, for his new assignment in September 1855, Grant was grubbing for a living at his farm named Hardscrabble a few miles away.

Grant married Julia Dent on August 22, 1848, upon his return from Mexico. His routine of garrison duty resumed, alternating between Detroit and Sackets Harbor on eastern Lake Ontario in upstate New York. As the army east of the Mississippi was without a mission, Congress had diminished its appropriations to the extent that garrison housing and buildings were dilapidated beyond repair. Every post was perdition for the families who accompanied their men. Unburdened with duties, officers alleviated the tedium with speculating or farming.

We wonder today why Thomas, Grant, and Lee remained in the army of the 1850s, enduring a life of inaction, humdrum routine, and distant, dreary postings. Although Grant was temperamentally unsuited to function as a quartermaster, the army retained him in that hapless role. In the army's niggling, nitpicky preoccupation with minutiae, the quartermaster general in distant Washington had to approve Grant's expenditures, however trivial. On one occasion, for example, Grant had to justify his purchase of hickory firewood because the department assumed that it cost more than maple or beech. His bookkeeping was slipshod, and his returns were chronically late. In one instance he failed to account for almost $40,000 in government funds.

In a mindless, irresponsible, almost impulsive act, the War Department ordered Grant's regiment to California in 1852. When their steamer left New York on short notice, the soldiers and their families knew neither where nor why they were going. Grant saved the lives of Julia and their first child, Frederick, by leaving them behind until he could send for them. When the regiment crossed the Isthmus of Panama, disease and heat killed most of the children and many of the women who had tried to accompany the men.

Grant ultimately landed at Columbia Barracks on the Columbia River in the Oregon Territory. There was no need for them to be there; the few natives were no threat. "[E]ven this poor remnant of a once powerful tribe," he reported to headquarters, "is fast wasting away before those blessings of civ- ilization 'whiskey and Small pox.' " The gold rush had so inflated the cost of living that Grant and his brother officers plowed ground and planted crops to augment their income. The labor and the wet climate cramped his arms and legs (a chronic health problem), and when a summer flood destroyed his crops, Grant tried speculating. His venture profits vanished in bad debts and unpaid loans. "I have lost from dishonesty of others," he lamented to Julia; it was but one instance of his everlasting poor judgment of character.

In the service promotion was everything, as it still is. With few exceptions (those ordered to the Second Cavalry, like Thomas), it came by seniority. Officers held sinecures for decades, until removed by death, infirmity, or senility. By tracking attrition-created vacancies, Grant predicted the timing of his promotion to captain, which, under the circumstances, he dreaded: the consequences of promotion would be a company command at Humbolt Bay, California, a post so remote, so forlorn, and so wretched that duty there was banishment to the outer darkness. It was, Grant wrote Julia, "a detestable place where the mails reach occationally."

Orders were orders, and Grant arrived there in late January 1854. "You do not know how forsaken I feel here!" he wrote to Julia. After three months he had received but a single letter, dated the previous October. "I sometimes get so anxious to see you, and the boys [a son Ulysses had been born]," he wrote Julia in early March, "that I am almost tempted to resign and trust to Providence, and my own exertions, for a living where I can have you and them with me. It would only require the certainty of a moderate competency to make me take the step. Whenever I get to thinking upon the subject how- ever *poverty, poverty,* begins to stare me in the face and then I think what would I do if you and our little ones should want for the necessities of life."

Grant was at the end of his rope three weeks later. "I do not feel as if it is possible to endure this separation much longer," he wrote Julia on March 25. He received his commission as a captain of infantry on April 11 and wrote his acceptance. In an apparently irrational act that reflected his emotional tur- moil, he simultaneously tendered his resignation, to take effect July 31.

When Grant returned to Missouri he worked the land adjacent to the farm of his father-in-law. Without capital to buy seed and equipment, he pleaded unsuccessfully with his father to lend him money. In desperation he cut fire- wood and hauled it into town, which so exhausted him that field work was neglected. Fever and ague sapped his strength even further. After four years of failure he sold out in 1858 and entered a real estate partnership in St. Louis with Julia's cousin. That too was a flop, as was his application for county engineer. Finally he moved to Galena, Illinois, in May 1860, a stranger, a thirty-eight-year-old father of four children. There he went to work as a clerk in his father's store.

Lee returned to Arlington from Mexico in June 1848, after an absence of nearly three years, to resume construction projects and serving on boards. It was as if the war in Mexico had never happened. His heartbeat slowed to the pace of peacetime routine. Once a gallant, Lee became a somber moralizer racked by moods of depression and disillusionment. When he received surprise orders appointing him superintendent at West Point, Lee protested that he was unsuited for the assignment. Perhaps he perceived a conflict of interest because his son Custis was a cadet. More likely he wanted to avoid the drawbacks of the position. The staff and faculty were unstable because officers avoided such duty, they delayed in reporting, and they were detached on short notice during the academic year. Funding was so anemic that the buildings and equipment were inadequate and inferior. The paperwork and political meddling would be more tedious than anything Lee had ever encountered. The cadets themselves were so ill disciplined that Lee may not have wanted to deal with them.

Yet Lee obeyed orders. He returned to the academy on September 1, 1852, after an absence of twenty-three years. During his ensuing two-and-a-half-year tour, Lee managed his post the old army way, conservatively and by the book, coming up to standards but cautious about changing the standards themselves. He squeezed every nickel and, with pen patiently scratching away, assaulted the piles of incoming paper.

Small victories emerged. Incremental appropriations allowed improvements both in instruction and facilities, like decent mounts and saddles for George Thomas. Reflecting his own exacting standards of behavior and duty, Lee's greatest achievement was to improve discipline in the corps—albeit temporarily—through tough and consistent punishment for disobedience of the regulations.

Orders from the War Department brought surprises. Congress had approved two additional regiments each of cavalry and infantry, and Secretary of War Davis announced that Lee would be appointed second in command of the new Second Cavalry Regiment. There were two immediate effects of this order. First was the explicit requirement that Lee transfer from the corps of engineers to the infantry.* The second was promotion from captain to lieutenant colonel, bypassing the intermediate rank of major, a jump in seniority nearly impossible had Lee remained an engineer.

Leaving the corps of engineers was a drama. He wrote to his daughter that the act was a renunciation of personal desires, a yielding to the obligations of duty, honor, and conscience. In the end, he explained, it was a matter of obeying army orders and God's will. "Still in a military point of view I have no other course, and when I am obliged to act differently, it will be time for me to quit the service. My trust is in the mercy and wisdom of a kind Providence, who ordereth all things for our good."

His farewell letter to the chief of engineers foreshadowed his resignation letter to the general in chief of the army in 1861. "In thus severing my con-

---

* There is no apparent explanation as to why Lee did not transfer to the cavalry in light of his assignment to a cavalry regiment.

nection with the Corps of Engineers, I cannot express the pain I feel in parting from its Officers, or my grateful sense of your constant kindness and consideration. My best exertions have been devoted to its service, and my warmest feelings will be cherished for its memory."

Having disposed of his obligations at the Military Academy, Lee left for Texas and his first command.

4

TAKING SIDES: THE CIVIL WAR BEGINS

———◆———

President-elect Abraham Lincoln arrived in Washington in March 1861 under cover of darkness. "[S]muggled into the capital," Grant later said. "[H]e would have been assassinated if he had attempted to travel openly throughout his journey." Since Lincoln's election the previous November, talk about secession and a civil war had intensified. The Northern states were ambivalent in their response to the crisis, and the administration of James Buchanan had been hapless.

Seven Southern states had seceded from the United States of America before Lincoln was inaugurated on March 4, 1861. South Carolina's troops attacked Fort Sumter, in Charleston Harbor, on April 12. The fort and its flag represented American sovereignty. The assault on the fort and its surrender the next day were a national catharsis. Northerners were outraged, Southerners were jubilant, and moderates were silenced. Four more Southern states seceded. The war was on.

Ulysses Grant had no quarrel with the institution of slavery, and, like many Northerners, he speculated that the war would be brief and that slavery would end as a natural consequence. "[A] few decisive victories in some of the southern ports will send the secession army howling and the leaders of the rebellion will flee the country," he wrote his father in early May. "All the states will then be loyal for a generation to come, negroes will depreciate so rapidly in value that no body will want to own them and their masters will be the loudest in their declamations against the institution in a political and economic view. The nigger will never disturb this country again." He foresaw a possible slave rebellion, and if one materialized, a Northern army would go south to suppress it "with the purest motives."

Lincoln intended to fight, and he needed soldiers in orders of magnitude beyond the tiny regular army. His call for volunteers extended to Galena. "Business ceased entirely," Grant wrote. Like all the people in the town, he was intensely excited. He left his store, never to return, and with rising agitation walked the streets swarming with angry men. Posters announced an evening meeting in the courthouse, and Grant squirmed his way into the crowd. At first all was disorder, and then his name was called to preside when it was remembered that he had once been an army officer. Squaring his shoulders and rubbing his shoe tops on the back of his trousers, Grant strode to the bench and with eyes gleaming turned to the throng.

After patriotic speeches the people resolved to raise a company of volunteers and to elect officers and non-commissioned officers. Before the balloting Grant announced that he did not want to be the company commander but would help otherwise. He would wait for greater opportunities.

The governor of Illinois, Richard Yates, was in a lather as companies of raw volunteers descended upon Springfield. Desperate for help, he heard stories about a West Point graduate who had accompanied the Galena company to the state capital and had shown a flair for military organization. After seeing Grant for himself, the governor asked him to remain to help train and equip ten regiments of volunteers. Grant agreed. He wanted to be in the war by then but was uncertain how to proceed. Appalled by the widespread political logrolling for commands and commissions, he played it straight with a regulation letter to the adjutant general in Washington asking for a regimental command.

The army never replied. Swallowing his pride, Grant went to Cincinnati a few weeks later for an audience with George B. McClellan, whom he had known at West Point and in Mexico. Three years Grant's junior at age thirty-six, he had graduated second in his class, and his army career had been brilliant. McClellan had resigned after eleven years of service and had risen to the presidency of a railroad. He had returned to the army as a major general and would soon be its ranking officer. Unable to get past the orderly, a gloomy Grant returned to Springfield.

While Grant was cooling his heels in Cincinnati, Lincoln issued a second call for volunteers. All ten Illinois regiments were immediately placed in Federal service. One of them, the Twenty-first Illinois Infantry Regiment, consisted of ruffians who embarrassed both the governor and the state. When Grant returned to Springfield, he learned that the governor had appointed him colonel of the regiment.

Men had enlisted to preserve a democracy, and it was the democratic way, they felt, for them alone to decide whom they would obey and when. They considered an officer equivalent to an elected official, and obedience to his orders discretionary and conditional. Some officers of the old army never learned how to adapt to these new conditions, while the behavior of the volunteer officers ranged from bluster to fraternization.

The appointment to colonel and command transformed Grant. After drilling volunteers he knew what to expect and asserted himself immediately, supported by his lieutenant colonel and major—humorless, abstemious men ready to enforce discipline. As the ranks had been skipping into town and raising hell, Grant immediately ordered that no one would leave camp after sunset without his authority. Some tried. Grant arrested them, and the guardhouse overflowed. Gradually the men behaved.

When Grant found his officers lax about mustering with their companies, he ordered them to be present at reveille and throughout the day. Drills and a regular routine went into effect. The disobedient were punished, but Grant was lenient if circumstances warranted. A month after his taking command, the Illinois papers and letters home reported high morale. Grant was making the men soldiers.

Influenced by both humanitarian and practical motives, Grant thought ahead to the time when his soldiers inevitably would encroach into civilian domains, South and North. He knew that secessionists feared an avenging Federal army; Northerners too had trepidations about the proximity of large encampments and footloose soldiers. Exhorting his men to behave with restraint and respect, Grant was in tune with much of the army's leadership, which believed that soldiers could contribute to victory not by guns alone, but also by good conduct. When the war escalated in scope and savagery, however, Grant abandoned such principles and resorted to the seizure and destruction of personal property.

In early July, three weeks after taking command, Grant took his regiment west into central Missouri to protect the railroads from guerrillas who were burning bridges. Missouri was a border slave state that Lincoln was trying to keep under Federal control, and the military and political balance was precarious. While other regiments went by rail, Grant marched his men to toughen them, and he commended them for acting like veterans.

Despite a fruitless search for guerrillas, Grant was pleased with the deportment of his troops. "When we first come here there was a terrible state of fear existing among the people," he wrote Julia. "They thought that evry horror known in the whole catalogue of disa[sters] following a state of war was going to be their portion at once. But they are now becoming more reassured. They find that all troops are not the desperate characters they took them for. . . . I am fully convinced that if orderly troops could be marched through this country, and none others, it would create a very different state of feeling from what now exists."

Eventually, however, his men would have to fight, and Grant had to be able to control their movements so that they massed and coordinated their gunfire, stood fast under enemy fire, and did not give way to stress and panic. As a cadet Grant had been inept in tactics instruction, and he had not read a manual since. The latest textbook, considered the authority by volunteer officers trying to learn soldiering, was *Rifle and Infantry Tactics*, written by William J. Hardee, now a Confederate general officer. After reading it, Grant decided that he could do better and tossed the manual aside.

Grant never would lead a regiment into combat. He was promoted to brigadier general in mid-August 1861, thanks to a recommendation to Lincoln from the Illinois congressional delegation, foremost among them Congressman Elihu B. Washburne. Grant learned the news by reading the papers. He was intensely proud of his two-month tenure as a regimental commander and believed that his record justified his promotion. Although Grant's command experience had been too brief for adequate seasoning, Lincoln needed people in a hurry, permitting Grant to soar from clerk to general in a twinkling.

Grant now needed a staff. By law it could number five men. The adjutant would be the principal administrator and chief of staff. The quartermaster would handle the accounts, pay the men, and procure equipment. The commissary officer would feed the men. Two aides-de-camp would carry out miscellaneous duties, often as couriers in battle.

Grant's first choice would be his best. John A. Rawlins, a thirty-year-old Galena lawyer who had risen from poverty to means because he was smart, tough, decisive, and principled, became Grant's adjutant. Grant had admired Rawlins's fierce, patriotic oratory and his smoking profanity when he talked about the secessionists. At first Rawlins knew nothing of military matters, but he knew men and learned fast. Intensely loyal, he quickly became Grant's confidant, conscience, and alter ego. He would remain with Grant throughout the war and afterward, unselfishly subordinating himself to his chief yet blistering Grant if need be, as no one else dared. As Rawlins was a recent widower and free from family obligations, he dedicated himself wholly to the general.

Before Rawlins arrived, Grant had selected two misfits, primarily for companionship. One was C. B. Lagow, an alcoholic lieutenant in his regiment. Another was William S. Hillyer, a St. Louis lawyer who had done Grant a favor several years before. The son of an alcoholic, Rawlins raged against drinking and tried to jettison the riffraff, with limited success. The upshot was a staff that would be hindered with incompetent officers throughout the war.

Grant received orders commensurate with his new rank in early September. He was to take command of the District of Southeast Missouri, with headquarters in Cairo, Illinois. The city was the strategic center of the most critical political and military theater in the west. Rivers were the region's most vital feature, serving as avenues for invasion, barriers to armies, and transportation routes for men and supplies. Cairo itself was located at the junction of the Mississippi and Ohio Rivers, and the mouths of the Tennessee and Cumberland Rivers were less than forty miles to the east.

The whole of southeastern Missouri and western Kentucky, embroiled in internal factional warfare, was also under Grant's jurisdiction, as were portions of Illinois and Tennessee. Kentucky had tried to maintain an armed neutrality, which was soon to unravel. The Confederate army was about to invade, and Grant would be faced with his first test as a general officer.

During the tumultuous presidential campaign in the summer and fall of 1860, George Thomas continued on duty with the Second Cavalry, scrapping with the Comanche in the badlands of southwestern Texas. Thomas was desperate for leave. (In some twenty years of service he had taken leave but twice.) Frances had come to Texas but later returned to New York, and Thomas wanted to be with her. He began his journey to New York a week after Lincoln's election. In the months before his departure, the regiment's Southern officers had discussed the implications of secession and what they would do in the event their home state withdrew from the Union. While seven states seceded soon after the election, Virginia waited. If Virginia seceded, Thomas's Southern relatives and the state government expected him to resign and pledge his allegiance to them.

The journey from Texas to New York gave Thomas time to think without distractions. Bad luck took him down in Lynchburg, Virginia, however; stepping off the train to stretch his legs, he lost his footing and tumbled down an embankment. The accident painfully wrenched his back. In Norfolk he went to bed and summoned Frances.

Meanwhile the tempo of secession intensified, and the Buchanan administration in its last days was paralyzed. The lame-duck president went before Congress on December 12. While the states had no right to secede, said Buchanan, the Constitution gave the government no power "to coerce a State into submission which is attempting to withdraw . . . [t]he sword was not placed in the hands of Congress to preserve the Union by force."

When Thomas was able, he continued to Washington and called upon another Virginian, Winfield Scott, his elderly general in chief, who told Thomas that he intended to remain loyal to the government of the United States. Afterward Thomas went to New York City to resume his leave of absence and to consider his alternatives. Northern officers would soon be in charge of whatever remained of the Federal army. If Thomas remained, he would be a solitary, suspect Southerner. When the influential Virginia delegation withdrew from Congress, he would be without patronage—a man without a country. Disgusted with the weakness of the government, anguished that his beloved army was fracturing, Thomas lay in his hotel room in the bleakness of winter, the pain exacerbating his emotional turmoil.

In mid-January 1861 Thomas applied for a faculty opening at the Virginia Military Institute. "[F]rom present appearances," he wrote to the superintendent, "I fear it will soon be necessary for me to be looking up some means of support." He was passed over. After his death, Southern critics said that this letter proved that Thomas wanted to join the Confederacy. It is true that he would have found himself south of the lines when the war began, but, to give him the benefit of the doubt, Thomas was looking for employment wherever he could find it. The war was not yet a foregone conclusion, nor had Virginia yet seceded.

Virginia remained uncommitted, and Thomas remained on leave of absence. On March 1, three days before Lincoln's inauguration, Thomas dispatched a letter to the adjutant general requesting assignment as superintendent of the mounted recruiting service for two years. His request was contrary to the custom of returning to one's regiment after a leave of absence. "I am still quite lame," he explained. "I fear that I shall not have sufficient strength to perform every duty which might be required of me if with my regiment." Thomas probably never fully recovered from his injury, losing the agility he once had as a hard-riding cavalryman. Men like Grant would scornfully associate his physical handicap with sluggishness in making war. "Thomas's movements [were] always so deliberate and slow, though effective in defence," said Grant in his memoirs.

While Thomas waited to hear from Washington, Virginia authorities asked if he would resign his commission and accept a position as chief of ordnance of the state's armed forces. Thomas declined. "[I]t is not my wish to leave the service of the United States as long as it is honorable for me to remain in it." But then he added contradictory and ambiguous conditions: "[A]s long as my native State remains in the Union, it is my purpose to remain in the army, unless requested to perform duties alike repulsive to honor and humanity." What exactly did he mean? Would he reconsider his decision if Virginia seceded? As we shall see, the similarity to Lee's contemporaneous choice of words is extraordinary.

The Second Cavalry had meanwhile been surrendered to Texas authorities through the complicity of an elderly brigadier general of the regular army, David E. Twiggs, a Southern sympathizer who commanded the Department of Texas. The men and the officers remaining loyal to the Federal government subsequently returned to New York. Orders reached Thomas on April 6 to meet them upon their arrival, take command, get them transported to Carlisle, Pennsylvania, and prepare them for active duty. While he was en route to Carlisle, the news arrived that Fort Sumter had been attacked. Five days later, Virginia seceded.

Thomas remained with his regiment and the United States Army. During the war Virginians were largely indifferent to his allegiance, especially as Thomas fought in the distant western theater. Had not Thomas distinguished himself, Southerners would have forgotten him.

His siblings were another matter. Although he rarely had gone to Southampton County during his army career, Thomas was a brothers' keeper for them all. In the prewar years he had exchanged letters, acted as both mediator and counselor, and freely lent them money. How wrenching then when his sisters shunned him for remaining in the United States Army. (Oddly enough, they kept his splendid ceremonial sword and gave it to the Virginia Historical Society.) Thomas never returned to Southampton County but still welcomed family news.

Controversy over Thomas's allegiance erupted after his death in 1870. Confederate general Fitzhugh Lee asserted in a Richmond newspaper that Thomas had remained with the Union not out of loyalty, but out of pique because Virginian authorities had not offered a position of suitable rank. Thomas's supporters reacted with fury, and the debate went on for years.

When Robert E. Lee accepted the assignment to the Second Cavalry in Texas in April 1855, he commanded troops for the first time in his career. He rarely saw them, for, like a traveling circuit judge, his primary duty was to preside over tedious courts-martial convened at distant sites. He had but one opportunity to lead troops afield, an expedition that lasted forty days and covered 1,600 miles without seeing an Indian.

Frontier duty was lonely monotony. Mary was an invalid, his daughters were unmarried, and his sons were unsupervised. His family lived at Arlington, thanks to the indulgence of Lee's father-in-law. On the face of it, Lee had little to show for a dedicated life of denial and sacrifice. He had no future, no hope of respite. Melancholia, pessimism, and a bleak fear of failure clouded his mind.

After nineteen months of tedium, Lee replaced A. S. Johnston as the regimental commanding officer. He moved to the headquarters in San Antonio, but nothing of consequence changed. Life droned on. Word was received that his father-in-law had died, and Lee took leave to return to Arlington to act as executor.

"So Lee settled down in the winter of 1857–1858 to become temporarily a farmer," wrote Freeman, "with scant equipment, little money, many debts, and indifferent help. He had often longed to lead the life of a planter, but now that he had to do so he entered upon one of the darkest, most unhappy periods of his life. Should he stay in the army, or was it his duty to resign and devote himself to Arlington?" His leave was extended and then extended once again, and soon he was out of touch with the army, totally absorbed with domestic affairs.

John Brown shook Lee out of the doldrums in mid-October 1859 when he seized the Federal arsenal at Harpers Ferry, Virginia and took hostages. Rumors that Brown intended to arm slaves and incite rebellion outraged and terrified the countryside. Lee was recalled to active duty, given the command of troops, and ordered to quell the insurrection. After a tussle, Lee delivered Brown and his cohorts to the authorities for hanging.

Lee returned to Texas and stewed in San Antonio through the fall of 1860. Lincoln was elected in November, and the secessionist movement began. Like other officers of the regular army, Lee had to take sides. His letters and remarks have since been studied intently by scholars, apologists, and critics in efforts to divine and rationalize his thinking and motivations. His words and actions can be interpreted in many ways, and they have been, depending on the point of view of the interpreter.

The letters express a leitmotif of conflicting loyalties and a fatalistic obedience to God's will. Lee would accept things as they came; he would not control events, but events would control him. His principal theme was to avoid involvement in the looming war and not to bear arms save in defense of his native state. Contradictory and ambiguous, Lee kept everyone guessing about his intentions.

The War Department ordered Lee to come home in February 1861. When he arrived in Washington, he spent several hours talking with his mentor, Winfield Scott. Their conversation is unrecorded, but Scott no doubt counseled Lee, as he had Thomas, to remain loyal to the United States. Lincoln was inaugurated on March 4, and suitors soon came to Lee with inducements. By March 30, Lee had accepted a promotion to colonel in the regular army and command of the First Cavalry Regiment. Apparently he was holding firm, especially in light of rumors that he had been offered a position as brigadier general in the new Southern army then being raised.

When Fort Sumter was attacked on April 12, North and South erupted with emotion and men volunteered to fight by the tens of thousands. Lee sat tight. From his front porch at Arlington he could see the White House and the Capitol. If Lincoln stood on his balcony, he could look to his right and see the columns of Arlington on the hill overlooking the Potomac. Days passed. A convention was underway in Richmond, and it was evident that Virginia was about to secede. Richmond authorities and Lee began surreptitious negotiations to coordinate how he would resign from the United States Army and come aboard as the commanding general of the Virginia armed forces.

The Lincoln administration wanted Lee to commit himself. Federal authorities summoned him six days after the attack on Fort Sumter, and he crossed the Potomac for the last time as an officer of the United States Army. First he went to Bethesda to see Francis P. Blair, Sr., an influential adviser to Lincoln. It is generally believed that Lincoln had authorized Blair to offer Lee command of the 75,000-man volunteer army then being mobilized, but such an offer would have been frivolous. It was absurd to think that Lee would have led an army against the state of Virginia, populated as it was with his cousins and kindred. And regardless of Lee's perceived qualities as a military commander, it is inconceivable that a Congress of Northern politicians would have approved such a powerful appointment to a quintessential Virginian. It was foreordained that Lee and Blair would simply go through the motions of an offer made and declined.

Lee then called once more on Scott. It is generally believed that Scott delivered an ultimatum that Lee had to take a side. Lee returned to Arlington. The next day, April 19, Virginia seceded. Lee "tendered" (that is, formally offered) his resignation, dated it April 20, and dispatched it to Secretary of War Simon Cameron. In a separate letter to Scott, he wrote that leaving the army was such a struggle that he had delayed a final decision until then.

Lee left on the morning of April 22 for the Virginia capital. Crowds called his name along the way, and Lee waved and bowed. When Lee arrived, the Richmond scenario went off as planned. The governor met Lee and advised him that on April 19 the state convention had authorized the appointment of a major general to command the military and naval forces of the state. An advisory council had recommended that Lee receive the appointment.

Lee accepted immediately. The governor then sent a note to the convention asking that Lee be confirmed, and the convention unanimously approved. At that moment Lee was both a colonel in the United States Army and a major general commanding the Virginia armed forces, who even then were attacking the Harpers Ferry arsenal that Lee had rescued from John Brown fifteen months earlier. Northern leaders would never forgive Lee for his rush to Richmond, considering it treason.

Lee's conduct and intentions in the matter of his resignation were debated on the floor of the U.S. Senate in February 1868, almost three years after his surrender at Appomattox. According to Cameron, then a senator of not unblemished reputation, Lee had pledged his loyalty to the Union and had requested command of the Federal army. "He never gave us the opportunity to arrest him; he deserted under false pretenses," said Cameron.

Senator Reverdy Johnson of Maryland responded in Lee's defense. "I doubt very much its truth," he said. "It is not in keeping with Lee's character."

The Senate erupted with laughter.

Lee promptly wrote to Senator Johnson with his version of the events with Blair and Scott on that April 18. "At that time," he wrote, "I hoped that peace would have been preserved; that some way would have been found to save the country from the calamities of war; and I then had no other intention than to pass the remainder of my life as a private citizen."

Lee's statement did not square with the facts, and, together with his other letters, it intensified the North's institutional animosity toward him. Lee's partisans have freely acknowledged that he drew his hitherto reluctant sword with celerity and offer arguments that he was justified in doing so. When all is said, the eye of the beholder has largely governed the judgments rendered on Lee over the past century.

However he felt about his duty to the United States Army or to Virginia, it is not surprising that Lee went to war with such vigor. He had been a frustrated career soldier from a once noble and prosperous Virginia family. Lee's father as well as his brother had squandered the family wealth and had disgraced its reputation. Except for the Mexican War, his military career had been drudgery. Despite Mary's deteriorating health, it was his decision to be absent from his family for such prolonged periods that the children hardly knew their father. Altogether Lee's life was made miserable by doubt and depression.

The looming Civil War was a grand opportunity for redemption. Military and political leaders of both sides were beseeching him to accept a high command in the spring of 1861. The transition from obscurity to prominence was exhilarating. Richmond greeted him with ovations, and suddenly he was the most important man in the state he loved. His fellow Virginians looked to him for their survival in the coming war, a savior in arms in the most glorious tradition of Southern chivalry. In the end, however, Lee's fighting spirit would unleash forces that would devastate the state he had pledged to protect.

John Hood's service in the Second Cavalry, like Lee's, was routine and tiresome. He had joined the regiment in 1855 after his first two years of commissioned service in California. His restlessness for action resulted in but one combat experience, a skirmish in the summer of 1857. It had begun like so many other forays in those days as an extended search for Indians who did not want to be found. Hood, however, discovered some promising sign and charged off in a reckless pursuit that exhausted men and mounts. Shots were exchanged, both sides suffered several casualties, and Hood was mentioned in dispatches.

Hood twice availed himself of the army's liberal leave policy, once to visit his ailing father in Kentucky, and again in September 1860 when he began an eight-month leave of absence. En route to the east he received orders to the

Military Academy as chief of cavalry. Like many young officers before him, Hood did not want such an assignment, perhaps because of unhappy memories. He went to Washington and got the orders canceled. Still on leave, Hood returned to his regiment in January 1861. Thomas had gone; Lee was in command but left on February 13. Five days later Twiggs—the Benedict Arnold of the Civil War—surrendered all troops and Federal property to Texas authorities. Those in the regiment loyal to the United States Army returned to the North.

Hood went his own way to await developments and seek opportunities. "Kentucky being the land of my nativity," he wrote in his memoirs, "I deemed it right I should first tender my services for her defence." But Kentucky was a border state trying to stay neutral and unlikely to join the Confederacy. Hood waited and fretted. He had been in limbo for almost seven months when the war began with the attack on Fort Sumter on April 12. He tendered a terse, one-sentence resignation four days later.

The Knight-Errant was driven by ambition and opportunism and would become an ingratiating social climber. Lee advised him from time to time on such matters as marriage. Hood recalled riding with Lee on a balmy, beautiful day in Texas before the war. "[T]he conversation turned to matrimony," wrote Hood, "when he said to me with all the earnestness of a parent: 'Never marry unless you can do so into a family which will enable your children to feel proud of both sides of the house.' He perhaps thought I might form an attachment for some of the country lasses, and therefore imparted to me his correct and at the same time aristocratic views in regard to this very important step in life."

Like Lee, Hood did not wait for a reply to his resignation from the secretary of war. He went to Montgomery, Alabama, a city ablaze with war fever. There he accepted a commission as a first lieutenant of cavalry in the Confederate regular army.*

John Gordon felt no ambiguity about secession and slavery. He believed passionately in both.

After leaving school he had tried his hand as an attorney in Atlanta, followed for a short time as a journalist in the Georgia capital of Milledgeville. It was his first sustained contact with politicians, and the experience was stimulating. He also discovered that his gift of oratory got him noticed.

There was a future for him in politics, but he first had to make a living. At the time that Lee, Thomas, and Hood went to Texas with the Second Cavalry, Gordon went to the mountains of northwestern Georgia with Fanny and their infant son. His father operated coal mines in Dade County, near the Alabama and Tennessee borders, and Gordon joined him there as a junior partner.

---

* See Appendix E, "Confederate Ranks and Organization," for an explanation of the Confederate regular and volunteer commissions.

His reputation as an orator brought invitations to rallies and gatherings. He talked not about local concerns but rather about national issues. His principal themes were that the slavery of black people was good and that the South needed a free hand to exploit its peculiar institution. Gordon's neighbors listened because he entertained them, but his ideas were irrelevant among the isolated, independent mountain people. They had little in common with the lowland plantations so dependent on enslaved black labor.

Figures like William L. Yancey, the most prominent Democrat in Alabama and an ardent, influential advocate of secession and slavery, shaped Gordon's political thinking. On July 18, 1860, Gordon spoke as Yancey's surrogate during commencement at Oglethorpe University near Milledgeville. His speech, entitled "Progress of Civil Liberty," was delivered before the university's literary societies. "African slavery," said Gordon, "is the mightiest engine in the universe for the civilization, elevation and refinement of mankind—the surest guarantee of the continuance of liberty among ourselves. Then let us do our duty, protect our liberties and leave the consequences with God, who alone can control them."

Gordon had a dream. "Do this and the day is not far distant," he said, "when the Southern flag shall be omnipotent from the Gulf of Panama to the coast of Delaware; when Cuba shall be ours; when the western breeze shall kiss our flag, as it floats in triumph from the guilded turrets of Mexico's capital; when the well clad, well fed, Southern Christian slave shall beat his tamborine and banjo amid the orange-bowered groves of Central America; and when a pro-slavery legislature shall meet in council in the Halls of Montezuma. And our foreign population, too, shall be encouraged by a successful resistance, on our part, to the aggressions of these Northern aggressors."

This was Gordon's credo: white liberty was dependent upon black slavery in perpetuity. The *Southern Recorder* accorded his speech a measure of attention. "Mr. Gordon was for protection to our slave property in its broadest sense, and was for expansion and extension. . . . He was an unadulterated 'filibuster.'* . . . A distinguished friend in commenting upon it, said that it commenced with an eulogy upon liberty, but wound up with an eulogy on slavery. But, upon the whole, we liked the speech."

During the presidential campaign Gordon went on the stump in Georgia and Alabama for John C. Breckinridge, the proslavery Democratic candidate, occasionally sharing the platform with Yancey. When Lincoln won, secession was certain. A special convention convened in Montgomery, Alabama, on January 11, 1861, and voted to secede. Crowds hurrahed, cannons roared, and church bells pealed. Orators, Yancey among them, whipped the crowds into delirium. Gordon too came before them. The act of secession was repeated eight days later in Milledgeville amid rejoicing. Gordon harangued the shrieking Georgia crowd.

---

* Defined in the mid–nineteenth century as a person who favored expansion of slavery, usually by force and often by private effort.

When the war began in mid-April, Gordon raised a local company of eager volunteers, a raucous conglomeration of mountain rustics in coonskin caps—the Raccoon Roughs, they called themselves. They elected Gordon their captain, but he was as ignorant as they in rudimentary military skills. After reading manuals he got them to obey orders and move in unison. Gordon first took them to Georgia to enlist, but the governor, swamped with volunteers, told them to await his call at home. Gordon sent telegrams, the governor of Alabama accepted his offer, and the company went to Montgomery and was incorporated into the Sixth Alabama Regiment of Infantry. Gordon was elected its major and commissioned on May 14, 1861.

As Virginia was about to be invaded, Gordon and the regiment went north as reinforcements in early June. Fanny went with him, leaving their children with relatives. She would follow him throughout the war.

Francis Barlow was practicing law in New York City when Fort Sumter was attacked. The outrage in the North incited a rush to answer Lincoln's call for 75,000 volunteers. Barlow was among them, enlisting as a private in the engineer company of the Twelfth Regiment of the New York State Militia on April 19, 1861, a week after the attack. The next evening, now in uniform, he married Arabella Griffith at St. Paul's Chapel. "Barlow . . . left her at the church door," wrote George Templeton Strong in his diary, "and went to Washington." The disorder and confusion of a great city mobilizing for war had disillusioned Strong; it had not seemed a noble undertaking. The example of Barlow and Arabella, however, had perked his spirits as he finished his diary for the day. "I have done this people injustice in my thoughts," he wrote. "We are *not* utterly corrupt and mercenary."

Barlow was reticent as to his reasons for going to war. Not until thirty years later did he make an unequivocal, unambiguous statement, when he wrote a long letter, published in the *New York Evening Post,* that read like a legal brief. Barlow was outraged over a law recently enacted to pension Union veterans indiscriminately, regardless of their record or length of service. As he had throughout the war, Barlow damned and condemned the cowards and shirkers, the malingerers and slackers, who now would receive pensions together with the combat veterans who had served honorably and well.

Barlow's sense of patriotism burns so fiercely in the letter that we may confidently conclude it to have been his principal motive for taking arms. "In all ages of the world," he wrote, "it has been supposed that it is the duty of citizens to come to the defence of their country. For thousands of years the people of other nations have defended their liberties and the integrity of their fatherland, without supposing that any reward was due to them for so doing, except the repairing of such damages as they and their families had suffered. Shall we be the first nation to admit that those who come to its defence . . . are to be paid for their patriotism? Is this patriotism? Will not this mercenary spirit in time come perilously near Dr. Johnson's definition that 'Patriotism is the last refuge of a scoundrel'?"

Not until the end of his letter does Barlow allude to his feelings of revulsion toward slavery. "The right or wrong of the war is not involved in this question," he continued. "No one rejoices more than myself in the overcoming of a rebellion the design of which was to destroy this Government for the purpose of maintaining the monstrous institution of slavery." Still, he acknowledged, the Southern soldiers defended "what they thought to be a good cause, though no one condemns the cause for which they fought more than I do."

The decisions facing Barlow and Gordon were clear-cut, because their loyalties lay squarely within the distinct regions that had formed their values. Most civilian volunteers, in fact, had few qualms when taking sides. The career army officers, in contrast, were often torn by insoluble conflicts. They had sworn to defend and support the Constitution of the United States, yet the very substance of the Constitution itself was clouded in the raging debates over the right to secede.

Could an officer of conscience make war against the national flag he had served and saluted? If he resigned to join the Confederacy, he faced the additional possibility of being charged with treason. On the other hand, state loyalty was deep-seated. Could an officer from the South make war on his family and neighbors?

PART II

EASTERN
THEATER,
1861-62

5

CONFEDERATE FIRST
ENCOUNTERS

*The Southern Confederacy was carried for four long years on the
bayonets of its armies. This is a common enough observation, but a
true one. Although the South's effort to achieve independence par-
took of the nature of a revolution . . . the Confederacy had no
administrators and statesmen comparable to those in our earlier
common War for Independence. . . . With few exceptions her civil
officials were mediocrities; and in many respects the President himself [Jefferson Davis] was but ill-adapted to the gigantic problems
with which he was confronted. . . . The South was at war, and the
flower of its manhood embraced the profession of arms.*

Ezra J. Warner, Generals in Gray

The size and topography of Virginia was both its strength and its weakness. In terms of population, agriculture, and industrial capacity, and
in the intrinsic influence of its leadership and prestige, it was the most
powerful state in the Confederacy. Rivers were its greatest vulnerability. The
Potomac River flowed past a hundred miles of Virginia shoreline, an avenue
for waterborne Federal forces and supplies. Three major rivers pierced Virginia's interior from Chesapeake Bay: the Rappahannock, the York, and the
James. Each provided ingress for Federal invasion forces, protected by the
Federal navy.

The state's land perimeters were also vulnerable. Some three hundred
miles bordered Ohio and Pennsylvania. The Allegheny Mountains in Virginia's western area were perhaps a physical barrier to an invasion, but the
mountain people of the region, opposed to secession, would welcome Federal forces.

Pageantry and high emotion had erupted in Richmond when Lee accepted
the commission of major general from the Virginia special assembly. The
crowds cheered as he left the Capitol. The next morning Lee had to deal with
bleak reality: an empty office, no staff, and a world in chaos. The Virginia

45

legislature had authorized but three assistants, while he desperately needed a professional staff to free him from distractions and details and allow him to concentrate on strategy and tactics.

Lee would be either unwilling or unable to assemble such a staff in the next four years, in part because ambitious officers considered such assignments inferior to the line. For Southerners, glory was on the battlefield. The tedium of staff duty was left to the drudges. As a consequence, the Confederate army would suffer shortages and deprivations throughout the war. Lee himself was no logistician, as Hood saw early on when he entered Lee's office jammed with cobblers, intently watching a hunched figure instructing them in making cartridge boxes and knapsacks. "Sir?" said Hood. The face that turned toward him was flushed and weary. It was Lee.

Lee returned to his desk, slumped in his chair, then brightened at Hood's eagerness to seek action. Lee preferred regular officers like Hood, but there were not nearly enough of them, and volunteers had to augment the professionals. The ink on their Virginia commissions had hardly dried, however, when the Confederate government established a national army that incorporated the individual state armies. A commission in the Virginia army became superfluous. The confusion intensified as out-of-state regiments augmented Lee's indigenous army. Although on Virginia soil, their officers took orders solely from the Confederate War Department. Disputes over jurisdiction and precedence made Lee's head spin. Within days of becoming a major general, Lee was soon to be without an army to command and shorn of all authority.

A remedy was promptly applied by commissioning Lee as a brigadier general in the Confederate regular army, which superseded his commission as a major general in the Virginia army. Thus he assumed command of all the armed forces in Virginia, regardless of origin. This reprieve, however, was temporary. When Jefferson Davis arrived in Richmond in early June to take command of all the Confederate armed forces, he consigned Lee to the ignominy of acting as his military aide.*

During the first four weeks of Lee's command, Virginians still had not voted to authorize secession, but the outcome was certain. Meanwhile, until secession was official, the Federal army remained across the Potomac. When the vote was in, Lincoln would order the army to invade Virginia. But where? And how? Lee did not know, for, other than reading Northern newspapers, he was without the means to gather intelligence, as he would be throughout the war. Having drawn his sword to defend Virginia, Lee waved it in futility.

A plebiscite approved the ordinance of secession on May 23, 1861. The next day Federal troops occupied Alexandria and the Virginia side of the

---

* For further discussion on the makeup of the Confederate armed forces, see Appendix E, "Confederate Ranks and Organization."

Potomac. Arlington passed out of the Custis family forever.* Mary and their daughters scattered among friends and relatives. Two sons entered the Confederate service, but Lee ordered his third and youngest son to remain a university student.

The four-year struggle for Virginia—and for Richmond—had begun. Until the city became the Confederate capital on May 20, 1861, its loss would not have been fatal, but now it had become the political symbol of the Confederacy. Many believed that if it fell the Confederacy could not endure. The eastern theater became defined as the hundred miles or so of Virginia soil between Washington and Richmond, where armies would converge and ravage Virginia's villages, farms, and fields. Even when Lincoln decreed Lee's army as the sole objective of Federal forces, Richmond loomed large until the end.

The war, said Lee in a self-fulfilling prophecy, would be long, bloody, and devastating.

Lee left Richmond to tour the lines a month after taking command. During his absence Jefferson Davis arrived to take charge of the Confederate government and its armed forces. Southerners hoped that Davis—West Point graduate, colonel in the Mexican War, secretary of war, and United States senator—would be the soldier-statesman to lead the Confederacy to independence. No man believed more passionately in the cause of the Confederacy than he. No man had more impressive military credentials.

Yet Davis splintered the political and military infrastructure of the Confederacy. Thin-skinned, quarrelsome, and intolerant, Davis assailed his antagonists—his generals among them—throughout the war. As commander in chief he intended to function as the imperial head and grand strategist of the Confederate army. His secretary of war would be solely an administrator, expected to recruit, feed, equip, and pay the army, tasks for which the five incumbents would utterly fail.

The department heads were functionaries of Davis's choosing and were notable for their ineptness. There was one exception, in an area that counted. Southerners understood the need for guns. Chief of Ordnance Josiah Gorgas was an officer of exceptional competency. Born a Yankee and a twenty-year army veteran, he exercised ingenuity and foresight in mobilizing armories and powder factories to produce modern firearms. Bolstered with his own fleet of blockade-runners, Gorgas either built or bought the tens of thousands of percussion-cap rifled muskets, together with the heavy

---

* The Federal government seized Arlington for delinquent taxes in 1862. The burial of the dead from Washington hospitals was so haphazard that Lincoln ordered Quartermaster General Montgomery Meigs to establish a permanent national cemetery to receive the thousands of bodies. In 1863, Meigs selected two hundred acres surrounding the Arlington mansion. Over 17,000 dead, both Federal and Confederate and including Meigs's son, were buried there by the end of the war. Under the circumstances Arlington could never be returned to Lee after the war, and Meigs planned it that way.

ordnance and the ammunition, that sustained the Confederacy's capacity to make war.

Frustrated and apprehensive, Lee stayed on, an aide without portfolio to Davis. It was a time when the two men established a relationship that prevailed throughout the war: Lee correct and restrained, well mannered and deferential, occasionally unctuous; Davis aloof, cool, and official. Expressions of respect were commonly exchanged, but cordiality never.

After a month Lee despaired as to Davis's intentions. "Where I shall go I do not know," he wrote to Mary, "as that will depend on President Davis." Lee's humiliation deepened when Davis kept him in Richmond while Davis himself went to the front for the Battle of Manassas on July 21.* P. G. T. Beauregard and Joseph E. Johnston were the heroes of the Confederate victory, and as their stature rose, Lee disappeared from public view altogether.

Davis dispatched Lee in late July on a forsaken rescue mission to soon-to-be West Virginia, where his government was losing its grip under Federal military pressure, Confederate ineptitude, and pro-Union sentiment. Major General George McClellan had whipped the hapless Confederate forces in the region before being summoned to Washington, and one more Federal victory would win the area irretrievably. Davis expected Lee to pull together the Confederate irregulars scattered among the mountain passes and drive away the Federal forces.

Lee found himself entangled in a morass. Two of the local generals were former Virginia governors, rivals still and not disposed to listen to the intruder from Richmond. Lee's efforts at conciliation were dismissed as weakness of character, and the generals ignored him. Rain fell for twenty successive days on the wretched, ill-equipped men, soldiers in name only. An epidemic of measles ravaged the farm boys, who came from homes so remote that the disease had been unknown to them as children. "[T]hose on the sick-list would form an army," Lee wrote to Mary.

Lee finally fashioned an intricate plan to divide the Confederate troops into isolated columns that would converge on the Federal positions at Cheat Mountain and then issued a general order reminiscent of Washington about to cross the Delaware. When read to the sodden, shivering soldiers prostrate in pools of water, it bordered on the ludicrous.

> *The forward movement announced to the Army of the Northwest in special Orders, No. 28, from its headquarters, of this date, gives the general commanding the opportunity of exhorting the troops to keep steadily in view the great principles for which they contend and to manifest to the world their determination to maintain them. The eyes of the country are upon you. The safety of your homes and the lives of all you hold dear depend upon your courage and exertions. Let every*

---

* Also known as First Bull Run.

man resolve to be victorious, and that the right of self-government, lib-
erty, and peace shall in him find a defender. The progress of this army
must be forward.

Slipping and sliding over rain-soaked mountain trails, the Confederates engaged in sporadic skirmishes, but most of them either caved in from exhaustion or lost their way. Lee stood speechless in the downpour, icy water streaming from his cap brim, as files of soldiers with vacant eyes shuffled out of the mists and passed him to the rear. Lee afterward explained the failure to Mary as an act of God. "I had taken every precaution to ensure success and counted on it," he wrote. "But the Ruler of the Universe willed otherwise and sent a storm to disconcert a well-laid plan."

This was the first instance of Lee's rationalizing that God was accountable for the end result of every combat—not Lee, nor his generals and colonels, nor his Federal enemies. God alone determined outcomes. Moreover, Lee time and again would predicate his plans on conditions as he wished them to be; when conditions were otherwise, as so often happened, Lee was without contingency plans.

The mortal danger to this kind of fatalism, of course, was that Lee could not learn from his mistakes, since in his mind he had made none. In a confidential letter to Virginia Governor John Letcher, Lee would admit to no errors in either his plan or its execution. "But for the rain-storm," he wrote, "I have no doubt it would have succeeded." Lee urged Letcher to say nothing, and he wrote nothing to Davis. Nor was Lee alone in his silence. Such was the shame that not one of the Confederate participants submitted an official report. Southern newspapers, ignorant of the facts, announced it as yet another victory. When the truth became known, Lee's credibility vanished.

The futile campaign neared its end. As a Federal army under Major General William S. Rosecrans made its way into the Kenewa Valley of western Virginia, Lee concentrated the Confederate forces with their squabbling political generals and their retinue of journalists. Each army dug in opposite the other and waited for the other to move.

It was now October in the mountains. Rain and frigid weather tortured Lee's forces. Men and animals were in misery for want of supplies, but Lee sent no request to repair roads or to send wagons. He confessed to another general that his army was already beaten for want of provisions. Lee awoke the morning of October 6 to discover that under cover of darkness the Federal troops had withdrawn to winter quarters.

Lee ordered his feeble soldiers, scarcely able to walk, to advance toward the Federal troops, but they could not. In a final spasm of fantasy, Lee conceived a plan for an offensive to drive the Federal troops out of western Virginia, but it was no more than ink on paper. By October 20 he called it off.

Eleven days later Lee returned to Richmond. His first field command as a general officer had been, in his words, a "forlorn hope expedition," a nineteenth-century colloquialism that reveals his feelings of shame, for in his mind he had been sent to perform an unusually perilous mission from which

he had been expected either to have emerged a live hero or to have died heroically. To have done neither was unforgivable. The Federal government had
retained control of what would become, in December 1863, the state of West
Virginia, lost forever to Virginia and the Confederacy. Lost, worse yet, by
default, for there had been no fighting of consequence in the three months
Lee had been present. Weather, politics, and logistics had whipped Lee. The
city that had cheered him now scorned him.

The loss of western Virginia would have profound consequences within
such border states as Kentucky, Missouri, and Maryland, whose divided loyalties were courted both by the Federal and Confederate governments. When
38 percent of Virginia's land area had pledged its allegiance to the United
States, Federal loyalists in such regions as eastern Tennessee and northwestern North Carolina would also be encouraged to break away from the Confederacy. Whatever the ultimate developments, it would be remembered that
such defections began when Lee lost western Virginia.

Lee was a huge political embarrassment to Davis, for Lee still had powerful friends who would precipitate awkward questions as to the extent of his
responsibility for the loss. Did not Davis and his administration bear some
measure of accountability? Lee told Davis privately that the tangled command relationships and lack of material support had been insurmountable
handicaps. In so many words, Davis had bungled his responsibility to support Lee afield. The less said the better, for both men.

Another embarrassment was that Lee had been promoted to full general
while he was in western Virginia and was now the third-ranking officer in
the Confederate army.* A public denouncement so soon after his appointment would repudiate Davis's judgment in selecting his generals, his most
politically sensitive prerogative as commander in chief. Nor would Lee
oblige Davis by resigning, for he was too proud to quit. The only question
for Davis was where to stash him.

The Federal navy provided the answer. A movement of the fleet southward raised fears of an imminent invasion at some point on the coast from
the Carolinas to Florida. As the Confederacy had neither ships nor coastal
defenses, the Federal forces could land almost at will at places of their choosing. Davis reacted by establishing a military department encompassing the
threatened coastal region and named Lee as its commanding general.

Six days after Lee's arrival in Richmond, the new orders came without
warning. Coastal residents, with small reason to hope that Lee could protect
them, protested to Davis. Lee probably had mixed emotions; while this was
an opportunity for redemption, he again would be without resources and at

------

* On May 16, 1861, the Confederate government had authorized a total of five full generals,
and Lee was confirmed in that rank on August 31. In order of seniority, the generals were
Samuel Cooper, Albert Sidney Johnston, Lee, Joseph E. Johnston, and P. G. T. Beauregard.
Joseph Johnston bitterly resented being ranked fourth in seniority, for he had been senior to the
other five in the United States Army. He blamed Davis for the affront, which started the long-
standing animosity between the two men that continued throughout the war.

the mercy of local interests. After two weeks of assessing conditions in his new command, his misgivings intensified. "Another forlorn hope expedition," he wrote his daughter from Charleston, South Carolina. "Worse than West Virginia."

Lee remained on the coast for four months. While the Federal fleet blockaded the major ports, there were no landings in force that threatened Confederate security. Lee was again an engineer, supervising the construction of fortifications as he had as a captain.

Gordon and the Sixth Alabama were among the out-of-state troops that swarmed into Virginia in June 1861. For all their free spirits and impetuous independence, Gordon's men would follow his inspirational leadership. Of elegant bearing and resonant voice, he looked and acted like the quintessential Southern officer, a gentleman and warrior in one. Once an overseer of a coal mine, Gordon was accustomed to exercising authority over the working class. As a rising politician he knew how to get votes by telling the people what they wanted to hear, and by vote the volunteer army determined who would lead and who would follow.

Gordon was of the people, as given to impulsiveness as they, and yet apart. Frenzied crowds, shrieking and chanting incoherently, gathered when the regiment passed through towns en route to Virginia, then fell silent when Gordon raised his arm to speak. Articulating their babbling into a single voice, his voice, he captured what they were feeling and trying to say, until finally his listeners would explode with a roar. This was giddy stuff for Gordon. "In the midst of this wild excitement and boundless enthusiasm," he wrote, "I was induced to make some promises which I afterward found inconvenient and even impossible to fulfill."

Gordon missed the action but saw the chaos at Manassas. Assigned to a brigade commanded by Brigadier General Richard B. Ewell, Gordon led his awkward, stumbling company forward to reconnoiter. It was an exposed and precarious position, and Ewell recalled Gordon before he could get in trouble. Beauregard, who fancied himself a mastermind, had planned the battle on a broad and sweeping scale, yet it was decided in a series of sporadic, spontaneous encounters of opportunity. The Federal troops fled the battlefield by late afternoon, and the Confederacy had its first major victory.

It was Gordon's first experience with battlefield hysteria; he watched in wonderment at the "wild panic which seized and shook to pieces the Union army at Bull Run, scattering it in disorganized fragments through woods and fields and by-ways, and filling the roads with broken wagons and knapsacks, and small arms—an astounding experience which was the prototype of similar scenes to be enacted in both armies in later stages of the war. No better troops were ever marshaled than those who filled the Union and Confederate ranks. Indeed, taking them all in all, I doubt whether they have been equaled. How courage of the noblest type, such as these American soldiers possessed, could be converted in an instant into apparent cowardice is one of the secrets, unsolvable perhaps, of our being."

And so the Federal army had fled. Davis joined Beauregard and Johnston, who had shared the Confederate command, urging them to pursue along the open road to Washington. But pursuit would rarely be undertaken in this war; losing armies would remain intact and prolong the conflict. Beauregard and Johnston decided to stay put and hold what they had, and Davis acceded.

Afterward there was some brief, wishful speculation that the Federal government would allow the South to go in peace, but when Lincoln fired Irvin McDowell and appointed George McClellan in his place, it was clear that the war would continue. The Federal forces, having endured the first of many humiliations in Virginia, began regrouping for the next campaign.

The glow of success rapidly faded for the Confederate leadership in Virginia. While the Federal government systematically prepared for a long war, Confederate leaders bickered and squandered opportunities. Beauregard's self-aggrandizement got him shipped off to the western theater as a subordinate to A. S. Johnston.

With both Beauregard and Lee in exile, Joseph Johnston became the undisputed military head of the Confederate forces in Virginia. When winter came, his army was scattered about the countryside, their condition wretched for want of food, clothing, and shelter. Knowing nothing of sanitation, the soldiers fell victim to diseases that they could neither prevent nor cure. Diarrhea afflicted Gordon in February, and he remained on the sick list for six weeks while Fanny nursed him back to health.

While McClellan was shaping up the Army of the Potomac across the river, Johnston attended solely to politics and the question of supremacy between military and civil authority. Neither Davis nor Johnston would budge. No one in authority could mediate; Secretary of War Judah Benjamin and Johnston found each other insufferable. The repercussions of such high-level tantrums were the institutional neglect of the sick and hungry soldiers, shivering under the snow in their shantytown encampments.

Spirit was about all that sustained Gordon and his troops that winter. The only good news was his promotion to lieutenant colonel. He was now second in command of the regiment.

When Hood had reported to Lee in Richmond in May 1861, Lee dispatched him to Yorktown, where the Confederate forces were constructing defenses at the mouths of the York and James Rivers. Both rivers and the land between them—universally termed the Peninsula—led to Richmond. The Federal army held Fort Monroe on the tip of the Peninsula, where it jutted into Hampton Roads near Norfolk and the entrance to Chesapeake Bay. The Federal strategy was self-evident. Staging out of Fort Monroe, a Federal army, its flanks protected and its supplies provided by the navy on either river, could march up the Peninsula toward Richmond seventy miles distant.

The threat seemed so imminent that Lee had expedited men and weapons to the commander of the peninsular defenses, Colonel John B. Magruder. A flamboyant career army officer, Magruder was daily in the prayers of apprehensive Virginians. A Federal invasion was expected momentarily, and Magruder had to stop it with scratch volunteers.

Hood arrived in Yorktown just before dark, finding lines of troops dug in and preparing for combat, and the officers, he later wrote, "delivering stirring and warlike appeals to the men. The following morning it was ascertained that the Federals were not within thirty miles of this line bristling with bayonets. The excitement therefore soon subsided, and the soldiers returned to their respective bivouacs. Such was my first night of service in the Confederate Army."

To a beleaguered Magruder, First Lieutenant Hood was a godsend, a bona fide professional with a tough, towering physique, whose voice had a militant timbre that tingled the spine. Here, said Magruder, is my cavalry commander. Hood would need commensurate rank, as he was junior to the cavalry captains. To avoid questions of precedence, Magruder expediently promoted Hood to major. Whether Magruder had such authority was irrelevant. There was a war on, and Hood's field promotion was uncontested and confirmed.

Hood was in his element, leading patrols into enemy lines in much the same way he had stalked Indians with the Second Cavalry in Texas. In early July, Hood and his troopers skirmished with Federal soldiers and brought prisoners back to base as trophies. Later such scrimmages would not have merited a notice, but in those early days, when not much was happening, Hood's little victory got him publicity and official attention in Richmond.

The war was providing opportunities undreamed of in times of peace. Quickly, almost effortlessly, Hood had become a major. He returned to Richmond to see the right people, who told him that Texas was sending troops to Virginia. Competition for the honor of commanding the two new Texas regiments became intense.

The headquarters of the Fourth Texas Regiment published a general order on October 1, 1861, announcing that *Colonel* Hood had assumed command. Again he had jumped two grades, bypassing the rank of lieutenant colonel. The officers selected for his staff reflected Hood's debut into new political and social spheres. His second in command was John Marshall; although twenty years Hood's senior and a military neophyte, he was a prominent Texan with connections and a friend of Jefferson Davis. The major was Bradfute Warwick, a young soldier of fortune and Richmond socialite who introduced Hood to the drawing rooms and ladies of the smart set. When Warwick was killed the following spring, Hood started a romance with the dead man's sweetheart, Sally Buchanan "Buck" Preston.

The three Texas regiments and the Eighteenth Georgia Regiment merged into the so-called Texas Brigade in late October, commanded by Brigadier General Louis Trezevant Wigfall, a hard-drinking, bombastic secessionist who before the war had been a United States senator from Texas. Hood's regiment left Richmond in early November and headed north to rendezvous with the remainder of the brigade in a squalor-ridden village named Dumfries, located near the Potomac River about thirty miles south of Washington. The bleak surroundings were a jolting change from the pleasures of Richmond, but such was the life of a soldier, and Hood settled in for the winter.

Richmond felt relieved when the Texas barbarians left. They had come to Virginia in small, restless groups looking for adventure and someone to fight, and their cocksure belligerence shocked and offended the mannerly easterners. Their brawling encampment transformed the somnolent countryside into bedlam. Many of the officers—including Wigfall—were mavericks in their own right, functionally incapable of imposing good order and discipline upon themselves, much less the enlisted men. The suspicion and distrust of authority were so instinctive that several senior officers were dismissed for want of approval by the ranks.

Hood acted to bring his regiment under control. Full bearded and towering physically over his men, he had a messianic figure that radiated a powerful sense of purpose and authority. Behave yourselves now, he lectured them, and unleash your thunder upon the enemy in battle. His style of fighting, as he explained it, would be violent: close with a rush so as to shock and then shatter the enemy's line. With glistening eyes, he rhapsodized on the glory of battle, and his men were spellbound by his imagery. Hood had them in hand.

The ineptness and indifference of the Richmond authorities exacerbated their hardships that terrible winter. Lacking shelter of any kind, the soldiers scrounged materials for makeshift huts and hunkered down against the cold. Without warm clothing or adequate food, they scavenged the countryside, and farmers loathed them. Disease—measles again—set upon them. Diarrhea leveled Hood for a time. Patiently, he and his soldiers waited for spring and the time for fighting.

The Confederate army pitched its winter headquarters at Centreville, some twenty miles west of Washington. As the front grew quiet and the snow fell, the generals had time to think about the identity of their army and their expectations for the Confederacy. A flag was the most profound symbol of national purpose, whether flying from the Capitol at Richmond or in battle with army and regiment. A mystique infused the Confederate colors, because they were made by Southern women who presented them as a sacrament, and soldiers rallied around the sacred colors in battle. As the colors went, so went the regiment. Progressively the names of battles would be stitched on the red field rent by shell and shot. To lose the holy banner was a disgrace. To seize enemy colors was a triumph.

The motif of the original Confederate national flags so resembled the Stars and Stripes that it was indistinguishable in the smoke and distance of the battlefield. The Confederate army wanted its own distinctive flag. Beauregard advocated a design of a blue diagonal cross with stars upon a red field in the fall of 1861. Johnston approved, and three Richmond women made the first three for Beauregard, Johnston, and Major General Earl Van Dorn. "The banners were received with all possible enthusiasm," Constance Harrison wrote in her diary. "[W]e were toasted, feted, and cheered abundantly."

The army ordered some 120 silken flags for the regiments serving in Virginia, and they were presented in a moving December ceremony. "The day for our division went off admirably," recalled staff officer G. Moxley Sorrel. "It was brilliant weather, and all were in their best outfits, and on their best mounts. The troops looked well as the colonels successively received their colors to defend. . . . Confederate uniforms were in great number. . . . We were then bravely dressed in the bright and handsome Confederate gray."

Afterward the generals adjourned to a great feast. James Longstreet had been promoted to major general and division command. Major John W. Fairfax, a wealthy staff officer who provided Longstreet's mess with abundant provisions, arranged the celebration. "Everything was plentiful in that stage of the war," remembered Sorrel, "and much liquor and wine were consumed. Johnston, G. W. Smith, Van Dorn, Beauregard, and others of high rank were present, and we had great merriment and singing."

During the banquet the talk turned to the need for a national anthem of corresponding grandeur to the new battle flag. The opera *I Puritani* by Vincenzo Bellini was popular at the time, and it was about another civil war, between Oliver Cromwell and the English monarchy. One of the most impassioned passages was known as the "Liberty Duet," sung by two basses who portray stalwart Puritans in Cromwell's army. Van Dorn loudly advocated that it be adopted for the Confederate anthem, and he began to sing.

"Up on the table and show yourself," bellowed Longstreet. "We can't see you!"

"Not unless you stand by me," shouted Van Dorn.

In a moment Van Dorn, Longstreet, and Smith, three West Point classmates and the three senior major generals in the army, stood precariously on the narrow table with arms clasped. Their voices filled the room and drifted across the darkened Virginia countryside and the soldiers in their shelters.

> *Let the words Country, Victory, and Honor awaken terror in the enemy.*
> *Let the trumpet sound and fearlessly I'll fight courageously.*
> *It is a fine thing to face death crying "Freedom"!*
> *Love of one's country undaunted reaps bloodstained laurels.*
> *Afterwards let mercy dry honorable sweat and tears.*

Not one among the revelers recognized that the Confederacy had nothing in common with Cromwell's Puritans. While they fancied themselves as revolutionaries, in fact the generals were protecting a reactionary oligarchy whose time had passed. Just as the Stuart monarchy had succumbed to Cromwell's Puritans during the English civil wars of the seventeenth century, the Confederacy's crumbling foundations would collapse beneath the storms of change.

6

BARLOW BECOMES A SOLDIER

Even when things went well, he couldn't really be joyful. They had gone wrong so often, they would probably go wrong again soon. Why make such a show of gladness? . . . It was a proud displeasure, firmly condemning and rejecting everything that was wrong: but though almost everything might be wrong, the inner oracle that condemned and rejected was sure of being itself right, and was not in the least dismayed.

George Santayana, The Last Puritan

Washington and Richmond were each in mutual dread of the other in the spring of 1861. Those in Washington, Lincoln not least among them, imagined the battle cries of an approaching army from the Virginia side on the Potomac, with Lee at its head, coming to protect his Arlington plantation and to occupy the capital. The Federal regular army could muster no more than a corporal's guard in defense.

Maryland was the other threat. A border state with slaves and Southern sympathies, it could very well align with the Confederacy. Baltimore mobs already had attacked Massachusetts troops en route to Washington. Maryland encompassed Washington from the east, and with a hostile Virginia to the west, Washington would be surrounded and isolated unless it were quickly reinforced.

Lee, however, had planned no offensive against Washington and had written off Arlington as indefensible. Federal troops suppressed the Baltimore insurgents, Lincoln pressured Maryland to remain neutral, and the threat to Washington diminished as volunteer troops arrived. Among them was Private Francis C. Barlow of the Twelfth New York State Militia Volunteers, who had married in uniform only to leave his bride at the church door to join his regiment already in motion. As the regiment was to serve but ninety days, he expected to return to Arabella and New York by late summer.

Barlow (seated far right) began the war as a private in the Twelfth New York State Militia Volunteers but soon was promoted to lieutenant of the engineer company. The well-turned-out soldier standing at his immediate left illustrates Barlow's insistence that his men conform to regulations. "I have commanded the Co[mpany] with credit during the past week & feel quite competent to be Capt[ain]," he wrote his brother, "with the exception of one thing - that is I have not the desire to make the damned scoundrels like me & I do not think they do especially. . . ." (Library of Congress)

Barlow went from private to first lieutenant in two weeks, the second in command of a company. "[Barlow] was not at first sight an impressive looking officer," recalled a soldier. "He was of medium height, of slight build, with a pallid countenance, and a weakish drawling voice. In his movements there was an appearance of loose jointedness and an absence of prim stiffness." Such first impressions lasted a day. Barlow zealously accepted army regulations as dogma and became their ruthless enforcer.

"This sort of life is not pleasant," the new lieutenant wrote to his mother, Almira, "but I did not come for pleasure and can endure anything for 3 months. An active campaign would be much preferable." Later he wrote his brother that his duties as acting company commander had been arduous. "For the last week I have hardly had time to eat." But he had gained confidence as an officer. "I have commanded the Co. with credit during the past week & feel quite competent to be Capt - with the exception of one thing - that is I have not the desire to make the damned scoundrels like me & I do not think they do especially. . . . You will see me in New York the moment our time is up & I shall not enlist again at least for the present - I am sick of this damned regiment."

The Puritan's feelings toward his regiment—and in a larger sense the army—were consistently ambivalent: now contempt, then pride. Troops by the tens of thousands passed in review before Lincoln and Winfield Scott on July 4. "Our Regt surpassed them all," he wrote Almira. "Genl Scott said 'they are really magnificent' - I was in command of my Company the Capt being on guard. . . ." When they later moved into the field, he compared his regiment to others in their brigade. "When along side of other Reg'ts I see the superiority of ours. Our camp was laid out with regular streets according to military rules. The others were all straggling and unmilitary. The other Reg'ts had not heard of dress parades apparently and began them after our example, apparently being shamed into it."

With less than a month of Barlow's obligated time remaining, McDowell's army, burdened with impedimenta, left Washington and struggled toward Manassas, where Beauregard waited. Barlow's regiment went to Charles Town, Virginia, some sixty miles northwest of Washington, where Confederate forces under Joseph Johnston protected the northern access to the Shenandoah Valley. Encumbered with lumbering wagons filled with extraneous supplies, the other regiments shambled across the countryside. Barlow's regiment moved smartly.

Once in Charles Town they merged with the Federal forces of 18,000 men assembling under Major General Robert Patterson, an ancient officer of the regular army. His mission was to pin Johnston in place to prevent his reinforcing Beauregard at Manassas. With fighting apparently imminent, Barlow confessed his ignorance of battlefield tactics. "You ask of my duties in battle," he wrote his brother. "Our duties are comparatively simple - As for fighting we ordinarily stand in the rear of our Companies & of course if the firings are there. In charging a battery or in charging bayonets I suppose the officers or at least the Commandant of a Company leads his men up to the object or the enemy to be attacked but he must fall back, I should think, before bayonets are crossed, as he would stand little chance with his sword Agt. a bayonet. I confess I understand but little of the practical duties of an officer in battle & no one else here does."

There would be no fighting that day. Johnston bluffed Patterson and left the field unopposed to join Beauregard in winning the battle at Manassas. When his militia regiment mustered out of Federal service, Barlow resumed his law practice, applied for a volunteer commission as a major, and expressed indifference as to the outcome. The commission finally arrived. It was as a lieutenant colonel, more than he had bargained for.

Charles A. Fuller, a college student in upstate New York, and his buddies eagerly volunteered to go to war for the Union in the summer of 1861. A company was formed, and they came together with about a thousand other like-minded men on Staten Island to create the Sixty-first New York Infantry Regiment. It was a mixture of Northern social classes, some from fancy New

York City militia companies, others from the provinces. Altogether they were a composite of the state that would provide the largest measure of Union manpower.

Their colonel, Spencer W. Cone, was a posturing journalist. His officers kicked him out of camp, then learned that Cone was returning with authority to arrest the mutineers. "There was a great scampering on the part of these officers," wrote Fuller, "and soon they were conspicuous by their absence." Cone granted amnesty and resumed his command.

It was the first and last time that the Sixty-first would be at its nominal full strength of a thousand. Two hundred disillusioned volunteers deserted in the following weeks. The disgruntled men of the regiment transferred to Washington in early November, to an open field called Kendall Green, within view of the Capitol. Barlow greeted them. He would be their second in command in name only. "[Cone] is not fit to command a drove of hogs," Barlow wrote Almira.

The division commander was Brigadier General Edwin V. Sumner, a forty-two-year veteran of the regular army who had distinguished himself in combat in the Mexican and Indian wars. His energy undiminished by age, his loyalty devoted to the Union, Sumner poured himself into the task of shaping the thousands of volunteers into fighters. Barlow was delighted to be serving under the old warhorse. "We are . . . under strict rule which I much like. . . . I am busy the whole time overseeing the whole camp getting things straight - I am supreme here & my position is a most pleasant one. . . . Genl Sumner says he shall not be so strict when we become better drilled."

What Sumner wanted, Barlow provided with a vengeance. Camp routine was executed with precision. When Barlow's watch malfunctioned, he sent it off for repair and wrote Almira, "I want the watch changed unless it goes perfectly correctly." Days started early and ended late. At six o'clock the bugle sounded reveille. When the men stumbled from their tents into the dawn, Barlow was waiting for them, his saber unsheathed. Six hundred soldiers assembled under arms in a single rank on the color line, officers and sergeants in the front. Voices barked roll call, and reports accompanied by swords flashing in salute went up the line to Barlow.

Barlow held relentless drills, training the men to load and fire in unison and then to reload their weapons so that the complicated steps became instinctive. His hoarse voice controlled every movement of the regiment, and no man dared disobey. A dress parade at four o'clock preceded supper. In the evening Barlow instructed the lieutenants. His day ended with further reading of military manuals.

"[W]hoever comes under me will have to submit to severe discipline for I keep them all right in my hand," Barlow wrote to Almira and his brother Edward some six weeks after his arrival. "What takes up my time is the making of rules and regulations and following them up throughout the Regt. from highest to lowest. Neither the Col. [Cone] nor Major have any capacity whatever for doing this or for overseeing or commanding a Regt. and I do it all. I could not have desired things to go on better than they have done and I am perfectly satisfied."

Fuller later recalled how the regiment responded to Barlow's leadership. "He knew the details of his business; he had the military instinct; and he was fearless. At first, from his exacting requirements and severity he was quite disliked, if not well hated; but, as time went on, and it was seen that he knew more than any other man, or set of men, in the regiment—that he knew how to work his men to the best advantage, and would see that they had what the regulations prescribed, and, that, when danger was at hand, he was at the head *leading* them, this animosity was turned into confidence and admiration."

As cold weather set in, a chorus of coughing reverberated from the tents at night. Measles again descended upon the encampments, and men died daily. On Christmas Eve a quarter of the regiment was hospitalized. But the Puritan thrived on physical hardship. "I have been remarkably well," he wrote Almira in early December. "I always stand fatigue and exposure better than much stronger people. . . . I do not want any more or thicker shirts or drawers."

Barlow took pride in shrugging off pain, as when a clumsy doctor tried seven times to extract a tooth. "He has however broken off everything which can be seen or appears above the gum," wrote Barlow, "besides cutting into the gum largely & he's now given it up in despair & I am to grin & bear it until I return to civilised parts. His instruments are of a rude character & it hurts like hell & I have now got so used to the operations that it is a pleasure."

He had built himself a small, snug log cabin with a brick fireplace, he slept on a pile of straw under five blankets, and a servant cooked his meals. Like many wives, Arabella lived nearby, and Barlow would take an evening with her before returning to his quarters. Her friends were convinced that she was her husband's motivation for becoming an officer. "Arabella tried to speak deprecatingly of the fate of a soldier's wife," a friend recorded, "but I know that in her heart it is just the thing she would choose and has, no doubt, had much to do in urging Frank to return."

Now Barlow was on top of the world. "I am probably the strictest disciplinarian in the Brigade but not despotic," he wrote to Edward after two months with the regiment. "My men I think like me." And to Almira he wrote, "It begins to be rather dull here. I have got used to the routine & learned nearly all that is necessary to enable me to discharge my duties. I shall now peruse the higher branches of the Art of War."

7

LAUNCHING THE PENINSULAR CAMPAIGN

———◆•◆———

T he political enemies of Jefferson Davis were howling for his neck in the spring of 1862. His generals had lost Kentucky and half of Tennessee and could not explain why.* In the east, eight months had passed since the victory at Manassas, yet the army in Virginia had been stagnant. Rumors were that McClellan was forming a huge army that would overwhelm the outnumbered and poorly equipped Confederates. Joseph Johnston, commanding the army in Virginia, wanted to withdraw from his exposed lines so near Washington. Ever secretive, especially to his commander in chief, whom he despised, Johnston would not tell Davis when and whether such a withdrawal would occur.

Davis needed help and recalled Lee from his coastal exile on March 2. What Davis expected of him was ambiguous, but Lee's presence alone fanned the political uproar. Judah Benjamin was dismissed as secretary of war, and the Confederate Congress passed an act that authorized a general to hold the position while retaining his rank. Many regarded it as an invitation for Davis to appoint Lee. Although Davis signed the legislation, he made no appointment. Other proposed legislation went back and forth, the gist of it being that the Congress wanted an autonomous general in chief to head the war effort. Again it was understood that Lee was the most likely candidate.

Unalterably opposed to any such legislation, Davis vetoed the bill and kept Lee under his thumb. Presently Davis shuffled his cabinet, appointing Benjamin secretary of state to preside over the Confederacy's futile foreign policy. George W. Randolph, a Virginia blue blood, replaced him as secretary of war. For the next three months Lee labored at menial things that Davis foisted upon him.

---

* This is the topic of chapter 14.

Life in Richmond "seemed gay and happy," remembered staff officer G. Moxley Sorrel, "with but little outward sign of apprehension or anxieties for the future. . . . Most of the troops passed through Richmond en route to the Peninsula, and there was much excitement and cheering. Main Street was thronged with people shouting wildly as the regiments marched down to . . . take the boat for part of the route."

Forfeiting what had been won at such cost the summer before, Johnston began his retreat on March 8, but Davis did not learn about it until four days later. For the only time in the war, the Confederate army had accumulated an abundance of food for its soldiers and had unwisely stored it near the front lines; as a consequence vast quantities were left behind. Davis blamed Johnston for abandoning the stores, and in turn Johnston blamed Davis for having allowed it to accumulate where it was unprotected.

Hood's career had advanced handsomely during the winter. Texas had elected Louis Wigfall to the Confederate Senate, and he relinquished his brigade command in February 1862. Hence Davis had the opportunity to designate a new brigadier general to lead the Texans. It was presumed that he would select one of the regimental commanders, two of whom were senior to Hood. Nothing had been heard officially when the brigade broke camp in early March to begin the dreary march to the rear. "[G]reatly to my surprise," wrote Hood, "I received information of my appointment as Brigadier General, and of my assignment to command of the Texas brigade."

So there he was, from first lieutenant to brigadier general in eleven months, with the war in the east hardly begun. The Knight-Errant was thirty years old. He had been obscure and undistinguished until he had arrived in Virginia. His total combat experience had been a cavalry skirmish the previous summer and an Indian raid years before. Now he commanded a brigade of almost 2,000 officers and men that daily grew in strength. They would be known simply as the Texas Brigade, and would become a premier fighting force in the Army of Northern Virginia.

Johnston's withdrawal to the Rappahannock River relinquished the northeastern part of the state to the Federal army. Officers had to explain to the soldiers why they had broken camp to start the 1862 campaign not with an advance, but with a galling retreat. Hood heard the murmuring and knew that he had to rationalize their turning from the enemy. He assembled his men and addressed them:

> Soldiers—I had hoped that when we left our winter-quarters, it would be to move forward; but those who have better opportunities of judging than we have, order otherwise. You must not regard it as a disgrace—it is never a disgrace when the welfare of your country requires such a movement. Ours is the last Brigade to leave the lines of the Potomac. Upon us devolves the duties of a rear guard, and in order to discharge them faithfully, every man must be in place, at all times.

> *You are now leaving your comfortable winter quarters to enter upon
> a stirring campaign—a campaign which will be filled with blood, and
> fraught with the destinies of our young Confederacy. Its success or fail-
> ure rests upon the soldiers of the South. They are equal to the emer-
> gency. I feel no hesitation in predicting that you, at least, will discharge
> your duties, and when the struggle does come, that proud banner you
> bear, placed by the hand of beauty* in the keeping of the brave, will
> ever be found in the thickest of the fray—Fellow soldiers—Texans—let
> us stand or fall together.*

Those who listened to him that day recorded that the men cheered.

Having recovered from diarrhea, Gordon rejoined the Sixth Alabama Regiment as it boarded a train in early April bound for Yorktown. McClellan had
landed his army at the tip of the Peninsula and had begun his march toward
Richmond; Gordon's regiment was among those sent to reinforce Magruder.
A collision en route demolished his train, but Gordon, his ever present
Fanny, and most of his men survived. At Yorktown the soldiers furiously
erected fortifications, while McClellan brought up his siege guns. New elections were held in the regiment on April 28, and the soldiers chose the Cavalier as their colonel. His first order as regimental commander was to
abandon the fortifications they had so laboriously constructed. The Sixth
Alabama evacuated Yorktown on the night of May 3 and began its march to
Richmond, fifty miles to the rear.

Barlow would remember the late winter and early spring of 1862 as a time
of waiting in the mud for something to happen. He brooded often about
country and cause. "[O]n the whole it is a damned stupid life," he wrote
Almira. "I hardly think this disgusting country is worth fighting for." Feck-
less Colonel Cone had finally gone. Barlow was promoted to colonel on
April 14 and given command of the regiment.

The city boy was at home in the elements. "I can sleep comfortably in a
pouring rain," Barlow wrote nonchalantly. He wrote Edward on May 15
from "a damned little hut made of an India rubber blanket, in a wood in a
pouring rain . . . [A]s usual it rained like Hell & after a good wetting we
were dumped in this wood for the night. My quarters are contracted, but tol-
erable dry. Our forces are gradually concentrating on Richmond." In an act
of compassion that would have astonished his regiment, Barlow enclosed
money in the letter and instructed his brother to help a boy in a homeless
shelter, the son of one of his soldiers.

Barlow's regiment had closed up on Richmond by mid-May, and he speculated on the upcoming battle. "[I]f we are beaten," he wrote, "I think the

---

* Wigfall's daughter Louise, who had a crush on Hood, had presented him with a battle flag
inscribed with the words "Fear not, for I am with thee; say to the North give up, and to the
South, keep not back," a paraphrase of Isaiah.

Army Encampment by Winslow Homer. In the first stages of the Peninsular Campaign, Barlow's soldiers wore heavy overcoats against the chill of early April. When they marched in earnest against Richmond in the warmer days of May, their coats were left behind. Barlow was at home in the elements. "I can sleep comfortably in a pouring rain," he wrote nonchalantly. (Cooper-Hewitt Museum)

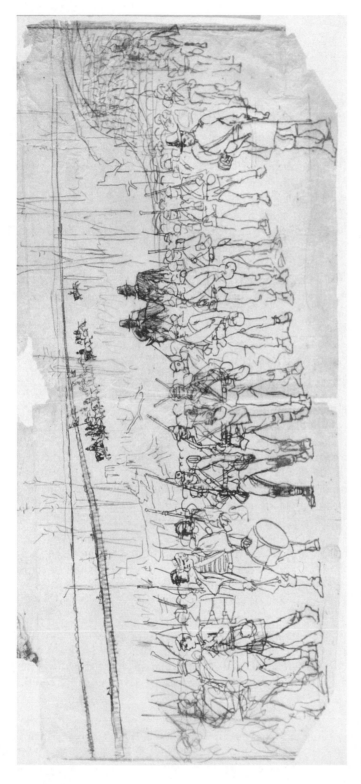

Infantry Columns on the March by Winslow Homer. Because they are smartly dressed and marching in step to the beat of a drum toward Richmond, these soldiers are probably from Barlow's Sixty-first New York Infantry Regiment. After the Seven Days, the regiment's survivors would be staggering from shock and fatigue. (Cooper-Hewitt Museum)

North will give up. . . . As for myself, I shall try to get out of the service just as soon as we have had a good battle - I think this must be quite soon. . . . I should like to be wounded slightly just enough to enable me to come home for a while."

Johnston again surprised Davis and Lee by secretly withdrawing from the Peninsula. As before, the withdrawal was so precipitate that supplies and equipage remained behind. The Portsmouth shipyard was also abandoned, together with its naval stores and cannon. The Confederacy's ability to build warships to oppose the Federal navy was lost forever.

By late May, McClellan had advanced to the outskirts of Richmond with an army of 150,000, well led at every level, well equipped, soundly staffed, and seemingly invulnerable. Johnston, with no recognizable staff organization, had perhaps 72,000 indifferently armed soldiers led by the flower of Southern field grade officers. Although Johnston concealed his intentions from Davis and Lee, they expected a battle momentarily. Lee went to army headquarters on May 31; too distracted to talk, Johnston left when Davis unexpectedly arrived.

After Johnston's orders launched the Battle of Seven Pines eight miles east of Richmond, Lee and Davis heard gunfire moving toward them and became engulfed in crowds of dazed and routed troops. Davis ordered regiments here and there and dispatched couriers for reinforcements, doing what Johnston should have done but had not. Johnston had gone to the front, forfeiting control of his army and exposing himself to enemy fire. In the early evening he was hit and borne to the rear.

Seven Pines was a day of hell for Gordon's regiment. Its parent brigade, commanded by Brigadier General Robert E. Rodes, had been detached from its division. Commanded by Major General D. H. Hill, the division, in dense wood and swamp, was to attack the center of the Federal line, supported by flanking attacks. When the support did not materialize, Hill decided to go it alone and ordered Rodes to rejoin on the double, a distance of two miles. Gordon led the way on his charger, through mud that sucked at the soldiers' legs. A bridge had been washed out, and the soldiers plunged into the water, some disappearing altogether, all trying to keep their powder dry. When the gasping men staggered into the staging area, Hill already had begun the attack.

Rodes yelled for Gordon to lead the way with his regiment. As his men scrambled into position, Gordon exhorted them in the name of Southern womanhood. "[I] reminded them of the proclamation of the infamous Butler,*" he later reported, "and the fate which awaited us if defeated, [and

---

* The Union general Benjamin F. Butler, the military governor of New Orleans, had two weeks earlier issued his notorious General Order 28, proclaiming that Southern women who verbally harassed Federal troops were to be treated as prostitutes.

then] deployed them as skirmishers in front of the brigade." The Cavalier led his six hundred onto a killing ground. For five horrible hours his men grappled with dense growth, muck, and water.

Undisturbed at their flanks and rear, the Federal troops massacred the struggling infantry. His horse shot away, Gordon led a final charge into a marsh that, he later reported, was "covered in water 2 or 3 feet deep, in which the vines, briers, and felled timber made an almost impassable barrier." Alone and exposed, the Alabama regiment writhed under a sheet of point-blank rifle fire that had "his officers and men falling thick and fast, if not killed outright possibly to drown in the water in which they stood." Rodes finally recalled them, said Gordon, as "the few survivors were loading and firing, all undaunted, amid their fallen comrades." Gordon's enemy had wiped out 60 percent of his command. He reported proudly that his men had never wavered.

Fanny Gordon had watched and listened from nearby Richmond, accompanied by an elderly uncle. "The battle in which Mrs. Gordon's husband was then engaged," he wrote, "was raging near the city with great fury. The cannonade was rolling around the horizon like some vast earthquake on huge crushing wheels. . . . [I]t was evident that her anxiety became more and more intense with each passing moment. She asked me to accompany her to a hill a short distance away. There she listened in silence. Pale and quiet, with clasped hands, she sat statue-like, with her face toward the field of battle. Her self-control was wonderful; only the quick-drawn sigh from the bottom of her heart revealed the depth of emotion that was struggling there."

Fanny collapsed when she learned that her husband was safe.

Johnston had hoped that the rain-swollen Chickahominy would sweep away the bridges to prevent the passage of reinforcements. But the partially submerged bridges held, and two corps of Federal reinforcements, Barlow's Sixty-first New York among them, crossed the river.

The two armies renewed their combat south of the Chickahominy on the morning of June 1, neither with its commanding general on the field. Johnston lay wounded in Richmond; McClellan remained on the north side of the Chickahominy, out of touch with his three corps on the opposite shore. In the absence of plans, the fighting resumed spontaneously with a roar of musketry when soldiers collided in the brush and thickets.

The sound of battle summoned Barlow and his regiment at seven o'clock in the morning. Along the way they passed Federal soldiers crouching under bushes. "I spoke to several," wrote Barlow, "and asked them why they did not go on. They said they had lost their guns. I pointed them out to my men as examples of what a coward is." Emerging from the woods, Barlow's regiment came upon a railroad, but no enemy. Barlow went into the woods to reconnoiter. In his absence stray bullets knocked down a man or two. Instinctively several men flattened on the ground, and the entire regiment followed suit. All were prone when Barlow returned. "Who ordered you to lie down!" roared Barlow. "Get up at once!" They scrambled to their feet.

When a volley discharged from the woods, an adjacent regiment ducked and fell back. Barlow's regiment remained standing. A brigade commander ordered the two regiments to advance, and Barlow rode in the front, not looking back to see if anyone had fallen, confident that his 417 men were following immediately behind him as he had trained them to do. The Confederate soldiers ahead of him fell back. Barlow advanced to a clearing on the crest of a hill and stopped to dress his line.

Suddenly a crash of fire erupted from the woods. "[A] most violent firing began on both sides," Barlow later reported. "The singing of the balls was awful. In about three minutes men were dying and groaning and running about with faces and arms shot, and it was an awful sight." Barlow's company officers fell one by one, alongside the soldiers who stood fast and kept firing, their ramrods flashing, until they too fell. After ten minutes the Confederates withdrew.

The discipline and behavior of Barlow's soldiers delighted him. "A few of the men at times would crouch down during firing and shirk to the rear," he later wrote, "but were brought up again by their officers, and were few in number. The greater part of the men stood firm and erect during the firing, and only stooped or went down when ordered to do so. . . . The men were certainly cool and obedient to orders and did not break at all."

Heroic death merited Barlow's praise: "He behaved most bravely and there is no doubt of his perfect contempt for danger," wrote Barlow in an epitaph to one of his fallen officers. It was what he expected, of himself, of everyone under his command. By his measure soldiers were either brave or cowardly; he recognized no other category.

Barlow dismissed the possibility of his own death. "I am a lucky person you know," he wrote, "and was not born to be killed in battle. . . ." But many others had died: a fourth of his regiment had been casualties, a figure that he noted was double the proportionate losses of Napoleon at Borodino, the Corsican's most costly battle. Carnage was a fact of war that he accepted fatalistically, with neither sentimentality nor remorse. "We have got entirely accustomed to dead, wounded & decayed men," he wrote later in the war. "It is singular how soon men become used to such horrid scenes. You see the dead and wounded carried past without any emotion."

Barlow had no doubt that his way of fighting, standard among most regiments, got the best results, albeit at great cost. It was centuries old, a taut infantry phalanx with massed weapons that traded heavy blows at close range. Casualties would be even worse if Barlow tried it against artillery. Whatever the tactics, the behavior and morale of his troops was paramount. "The men cheered me violently during the fight and when we came out," he wrote Almira. "I have just been down to the Hospital to see my men who were very glad to see me. . . . My men are very pleased with me since the action." Discipline, however, remained unrelenting. "I now have several walking before me for various offenses."

It was important to Barlow that he and the regiment get their full measure of credit. "The Regt. is praised on all sides," he wrote. "We are generally considered here as being the crack Regt. in this fight." He carefully read every

Infantry Rifle Drill by Winslow Homer. Like most Federal and Confederate officers in the early part of the war, Barlow trained his men to remain upright while firing; to seek cover was disdained as cowardly. Hence the soldiers were conspicuous targets and suffered grievous casualties. The soldiers' arms were vulnerable under any circumstances, for they had to be raised high to ram home bullet and powder. Later Barlow would make skirmishing a fine art. Gordon, however, would continue to keep his men in ranks when advancing during combat. (Cooper-Hewitt Museum)

nuance of whatever was written about him officially and in the papers, and on the whole he was pleased with the way he was viewed, although normally he considered the newspapers' reporting of the war as biased and distorted.

His sense of satisfaction was abruptly shattered a week after the battle. Someone (perhaps his law partner) published his confidential letter to Almira, which would be read as bragging about his own regiment and himself, and in which he had too freely criticized other regiments in the battle, criticisms that he subsequently found he had exaggerated. "It is damned outrageous to have published the letter," he fumed to his mother. "Who in Hell had my letter published?"

As the euphoria of battle faded, his mood was again sour. The Richmond front stalemated as McClellan systematically entrenched for a protracted siege. "I don't know if we are to be the attacking or the attacked party," Barlow seethed to Almira. "We are frequently turned out by alarms but no enemy appears. I am sick of this damned life and have no idea of beginning to drill and discipline a Regt. over again which will have to be done if this is recruited up. . . . We are now encamped behind the works which have been thrown up along the whole line of our front. One would think we were acting on the defensive instead of the offensive. . . . I shall certainly resign as soon as we get to Richmond."

Seven Pines was a Confederate fiasco; less than half of Johnston's army got into the fight. The remainder listened to the sound of the guns but stayed where they were. Because the generals were amateurs and their staffs novices, the muddling would continue throughout the entire Peninsular Campaign.

Beyond the shortcomings of generals and staffs, the institutional defect that would most impede the Confederate operations during the spring of 1862 was the wholesale ignorance of roads and terrain in Henrico County, surrounding Richmond. It was a treacherous place to maneuver: narrow roads and cow paths; swamps, forests, and thickets; streams that became unfordable torrents in the spring rains; rickety bridges that could handle no more than a single file of infantry, or cavalry and artillery not at all. Some brigades took roads that led nowhere, while others congested the roads that led somewhere. As getting troops into position on time was impossible, coordinated morning attacks would be a dream never attained.

One of the most puzzling features of Lee's generalship in the war was that he must have forgotten or dismissed entirely his Mexican War experience, when he had reconnoitered the terrain to find the best routes. Consumed as he was in preparing the defenses of Richmond while on Davis's staff, Lee had not thought to order topographical surveys and to make maps. It was a vital task he could have done on his initiative as a seasoned engineer, and without asking Davis's permission. The few crude maps that were available were useless. On June 21, Lee finally got himself a decent map of Henrico County, apparently the only copy available in the Confederate army. Ironically, the Federal army also got a copy and quickly integrated it into its own campaign maps.

Thomas J. "Stonewall" Jackson's army had the finest cartographer in the Confederacy, Jedediah Hotchkiss, and his excellent maps were crucial to Jackson's early 1862 successes in the Shenandoah Valley. When Jackson reinforced Lee at Richmond, Hotchkiss stayed behind. There was no one like him in Richmond, and Jackson's generals, including Richard Taylor, felt the difference. "The Confederates knew no more about the topography of the country than they did about Central Africa," Taylor wrote. "Here was a limited district, the whole of it within a day's march of the city of Richmond . . . and yet we were profoundly ignorant of the country, were without maps, sketches or proper guides, and nearly as helpless as if we had been transferred to the banks of the [Congo]."

The Federal army was better supplied and always would be. When it had first landed, the Peninsula was terra incognita. Existing maps were useless. Brigadier General Andrew A. Humphreys, a topographical engineer of great competence with thirty years experience in the regular army, quickly remedied the deficiency.* Under Humphreys's direction a staff of topographers,

---

* Humphreys would become chief of staff to George G. Meade when Meade commanded the Army of the Potomac and would command the Second Corps in the last months of the war.

engineer officers, and their assistants surveyed and reconnoitered the countryside from Fort Monroe to Richmond as the Confederates withdrew. From these data, accurate, detailed maps were produced and photographed, and copies were distributed to the field commanders and their staffs. As a consequence the Northerners knew the Virginia roads and countryside, and the Virginians did not. The maps would time and again determine the outcome of the battles that were to follow in the Seven Days.

Davis appointed Lee to command the Virginia army on the morning of June 1. Lee was fifty-five years old, with three decades of military service, largely as a civil engineer working on river and harbor projects or as a staff officer. Except for his brief and failed experience in western Virginia, he had not commanded troops in combat, and Davis had persistently refused to entrust Lee with responsibility commensurate with his senior rank. But Davis was now in extremis and had no alternative. Moreover, he could take comfort in the knowledge that Lee's political and social connections would deflect any serious objections to the appointment.

Davis, however, did not yield an iota of his own authority in the process. As a consequence the appointment was demeaning and restrictive for Lee. Johnston's disability, wrote Davis, "renders it necessary to interfere temporarily with the duties to which you [Lee] were assigned in connection with the general service, but only so far as to make you available for command in the field of a particular army." Davis had affirmed that he was still in charge of the armies at Richmond and throughout the Confederacy, and by no means was anyone to interpret Lee's assignment as other than an unavoidable expedient.

Lee expressed his usual disclaimers about his fitness for the assignment. "I wish that [Johnston's] mantle had fallen upon an abler man," he wrote his daughter-in-law. Among his first acts was to name his army, for it never had received an official designation. In a grandiose general order he wrote, "The presence of the enemy in front of the capital, the great interests involved, and the existence of all that is dear to us appeal in terms too strong to be unheard, and he [Lee] feels assured that every man has resolved to maintain the ancient fame of the Army of Northern Virginia and the reputation of its general [Johnston or Lee?] and to conquer or die in the approaching contest."

The claim to "ancient fame" was absurd, because the newly christened Army of Northern Virginia was but a year old. To be sure, its name would become legendary, but the immediate reaction in Richmond to Lee's appointment ranged from indifference to contempt. Within the Federal army, few knew and fewer cared that Lee was in command. Lee's army would grow in size to some 90,000 men during the month of June 1862. It would never again be as large. It would suffer more than 20,000 casualties in the first two months of Lee's command, among them irreplaceable young leaders.

The rain persisted. McClellan was mired in mud, giving Lee time to think. Reverting to his instincts as an engineer, he first thought in terms of static warfare in elaborate fortifications. Such a strategy, however, would be self-defeating on several counts. Southerners wanted to fight and felt manual labor demeaning; they indignantly refused to stack arms and take shovels. And to remain behind barricades under any circumstances forfeited the initiative to McClellan. His Army of the Potomac was the stronger and would remain so. Thus allowing McClellan to establish the timetable and to fight on his terms would be a mistake.

Lee wisely changed his thinking and decided to attack preemptively. His two greatest allies were the Chickahominy River and Lincoln's sensitivity to defending Washington. Surging above its banks, the river had immobilized McClellan's army by splitting it apart, and it could be crossed only with exertion. Roads were flooded, the countryside awash. Meanwhile, to the north, Jackson rampaged in the Shenandoah Valley and threatened Washington, engaging Federal troops that otherwise could augment McClellan. Lee reckoned that Jackson could serve a dual role as both decoy and reinforcement. A convincing demonstration toward Washington would suck troops from McClellan; Jackson could then quickly transfer to Richmond to help Lee's attack.

Jackson had other plans. Given enough troops, he maintained, he could invade Pennsylvania and end the war. He cherished his independence and had no incentive to bring his valley men into the Richmond morass. If he came to assist Lee, he would come reluctantly. Come he must, Lee insisted, but arranging how and when became confusing. The two generals communicated by letter and courier, which so often crossed paths that the messages they conveyed puzzled rather than clarified. Telegraph lines were available, but as the Confederate army had a crude cipher system, it did not entrust its secrets to the wires. The predictable result was that Lee knew neither Jackson's movements nor his intentions.

Three weeks after Lee had taken command, Jackson arrived unannounced at Lee's headquarters and reported that his Army of the Valley was en route by rail for Richmond. Lee summoned a council of war to explain his plan, which Davis earlier had blessed. (Davis was delighted that Lee consulted with him, a welcome change after Johnston's reticence.) Of forty-nine general officers in his army, Lee invited but four, Major Generals Jackson, James Longstreet, D. H. Hill, and A. P. Hill. These four would command the 56,000 troops that were to attack the single Federal Fifth Corps of 28,000 soldiers under Fitz John Porter, isolated north of the Chickahominy River.

Lee explained that Jackson would come down surreptitiously from the north and kick off a surprise attack, hitting Porter on the flank and rear. Simultaneously the other three commanders would attack Porter's front. Together they would crush Porter's corps, then sweep down and occupy the north bank of the Chickahominy. Ultimately they would sever McClellan's railway line of communication with his principal base at White House on the Pamunky River, over which some six hundred tons of supplies came daily to the army at Richmond.

The flaw in Lee's strategy was that the remaining four corps of McClellan's army would be intact south of the river, while the bulk of Lee's army was on the north shore. Lee had no plan as to what he would do once he and McClellan were on opposite shores. If McClellan exercised the initiative while the river protected his northern flank and rear, he might well attack Richmond in the absence of Lee's army. But whatever the outcome, Lee ensured that he and Davis were in it together, for Davis had approved Lee's plan.

Lee also did not realize that his plan would expedite what McClellan already intended to do: abandon White House and the north bank of the river. McClellan had kept his troops there hoping for reinforcements from Washington. When he realized that none were coming, he began moving southward. As his north bank troops got fewer, McClellan had foreseen that an attack on the rear guard was likely.

Confederate activity confirmed McClellan's suspicions. Lee earlier had sent cavalry Stuart on a reconnaissance, but Stuart had raided instead, so alarming McClellan that he had accelerated his movement to the James River. Likewise, Jackson's approach from the north, which Lee hoped would be a surprise, was so slow and so obvious that it alerted everyone of the imminent attack.

Such forewarnings intensified the hazards of tackling Porter's corps. Porter knew exactly where he was going to fight, he had good defensive positions to fall back on, and the Federal engineers had built bridges across the Chickahominy, which would allow him to cross and join the remainder of the Federal army when the pressure got too great.

Lee knew none of this when he presented the concept of his plan to the four generals; as in western Virginia, his thinking was predicated on conditions as he wished them to be rather than as they were. Lee did recognize that he was out of his element as a field commander, with neither a competent staff nor the personal experience to take a plausible plan and develop the details. So he would rely on the four generals, who he trusted had the talents lacking in himself and his staff. He would leave them for a time, he said, to function as an ad hoc planning staff. If they had to execute the plan, thought Lee not unreasonably, they would thrash out the details to their own satisfaction. And if they were confident that they could execute his plan, reasoned Lee, then the odds of success were improved. Lee was exercising a classic principle of leadership that allowed his subordinates a wide latitude of initiative. His great error was that he could justifiably delegate authority, but not responsibility.

Before Lee left the generals to puzzle out the specifics, he told them certain of his expectations. The 56,000 soldiers were to attack en echelon—that is, individual segments of the battle line, usually a division or brigade, were to attack sequentially, starting at one end and rippling progressively along the line so that the alignment would be like a staircase. The potential advantage of such a maneuver was to prevent the opposing commander from shifting the uncommitted portions of his line for fear of exposing a flank to the advancing forces; it also had the potential of allowing an assault force, inferior in numbers, to defeat a numerically larger force.

Timing and coordination were critical, for a given segment would not attack until its neighbor had attacked. If the neighbor either canceled or delayed for whatever reason, or if it could not be determined if the neighbor had indeed begun his attack, the coordination would disintegrate. For the maneuver to succeed, therefore, the assault forces must be in place, on time, and able to communicate with one another. The attack en echelon was often the Confederate maneuver of choice throughout the war, but in practice such attempts were often clumsy, uncoordinated, and costly.

For generals in combat, the devil is in the details, a condition that Clause-witz called "friction in war." He explained it this way:

> *Friction, as we choose to call it, is the force that makes the apparently easy so difficult. . . . Everything in war is very simple, but the simplest thing is difficult. The difficulties accumulate and end by producing a kind of friction that is inconceivable unless one has experienced war. . . . [A] battalion commander's duty is to carry out his orders; discipline welds the battalion together, its commander must be a man of tested capacity, and so the great beam turns on its iron pivot with a minimum of friction.*
>
> *In fact, it is different, and every fault and exaggeration of the theory is instantly exposed in war. The battalion is made up of individuals, the least important of whom may chance to delay things or somehow make them go wrong. . . . Fog can prevent the enemy from being seen in time, a gun from firing when it should, a report from reaching the commanding officer. Rain can prevent a battalion from arriving, make another late by keeping it not three but eight hours on the march, ruin a cavalry charge by bogging the horses down in mud. . . .*

Friction lurked everywhere for Lee. The few maps were useless, so the generals—especially Jackson—could only guess at the marching time to bring troops onto the field. Locations of landmarks and reference points were wrong. The nature of the terrain was a mystery. The reputation of Jackson and his army masked their want of discipline in the march. For lack of intelligence, the generals had no knowledge of the strength or deployment of Porter's corps. All of the factors that had so disrupted Johnston's attack at Seven Pines were unchanged.

Friction, wrote Clausewitz, cannot "be reduced to a few points, [it] is everywhere in contact with chance, and [it] brings about effects that cannot be measured, just because they are largely due to chance." It is dealing with friction, wrote Clausewitz, that marks the great general.

> *[H]e will need the greatest skill and personal exertion, and the utmost presence of mind, though from a distance everything may seem to be proceeding automatically. . . . An understanding of friction is a large part of that much-admired sense of warfare which a good general is supposed to possess. . . . The good general must know friction in*

order to overcome it whenever possible, and in order not to expect a standard of achievement in his operations which this very friction makes impossible. Incidentally, it is a force that theory can never quite define.

Even if it could, the development of instinct and tact would still be needed, a form of judgment much more necessary in an area littered by endless minor obstacles than in great, momentous questions, which are settled in solitary deliberation or in discussion with others. As with a man of the world instinct becomes almost habit so that he always acts, speaks, and moves appropriately, so only the experienced officer will make the right decision in major and minor matters—at every pulse- beat of war. Practice and experience dictates the answer: "this is possi- ble, that is not." So he rarely makes a serious mistake, such as can, in war, shatter confidence and become extremely dangerous if it occurs often.

As Lee and his newly minted generals had neither practice nor experience, it was foreordained that friction would wreck Lee's plan.

Lee rejoined his four generals to hear their recommendations. The attack, they told him, should be launched at Mechanicsville, north of the Chicka- hominy, on June 26, the earliest date that Jackson could arrive with his troops, then in transit. When the meeting adjourned in the evening, Jackson returned to his saddle to rejoin his distant command. He left before Lee wrote his operation order, so that Jackson had nothing in writing, and his exacting role in the success of the attack was imperfectly understood in his fatigue-numbed mind.

In creating an operation order, a Civil War general could express himself as he chose. An experienced staff could draft one, but as Lee's staff had not participated in the planning, Lee had to write his own. Other than the fiasco in western Virginia, Lee had never before written such an order, and now he had to write one that would take 56,000 men into action against a danger- ous enemy. Lee had not participated in the discussions among his four gen- erals, so he was uninformed as to their considerations and could not include them in his order. Instead, he wrote it based upon what he remembered they had told him afterward.

In many ways the order that Lee wrote resembled Napoleon's operation order for his attack against the Russians at Borodino. "These instructions," wrote Tolstoy in *War and Peace,* "which strike one as exceedingly confused and obscure, if one ventures to throw off the superstitious awe for Napoleon's genius in treating of his disposition of his troops—may be con- densed into four points—four commands. Not one of those instructions was or could be carried out."

So too for the instructions contained in Lee's orders. The ambiguity and omissions of his orders would wreck Lee's plan even before the first gun had been fired.

8

THE SEVEN DAYS

Conspicuous feats of valor there had been on the part of regimental and company officers, feats that had in some instances cost the lives of rising men. In the ranks, the soldiers had done everything that could reasonably have been demanded of them. It was the high command that had failed. None could deny that.
        Douglas Southall Freeman, *volume 1 of* Lee's Lieutenants

DAY ONE, JUNE 25: THE LONGEST MARCH

When Jackson returned to his army north of Richmond on June 24, he found it strung out and stationary. Fatigue, muddy roads, and lack of maps had brought it to a halt. Jackson himself seemed in a torpor. It had been understood at the planning conference that Jackson would converge with the remainder of Lee's army by sunset on the twenty-fifth, but Jackson invoked no sense of urgency upon his listless columns. His men would never rendezvous with the remainder of Lee's army in time for the attack at Mechanicsville on Day Two.

DAY TWO, JUNE 26: THE ENGINEERS AND THE SIGNAL CORPS

Davis and his Richmond entourage watched Lee's humiliating attempt at generalship at Mechanicsville. Of 56,000 men at his disposal, Lee brought but 14,000 into action, and those incrementally. Jackson had not appeared to attack the rear and flank; Lee sent no one to find him and went to bed still uninformed as to Jackson's whereabouts.

Porter and McClellan meanwhile pondered alternatives. Reinforce Porter and fight it out on the north bank of the Chickahominy? Let Porter hold the fort while the four unengaged corps attacked Richmond? Withdraw to the James? The crusty, outspoken chief engineer, Brigadier General John G. Barnard, heard all the arguments and sensed indecision.

Barnard was a distinguished veteran of three decades of army engineering duty, and he was unhappy with the treatment of his once elite branch. For one thing, engineers were not getting promotions commensurate with the combat arms. War had changed roles and perceptions. Washington politicians—and most generals—associated engineers with fortifications and static warfare and thought them unnecessary. Congress wanted its armies to move fast and to attack. Unable to equate offensive mobility with engineers, Congress refused to augment the corps. The shortage of engineers in the field armies was exacerbated because as many as a third of the scarce regulars remained in peacetime assignments.

McClellan—an engineer himself—knew that they were indispensable and tried unsuccessfully to get help from Congress. Unwilling to wait, McClellan took the initiative and organized his own pioneers: a battalion of regular engineers and a brigade of volunteer engineers. When the fighting started, his pioneers were prepared to build, repair, and maintain (and destroy when necessary) bridges, pontoon causeways, corduroy roads, and fortifications; to site artillery and infantry positions; to reconnoiter enemy positions; and to route and guide troop columns and supply and artillery trains across the terrain. "The movements of the whole army," wrote Barnard, "were determined by the engineers."

Lee's army was nearly barren of engineering talent. Only thirteen engineers of the regular army had resigned their commissions in favor of the Confederacy. As the South was largely agrarian, less than a hundred engineers, of doubtful competence, were recruited from the volunteers. The senior engineer in the Army of Northern Virginia was but a major. Lacking pioneer companies, the engineer officers had to beg for temporary help.

"Our people are opposed to [manual labor]," Lee wrote to Davis. "Our troops officers community & press. It is the very means by which McClellan has & is advancing. Why should we leave to him the whole advantage of labour. Combined with valour fortitude & boldness, of which we have our fair proportion, it should lead to success. What carried the Roman soldiers into all Countries, but this happy combination. The evidences of their labour last to this day. There is nothing so military as labour, & nothing so important to an army as to save the lives of its soldiers."

Lee and the Confederate armies would never have a Barnard to build roads and bridges or a Humphreys to make maps.* And perhaps Lee simply gave up trying to get the Southerners to do what they would not do by their culture and inclination. In the end, all would depend on the Confederate foot soldier doing what he did best.

McClellan had sent Barnard on the afternoon of Day Two to select bridgeheads that could be held on the north shore of the Chickahominy. Lieutenant George A. Custer from McClellan's staff belatedly joined him and told

---

* The Confederate Congress finally tried to remedy the deficiency by authorizing a corps of engineers in May 1863, comprised of one engineer company per division from volunteers within the division. Lee, however, suspended the general order in the Army of Northern Virginia shortly after Gettysburg (July 1863), probably because he wanted his few remaining soldiers to carry weapons and not tools.

Barnard that McClellan wanted him to reconnoiter the north bank plantation of a Dr. Gaines as a possible defensive position. Custer asked for Barnard's map and drew the line that McClellan had in mind, about four miles downriver from Porter's position behind Beaver Dam Creek. The pencil line followed the contour of Boatswain's Creek, a narrow, meandering watercourse with steep ridges on either bank. Several bridges behind the line would allow Porter to withdraw across the Chickahominy if the time came to do so.

Barnard rode about the area, carefully noting fields of fire and potential artillery and infantry emplacements. The sounds of furious battle from upstream reminded him that Porter and his 26,000 men might be moving into the area at any time and would need to know where to go. After sunset Barnard returned to McClellan's headquarters. McClellan had gone to see Porter, and Barnard awaited his return. The telegraph chattered in the communications center at about ten o'clock, summoning Barnard to join McClellan and Porter on the north shore. Barnard crossed the river for the third time. He met the two generals at about midnight. Porter's headquarters equipment had already left for the south side of the river.

The telegraph that summoned Barnard was yet another technological innovation that McClellan and the Army of the Potomac brought to the battlefield. A New York inventor had developed a field telegraph that used small, portable permanent magnets for power instead of cumbersome wet cell batteries; a pointer with an alphabet dial allowed messages to be sent and received by anyone not trained in the key. Industry produced reels with miles of insulated wire, impervious to moisture, that could be quickly laid from one headquarters to the other—the greatest problem was curious soldiers who cut the wire for souvenirs. To supplement the telegraph, signal officers were specially trained in such visual communications techniques as the semaphore, rockets to warn or to coordinate attacks among separated forces, and torches for night signaling. One way or another, the Federal army could communicate across miles of wild and hostile terrain.

Lee and his generals, in contrast, rarely knew one another's locations. Communications in the Army of Northern Virginia were primitive, occasionally carried by telegraph, but most often by courier. Lee would never be certain whether his messages had been received or whether he had received messages from others. A modest signal detachment had neither the numbers nor the sophistication of its Federal counterparts, and its usefulness was marginal.

Barnard met with Porter and McClellan around midnight and explained his survey of the area. They talked, then McClellan left without deciding whether to stay at Beaver Dam Creek or to withdraw to Boatswain's Creek. While waiting to hear from McClellan, Porter asked Barnard for advice. The engineer said simply that in any event Porter needed to have a way to cross the river. Then a telegram from McClellan told Porter to move back to the Gaines plantation, behind the natural barrier of Boatswain's Creek. Quickly and quietly, Porter's troops moved four miles to the rear. As daylight broke, Barnard and Porter rode about the region of the new line and discussed the best locations for defending themselves. Barnard left, and Porter continued to move his corps into their new position.

DAY THREE, JUNE 27: GAINES'S MILL

A Confederate attack of sorts lurched off by midmorning toward Porter's assumed position, but the abysmal maps sent the soldiers in all directions. Jackson finally checked in with Lee; his two divisions, he reported, were perched north of the battlefield. The two talked privately, out of the hearing of their staffs; Lee seemed calm, and their voices were subdued. Jackson's basic orders were unchanged: get around and behind Porter's right flank and attack in support of comrades flying into the teeth of the Federal line.

As Lee did not know where Jackson was, or where exactly he was to go, or which roads to take to get there, Lee could not estimate how long it would take Jackson actually to attack anyone. So his directive to Jackson was necessarily vague, and Lee had to hope that Jackson's initiative—missing so far—would help him muddle through. Jackson left, and he and his troops disappeared incommunicado until the last hours of the day, removed yet again from the fighting.

Porter's position was a blank spot on Lee's map, so he knew nothing of Boatswain's Creek and its hardwood forest or its steep, treacherous terrain. Lee had neither engineers nor signal officers to reconnoiter, nor would he use his cavalry to see what lay ahead. Porter's fire was so hot that Lee was certain he was facing the whole of McClellan's army and not just a corps. Hoping, unreasonably it would seem, that Jackson would momentarily appear so that the Army of Northern Virginia could surround and destroy the entire Army of the Potomac, Lee ordered A. P. Hill and his single division into a wild, piecemeal attack to pin down the main Federal line until Jackson got into place for the coup de grâce.

The attack began without artillery support, and Lee watched Hill's brigades crash into the forest and disappear, ten thousand men attacking twice their number. The sound of ordnance erupted, smoke writhed from the forest canopy, and then there was disaster. Panicked soldiers stampeded back and told Lee and his staff of the horror: they had struggled through bogs and ditches, in water and underbrush, across ravines and embankments, and when they had emerged from these, the Federals, protected from behind their fortifications, had swept them away with rifle and artillery fire. Barnard had laid out the line with deadly efficiency. The attack was over by four o'clock. Porter had mangled Hill's division. Of five divisions at his disposal, Lee had gotten but one in motion and had flung it against the whole of Porter's corps.

Lee ordered renewed afternoon attacks by Longstreet on the right and by elements of Jackson's forces on the left as they straggled onto the battlefield. Porter, his back to the river, was making his stand, and Lee continued to throw troops into the inferno incrementally, regiment by regiment, and each was in turn consumed by the fire. In the late afternoon Jackson sauntered into Lee's command post, without apology for having missed the fight and for not having supported his comrades. After a chat with Lee, he again rode away and disappeared into the mists.

Jackson's and D. H. Hill's columns—the soldiers that Lee in the morning had thought would smash into the enemy's rear as a mighty hammer—presented themselves in late afternoon. After a babble of conflicting orders from Hill and then Jackson, the Confederate troops crashed into the thickets in a snarl of hopeless disorder.

Among the tortured troops was Rodes's brigade, including Gordon's tattered Sixth Alabama. Alone and unsupported, Gordon had advanced with his men to an open field, exposing themselves to the muzzles of Federal cannon and rifle, which delivered a barrage upon them. They hugged the ground. Unable to go further, they later withdrew and went to the rear. Nothing came of further spasmodic attacks by Jackson and Hill except more casualties.

Desperate to salvage something, Lee ordered a charge by William H. C. Whiting's division of two brigades under Hood and Evander M. Law, which had been stranded with Jackson but had finally come to the field. Shrieking primordial screams, Hood's Brigade and Law's Brigade streaked across the battlefield. The Federal guns tore their ranks, but the apparition was so terrifying that the Federal soldiers finally broke, and the Confederates raised their rifles and fired into the backs of the fleeing men. Again they moved forward, mounting one barricade and then another. Other Confederate brigades made their last, maddened charges, and the Federal troops were squeezed into a tighter knot. And then came darkness, and exhaustion fell on the battlefield and brought all to an end.

Hood asked his division commander to spare his brigade from further action because its casualties had been so severe. Gordon would fight again.

Lee reported that night to Davis that God had blessed the Confederate army:

> Profoundly grateful to Almighty God for the signal victory granted to us, it is my pleasing task to announce to you the success achieved by this army today. The enemy was this morning driven from his strong position behind Beaver Dam Creek [Lee was unaware Porter had withdrawn before Lee's attack] and pursued to that behind Powhite Creek [he never did realize that Porter was a half mile farther east behind Boatswain's Creek, which was not on Lee's map], and finally, after a severe contest of five hours, entirely repulsed from the field [Porter still held his ground north of the river]. Night put an end to the contest. I grieve to state that our loss in officers and men is great [some 8,000 casualties, at least a fourth of his soldiers who saw combat that day]. We sleep on the field, and shall renew the contest in the morning.

The battle had been a near thing for Porter. He had asked McClellan for reinforcements. Those that came were few and late, but they helped Porter to survive. His dead and wounded were half that of Lee's. After dark he withdrew his corps to the south bank of the Chickahominy and burned his bridges behind him. The whole of the Army of the Potomac was now south of the river, while the bulk of the Army of Northern Virginia was to the north.

DAY FOUR, JUNE 28: THE PAUSE

Day Four was the quiet day. Lee had accomplished what he had set out to do, incomplete as it was. He had cleared the Federal army from the north bank and could now sever the abandoned rail line to White House. But his situation apparently was no better, perhaps even worse, than it had been before the battle at Gaines's Mill. McClellan occupied the south side of the river, his army still largely intact and threatening Richmond. What Lee did next would in large measure depend upon McClellan.

Although Lee did not know it, he had whipped McClellan. No longer was Richmond in danger. The ferocity and violence of the attacks on Days Two and Three, at Mechanicsburg and Gaines's Mill, had broken McClellan's spirit. However backward in terms of technology and organization, Lee's army had proven that it could fight. The Federal army had proven that it could fight equally well if McClellan would allow it, but he would not, because there was no fire in his belly.

McClellan seemed not to grasp the fact that his army was superior in the sinews of war—engineering, mapping, communications, logistics, transportation, artillery, and staff organization—and that his infantry was as well led and with equivalent fighting skills. McClellan calculated the relative power between the armies solely by head count. His Pinkerton agents had readily convinced him that Lee outnumbered him two to one.* Lee had to have unlimited manpower, reasoned McClellan, because he had attacked with such abandon and disregard for casualties.

McClellan decided on the night of June 27–28 to withdraw his army from Richmond to the protection of the navy's gunboats on the James. His engineers recommended Harrison's Landing, a river plantation fifteen miles south of his position at the time. To get the army there they planned either to build or to improve roads and bridges across the marshland. The wagon trains began rumbling toward the James before daybreak. Such a withdrawal was an enormous risk if Lee pursued the vulnerable retreating columns.

Lee had not dispatched his cavalry to reconnoiter, and because the forests and rivers screened McClellan's movements, Lee issued no orders for pursuit during Day Four. Only the isolated divisions of John B. Magruder and Ben-

---

* Generals got their intelligence from many sources. McClellan depended on the Pinkerton private detective agency, which one might even suspect was a double agent for the Confederacy. Although field generals usually overestimated enemy strength, McClellan was an extreme example.

jamin Huger were near the Army of the Potomac south of the Chickahominy. Expecting a massive attack from McClellan, the two Confederate generals hunkered down, unaware of the Federal withdrawal. They would undertake a belated pursuit on the morning of Day Five.

While Lee idled, Federal forces worked furiously. As the Federal navy moved its gunboats to the James River, McClellan's engineers sited emplacements for artillery batteries around Harrison's Landing; his quartermasters transferred stores from White House and all points north of the Chickahominy; and his engineers surveyed routes for moving the wagon trains south. White Oak Swamp was a big obstacle, and to span it the efficient Federal engineers had built a corduroy road that would move heavy traffic when the time came. Thanks to their comprehensive topographical survey of the countryside, McClellan's staff already had planned the marching routes for each corps, and they knew the best terrain for placing the artillery and infantry.

DAY FIVE, JUNE 29: THE PURSUIT

Finally aware of McClellan's withdrawal in the morning, Lee ordered a pursuit that was bungled from the beginning. "At Lee's temporary headquarters there was the same 'fog of war' that somehow had prevailed from the beginning of the campaign," wrote Freeman. "Few couriers came and those few brought little news. Either the majority of the division commanders did not appreciate the necessity of keeping G.H.Q. informed, or else each of them was acting as if he were exercising independent command, and under no necessity of coordinating his movements with the others." At nightfall some skirmishing went back and forth, but the Army of the Potomac was still well ahead of its thrashing pursuers. "The day's operations," wrote Freeman, "had been a failure, not to say a fiasco."

Nonetheless, Lee hoped that White Oak Swamp would so impede the Federal army that he could come to grips with it on Day Six. Foremost in his mind was the need to prevent McClellan from reaching the James River and the protection of the gunboats. That evening Lee issued yet another set of orders that were simple in concept. Each division was to march down one of five specified roads. As the roads converged, so too would the Confederate divisions converge on the retreating Federal columns.

DAY SIX, JUNE 30: FRAYSER'S FARM

Not one aspect of Lee's plan was executed.

Major General Theophilus H. Holmes, a cautious, chivalrous West Pointer from the old army, was the southernmost division commander. Lee had ordered him to intercept the columns of Federal wagons and troops headed for Harrison's Landing via Malvern Hill, the high ground interposed between White Oak Swamp and the James River. Holmes advanced to a junction of two roads on the west side of Malvern Hill, and there he waited for the enemy to appear.

In late afternoon an engineer officer invited Holmes's attention to the Federal forces passing unmolested by his front. Holmes carefully moved forward a few miles, where Lee found him and suggested that he attack the enemy. Holmes decided that artillery alone was sufficient. He moved closer to the hill, wheeled his batteries into place, and his guns began firing.

A Federal signal officer on the crest of Malvern Hill spotted Holmes's positions and reckoned that the Confederates were within range of the gunboats. He wagged his semaphore flags to alert the army signal officers in the mast tops afloat. "Come on and shell the enemy," he signaled, and the gunboats chugged toward shore. Further instructions followed. "Fire one mile to the right." "Good shot." "Fire low and into the woods near the shore." (This was probably the first instance of indirect naval gunfire support controlled by spotters ashore. It would not again be revived until the amphibious campaigns of the Second World War.) Field batteries on Malvern Hill also opened on the Confederate positions; signal officers spotted their fire as well, with red signal flags for artillery instructions and white flags for general service. The Confederate batteries quit firing and Holmes retreated, allowing the Federal troops to resume their passage undisturbed.

Huger's role was to march down the Charles City road from Richmond and intercept the Federal columns exiting White Oak Swamp. As Huger was closest to the Federal troops, Lee assumed that he would be the first to attack. His firing would be a signal for the other converging divisions to attack as well. Lee did not know that Federal engineers had felled trees across the road, compelling Huger to hack his way through them. Toward evening the Confederate column caught up to the Federal engineers, still swinging their axes, and, Huger reported, his troops drove them off. As a consequence of the delay, Huger never made the signal to start the converging attack.

Magruder's task—explained to him by Lee personally—was to withdraw his division from the Richmond trenches, march to the rear, and then act as a general reserve once the converging divisions began their attack somewhere south of White Oak Swamp. Magruder marched up one road and down another and came to rest somewhere in the rear to await orders. Late in the day Longstreet ordered Magruder to support Holmes on River Road. As Magruder had no map and only a vague notion as to Holmes's location, his columns got lost and marched randomly until darkness.

Lee had met Jackson early in the morning and explained that his Shenandoah Valley army, together with Whiting and D. H. Hill, were to cross a bridge over White Oak Swamp and attack the enemy in the rear. Advancing lethargically, Jackson allowed the withdrawing enemy time to clear the swamp and the bridge, which the Federal engineers then had the foresight to destroy, stranding Jackson's infantry. The action was confined to an exchange of artillery fire.

Lee was desperate. Jackson was not going to cross the swamp; Huger, Magruder, and Holmes were disengaged. Davis was at his elbow, another damnable distraction. The time was five o'clock, and McClellan was slipping away from him. Lee resignedly ordered his only near-at-hand troops (those of Longstreet and A. P. Hill) to attack at a place called Frayser's Farm.

It is charitable to call this an attack at all, for the term implies some sense of orderly maneuvering, a plan perhaps, some measure of coordination by a commanding general. Such was not the case on the evening of Day Six. Let us call it instead a massive free-for-all, a melee of grand proportions in the shadows of the hot setting sun.

Barlow and his little regiment rushed to the sound of the guns, a maelstrom sucking in troops of both sides. As the light faded, the Federal troops fired on one another, and in the confusion Barlow's regiment separated from its brigade. Looking for orders, Barlow found a brigadier general who told him to charge across a field.

It was almost dark. Smoke obscured his vision still further. Barlow ordered his 230 survivors to their feet, and they marched into the gloom with fixed bayonets. Enemy soldiers dimly seen disappeared into the murk, leaving behind their regimental banner. Once on the field, Barlow wheeled the regiment toward the woods on the far side.

"What regiment is that?" demanded a voice from the woods.

"Every heart stood still," a company officer remembered. "Who would answer? And what would he say? To my astonishment and dismay one of our men piped out, 'Sixty-first New York!' "

"Throw down your arms or you are all dead men," said the voice from the woods.

"Open fire!" roared Barlow.

Again his men stood to fire, unprotected in the field, as Barlow had taught them to do. Confederate and Federal soldier alike fired at gun flashes that became in turn new targets. Barlow's men dropped dead and wounded around him; his regiment was near annihilation. Unwilling to withdraw without orders, Barlow sent a staff officer for reinforcements, who returned to report that none were available. Then came a savior, Captain Nelson A. Miles of the brigade staff, looking for Barlow to try to help. Miles returned with the Eighty-first Pennsylvania, and Barlow took command of both regiments. Finally ordered to withdraw, Barlow had to leave his wounded, including six of his eight remaining field officers. One had a shattered leg that would have to be amputated.

"Colonel Barlow came to me," the field officer later wrote, "when the fighting was over, and showed all the tenderness of a brother, letting me see a side of his nature that I had never known anything about before. He deplored the fact that there was no way by which he could have me carried off and kept within our lines. And so, after having me moved to the side of the road, and after my friends had come and talked to me and bade me good-bye, that splendid little regiment marched away about two o'clock in the morning, and left me to reach home, nearly dead, after about twenty-four days, by the way of Libby prison."

Barlow took consolidated command of his regiment and two others, and he prepared to hold the parapets with bayonets because his ammunition was expended. But no one attacked, and the men slept fitfully.

DAY SEVEN, JULY 1: MALVERN HILL

Barlow awakened his men in the darkness. With whispered orders they silently withdrew, the last of the rear guard. They marched rapidly, their throats dry, their canteens empty. Barlow walked with his men. "Billy," his steady old bay, had been shot dead. In the morning twilight Malvern Hill loomed before them. They ascended the slope to the plateau, threw themselves on the ground, and slept again. Troops and horses were everywhere about them. They were once again with the Army of the Potomac, and faithful Charles Fuller of the Sixty-first New York desperately hoped that the fighting was finally over.

Lee surveyed what he could dimly see of Malvern Hill. Federal artillery stood hub to hub on the higher elevations, with clear fields of fire over the sloping terrain below. Colonel Henry J. Hunt, chief of artillery for the Army of the Potomac, had supervised the placement of his weapons. Hunt was regular army and had written the book on artillery tactics and employment. Tactical command fell to Porter, who had worked closely with the engineers to station the infantry behind barricades of earth and felled trees. McClellan would come and go between Malvern Hill and the gunboats.

A flanking attack was impossible. To Lee's right the terrain was too steep to scale, and Federal gunboats could saturate any attacks from that direction. Cliffs and creek beds to Lee's left were equally inaccessible. The only way to the top of the hill was up the open slopes facing to the north, where the Federal guns waited. "Had the Union engineers searched the whole countryside below Richmond," wrote Freeman, "they could not have found ground more ideally set for the slaughter of an attacking army."

Slaughter it would be. Unaccustomed to a grueling field campaign, Lee had shot his bolt by Day Seven. He had but a slight understanding of conditions on Malvern Hill—trees in the valley limited his field of vision, and he made no attempt to reconnoiter the terrain. As his worn-out soldiers shuffled past him and his staff hovered uselessly nearby, Lee experienced Day Seven as a blur of noise and motion.

Having driven McClellan from Richmond to the James River, Lee had accomplished all he had set out to do. But the Army of the Potomac had not broken, and it would not break now under the protective umbrella of the gunboats. Large portions of Lee's army were too battered for further combat, and its organizational defects had proven grievous beyond redemption. There was every reason to say, "Stop. We shall go no further," but Lee gave no such order.

And so it would go on. Jackson, Magruder, and Huger had missed the earlier combat. (Three of Jackson's four brigades had no more than skirmished at Gaines's Mill and had suffered perhaps a hundred casualties.) Today they would fight. The troops of Longstreet and A. P. Hill had been so badly savaged the day before at Frayser's Farm that Lee put them in reserve. As Longstreet was handy, Lee seconded him as his acting chief of staff, someone to lean on in his state of fatigue.

The soldiers of Jackson, Magruder, and Huger congested the sole road that led to the base of Malvern Hill. The name of the road itself was confusing; some said Quaker Road and others said Willis Church. A second road that led away from Malvern Hill was also called Quaker Road. Local guides took Magruder down the latter. Arguments from Longstreet and others ultimately convinced Magruder to countermarch.

Longstreet came to the weary Lee with a recommendation: He had found elevated sites where the Confederate artillery could suppress the Federal artillery as a prelude to the infantry attack. Magruder's artillery would fire from the right, Jackson's from the left, and together they would pour a cross fire into the Federal lines. Perhaps the reserve artillery could be brought into play. Lee assented, and Longstreet hustled off to execute his plan.

Longstreet's plan to use artillery was impossible to execute, in large measure because Lee had not foreseen a need for artillery in the campaign. A month earlier Lee had advised the secretary of war that he had all the artillery he needed and recommended that light, mobile artillery batteries then being organized be "changed to some other branch of the service, where the horses and men could be used to greater advantage." As Lee had limited knowledge about artillery, it was his additional misfortune to be poorly served by his chief of artillery, Brigadier General William N. Pendleton, a likable man and an intimate of Lee. A West Point graduate, Pendleton had been an Episcopal priest for twenty-four years. His ineptness as chief of artillery in the Army of Northern Virginia was as profound as the competence of his opposite number in the Army of the Potomac, Henry Hunt.

The disparity between the artillery arms was clear at Malvern Hill. Pendleton was out of touch. Even had he known that Lee wanted the reserve artillery brought forward, the few roads were so clogged that movement would have been impossible. Divisional artillery near at hand required extraordinary effort. Magruder's artillery on the right was dragged through swamps, and as the individual batteries heaved into sight, the massed Federal guns smothered each in turn. On the left, Jackson's artillery commander was sick; the battery commanders went it alone, uncovered their weapons, and the long-range Federal cannon summarily crushed them. D. H. Hill had sent his batteries to the rear for want of ammunition.

A plan had to be devised to determine when the Confederate artillery had done its (impossible) job and a signal given to begin the infantry assault. Such an assessment and such a signal was wholly Lee's responsibility, wholly his obligation to the troops who had to assault the hill, and wholly his prerogative as commanding general of the army in the field. Lee, however, delegated his responsibility to a brigadier general named Lewis A. Armistead, commanding a brigade on the right wing of the Confederate line. Armistead was to observe the effect of the artillery fire, and when in his judgment it had sufficiently weakened the Federal line, his brigade was to attack with a yell. When the other commanders along the length and breadth of the line heard the yell, they too were to attack. Lee would be a bystander.

Couriers dashed off on plunging horses into the bewildering forests to try to deliver the orders. Huger's brigades struggled into position, uncertain as to whether they were to obey Huger or Magruder. Lee had restrained the fuming Huger, while Magruder, having returned from his misadventure down the wrong Quaker Road, hustled into position. Hence no one commanded the right wing, where the attack was to originate.

Lee's plan was overtaken by events by midafternoon. Word reached Lee that the Federal forces were withdrawing and that Armistead was advancing on the right wing. This information was false. The Federal troops were not retreating; Armistead was stalled and going nowhere. But Lee wanted to believe that his enemy was retreating, and that now was the time for everyone to attack. Orders were issued, and couriers again rushed off to uncertain destinations.

Magruder got the order at about four o'clock. He was one of the few generals who obeyed Lee to the letter, even when the letter rested upon fallacies and wholesale ignorance of conditions. Fifteen thousand of his soldiers advanced on the right wing through hellish terrain into the teeth of the Federal artillery. The result was carnage. To the rear Lee ordered more and yet more regiments into the attack, and, like all that had gone before, they too were consumed. Jackson on the left wing remained disengaged, consistent with his apathy throughout the Seven Days.

Barlow now commanded the consolidated fragments of the Sixty-first New York and Eighty-first Pennsylvania regiments.

At midmorning the Puritan's soldiers went into line on the Federal right wing, opposite Jackson's left wing. Intense heat prostrated many. They watched a Confederate battery unlimber in full view, it loosed some shells in their direction, and then their own artillery smashed it down. One of Barlow's captains distributed ammunition, instructing the soldiers to take additional rounds in their knapsacks. Another major battle seemed imminent.

One of the regiment's misfits approached Barlow, pleading sickness and begging permission to go to the rear. Fuller always remembered what came next, because it was so typically Barlow. "The Colonel was not in an amiable frame of mind," wrote Fuller in his memoirs.

> He was on foot, old "Billy" had been killed the night before, and he felt like having a dialogue with someone. He asked this man some questions which satisfied him he was a coward. His wrath broke out vehemently. He cursed and swore at him and called him a variety of unpleasant and detestable things and then he began to punch him with his fist wherever he could hit.

Finally he partly turned him around, and gave him a hearty kick in the stern and said: "Damn you, get away from here! You're not fit to be with my brave men." The fellow departed as fast as his short legs would carry him. I knew of no other man presenting an excuse or asking for leave of absence that day. I believe every man of us preferred to meet the rebels rather than the vocal scorn and denunciation of Barlow. I believe he did not know what personal, bodily fear was, and he had no consideration for a coward.

As Jackson did not release his infantry against the Federal right wing, Barlow and his troops were initially unengaged, leaving them available to reinforce the center of the Federal line when Magruder and D. H. Hill began their attacks in late afternoon. The Confederate artillery fire was more intense than is generally credited, or at least it seemed so to Barlow's men, who had to endure it. By late afternoon they had moved to the rear of the massed artillery that dominated the northern slope, near a house and barn owned by a farmer named West. A soldier of an adjacent regiment remembered that Barlow seemed to be coolly maneuvering the entire brigade. Hill's division was a mile away, where its commander was fretting about the preemptory order to attack on Armistead's yell.

Artillery tactics had changed extensively since the start of the war. Cannon once outranged the smoothbore muskets, permitting mobile batteries to unlimber close to enemy infantry without the fear of small arms fire. The rifled musket changed everything. It had become so accurate and its range had so increased that infantry could hit the exposed gunners serving their pieces on the front line. For the artillerymen to survive, it had become common practice in both armies for one or more infantry regiments to protect their artillery batteries from enemy infantry. Barlow and his men got the job. The infantry hated such an assignment because they got a good share of the counterbattery fire.

Hunt had positioned the Federal artillery on the crest of Malvern Hill, a position dominating the open fields of the northern slope, a gradually rising avenue of approach that funneled Hill's infantry into a front perhaps 1,200 yards wide, upon which the barrels of the artillery converged. The artillery line intersected two conspicuous sets of farm buildings, on the left what was known as the Crew house, and on the right a quarter mile distant, the West house. Both houses were a conspicuous point of aim for those few Confederate batteries resolute enough to take on Hunt's ordnance. As long as the Confederates could fire, Barlow and his men took their barrage on the chin.

It was terrible to endure. "The fragments of the exploded shells came showering down upon and about us," Fuller later wrote. "Every now and then along the supporting line a man was knocked out, . . . a Hamilton boy, and another lying beside him had their brains knocked out by these shell fragments. They were but a few feet from me and I saw the whole bloody business."

One of Barlow's captains was blown to the ground and yelled piteously for help. Barlow ordered the quivering body taken to the rear, where the officer miraculously revived, as only his coattails had been hit. When the man shambled back to the front line, Barlow was astonished. "Men," cried Barlow, "give Captain Broady three cheers. He's a brave man." The ragged line cheered with gusto, then ducked as more rounds zeroed in. Another order moved the regiment nearer yet to the West house. "We again lay down," Fuller remembered. "The enemy were shelling these buildings at a terrific rate; the rattle and crash of the shells into that woodwork made the hair fairly stand on end."

Gordon now commanded Rodes's brigade in the absence of its wounded brigadier. Under orders from D. H. Hill, the Cavalier had moved forward trying to join the Confederate batteries that blasted away at the West house. Working his way through dense woods, he discovered them still firing and positioned his own troops behind the cannon. That was a mistake, for the Federal artillery fire smashed into his troops as well as the Confederate battery. Gordon pulled his troops clear of the doomed battery and watched it get splintered. The Federal artillery, in plain view, seemed untouched and indomitable. Next he saw Federal soldiers, Barlow's soldiers, taking position on the flank of the artillery line, standing erect, waiting for the Confederate infantry charge whenever it might come.

When Magruder on his right began his disjointed attack in late afternoon, Hill assumed that Armistead had kicked off the action, obliging him to follow suit. As his brigades headed up the slope, they one by one peeled off, stopped, and then fell away from the killing ground. Hill was blunt about the disintegration. One brigade "retreated in disorder," another was "streaming to the rear," a third was "suffering heavily and effecting little." "[I]t was not war—it was murder," he later wrote. Gordon and his brigade alone kept moving forward.

Hill had told Gordon to take the Federal batteries, promising support on both flanks as he ascended the slopes. "I made the advance," Gordon later wrote, "but the supports did not come. Indeed, with the exception of one other brigade, which was knocked to pieces in a few minutes, no troops came into view." Gordon pressed on across the plain as shell and shot tore his brigade to pieces, while he seemed invulnerable in their midst. Finally the remnants took shelter in woods, a place of temporary safety as the Federal artillery was aiming over and beyond them.

Gordon ordered his men to fire at Barlow's standing lines of infantry perhaps a hundred yards away, and it looked to the Federal troops as if Gordon's officers were preparing to attack. Barlow's infantry poured in fire with coordinated volleys. As one rank fired, the other reloaded, so that the rifle fire was massed and continuous. Eventually Barlow ordered them to fire at will. The gun barrels got so hot that the soldiers could hardly aim or ram their rounds through the black powder residue.

Gordon's men kept firing. Again Nelson Miles came to Barlow, then returned with a battery that blasted into Gordon's troops at the edge of the woods. "Here the canister and musketry mowed down my already thinned ranks so rapidly," Gordon later reported, "that it became impossible to advance without support; and had it been possible to reach the batteries, I have high authority to back my own judgment that it would have been at the sacrifice of the entire command."

Gordon expected Barlow's infantry momentarily to overwhelm his remaining soldiers. He looked to his rear for reinforcements. Nothing. Abandoned and forsaken, he could neither go forward nor retreat. Even raising his head could be fatal. His uniform shredded, his ears ringing, dirt and gravel embedded in his skin, Gordon hugged the ground to wait for darkness.

As darkness came, Barlow's regiment ran out of ammunition. Under such circumstances a conventional commander would have withdrawn, but Barlow held fast and ordered fixed bayonets. Out of the darkness came the sound of movement, then the Rebel yell. Barlow's men leaped to their feet, and an adjacent regiment fired the last of its ammunition. The Confederate soldiers turned away. Barlow afterward went along the line with water for his wounded, and he found Gordon's soldiers among his own, "so near had they got to us in their charge." "The batteries were not taken," Gordon later reported, "but, without detracting anything from the action of other troops, justice to these men compels me to say that the dead of this brigade marked a line nearer the batteries than any other."

The shooting finally stopped. Groans and cries rent the darkness. Slowly Gordon withdrew his shivering survivors down the hill, stumbling over bodies until they reached the safety of the rear area. Barlow and his men lay quietly, enveloped in fatigue. Thunder and lightning broke above them, and rain lashed them as they lay.

EPILOGUE: JULY 2

The next morning Moxley Sorrel wandered on the slopes of Malvern Hill, pausing when he heard groans from within a farmer's shanty. Opening the door, he saw heaped bodies, among them brigade commander Richard Ewell. Sorrel knew and admired Ewell, a distant relative with a speech impediment, an old army man of bravery and skill, but now doubled up on the floor, hands covering his head. "Raising himself up," Sorrel wrote, "he instantly recognized me, and lisped out, 'Mather Thorrel, can you tell me why we had five hundred men killed dead on the field yesterday?' That was all; the soul of the brave General was fit to burst for the awful and useless sacrifice. It was a fearful blunder somewhere and has not yet been boldly and clearly lighted up."

9

THE SEVEN DAYS IN
RETROSPECT

———◆◆———

McClellan abandoned Malvern Hill during the night and occupied Harrison's Landing on the James River. Rain fell, as it always seems to do in any age following a battle, a motif of final agony and suffering. The Army of the Potomac was close to cracking.

Lee for a time suspended throwing soldiers into the guns. McClellan retreated no further. Federal warships protected the Army of the Potomac, and riverboats provided unlimited logistical support. Lee conceded that he could do nothing more. A single sentence pronounced his decision in a letter to Davis on July 9: "I have caused the army to fall back to a position higher up the river, in order to meet the enemy should he again advance on Richmond, leaving the cavalry to watch his movements below." Lee said nothing else about the campaign until his official report nine months later.

"It is wonderful how I have escaped without a wound," Barlow wrote to Almira just afterward. "I had a ball through my coat which is the only mark upon me. (I just heard one of the men say outside as I am writing 'The Col. will be shot in the next fight and then every man will go for himself.')" Years later he and Fuller met at a veterans' reunion. Fuller remarked, "I never went into battle without an effort of my will, and always expected to be wounded or killed." In his quiet way Barlow responded, "I never felt so. I never had an impression I was to be hurt." Gordon felt much the same. "I was never in a battle," he later wrote, "without realizing that every battle might be my last; but I never had a presentiment of certain death at a given time or in a particular battle."

Though both had been civilians just months before, Barlow and Gordon proved dynamic leaders in battle. Their voices moved men. Gordon was an orator. Slim and erect on his mount, he invoked God, country, and honor as the prelude to every battle. Barlow, in contrast, hated public speaking per se. At the end of the war a Harvard professor asked him to speak in Cambridge, and he desperately begged off. "Sometime - when I have something to say to the world I have faith that the gift will come," he wrote, "but now I have it not . . . the thought of a *speech* is dreadful to me. I have never yet put myself where it would be expected of me & I cannot & will not do it." But his voice could lash and command troops.

As neither Gordon nor Barlow experienced fear in combat, they expected their soldiers to behave as they did, and their powerful moral authority conditioned their men to act with discipline. But casualties were severe. Once engaged, their men advanced in formation, stood erectly at point-blank range, and blasted away. This way of fighting killed men in droves. In time Barlow would become a master at skirmishing and using cover. Gordon, however, would forever maneuver with his men fully exposed.

Gordon's Sixth Alabama had started with 600 men. After Seven Pines, 232 remained; after the Seven Days, 169. Of the 2,200 men who had started with Rodes's Brigade, 636 emerged still able to fight. Half its numbers were lost at Seven Pines and at Gaines's Mill. Gordon led the thousand remaining in the brigade at Malvern Hill, with 40 percent casualties. Gordon's only quarrel was that he had not been supported, that his brigade alone had closed with the enemy and had been left in extremis. He blamed no one by name, but he wanted it understood that he had followed orders to the extent it was humanly possible.

Barlow had started with something over 400 men in the Sixty-first New York. After the Seven Days he was down to 149 men fit for duty. A month later the number had dwindled to 126, the smallest regiment in Sumner's Second Corps. McClellan reviewed the corps and stopped to talk with Barlow. "Our extreme smallness must have struck him," Barlow wrote Almira. "It is very sad to see my Regt. so much reduced. Almost every officer who started with us is gone. I miss them sadly."

That he missed his men was a rare admission of sentiment for Barlow. The postwar Cambridge gathering to which he had been invited was intended as a memorial for the Civil War dead. "I would like exceedingly to come," he wrote, "to look tenderly upon the 'gathering of women', listen to the music, share the enthusiasm, *feel* the tears, which is not given to man to shed. But I know I would be called upon to speak & so I must keep away as I have done from so many similar meetings & been called heartless for doing so. If I could come in a quiet way & look on I would enjoy it & *feel* it."

As Barlow and his tiny regiment waited in the heat and pestilence of the huge Federal encampment by the river, it became obvious that McClellan was going to withdraw from the Peninsula. Sensing that Davis and Lee had prevailed, he wrote bitterly to Almira and Edward, "We shall have to acknowledge the S[outhern] Confederacy in the end."

Hood's combat experience had been brief but intense. His brigade had been like a bomb that, exploding with great destruction, could do its damage but once. After breaking the Federal line at Gaines's Mill in the afternoon of Day Three, his soldier-zealots had disintegrated into knots of hunters pursuing their prey. Such tactics fractured the brigade's cohesion and exhausted its momentum.

Hood had personally exulted in the excitement of combat. Those who saw him remarked how his eyes had glowed, how the battle had visibly transformed him into a terrifying warrior whose fighting spirit enraptured his entire brigade. They had returned with prisoners, cannon, and battle flags, the trophies of war by which Hood measured his success as a leader.

Battle reports flowed in from all echelons of the Army of the Potomac. Judging from their tenor, the army had recovered from its demoralizing retreat and was ready to fight again. Commanders freely admitted mistakes in organization, administration, and tactics, and they advocated remedies. Henry Hunt, the army's artillery genius, described how the frequent mishandling of supporting infantry sometimes interfered with the batteries. Ways had to be devised, he said, to better coordinate the two combat arms. He was, nonetheless, generally satisfied that the artillery had been well managed.

McClellan prepared an extravagant report that exculpated his failed campaign. Its gist was that he had been unable to seize Richmond for two reasons: Lee outnumbered him, and the Lincoln administration withheld troops. The second had some truth to it, but the first was false. Other reports treaded lightly as to McClellan's leadership, reflecting an institutional reluctance to enter disapproval and criticism on the record.

The army's chief engineer, John Barnard, was an exception. The old warrior scorched both the administration and McClellan for bungled opportunities, unwarranted delays, want of initiative, and waffled thinking and reasoning. Barnard's report was the antithesis, the stinging rebuttal, to the special pleading and equivocation of McClellan's report. But it has rarely been cited by historians and has not been published intact beyond volume 11 of the *Official Records*.

The Confederate reports were fewer and less complete. Casualties were always difficult to assess. Six weeks after the Seven Days campaign, Lee's medical director lamented the lack of data because of incomplete or missing reports, particularly from Jackson, who edited his reports interminably, disregarding the passage of time.

The Confederate reports, like Jackson's, were chiefly circumspect, lacking analyses and recommendations for improvement. Discretion prevailed. If a brigade, for example, had faltered, neither the brigade nor its commander would customarily be identified. An assertion that an officer had wavered was tantamount to a glove across the face. At the least a blizzard of charges and accusations would erupt, with demands for courts of inquiry and hearings before higher authorities. At the worst, a duel.

Gordon spoke glibly of one such *affaire d'honneur* in his memoirs. In the confusion during the Seven Days, he recalled, there were "many amusing mistakes as to identity, and some altercations between officers which were not so amusing and not altogether complimentary. . . . Early the next morning a challenge was sent, but the officer who had given the offence was in a playful mood when the challenge reached him; so, instead of accepting it, or answering it in the formal style required by the dueling code, he replied in about these words: 'I did not volunteer to fight you or any other Confederate, but if you and your men will do better in the next battle I will take back all I said to you last night.'

"[H]ow easy it was," Gordon concluded, "to get up a fight in the sixties, if one were so disposed, either in a general mêlée with the blue-coated lines, or single-handed with a gray-clad comrade." Because of this Southern tradition, neither Lee, with his aversion to controversy, nor any temperate general officer would challenge the performance of a colleague if it could be avoided.*

D. H. Hill was the only general of stature who criticized and condemned his brethren. He rendered things as they were—even the blasphemy that the Confederate losses had been the greater. "The battle at Malvern Hill might have been a complete and glorious success," Hill wrote. "So far as I can learn none of our troops drew trigger, except McLaws' division, mine, and a portion of Huger's. Notwithstanding the tremendous odds against us and the blundering management of the battle we inflicted heavy loss upon the Yankees."

Two weeks after Malvern Hill, Davis assigned Hill to a departmental command in North Carolina. Hill's department extended to the south side of the James, and he had the nominal responsibility of watching McClellan's movements. In August, McClellan skillfully extracted his army from Harrison's Landing with interference neither from Lee nor Hill. Both generals looked foolish, but Lee exploited the opportunity to dispose of Hill. In a letter to Davis, Lee wrote, "This induces me to say what I have had on my mind for some time. I feel General Hill is not entirely equal to his present position. An excellent executive officer, he does not appear to have much administrative ability. Left to himself, he seems embarrassed and backward to act."

And so D. H. Hill, whose initiative had been unmatched, was for want of initiative officially disgraced and dismissed into obscurity. Circumstances later in the year would require his temporary recall, but he would never again be numbered among Lee's lieutenants.

With neither apology nor explanation for nine months of silence since the Seven Days, Lee submitted his official report to Davis on March 6, 1863. His explanations as to why his plans had failed to materialize were enigmatic. When Jackson did not arrive to turn the flank at Mechanicsville, it was a "consequence of unavoidable delays." When Jackson again failed to attack at Gaines's Mill, it was because he had been "delayed by the length of [his] march and the obstacles he encountered." J. E. B. Stuart's cavalry had been unengaged during the Seven Days "[o]wing to the nature of the country." The Battle of Frayser's Farm would have been a more decided victory

---

* This canon would be disregarded later in the war when disasters could no longer be disguised as victories. Bragg and Hood would be among the most notorious of the senior generals who would blame others for the calamities of a campaign.

"[c]ould the other commands have co-operated in the action." The nature of the terrain at Malvern Hill had disrupted what would have been a coordinated attack.

"Under ordinary circumstances the Federal Army should have been destroyed," Lee concluded. "Its escape was due to the causes [the unmapped and hazardous terrain] already stated." His non sequitur meant that nothing needed to be fixed. Not even better maps. Lee considered his strategy and tactics as perfectly sound, having failed only because conditions were not as he had wished them to be. In reality, McClellan had survived in great measure because of inept leadership within the Confederate high command, inferior staffs, faulty tactics, and mediocre matériel. Perhaps more could not be expected of a Confederate army so large, so immature, and so captive of its culture.

By the time Lee wrote his report, he well knew what Hill had said about "blundering management of the battle." That had stung. It could not be left unanswered, and Lee included a belated riposte. "To the officers commanding divisions and brigades belongs the credit [and by implication discredit] for the management of their troops in action. The extent of the fields of battle, the nature of the ground, and the denseness of the forests rendered more than general directions impracticable." In other words, Lee had removed himself from the battlefield. The plan had been his. The execution of his plan, for better or worse, had not been his responsibility.

The outcome of the Seven Days was, of course, not entirely dependent on what the Confederate army did wrong. The Army of the Potomac did many things right, making it an army of such immense power that Lee could never destroy it. Lee would knock it about, but it would always rebound. It would win in the end because it had the military sinews—especially engineering—that the Army of Northern Virginia never would have.

In contrast, the Confederate engineers, such as they were, could not cope with the impediments thrown their way by the Federal engineers. Jackson, for example, had frittered away an entire day trying to repair the Grapevine Bridge across the Chickahominy. The Federal engineers felled trees to block a road, and Huger's engineers had been unable to remove the obstacles. How ironical that Lee, after decades as an engineer, would time and again be frustrated by the engineers of his enemy.

Combined Federal operations were another aspect of modern warfare that would batter Lee and his army. The Federal army and navy worked well together, not only against Lee but also on the coast and on the western rivers. Whenever a Federal army worked within the range of naval gunfire, its soldiers found safety. The Army of the Potomac would always have secure lines of communication and excellent logistical support thanks to the navy's control of the rivers. With the loss of the Portsmouth shipyard, the Confederacy was impotent afloat.

Lee recognized that he had to deal with these powerful advantages and do better next time. With its esprit de corps the infantry would continue to be the queen of battle, the very essence of his army, although Lee would reorganize its divisions into corps for better command and control. Cavalry would be largely employed in raids, skirmishing, and other detached operations, making it an arm without substance on the battlefield. Artillery would undergo incremental improvements but would remain inferior to its Federal counterpart. Engineering, cartography, communications, intelligence, and logistical support would persist in being consistently mediocre.

Staff organizations—including his own—were unchanged, and Lee increasingly did more of the staff work himself. He was planning for the short haul, trying to win the war by doing what Confederate soldiers did best, and not attempting long-term improvements that would require time and resources he did not choose to commit.

A recurring theme in most analyses of Lee's leadership is that his lieutenants too often did not do what he wanted done. If only they had obeyed his orders, goes the argument, if they had carried out his plan, had conformed to his intentions, the Army of Northern Virginia would have won more, if not most, of its battles. It is true that in many instances his generals were disobedient, although to an extent because of shortcomings in Lee's style of leadership.

Lee's lieutenants were typically proud, independent, fractious, egotistical, confrontational, and thin-skinned—attributes of fighters, sure enough, but pure hell to deal with when Lee needed conformity and cooperation. All his life, Lee had avoided confrontation. He was a mediator, a conciliator, instinctively deferential. It was Lee's way to speak in quiet, civil tones, to use the self-deprecating understatement, to employ circumlocution to avoid unpleasantness.

In his new role Lee was at a loss in disciplining a stubborn general who crossed him or in discarding a stupid general without hurting his feelings. At times he may have wanted to throttle Jackson or Stuart, but instinctively he handled them gently, suppressing his anger and keeping a firm hold on his self-control. Such problems were not confined solely to Lee, for not one general of full rank achieved an ascendancy over his subordinates.

Lee was sometimes able to use his special relationship with Davis to get the generals he wanted and to slough off those he did not want. Magruder, for example, got sent to the far west, and Huger was similarly relieved of duty within the Army of Northern Virginia. On the other hand, Davis was no great judge of character and would foist generals upon Lee whom Lee would otherwise have rejected. Yet Lee would not, could not, change his style of leadership, not then, not ever. He was who he was.

1 0

SECOND MANASSAS

Lee was bold and bloodthirsty when striking.
Confederate general Stephen D. Lee in a postwar letter

The two great armies reposed, McClellan and the Army of the Potomac at Harrison's Landing, Lee and the Army of Northern Virginia twenty miles away at Richmond. As both armies recuperated and refitted, Lee pondered the future. So long as McClellan remained nearby, Lee's army had to remain in Richmond. McClellan's army was so well protected by the warships and so well supplied by the river steamers that he could threaten Richmond indefinitely. Lee could never hope to attack him under the circumstances.

But neither government could tolerate the prolonged immobilization of its armies. Fresh initiatives were inevitable. The Federal government formed a new army in northern Virginia under John Pope, who had performed credibly in the western theater and had been summoned east. He now commanded the Army of Virginia, a conglomeration of once scattered independent corps and divisions. Pope spoke rashly of whipping the Confederate army and devastating and pillaging the people and property of Virginia. Lee had to find a way to deal with him, but as Davis had the last word on what brigades went where, Lee was constrained in the movement and deployment of his army.

Lincoln and Davis thought alike in the defense of their capitals, protecting them with permanent garrisons while simultaneously threatening the enemy's capital. Davis would never have enough troops to do both; Lincoln would have enough, though not an unlimited number. Lee's proposed remedy substituted trenches for men: tougher fortifications required fewer soldiers to defend Richmond, releasing more men for distant service.

Pope's Army of Virginia did not immediately threaten Richmond, but by July 12 it was within striking distance of Gordonsville, a railroad terminus through which passed the Virginia Central Railroad, an east-west trunk line that connected Richmond with the Shenandoah Valley. If Pope severed it, the valley and its abundant resources would be isolated from Richmond and Lee's army. Lee had to defend the railroad.

Lee also had a personal motive. He despised Pope for his threats, for the Aristocrat still held to an idea of warfare constrained by chivalry and honor. To Lee, civilian property and lives were exempt from confiscation and harassment. Having proclaimed that he had taken the sword against his government to protect the people of Virginia, Lee was honor bound to act against Pope.

But Lee could not stem the growing brutality of the war. Raids, reprisals, spying, assassinations, and sabotage were common in border states and occupied territories, where civilians made war on one another and against uniformed troops. Generals on both sides retaliated harshly, following their own rules. Cabinet officials—both in Richmond and in Washington—encouraged them by loudly condemning as traitors all those who would not pledge allegiance to their respective governments. While Pope reflected the war as it was, he rankled Lee. "I want Pope to be suppressed," Lee told Jackson. "The course indicated in his orders . . . cannot be permitted and will lead to retaliation on our part. You had better notify him the first opportunity."

The need to deal with Pope had arisen by mid-July, too brief a time to mend the combat readiness of Lee's army. The officers and men he had squandered in the Seven Days were irreplaceable. Sorting out the surviving combat leaders had to be done swiftly. The seven division commanders who had fought in the Seven Days had been independent warlords, defying Lee's directives and unwilling to cooperate. Some, impatient for glory, had recklessly attacked; others, from sloth or sulking, had avoided battle.

As contending with such unruly people was distasteful, Lee's remedy was to create corps commanders to do it for him. He would appoint two or perhaps three of them, people he trusted, and they could deal with the other fractious generals. He would remain above the fray, maneuvering his forces into the most advantageous position for fighting the enemy, then passing responsibility for the outcome to the corps commanders. "[W]ith that I have done my duty," Lee told a German observer. "As soon as I order the troops forward into battle, I lay the fate of my army in the hands of God." Lee's doctrine would prove impossible to carry out. As he would discover, the commander of an engaged field army could not remain aloof from unfolding developments.

The Confederate Congress had authorized neither the organization of corps (two or more divisions comprised a corps) nor the commensurate rank of lieutenant general, so Lee acted without legislation, making Jackson and Longstreet de facto corps commanders while retaining their rank of major general. Command of their respective divisions quietly passed to the senior brigade commanders.

The two divisions commanded by the Generals Hill were immobilized for political reasons. In late July, of course, Lee had gotten Davis to transfer D. H. Hill to a district outside his jurisdiction. The banishment backfired when legislative problems with the numbers and seniority of major generals prevented naming a replacement. Hill's division languished without a leader.

The other loss was incongruous yet typical of the Southern command system. It began when Longstreet resented the praise lavished on A. P. Hill by a Richmond newspaper, and Longstreet sent a letter of rebuttal to a rival paper. Hill was so angered that he refused to take orders from Longstreet, who arrested Hill in retaliation. A replacement was unavailable, and Lee would neither lift the arrest nor deploy Hill's division without him. In few other armies could one general arbitrarily arrest another and so immobilize an infantry division in an emergency. (Federal generals had the power to arrest but not as willfully as did the Confederates.)

Lee would now have to provide sustained logistical support for a mobile army maneuvering in the field. Arrangements hitherto had been straightforward, using stores in and near Richmond, and supply trains had arrived unimpeded from other regions. Lee's logistical planning began and ended with the stroke of his pen dispatching an order to Richmond officials, for he had neither the time nor the inclination to get involved, and no one on his minuscule staff was qualified to coordinate logistics.

Logistical support for Lee's army was handicapped by a system of institutional evils. Transportation was the most telling impediment. Food and supplies had to reach the soldiers either by rail or wagon, for the Federal navy controlled the rivers. (Beef on the hoof was the one commodity that provided its own transportation.) The incapacity of the primitive Virginia roads made wagon trains an encumbrance to the fast marching corps, who routinely left behind their cargoes of food and forage. Orders to cook rations for three days were a sure sign that soldiers soon would be fighting and starving.

Railroads therefore were essential for delivering military cargo, but the lines in Virginia were a hodgepodge of seventeen private companies, with track lengths ranging from 8 to 205 miles. The single-track lines had few sidings for passing trains, limiting their carrying capacity. Davis would not allow the government to control the railroads, so they did as they pleased. The companies were competitors, their lines rarely connected, and each was operated to make a profit regardless of wartime emergency. While the owners gave lip service to the war effort, the first priority went to the customer who paid the most, often excluding the government as a consequence.

Choosing not to contest the pervasive indifference and ineptness of civilian authorities, Lee tried to improvise as he went north toward Pope. He remembered northern Virginia as a fertile country and considered it feasible to remain in the region and live off the land indefinitely. "I think I can feed the whole army here if Col Northrop* will give the necessary directions about collecting beef," he wrote Davis, "& if we can secure this country the millers will give us flour. At first there will be difficulties, but they will be softened as we advance & we shall relieve other parts of the country & employ what would be consumed & destroyed by the enemy. The theatre of war will thus be changed for a season at least, unless we are overpowered."

---

* Colonel Lucius B. Northrop was the maladroit commissary general for the Confederate War Department and a terrible liability. Davis kept him in office during most of the war.

Such was the gist of Lee's logistical support plan in the last days before Second Manassas.* It would fail. Hunger, not Federal soldiers, would ultimately halt Lee's army. The empty bellies of his men and horses would sap their combat power and drive Lee into desperate expediencies. The recourse of living off the country might have worked for Napoleon, and it would succeed for Grant at Vicksburg, but often as not it was wishful thinking for the Army of Northern Virginia.

Pope could not be allowed free rein in northern Virginia. Part of Lee's army protecting Richmond had to be detached and sent north. Jackson was the general to do it, for he relished his independence and needed to restore the reputation splattered by his performance during the Seven Days. Accordingly, Lee sent him with two divisions by train to Gordonsville in mid-July 1862. Pope outnumbered Jackson, but Jackson had outsmarted larger Federal forces in the Shenandoah Valley before. He could not repeat his success, however. Within days Jackson wanted reinforcements. Lee persuaded Longstreet to suspend A. P. Hill's arrest and sent Hill on his way with his division.

Major General Henry W. Halleck ended the impasse in late July when he assumed command of all the Federal armies after his successes in the west. He found the situation in Virginia to be intolerable. Lee was operating on interior lines between the widely separated armies of McClellan and Pope. Halleck's instinct was to consolidate, and he ordered McClellan to move north and reinforce Pope. When he saw McClellan evacuating Harrison's Landing, Lee realized the danger to Jackson.

The speed with which Lee and McClellan reinforced Jackson and Pope respectively would govern the outcome of the northern Virginia campaign. It was no contest. Lee was masterful in prying soldiers out of Davis and won the race. McClellan flouted Halleck's orders, and he so obstructed the transfer of his divisions that not one would arrive to assist Pope until it was too late to affect the outcome.

With his army reunited at Gordonsville on August 15, Lee confronted Pope, who had a dangerous and capable army of perhaps 70,000 men some twenty miles up the Orange and Alexandria Railroad line at Cedar Mountain and behind the shallow Rapidan River. Pope was exposed, the Rappahannock River to his rear. His only line of withdrawal across the river was at the railroad bridge at Rappahannock Station. If Confederate cavalry could circle around Pope's forces and destroy the bridge, Lee could pin Pope against the Rappahannock. Haste was essential, as Lee expected McClellan momentarily. He decided to attack three days later, on August 18, and wrote his orders accordingly.

Again Lee had ordered the impossible. His soldiers needed to eat before attacking, but there was no food on hand by the eighteenth; Lee's whimsical

---

* Also known as Second Bull Run.

logistical planning had already hampered operations. The plan to have the cavalry destroy the Rappahannock Station bridge was a fiasco. J. E. B. Stuart's whereabouts were unknown. After Lee postponed the attack, Stuart sheepishly came to Lee's headquarters with the news that he nearly had been captured by Federal cavalry.

Lee rescheduled the assault for August 20, but by then Pope had realized Lee's intentions and withdrew behind the Rappahannock. By the twenty-fourth its waters and steep banks still separated the armies. Lee was losing time, and he knew it. Secure behind the river, Pope daily grew proportionally stronger than Lee.

Lee's thinking for the next six days is hard to fathom. He wrote Davis that he intended to avoid a general engagement through maneuvering. Having said this, Lee maneuvered his army to provoke a general engagement. He ordered Jackson to take three divisions of 23,000 men, circle around Pope, and then cut his communications with Washington on the Orange and Alexandria Railroad. Meanwhile, Longstreet would occupy Pope's attention.

As Lee's instructions were oral and unrecorded, we do not know what he expected Jackson to do afterward or what he expected of Longstreet. Diametrically contradicting the textbooks by dividing his army, already numerically inferior, Lee operated on exposed exterior lines and became even weaker in the face of the enemy. Pope could maneuver on shorter, protected interior lines and could fall upon either Jackson or Longstreet while each was out of supporting distance of the other. It was also certain that the Federal army would react to restore the railroad line. How long, then, was Jackson to hold on? If Jackson stayed on or near the railroad, he could be caught between Pope and reinforcements coming from Washington.

Lee was wagering that Pope would panic and do something stupid which would allow Lee to get away with his audacity. Lee had confounded and intimidated McClellan by being aggressive and unpredictable; perhaps he could do the same to Pope. He would baffle other Federal generals, too, not by genius, but by his readiness to fight by unorthodox rules and to exploit developing opportunities. Winning and losing ultimately became a battle of willpower between Lee and the Federal generals. In the first two years, Lee sometimes won and always survived to fight again. All would change when Grant came east in 1864.

Jackson marched fifty-four miles in two days, redeeming his sloth of the Seven Days. He descended upon the Orange and Alexandria on August 27, well to the rear of Pope's lines. Seizing tons of undefended stores at Manassas Junction, his troops fell ravenously upon the food, for they had only crumbs in their haversacks. Jackson allowed them to gorge for a day. He could not remain, for his position was indefensible, and he could not take the stores with him to feed his army on the morrow, for he had no wagons. Putting the torch to the remaining food, Jackson withdrew ten miles to the north and dug in behind an unfinished rail embankment at the foot of a hill known as Stoney Ridge. Presumably he expected Lee and Longstreet to join him there, but whether Lee and Jackson had made such prior arrangements remains a mystery.

Lee had no knowledge of what Jackson had done or where he was, for they had no rapid way to communicate. Gauging developments by observing Pope's movements on the other side of the Rappahannock River, Lee convinced himself that Pope was withdrawing, and he ordered Longstreet to join Jackson with all speed, wherever he might be. Longstreet's corps was underway by the afternoon of the twenty-sixth. The next day Lee received a dispatch from Jackson that he had seized Bristoe Station and Manassas Junction. Lee now knew Jackson's approximate location.

While Pope's army thrashed about trying to find him, Jackson lay under cover at Stoney Ridge. Unwilling to remain concealed until joined by Lee and Longstreet, Jackson ambushed a passing column of Federal soldiers in the late afternoon of the twenty-eighth. It was a grievous mistake. He unwittingly had attacked a tiger, the Iron Brigade commanded by John Gibbon, a regular army veteran and one of the finest of all the Federal generals. Gibbon held his ground and fought back until darkness, when he withdrew. The consequences of the battle were twofold: Jackson's corps had suffered its worst proportional casualties of the war, and he had disclosed his position before an army superior in manpower. The Stonewall Brigade had lost so heavily that it was reduced to the size of an average regiment. Two of Jackson's three division commanders, Richard Ewell and William B. Taliaferro, were badly wounded.

The next day, August 29, Pope's army drew up before Jackson in two wings, prepared to attack from both the east and west. Jackson's impetuousness had made his position desperate. Many regiments were no larger than a company or even less, and others were led by only one or two officers. The Federal attacks began in the morning, but they were not well coordinated and Jackson hung on. Lee and Longstreet arrived while the fighting raged on Jackson's front, and by noon Longstreet's divisions were in place to the right of Jackson. Pope did not realize that Longstreet had arrived, and he continued to attack Jackson with increasing intensity throughout the afternoon.

It was obvious to Lee that Longstreet should immediately attack to relieve Jackson; that had been the point of Longstreet's forced march to get there. But it was not Lee's way to order Longstreet to attack. Rather, he suggested that Longstreet consider an attack to ease the pressure on Jackson. Longstreet gathered from Lee's voice and choice of words that Lee was not sure, that he did not entirely trust his own judgment after the blunders of the Seven Days. Lee had said that the conduct of the battle would be up to his generals. Well then, reasoned Longstreet, he was free either to adopt or disregard Lee's suggestion.

Longstreet knew neither the terrain in front of him nor the location of the Federal forces, and he suspected that a good number of the enemy were approaching his front and flank. During the Seven Days, Lee impetuously had ordered attacks under similar circumstances, and Longstreet's men had been devastated. The mistake would not be repeated. Trusting his judgment before Lee's, Longstreet sat passively throughout the twenty-ninth while Jackson got mauled a mile away.

Longstreet was also nursing a grudge. During the Seven Days, Longstreet had done the fighting. He had again and again anticipated Jackson's support, but Jackson had stayed out of the fighting and allowed Longstreet to get beaten up. Now it was Jackson's turn to take it on the chin. In any event, Jackson seemed determined to go it alone, as if Longstreet's troops were superfluous. Lee remained above the fighting and allowed Jackson and Longstreet to do things their way. At sunset Jackson still held on. In the late afternoon Longstreet had sent Hood forward in a reconnaissance in force that met a hard fight with Federal troops at the front. Hood returned and recommended against an attack the next day. Longstreet remained a spectator while Jackson did the fighting.

Lee issued no instructions for the morning. Hood withdrew his troops from their exposed salient and redeployed them within Longstreet's lines. It was understood that Jackson and Longstreet would stay where they were and await developments. All was quiet the next morning, August 30, and Lee had time to write to Davis. His letter was incongruous. He had maneuvered his army into the midst of a huge Federal army about to attack him, yet he scribbled on his stationery, "My desire has been to avoid a general engagement, being the weaker force." Jackson had weathered two fierce and costly battles on the twenty-eighth and twenty-ninth, but Lee casually referred to them as "partial contests." He closed with a request for more reinforcements and supplies: "We have no time to lose & must make every exertion if we expect to reap advantage."

Pope finally attacked in the late afternoon, so oblivious to Longstreet that the latter could no longer restrain himself. With Hood leading the way, Longstreet's corps crashed into the flank and rear of Pope's army. "Onward it swept toward Bull Run," Hood later wrote nostalgically, "driving the enemy at a rapid pace before it, and presenting to the view the most beautiful battle scene I have ever beheld." Hood's soldiers whooped on ahead like wolves after quarry.

Jackson made another of his wild excursions to the rear of Pope's army, but exhaustion slowed him and the Federal rear guard stopped him. Pope fell back in disorder, not stopping until he got to Washington, where Lincoln fired him. Lee held the field. He had swept the Federal army from all of Virginia. The Federal army, it was felt on both sides, was trembling so in Washington that there was wild speculation that Lee might seize the capital itself.

Lee released his victory dispatch to Davis on the evening of August 30, so brief as to say nothing in detail. A short letter to Davis on September 3 was similarly vague. He did manage in a single sentence to summarize what had been achieved, and he said it well: "The great advantage of the advance of the army is the withdrawal of the enemy from our territory, & the hurling back upon their capital their two great armies from the banks of the James & Rappahannock Rivers."

He had whipped them. He had really whipped them. He felt no need to explain how he had done it. His formal report was submitted nine months later. Like his earlier report on the Seven Days, it neither explained nor complained.

The Army of Northern Virginia had begun to assume its distinctive character. Its mobility seemed unmatched by the Federal armies in Virginia. The cavalry could roam at will over distances, but Stuart, its flamboyant commander in cape and plumed hat, was too often distracted into raids which although momentarily spectacular, like a fireworks display, added little to intelligence gathering or to the army's hitting power.

The infantry moved rapidly when unhindered by wagons of baggage, food, and forage. But its energy was transient—it could hit hard when it was fed, but its staying power depended on food either foraged or captured. When neither source could satisfy hunger, the army slowed to a walk or stopped altogether. Lee's dream of living off the abundance of northern Virginia was only that, and supplies from depots further south rarely reached his soldiers north of the Rappahannock.

There would be endless speculation as to whether Lee had planned to seize Washington and so end the war in favor of the Confederacy. Lee is reported to have said that his men were too hungry to sustain an assault on the Washington forts and that he went into Maryland to find food for them. Yet Virginia was not entirely destitute of supplies, and his army could have been fed had it remained in the state. In reality, Lee had greater goals in mind when he sent the Army of Northern Virginia northward across the Potomac.

1 1

ANTIETAM

Up from the meadows rich with corn,
Clear in the cool September morn,

The clustered spires of Frederick stand
Green-walled by the hills of Maryland.

Round about them orchards sweep,
Apple and peach tree fruited deep,

Fair as a garden of the Lord
To the eyes of the famished rebel horde,

On that pleasant morn of the early fall
When Lee marched over the mountain-wall;

Over the mountains winding down,
Horse and foot into Frederick town.

John Greenleaf Whittier, Barbara Frietchie

The Second Manassas campaign ended on September 1 as Jackson's exhausted force and Pope's rear guard disengaged at Chantilly. The next day the Army of the Potomac and the short-lived Army of Virginia were united in the fortresses surrounding Washington, and Lee withdrew. When Lincoln relieved Pope, McClellan again commanded the consolidated armies.

Lee was exactly where he had said he wanted to be, north of the Rappahannock River in the land of plenty. The Virginia Central Railroad, the east-west trunk line that connected Richmond with the Shenandoah Valley, was now secure. The despised Pope had been disgraced and dismissed. Richmond was secure, free of Federal troops. A new offensive led by the cautious McClellan would take months to organize. It was altogether a time to think clearly about the future in concert with other minds, to refit the Army of Northern Virginia, to restore interior lines of communication, and to conserve the most precious resource of the Confederacy: its emaciated, ill-clothed, bone-weary infantry soldiers.

Why, then, did Lee immediately lunge into Maryland less than a day after successfully concluding the Second Manassas campaign? His decision arose from misjudgments, both about the capacity of his army and about the extent of a latent body of Confederate support within the state. The Baltimore riots early in the war had given rise to expectations of secession in a state with 86,000 slaves. Its soldiers fought in the Confederate army, and the evocative song "Maryland, My Maryland" was often advocated as the South's national anthem. Lincoln, acting with determination, had stationed troops within the state and suppressed Southern sympathizers. Such measures, together with the support of business and commercial interests, brought Maryland into line with other Union states.

Lee, like many in the South, surmised that Maryland longed for independence from the tyranny of the Federal government. The question of invading Maryland was, of course, a political decision with many ramifications, and it was solely the prerogative of Davis and the Confederate government. Such a decision could take months, perhaps longer, and Lee felt that haste took precedence. He would not wait for the political process. Compelled by the certainty of his views, Lee chose to preempt Richmond and move so swiftly that Davis would be overtaken by events and forced to go along.

While Lee wrote profusely to Davis to explain his ideas, Lee nonetheless did as he pleased before Davis could respond. Lee's first letter was written while his gun barrels were scarcely cooled from Manassas. "The present seems to be the most propitious time," he wrote, "since the commencement of the war for the Confederate Army to enter Maryland." He ticked off the reasons: the Federal army was weakened and demoralized; Maryland longed to join the Confederacy; if he went into Maryland, the enemy would have to operate north of the Potomac; and Virginia would not be a battleground. Seeking food for his army was not among his stated reasons.

Lee admitted that his army was "not properly equipped for an invasion of an enemy's territory." Having said that he was not ready to invade Maryland, Lee then explained why he intended to do so: "[W]e cannot afford to be idle, and though weaker than our opponents in men and military equipments, must endeavor to harass if we cannot destroy them. I am aware that the movement is attended with much risk, yet I do not consider success impossible, and shall endeavor to guard it from loss."

The next day, September 4, Lee's army began crossing the Potomac into Maryland. Another letter reported the fait accompli. "I am more fully persuaded of the benefit that will result from an expedition into Maryland, and I shall proceed with the movement at once, unless you should signify your disapprobation." Lee either was being disingenuous, which was unlikely, or preemptory, which is more conceivable. By the time Davis got the letter Lee would have committed his army and, by association, the Confederate government. Davis could not order him to return to Virginia under those circumstances.

Lee's mind soared with possibilities. His sword, he was convinced, made Lincoln tremble, and he spoke headily of threatening Washington and Baltimore, and of invading Pennsylvania. So confident was Lee of Confederate

Lee invaded Maryland on September 4, 1862, by first crossing the Potomac River. His strategy was based on the mistaken premise that the state was sympathetic to the Confederacy and would welcome the Army of Northern Virginia as friends and allies. Instead the people shunned his army, and his starving, footsore soldiers deserted by the thousands. Combat artist Alfred Waud rendered hundreds of excellent sketches of Civil War scenes to illustrate newspaper accounts of battles and campaigns. (Waud—Library of Congress)

ascendancy that he urged Davis to propose to the Federal government that now was the time to recognize the Confederacy.

But Lee was no statesman, only a soldier playing with political fire in an arena where he did not belong. The repercussions of his invasion would be disastrous to the Confederacy. Even then, Lincoln was waiting for propitious conditions to announce the Emancipation Proclamation, the first step in forever abolishing the institution of slavery that Lee and the Confederate army were fighting to preserve. Recognition by foreign powers was also at stake, and the governments of England and France would decide once and for all not to endorse a losing cause after the battle at Antietam.

Lee's grandiose intentions alarmed his generals. The soldiers were spent from the fighting and marching and from their hunger. They wanted—deserved—rest and nourishment. One potential crisis was that the ravenous troops would pillage to feed themselves. Moreover, Lee's proposed invasion offended their principles. His soldiers were willing to defend Southern soil from invading Northerners, but not to become invaders themselves. Talk of desertion was widespread in the ranks.

Both as a precaution and as a remedy to the discontent, Lee issued a general order on September 4. Liberators, he lectured, do not plunder the people they are liberating. If they stayed in ranks, Lee assured them, food would be forthcoming: "Quartermasters and commissaries will make all arrangements for purchase of supplies needed by our army, to be issued to the respective commands upon proper requisitions, thereby removing all excuse for depredations." The quartermasters and commissaries had been unable to feed the army in Virginia. Even the gullible wondered how they could purchase supplies in Maryland, where Confederate currency was not the coin of the realm.

Lee had two ways to deal with potential desertion and straggling. One was to appeal to the loyalty and goodwill of the soldiers. The other was coercion. Lee chose the latter alternative, establishing a provost guard to sweep laggards into ranks. No one was exempt, neither the halt nor the feeble. Threats and brute force would keep the soldiers marching. Yet a third of Lee's army would desert in a period of two weeks.

Lee's generals, D. H. Hill, for example, seemed baffled as to why. One reason was apparent, for as Hill later wrote, "Doubtless the want of shoes, the want of food, and physical exhaustion had kept many brave men from being with the army." But what about the others? Why did they fight during the Seven Days and Second Manassas, but not in Maryland? Hill could only fulminate that "thousands of thieving poltroons had kept away from sheer cowardice. The straggler is generally a thief and always a coward, lost to all sense of shame; he can only be kept in ranks by a strict and sanguinary discipline."

Francis Barlow would have agreed. Federal soldiers too would straggle and malinger, though to a lesser extent, because they were fed, clothed, and sheltered. But in an army in any age, the weak in body and spirit try to dodge the bullet. Never could a Federal regiment muster all the men on its rolls. Barlow's remedy was both brutal and effective. He posted a rear guard of his meanest and most reliable soldiers, whose bayonets dislodged stragglers from alongside the road. Underbrush and thorns aggravated the guards' already foul moods, and they became merciless. In a published letter to a newspaper editor after the war, Barlow discussed those who fought and those who did not.

> [T]here were cowards, stragglers, and shirks in the army. . . . I was
> wounded at the battle of Antietam, and as I was brought out I

*was amazed to see the numbers of stragglers who were amusing them-
selves in the rear of the troops who were fighting in the front. The
country in the rear was filled with soldiers broken up and scattered
from their commands, who were having "picnics." They were lying
under trees, sleeping, cooking their coffee or other rations, and amusing themselves outside of the enemy's fire. This was by no means confined to the enlisted men, but I saw officers of various ranks, and even
of high ranks, and of different corps and divisions, who had thus
deserted their comrades in the front. . . .*

*War is a savage business, and it is idle to try to introduce tenderness
into it, except so far as relates to the care of soldiers and the treatment
of the sick and wounded. If, after every action, each regiment should
condemn to death every man who had fallen out without urgent reasons, or had flinched in battle (and a man's comrades, after awhile,
understand these things), it would establish a discipline and a spirit
which would have saved thousands of lives. Harsh as this may seem, it
would in the end be the greatest humanity, for when cowards and
stragglers are pardoned or honored, it is at the expense of brave and
faithful soldiers.*

Lee and his army reached Frederick, Maryland, about eighty miles northwest of Washington, by September 7. His army of liberation was dismal to
behold. Even Lee could not dignify the occasion. Unable to ride (his hands
had been injured at Manassas), he used an ambulance. Maryland, he discovered, considered him unwelcome. "I do not anticipate," he wrote Davis,
"any general rising up of the people in our behalf."

Wholesale desertion began. Lee pleaded with Davis for legislative help. Discipline within the army, he said, was collapsing owing to the need for forced
marches and hard service. Lee proposed a commission of inquisitors to accompany the army that would hear cases and authorize punishment en masse. A
provost marshal and staff would "execute promptly its decisions." "I assure
you some remedy is necessary," he concluded, "especially now, when the army
is in a State whose citizens it is our purpose to conciliate and bring with us.
Every outrage upon their feelings and property should be checked."

Lee had entered Maryland waving an olive branch, but he was treated like
a plague. It was quickly apparent that his troops were not being welcomed
as liberators. The quartermasters and commissaries, with neither money nor
credit, were empty-handed. Farmers had taken their livestock into the hills,
merchants had locked their doors, and wheat was still on the stalk. At
Sharpsburg, a Maryland homeowner would remove the pump handle from
his well to prevent the soldiers from getting water. Desperate with thirst, they
would fill their canteens from a barnyard mud hole.

In a last effort to salvage goodwill, on September 8 Lee issued a proclamation addressed to "The People of Maryland." They were, he said, a people with strong ties to the South, whom the Federal government had
"deprived of every right and reduced to the condition of a conquered
province." Lee reeled off a list of alleged grievances that he had come to

Rec'd A.A.G.O. Sept 16 */16/62*

HEAD-QUARTERS ARMY N. VA.,
NEAR FREDERICK TOWN, 8th September, 1862.

TO THE PEOPLE OF MARLAND:

It is right that you should know the purpose that has brought the Army under my command within the limits of your State, so far as that purpose concerns yourselves.

The People of the Confederate States have long watched with the deepest sympathy the wrongs and outrages that have been inflicted upon the citizens of a Commonwealth, allied to the States of the South by the strongest social, political and commercial ties.

They have seen with profound indignation their sister State deprived of every right, and reduced to the condition of a conquered Province.

Under the pretence of supporting the Constitution, but in violation of its most valuable provisions, your citizens have been arrested and imprisoned upon no charge, and contrary to all forms of law; the faithful and manly protest against this outrage made by the venerable and illustrious Marylanders to whom in better days, no citizen appealed for right in vain, was treated with scorn and contempt; the government of your chief City has been usurped by armed strangers; your Legislature has been dissolved by the unlawful arrest of its members; freedom of the press and of speech has been suppressed; words have been declared offences by an arbitrary decree of the Federal Executive, and citizens ordered to be tried by a military commission for what they may dare to speak.

Believing that the People of Maryland possessed a spirit too lofty to submit to such a government, the people of the South have long wished to aid you in throwing off this foreign yoke, to enable you again to enjoy the inalienable rights of freemen, and restore independence and sovereignty to your State.

In obedience to this wish, our Army has come among you, and is prepared to assist you with the power of its arms in regaining the rights of which you have been despoiled.

This, Citizens of Maryland, is our mission, so far as you are concerned.

No constraint upon your free will is intended, no intimidation will be allowed.

Within the limits of this Army at least, Marylanders shall once more enjoy their ancient freedom of thought and speech.

We know no enemies among you, and will protect all of every opinion.

It is for you to decide your destiny, freely and without constraint.

This army will respect your choice whatever it may be, and while the Southern people will rejoice to welcome you to your natural position among them, they will only welcome you when you come of your own free will.   R. E. LEE, General Commanding.

When Lee and his army entered Maryland he issued this proclamation explaining his intentions. To his dismay, the people of the state shunned him. "I regret that the stay of the army in Maryland," he wrote the secretary of war on September 30, 1862, "was so short as to prevent our receiving the aid I had expected from the State." (National Archives) redress. "[O]ur army has come among you, and is prepared to assist you with the power of its arms," he assured them, "in regaining the rights of which you have been despoiled. . . . We know no enemies among you, and will protect all, of every opinion. It is for you to decide your destiny freely and without constraint."

Lee made his proclamation—like all his other actions—without consulting Davis. It backfired. A few days later Lee received a proclamation from Davis, with orders to announce it as official policy. The proclamation was the antithesis of Lee's declaration, as Davis obviously did not expect the people to arise in sympathy. Maryland, said Davis, was an enemy of the Confederacy. It could either convince Washington to end the war or conclude a separate peace with the Confederacy, which would "secure immunity from the desolating effects of warfare on the soil of the State."*

Lee was in a dilemma of his own making, as he had already sent Davis a copy of his own conciliatory proclamation. He decided to bluff it out. "You will perceive by [my] printed address to the people of Maryland," he wrote brazenly, "that I have not gone contrary to the views expressed by you on the subject. Should there be anything in it to correct, please let me know." Davis let it stand.

Lee lingered in Frederick, trying to decide where opportunities lay. His lines of communication governed his strategy. Ammunition and other supplies came from Richmond, and Lee already had planned to have it routed through the Shenandoah Valley. The other great need was food. As Maryland had locked its cupboards, the only alternative source was the Shenandoah Valley. Food and all else went by railway line north and terminated at Harpers Ferry, occupied, unfortunately for Lee, by a Federal garrison of some 12,000 men. Lee had hoped that the garrisons would abandon Harpers Ferry and the nearby railroad town of Martinsburg, but they did not cooperate and remained astride his sole line of communication from Virginia. Hence Lee had to seize both places.

Lee issued his notorious Special Orders No. 191 on September 9. Half of his army, under Jackson, would split into three groups and later converge on Harpers Ferry, twenty miles to the west on the Potomac River. The other half, under Longstreet, would head northwesterly, fifteen miles up the road to Boonsboro, and await further orders. D. H. Hill (who had been restored to command of his division and had rejoined the Army of Northern Virginia) would guard the rear against any Federal troops coming from the east. Lee was, in effect, moving away from Washington. McClellan would not be an immediate threat.

Hill was unclear as to whom he reported, Lee or Jackson. The confusion was compounded when he received two copies of the special order, a dupli-

---

* Davis sent an identical proclamation to Bragg, who simultaneously invaded the border state of Kentucky on a similar mission. See chapter 16.

cate from Jackson and an original from Lee. Hill snorted at the inept staff work of the high command and tossed away the redundant order. A staff officer retrieved the document and used it to wrap his cigars. When Hill and Lee's army got underway the next morning, September 10, the package was left behind. A Federal soldier rummaging through the campsite found the cigars, and Lee's order was delivered to McClellan when he arrived in Frederick on September 13.

Rather than staying in Washington as Lee had hoped, McClellan moved his army in search of Lee. "Had Lee whispered into the Federal General's ear his inmost plans," Moxley Sorrel later wrote, "the latter could have asked for nothing more than the information brought him on that fatal paper." McClellan decided that the document was authentic and not a plant. He accelerated his pursuit.

Gordon was once again a regimental commander. Rodes had recovered from his wounds and had resumed command of his four-regiment, 1,200 man brigade in D. H. Hill's division. The soldiers marched first to Frederick, and on September 10 they continued to the northwest behind Jackson and Longstreet. Ahead they saw a range of high hills, called South Mountain, through which they passed via a valley called Turner's Gap. Once through the gap they encamped at Boonsboro, on the western side of the mountain range. A village called Sharpsburg and a creek named Antietam lay seven miles to the southwest. Lee had heard rumors (false, as it turned out) that a Federal force was descending from Pennsylvania toward Hagerstown, ten miles further up the road, so he and Longstreet marched on to intercept them there. Hill remained in Boonsboro. Jackson meanwhile had veered farther west, on a circuitous journey to Harpers Ferry. Never before had Lee's army been so fragmented and out of touch. It was ripe for defeat in detail.*

Lee realized that his plans were falling apart. He had heard nothing from Harpers Ferry, and he received reports that McClellan was following on his heels instead of staying in Washington. Somehow McClellan had to be slowed to give Lee time to reassemble his army. Turner's Gap seemed defensible if the Confederate troops could hold the high ground; perhaps Hill could slow McClellan's army from pouring through the gap onto the open farmland west of the mountains.

Lee asked the impossible. Hill's small division of 5,000 men had to cover five roads on a three-mile front against two Federal corps. The Federal front was so wide and deep that it threatened to envelop and swallow Hill's division. Rodes's brigade held the left of the Confederate line, and Gordon's regiment was the farthest left of all. Federal troops swung around and behind Gordon, threatening to come upon a road that would lead to the rear of Hill's entire division. As Rodes moved even farther to his left, his brigade

---

* "Defeat in detail" occurs when a massed, larger force converges on a smaller segment of a dispersed enemy army, defeats it, and then goes on to another segment.

became isolated and nearly surrounded. Its regiments, scattered among the gorges and gullies, were flushed and routed like coveys of quail. Rodes gathered them for a final stand atop a mountain peak.

"This enabled me to face the enemy's right again," Rodes later reported, "and to make another stout stand with Gordon's excellent regiment (which he had kept constantly in hand, and had handled in a manner I have never heard or seen equaled during the war), and with the remainder of the . . . Regiments." The Federal attack intensified, and Federal troops poured fire upon Rodes's brigade from nearby hills. Rodes's soldiers neared collapse. Gordon alone did not break, and his disciplined soldiers were the only regiment still intact and fighting. They were still fighting when the sun set.

Hill had been everywhere that day, cursing Lee for having separated the army and wondering if Longstreet would return in time to keep him from being overwhelmed. Hill thanked God that he had fighting generals like Rodes, who had held the line against the "restorers of the Union," as he contemptuously called the Federal troops. Rodes had been splendid, Hill later reported, and Gordon the best of all. "Colonel Gordon, the Christian hero," he wrote, "excelled his former deeds at Seven Pines and in the battle around Richmond. Our language is not capable of expressing a higher compliment."

Lee saw the peril of his divided army the night before the battle on South Mountain. Harpers Ferry still had not surrendered, and, as he wrote Davis, "the enemy was advancing more rapidly than was convenient" from Frederick. Lee ordered Longstreet to leave Hagerstown in the morning of the fourteenth to reinforce Hill. Longstreet got underway on a forced march of twelve miles. Lee was again mounted although his hands were still in pain, and he could barely grasp the reins. In the afternoon the sounds of battle came from the mountains ahead of them, and a message from Hill urged haste. Officers spurred the weary soldiers. As the Texas Brigade hurried by Lee, they yelled at him to give them Hood.

Hood was under arrest. He and an evil-tempered general named Nathan G. "Shanks" Evans had argued over the ownership of captured ambulances shortly after Second Manassas. Evans had arrested Hood for insubordination, and Longstreet had ordered him to remain in Virginia to await court-martial. The power of arrest was sacrosanct, and Lee would neither intercede nor overrule Evans, thus allowing a petty feud with an alcoholic misfit to remove one his best fighting generals from command in a time of crisis. Hoping that Hood and Evans would be reconciled, Lee compromised to the extent that he permitted Hood to bring up the rear of his division.

Hood's soldiers now jarred Lee into action. Calling Hood to his side, Lee asked him to apologize so that, with battle imminent, he could lift the arrest and allow Hood to resume his command. Hood refused, but Lee persisted. When Hood would not back down, Lee gave in to expediency and "temporarily suspended" his arrest. Hood galloped to the head of his division, which then joined the other panting brigades of Longstreet's command that were scrambling into the mountain fighting. Lee, still a semi-invalid and unable to keep his seat in the rough terrain, stood clear of the battlefield. The gunfire finally ended at nightfall.

Lee took stock on the night of September 14–15. He had begun his Maryland campaign with some 55,000 men. Because he had dispersed them, and through desertion, the army under his immediate command near South Mountain had dwindled to perhaps 18,000 starving, ragged men whom he could not feed. Jackson and John G. Walker were still at Harpers Ferry, and Lafayette McLaws was about to be trapped near the Potomac River. A Federal army of perhaps 85,000 men would surge through South Mountain in the morning. To avoid annihilation, Lee would have to withdraw from Maryland and cross the Potomac back into Virginia. Before the gunfire at South Mountain had entirely ceased, and before he could talk to Hill and Longstreet, Lee was ready to quit.

Others wanted to fight it out. Hood wrote in his memoirs that he and Hill went together at about 10 P.M. to headquarters to join Lee and Longstreet. "After a long debate," he later wrote, "it was decided to retire and fall back towards Sharpsburg." The commanders and their staffs rounded up their troops and put them on the road to Sharpsburg. It was the first time since Lee had taken command four months before that he had had to retreat after a battle.

Sometime during the evening Lee got more bad news. Federal forces—William B. Franklin's Sixth Corps—had brushed aside a cavalry force and were pouring through another opening in South Mountain, called Crampton's Gap, about ten miles south of Turner's Gap and seven miles north of Harpers Ferry. Franklin was now between Lee and McLaws and could likely trap McLaws against the Potomac River. Jackson and Walker were south of the Potomac, still trying to seize Harpers Ferry. Worst of all, Franklin was closer to the Potomac River than were Lee's forces evacuating South Mountain. Lee's line of retreat into Virginia was broken. The specter of defeat in detail was about to become a horrifying reality. McClellan had run him to ground.

Lee had but two alternatives. First, he could fight his way through. Second, he could try to evade the trap and escape to Virginia, a distasteful alternative. When Lee had invaded Maryland, he had conspicuously pronounced that he intended to stay there and liberate the state. To flee ten days later, tail between legs, before an army Lee had whipped both on the Peninsula and at Second Manassas, would humiliate Southern pride and prestige. Southern arrogance was another consideration. Combat leaders like D. H. Hill despised the Northern enemy and passionately believed that they could whip any Yankee force regardless of numbers. Lee would lose face if he retreated without fighting.

Lee chose to take a stand at Sharpsburg and pray that McClellan would delay an attack long enough for him somehow to reunite his army. While Lee afterward maintained that McClellan was the best general he faced during the war, he knew that McClellan was chary and slow in pursuit. Perhaps he could bluff him once again. By 10:15 P.M. Lee had silently reversed his decision to retreat to Virginia.

Sharpsburg was not a good defensive location for several reasons, though under the circumstances Lee had few choices. If a general must act defensively, it is far better to have a river at the front as a natural barrier to the attacking army. By remaining in Sharpsburg, Lee had the Potomac River at his immediate rear, a barrier to his own army and not to McClellan. If the battle went against him, Lee could not withdraw to the safety of Virginia, unless McClellan allowed him to cross the river without opposition.

One minor water barrier, Antietam Creek, flowed between the two armies, but it could be forded in most places without difficulty. The countryside around Sharpsburg was open, gently rolling farmland, which would allow the longer-range Federal artillery to bombard the Confederate lines. The Federal army would have ample room to maneuver. High casualties on both sides were inevitable for lack of natural cover.

McClellan allowed Lee forty-eight hours of grace before he attacked, time enough for Lee to consolidate his scattered army at Sharpsburg. The Confederate soldiers were too weak to entrench and, in any event, were without tools. As someone had sent away the wagons, their only food was green corn and green apples, weakening them further with diarrhea. A Union visitor walked the battlefield afterward. "We traced the position in which a rebel brigade had stood or bivouacked in line of battle for half a mile by the thickly strewn belt of green corn husks and cobs," he later wrote, "and also . . . by a ribbon of dysenteric stools just behind."

The Second Corps under Major General Edwin Sumner, responding to Lee's invasion, crossed into Maryland with the Army of the Potomac in early September. Barlow's Sixty-first New York had left its tents and blankets behind in the rush to get from Washington to Manassas, but the well-oiled Federal transportation system reunited men and equipment in Maryland. They were, said Charles Fuller, "received with thanks. Campaigning in August and September . . . without shelter and blankets was a hardship." Maryland was good to the Federal army marching toward Sharpsburg. Food was plentiful, and the soldiers ate well.

Arabella followed as a volunteer nurse, the only cheerful aspect of Barlow's otherwise gloomy frame of mind. His spirits were also helped by the promotion of Nelson Miles to lieutenant colonel and his assignment as second in command, a position Barlow had long advocated, for Miles had proven a courageous comrade in the Peninsular Campaign and had become a close friend. (Years later Miles would become general in chief of the army.) But there was not much to command. The Sixty-first, once numbering over 500, had been reduced to 105 soldiers in three companies. New York would not send replacements that could be trained and assimilated by the surviving veterans, raising instead raw, new regiments without benefit of combat experience and leadership. Fortunately, the Sixty-fourth New York, with 200 men, had augmented his command, so that Barlow and Miles would take something over 300 riflemen into combat.

Frederick was typical of the welcomes they experienced. The soldiers always remembered its beauty and tranquillity and the townspeople who greeted them as liberators as they marched in smart, disciplined formations on the heels of Lee's scruffy hordes retreating to the west. The regiment camped west of the town, spectators to the battles on South Mountain. Afterward they went with the remainder of McClellan's army to Sharpsburg, where Lee and Hood and Gordon waited for them.

Barlow and his regiments were part of the military spectacle that unfolded before Gordon, stationed on a sunken road near the crest of a hill a mile and a half northeast of Sharpsburg. The Cavalier remembered the panorama of impending battle. "From the position assigned me near the centre of Lee's lines, both armies and the entire field were in view. The scene was not only magnificent to look upon, but the realization of what it meant was deeply impressive. Even in times of peace our sensibilities are stirred by the sight of a great army passing in review. How infinitely more thrilling in the dread moments before the battle to look upon two mighty armies upon the same plain, 'beneath spread ensigns and bristling bayonets,' waiting for the impending crash and sickening carnage!"

Hood's memories were less romantic. Joseph Hooker's corps crossed Antietam Creek late on the sixteenth and made a threatening approach to the Confederate left wing. Responding, Hood's tiny division rushed to a white building called Dunker Church. Federal artillery shells fell among his exposed troops, and at a late hour they got in a firefight against Hooker's corps that lasted until nightfall. In the darkness Hood heard the sound of thousands of enemy troops massing nearby.

"The extreme suffering of my troops for want of food," Hood later wrote, "induced me to ride back to General Lee, and request him to send two or more brigades to our relief, at least for the night, in order that the soldiers might have the chance to cook their meager rations. He said he would cheerfully do so, but he knew of no command which could be spared for the purpose."

Lee suggested that Hood find Jackson to seek relief. Hood rode about in the darkness and found Jackson asleep. Jackson agreed to let Hood withdraw with the understanding that he would be on instant recall. Hood had not sent his food wagons across the river with the others, and he tried to get them and their flour to his men, but before the dough was in the ovens, the Battle of Antietam had begun. " 'To arms' was instantly sounded," he wrote, "and quite a large number of my brave soldiers were again obliged to march to the front, leaving their uncooked rations in camp."

If McClellan had hit Lee with a full-scale coordinated attack on September 17, the massed power would have overwhelmed and destroyed the whole of Lee's emaciated army. Instead, McClellan committed the Army of the Potomac incrementally from right to left, allowing Lee wiggle room to shift blocks of troops to the points of the severest action. McClellan issued no plan, no order, and his later report of what he intended to do was so vague that confusion and misunderstanding were assured. His one contribution to the outcome of the battle was to delay the forward movement of his individual corps in such a way as to assure that they would arrive piecemeal on the battlefield.

Once he had released them at random intervals, McClellan delegated the deployment of the troops to the corps commanders, who brought their divisions on line at different times and at places of their choosing. The corps commanders went to the front, where they became so involved in the immediate fighting that they lost control of their corps. When Hooker was wounded and Joseph Mansfield killed, the division commanders on the right wing were on their own in a free-for-all.

The momentum of the Federal assault collapsed Jackson's left wing into a bloody heap as Hood was still moving toward the front. When he saw the unfolding disaster across the open countryside, Hood acted without hesitation, galloping among his advancing troops, sword drawn and voice resounding, impelling them to rush forward into a wall of fire. "[W]hole ranks of brave men . . . were mowed down in heaps to the right and left," he later wrote. "Never before was I so consciously troubled with fear that my horse would further injure some wounded fellow soldier, lying helpless on the ground. This most deadly combat raged until our last round of ammunition was expended."

Hood sent messages to the rear, pleading for reinforcements, but none came. So intense was the volume of fire that he had to withdraw, and his survivors fell back to the comparative shelter of woods behind Dunker Church. McLaws's division, still panting from its march from Harpers Ferry, came up from the rear. Hood told him the location of the line, and McLaws plunged into the maelstrom that had demolished Hood. Hood moved his few remaining soldiers to the rear and fought no more, although he continued to direct reinforcements as they arrived.

It had been Hood's finest hour. He and his soldiers had held the left wing against enormous odds, and he had rallied troops from other brigades. Hood's own division was shattered, and he would be forever bitter. The high command had betrayed his soldiers. Lee had got them into a position of peril without the means to defend themselves. Hood had asked Longstreet for help, but Longstreet had ignored him. So he had gone to Lee, and Lee too had ignored him and had passed him off to Jackson, whom he had found asleep. The worst had come, as Hood had predicted it would, and his men had suffered for it. When he had been thrust into the fighting, he had gone in alone; pleas for reinforcements to save his division from annihilation had been "ineffectual," and when the ammunition was gone, he had pulled out.

Hood could have been reinforced. McLaws had arrived early that morning from Harpers Ferry, his troops groggy from hunger and forced marching and want of sleep. All was confusion as to his orders. At first McLaws could not find Lee, and when he did, Lee had unaccountably held him back for an hour before sending him a mile to the left. None of Lee's staff went with McLaws to guide him over the unknown terrain or to find his place in the line. Finally one of D. H. Hill's staff officers pointed out a destination. (Where was Jackson, presumably in charge of the left wing?) McLaws ultimately came upon Hood hunkering down behind Dunker Church and entered the battle.

The leadership and staff work of the high command had been horrendous. There is a story of an exchange between Lee and Hood that evening, which is perhaps apocryphal but nonetheless in the spirit of the events.

Lee asked, "Where is your brigade?"

"They are lying on the field where you sent them," Hood replied.

D. H. Hill and his tattered division of 3,000 men held the center of the Confederate line immediately to the right of Hood and Dunker Church. He had assembled some artillery pieces, but wherever he placed them Hunt's guns pounded them down from across Antietam Creek. When the first phase of the battle had begun on his left, Hill had dispatched three brigades to the inferno, and they had been consumed. His other two brigades, perhaps 1,600 men, were all that remained intact.

By midmorning he had stationed them "in the bed of an old road," which for years had served as a shortcut bypassing Sharpsburg to the northeast and connecting Hagerstown and Boonsboro Pikes. Traffic and erosion had worn it deep enough to shelter crouching infantry. Its most prominent feature was a section shaped like a broad arrowhead, pointing across the undulating fields over which the Federal soldiers had to come after crossing Antietam Creek. The two cutting edges of the arrowhead were each five hundred yards in length, atop a moderate rise. Rodes's brigade of 800 men took the left half of the road, and G. B. Anderson the right. Gordon and his regiment were at the tip of the arrow.

Gordon had watched the battle unfolding on his left since early morning. The two armies had collided in the open fields near Dunker Church and beyond it in a cornfield surrounded by woods on three sides, from which soldiers would emerge and surge and then retreat. The Confederate line held. A third Federal corps entered the arena, Sumner's Second Corps, delayed for hours by McClellan. After fording Antietam Creek it moved southwestward toward the battle line. Sumner joined his leading division and led it into an ambush. The two trailing divisions under William H. French and Israel Richardson, including Barlow's regiment, went their own way.

French veered his division away from Sumner and toward the Confederate center. Some of his regiments got tangled with Confederate strong points, while others formed up in three parallel ranks to attack the Confederate soldiers crammed into the sunken road. Henry Hunt had pounded the Confederate artillery into silence, so that the marching Federal lines were undisturbed. Gordon's voice rose above the clangor: steady now, stand steady. The Confederate soldiers frantically piled fence posts in their front as the Federal lines disappeared behind a hill and reappeared on the crest, less than a hundred yards away, still coming, their buttons bright on blue uniforms, led by an officer on a great horse as if on parade. What a magnificent sight, thought Gordon, and then the two Confederate brigades began firing. The Federal soldiers stood and fought, charged, then retreated and charged again. Finally they sought cover and returned fire.

The first Federal volley struck Gordon in the leg and killed the commander of the adjacent regiment standing with him. A second bullet hit the same leg, leaving Gordon staggering but still erect. A third and then a fourth bullet tore into his arm and shoulder. A fifth bullet smashed his jaw, and he fell paralyzed, facedown in his hat. Gordon gagged as blood from his facial wound filled the hat. I will drown in my own blood, he thought, but it drained through shrapnel holes in the crown, and he thanked God that he could still breathe. Before he fainted from shock and pain, he felt himself being lifted and carried away.

Longstreet meanwhile ordered Rodes to attack the Federal troops in the field. When Rodes's few hundred men sallied forth, the Sixth Alabama was too paralyzed to follow. Gordon had seemed immortal to the soldiers, and now he was gone, drenched in blood, probably dead. The regiments that did go forward came reeling back, and Rodes could barely contain them in the road, for they were near panic. The road was a death trap. Some of the nearby hills were higher than the road, and the Federal troops could fire into the men packed into it. Hill and Rodes became desperate. "I sent several urgent messages to General Lee for re-enforcements," wrote Hill, but none had arrived when French's division paraded onto the road. Where were reinforcements? Were there reinforcements?

Reinforcements had been available for several hours. None came in the beginning because Lee and the high command continued to bungle the deployment of the two divisions that had arrived that morning from Harpers Ferry. McLaws, of course, had been held in place for an hour before going helter-skelter to the left wing. The other division of 3,400 men belonged to Richard H. Anderson. There is no record of where it was for several hours after it had arrived. At the eleventh hour, with Hill near collapse, either Lee or Longstreet finally sent Anderson to Hill, but because of the delay Anderson's division had to pass through a barrage from Hunt's artillery and French's muskets. Anderson went down. Some of the survivors tumbled into the road, adding to the piles of bodies already there. Others lay in the cornfield to the rear of the road, absorbing the full fury of the Federal fire.

The battle was testing the Federal troops as well. Richardson's division came onto the field and went left to support French. The arrow in the road still held, bulging with bodies, some firing, some inert or twitching. Barlow and his men rushed the road, stopped, and poured fire at and around the point where Gordon had gone down. Gordon's second in command tried to retreat; in the roar of battle words were garbled and orders misunderstood. When Gordon's regiment pulled back, the entire brigade—the left edge of the arrow—went with it. As they fled through the cornfield toward the shelter of farmer Piper's orchard, the fire from Barlow's rifles tore into their backs. Gordon's regiment ceased to exist.

Anderson's soldiers in the other half of the arrowhead still crouched in the road. "[W]e pressed on," wrote Sergeant Isaac Plumb of the Sixty-first New York, "until we reached a ditch dug in the road in which the enemy lay in line and the few who did not surrender did not live to tell the tale of their defeat." Fuller wrote, "The result was terrible to the enemy. They could do us little harm, and we were shooting them like sheep in a pen." The frantic soldiers in the pit waved white handkerchiefs, but Barlow's soldiers kept firing until his officers forcibly knocked their guns aside. Some three hundred prisoners crawled out of the road. Bodies were stacked everywhere. Barlow's soldiers went among them, pulling the dead off the wounded and giving the wounded water.

Barlow had broken the very center of Lee's line.

Other regiments joined Barlow, and together they tramped across the cornfield toward the orchard and Piper's farm. Hill saw them coming and threw together scratch companies that went down the Hagerstown Pike, on the right flank of the approaching Federal soldiers. Barlow saw Hill's soldiers assembling on his right, and as if on a parade ground he barked orders, "Right shoulder. Shift arms." He then gave orders to the right oblique, and the troops advanced three hundred yards, where the enemy crouched behind a stone wall. Again Barlow ordered his soldiers to fire, and the Confederate soldiers fled.

Barlow shouted more parade ground orders, and the regiments again marched toward the orchard and the Piper farm beyond. The veterans had indelible memories of Barlow that day. A year later Fuller swapped stories with a wounded Pennsylvania soldier. "When he learned I was of Barlow's regiment, he told me that about the finest sight he ever saw on the battlefield was seeing Barlow lead his command in to action at Antietam. He was where he had a full view of the display. The regiments were in line of battle, and [Barlow], with sabre in hand, was ahead of the line. Such is the plain fact, as all who were there can testify."

Hill found two cannon and pointed them toward Barlow, whose regiment had forged ahead of the others. A canister ball hit Barlow's groin, and he went down. Miles assumed command. Barlow, still conscious, was taken to the rear. Richardson, too, had been wounded—the wound would be fatal— and the leadership needed to sustain the attack was gone.

The decision whether to resume the attack belonged to the corps commanders, for McClellan was in his headquarters at the Pry house, across Antietam Creek, removed from the battle. Franklin had come forward with his fresh corps ready to exploit the collapse of the Confederate center, but Sumner was the senior corps commander. Still shell-shocked, the old man wanted no more fighting and forbade Franklin to attack. Franklin appealed to the distant McClellan, who naturally agreed with Sumner.

The third and final phase of the battle progressed on the left wing. Exercising blundering leadership that resulted in hours of delay, Ambrose E. Burnside had finally gotten his corps across his infamous bridge spanning Antietam Creek. A. P. Hill arrived from Harpers Ferry at the critical moment to pin him down. Lee's army had survived.

Both armies remained immobilized, in shock, and on the eighteenth, the generals began beating their chests and contriving excuses to explain away their inertia for the benefit of history. In reality, no one was ready to shed any

The sunken road at Sharpsburg was the scene of one of the fiercest battles of the war. Here Gordon tried to hold the center of the Confederate line against the Federal assault. Barlow's regiments fired point-blank at the Confederate defenders, killing and wounding so many that their bodies lay stacked in the road. His body torn by bullets, Gordon nearly drowned in his own blood, and the Sixth Alabama was demolished. After the breakthrough, Barlow, too, was grievously wounded. (Massachusetts Commandery Military Order of the Loyal Legion and the U.S. Army Military History Institute)

more blood. Lee retreated across the Potomac that evening and returned to Virginia. McClellan neither opposed the withdrawal nor pursued. Lee would be free to reconstitute his army for the remainder of the fall.

The casualties of Antietam were the most severe of any American battle in any war. Many of Lee's regiments, like Gordon's Sixth Alabama, simply disintegrated. No one remained to report their losses. One entire division was so ravaged that it submitted not a single report. It is guesswork as to how many men even were present in Lee's army at Sharpsburg, but a reasonable estimate is 33,000. His estimated losses—killed, wounded, and missing—were more than 10,000. In twelve hours Lee lost a third of his army to casualties.

We have to grope for some way to put these figures in perspective. For comparison, consider the Allied landing at Normandy on D-Day, a hard-fought and costly battle, during the Second World War. The losses of the Allied forces in that action were the same as Lee's at Antietam, about 10,000 men. Lee, however, began the Maryland campaign with only about 55,000 men. Perhaps 20,000 remained capable of fighting when he retreated over the Potomac back into Virginia. Thus, through combat losses at South Mountain, Harpers Ferry, and Sharpsburg and through the attrition of straggling and desertion, in two weeks Lee's army was reduced to but 35 percent of its original strength. By contrast, the Allied losses on D-Day amounted to about 6 percent of the total forces.

Federal losses were also severe. The generally accepted figure is something more than 12,000, about 25 percent of those who went into action. McClellan withheld a third of his army from battle.

Barlow's withered regiment lost another third of its men, six killed and thirty-five wounded. Of those soldiers who had been in continuous combat with Barlow from the beginning, only Fuller, Plumb, and one other had been untouched by gunfire.

Lee's Maryland campaign was a calamity for the Confederacy that would forever cripple its war aims. Civil war battles ultimately are fought for political objectives. No good reason existed to warrant an invasion of Maryland at that time and under those circumstances. Lee's soldiers certainly knew this, for they abandoned his army in wholesale numbers. His assumption that the people of Maryland would support him was correspondingly fallacious, but he clung to it even after the debacle. "I regret that the stay of the army in Maryland," he wrote duplicitously to the secretary of war on September 30, "was so short as to prevent our receiving the aid I had expected from that State."

Conceding his political miscalculations, some writers have tried to make the case that Lee had won a defensive victory at great odds. This argument disregards the question as to whether Lee should even have fought at Sharpsburg. It takes no genius to avoid defeat when fighting a Federal army commander who does not want to fight. Even so, the Federal ranks and artillery that did see action fought fiercely and well and might have annihilated the cornered Confederate army that Lee had exposed to peril. With no credit to Lee, the valor of his soldiers allowed two-thirds of them to survive the catastrophe.

Lee once had said that when he had maneuvered his army into contact with the enemy, he relinquished tactical control to his generals. But at Sharpsburg he was actively involved in decisions as the battle progressed. Exactly where Lee was, what he did, and when, cannot be accurately reconstructed, but the result of his activity was a haphazard and extemporaneous chain of command. Hood, for example, sought out Longstreet, Lee, and Jackson successively for reinforcements on the eve of battle. During the battle on the sunken road, Longstreet bypassed Hill and directly ordered Rodes to counterattack. Hill went directly to Lee, rather than Longstreet or Jackson, to ask for reinforcements. With such divided and confusing command relationships, with neither of the three principal generals fully aware of what the others had ordered done, it is small wonder that the Confederate army lacked cohesion and coordination.

D. H. Hill and John Hood were the two most important and effective Confederate generals of the day, because they brought a measure of coherence to the chaos at the center and left wing, respectively. It was they who perceived what was happening at their fronts and who called for reinforcements. And it was they who directed the reinforcements into position once they arrived. Now and again Longstreet interposed himself between Hill and his brigade commanders, but altogether Hill was the master of the center. Hood was particularly effective at the murderous left wing. His division prevented a collapse in the beginning, and as the other two division commanders were early casualties, the brigade and regimental commanders looked to Hood for direction.

As with the Federal forces, the ultimate outcome of the battle rested in the hands of the Confederate brigade and regimental commanders, fighting to survive with their backs to the river. The only permanent segments of the front line were the sunken road and Burnside's bridge. Otherwise the combat was fluid and swirling. Soldiers found temporary protection behind walls and trees and embankments, but the Confederate style of fighting demanded movement. The regimental commanders spontaneously led charges both frontal and at the flanks and rear.

When opposing regiments went head to head in the fields, the effect was brutally destructive. The winners—if there were any—were those regiments with the better discipline and firepower. Artillery was lethal, owing to the open terrain and hills. The Federal artillery was again superior, and it shattered Confederate formations and batteries at long range. All these factors contributed to the enormous casualties.

The underlying reason that the Army of Northern Virginia survived was because its commanders would not concede it could be beaten. Such an attitude was instinctive and invaluable, and it was the capital that Lee would draw upon until it was finally exhausted.

Lee claimed neither success nor failure in the formal report he submitted eleven months later. Nor would he admit to any error of thinking or leadership. Within days after withdrawing from Sharpsburg, he wrote Davis that he had intended to return immediately to Maryland and resume his offensive, but that the condition of his army had frustrated his plan. "In a military point of view," he temporized, "the best move, in my opinion, the army could make would be to advance upon Hagerstown and endeavor to defeat the enemy at that point. I would not hesitate to make it even with our diminished numbers, did the army exhibit its former temper and condition; but, as far as I am able to judge, the hazard would be great and a reverse disastrous. I am, therefore, led to pause."

Such explanations were good enough for Davis. He and Lee shared a disdain for critics. "I am alike happy," Davis wrote Lee on September 28, "in the confidence felt in your ability, and your superiority to outside clamor, when the uninformed assume to direct the movements of armies in the field. . . . In the name of the Confederacy, I thank you and the brave men of your army for the deeds which have covered our flag with imperishable fame."

New York diarist George Templeton Strong had gone to Sharpsburg to help with the wounded. "In the crowd of ambulances, army wagons, beef-cattle, staff officers, recruits, kicking mules, and so on," he wrote, "who should suddenly turn up but Mrs. Arabella Barlow, . . . unattended, but serene and self-possessed as if walking down Broadway. She is nursing the colonel, her husband (badly wounded), and never appeared so well. Talked like a sensible, practical, earnest, warm-hearted woman, without a phrase of hyperflutination."

Arabella had found a haven for her husband at a farmhouse east of Sharpsburg. The surgeons had removed a large canister ball from his wound, and Arabella took it as a souvenir that she delighted in showing to visitors. Barlow, of course, would not admit to pain, but his sense of relief that Arabella was there to care for him was unmistakable. He lay on the same stretcher that had brought him from the field hospital, perhaps because of his stoicism or because beds were scarce.

Several weeks after the battle a travel-stained Sergeant Plumb from the Sixty-first New York arrived at their doorstep to deliver an official document. Arabella broke the seal, read it, and smiled. "Frank," she said, "you're a general!"

Eager to celebrate, Arabella went into Boonsboro astride the sergeant's gaunt, ancient horse to buy food, with the sergeant in tow. The townspeople gaped when she arrived, dismounted briskly, and strode from store to store. They were still staring when she rode away, Sergeant Plumb lugging an overflowing basket behind her.

Arabella invited Plumb to stay for dinner, set a bench on the back stoop, and fed him generously. Plumb chuckled at the incongruity of it all. He was a common infantryman, a boy really, whose uniform was filthy with red dust, and his toes poked out of his shoes. Yet this splendid lady and the new general had made him their guest. Inside the house Arabella sat beside her husband, and his face looked as young as the sergeant's. You will get well, Frank, she said brightly; you will wear your general's star and fight again.

Barlow's promotion was a reward for his bravery and leadership during the Seven Days. Excellence alone, however, was no guarantee of the recognition and advancement that Barlow sought; it often took friends in high places to ensure a nomination. Barlow was no exception, and he was astute enough to know who had been his advocates and to express his gratitude.

One such person was Judge Charles Daly of New York, whom Arabella invited to visit with his wife Maria. "He was very earnest in his thanks to Charles for his exertion in procuring him his brigadiership," Maria Daly wrote, "and Charles was equally earnest in his professions of having done very little."

Barlow spoke readily of his experiences at Antietam and of his feelings about the enemy. "He admired the rebels," Maria Daly wrote, "what constancy, endurance, and discipline they showed, with what bravery they fought. Their long grey lines, he said, their shaved heads, their lank, emaciated forms and pale, cadaverous faces made them seem like an army of phantoms awaiting you. They were terrible, he said, and fearful from their fierce hate."

Months of recuperation would pass before Barlow returned to the war.

The surgeons had given up on the shattered body lying on the dirty straw in the makeshift hospital. Its face was gruesome, black and swollen, with eyes squeezed into slits, a leg and an arm bandaged and propped on pillows. Then Gordon awoke. The surgeons murmured as to the gravity of his wounds, but Gordon refused to listen. "Mrs. Gordon is outside," said the surgeons, "but we are concerned whether the colonel's lady is entirely prepared to withstand the possible shock under the circumstances."

Now more fully conscious, Gordon scoffed. Let her come in, he said.

Fanny entered the room, looking about for someone she recognized. "Here's your handsome husband," said the ghastly figure. "I've been to an Irish wedding." Fanny stifled a scream, then calmly kneeled beside her husband. Here I am, she said, your Fanny is with you now.

Then she nursed her husband to recovery. His jaw was wired and immobile, and Fanny funneled liquids through his clenched teeth. The wounds festered and drained pus that Fanny wiped away. Even Gordon lost hope when erysipelas, a usually fatal streptococcus infection, attacked his arm. A deep red inflammation spread up the skin toward his body.

Fanny spoke with the physicians. The only hope, they counseled, was to apply iodine above the wound several times a day. "She obeyed the doctors," Gordon later said, "by painting it, I think, three or four hundred times a day." The infection receded, but month after anxious month other crises arose and eventually abated under Fanny's meticulous nursing.

The prolonged and agonizing recovery created a profound change in Gordon's identity. Once fiercely self-contained, his very life became wholly dependent on the love of a woman whose courage equaled his own. Prayer, intense and devout, had healed as well, and his Christian faith was born again. It would be a humbled and pensive Gordon that returned to the Civil War battlefields.

1 2

FREDERICKSBURG

———•◦•———

Antietam reduced the Army of Northern Virginia to a mob of vandals. Defeated and disillusioned, its officers and men had lost confidence in Lee's leadership and judgment. Thousands of deserters and stragglers, in growing numbers, roamed at will, and officers no longer exercised military order and discipline. The disintegration of his army devastated and bewildered Lee. "I have taken every means in my power from the beginning to correct this evil," he wrote to Davis three days after he had retreated across the Potomac into Virginia, "which has increased instead of diminished. A great many men belonging to the army never entered Maryland at all; many returned after getting there, while others who crossed the river kept aloof."

Lee would never confess to his responsibility for the debacle. Antietam, he reported, while not a victory, had not been a defeat; his men should have been proud to have fought a larger army to a standstill. "It is true that the army has had hard work to perform," he wrote Davis, "long and laborious marches, and large odds to encounter in every conflict, but not greater than were endured by our revolutionary fathers, or than what any army must encounter to be victorious."

Lee's Army of Northern Virginia ransacked the northern Virginia countryside. "[T]he destruction of private property by the army has occupied much of my attention," wrote an anguished Lee to Davis. "A great deal of damage to citizens is done by stragglers, who consume all they can get from the charitable and all they can take from the defenseless, in many cases wantonly destroying stock and other property. . . . It is impossible as the army is now organized to prevent these acts by orders. When such orders are published they are either imperfectly executed or wholly disregarded."

The anarchy, as Lee saw it, was a consequence not of his leadership but of the leniency of the laws and regulations governing military conduct, the responsibility for which lay with Davis. Lee beseeched Davis for legislative relief that would allow him to punish and purge the unfit. As a stopgap, Lee requested the assignment of two field grade officers to act as a military inquisition.

Lee knew well enough, however, that if he were to salvage his army he would have to do it himself. He began with harsh orders to Longstreet and Jackson, reminding them of their accountability. "The depredations committed by this army," he wrote, "its daily diminution by straggling, makes it necessary for preservation itself, aside from considerations of disgrace and injury to our cause arising from such outrages committed upon our citizens, that greater efforts be made by officers to correct this growing evil."

Lee was appalled when he received the first head count. "This return is very imperfect," he noted before submitting it to Richmond. Nonetheless it reflected "the woeful diminution of the present for duty in this army. The absent are scattered broadcast over the land." The most immediate remedy was to restore morning roll call, at *reveille* Lee emphasized. Once roll calls were in hand, Lee could begin to determine how many men remained in his army.

To get more accurate muster reports, Lee lectured Longstreet and Jackson like second lieutenants. "As half a quire of foolscap paper will last one year for a morning report," he admonished, "containing, as it does, thirty-two lines, and it is the labor of half an hour to rule the columns of a morning report for one month, the morning report will be made every morning to the regimental or battalion commander and sent through brigade to division commanders."

Lee's search parties scoured the countryside for stragglers and hauled them in. "How long they will remain with us," he wrote Davis, "or when they will again disappear, it is impossible for me to say." He insisted that convalescents be returned to duty promptly and refused to allow them furloughs. If soldiers did somehow get home on authorized leave, Lee did not want them paid while absent. When they needed money, he reasoned, they would return to their regiments.

Lee's greatest reliance was on conscription, because most Southerners had lost their zeal for volunteering. "Although he had gone to war to prevent coercion of a state by the national government," wrote James McPherson in *Battle Cry of Freedom*, "Lee now believed the war would be lost unless the government in Richmond obtained the power to coerce men into the army." The Confederate government passed legislation in April 1862 making able-bodied white males between eighteen and thirty-five (soon amended up to forty-five) liable to three years of service. Those already in the army remained in uniform for at least three years (later extended for the duration of the war). The Confederate Congress amended and enlarged the laws as the war progressed, although loopholes and exemptions remained.

As the Army of Northern Virginia replenished its manpower by one means or another, Lee reorganized its still cumbersome structure. Heretofore several divisions had been loosely collected into de facto corps, commanded by Longstreet and Jackson by virtue of their seniority. Shortly after Antietam, Davis notified Lee that the Confederate Congress had authorized permanent corps whose commanders would have the rank of lieutenant general. Davis asked Lee to nominate generals for the new position, together with recommendations for promotion to the ranks of general.

Lee promptly recommended Longstreet and Jackson for lieutenant general.* Later he would assert that the two corps, each with four divisions, were too large and cumbersome. Three smaller corps were preferable, but no other generals were thought competent for the third corps command.

Lee deferred to Davis to pick and choose the major and brigadier generals from a list that Lee already had provided. The promotion of general officers had become so contentious and politicized that Lee wanted to remain at arm's length, even at the risk of allowing Davis to make bad selections, as he so often had done in the past.

Davis tried and gave up. Promotions in the Confederate army were predicated upon vacancies in command positions, but Lee's organization was a maze to Richmond. No one knew with certainty how many divisions and brigades existed and, given the casualties at Antietam, who, if anyone, commanded them. The secretary of war passed the buck back to Lee.

Lee had a hell of a mess. While combat attrition had diminished the number of officers competent for higher command, the survivors' ambition for promotion was intense and shamelessly overt. To add to the predicament, statutes prevented Davis and his War Department from relieving or removing the incapacitated and incompetent from command. Given the casualties of the summer's campaigns, many unqualified officers had risen to higher command by reason of seniority, and a disabled officer could retain his nominal command indefinitely.

Davis nudged the Confederate Congress into granting him a measure of latitude, but in the main Lee was forced to juggle his generals by persuading them to cooperate voluntarily. When the sorting out was concluded, Lee submitted his recommendations. Hood was recommended for permanent division command and promotion, becoming, at age thirty-one, the youngest of nine major generals of infantry.

Gordon too made the list. Although an invalid, with his return to duty conjectural, Gordon was recommended for brigadier general. He would have to wait, however. The previous commander of the brigade intended for Gordon unexpectedly returned to reclaim his brigade, closing the vacancy. Gordon's promotion was deferred, awaiting his recovery.

With few exceptions, Davis and the Confederate Senate approved Lee's recommendations.

Winter was approaching, and Lee's soldiers were in rags. Shoes and blankets were among their greatest needs, and there were never enough. When his son Rob visited Lee at his headquarters, they had to sleep together and share Lee's only blanket. Lee bombarded the Richmond authorities with requests

---

* The Confederate Senate confirmed a total of seven lieutenant generals in mid-October 1862. Grant would be the only lieutenant general in the Federal army; his promotion would come in March 1864.

for support. "The number of barefooted men is increasing daily," Lee wrote Davis after the retreat from Antietam, "and it pains me to see them limping over the rocky roads." Lee's concern for the horses was equally intense, and he issued detailed orders for maintaining their health.

The Confederate supply system was in its customary disorder. Speculators, many of them in uniform, sold provisions and supplies to their comrades at exorbitant prices. In mid-November 1862 the secretary of war confirmed that Lee's army would have to subsist on reduced rations for the foreseeable future. Forsaking the possibility of reforms in the administration of supply at the seat of government, Lee improvised, sending cavalry raiders to grab cattle and leather and his quartermasters to expropriate cloth at factories. Such expedients alleviated the most grievous shortages, but in the long term many of his soldiers trod the snow in bare feet, and with empty stomachs they slept in freezing weather without blankets. That they still could, and would, fight well was the miracle of the Army of Northern Virginia.

Fighting was what Lee's generals did best. As administrators they were largely slack and indifferent. Hood was typical of their inattention to matters of organization and supply. Several weeks after Hood's promotion to major general, Lee's inspector general scrutinized the division. He found the soldiers badly clothed and shod, with hundreds barefoot—problems that could not be laid entirely to Hood. His horses, wagons, and artillery seemed in good shape. On the other hand, many of the soldiers were without arms, which always were available and needed only to be requisitioned. A number of companies had arms of mixed caliber and poor condition, which complicated the supplying of ammunition. By a simple redistribution each company could have identical rifles and a common-size bullet. Nothing could have been more important than well-armed infantry, yet Hood had not acted on the flagrant deficiencies.

When Lee read this and similar reports, he knew that his army had not recovered from the psychological and physical ravages of the Maryland campaign. He would have to sit tight, as close to supplies as possible, and react to McClellan. If McClellan did not bestir himself before deep winter halted all operations, Lee would not disturb him.

In early November, Washington bludgeoned McClellan into undertaking a new campaign. When Lee received reports of massive troop movements, he confirmed his strategy of avoiding battle in a letter to Secretary of War George Randolph. "The enemy, apparently, is so strong in numbers," he wrote, "that I think it preferable to attempt to baffle his designs by maneuvering, rather than to resist his advance by main force. To accomplish the latter without too great risk and loss would require more than double our present numbers."

This was a new Lee talking, a chastened Lee, cautious and conservative instead of combative. For the first time, he advocated a scorched-earth policy that destroyed roads and railroads to retard the enemy's approach, a thought hitherto unimaginable. Moreover, he was prepared to concede areas south of the Rappahannock River all the way to Richmond. "I am loath to add to the devastation of the country," he wrote to the secretary of war on November 14, "which had already occurred by the ravages of war, and yet think it prudent to throw every impediment to the progress of the enemy toward Richmond in his way." He would fight to the last with every means. The longer Lee fought, the more devastation Virginia would suffer. As the war inexorably escalated, its military guardian would in fact destroy the state to save the state.

Lincoln ordered Ambrose E. Burnside to replace McClellan on November 7 as commanding general of the Army of the Potomac. "Burnside was regarded by his military associates as a loyal, honest officer and gentleman," wrote historian E. J. Stackpole, "but none had any illusions on the score of his military competence." Burnside had many options and great resources for their execution. Lee would try to interpose his army in Burnside's path wherever it led. Jackson was in the Shenandoah Valley; Longstreet was on the Rappahannock. Eventually they would have to rejoin wherever Burnside chose for the decisive battle. For once, Lee had the benefit of good intelligence sources. He was certain by November 20 that Burnside was headed toward Fredericksburg on the Rappahannock, and ultimately Richmond.

The two armies converged on the lovely community from opposite sides of the river and prepared for battle. "Fredericksburg is one of the oldest and most aristocratic of the Virginia towns," wrote Moxley Sorrel. "At this time the place was the home of families of historical importance and present interest, with a thorough knowledge of good living, and still respectable cellars of old Madeira that had been imported by them many years before."

The Federal army demanded that the town immediately surrender or else be leveled. Lee negotiated a compromise allowing the inhabitants to evacuate their homes before the shooting started. The refugees in the rain were a scene of pathos. "I was moving out the women and children all last night & today," he wrote Mary on November 22. "It was a piteous sight. But they have brave hearts. What is to become of them God only knows. I pray he may have mercy on them." Their Madeira was distributed among the soldiers, who gulped it from tin cups.

The two armies squatted on the opposite shores for more than two weeks while Burnside waited for pontoons to bridge the Rappahannock. The delay allowed Jackson to rendezvous with Lee. Perhaps for want of tools or motivation, the Confederates did not construct fortifications but waited on the hills overlooking the town and the river. Eventually the pontoons were constructed, and, protected by artillery, the Federal army came unopposed to Lee's side of the shore. Peering through his ever present long glass, Lee gritted his teeth as he watched the enemy occupy and pillage the town with a cheerful will, while awaiting orders to begin the assault. Lee spoke briefly to an aide, and the Confederate artillery, seeking out the Federal soldiers among the buildings, completed their destruction.

Lee was both incredulous and relieved that Burnside's intentions were so obvious and so tardy in execution that he could counteract every cumbersome, protracted move. The Federal assault ultimately failed, according to Francis Walker in his history of the Second Corps, "from the utter absence of anything like a plan of operations. The troops were thrown over the river in a sort of blind hope that so splendid an army, in such overpowering numbers, would somehow achieve a victory."

Burnside's garbled orders on December 13 committed but two of his nine right-wing divisions to open the assault against Longstreet, who overlooked the town from Mayre's Heights. The Federal troops had to cross a drainage canal on its two rickety bridges, a splendid point of aim for Lee's artillery barrages. As Burnside had declared that the ditch did not exist, he made no provisions for engineers to build bridges across it.

The men who managed to cross the existing bridges threw themselves against Longstreet's infantry, protected by a stone wall along a road leading to the cemetery on Mayre's Heights. Further downriver, Burnside's left wing had no better luck against Jackson. The Federal soldiers had been condemned from the beginning. As early darkness fell, both armies still occupied what they had held when the battle began.

And, as at Antietam, the beaten army was allowed to escape. Sorrel, still on Longstreet's staff, was baffled. "A thick fog or mist also arose and enveloped the enemy's movements in strangeness and uncertainty," he later wrote. "They were actually started on hastily recrossing the river, but we don't appear to have known it. Most of the day of the 14th it was thick and misty, veiling successfully the enemy's movements, but all the time he was preparing for his retreat. He was not attacked while in this exposed position. Why not? It is generally thought it would have been fatal to the Federals and it is indisputable that they were in hourly dread of it. But why did we not attack on the 14th in daylight? It is not my part to attempt this explanation, but it looks as if we were 'building a bridge of gold for the flying enemy.' "

The fact was that Lee did not want to fight if he could avoid it, a drastic departure from his principle of fighting for the sake of fighting. Conserving his army was paramount. His only explanation was that he did not want to get within range of the Federal artillery. Burnside recrossed without opposition to the opposite bank of the river, taking with him all that he had brought, except his dead.

Lee was astonished that Burnside had given up so easily. God himself had spared the Army of Northern Virginia from further fighting, he told Mary. "[God's] discomfiture of our numerous foes," he wrote three days after the battle, "& obliging them to recross the river was a signal interference in our behalf for which I feel I cannot be sufficiently grateful." Lee let them go in peace. "They went as they came," he wrote, "in the night."

One indication that the fighting was over was a messenger that Lee sent to Burnside. Moxley Sorrel crossed the river under a flag of truce. He walked through the abandoned town, now in utter destruction. "[A]ll that went to make up those comfortable old homes," he wrote, "were strewn helter skelter, broken and ruined around the streets. The streets were filled with distressed women and children, both black and white. But we passed on—'C'est à la guerre comme à la guerre!' "

Sorrel delivered a request that the Federal army bury its dead lying behind the Confederate lines, stripped naked by Confederate scavengers. A Federal officer asked how many bodies there were, so that adequate burial parties could be sent. When Sorrel guessed at the number, the officer groaned. The burial details were so careless and indifferent that Lee sent Sorrel a second time. He was detained overnight and ate supper from a Federal mess. The contrast with his usual fare was overwhelming.

"To see what they had, its quality, its abundance," Sorrel later wrote, "filled one's heart with envy when contrasted with the doled-out, bare necessities of life the lot of our own uncomplaining fellows. Here in this great kitchen were huge swinging vessels of odorous real coffee; immense chunks of fat, fresh beef of all parts of the animal; great slabs of desiccated vegetables, which, when thrown with knuckles of meat and good flesh into the boiling cauldron, puffed out, swelling each vegetable into something like freshness, and then with free dashes of salt and pepper, behold, a soup of strength and tastiness fit for Faint Heart himself to fight on. They gave me of it all and I tasted all, sleeping well and early up."

Lee moved his headquarters and army to the southern bank of the Rappahannock, across from Fredericksburg, for in the spring the Army of the Potomac would again descend upon him from the north. His tent was pitched in the twilight of swirling snow, and he slowly moved inside to his chair as his servant lighted a fire. Lee knew that he was unwell; his very hands were weakening, making it difficult to grasp the reins while riding. The servant murmured and handed Lee his meager supper on a tin plate.

PART III

WESTERN

THEATER,

1861-62

1 3

GROPING IN THE
HEARTLAND

*Next to Virginia, Tennessee was tramped by more soldiers, plowed
by more projectiles, plagued by more guerrillas and consequently
bred more military problems than any other state.*
Francis F. McKinney, Education in Violence

Tennessee campaigns occupied George Thomas throughout the war,
Ulysses Grant in the war's beginning, and John Hood at its end.
Thomas knew the state well. It occupied a central geographic location and was surrounded by eight other states. Six of them were in the Confederacy: Arkansas to the west; Mississippi, Alabama, and Georgia to the
south; North Carolina to the east; and Virginia to the northeast. The border
slave states of Kentucky and Missouri lay on Tennessee's northern and
northwestern boundaries. Hence Tennessee could be used as a base of operations by the Union for offensive operations southward and for Confederate
expeditions northward.

The state was politically divided. True believers in the Union lived in East
Tennessee, and Confederates elsewhere. The distribution of slaves reflected
the schism: they were numerous in western Tennessee and somewhat less so
in the central region, with few living in the mountainous east. A plebiscite
rejected secession on February 9, 1861, but Lincoln's call for troops after
Fort Sumter allowed pro-Confederate politicians to harangue voters to
approve secession by a two-thirds majority on June 8, 1861.

East Tennessee refused to join the Confederacy, and so the state had political representatives in the congresses of both the United States and the Confederate States. Each government claimed Tennessee as its own. U.S. Senator
(and later Vice President and President) Andrew Johnson and Representative
Horace Maynard—both from East Tennessee—exerted unremitting pressure
on Lincoln to occupy East Tennessee as an act of deliverance to the Union
faithful in the region.

Tennessee's population contained large numbers of potential soldiers, and
its volunteers fought for both the North and the South. The Army of Ten-

nessee was the principal army of the Confederacy in the west. Its commanders included A. S. Johnston, P. G. T. Beauregard, Joseph Johnston, Braxton Bragg, and Hood. The Federal Army of the Tennessee was active but not so large; its organization varied over time, and its commanders included both Grant and Sherman.

Time and again both the Federal and Confederate armies undertook massive offensives that swept the state from top to bottom. The Federal army of occupation, nervous and insecure, dispersed its troops in garrison duty throughout the state, because guerrillas attacked lines of communications and depots. Forced to retreat into the Deep South, the Army of Tennessee always sought to return to the state, like Crusaders liberating the Holy Land.

Chattanooga, located in the southeastern corner of the state, was the strategic heart of the western Confederacy and a gateway to the Deep South. Its railroads radiated in all directions. One line went off into the mountains, finding its way by following the Tennessee River valley through Knoxville and into Virginia; it was this contested route that allowed the rapid shifting of Confederate troops between the eastern and western theaters and the transport of foodstuffs, supplies, and raw materials for Lee's Army of Northern Virginia. Another line went southward to Atlanta. A third major trunk line went directly west to Memphis on the Mississippi, and the fourth went northwest to Nashville in north central Tennessee.

Nashville, the Tennessee capital, rivaled Chattanooga in importance. Possession by either side was politically symbolic. Confederate dreams of seizing and holding Kentucky and Missouri made Nashville the principal Confederate operating base in the early phases of the war. The city lay within the most productive agricultural region of the state, and its railroads shipped supplies in all directions. The Cumberland River flows from the northeast, changes direction at Nashville, and proceeds northwest toward its confluence with the Tennessee and Ohio Rivers, facilitating waterborne transportation and distribution. The city's manufacturing facilities and huge supply depot, the Confederacy's largest in the western theater, supported the Army of Tennessee. When Nashville came under Thomas's control, it became the largest supply depot in the war, sustaining all of the western Federal armies.

Tennessee's rivers served both as avenues of invasion and as barriers to advancing armies.

• The Mississippi flows southward along Tennessee's western border. When Memphis fell to Federal forces, it opened the river downward to Vicksburg, the site of Grant's July 4 victory in 1863, coincident with the victory at Gettysburg.

• The Tennessee flows westerly through upper Alabama after passing Chattanooga and then turns northerly back into west central Tennessee. After Grant took Fort Donelson, the river allowed his army to attack Shiloh and to occupy the most fertile regions of the state.

- The Cumberland, flowing east to west, impeded either army from moving north or south, but Thomas used it to get men and supplies into Nashville throughout the war.

Finally, Tennessee was the principal supplier of horses, mules, beef, pork, corn, and grain to the Confederate armies, providing, for example, 78 percent of the army's pork and two-thirds of its beef by early 1862. Mines in the East Tennessee mountains provided two-thirds of the minerals and ores that were critical to the manufacture of Southern armaments; especially important were niter, used for gunpowder, and copper from a large mine in Ducktown, sixty miles east of Chattanooga. In his work *Confederate Supply,* Richard D. Goff wrote that, together with Virginia, Tennessee provided "nearly all of the significant iron mills, coal mines, flour mills, grain fields, and slaughterhouses of the Confederacy."

Given all this, the strategic objectives of both sides were elemental. At the minimum, the Confederacy had to hold Tennessee in order to feed and equip its armies and as a source of recruits. Only Virginia provided more Confederate soldiers than Tennessee, and Tennesseeans were enthusiastic fighters who had turned out in such numbers for the Mexican War that the state nickname had become the Volunteer State. Beyond that, Confederate strategists planned to have the Army of Tennessee invade Kentucky and Missouri, slave-holding border states that could provide additional manpower and matériel. These states could strengthen the Confederacy enough to avoid defeat and to gain recognition by European powers. The Confederacy would then have achieved its independence. Tennessee was the crux.

Federal strategy clashed between political and military motives. President Lincoln wanted to rescue Union supporters in East Tennessee by kicking out the Confederate army, pacifying the rebel civilians, and holding the region for the duration of the war. His generals, however, resisted such a strategy because of the logistical difficulties of mountain warfare. Their prime objectives were the seizure of Nashville and Chattanooga, control of the rivers and railroads, and the occupation of central and western Tennessee.

Such was the genesis of the western strategies when the war began. Some aspects persisted as unshakable dogma, especially the Confederate crusades into Tennessee and Kentucky. The Federal government eventually realized that capturing *places* would not end the war. The only sure way to victory was to destroy the western Confederate army, an undertaking that for years proved impossible to achieve.

A political apocalypse raged in Kentucky in the summer of 1861, because it was a slave state divided between loyalists and secessionists. Arming themselves for a fratricide, both camps schemed, blustered, and intimidated. Frantic to prevent incipient bloodshed, the governor and the legislature declared that Kentucky had chosen a policy of armed neutrality, that it would ally itself with neither the Federal nor the Confederate governments, and that troops from neither side would be allowed on Kentucky soil. Kentucky would live in peace, aloof from the Civil War.

It was absurd and wishful thinking. No state could be neutral. Geographically, Kentucky was an avenue for troop movements between the North and South and could not long remain a huge no-man's-land. In political terms, Kentucky had set itself apart as a de facto third country; that is, it had broken away from the Union just as surely as had any Confederate state. From Lincoln's point of view, any state that did not support the preservation of the Union was traitorous regardless of declarations of neutrality. All states had to declare their loyalty and fealty to the government of the United States. There were no exceptions. That was the war aim of the United States.

The governor realized this in late August 1861 when he wrote to Lincoln protesting that the Federal army had established Camp Dick Robinson near Lexington in violation of Kentucky's neutrality. Lincoln dismissed the governor's complaint, then concluded ominously: "It is with regret I search and can not find in your not very short letter, any declaration or intimation that you entertain any desire for the preservation of the Federal Union."

Still, in the beginning, Lincoln respected Kentucky's dilemma and tried to win the state's allegiance through political means. The Confederacy, too, avoided overt military action from out of state, planning instead surreptitiously to arm and mobilize a Kentucky militia led by secessionists who would seize political control by a coup d'état. A navy lieutenant, William Nelson, warned Lincoln of the threat. Although a junior officer, Nelson was of a prominent Kentucky family whose political connections gave him direct access to the President. Lincoln authorized Nelson to provide arms and ammunition to Kentucky loyalists, which Nelson did with such dispatch that the secessionist militia abandoned its conspiracy. Its leaders fled into Tennessee to try again later.*

While Kentucky wavered, Brigadier General Grant arrived in Cairo, Illinois, without his new uniform. Still in civilian clothes, he entered the district headquarters. Not recognizing Grant, the colonel in command ignored him. Grant sat at a table. His pen scratched on a sheet of paper, which he gave to the colonel. It was an order announcing that Grant had assumed command.

A bullheaded Confederate Episcopal bishop ended the sham of Kentucky's neutrality on September 3, 1861. Acting without authority, Bishop-Major General Leonidas Polk, with headquarters in western Tennessee, ordered Brigadier General Gideon J. Pillow to enter southwestern Kentucky and seize the Mississippi River town of Columbus, closing the river to Federal traffic. As Columbus was also the northern terminus of the Mobile and Ohio Railroad, it was reasoned that the Federal army would be unable to use it for points south. The Confederate momentum, it was believed, might extend to the Ohio River, Kentucky's northern boundary with Illinois.

---

* Nelson became a major general of volunteers in the Federal army, the only naval officer to do so. Another Federal general shot him dead in a quarrel.

Grant had to act. To do nothing, to allow the Confederates to seize western Kentucky and to threaten Illinois—Lincoln's home state—was unthinkable. Control of the rivers was imperative. Paducah, Kentucky, at the confluence of the Tennessee and Ohio rivers, was one such control point. It was forty miles up the Ohio River from Cairo and could be easily reached by steamer. Ten miles farther upriver lay Smithland, Kentucky, and the mouth of the Cumberland River. Both river cities had to be seized before the Confederates got to them.

Grant's obstacle was not the Confederates but rather Major General John C. Frémont, his superior in St. Louis. Frémont had been a celebrity before the war and the Republican presidential candidate in 1856. Lincoln had commissioned him in the regular army and had sent him west as supreme commander, a position in which Frémont proved incompetent. Already frenzied by reports of guerrillas in Missouri, Frémont panicked yet further at news of the Confederate invasion of Kentucky. In confusing, long-winded letters and dispatches, he ordered Grant to fortify both banks of the Ohio River and to deploy troops helter-skelter. Grant lunged in the traces when he realized that Frémont had actually given him a free hand. Two days after Polk's invasion, Grant telegraphed Frémont that he was ready to seize Paducah. Frémont readily approved, but in an act of madness encrypted his authorization message in Hungarian.

A flotilla of transports and gunboats awaited Grant's command to get underway. Grant came aboard in the darkness and joined navy Captain Andrew H. Foote. The boats cast off and steamed upriver, the first of Grant's many combined operations with the Federal navy. Paducah came into sight, flying Confederate flags, on the morning of September 6. Confederate soldiers scurried out of town as the boats approached the landing, and the flags disappeared. The uneventful occupation of Smithland followed. Grant controlled the Kentucky bank of the Ohio River.

The Kentucky governor and legislature finally had to take sides. New elections in the state had favored the United States, and as the Confederacy had been the first to occupy Kentucky, the state government declared for the Union. Kentucky was now open for the Federal army to move south into Tennessee and beyond. Whether they would move was another matter.

Months before Grant had set his military foot in Kentucky, Federal regiments had recruited Kentucky volunteers, but, owing to the precarious political considerations, they had kept their encampments across the Ohio River in Indiana and Ohio. Local political leaders insisted that Kentucky volunteers had to be based in the state, and in July 1861 they established Camp Dick Robinson in the dead center, thirty miles south of Lexington. Nelson was in charge. Two thousand volunteers assembled, and more would follow. The secessionists were enraged, timid politicians feared all-out war, and as we have seen, the governor protested in vain to Lincoln. The navy lieutenant stayed put with his men and awaited arms and supplies from the Federal government.

The nearest Federal army authority was in Cincinnati, 100 miles to the north. Since May, Brigadier General Robert Anderson, a Kentucky native and late commander of Fort Sumter, had commanded the Department of Kentucky, the name a paradox for he had not a soldier in the state. He needed help. A Confederate invasion from Tennessee was considered imminent. Camp Dick Robinson needed immediate support, and regiments from the midwestern states had to be assembled and organized. As a bargain for accepting his assignment, Anderson in return had the prerogative of selecting four brigadier generals to command in the field. George Thomas, William Tecumseh Sherman, Don Carlos Buell,* and Ormsby M. Mitchel were duly promoted and assigned to the western theater.

Thomas was ready to move. He had been in Carlisle, Pennsylvania, when the war began in earnest in April 1861, attempting to equip and remount the Second Cavalry Regiment, which had left Texas betrayed and in disgrace. Two successive promotions, to lieutenant colonel and then colonel, arrived in late April and early May to fill the vacancy created by Lee's resignation. Commanding the regiment, Thomas joined the forces of Robert Patterson, assembling at the Virginia-Maryland border to pin down Joseph Johnston and prevent him from reinforcing Beauregard at Manassas. As a consequence, Thomas invaded his home state in command of a brigade and skirmished with Stonewall Jackson, but Patterson's caution allowed Johnston and his army to go to Manassas to share in the Confederate victory.

While Grant was busy in western Kentucky and Thomas was in transit from the east, Confederate General A. S. Johnston arrived to take command of the western theater. A man of whom much was expected, he was a friend of Jefferson Davis from the old days. Johnston soon discovered, however, that Davis had sent him on an untenable assignment. Tennessee's governor, Isham Harris, for example, had fortified the Mississippi River to the exclusion of the remainder of his state. Generals Polk and Pillow were similarly transfixed on the river. Tennessee's northern border with Kentucky had been left open on the naive assumption that Kentucky's neutrality would be a buffer against Federal attack. Nashville was defenseless. Polk's insane invasion of Kentucky had opened the door for Federal troops to swoop across Tennessee's 300-mile border, defended by the handful of Confederate troops not otherwise engaged on the Mississippi River.

Johnston decided to attack to keep the Federal army off balance while he consolidated his position with arms and reinforcements. Confederate soldiers swarmed into Kentucky. Brigadier General Simon B. Buckner took a trainload of troops sixty miles up the line from Nashville to Bowling Green, Kentucky, and there was speculation that he planned to seize Louisville and Lexington. Sherman scraped troops together in Louisville and raced forty miles down the railway to derail Buckner, the first of many instances when a western campaign followed the line of a railroad. To the east, Confederate Brigadier Gen-

---

* No relation to the author.

eral Felix Zollicoffer simultaneously invaded southeastern Kentucky near the vital Cumberland Gap, the mountain passage at the convergence of Kentucky, Tennessee, and Virginia. Johnston's bluff worked. His numbers were few, but they loomed large. Anderson and Sherman were stunned.

Thomas arrived at Camp Dick Robinson in mid-September, just as the Confederates began their Kentucky invasion. Relieving Nelson of command, Thomas inspected the squalid encampment and talked to the men. It was readily apparent that they were confused, despairing, and rebellious, many of them sick with measles. Thomas was appalled. Where were the supplies, the equipment, the funds, the transportation? he asked. There were none, he discovered, for the camp was without a single staff officer, neither paymaster nor quartermaster. For two months the volunteers had endured the hostility of secessionists and prayed for relief. By an act of faith they had stuck it out, waiting for someone in authority to lead them, to make soldiers out of them, and to provide them guns and ammunition and food. Such were their expectations of deliverance from the stout officer who came in the name of the United States Army.

Thomas fired off a requisition for winter supplies and the first of many pleas to Quartermaster General Montgomery Meigs for staff officer support. In the interim, he performed the functions himself. In early November help arrived. A regular army officer, Captain Alvan C. Gillem, a Tennesseean and a West Point graduate, reported as Thomas's quartermaster, a man of such competence that he became a general officer and one of the most influential figures in Tennessee government. He brought his protégé with him, a civilian quartermaster clerk, John W. Scully, a former enlisted artilleryman. Both men were old army and had served in Texas.

Scully was an intelligent, literate, ambitious Irishman who desperately wanted the status and prestige of a regular army commission. To Scully's delight, the officers treated him as an equal. His letters to his wife provide the best description of Thomas and of events in the early days of the war in Kentucky and Tennessee. When he first arrived at Thomas's headquarters, his eye caught the situation immediately. "It would astonish you to see the Volunteer officers," Scully wrote his wife. "[They] bother the life out of the General." When Gillem first introduced him to Thomas, the general's eyes gleamed when he learned that Scully had served in Texas. "[Thomas] said he wished I had a commission and he would place me on his staff," wrote Scully. "He said he has had to act [as] adjutant and every thing else himself."

Scully and Gillem found a frightful mess. "The Quartermaster Department was in such a state when we came in to this division," Scully wrote, "that General Thomas had serious notions of sending in his resignation several times. There was upwards of six million of dollars expended in this part of Kentucky alone, and no account taken of it, until we came here and straightened it up."

Thomas began to organize the nucleus of a proper army. From the crowd at Camp Dick Robinson he formed four regiments of Kentucky Union men and two regiments of volunteers from East Tennessee. And from these six regiments Thomas established the First Kentucky Brigade, the embryonic beginning of the Army of the Cumberland, which would become the most professional and modern of all the armies in the Civil War.

While Thomas shaped up his command, delegations from Lexington beseeched him to defend the city from the approaching Confederates, who were brushing aside the scattered irregulars. Thomas stood fast, believing—as we know now correctly—that the threats were largely imaginary and that to go off half-cocked would be, in his words, a "disaster." Sherman had stopped Buckner at Bowling Green, and Thomas's outposts kept Zollicoffer at bay in the southeast. The front had stabilized by the end of September.

Meanwhile, Anderson had asked to be relieved for reasons of health, and Sherman, himself erratic and distraught, briefly took his place. The first of many operations into East Tennessee soon began, for Andrew Johnson and Horace Maynard had convinced Lincoln by mid-October that if a Federal army entered the region, the loyal partisans would revolt against the Confederate authorities and secure East Tennessee for the Union. Having received Lincoln's backing, Johnson and Maynard were blunt with Sherman and Thomas. Federal forces had to go into East Tennessee. If they refused, whatever their misgivings about lack of readiness, Lincoln would relieve them. It was compelling logic.

The politicians explained their plan to destroy the bridges on the East Tennessee railway that went northeast from Chattanooga and Knoxville into Virginia. The partisans would infiltrate and seize the bridges, and Thomas's troops would rush to their support. Thomas got underway, but as he got closer to his rendezvous, Sherman succumbed to panic and, imagining that Thomas was about to be trapped, ordered him to withdraw. Johnson, who was with Thomas, became furious, demanding that the East Tennessee regiments (sensing betrayal and verging on mutiny) be placed under his command. If Sherman and Thomas did not have the guts to do it, shouted Johnson, he would take them in. Thomas had tried to dissuade Sherman, but, failing that, he told Johnson that he had to obey orders. He would not relinquish his authority to the livid Johnson and threatened to arrest him if Johnson persisted. His voice and face expressionless to mask his emotional pain, Thomas ordered an about-face. Mounting his horse, he turned away from the partisans, who thought that he was coming.

Left on their own, the partisans burned several bridges. The result was first hysteria and then retaliation. "The burning of the railroad bridges in East Tennessee shows a deep-seated spirit of rebellion in that section," Governor Harris wrote to Jefferson Davis. "Union men are organizing. The rebellion must be crushed out instantly, the leaders arrested and summarily punished." Troops rushed in, arresting civilians suspected of Union sympathy. A colonel in Knoxville asked the Confederate secretary of war, Judah Benjamin, what to do with them. "I proceed to give you the desired instructions," Benjamin replied, "in relation to the prisoners taken by you among the traitors in East Tennessee. [A]ll such as can be identified as having been engaged in bridge burning are to be tried summarily by drum-head court-martial, and if found guilty, executed on the spot by hanging. It would be well to leave their bodies hanging in the vicinity of the burned bridges."

In the North there was predictable outrage. Sherman's behavior had been so bizarre that Secretary of War Simon Cameron said that he was crazy and fired him. As Thomas had been involved and had crossed Johnson, he undoubtedly assumed that he too would be dismissed. Although Johnson had opposed his appointment from the first, their relationship began to improve, perhaps out of mutual respect. As it was evident that Thomas had done his best to carry out the plan, he remained in place. East Tennessee remained under Confederate control, and the trains continued to roll through the mountains and over the bridges past the hanging bodies.

From the standpoint of both the Federal government and the Confederacy, the incoherence of civil-military affairs in the west cried out for resolution. As agendas and geographical jurisdictions rarely coincided between regional political leaders and commanders of the military departments, a paradox arose: coordination was both paramount and unachievable. Nonetheless, both sides tried. The Confederate government had established a unified command under A. S. Johnston, that is, under one officer of high rank with commensurate authority to unify disparate forces over a large geographical region. The position, however, was beyond Johnston's functional capacity.

George McClellan, the Federal general in chief, attempted to achieve coordination through the voluntary cooperation of two senior generals, Buell and Henry W. Halleck, each commanding a portion of the theater. Buell relieved the disgraced Sherman in early November and became Thomas's immediate superior in the Army of the Ohio. His jurisdiction included Kentucky east of the Cumberland River and all of Tennessee. Halleck relieved Frémont, the political animal who had bungled military affairs and had embarrassed the administration with pronouncements of emancipation. Grant's new boss now commanded the Department of the Missouri and the region west of the Cumberland.

Halleck had graduated from West Point some twenty-two years before and had proven himself at once an intellectual, a writer and a published military theorist. He had resigned from the army in 1854 and established himself in California as a successful lawyer, businessman, and author. When the war began, Lincoln appointed him the fourth ranking general in the army. Halleck went to St. Louis and found Missouri in anarchy. Until he restored order there, an aggressive movement into Kentucky was out of the question, McClellan's wishes notwithstanding.

Buell, too, had come from California, where he had been stationed with the regular army. Commissioned a brigadier general of volunteers, he had served briefly with his friend McClellan in organizing the Army of the Potomac before his posting to Louisville as Sherman's relief. Both Lincoln and McClellan had given Buell parting instructions to seize East Tennessee, each for different reasons. Lincoln wanted to rescue the Union loyalists suffering persecution after the abortive bridge burnings. McClellan had military objectives: to destroy the Tennessee railroads leading into Virginia, then to invade western Virginia concurrently with McClellan's projected invasion of eastern Virginia with the Army of the Potomac.

Buell had no intention of complying with either Lincoln or McClellan. Like Halleck, his first priority was to organize and train his ragtag volunteers. While the Confederate forces in southeastern Kentucky under Generals Zollicoffer and George B. Crittenden were annoying, they did not threaten Buell's army. Thomas, he felt, could neutralize them with a brigade or two. Buell had his eye on the main Confederate army, Johnston's forces at Bowling Green. If it were smashed, the feeble Confederate line across Kentucky would collapse, Tennessee would be opened, and Nashville would surely fall. Do this first—Buell urged in telegrams to McClellan—together with supporting operations from Halleck, and then East Tennessee could be attended to in the fullness of time.

With neither Halleck nor Buell ready for an immediate offensive, the year 1861 came to a discouraging close. Aloof from each other, the two generals were also so reticent with Washington that Lincoln and McClellan remained unaware that their western armies were stationary and would remain so indefinitely.

The two men's inertia was a reprieve to Johnston, who despaired of his future once the Federal army bestirred itself in his direction. Yet Johnston failed to convey a sense of urgency to Richmond, either because he was unaware of the alarming degree of unreadiness within his scattered department, or perhaps because he felt obliged to spare Davis bad news. In any event, Davis and Benjamin gave first priority to Virginia, trusting that Johnston, reputed to be a master soldier, miraculously would find a way to make do. Not only did Richmond fail to bolster Johnston's army, in many instances the government weakened it with ill-advised policy directives. The most glaring deficiency was weaponry. Many of Johnston's regiments were destitute of arms, and they were likely to remain so. Richmond simply ordered the regiments disbanded, over Johnston's protests that he wanted to retain them, even though weaponless, to deceive enemy intelligence.

Nevertheless, Johnston could have done more on his own initiative. Complacent Nashville dug not a spadeful of dirt in self-defense. Neglecting to see for himself, Johnston reported that the city was behind robust ramparts. He similarly deceived himself about Forts Henry and Donelson, ostensibly guarding the Tennessee and Cumberland Rivers at the Tennessee border. An inspection would have revealed that apathy had rendered the forts contemptibly inadequate. Rather than walking around, Johnston remained anchored in Bowling Green for four months, deluding himself and Richmond as to his readiness for sustained combat.

A mental fog descended over Kentucky and Tennessee that clouded the thinking of the local commanders, whose vision extended no farther than the hands before their faces. Distance and winter weather distorted estimates of enemy strength and capabilities, while internal mistrust and feuding further distracted the generals from developing coherent plans and strategies. Each side so feared the other that neither grasped the nettle. So it was a most peculiar stalemate: front lines separated by scores of miles of misty, soggy countryside, and generals composing telegrams to Washington and Richmond explaining away their paralysis and their apprehensions about the distant enemy they could not bring themselves to confront.

After his brisk occupation of Paducah, Grant returned to his headquarters at Cairo in early September. Its living conditions were, according to a contemporary, "an abomination . . . the streets were without bottoms and the walks were on stilts." Mud was everywhere, mixed with a slop of garbage and refuse, its stench so overpowering that the city could be smelled before it was seen. Saloons were the principal business. "Bunyan's Slough of Despond," wrote a war veteran, "into which all the filth and slime of this world settled, was nothing beside the slough of Cairo."

Grant's uniform had finally arrived, and he delighted in it. Plumes decorated his snap-brimmed hat, and a sword and gold sash accented his ensemble. His flowing beard touched his chest. He liked what he saw and sent portrait photographs to relatives. Eventually he had second thoughts. Possibly Julia scolded him for being ostentatious. Perhaps he remembered how he had been humiliated showing off his uniform as a junior officer. For whatever reasons, Grant trimmed his beard and wore the simple field uniform so familiar in his later photographs.

The tedious details of administration consumed Grant's attention. Some 20,000 soldiers in his district were scattered along the rivers, and he organized them into proper military entities, five brigades in all. As a former quartermaster, he was accustomed to procuring necessities for his men and animals, but his requisitions to St. Louis languished in Frémont's headquarters, a place of corruption. Frémont also withheld funds for paying the troops and purchasing goods and services, forcing Grant to use credit, and eventually the contractors balked. He could not even buy coffins.

It was under these circumstances—typical on both sides—that Grant first distinguished himself from most other generals. He neither complained nor threatened, nor did he fight the system. Rather, he ordered through regular channels, explaining simply why he needed the order, so that his requests seemed neither unreasonable nor inflated. He would never cite shortages, as others would, as an excuse for inaction. Grant's way would please Lincoln, who suffered from generals who demanded more of everything rather than fight with what they had.

Yet Grant would not passively accept whatever the system imperfectly provided. If he could not get what he wanted by the book, he would impulsively try other ways, getting things done by resourcefulness and brute force. For Grant, doing nothing was intolerable. Doing something, anything, regardless of risk and wasted motion, was compulsory. When Frémont sent him defective muskets, for example, Grant went to Springfield to seek arms and artillery from the Illinois state government. On another occasion he sent his quartermaster to St. Louis to find hospital blankets.

Frémont's mismanagement became so scandalous that Illinois congressman Elihu Washburne and a congressional committee investigating fraud came to Cairo in late October to query Grant about procurement practices. Without mentioning Frémont by name, Grant confirmed the allegations. Washburne beamed at his protégé. In a letter the same day to Secretary of the Treasury Salmon P. Chase, he wrote that Grant needed both reliable arms and operating funds. Then he gave the good news: "Genl Grant . . . is one of the best officers in the army, and is doing wonders in bringing order out of chaos. He is as incorruptible as he is brave."

The nice words from his mentor masked a dilemma. Grant's career was stagnating, even though Washburne was talking him up for promotion to major general. Grant knew that he did not merit advancement until he was combat proven. "Let service tell," he wrote his sister, "who are the deserving ones and give them promotion." In fact, Grant had been a brigadier general in command of troops in sight of the enemy for three months, but he had not moved against the Confederate stronghold at Columbus, so close that he could spit on it, only twenty miles downriver from Cairo. The newspapers were complaining, and he looked bad. "What I want is to advance," he wrote Julia on October 20. But he knew the numbers, and they favored the Confederates behind their fortifications.

The opportunity came on November 2, two days after Washburne and his colleagues had left Cairo. In a last hurrah, Frémont had ordered Grant to dispatch troops into Missouri to chase down troublesome guerrillas, and Grant had put several regiments into motion. Now, though, Grant saw a chance to move on his own, because the St. Louis headquarters was a vacuum: Frémont had been sacked, and his interim relief, Major General David Hunter, was a nonentity who took days to find the front door. With no interference from above, Grant could interpret Frémont's final orders in a way that would allow him a free hand.

As a consequence, Grant decided to try an opportunistic, hit-and-run attack against the enemy encampment at Belmont, Missouri, across the Mississippi River from Columbus. Belmont had been on his mind before; when Washburne had visited Cairo on October 31, Grant and Brigadier General John A. McClernand (a brigade commander and coincidentally an Illinois congressman) had told Washburne that there should be an offensive down the Mississippi, starting with an attack on Belmont and going on from there. But now Grant put the grander scheme aside, limiting his objective solely to Belmont: he and McClernand would take a force of infantry, together with modest artillery and cavalry support—about 3,000 men in all—downriver in transports supported by two gunboats. They would land in the early morning and assault whatever forces they chanced upon. Beyond that, Grant would capitalize on unfolding opportunities.

Grant covered himself for the record by writing that the military objective was to prevent Confederate forces at Columbus-Belmont from interfering with his operations in Missouri; that is, the Belmont operation was simply an extrapolation of Frémont's November 2 directive. What Grant really intended is uncertain, perhaps to get favorable attention, possibly to relieve the abominable boredom. By attacking Belmont he indirectly attacked the Confederate fortress at Columbus, but at less risk. Perhaps he hoped that the gunboats could isolate Belmont from Columbus and prevent reinforcements from crossing the river once the fighting started.

In any event, there were no Confederate gunboats to threaten his own transports; the Federal navy controlled the rivers, as it would throughout the war. Furthermore, Gideon Pillow—whom Grant scorned—commanded at Columbus and was thought unlikely to threaten. Whatever happened that day, Grant had too few men to hold Belmont, so the best hope was a brisk fight in which he caused more casualties than he received. He would have to reembark his troops when the time was right, return upriver, and then some-how explain how a withdrawal in the face of the enemy was a victory.

At first Grant's Belmont raid succeeded. His men drove the Confederates from their camp, but then fell to looting. When Confederate reinforcements got across the river from Columbus, Grant and his troops, with bullets whistling around them, had to hightail it back to their transports. The troops clambered on board, dragging captured horses and a few artillery pieces. The boats withdrew in a fusillade from the pursuing Confederates. It was a close call.

Grant's casualties were grievous, over 600—some 20 percent of his force—although he originally claimed but 250. The Confederates had suffered losses in like proportion. Now it was time to explain in the most favorable terms what he had done. Grant wired Hunter a terse, noncommittal report upon his return to Cairo; Hunter had to have been bewildered when he read the telegram. What had Grant been up to? What about the "heavy casualties"?

Grant sent Hunter a follow-up telegraphic report the following day, November 7. First things first: "The victory was complete." Next, Grant had been in the thick of action: "Gen. McClernand & myself had a horse shot under us." Finally, his raid had prevented the Confederates from interfering with his Missouri operations: "Prisoners taken report that a large force were prepared to start [to reinforce Missouri irregulars]. This move will no doubt defeat this move." Grant's latter assessment was either misinformation or an alibi. We now know that Polk and Pillow had entertained no such intention. They were anchored in Columbus and sending not a single soldier elsewhere.

Grant's first detailed report, on November 8, went neither to army head-quarters nor to Washington, but to his father. It was a glowing, self-serving account of sound military reasoning, bravery, sizzling action, and ultimate success. The letter was printed in the *Cincinnati Gazette* on November 11. Civilians in Ohio were the first to learn about what Grant now called the Battle of Belmont. Grant finally wrote to Washington on November 10. But questions lingered, and skeptics since have challenged Grant's motives and skewing of events. Grant could never shake the accusations and had to explain away Belmont until his death.

Belmont did establish precedents for the early phases of the war, for example, the disposition of prisoners, the dead, and the wounded. There were no rules of war; those would come later when Halleck was in Washington. For the nonce rules of chivalry sufficed. Grant had left men and bodies behind when he hastily evacuated Belmont, and now he was obligated to try to retrieve them. It would be tricky. Some days before, when Polk had proposed a prisoner exchange, Grant had patronizingly replied, "I can, of my own accord, make none. I recognize no Southern Confederacy myself."

Polk still might be sore, and the battlefield was his territory, so Grant chose his words with discretion. "In the skirmish of yesterday," wrote Grant on the eighth, "in which both parties behaved with such gallantry, many unfortunate men were left upon the Field of Battle who it was impossible to provide for. I now send in the interest of humanity, to have these unfortunates collected and medical attendance secured them." As the "unfortunates" were all wounded Federal soldiers he had abandoned, Grant offered a quid pro quo. "I at the same time return sixty four prisoners taken by our forces who are unconditionally released." That was good enough for Polk. A flag of truce was arranged, sixty-eight Federal corpses were buried, and officers from both sides conferred in quiet, courtly negotiations on the riverside for the exchange of the wounded and prisoners.

By then, the Confederates thought that they had assessed Grant. In the aftermath of Belmont he seemed like one of them, courteous and gallant, a man who regarded a battle as a joust with no hard feelings afterward. And they were getting to know him socially, for Grant and his staff earlier had met the Confederate officers in neutral waters on the river, passing the time with drinks and conversation. It was a time of innocence that would not linger. The war would become so brutal, so absolute, that by the third year Grant would neither exchange prisoners nor agree to a truce to save the wounded. Yet his fondness and respect for old friends in Confederate service never changed.

Good did come to Grant from the Belmont experience. He was, for example, learning how to work jointly with the navy. The war in the west would be governed in large measure by the rivers, where troops and supplies in quantity could be transported swiftly, independent of the crude and undeveloped roadways. The Federal navy controlled these waters from the beginning, except for Confederate strong points like Vicksburg. Shipyards on the Ohio produced protected gunboats—mobile artillery batteries that provided naval gunfire support for troops ashore and could slug it out against shore batteries. There was an enormous potential if the army and the navy worked together in combined operations, which Grant recognized early on. He was on good terms with the naval officers in his district, even providing them food and supplies from his own stores.

Another longer-term benefit for Grant was that the Belmont episode had so rattled Polk that he feared an imminent assault on Columbus. He drew his defenses more tightly about him, disregarding the remainder of the Confederate line stretching eastward. Johnston, peering anxiously for the approach of Federal troops, remained similarly immobilized at Bowling Green, 150 miles to the east. Between them flowed the Cumberland and the Tennessee, the vulnerable ingress to the vitals of the western Confederacy, a way whereby the Federal forces could with impunity steam past their flanks and into their rear; yet so mentally and physically entrenched were the two Confederate generals in their isolated Kentucky citadels that the defenses of the rivers languished for want of attention.

There was one other unintended consequence of Belmont. Grant had dazzled the Washington authorities with his claims of victory. In the eyes of Lincoln and McClellan, it seemed that Belmont was a prelude to bigger things, and Washburne remembered that Grant had spoken of Belmont as a first step to operations down the Mississippi. Hence, they were given to believe that, if they got Grant the additional arms and equipment which Frémont had denied him, a major offensive was imminent.

Imminent offensives were far from Halleck's mind when he took command of the western district on November 19. Frémont had left him a mess that would take months to unsnarl. Indeed, Halleck could hardly communicate downriver between St. Louis and Cairo; the secessionists who controlled the Missouri shore of the Mississippi hijacked riverboats with impunity, while smugglers sympathetic to the Confederacy brazenly landed supplies. Secessionists ransacked Union farms, and their owners became refugees. Until Halleck rid southeastern Missouri of guerrillas and irregulars, there was small chance that he would undertake an offensive through Kentucky.

Meanwhile, Grant had discarded his idealistic policy of toleration toward civilian secessionists. "There is not a sufficiency of Union sentiment left in this portion of the state to save Sodom," he advised Halleck on the twenty-second. Infuriated by the slaying of four of his soldiers in early January 1862, Grant ordered reprisals and the roundup of civilian suspects. The brigade commander took Grant's orders literally. "I shall probably have a hundred in tonight," he reported. "Will General Grant please give me more definite instructions. I think I shall find out who shot the pickets and when I do I shall shoot the guilty parties on very short notice." But feeding, housing, and guarding a horde of hostile civilians, including women and children, got so distracting that Grant gradually abandoned his purge.

Grant fretted that brigadier generals his senior coveted his command, and that he might soon be sent packing. That apprehension intensified when Halleck became his new boss. Grant immediately proposed that he go to St. Louis to brief Halleck, but Halleck told him to stay away. Thereafter, communications became infrequent, limited largely to administrative matters, and Grant had to address all of his correspondence to Halleck's adjutant.

Grant soon felt snubbed, with good reason: Halleck distrusted him. Grant was too ambitious, too chummy with Washburne, who had clout with Lincoln; Halleck expected subordinates to report to him and not trade secrets with politicians. And Grant had used poor judgment at Belmont, had gone off half-cocked, and then had covered it up with self-serving reports. Halleck would keep Grant under his thumb so that he could not derail Halleck's own agenda.

Halleck was also contemptuous of Grant's abysmal record as an administrator. Washburne's accolades following his October 31 inspection had blinked away reality, because newspapers now published headlines about the "Cairo Fraud." Grant's quartermaster, Reuben B. Hatch, had taken kickbacks and had stolen government property, and his clerks were racketeers. Competitive bidding, when there had been any, often went to the highest bidder, typically friends and relatives. The stench of scandal found its way to Washington, and Quartermaster General Meigs directed Grant to arrest Hatch and convene a court-martial. Grant was in a bind. Hatch was crooked, but he also had strong political connections in Illinois. Then Lincoln himself got involved. He knew Hatch personally, thought kindly of him, and said so. Under the circumstances the buck passed between Washington, St. Louis, and Cairo. Nothing came of the charges, and Hatch returned to duty.

Business with the riverboats was similarly corrupt. The craft were essential to the army, the boat captains knew it, and they squeezed the government for all they could get. Grant foolishly had negotiated some of the worst of the contracts himself and had signed vouchers for leasing riverboats at exorbitant prices. To remedy the problem, McClellan and Edwin M. Stanton, the Federal secretary of war, sent a cantankerous river captain named William J. Kountz to Cairo with the authority to charter riverboats on Grant's behalf. Kountz was honest but tactless. When he challenged the going rates, the captains rebelled and petitioned Grant to replace Kountz with one of their own. Grant and Kountz had words, and in mid-January 1862 Grant arrested him for insubordination.

The move backfired spectacularly, and Grant almost got himself court-martialed when Kountz formally charged him with having been "beastly drunk" while in company with the Confederates under a flag of truce. Other formal charges followed, alleging that Grant staggered drunk in public. The charges—drawn up in regulation style and signed by a cloud of witnesses— found their way to Washington via Halleck.

Grant instinctively turned to Washburne and sent an emissary, Algernon S. Baxter, to plead his case. "Capt. Baxter can tell you of the great abuses in his Department, here," wrote Grant, "and the efforts I have put forth to correct them, and consequently the number of secret enemies necessarily made." Even before Baxter arrived, Washburne had heard rumors and allegations. He could look the fool for supporting Grant, who was now potentially a political liability. Washburne anxiously wrote to John Rawlins for reassurance.

Grant's chief of staff replied to Washburne with a rambling, contradictory, passionate apologia. Grant was "a strictly total abstinence man," although it was true, Rawlins wrote, that Grant had a drink now and then. But never had he been drunk or out of control. Such charges stemmed from malice, wrote Rawlins. Assuring the politician of Grant's fidelity, he ended with a pledge: "Should General Grant at any time become a intemperate man or an habitual drunkard, I will notify you immediately, will ask to be removed from duty on his staff (kind as he had been to me) or resign my commission. For while there are times when I would gladly throw the mantle of charity over the faults of friends, at this time and from a man in his position I would rather tear the mantle off and expose the deformity."

Although Washburne was placated, in early February Stanton sent his assistant secretary of war, Thomas A. Scott, to Missouri and Cairo to investigate and report. The condition of affairs in Grant's quartermaster department, wrote Scott, were "about as bad as could well be imagined . . . a regular system of fraud appears to have been adopted." A complete reorganization of the Cairo post was essential. With an obvious swipe at Grant, he continued, "I am prepared to recommend . . . that an efficient Brigadier General—a regular officer and a good business man—be sent here."

It was small wonder that Halleck viewed Grant with suspicion and hostility. Nonetheless, although Grant's ineptness in business practices had carried over into his military administration, Halleck as yet could not remove Grant for cause. As the new year arrived, Grant felt that he had to see Halleck to explain what was happening. Grant sent a telegram on January 6, 1862, begging for an audience. Halleck ignored him.

Soon, however, Halleck would be overtaken by events, and he would be forced to deal with Grant. Fighting was about to begin.

14

KENTUCKY AND THE
FORTS

A s the first winter months of the war descended upon the western theater, the generals on both sides struggled toward combat readiness.
Eventually one side or the other would consider itself ready to make
war and venture hesitantly to confront the enemy. Strategic planning on the
Confederate side was largely ad hoc. A. S. Johnston was a theater commander in name only, exerting so little authority that his subordinate commanders acted autonomously. Absent a firm hand, their squabbling forestalled
coordination. The Confederate objectives defaulted to holding what had been
seized in Kentucky in September.

Halleck and Buell were stiff-necked generals who disdained directives from
Washington as ill-considered political expediencies. Their problem was the
anarchy left them by Frémont and Sherman. Sorting out the wreckage was
daunting. Militias had to be sworn into Federal service and properly equipped.
Haphazard companies had to be assigned to regiments, regiments formed into
brigades, and brigades formed into divisions, levels of organization never contemplated in the prewar army. Commanding officers had to be selected and
assigned. Volunteers needed arms and equipment, especially rifled muskets
that provided longer range and greater accuracy. Efficient staff organizations
were required for logistical support and medical services. Despite demands
from Washington, immediate offensives were out of the question.

Buell organized his Army of the Ohio into brigades and divisions in early
December.* Thomas took command of the First Division, which incorpo-

---

* The Federal and Confederate armies differed in the ways in which brigades and divisions were
designated. The Confederates identified each unit by the name of its first permanent commander (e.g., Hood's Brigade, Cleburne's Division), and the designation was retained even
though a succession of officers might subsequently serve in command. In contrast, the Federal
army used a straightforward numbering system.

rated four brigades of four regiments each, together with miscellaneous cavalry regiments and squadrons and several artillery batteries. Whenever possible, a Federal division included a "regular brigade," one whose officers were largely from the professional army. Considered the most reliable and battleworthy, this brigade would be given the toughest assignments.* Such would be the framework of Federal divisions throughout the war. Attrition—casualties, sickness, desertions, expired enlistments, and miscellaneous absentees—governed the strength of a typical division. In this instance, Thomas's division probably numbered about 5,000 able-bodied men at the end of 1861.

Moving the men into action was laborious. It was easy for Lincoln in far-off Washington to press for immediate action in East Tennessee, but he could not envisage the impact of weather and topography. An army division, dragging its logistics tail behind it, quickly churned the few miserable roads into mud pits. This was a self-evident truth to every soldier who had ever wrestled a laden wagon mired in muck, its team floundering in rain and sleet.

Nashville, on the other hand, made strategic sense to Buell. It was the focus of Confederate activity in Tennessee and could be approached on the Cumberland River from either the east or the west, making roads unnecessary. As Nashville was close to Halleck's bailiwick, his Department of the Missouri could support Buell. With these considerations in mind, Buell urged Lincoln to defer operations toward East Tennessee and to give him permission to advance on Nashville.

Assigned to the area of eastern Kentucky, Thomas had an ambiguous mission. He was supposed to prepare to advance into East Tennessee, yet Buell restrained him, awaiting Lincoln's blessing on his Nashville scheme. By December 1861, Thomas had scattered his brigades in southeastern Kentucky primarily to thrust and parry with Felix Zollicoffer's forces. In anticipation of Lincoln's approval, Buell began to withdraw these brigades so that they would be ready for Nashville. Zollicoffer filled the vacuum, battering Thomas's outposts and extending his span of control within the state. By giving Zollicoffer a free hand, Buell had created a predicament that could not be explained away to Washington.

On Christmas Day, Thomas got the job to find and hammer Zollicoffer. Such an effort required an efficient staff, and by the time the troops were underway Thomas had assembled the people he needed. The adjutant general was the staff administrator, who found Thomas meticulous in completing his paperwork on time and in proper format, regardless of distractions. The trustworthy Scully was the scribe for Thomas's confidential letters. Alvan Gillem had become, according to Scully, Thomas's right hand man. With the

---

* Grant deplored grouping the professional officers into elite units and instead believed that they should be distributed throughout the entire Federal army as leavening. As the Confederacy had no regular army, by default its professional officers were integrated into the provisional army, whose volunteers benefited from their competency and experience.

services of supply under control, Thomas's troops undertook their first campaign well fed, shod, equipped, and armed, and they were healthy. When smallpox began to appear, the staff arranged vaccinations that helped to an extent. Although the disease felled many, it could have been worse had Thomas done nothing out of ignorance or indifference. Most generals practiced the self-inoculation of camp life.

The staff gathered in Thomas's mess tent for supper on the first night of the march. Seating arrangements were a matter of precedence, and Thomas assigned each to his place. The adjutant general sat at Thomas's right hand, the place of honor and seniority, and Gillem took his traditional place as mess treasurer at the foot of the table. Two aides-de-camp remained standing, together with Scully, who instinctively deferred to the younger officers. "Come Scully, you're the oldest soldier," said Thomas. "You take my left ahead of the volunteer aides." Scully was touched. "I think he done it," he wrote his wife, "to show them he placed me on a footing with any of them."

Thomas was stoic, stolid, businesslike, and always visible to his troops. "[W]henever and wherever they saw him, they knew that all was right," wrote an army veteran. "So, also, on the march nobody ever saw him, with an escort trailing behind him, dashing past a moving column of troops, throwing up dust or mud, and compelling them to leave the road to him. If anybody had the right of way, it was they and not he. He would break through the woods, or flounder across a swamp, rather than force his men from the road, and so wear them out by needless fatigue.

"He sometimes had terrific outbursts of temper," recalled the veteran. "It was usually under complete control, but when it did break out it was volcanic. He once so alarmed a teamster who, when his mules were stalled, was beating them over the head with the butt of his whip, that the poor fellow took to the woods to escape he knew not what fate. . . . The violation of a flag of truce . . . led him to such vehemence of language as even treason to the flag did not call forth. [Thomas reacted similarly to guerrillas who ambushed his soldiers.] But such outbursts were very infrequent, only often enough to show it would not do to trifle."

And as time passed, Scully perhaps best expressed the feeling that grew and would last between Thomas and his soldiers. Months after Scully had left the staff, Thomas came upon him along a road and reined in to chat for a moment. "Scully," chuckled the general, "you are getting positively stout." It was a tender moment for the young Irishman. "I love old General Thomas," he wrote his wife.

The mud and miserable weather were hard on the men, but spirit transcended pain. The Kentucky and Tennessee regiments lusted for a fight because of their hatred for Zollicoffer. Thomas further sparked morale by assuring them that conditions were in their favor. "We are confident of whipping [Zollicoffer]," wrote Scully, "as we have more men and better equipment than he."

The brief campaign in southeastern Kentucky was the first instance of Thomas infusing his troops with the "spirit of the army," a concept expressed by Tolstoy in *War and Peace*. Tolstoy's words were about the Russian army, but they bear repeating here, as the concept is universal.

> *And through the undefinable, mysterious link that maintains through a whole army the same temper, called the spirit of the army, and constituting the chief sinew of war, Kutuzov's words, his order of battle next day, were transmitted instantaneously from one end of the army to the other.*
>
> *The words and phrases of the order were by no means the same when they reached the furthest links in the chain. There was, indeed, not a word in the stories men were repeating to one another from one end of the army to the other, that resembled what Kutuzov had actually said; but the drift of his words spread everywhere, because what Kutuzov had said was not the result of shrewd considerations, but the outflow of a feeling that lay deep in the heart of the commander-in-chief, and deep in the heart of every Russian.*
>
> *And learning that tomorrow we were to attack the enemy, hearing from the higher spheres of the army the confirmation of what they wanted to believe, the worn-out, wavering men took comfort and courage again.*

Civil War armies both the North and South had at first an abundance of fighting spirit. In those armies where it was nurtured, that army grew in strength, the foremost example being the Army of the Cumberland. In other armies much of it was betrayed and wasted in inverse proportion to the quality of leadership of the generals, most grievously in the Army of Tennessee, less so in the Army of the Potomac and the Army of Northern Virginia. The wise general used the spirit of the army with prudence and discretion, and his army responded with triumph against incredible obstacles and with steadfastness in crises. Less wise generals squandered it trying to compensate for failures in planning, or in logistics, or in battlefield coordination, and their armies suffered tragedy either with Pyrrhic victories or devastating defeats.

Near Mill Springs, Kentucky, on January 17, 1862, the vanguard of Thomas's mud-clogged column staggered to a halt some ten miles north of the Confederate encampment. An advance brigade commanded by Brigadier General Albin F. Schoepf stationed nearby had watched Zollicoffer, and Thomas conferred with Schoepf as to their next move.

The Confederates were trapped by their own hand on the north bank of the Cumberland River. The river immediately behind them was so deep and strong that they could scarcely cross over should they be forced to withdraw. They must have known for days that Thomas was coming, yet they had remained rooted in place. They obviously intended to fight where they were, or else they would not have waited for Thomas to get there.

Thomas too had come to fight, but not before he was ready. Zollicoffer was not going anywhere, not now. With his own winded forces stretched for miles behind him, Thomas decided to bring up his rear and to consolidate with Schoepf's brigade before attacking Zollicoffer and pushing him into the river. In the meantime, precautions were necessary. Zollicoffer might attack him first—attacking was the Confederate way of war. And a commander surrounded in any war often tried to break out and escape. Anything could happen. Thomas spoke to his commanders. Presently cavalry and infantry pickets trotted toward the Confederate encampment with orders to sound the alarm if the enemy came into view.

In the Confederate camp, Zollicoffer was no longer in command. Jefferson Davis had assigned Major General George B. Crittenden, a professional officer, to command the eastern Kentucky district; Zollicoffer the politician was now his subordinate. Crittenden had arrived at Mill Springs on January 2 and was horrified to find Zollicoffer on the wrong side of the river, dangerously exposing his camp. Time did not permit the Confederates to move across to the defensible riverbank before Thomas arrived. Acting in desperation, Crittenden chose to attack Thomas preemptively.

Crittenden's decision was ill considered. The Confederate arms dated from the War of 1812; rain rendered the flintlock muskets even more unreliable. The troops were country boys, accustomed to hit-and-run raids in small groups, untrained to fight as disciplined regiments. Crittenden sent these men, with Zollicoffer to lead them, down the muddy trail and through the underbrush in a midnight downpour, forsaking the familiarity of their fortifications to meet Thomas's disciplined troops on strange terrain.

Zollicoffer first made contact with Thomas's cavalry pickets and then with the infantry outposts in the misty, drizzling morning twilight of January 19. The sound of musketry reached the Federal encampment, and excited soldiers rapidly mustered under the barking of orders from their officers. Their first battle of the war was upon Thomas and his troops.

Thomas had but two infantry regiments immediately at hand to confront an enemy attacking in unknown numbers. They would have to hold the line until Thomas could throw in reinforcements. Their brigade commander, Colonel Mahlon D. Manson, galloped up to report his preparations to meet the enemy. His uniform disheveled, his body shaking with tension, his voice gabbling, Manson momentarily was unfit to lead the nervous troops. "Sir," roared Thomas. "Return to your command." Manson straightened his back, wheeled, and returned to the front.

Thomas took his staff forward to assess developments and saw that one of Manson's regiments was still in ranks, awaiting orders. Calling the regimental commander to his side, Thomas put his arm on the colonel's shoulder, pointed toward the sound of gunfire, and quietly instructed the shivering young officer where to deploy his men. Steadied now by Thomas's composure, the colonel issued brisk orders, and Thomas watched approvingly as the regiment trotted into the dripping woods.

Nearer to the front, peering through the rain, Thomas saw enemy soldiers in a cornfield attempting to turn his flank. "Gillem, bring up a battery," said Thomas, and their fire swept away the Confederates. Scully later wrote to his wife that Gillem was "man of all work" in the fight, guiding regiments into line, replenishing their ammunition, coordinating the other staff officers, acting altogether as Thomas's indispensable lieutenant.

In the beginning the Confederates outnumbered the Federal troops, but the flints on many of their muskets were too wet to strike an ignition spark. The Federal soldiers had the more modern percussion-cap rifles. That evened the odds. The Confederate artillery never did enter the fight. "The rebels fought like tigers for about an hour," wrote Scully, "during which there was an incessant roar of musketry." Two more regiments reported to Thomas for orders. Thomas pushed them forward just as the two frontline regiments exhausted their ammunition.

Three more regiments of Federal troops arrived, and Thomas threw them into the enemy flanks. An Ohio regiment commanded by Robert L. McCook charged straight ahead with bayonets. Scully was amazed that a German-American regiment could act so bravely, as it was commonly believed that they were not good fighters. "[A] more splendid thing I never witnessed," Scully later wrote. "The Colonel was shot in the leg, and as I passed by him he sang out, 'Scully, I'm shot in the leg, but I'm good for the day anyhow.' [H]e rode all day without having his wound dressed."

The Confederates collapsed under the pressure, running pell-mell for the river ten miles away, littering the road with the debris of the panic-stricken. There was no one to rally them; Zollicoffer had been shot dead when he wandered into the Federal lines. Thomas replenished and realigned his regiments, and they marched toward the river in pursuit. "[T]he line was kept up as uniform as I ever saw at a drill," Scully later wrote, "every regiment and battery in its proper place, that one would imagine he was at a grand review instead of a terific battle. All through the General was as 'Cool as a Cucumber.' "

The troops arrived at the Confederate base by midday and found its men, with their backs to the river, crouched for a last-ditch stand. Thomas knew that his men were exhausted by the morning's fighting and the pursuit afterward, nor had they eaten. If he attacked the entrenchments before nightfall, he would suffer unnecessary casualties. Better, he thought, to wait until morning and meanwhile let his artillery soften things up. His men would be fed and rested, all his troops would have arrived, and he could launch a powerful, coordinated attack.

When day came, he discovered that during the night Crittenden and his survivors had fled over the river on makeshift watercraft. Guns, wagons, cannons, and garrison equipage, a thousand or more horses and mules— everything had been abandoned in the mad rush to escape from Thomas's troops. The wounded had been left groaning where they lay. Even the sacred regimental colors had been left behind. On the opposite side of the river the shocked and ragged bands of survivors had disappeared into the countryside. Thomas stayed where he was to savor his triumph.

Colonel Speed S. Fry, a regimental commander who, incidentally, had shot Zollicoffer, was puzzled. "General," he asked, "why didn't you send in a demand for surrender last night?"

The question seemed to startle Thomas, and then he meditated for a moment. "Hang it all, Fry. I never once thought about it."

The victory was stunning, the first since the Federal debacle at Manassas six months before. For the Federal side, Mill Springs was a dramatic role reversal. Federal soldiers had gone head-to-head with a larger Confederate force that had been unchallenged in southeastern Kentucky for months. In a masterstroke, Thomas had reclaimed a third of the state for the United States and, in a day, utterly destroyed a Confederate army.

Bravery had not been a factor in the outcome at Mill Springs. Combatants on both sides would always be brave in equal measure. Victory came rather from superior leadership and weapons technology.

Thomas was the better general. He had coolly directed his regiments and kept them steady under fire. Crittenden, on the other hand, had disgraced himself, not by attacking, but by his panicked flight afterward. He never again held a command and resigned his commission. The befuddled and blundering Zollicoffer had not recognized the enemy and had gotten killed as a consequence.

The edge in technology had been with the Federal small arms. The obsolete Confederate flintlock muskets had been disastrous. Even when they did work, the Federal soldiers could thumb their noses at their opponents from two hundred yards away. Josiah Gorgas, the enterprising Confederate chief of ordnance, would shortly get proper weaponry into the army, rifled muskets with percussion primers that could match the Federal arms for range, accuracy, and reliability. It would be the only Confederate war-making technology equal to the Federal army. In all other respects, as we shall see, the Northern technology would provide a potentially decisive advantage for those generals who understood how to employ it.

Finally, the Federal artillery had been superior by orders of magnitude, for it had been both deadly and mobile. Thomas knew how to use it, how to place it where it was most needed, and when and how to reposition it as situations unfolded. Its effect on the enemy was dramatic. "Their artillery," wrote a Confederate brigade commander afterward, "having been brought into play, swept the entire field, throwing shell, grape, and canister shot into our very midst." The Confederate artillery never unlimbered. Thomas's devastating use of combined arms—coordinated and mutually supporting artillery and infantry (and later cavalry)—would become his trademark in this and future battles.

News did not travel rapidly from that remote and lonely corner of Kentucky. Johnston, in Bowling Green, did not learn that his right flank had disappeared until Crittenden finally got to a telegraph in Nashville. Thomas, again technologically superior, had laid wire as he advanced, so that Washington quickly got the word by telegraph, where it was received with elation.

But Stanton's victory proclamation cited no names, not Thomas, not anyone. When the official reports had been received, said Stanton, rewards would be forthcoming. Lincoln and Stanton were as good as their word.

Within a month after receiving the official reports, Lincoln nominated Thomas for promotion to major general of volunteers. The Senate confirmed the nomination on April 25.

Thomas's victory opened the way to East Tennessee, giving Buell the best opportunity of the entire war to occupy and consolidate the region and to achieve Lincoln's highest priority in the western theater. But like Sherman before him, Buell ordered Thomas to return. Regardless of what Lincoln wanted, Buell was still set on taking Nashville, and he needed Thomas's division to do it. Turning their backs on their field of victory—and on East Tennessee—Thomas and his men returned to central Kentucky over the same muddy path they had just traveled. Within weeks, Confederate soldiers reoccupied the vacuum.

Thomas would always remember the campaign with a smoldering rage. Twice he had had East Tennessee in his grasp. Twice he had been recalled. Throughout the remainder of the war the Confederates would use the area to threaten Federal communications and to send troops and supplies between the eastern and western theaters. Federal forces would try time and again to seize the area, always with failure, until the war was nearly over.

By January 1862, the inertia and lack of cooperation between Halleck and Buell had exhausted Lincoln's forbearance. McClellan had been unable to budge the two generals, and when he took sick and was confined to bed, Lincoln dealt directly with the field commanders. A series of messages hummed on the telegraph wires. Lincoln pressed Buell and Halleck to work in concert, to talk to each other, and to produce a plan they both agreed upon.

In response, Buell sent a lengthy proposal to Halleck on January 3, suggesting that they combine forces for any hope of dealing with Johnston's forces in central and western Kentucky. Halleck responded three days later that he was still dealing with insurgents in Missouri and "it would be madness" to undertake offensive operations in Kentucky. He would be unable for some weeks to cooperate with Buell in any way. Thereafter the two generals exchanged not another word until the end of January. Lincoln's hopes for coordination between the two generals were fruitless.

Having told Buell that offensive operations in Kentucky were impossible, Halleck immediately began offensive operations by ordering Grant to undertake a purposeless demonstration toward Columbus, Kentucky. Grant's forces flailed about in the muck and rain for two weeks, their suffering worsened for want of logistical support, as Grant had arrested quartermasters Reuben Hatch (the crook) and William Kountz (the disputatious riverboat captain). Grant brought the debacle to an end on January 18.

Grant had managed, however, to gather important information concerning Fort Henry, just over the Tennessee border and presumably guarding the Tennessee River. Brigadier General Charles F. Smith had steamed up the river and assessed the fort's condition. It looked less than formidable. "I think two iron clad gun-boats could make short work of Ft. Henry," he wrote to Grant on January 22.

Grant had the letter in his pocket when he left for St. Louis on the twenty-third to see Halleck, who finally had granted him an audience. Face to face, the imperious Halleck easily established his moral ascendancy, for Grant came as a supplicant, susceptible to browbeating, which Halleck dished out in good measure. (For all his aggressiveness on the battlefield, Grant would often defer to people accustomed to exercising power and having their way, as the politician Benjamin Butler would later prove during the 1864 Virginia campaign.)

The subject of Fort Henry was put on the table, perhaps by Grant, perhaps by Halleck. It was not an original idea—other reports to Halleck had confirmed it as a desirable objective. As the Confederates had sat tightly in Columbus when Grant had tweaked their nose during his demonstration, they just might allow Fort Henry to fall without sending reinforcements. And as Lincoln was pounding on Halleck to do something immediately, Halleck was readily convinced that the time had come to proceed.

Despite Halleck's reservations, Grant would command the land forces, for Halleck had no alternative commander. Given the condition of the roads, the attack would have to be made by water, a combined army-navy operation. Andrew Foote would have to agree, and Halleck trusted Foote to keep Grant out of trouble. When Grant returned to Cairo on the morning of the twenty-eighth, he conferred with the naval officer, then each fired a telegram to Halleck recommending action.

Halleck sent his approval to Grant on January 30. Given the impossible roads, Grant was to move by steamer. Once Fort Henry had been captured, Grant was to send cavalry to destroy a nearby bridge crossing the Tennessee, severing Confederate rail communications between their main bodies at Bowling Green and Columbus. Halleck said nothing about Fort Donelson, eleven miles to the east of Fort Henry.

Grant energetically prepared for the campaign, requisitioning every steamer on the river, but so few were available that Grant found it impossible to transport his force of 15,000 men in one lift, nor could he take any supplies or equipment beyond rations for men and horses plus ammunition. Scribbling out plans and directives, Grant organized independent regiments into brigades and shrugged off inflated estimates of enemy intentions and strength at Fort Henry.

The armada carrying the first wave of troops chugged fifty miles up the Tennessee toward Fort Henry on February 4, with Foote's gunboats in the van. Grant wanted to land near the fort but beyond range of its artillery, and he sent a gunboat to draw enemy fire. The Confederate smoothbore rounds fell short, and Grant picked a likely landing site just beyond the impact point. Suddenly the fort fired a rifled cannon, and the projectile crashed through the deck. Grant promptly changed the landing site farther downriver.

The transports snuggled against the shore, and three miles below the fort 8,000 troops under McClernand sloshed ashore into water and tangled woods. The 2,500 Confederates under Brigadier General Lloyd Tilghman watched apprehensively from their fortifications. Tilghman made no move to oppose the landings, in large measure because the gunboats protected the landing area. McClernand quickly deployed his troops against possible counterattack and inched his way toward the fort.

That evening Grant went the fifty miles downriver to Paducah, leaving McClernand and his first wave mired near the guns and soldiers of Fort Henry. The next day he returned with the remainder of his forces. The end came unexpectedly. The naval bombardment was so fierce that Tilghman surrendered before Grant's troops got to the fort. Except for Tilghman and a few artillerymen, the fort was empty. The Confederate infantry had fled to Fort Donelson, eleven miles away. The navy had won the battle.

The Yeoman had to decide on his next courses of action. One was immediate: a gunboat scurried twelve miles upriver to destroy the Memphis and Ohio Railroad bridge spanning the Tennessee. With it down, reinforcements no longer could shuttle between Columbus and Bowling Green, although Johnston and Polk in their paralysis had no such intention. Eleven miles to the east of Fort Henry lay Fort Donelson, tantalizingly close, but Grant needed Halleck's approval to go there.

Grant used words of discretion to coax Halleck's sanction. It would be more of a raid, said Grant, than an assault and occupation. "Fort Henry is ours," he reported on February 6. "I shall take and destroy Fort Donaldson* on the eighth and return to Ft. Henry." Grant next sent a letter suggesting that an attack on Fort Donelson was a natural extension of the Fort Henry operation, but that its extent was conditional. He would be prepared to withdraw, he assured Halleck, in the face of superior forces from Bowling Green.

Grant's idea of attacking two days after seizing Fort Henry was fantasy, for he had brought neither equipage nor transportation to move overland to Fort Donelson. The winter weather was pummeling his men, deprived of tents and food, and the countryside between the two forts was a morass. Grant champed at the bit, fretting at the lack of word of either approval or disapproval from Halleck. The longer he delayed, the greater the possibility that Halleck would somehow interfere, and surely the Confederates by now were reinforcing Fort Donelson.

"I intend to keep the ball moving as lively as possible," Grant wrote his sister on February 9. Administrative and logistical matters consumed his time and energy, for his fumbling staff could not orchestrate the exacting movement of troops and supplies by water and land in the proximity of the enemy. Discipline wobbled as famished soldiers looted and pillaged; Grant reacted fiercely and threatened harsh punishment if it continued; still he could neither feed nor shelter the men.

"You have no conception of the amount of labor I have to perform," he wrote his sister. "An army of men all helpless looking to the commanding officer for every supply. Your plain brother however has, as yet, had no reason to feel himself unequal to the task and fully believes that he will carry on

---

* Grant consistently misspelled "Donelson."

a successful campaign against our rebel enemy." Part of Grant's confidence was the knowledge that Gideon Pillow was commanding troops at Fort Donelson. "I had known General Pillow in Mexico," Grant later wrote, "and judged that with my force, no matter how small, I could march up to within gunshot of any intrenchments he was given to hold."

Grant finally was ready to go on February 12, six days after Fort Henry. His woeful soldiers, carrying rations for two days and forty rounds of ammunition, would march the eleven miles. Road conditions prevented the passage of wagons, so tents, baggage, and additional food and ammunition were left behind, to go by steamer roundabout over 150 miles of river to reunite with their owners at Fort Donelson. Logistics continued to be a predicament for Grant as the Donelson phase of the river campaign unfolded, in large measure because Grant's staff was in its usual disarray.

Superb support at the mouths of the two rivers compensated for the imbroglios. Generals Sherman in Paducah and George Washington Cullum in Smithland funneled supplies and reinforcements upriver and sent encouraging letters. Only trickles got to Grant's men in the trenches, however, as he was without teams and wagons to move matériel from the landing below Fort Donelson. Without tents, many without blankets or overcoats, on short rations and short of ammunition, Grant's soldiers took a beating from the weather.

Grant's 15,000 men marched to Fort Donelson on two primitive roads separated by two miles of swamp and forest. Under such perilous conditions his officers desperately needed guidance and assurance, but Grant's instructions to his brigade commanders comprised but six sentences barren of detail. He specified the order of march and said that, when the two columns arrived at Fort Donelson, they were simply to fan out and encircle the fort. "The force of the enemy being so variously reported," Grant wrote in his concluding sentence, "it is impossible to give exact details of attack but the necessary orders will be given in the field." It was an unconscious admission that he was acting on incomplete intelligence, a self-inflicted predicament that persisted throughout the war.

The potential dangers were frightful. If the Confederates had attacked the columns with heavy blows while they were separated and beyond mutual support, Grant never would have gotten to Fort Donelson. Fortunately for Grant, the Confederate command was paralyzed, if only temporarily. In less than a week, two new commanders had arrived at Fort Donelson, first Brigadier General Bushrod R. Johnson on February 7, who was then superseded on the ninth by Pillow, with Simon Buckner and the first wave of reinforcements from Bowling Green in tow.

Grant's forced march got his men within sight of Fort Donelson before Pillow could react. The Federal soldiers brushed aside a smattering of Confederate cavalry and pickets and then dug in without opposition. That night, February 12–13, Brigadier General John B. Floyd arrived at Fort Donelson with another large body of troops, bringing the total garrison to no less than

15,000 men and perhaps as many as 20,000. Floyd was now the senior general at Fort Donelson, but he was no more willing to venture beyond the ramparts than his predecessors had been. The loudest Confederate activity was the bitter arguments among the generals.

Smith's division on the left wing and McClernand's division on the right wing joined in a two-mile, semicircular front around the fort and the adjacent village of Dover on the morning of the thirteenth. Grant sent a brigade to test the abatis defenses,* and after an intense firefight it retreated with losses. Freezing rain and sleet pelted his men exposed in the field, and Grant peered anxiously downriver for the sight of gunboats and transports. A single gunboat came into view, and at Grant's request it exchanged fire with the fort and then withdrew.

Grant's intentions were as unknown to his commanders as they were to the enemy. "Without asking for any information not proper to be communicated," McClernand wrote to Grant, "I would be pleased to be advised of any plan of operations and attack which you may have digested and decided upon." Avoid any action, Grant answered, that would provoke a strong reaction from the Confederates. That night the Federal soldiers huddled in their shallow trenches in a shrieking blizzard, their stomachs empty, so close to the enemy lines that they were forbidden to make fires. "[T]here was one universal wish," wrote a brigade commander, "to meet the enemy, to carry the fort, and to end the sufferings of the men."

Conditions incrementally improved on the fourteenth. Foote and six gunboats arrived, escorting twelve transports carrying Lewis "Lew" Wallace's division and limited supplies. Even when Wallace's troops augmented the encircling Federal line, gaps remained for Confederate supplies and reinforcements. Grant foresaw a protracted siege and telegraphed Halleck that the abatis prevented carrying the fort by storm. That afternoon Foote's flotilla attacked; after an hour of cannonading the heavily damaged gunboats withdrew. The fort remained intact.

"When this is to end is hard to surmise," Grant wrote Julia on the fourteenth, "but I feel confidant of ultimate success." Grant again ordered that the Confederates were not to be provoked. For the third straight night Grant's soldiers endured the weather with neither food, nor shelter, nor fires for warmth. "All night long we could hear [the Confederates] felling trees and using picks and shovels to strengthen their defenses," wrote a Federal colonel.

Still awake in the early morning hours of the fifteenth, Grant scratched out a report to Halleck: "Appearances now indicate that we will have a protracted siege here. The ground is very broken and the fallen timber extending far out of the breast works I fear the result of attempting to carry the place by storm with raw troops. I feel great confidance however of ultimately reducing the place."

---

* An abatis is an obstacle or barricade of sharpened trunks and branches directed toward an enemy. During the Civil War it was a common fortification wherever trees were readily available.

A messenger entered his tent at four in the morning with a message that would cause Grant to commit a near fatal blunder. It was a request from Foote to come to his flagship to confer about the disabled gunboats. (Foote was wounded and unable to walk.) Leaving his headquarters in the face of the enemy, Grant went downriver to see the mariner. Compounding the muddle, Grant failed to notify his division commanders that he would be incommunicado. His staff failed him yet again by not realizing the danger of his silent departure, for they too said nothing to the field commanders. McClernand, Wallace, and Smith were on their own.

We can only speculate as to what prompted Grant's thoughtlessness. He might have been too fatigued to think clearly; perhaps he had a headache, for headaches came upon him when he was exhausted. Perhaps he had been drinking. Or perhaps he held Pillow and Floyd in such contempt that he assumed they were unlikely to attack. Whatever the reasoning, his journey downriver could have been disastrous. He had conditioned his generals not to act without his permission, and now his voice of authority had disappeared around the river bend into the morning twilight.

The unexpected Confederate attack erupted against the vulnerable right wing just as Grant's boat passed beyond the sound of the guns. McClernand rushed to the front and found that he was in a fight for his life. The Confederates pounded his line and swept around and behind his exposed right flank, and it seemed likely that he was about to be annihilated. Surely, he thought, Grant would hear the din of battle and send reinforcements, ammunition, and artillery support, but when none came, he sent messengers to Grant's headquarters. They returned, shocking McClernand with the news that Grant had gone down the river.

McClernand pleaded with Wallace and Smith for help. Smith refused. Even though his front on the left wing was quiet, Grant's last orders had been to stay put. Smith was a professional soldier who obeyed his last orders. He would not move. Wallace was an amateur soldier, and to his great credit he withdrew a brigade from the center, shifting it right. The Federal line, now at right angles to its original position, held on. Then the roar of battle began to subside, the firing ceased, and the Confederates receded. The Federal troops took deep breaths, those living thanked God, and an interlude descended upon the battlefield. The time was about one o'clock.

Serenely unaware of developments, Grant returned to the landing following his talk with Foote, who told him that the gunboats were unfit for further combat. After a frantic aide met him at the landing, a suddenly stunned Grant galloped back to the battlefield. It was early afternoon. He had been gone for at least eight hours.

On lathered horse, Grant first came upon Smith's division on the left wing, still intact as it had remained unengaged. Further along he found McClernand's soldiers dazed and milling about, with bodies strewn in the open fields. His face expressionless, Grant listened to McClernand describe how the battle had developed, his frustrated attempts to locate Grant, and the fact that his division might have gone under had not Wallace stabilized the line. Casualties were uncertain. The hiatus could not last indefinitely. Although the enemy had inexplicably withdrawn just when the Federal troops were on the ropes, they could attack again.

Grant would deal with countless crises throughout the war. His invariable reaction was to remain poised and to seize or to regain the initiative. Regardless of how badly he had been mauled, he instantaneously would hit back harder, often when his opponent least expected it. He was rarely brilliant or capable of careful planning, but this behavior, brutally effective, distinguished Grant from lesser generals and saved him time and again from straits of his own making.

In this instance Grant had three options. One would be contrary to his nature: he could withdraw, but that would be unthinkable, for such an admission of defeat—coupled with his prolonged absence from the battlefield—would end his career in disgrace. A second option was to dig in, but that was the equivalent of "doing nothing," a condition he abhorred and which could well lead to an extended stalemate discrediting his generalship.

As a quick victory was Grant's sole objective, the only suitable option was to attack on the presumption that the Confederates had suffered the worst. They had, after all, retreated back into the fort, their morale and cohesion had to have been damaged, and they might well be unprepared to receive a counterattack.

Grant's mind raced for an acceptable plan of assault. The gunboats, he thought. He needed the gunboats to rally his troops and to intimidate the enemy even though Foote had just told him they were heavily damaged. But Grant was desperate, and he begged Foote for a show of force to inspire his soldiers. Two gunboats limped back up the river and demonstrated, but their presence was immaterial to the outcome. The Federal foot soldier had to grasp the nettle. Grant ordered Smith, hitherto unoccupied, to attack with his division on the left wing, and at two o'clock it swept forward and seized the outer line of fortifications. Confederate troops rushed toward Smith and prevented him from carrying on to the fort proper.

The situation was less straightforward on the right wing. After seven hours of combat the ranks were still reeling. Troops were scattered and intermixed between McClernand's and Wallace's divisions, many were out of ammunition, and others had not eaten for several days, leaving them shivering, bewildered, and confused from the fury of the morning. Grant, McClernand, and Wallace conferred. Two of the least-mangled brigades went forward in midafternoon, pushed back the Confederates, and reoccupied their original line. By nightfall the bloodied Federal forces were where they had been in the morning, when Grant had gone downriver.

The near certainty of failure descended with the darkness upon Grant. His plan—his campaign—had foundered, and his troops lay gasping. Destitute of fresh ideas, Grant told his dejected generals to resume the assault in the morning and then dismissed them. As he sat staring at the wall of his tent, a staff officer entered with a message from Buckner, delivered under a flag of truce. Breaking the wax seal, Grant smoothed the paper on the table beneath the candlelight.

Sir: In consideration of all the circumstances governing the present sit-
uation of affairs at this station I propose to the commanding officers of
the Federal forces the appointment of commissioners to agree upon
terms of capitulation of the forces and post under my command, and in
that view suggest an armistice until 12 o'clock to-day.

A gift had been placed before Grant: the Confederates had cracked. The irresolute Floyd and the despicable Pillow had apparently bailed out and left a humiliated Buckner holding the bag. Buckner was of the old school, and he had written a conventional proposal in the belief that Grant surely would be magnanimous enough to allow him to save face.

There was reason to believe as much. Grant and Buckner had been cadets together at West Point, both had been in the Mexican War, and their past associations had been pleasant. During the quiet days at Cairo, Grant had exchanged decorous letters with Polk for the exchange of prisoners, he had been chivalrous on the Belmont battlefield when the wounded had been retrieved, and he had socialized with Confederate officers under a flag of truce on the river, swapping stories with drink in hand. Surely Grant would be reasonable.

But Grant had no such intentions. A major facet of his extraordinary transformation since rejoining the army was the adroitness he had acquired in dealing with political matters both in Illinois and in Washington, and his sensitivity to the influence of the press. Thus he now recognized his opportunity for a public relations bonanza. The nation was watching, waiting, wondering at the outcome of this epic battle for the river forts. Grant's reply would be for public consumption and only incidentally for Buckner. Whatever Grant wrote would become instant news, crackling across the telegraph lines to every newspaper editor North and South. It would have to play well with Lincoln and the fire-breathing Stanton, and to the extent possible it would also have to intimidate Southerners and secessionists. As it would transcend official reports and personal letters, Halleck could not sit on it, the jealous generals coveting his command could not suppress it, and politicians and the press could not distort it.

With these considerations in mind, Grant wrote his reply, a masterpiece of pugnacity, so clear and succinct that its meaning was unmistakable. He showed it to Smith, the old warrior whom Grant had so respected ever since his cadet days. Then he wrote a copy to Buckner.

Yours of this date proposing Armistice, and appointment of commis-
sioners, to settle terms of capitulation is just received. No terms except
an unconditional and immediate surrender can be accepted. I propose
to move immediately upon your works.

Buckner had no choice. He was a beaten man. His will to resist had been broken. He was compelled, he replied to Grant, "to accept the ungenerous and unchivalrous terms which you propose." Cheers resounded in the Federal lines at the news, and the troops marched in to occupy Fort Donelson and Dover village.

The news of Grant's victory arrived in Washington on the same day. That evening Stanton placed Grant's nomination for major general before Lincoln. As he signed the document, Lincoln ruminated aloud. "If the Southerners think that man for man they are better than our Illinois men, or western men generally," said the President, "they will discover themselves in a grievous mistake." The Senate enthusiastically approved the nomination on February 19. A delighted Washburne telegraphed the grand news to Grant. It took small imagination for the newspapers to proclaim the winner as "Unconditional Surrender" Grant.

The behavior of the hungry, freezing Federal troops toward the 10,000 or so Confederate captives ranged from indifference to brutality. Despite Buckner's bitter and outraged complaints to Grant, the prisoners were stripped of equipment and outer clothing and herded like cattle. The pandemonium was beyond Grant's capacity to control. "In the midst of confusion there had been a great deel of plundering notwithstanding all the precautions taken to prevent it," he wrote to Cullum on the second day of occupation. "I ordered guards over all captured property before marching the troops into the works of the enemy but it seemed to do no good."

No one noticed, for the rewards of victory were stunning. Buckner's surrender of Fort Donelson started the dominoes tumbling. Johnston abandoned Bowling Green without a fight when the move against the fort began, and he moved his forces across the state line to Nashville. On the evening of February 15 Johnston received news of the Confederate victory at Fort Donelson, the next morning of defeat. His fear of gunboats coming up the Cumberland from the fort was so great that he immediately deserted Nashville and its tons of precious stores and supplies, and the mob fell upon the warehouses and stockpiles. To the west, Beauregard, then commanding along the Mississippi, recognized the peril at Columbus, and before Fort Donelson fell he received permission from Richmond to abandon the Mississippi River fortress.

Davis read of Federal triumphs in the Northern papers and fumed that he had heard nothing from Johnston. A courier letter of March 12 to Johnston demanded a report; Johnston finally replied in a letter dated March 18. Its contents were horrific. Like Lee after his debacle in western Virginia, Johnston had withheld the news of tragedy. "I observed silence," Johnston lamely explained, "as it seemed to me the best way to serve the cause and the country. The facts were not fully known, discontent prevailed, and criticism or condemnation were more likely to augment than to cure the evil."

Johnston's long retreat spanned more than two hundred meandering miles across Tennessee farmland that henceforth would not sustain the Confederacy. He and Beauregard finally rendezvoused at Corinth, a major rail junction in northeastern Mississippi, near where the Tennessee River turns ninety degrees toward the east. There they rested. Reinforcements began to arrive, as the shock of the disaster had jolted the Confederate government to strengthen their western forces. A river town named Shiloh Church lay twenty miles away, on the big bend in the Tennessee River.

The Federal high command could not comprehend the Confederates' total abandonment of Tennessee and was psychologically unprepared to exploit the opportunities. Halleck and Buell proceeded cautiously, tentatively into the vacuum. Grant and Foote wanted to move promptly upriver to Nashville, but Grant awaited approval and guidance from Halleck, who was preoccupied with empire building. When Fort Donelson had fallen, Halleck demanded 50,000 more men and unified command. Then he would be ready, he told McClellan, to lead his grand army south into Tennessee and beyond, Buell through Nashville, and Grant up the Tennessee River. Until Halleck heard from McClellan, he forbade Grant to advance up the Cumberland to Nashville and told him to be ready for an ascent up the Tennessee. Communications were so garbled and misconstrued, however, that misunderstandings and hard feelings were inevitable.

Nashville was in Buell's jurisdiction, and he gingerly approached the city from the east, unable to believe it was his for the taking. Meanwhile, Grant could not resist the lure of the open city. Against Halleck's orders, he audaciously entered first while Buell maneuvered on the outskirts. The two met in a stormy confrontation. Grant smugly dismissed any threat from the long-gone Johnston; an outraged Buell expected a counterattack momentarily.

Grant should not have gone to Nashville. He was needed at Forts Henry and Donelson to remedy the chaos of his command and the misery of his soldiers. The brutal weather lowered the resistance to disease, and smallpox broke out. McClernand warned Grant that the want of fresh meat and potatoes was causing scurvy; even though such supplies were plentiful fifty miles downriver, his staff could not organize the riverboats to make delivery. Once supplies were landed near Fort Donelson, Grant had neither transportation nor laborers to deliver them to the soldiers. A quartermaster had sent 176 teams to Grant, but they had somehow disappeared, and Rawlins belatedly issued a general order for commanders to report the numbers of teams in their custody.

Because of the lack of storage facilities ashore, boats were commandeered and immobilized as floating warehouses, worsening the shortage of water transportation. Cargo coordination was makeshift, in large measure because Fort Donelson was without a telegraph station. Potatoes sent to the fort returned downriver on the same boat. An infantry division had carefully conserved and sorted its ammunition, which was inadvertently loaded on a departing riverboat. The division commander, former naval officer William Nelson, sent a furious letter to Grant. If his ammunition was not returned, wrote Nelson, "I will endeavor to find the enemy with the bayonets of my division."

Grant had lost control. His soldiers, desperate for food and shelter, continued to ransack the countryside. Grant issued order after order, then orders to obey orders; still the looting persisted. Grant's staff was pitifully inadequate to attend to the needs of the 25,000 men under his direct command. Without a quartermaster, his other staff officers had no competence in logistical support, nor were officers of skill seconded from the regiments. Grant's characteristic reticence, his aversion to explain or complain, prevented the dispatch of help he desperately needed. Instead he stubbornly plugged along, slowly going under, often too sick to think clearly. "I am bearly able to be out of my bed," he wrote to Foote on March 3. "I have had a severe cold ever since leaving Cairo and it had now settled on my chest which, with a severe head ache, nearly destroys my energy."

The next day Halleck sent a withering telegram that shocked Grant out of bed. "Why do you not obey my orders to report strength & positions of your command?" It was a curious complaint, because Halleck had sent no such orders. On the other hand, Grant had sent no reports as to the strength and dispositions of his regiments, as he should have done without prompting from Halleck. Countermanding his orders to prepare for an ascent up the Tennessee, Halleck directed Grant to remain at Fort Henry and to put Smith in command of the expedition.

Three days later Halleck sent an even more damning wire. "Genl McClellan directs that you report to me dayly," said Halleck, "the numbers and positions of the forces under your command. Your neglect of repeated orders to report the strength of your command has created great dissatisfaction, & seriously interfered with military plans. Your going to Nashville without authority & when your presence with your troops was of the utmost importance, was a matter of very serious complaint at Washington, so much so that I was advised to arrest you at your return."

Grant realized he was fighting for his life; clearly Halleck and McClellan were conspiring to discredit and humiliate him. He knew that Halleck had never asked for reports on troop strength during the Henry-Donelson campaign; Grant in turn knew he had not reported his head count and combat readiness. If he perhaps suspected that Halleck had been stung by McClellan for not reporting to Washington, he would have been right. Smarting from McClellan's rebuke, Halleck had lashed out at Grant to deflect the heat from himself. Halleck had swung wildly and not well, and he was vulnerable.

Grant answered back with shrewd ripostes. Some were statements of fact:

> I have averaged writing more than once a day, since leaving Cairo, to keep you informed of my position; and it is no fault of mine, if you have not received my letters. . . .
> Evry move I made was reported to your Chief of Staff, who must have failed to keep you properly posted.

Grant explained away his foray into Nashville by implying that he had not been forbidden to go there, nor did he need permission. "My going to Nashville was strictly intended for the good of the service," he wrote, "and not to gratify any desire of my own." Then came the bluff. "I did all I could to get you returns of the strength of my command," he wrote, knowing full

well he had not. Moreover it was a glaring admission that he was uninformed as to how many of his men were fit for combat, facts that he as a
commanding general should have known day by day.

Grant's final gambit was an ultimatum. "If my course is not satisfactory
remove me at once. I do not wish to impede in any way the success of our
arms." He then concluded, "Believing sincerely that I must have enemies
between you and myself who are trying to impair my usefulness, I respectfully ask to be relieved from further duty in the Dept."

Halleck was on the spot, for he could not possibly relieve a man who had
just been promoted to major general. And the administration could never
explain a precipitous dismissal of a man it had just proclaimed a hero, one
who had won a victory such as no other general in the war. Congressional and
public outrage would have discredited the administration, and Grant knew it.
More telegrams passed between Halleck and Grant, and Grant exploited his
advantage. Grant bore in harder on March 13. "There is such a disposition to
find fault with me," he wrote Halleck, "that I again ask to be relieved from
further duty until I am placed right in the estimation of those higher in
authority."

Halleck capitulated. "You cannot be relieved from your command," he
replied. "There is no good reason for it. . . . The power is in your hands; use
it, & you will be sustained by all above you. Instead of relieving you, I wish
you, as soon as your new army is in the field, to assume the immediate command & lead it on to new victories."

Grant had survived. Halleck's hatred would not subside, but he was
shrewd enough to know that he had no alternative to retaining Grant. Halleck's chagrin was ameliorated by the welcome news that Lincoln had finally
agreed to give him command of the entire west. Having now gotten what he
wanted, Halleck could back off from Grant. For the moment Grant still had
his combat command, with a charter to move up the Tennessee. And after a
river journey of a hundred miles he would come to a place called Shiloh
Church.

15

SHILOH

G rant's victory at Forts Henry and Donelson forced the Confederates to abandon Nashville and the western half of Kentucky and Tennessee and jolted Richmond into reinforcing the western theater. The voice of urgency came from Beauregard, banished to the west because Davis had wearied of his posturing in Virginia. Once second in command in the east, Beauregard was now second in command under A. S. Johnston. Westerners had hoped he would bring reinforcements, but only his staff came with him. What he did bring was a sense of authority and purpose at a time of crisis. Like the Napoleon he thought himself to be, Beauregard had plans and a strategic vision. His call for men and matériel was clear and persuasive.

People of influence listened and responded. Davis sent brigades. Governors sent volunteers. Johnston was deferential and took his Bowling Green aggregation to Beauregard's headquarters at the railroad junction of Corinth, Mississippi, the new center of gravity. The town had to be held, for through it ran the Memphis and Charleston Railroad, the major east-west trunk line of the western Confederacy and its connection with the east. Another major railroad led due south into Mississippi.

Corinth's vulnerability to river-borne Federal forces was starkly evident. The Tennessee River rounded the corner—from north-south to east-west—at Shiloh Church, some twenty miles from Corinth. Then the river paralleled the Memphis and Charleston Railroad line for nearly a hundred miles. Federal forces could disembark from transports anywhere along the way, scoot overland a few miles, and sever the Memphis and Charleston at a thousand places, isolating the Mississippi River basin from the Confederacy eastward.

Beauregard saw the threat and mobilized an army to preempt Halleck at Corinth. Miraculously, the wheezing Confederate railroad system transported the necessary troops. "In less than two months," wrote Robert C. Black, "it had gathered nearly forty thousand men from points as distant as five hundred miles and had delivered them precisely where their presence would do the most good." Acting now as the unified commander, Halleck too moved large masses of men, Grant by water and Buell by foot. Grant took his Army of the Tennessee upriver and disembarked at Pittsburg Landing, near Shiloh on the west shore of the bend in the river and a day's march from Corinth. Buell was coming by foot from Nashville with his Army of the Ohio. (Thomas would bring up the rear because of his long journey from Mill Springs.) When Buell arrived, an attack on Corinth would follow. Apparently Halleck had achieved a coordinated operation.

Both Beauregard and Halleck intended to fight a decisive battle—the decisive battle—in the west with their swelling armies. The Confederates, however, never could match the Federal forces in manpower. The longer they waited, the greater the Federal advantage, and when Buell arrived, the Federal superiority would be overwhelming. Although the hastily assembled Confederate army was not ready for combat, Beauregard convinced Johnston and the Confederate high command on April 2 to attack Grant preemptively at Pittsburg Landing on the fourth.

Beauregard conceived his elaborate battle plan in haste; Johnston would execute it in chaos. As if written for an abstract war game, the plan ignored reality. The troops were raw, and their officers understood dimly at best where they were going and why. The low-lying, undeveloped countryside on the way to Pittsburg Landing was unmapped, the condition of the primitive roads was unknown, and the nature of the terrain around Pittsburg Landing was a mystery. All was ripe for disaster.

Still, the Confederate soldiers had come to fight a war, and they left Corinth on April 3 with spirit and enthusiasm. "There was no attempt at concealment or surprise," said staff officer Joseph B. Cummings afterward. "We marched out with drums beating and flags flying." Because the exodus started late and the narrow roads soon were jammed, an attack the next day was patently impossible. By the afternoon of April 5 the clangorous Confederate army had untangled itself from the roads and surrounded Grant's bivouac at Pittsburg Landing.

As the sun descended behind him, a disheartened Beauregard watched his grand design disintegrate. The racket, he was certain, must have alerted the Federal troops. Three days of hunger and floundering in the mud had worn out the soldiers. Beauregard was ready to turn back, but Johnston pressed on, seeking redemption from the humiliations he had borne since taking command in the west. He would fight now, regardless of omens and impediments. The generals were still arguing on the following morning when they heard gunfire. The battle had begun spontaneously. Telling Beauregard to manage the rear areas, Johnston rode to the sound of the guns.

Its tents randomly pitched wherever dry ground was available, Grant's army—which now included a division commanded by Sherman—had loitered at Pittsburg Landing for two weeks. Grant remained at his headquarters twelve miles downriver at Savannah, Tennessee, waiting for Buell. Halleck had taken personal command and had instructed Grant to avoid a fight until Buell arrived. If the Confederates continued to reinforce their army at Corinth, so much the better. Halleck had been chasing rebels all over the western states. Now that they were concentrated in one location, he could destroy them in a stroke.

It was clear to Halleck, if to no one else, that the Confederates might attack before Buell arrived. The conditions were right: Halleck could quote them from his seminal work, *Elements of Military Art and Science*. A battle is acceptable, he had written, when one's enemy "is on the point of receiving reinforcements which will materially affect your relative strength." As Buell was about to reinforce Grant, it made sense for Johnston to launch a preemptive attack. Halleck undoubtedly reasoned, though, that he need not warn Grant. Having been caught unawares at Fort Donelson, surely Grant had learned his lesson. Would he not act prudently, watching the Confederates and fortifying Pittsburg Landing while awaiting Buell?

No, Grant and his generals were complacent, confident that the Confederate army would remain in Corinth until the Federal army chose to assault it there. Grant acted as if he were on peacetime bivouac; neither scouts nor pickets watched for the enemy, and nary a barricade or trench defended the perimeter. Enemy troops were probing and testing, but the Federal generals dismissed their significance. "We are constantly in the presence of the enemys pickets," Sherman wrote his wife as 40,000 Confederates marched toward his slumbering encampment on April 3, "but I am satisfied that they will await our coming at Corinth or some point on the Charleston road."

The Confederate army was within spitting distance of the Federal encampment by the afternoon of April 5. Cummings could hear music and voices. "Still the enemy was strangely unaware of our proximity," he wrote afterward. Grant remained downriver at Savannah, reading Sherman's latest report. His troops had had a fierce firefight with enemy cavalry, infantry, and even artillery, but Sherman shrugged it off. "I do not apprehend anything like an attack upon our position," Sherman concluded. Grant mulled over the news and then wrote his estimate of the situation to Halleck. It included a sentence he would forever regret: "I have scarsely the faintest idea of an attack, (general one,) being made upon us but will be prepared should such a thing take place."

The Battle of Shiloh began on the morning of April 6 when an armed mob of 40,000 assaulted the unsuspecting Federal encampments. The Tennessee River and two streams flowing into it enclosed the encampment on three sides. The Confederates came from the open fourth side, their backs to Corinth to the southwest. The initial collisions were random. Sounds of battle warned the clearheaded among the Federal troops to take arms and form lines. Others fled in terror and cowered by the riverbank.

Beauregard had chosen an unconventional battle formation that prevented the Confederate generals from controlling their commands, although that was not his intent. William J. Hardee's corps spread itself across the entire two-mile front opening to the southwest. Braxton Bragg's corps was similarly deployed somewhat to the rear of Hardee. Leonidas Polk and John C.

Breckinridge* remained behind the two leading corps to deploy their divisions as circumstances dictated.

The defects of such a plan should have been apparent. Hardee and Bragg could not communicate with their subordinates over so wide a front, and inevitably their two corps would entangle. Astoundingly, Beauregard did not position the bulk of the army on the right wing, intended to be the mighty hammer; most of the troops were on the left and center. Polk and Breckinridge would rush their reinforcements to the center of the line, where Federal general Benjamin M. Prentiss commanded. The outcome was a melee that bore no relationship to Beauregard's plan.

Grant was downriver at Savannah waiting for Buell's arrival. Grant hurt. His horse had fallen on his leg, and his ankle was swollen. When not mounted, he used crutches. The startling sound of battle from upstream was electrifying. There was a quick order, lines were taken in, and Grant's little steamboat chugged toward Pittsburg Landing. The roar increased as he approached. Grant could see soldiers huddled on the embankment; others ran about in confusion. From the intensity of the disorder at the landing, the situation at first seemed far worse than at Fort Donelson, but things always looked bad in the rear. The mettle of an army in combat, he firmly believed, resided at the front, and that was where he had to be.

Grant hobbled to his horse, mounted, squared his hat, and forced his way ahead. One by one he found his generals; unlike those at Fort Donelson, they were cooperating in his absence. Sherman, Prentiss, and McClernand had absorbed the first shock; although reeling and falling back, their divisions had not broken. William H. L. Wallace and Stephen A. Hurlbut were bringing their troops into line from the rear. Grant sent his staff scurrying to summon Lew Wallace, camped several miles upstream, and to hasten Buell's advance guard, soon to arrive across the river. By noon, some 60,000 Federal soldiers (more or less, considering casualties and shirkers) were fighting on a fluid front six miles wide and perhaps a mile deep.

Johnston directed the frontline traffic on the Confederate side for his first and last hurrah. He was where he wanted to be, among the smoke and bullets, but his influence on the battle was negligible. In the early afternoon a bullet severed a leg artery, and Johnston bled to death. Beauregard assumed command of the army.

Grant managed his side of the battlefront from a log building on top of a hill, from time to time visiting his division commanders to assess the situation and lend encouragement. Afterward Grant wrote that he did not have to stay long with Sherman. Once thought unstable and erratic, Sherman was fighting like a demon in his first combat as a division commander.

Too many soldiers—and officers as well—fled. They had to stop at the river, and from time to time Grant's cavalry rounded them up and returned them to the front. Buell arrived, talked with Grant, then raged at the hordes

---

* Breckinridge had been vice president of the United States under James Buchanan just before the war.

cowering on the landing. Grant was mortified that Buell judged his army by what he saw near the river, and he suspected that Buell doubted that Grant could hold on until Buell's own troops would arrive that night.

Grant established an unbroken line across his front, which slowly yielded under pressure on the flanks, but Prentiss held at the center, a place remembered in history as the Hornet's Nest. There the Confederates gravitated, until by late afternoon Prentiss was surrounded and surrendered his survivors, but by then he had given Grant time to recover. The Confederate attacks petered out as the first of Buell's reinforcements clambered ashore.

A night rain fell upon a landscape of horror and misery. Bodies were sprawled in a pattern that encompassed the width and breadth of the battlefield, some dead, others shrieking. Grant knew that his casualties numbered in the thousands. Numbed survivors huddled in the muck. They had trusted Grant when they had slept the night before in false security. There was no threat of attack, Grant had said repeatedly, and they had believed him. He had betrayed them. He knew it. They knew it. Somehow Grant had to make them believe in him again.

"It is the impact of the ebbing of moral and physical strength," wrote Clausewitz,

> of the heart-rending spectacle of the dead and wounded, that the commander has to withstand—first in himself, and then in all those who, directly or indirectly, have entrusted him with their thoughts and feelings, hopes and fears. As each man's strength gives out, as it no longer responds to his will, the inertia of the whole gradually comes to rest on the commander's will alone. The ardor of his spirit must rekindle the flame of purpose in all others; his inward fire must revive their hope. Only to the extent that he can do this will he retain his hold on his men and keep control.

"In the dreadful presence of suffering and danger," Clausewitz went on to say, "emotion can easily overwhelm intellectual conviction. . . . Action can never be based on anything firmer than instinct, a sensing of the truth." The truth, as Grant saw it, was that the Confederate army had expended its combat power. His own army was battered as well, but Buell had delivered tens of thousands of reinforcements, and Lew Wallace had arrived with his own division. Grant's instinct was to strike back, as he had done at Fort Donelson.

We can only speculate as to what extent Buell and Grant coordinated their two armies. Theoretically, Grant commanded the now combined armies by date of rank, a matter of a few weeks. Actually, Grant's seniority was immaterial. Grant had sensed Buell's contempt during their river meeting and perhaps felt that Buell—an old, respected soldier and a disciplinarian—would disdain orders from a man who had blundered. In all likelihood Buell saw himself as Grant's savior. Grant rejected any such perception. By his account,

Buell's 25,000 men were superfluous.* "Victory was assured when [Lew] Wallace arrived," Grant later wrote in his memoirs, "even if there had been no other support. I was glad, however, to see the reinforcements of Buell and credit them for doing all there was for them to do."

The staffs arranged matters. Both armies would attack in the morning. During the night Buell's army occupied the left wing, and Grant's divisions the right.

The Confederate army, too, spent the night attempting to restore order. The high command was wishfully confident, including Bragg and Hardee, whose corps had been in the thick of it. Beauregard reported to Davis of "a complete victory, driving the enemy from every position." One last push seemed all that was necessary to finish them off.

The Federal armies struck first, while the Confederates were still thinking about it. Grant and Buell independently fought their own battles; each coincidentally reinforced the other. Grant's assertion that he could have succeeded without Buell was fallacious: the Confederates, for all their fatigue and disorder, fought well and held their own until midafternoon. Finally Beauregard, in despair over seeing his grand plan reduced to shambles, ordered a retreat. Having left Corinth with banners and drums, the Confederate soldiers returned silently with regimental colors drooping.

Grant and Buell let them go, and the Battle of Shiloh was over. The Federal armies did not pursue. "I wanted to pursue," Grant rationalized years later, "but had not the heart to order the men who had fought desperately for two days, lying in the mud and rain whenever not fighting, and I did not feel disposed to positively order Buell, or any part of his command, to pursue. . . . I did not meet Buell in person until too late to get troops ready and pursue with effect; but had I seen him at the moment of the last charge I should have at least requested him to follow."

Grant's explanation is implausible, for in subsequent campaigns he pursued with a vengeance, regardless of the fatigue of his soldiers. Two days of hard fighting would be incidental when Grant later fought Lee in the 1864 Virginia campaign. Shiloh was one of the few instances in which discretion tempered Grant's impulse to press on. Perhaps he was simply relieved to have survived, especially as he and his staff considered themselves outnumbered, for as usual Grant had no hard intelligence on which to base his decisions. Buell, with the fresher army, should have pursued, but his conservatism constrained him.

Fundamentally then, neither Buell nor Grant cared to pursue, and each had an excuse. Halleck confirmed their decisions when he wired Grant to stay put until he got there.

---

* Grant's chief of staff, John Rawlins, thought otherwise. In a letter on April 8 to his mother, Rawlins said that he thought the Confederates had an army of 110,000 against less than half that number for Grant. "Just when they were needed," he wrote, "and not a moment too soon, Buell's advanced forces, ten thousand strong, arrived on the opposite side of the river, were quickly crossed to our side of the conflict, and checked the enemy."

The time had come to declare winners and losers. This was difficult to do. Each army occupied exactly the same ground it had occupied before the battle, and twenty miles again separated them. As nothing had been accomplished save the killing and maiming of more than 20,000 men, the leadership on both sides would be pilloried. The press would be particularly virulent. Salvaging reputations took high priority.

Naturally, both sides declared victory.

The Confederate government's pronouncements were both foolish and deceitful. Having received Beauregard's report of victory on the night of the sixth, Davis jumped the gun with an exultant message to the Confederate Congress on the eighth. "From official telegraphic dispatches," he advised the legislators, "I am able to announce to you, with entire confidence, that it has pleased Almighty God to crown the Confederate arms with a glorious and decisive victory over our invaders."

Beauregard waited five days to report the outcome of the second day's battle. Again he reported a victory. He had so badly crippled Halleck's army, Beauregard assured Richmond, that it could not possibly advance on Corinth. Beauregard had returned to Corinth, he explained lamely, because having whipped Grant and seized his stores, the plan had been to return to Corinth before Buell arrived. The charade continued until Beauregard evacuated Corinth in late May before the weight of Halleck's massive army. Bragg replaced Beauregard in late June as commanding general of the Army of Tennessee.*

The Federal government received similar misinformation. Grant telegraphed Halleck that, successively, the Confederates were completely repulsed, then badly routed, and finally forced to flee toward Corinth. Halleck in turn relayed to Stanton the story that the enemy had been repulsed and had suffered heavy losses. That was sufficient for the secretary of war to issue congratulatory orders to Halleck and all his generals in the west, "giving thanks for the recent victories and overthrow of traitors."

Knowing that Halleck was coming to Pittsburgh Landing, Grant wrote his preliminary report on April 9, two days after the battle had ended. As his report would be widely read, Grant fashioned it for the larger audience. It read like a clumsy press release. His opening paragraph purported that the Battle of Shiloh had sustained the vital interests of the Federal government:

> It becomes my duty again to report another battle fought between two great armies, one contending for the maintenance of the best Government ever devised[,] the other for its destruction. It is pleasant to record the success of the army contending for the former principle.

---

* Davis fired Beauregard on the pretext that Beauregard had taken a leave of absence without his permission.

His next paragraph was a bald fabrication intended to preempt the inevitable charges of negligence:

> *On Sunday morning our pickets were attacked and driven in by the enemy. [There had been no Federal pickets.] Immediately the five Divisions stationed at this place were drawn up in line of battle ready to meet them. [There was no line of battle. The Federal troops were entirely unprepared for the Confederate attack.] The battle soon waxed warm on the left and center, varying at times to all parts of the line.*

The remaining paragraphs summarized events and commended the division commanders—especially Sherman—as well as Grant's personal staff. Not a word was said as to why his army had been surprised, or indeed that it had been surprised. (Grant's apologia would always be that the battle had been a near thing because he was outnumbered three to one.) A brief, patronizing paragraph acknowledged that Buell's army had provided "efficient service."

Grant's honeymoon with the press was brief. Reporters talked to witnesses and heard from Buell's Army of the Ohio, which had, in its view, found Grant's Army of the Tennessee in extremis and about to go under. Letters written home also influenced public opinion. "I suppose they [the papers] will give all the glory to Grant," wrote John Scully, who was now on Buell's staff, "but I assure you, there never was a worse 'whipped' army on the face of the earth, than Grant's was on Sunday night; and were it not for the timely arrival of Buell, would be utterly annihilated."

Halleck arrived at Pittsburg Landing on April 11, four days after the battle had ended. He had heard the first rumors: Grant had been drunk, his soldiers were asleep in their tents, half his army had bolted. Washington demanded information. Halleck asked Grant for a fuller report, but Grant refused on the grounds that Halleck was not showing him reports from Buell and his generals.* Grant had become a pariah by then, a colossal embarrassment both to Halleck and to Washington. "I was ignored," he later wrote, "as much as if I had been at the most distant point of territory within my jurisdiction."

Meanwhile Halleck and Sherman undertook damage control by refuting the hostile published accounts of the battle. Congress was in an uproar over the casualty list, a figure thought to number between ten and twenty thousand.† It was also agitated about Davis's victory claims and speculation about Grant's drinking. Pressed for data and explanations, Stanton jogged Halleck on April 23 for a report and went to the root of the matter, asking Halleck "whether any neglect or misconduct of General Grant or any other officer contributed to the sad casualties that befell our forces."

---

* Grant wrote nothing more about Shiloh until his memoirs years later, to which he devoted a two-chapter apologia.
† The final figure was something over 13,000.

Halleck decided to cover up. He replied to Stanton that casualties were a part of great battles and could not be avoided. Grant was not to be blamed. The enemy soldiers, good and brave fighters, had caused the casualties, as had the poor leadership of volunteer officers unfit for their positions (a recurring Halleck diatribe against political appointments). Newspaper accounts that Grant's army had been surprised were false, Halleck continued, as each division had known of the enemy's intentions hours in advance. That was the party line, and to that line Halleck and his generals held. Why Grant had nearly been pushed into the river was left unexplained.

The Federal western army grew in size and strength throughout April. The remainder of Buell's Army of the Ohio, including Thomas and his division, assembled at Pittsburg Landing. John Pope and his Army of the Mississippi made rendezvous, bringing with them a series of successes against Confederate strong points on the river.

This was the first time that Halleck had commanded in the field. Escorted everywhere by his mounted Praetorian Guard, he found conditions appalling. Well over 100,000 men and their animals had congregated. Rain had been incessant, the stench of the army's refuse and rotting flesh was intense, and sickness worsened for want of sanitation. Even the robust Thomas was stricken with diarrhea. Grant's soldiers, in Halleck's view, were slovenly, and most of their officers lax. Small wonder, thought Halleck, that so many ran at the first sound of gunfire.

Halleck tore into Grant within seventy-two hours of his arrival at Shiloh. "Immediate and active measures must be taken," he wrote, "to put your command in condition to resist another attack from the enemy. Fractions of batteries must be united temporarily under competent officers; supplied with ammunition, and placed into position for service. Divisions and Brigades should where necessary be reorganized and put into position; and all stragglers returned to their companies and regiments. Your army is not now in condition to resist an attack. It must be made so without delay."

And so a wrathful Halleck pounded away to reform the slipshod practices that Grant had either ignored or tolerated. Orders and regulations issued from Halleck's headquarters; a purge scoured the regiments of officers, from colonel to lieutenant, who had failed to measure up. Harassed and humiliated, Grant was reduced to jumping to Halleck's ultimatums. Buell was in all likelihood pleased with Halleck's attitude, for it reinforced his own efforts in the Army of the Ohio.

Journalists also battered Grant's self-esteem. "I hope the papers will let me alone in future," he wrote forlornly to Julia. "I do not look much at the papers now consequently [I] save myself much uncomfortable feeling." His father and his aide-de-camp, William Hillyer, made the bad press even worse. Jesse Grant unwisely published a letter from his son in a Cincinnati newspaper, and Hillyer sent inflammatory letters to the elder Grant which also made the papers. Rather than admonish his aide, Grant recommended that Hillyer be promoted from captain to colonel, together with C. B. Lagow, and the War Department cooperated. Not until much later would Grant acknowledge their liabilities and discharge them.

Grant had reason to believe that he had survived the horrible publicity and would retain command of his army for the campaign against Corinth. Halleck announced on April 28 that he had organized his huge army into three wings and a reserve. Pope commanded the left with his Army of the Mississippi, Buell and his Army of the Ohio were in the center, and Grant commanded his Army of the Tennessee on the right. Two of Grant's divisions comprised the reserve under McClernand. "I am looking for a speedy move," Grant wrote Julia on the thirtieth, "one more fight and then easy sailing to the close of the war." Despite the abuse he had taken from Halleck, in his letter to Julia he spoke of "our Chief, Halleck, who I look upon as one of the greatest men of the age."

Grant deceived himself. As he had before the Fort Donelson operation, Halleck worked intently to remove Grant from command, but there were few qualified replacement candidates. Grant's relief had to be a major general, a West Point graduate, and someone not already engaged as an army commander. That eliminated Pope and Buell. McClernand was a politician. Halleck's choices narrowed to his two best brigadier generals, Thomas and Sherman, as they had been nominated for major general. Sherman was too close to Grant and under the circumstances would never agree to relieve him. That left Thomas. Halleck urged Stanton to get his nomination out of committee and on the floor of the U.S. Senate for immediate approval. The Senate approved Thomas's nomination on April 25, and a general order announced his promotion on April 30. The way was clear for Halleck to give Thomas command of the right wing and the bulk of Grant's army.

Grant was shocked when Halleck rescinded his April 28 order and gave command of the right wing—and with it Grant's Army of the Tennessee—to Thomas. Thomas did not know at the time that Halleck had expedited his promotion so that he could relieve Grant, and he undertook his assignment with the understanding that it had come about because of an emergency. Grant was relegated to second in command under Halleck, a meaningless position in which Halleck would snub him as before.

Thomas was in awkward circumstances when it became obvious that Halleck was using him to humiliate Grant. Halleck, for example, kept his own headquarters near Thomas and made Grant tag along. When Halleck ostentatiously asked Thomas for advice, he deliberately excluded Grant from the discussions. "For myself," Grant later wrote, "I was little more than an observer."

As the ponderous army made its glacial advance toward Corinth, Grant once made so bold as to recommend an envelopment by the left wing. "I was silenced so quickly," he bitterly recalled, "that I felt that possibly I had suggested an unmilitary maneuver." Grant felt that his predicament was so intolerable that on May 11 he asked Halleck either to restore his command or to relieve him of duty. Halleck responded bluntly: Grant had no reason to complain, as Halleck was acting in his best interests and protecting his reputation. Trust me, said Halleck, for I am your friend. With that Grant seemed resigned to his circumstances and fatalistic about his future. For the remainder of the campaign he was along for the ride.

Halleck's sole objective was to seize Corinth without a fight. Washington had complained about the casualties at Shiloh, and Halleck intended to demonstrate that battles could be won without bloodshed. Beauregard could find no weakness to exploit, and no way to impede Halleck's inexorable approach. Grant had anticipated a great battle. Instead Beauregard abandoned Corinth and withdrew from reach.

The victory at Corinth was empty. The war could not be won solely by capturing places. Conceding territory to fight another day, the western Confederate army remained intact. Indisposed to chase the withdrawing Confederates, Halleck fortified Corinth. The war seemed interminable, and the occupation of Tennessee and Kentucky had become a liability. Federal strategic thinking was stalled, for no one thought ahead. Halleck's huge and potent army swung its fists in empty space. But Halleck had at least done at Corinth what McClellan had failed to do at Richmond. As a reward, Lincoln called Halleck to Washington as general in chief of the Federal armies. No one replaced him, and unified command in the western theater vanished. The great Federal army dispersed into three independent armies as before.

Grant was restored to the command of his army and given the task of pacifying the Mississippi Valley from his headquarters in Memphis. Buell was ordered eastward toward Chattanooga, joined later by Thomas, once again in command of his division. By then Thomas probably realized that he had been used by Halleck, and it is likely that Grant blamed Thomas, by association, for his humiliation. Thomas took his demotion stoically, yet he was proud of his performance and said so months later in a letter to Halleck.

"Before Corinth," wrote Thomas, "I was intrusted with the command of the right wing of the Army of the Tennessee. I feel confident that I performed my duty patriotically and faithfully and with a reasonable amount of credit to myself. As soon as the emergency was over I was relieved and returned to the command of my old division. I went to my duties without a murmur, as I am neither ambitious nor have any political aspirations."

Grant contended with a thankless and frustrating task. His scattered garrisons tried to guard railroads and depots from raiders and guerrillas abetted by local secessionists, but the Confederates had easy access into his district and a free hand when they got there. Grant worried that what had been won would again be lost, not a major battle, but by attrition. "The most anxious period of the war, to me," he said in his memoirs, "was during the time the Army of the Tennessee was guarding the territory acquired by the fall of Corinth and Memphis and before I was sufficiently reinforced to take the offensive."

Grant's perspective on the war had changed dramatically. Before Shiloh and Corinth he had thought that the Confederate government would collapse should one or more of its major armies be defeated. Defeated they had been, first at Forts Henry and Donelson, then at Corinth, and they had lost some of their most valuable territory as a consequence. Still the Confederacy seemed to have a resiliency and a toughness that maintained its fighting spirit and its determination to carry on.

When this sank in, said Grant, "I gave up all idea of saving the Union except by complete conquest." From then on he would destroy not only armies, but also their source of supplies. Foodstuffs, horses, cattle, and crops in the field "within reach of Confederate armies I regarded as much contraband as arms of ordnance stores. Their destruction was accomplished without bloodshed and tended to the same result as the destruction of armies. I continued this policy to the close of the war. . . . This policy I believe exercised a material influence in hastening the end."

But to what extent Grant would influence the war was problematical in the summer of 1862. Memphis was in the western extremities, remote from Washington, and there was little reason to believe that he was being considered for further duty of any importance.

16

THE KENTUCKY
CRUSADE

———◆·◆———

Braxton Bragg, the new commander of the Army of Tennessee, remained in Tupelo, Mississippi, where his predecessor, Beauregard, had retreated from Corinth. The only active Confederate force was the cavalry roaming freely in the Kentucky and Tennessee countryside, destroying Federal rolling stock, bridges, tunnels, tracks, and depots with enthusiasm and abandon. The colorful, audacious horsemen tormented their enemies and enthralled the civilians. One such cavalry commander was John H. Morgan. Things had gone well for him in Kentucky during July 1862. Glowing from warm receptions and successful raids, he told Major General E. Kirby Smith that some twenty-five to thirty thousand Kentuckians were ready to join up. This news delighted Smith, one of a succession of department commanders in East Tennessee frazzled by Union sympathizers in the mountains.

Smith shared the unwavering self-delusion of many Southerners that Kentucky sympathizers would welcome and reinforce an invading Confederate army, help it to drive out the Federal army, and bring Kentucky into the fold. Smith yearned to lead such a crusade. The only problems were Buell and Thomas, headed slowly toward Chattanooga from Corinth in the west. If Bragg headed them off, Smith would be free to march into Kentucky.

By inspired improvisation the Southern railway system moved Bragg's 35,000-man army across four states in less than a week, bypassing the Federal army advancing on foot. The atmosphere was euphoric on the 800-mile train ride from Tupelo to Chattanooga. People cheered along the way. The war was going to be taken to the Ohio River, far away from the Southern heartland. God bless Bragg and his splendid army.

Bragg and Thomas had served together in Mexico, and Bragg had proven his bravery, but in later years he became a strange and angry man. Ailments had made him aged, thin, and haggard. His plans and strategy vacillated, and on the battlefield he became confused and indecisive. Subordinates despised him for his choleric behavior, often ignored him, and routinely disobeyed his orders. Through it all, his friend Jefferson Davis stood by him and allowed Bragg to lead the Army of Tennessee from disaster to disaster.

Bragg and Smith conferred in Chattanooga on July 31 and agreed to cooperate, parting with an understanding that their ultimate goal was Louisville on the Ohio River, Kentucky's northern border. Their cooperation was nominal, and each crusaded by going his own way. Victories came easily for Smith, who seized Lexington and the capital of Frankfort by the end of August. Historian Thomas Connelly described the spirit and expectations of Smith's men in the beginning:

> It was a difficult climb over the Cumberlands, and a strange Cromwellian zeal seemed to come over the entire force. Many were ragged and barefoot, and the stony roads, heat, dust, thin rations, the day and night marching, and the strain of hauling field pieces and wagons along the horse trails molded an almost religious fervor so powerful that the march to Barboursville [Kentucky] became almost a mass prayer meeting. Whole regiments prayed for their enemies, "that God may turn them from the error of their ways," and the desire was intense to carry flag and cross to Lexington.

But Kentuckians had not augmented his small army as Smith expected; on the contrary, bushwhackers had sniped at his columns in the Kentucky mountains. Bragg was out of touch, still in Chattanooga, and Smith lacked the strength to go on to Louisville or farther north. He stayed where he was to await developments.

Buell, meanwhile, abandoned plans for taking Chattanooga, and his army dissipated along railroad lines, at garrisons to guard depots, and in futile attempts to engage the Confederate cavalry. Embarrassed by his own idleness, Bragg headed north at the end of August, ostensibly to rendezvous with Smith as he had promised.

Bragg did not reach Louisville. Spurred by a sense of crisis, Buell and Thomas got there first, so Bragg pulled up in the Bluegrass Region. He found, as had Smith, that Kentuckians shunned him. "The arms in abundance, which Kentuckians were advised to grasp," Buell later wrote, "remained in the store-houses." Bragg decided to abandon his crusade fifty miles short of Louisville on September 22, less than a month after starting.

Political clamor broke loose in the North when Smith and Bragg invaded Kentucky. The debacle of Second Manassas and Lee's invasion of Maryland coincided with the western invasion and intensified the uproar. Buell had embarrassed Halleck by failing to take Chattanooga, and Lincoln thought that Buell was another George McClellan for having allowed Bragg to get into Kentucky. Powerful western politicians who had grudges against Buell—especially the governors of Illinois and Indiana—held him accountable and demanded his relief.

By the time Buell arrived in Louisville in late September, one step ahead of Bragg, the atmosphere was poisonous. The governor of Indiana, Levi Morton, was in town trying to wrest control of the Indiana volunteers from Buell. Legions of raw recruits had volunteered in response to the emergency and had waited impatiently for Buell to arrive in Louisville and take them in. Buell tried to integrate them into his veteran army while fending off Morton and simultaneously preparing to move against Bragg.

The worst of all days was September 29. Two of Buell's generals, Jefferson C. Davis of Indiana and the Kentucky hero William Nelson, argued violently in the lobby of Buell's hotel. Davis shot and killed Nelson, and Buell arrested him.* In the hullabaloo, Indiana and Kentucky partisans went at each other's throats. While Buell tried to restore calm, a courier from Halleck, Colonel J. C McKibbin, delivered dispatches to him and Thomas. They ordered Buell to relinquish command of the army to Thomas.

Shutting the door to muffle the bedlam, the two generals discussed the implications. Buell had no alternative to immediate obedience, but Thomas did not want to relieve him. The army, about to march into combat, was in crisis. An abrupt change of command would only add more instability. If Thomas relieved Buell, the situation would not improve and would probably worsen. The risk was too great.

But the orders from Halleck were mandatory. Buell considered himself relieved of duty and wired Halleck that he had turned over command to Thomas. Thomas simultaneously wired Halleck asking that Buell be retained in command, as the army was about to go into battle.

Halleck was stunned when he received their wires, because he had been praying that McKibbin would not deliver the orders, dated September 23. Halleck had convinced Lincoln to give Buell more time to redeem himself, and he had sent wires to McKibbin en route not to deliver the orders. Now Halleck had been overtaken by events. Thomas did not want to obey the orders that Halleck had not wanted delivered to him. Halleck explained the snafu to Thomas by wire. The orders were temporarily suspended, he said, and he would lay Thomas's telegram before the president and get instructions. Late that night, Halleck advised Buell and Thomas that the orders had been suspended.

The Army of the Ohio left Louisville in search of Bragg on October 1. Many had hangovers, because Buell had granted a holiday to reduce tensions. On October 8, Bragg allowed a portion of his scattered army to blunder into the path of Buell's force at Perryville, Kentucky, sixty miles southeast of Louisville. It was the strangest of battles. Buell was unaware that an entire corps of his army was in combat two miles away from him, for an acoustic anomaly muffled the sound of battle. Thomas commanded a corps south of the battlefield. He too was unaware of developments. The other Federal

---

* Nelson is remembered as the organizer of Camp Dick Robinson in Kentucky early in the war. Davis (not related to the president of the Confederacy) was never punished and returned to duty.

corps commanders did the fighting. They beat Bragg, and that night he began his withdrawal from Kentucky.

Nothing had worked for the Confederates in Kentucky. The humiliation was unbearable. They had started the campaign fervently hoping to bring salvation to their Kentucky kinsmen, but the Kentuckians had rejected them. Bushwhackers had been the most unbearable outrage. Seething with desire for revenge as they retreated south, the Confederate soldiers seized a dozen hostages and took them to a single noose suspended from a tree. One by one, they hanged the Kentuckians until all were dead.

By late October 1862 Buell's pursuit of Bragg had stalled, and Buell and Washington were again irreconcilable as to strategy. This time Lincoln meant to have his way.

Again the question arose in Washington as to who should replace Buell. It would not be Thomas. He was qualified, of course, or else he would not have been nominated a month earlier, but his refusal had added to the fiasco in Louisville. He would not be allowed a second chance to say yes or no. Instead Lincoln selected Major General William S. Rosecrans, a West Pointer who had trounced Lee in western Virginia the year before and had performed with competence in the western army since. Most recently a corps commander under Grant, he had beaten back a Confederate attack against Corinth and had won an earlier victory at Iuka, Mississippi. His achievements were nothing spectacular, but somebody in Washington liked him.

Rank was a problem. By statute, generals of the Federal army were either brigadier general (one star) or major general (two stars), with commensurate authority for brigade and division command. Hence the administration could not assign ranks commensurate with the command of corps and armies, i.e., lieutenant general (three stars) and general of full rank (four stars). Dates of rank, therefore, conferred seniority, and in lieu of promotion the administration simply changed the date of rank to make a new commander senior to his subordinates.

Rosecrans had only recently been promoted, with a date of rank that made him among the most junior. He had complained earlier on principle, but he remained on the bottom of the list—that is, until Lincoln decided that he would relieve Buell. As three of Buell's corps commanders—Thomas, Alexander M. McCook, and Thomas L. Crittenden*—were senior to Rosecrans, Lincoln changed Rosecrans's date of rank so that he jumped thirty-nine numbers.

The relief of Buell was as awkward and humiliating as it had been a month before. Halleck sent orders to Rosecrans, who was to tell Buell personally, but Buell already had heard rumors about being sacked. Thomas was in a fury. Seniority was sacred in the army, and generals knew their place precisely in

---

* Thomas L. Crittenden was the brother of Confederate general George B. Crittenden, whom Thomas defeated at Mills Spring.

the pecking order. Being forced to report to a junior was insufferable, and he protested to Halleck. Halleck responded that Rosecrans was now senior to him. And so the matter ended. Thomas would become Rosecrans's counselor and confidant on all matters in both combat and administration.

A disappointed administration in Washington soon realized that Rosecrans—like Buell before him—had no intention of entering the mountains of East Tennessee. Instead, he stayed in Nashville and besieged Halleck with demands for supplies and reinforcements, particularly cavalry to protect his communications from Confederate raiders. Halleck blustered that Rosecrans would be fired if he did not leave Nashville. "To threats of removal I am insensible," Rosecrans wired back, and he stayed where he was.

The rancor between Rosecrans and Halleck would persist for the year that Rosecrans commanded in the west. At its core was the administration's ignorance of conditions. Lincoln and Stanton could not comprehend the theater's vast distances and the vulnerability of its inadequate roads and railway lines; Halleck, although a veteran of the theater, apparently did not enlighten them. Feeding the army posed almost insuperable difficulties in the mountains, as the marginal farms could not supply forage and food. By contrast, Grant and Sherman later could live off the land in Mississippi and Georgia. In those regions the farms were bountiful and the people clearly secessionist. But in Tennessee and Kentucky the loyalties were divided, and army commanders like Thomas did not want to plunder from Union loyalists already stripped by the Confederates.

The greatest misunderstandings concerned cavalry. The Confederates, born to the saddle, galloped circles around the mounted midwestern farm boys. Rosecrans wanted more and better Federal cavalry to fight fire with fire, but Halleck was unmoved. Other measures would be necessary to counter the cavalry menace, which threatened to immobilize Rosecrans indefinitely.

Rosecrans would not budge from Nashville until he had accumulated sufficient supplies from Louisville, 160 miles to the north on the Ohio River. The railroad between the two cities, carelessly laid out and constructed for commercial enterprises, crumbled under the stress and pounding of military traffic. The Confederate cavalry worsened matters by closing tunnels, ripping up track, and destroying bridges. Supplies were reduced to a trickle.

Thomas developed a remedy. The key was to fix damage fast. At first Thomas used brute manpower, which opened the line within a month, so that supplies began to flow again. Over time he established repair shops at Nashville and Chattanooga, organized gangs of specialized workers, and located material where it would be readily available. Construction trains were held in readiness at strategic locations, and standard bridge trusses in sixty-foot sections could be dropped into place by mobile railway cranes. "Thomas could not prevent the damage," wrote McKinney, "but by his system for repairing it, he was able eventually to lay a new track as fast as a dog could trot."

The Roman began to create a modern, professional army. The War Department permitted Thomas to select his own staff, and the officers he gathered about him were experts and specialists. Eventually the staff numbered nineteen, large for the Federal army, but it was the size and composition needed for modern warfare: adjutant general, quartermaster, commissary of subsistence, inspector general, chief of artillery, chief topographical officer, signal officer, medical director, medical purveyor, and aides-de-camp. They formed a crisp, taut staff quartered in crisp, taut tents laid out with the precision of a surveyor's transit. Headquarters crackled with precision and purpose. Visitors felt it and buttoned their collars. Subordinate commanders and staffs got the message.

The saddle was Thomas's headquarters in combat. A blue command pennant accompanied him so that his staff and subordinates could see his whereabouts. Each staff officer had specific tasks in battle, whether it was the medical director establishing field hospitals or aides delivering messages. An elite infantry regiment served as Thomas's provost guard, protecting convoys, collecting stragglers and arresting skulkers, receiving prisoners, and maintaining security. A cavalry regiment provided his escort, scouts, and couriers.

Rapid and reliable communications systems allowed Thomas to control and coordinate his forces both in the battlefield and on the march. He had perhaps the first mobile command post in the American army, a specially equipped wagon with desks and file drawers for his clerks and telegraphers to send and receive dispatches. It was, according to an observer, "a model of convenience and utility." Generals in the Second World War would employ equivalent facilities.

Thomas used visual communications to the extent possible, but they were limited by weather and terrain. Hence his army turned to the telegraph. The telegraphers were well-paid, intelligent civilians; the soldiers sometimes shunned them because they resented their special status. During the Vicksburg campaign Grant could not tolerate the telegraphers' independence, tried to bring them under his personal control by arresting the district superintendent, and fought the system all the way to its Washington headquarters. Thomas, on the other hand, recognized their value, praised their work, and issued them blue uniforms to make them feel a part of his army.

Accurate maps were another critical requirement for command and control. Thomas used them to determine march routes, deployment maneuvers, defensive positions, and potential enemy moves. A master at logistical planning, Thomas was so familiar with the roads, bridges, and fords in his campaign theater that he could precisely calculate the tonnage that could be transported by wagons. "Map making was quicker and more accurate," wrote McKinney.

Sharp-eyed cavalrymen on Thomas' front reported to his headquarters on roads, streams, fords, forage, bridges, drinking water, defense positions and the other minutiae necessary to rapid maneuver over a

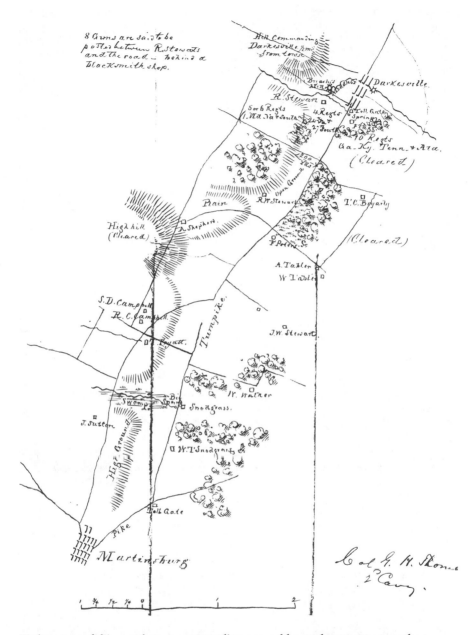

To be successful in combat, a commanding general has to be an expert on the
terrain, roads, and rivers in his theater of operations. George Thomas captured
these data on maps and notebooks so that he knew every feature of the countryside
where he would be fighting. This map, which he sketched during his initial
assignment in Virginia, illustrates his attention to detail. Thomas kept the map
folded inside the front of his map journal throughout the war. (National Archives)

These pages from Thomas's map journal are an example of his meticulous recording of the topography of the geographic areas where he would be operating. The breadth, accuracy, and diversity of his collected intelligence are astounding: distances between points, road conditions and carrying capacities, river crossings, landmarks, potable water, forage, cover—even the loyalties and trustworthiness of local residents. Information was gathered from many sources, ranging from military engineering surveys to spies and escaped prisoners. (National Archives)

strange terrain. This information, supplemented by the steady flow of material from Thomas' scouts and spies and infantry reconnaissance, was correlated at Thomas' headquarters into bulletins and simple two-dimensional maps. . . .

These detailed studies went to the topographical engineers who transferred the more important items to maps which were printed in the field and distributed throughout the army. The first edition would

Thomas had the first mobile command post in the American army, a specially equipped wagon with desks and file drawers for his clerks and telegraphers to send and receive dispatches. It was, according to an observer, "a model of convenience and utility." Generals in the Second World War would employ equivalent facilities. (Library of Congress)

> *be liberally sprinkled with little question marks, explained by a note which read, "Information is wanted where this (?) sign occurs. Engineers and officers are requested to send it in immediately to these headquarters." As fast as the information came in, more complete maps were printed and distributed.*

A professional army required sound administration when not in battle. Thomas demanded, for example, accountability of equipment and arms. His Chickamauga after-action report was a striking example. In addition to casualties, it listed every item of hardware destroyed or captured by the enemy, including small arms and accouterments; clothing, camp, and garri-

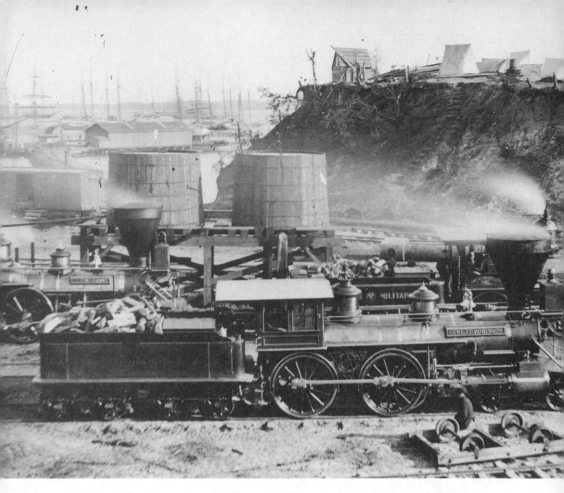

Logistical support for the Federal army in the west depended upon reliable rail transportation. Confederate cavalry tried continually to destroy bridges, tunnels, track, and rolling stock, but Thomas countered with ingenious ways to repair damage rapidly and thereby keep the supplies flowing. (Library of Congress)

son equipage; and such quartermaster stores as horses, mules, wagons, harnesses, and artificers' tools. Another report listed small arms and artillery ammunition expended. Such detailed accounting was extraordinary, especially as it was promptly submitted after a devastating battle, and it is a testament to the cohesion of Thomas's organization. Such comprehensive detail simply is not found anywhere else in the official reports of the Civil War.

To what extent did this focus on detail contribute to the combat readiness of Thomas's forces? Why did Thomas want to know how many wagon whips, currycombs, horse brushes, and linchpins were lost in battle, when most generals were satisfied solely with casualty statistics?

Thomas held that attention to detail paid off in combat. The following anecdote, perhaps apocryphal, illustrates this belief. One day Thomas inspected an artillery battery and found a defective linchpin. He explained to the battery commander that the linchpin might fail just when the team was straining to pull the battery into line. A broken linchpin could lose a battle.

In Thomas's mind every item of arms and equipment, however minor, had a purpose, and the soldier who understood his gun and his gear and cared for them had the best chance of survival. His soldiers were to know what they had and how to use it, and they were not to lose it in battle or elsewhere. Waste was intolerable.

Thomas created a mobile field hospital system that was unsurpassed in discipline, cohesiveness, and preparedness. It saved countless lives at Chickamauga, despite the chaos of that battle. The corps medical director summarized how his medical staff had prepared itself to handle battlefield casualties.

> *The regiments and batteries were all abundantly supplied with medicines and surgical instruments, the latter having, previous to the march, been thoroughly inspected and repaired by an expert.*
>
> *Aside from the usual regimental supplies, which are transported in the hospital wagons and accompany the regiments, we were provided with a reserve supply, consisting of hospital tents, blankets, sheets, hair pillows, shirts, drawers, bed-sacks, surgical instruments, bandages, lint, mess-chests (including cooking utensils), concentrated milk and beef, liquor, chloroform, and such other medicines, surgical apparatus, and hospital stores as experience has taught to be most needed and useful in emergencies in the field.*
>
> *These supplies were in possession of the medical purveyor of the corps subject to my order. They were transported in a train of fifteen army wagons. . . .*
>
> *The four divisions of the corps were each provided with a train of 30 light two-horse ambulances, under the general control of the corps and division medical directors. In addition to these, each regiment and each battery had permanently attached to it 1 ambulance, which is usually driven in the rear of these commands. This arrangement of our ambulances has operated more satisfactorily than any other that has yet been tried in this army.*

Conditioned, clothed, armed, and equipped, Thomas's men sensed that their general cared deeply for them and for their welfare. By providing them the wherewithal, the discipline, and the self-confidence to survive in combat and in the camp, Thomas transformed volunteers into warriors. In the process a special bond developed between general and soldier. Thomas was like a father, guiding, teaching, nurturing, expecting great things of them. "Old Pap," they began to call him.

17

MURFREESBORO

Tennessee had been the battleground of the west, politically and militarily, since the war began. As 1862 came to a close, neither the Federal nor the Confederate government confidently controlled its regions. Countless campaigns by both sides had ranged along its rivers and mountains and valleys. Battles of all magnitudes had been fought, from guerrilla skirmishes to massed infantry and artillery at Shiloh. Still all was flux.

Thanks to Thomas, supplies were flowing from Louisville into Nashville, and Rosecrans finally felt ready to seek battle with Bragg. Beforehand, Rosecrans had changed both the name and organization of his army. He now designated his force the Army of the Cumberland (no longer the Army of the Ohio), owing to yet another War Department redefinition of district and department boundaries. He divided the 45,000-man army into three sections, the left and right wings and the center, commanded respectively by Thomas Crittenden, Alexander McCook, and Thomas. Later these would be designated as corps.

This combat organization was shaped by Rosecrans's "strategy of maneuver," which he would employ against Bragg starting at Murfreesboro (Stones River) and continuing until it backfired at Chickamauga. The three corps would advance on a broad, flexible front, each within supporting distance of the other, enabling Rosecrans to exploit Confederate weaknesses and to turn the flanks of Bragg's Army of Tennessee. Sherman would employ an identical strategy in the 1864 Atlanta campaign.

While such a strategy was classic in the abstract, it faltered in practice under the hemorrhaging inflicted by the Confederate cavalry. The threat of Morgan's 3,000-man cavalry division rampaging through Kentucky and central Tennessee would force Thomas to employ twice that number to guard the rail lines leading into Nashville from the north. Another division would remain to garrison Nashville.

Thus, without firing a shot, Morgan would suck the equivalent of three divisions from Thomas's corps. His remaining troops would be two divisions under James S. Negley and Lovell H. Rousseau, plus a brigade under Colonel

Moses Walker. Of these seven brigades, three would be primarily engaged in protecting the wagon train from Confederate cavalry. The consequence was startling. Of a total of fourteen brigades in Thomas's corps, nine would be engaged in protecting near and distant lines of communication and depots. Only five would be available to fight Bragg's infantry at Murfreesboro. Such was the leveraged power of the Confederate cavalry: one cavalryman equaled three Federal infantrymen.

Rosecrans found Bragg thirty miles from Nashville, in the town of Murfreesboro on the Stones River. Bragg, too, was looking for a fight and had conveniently moved his 37,000-man army there during the fall. Unlike Rosecrans's deliberate preparations, Bragg had hastily planned his offensive, giving his army no time to recuperate from Kentucky. The impetus for immediate battle was a mania to recapture Nashville at all costs. Its occupation was insufferable. The dream and the passion could not be extinguished. Hood would be similarly enraptured on his tragic crusade two years later.

Bragg was eager to redeem his failure in Kentucky and had gone to Richmond in late October to discuss his plans to retake central Tennessee. Bragg's unreadiness for battle either was not recognized or was ignored by the high command. The common belief in Richmond was that Bragg had brought a wealth of stores with him from Kentucky, but, other than unclaimed guns and some cattle, the rumored plunder was illusory. His army wore rags, marched on bare feet, and ate reduced rations. Food raised in Tennessee was reserved for Lee by order of the Richmond government. Bragg had to glean the leavings.

Bragg's organizational efforts were as futile as Rosecrans's were effective. He and two other generals, Kirby Smith in East Tennessee and John C. Pemberton on the Mississippi, competed for troops and resources. His own Army of Tennessee was organized into two corps under Leonidas Polk and William Hardee. Polk, the bishop-general, was an imperious Tennessee patriarch with power both in Richmond and the army, and he cooperated with Bragg at his discretion. Bragg could not touch him because Polk was a close friend of Jefferson Davis, to whom he sent letters urging Bragg's removal.

Hardee, a respected tactician and professional soldier, despised Bragg with equal intensity. After Bragg returned from Richmond in early November, both Polk and Smith went there to urge that Bragg be relieved. Davis decided to stick with Bragg and to allow him to fight Rosecrans. "Never had a general begun a campaign in the west," wrote the historian Thomas Connelly, "with such little support from his lieutenants."

The one common recommendation that Davis had received from his western visitors was the urgent need for a unified commander, someone to coordinate Bragg, Pemberton, and Smith against the armies of Grant and Rosecrans, to allocate troops and resources, and to develop a coherent strategy. That commander would have to be a full general, necessarily limiting the candidates to Lee, Beauregard, Bragg, and Joseph Johnston. Lee, of course, would stay in Virginia. Davis had fired Beauregard from the western command in June and would under no circumstances reinstate him. Bragg had his hands full with his present command. This left Johnston, who by November 1862 had recovered from his wounds at Seven Pines. Davis and Johnston hated each other, but the western generals seemed willing to work for Johnston, and so on November 24 Davis appointed him commander in the west.

Though he had appointed a unified commander, Davis took care not to delegate any of his own closely held authority as commander in chief of the armed forces. The charter that Davis gave Johnston was sufficiently vague and ambiguous to inhibit him from exercising any meaningful authority. They could not agree on an appropriate strategy for the theater of operations, and Davis routinely bypassed Johnston by communicating directly with Bragg, Pemberton, and Smith.

Davis's snubbing of Johnston immediately became evident when Davis came to Murfreesboro in mid-December to see the troops and talk over plans with his generals. Johnston went along for the ride. Davis's visit was a grand occasion, and the regiments strove to look their best. Passing in review before Davis's misty eyes, they looked ready for battle, confirming what Bragg and his commanders were telling him.

Bragg was sure that Rosecrans would withdraw into Kentucky, because he mistakenly believed the Federal troops in Nashville were starving owing to the broken railroad line. In a matter of a few weeks, said Bragg, he would lead his army back into Nashville, and his officers boldly affirmed his predictions. Their self-deception was complete. Confident of success in Tennessee, Davis decided to send a fourth of Bragg's infantry to reinforce Pemberton at Vicksburg.

The holiday spirit and the ardor of soldiers suffused Murfreesboro and mesmerized Davis. Wives and sweethearts were in town for the balls and celebrations and horse races, and a banquet was held for the guest of honor. Morgan's marriage celebration added zest and gaiety to the festivities. Johnston returned to Chattanooga in a huff, and when the telegraph line to Murfreesboro went dead, he lost all touch with Bragg.

Still aglow from the holiday celebrations, Bragg was shocked on Christmas Day when he received reports of Federal troops moving on Murfreesboro. They were coming down many roads in large but unknown numbers, in terrible weather of sleet and rain. Given his braggadocio with Davis, Bragg had to fight. The terrain at Murfreesboro was unsuited for defensive purposes, and the Stones River sliced through the center of his lines, separating the two corps. Bragg decided that he would attack Rosecrans preemptively. By coincidence each general planned to attack with a powerful left wing, reducing the strength of the right wing in proportion.

Bragg was the first to strike, at daylight on the thirty-first, his left under Hardee against the Federal right under McCook. Bragg had contrived the usual Confederate plan of attack by divisions en echelon. As always, the plan was incapable of execution. Nonetheless, Hardee's assault crushed the right-wing Federal division under Richard W. Johnson. The Confederate cavalry brigade under Brigadier General John A. Wharton compounded the catastrophe by slamming into the rear of the Federal infantry and bagging 1,500 prisoners. Looking beyond his immediate front, Wharton saw an immense wagon train stretched along the Nashville Pike, guarded by Federal cavalry and infantry. There was his prize. His 2,000 horsemen, he later wrote, "were hurled on the foe. The ground was exceedingly favorable for cavalry operations, and after a short hand-to-hand conflict, in which the revolver was used with deadly effect, the enemy fled from the field in the wildest confusion and dismay, and were pursued to Overall's Creek [where] the enemy reformed out of range of our guns.

"The wagon train—consisting of several hundred wagons—many pieces of artillery, and about 1,000 infantry, who were either guarding the wagons or were fugitives from the field, were ours. The trains were turned round, and started back on the pike towards Murfreesboro."

We may wonder why this magnificent Confederate cavalry brigade broke off the pursuit at the creek, rather than continuing to rampage and disrupt. If the enemy re-formed "out of range of our guns," why did Wharton not close the range and tear relentlessly into the enemy "to do them all the damage I could," as Hardee had ordered him to do?

To come to the answer, we must appreciate conditions in the rear during combat, which the writer Ambrose Bierce, a cartographer and staff officer for the Army of the Cumberland, saw and later described:

> An army in line-of-battle awaiting attack, or prepared to deliver it, presents strange contrasts. At the front are precision, formality, fixity, and silence. Toward the rear these characteristics are less and less conspicuous, and finally, in point of space, are lost altogether in confusion, motion, and noise. The homogeneous becomes heterogeneous. Definition is lacking; repose is replaced by an apparently purposeless activity; harmony vanishes in hubbub, form is disorder. Commotion everywhere and ceaseless unrest. The men who do not fight are never ready.
>
> The battle intensifies. Shirkers, the wounded and the dazed, the orphaned companies alike, stream back from the front. Columns of reinforcements collide with careening ammunition wagons, artillery batteries, and ambulances. Amidst cries and shouts and screams and curses, artillery shells explode among the throngs. Enemy cavalry swoop in and out raising fresh alarms. Spur-of-the-moment efforts to quell the panic—often by generals and their staffs with sword and appeal—are usually futile.

Thomas's remedy was the provost guard, a force of sufficient steel to invoke order and security in the rear. Exercising characteristic foresight, Thomas had taken the best regiment he could find, the Ninth Michigan Infantry Regiment under Lieutenant Colonel John G. Parkhurst, and made it his provost guard.

Two hours after the battle at Murfreesboro had begun, Parkhurst was rounding up stragglers. Suddenly a deluge of cavalry, troops, and wagons came pounding down upon him, he later reported, "in the most rapid retreat, throwing away their arms and accouterment, and many of them without hats or caps, and apparently in the most frightful state of mind, crying, 'We are all lost.' I at once concluded it was a stampede of frightened soldiers, and before many had passed me I drew my regiment up in line of battle across the road, extending on either side, and ordered my men to fix bayonets, and to take the position of guard against cavalry. This was done with celerity, and with much difficulty. Without firing upon the frightened troops, I succeeded in checking their course, and ordered every man to face about. Within half an hour I had collected about 1,000 cavalrymen, seven pieces of artillery, and nearly two regiments of infantry. Among them was a brigadier general. . . . One colonel succeeded in escaping my lines, and passed on towards Nashville."

Parkhurst assembled his makeshift brigade and sent the cavalry back to rescue the wagons that Wharton had seized. After a series of swirling encounters, the Confederates took what they could and returned to their lines. Thanks to Parkhurst, Rosecrans still had the bulk of his wagons and was able

The elite Ninth Michigan Infantry Regiment served as Thomas's provost guard under these stern and competent officers. At Murfreesboro they and their men stemmed the panic in the rear, allowing the Army of the Cumberland to recover and eventually to win the battle against Bragg's Army of Tennessee. (Massachusetts Commandery Military Order of the Loyal Legion and the U.S. Army Military History Institute)

to replenish ammunition—albeit at the last minute—allowing the infantry and artillery to sustain combat. It had been a near thing. Had Wharton taken the train, the Federal army would have been annihilated when its ammunition was gone. It was men like Parkhurst who set Thomas's army apart.

The gritty Parkhurst could not contain the entire flood with but one regiment. Thomas got help from Colonel Moses Walker. Like Wellington at Waterloo, Walker had deployed his brigade in squares to repel cavalry. "I remained in this position but a few moments," he later wrote, "until another stampede of mules, negroes, fugitives, and cowards of every grade were seen swarming to the rear. At this moment Captain Mackay, of Major-General Thomas' staff, rode up and requested me, if possible, to check the stampede. I at once [formed] line of battle with my right resting upon the road. The appearance of this force appeared to reassure and give confidence to the runaways. Men and mules stopped."

Walker later went into the line, and his soldiers did well. "We have tried to perform our duty," he wrote at the conclusion of his report. "We have done the work assigned us in the best manner we knew how. We are in good condition to perform any service which may be required of us, and will do it cheerfully, whatever it may be, as we have ever heretofore done."

Who is it, when battle rages, that sees it in its entirety? Bierce explained that few really knew.

> The civilian reader must not suppose when he reads accounts of military operations in which relative position of the forces are defined . . . that these were matters of general knowledge to those engaged. Such statements are commonly made, even by those in high command, in the light of later disclosures, such as the enemy's official reports. It is seldom, indeed, that a subordinate officer knows anything about the disposition of the enemy's forces—except that it is unamiable—or precisely whom he is fighting.
>
> As to the rank and file, they can know nothing more of the matter than the arms they carry. They hardly know what troops are upon their own right or left the length of a regiment away. If it is a cloudy day they are ignorant even of the points of a compass. . . . [W]hat is going on in front of him he does not know at all until he learns it afterward.

The Roman was great among generals because he saw through the fog of battle. Among his gifts was an intuitive eye that envisioned terrain as a battlefield. Athwart this meadow was a field of fire that exposed the enemy, and yonder was a ridge that protected his own. And here was a plateau for an artillery site to enfilade exposed enemy flanks or to sweep its fronts. When circumstances either allowed him to advance or caused him to withdraw, he usually knew beforehand where he would reposition his artillery, or where he would form a new infantry line. Regardless of the stress of combat, he always thought clearly and logically in such terms.

As he approached Murfreesboro on the thirtieth, Thomas was therefore thinking about terrain and the battle that was about to unfold. A forest of cedar dominated the battlefield, so dense that men could barely squeeze through, artillery batteries and wagons not at all. When Thomas drew up his lines in anticipation of battle, the cedars were in the midst of his corps. Negley faced Murfreesboro to the east, with the cedars to his rear, while Rousseau, in reserve, had them on his front. The cedars could have isolated and immobilized individual regiments as much as river or ravine. Yet on the day of battle Negley and Rousseau freely maneuvered infantry and artillery through the thickets, because Thomas had ordered roads cleared the day before.

This, in turn, had been possible because Rosecrans and Thomas had had the foresight to establish a pioneer brigade commanded by engineer officers. To supplement this brigade, Rosecrans had instructed each regiment to have a self-sufficient pioneer detachment comprised of two men from each company. The pioneer organization had expanded to nearly 1,000 officers and men by the summer of 1863. They built and repaired railways and bridges, cut firewood for the trains, built storage platforms, repaired and operated steamboats and sawmills, and worked on roads and fortifications. When Thomas wanted roads through the cedars, the pioneers, under fire, cut trees and grubbed stumps. When the fighting began on the thirty-first, they lay down their tools and took up rifles.

As the battle progressed on the morning of New Year's Eve, Hardee pushed back McCook's corps about two miles, squeezing the Federal line into a salient. If Hardee could continue to compress the salient from the southwest, he would trap Rosecrans against the river to the east, while Polk rolled up the center and left. Rosecrans galloped behind the lines, shifting his unengaged divisions from the left and his reserve to restore the right wing. Thomas sent Rousseau to the right of Philip H. Sheridan, the sole general of McCook's corps whose division had remained intact, while Negley fought off Polk.

By late morning the Confederate brigades had lost their cohesion, but their piecemeal attacks continued as if their manpower was inexhaustible. Sheridan had devastated his attackers, but the firing was so intense that his soldiers had expended their ammunition. Because Wharton's attack had momentarily scattered the wagon train, there was no ammunition for immediate replenishment.

It was a macabre kind of warfare. The Confederates had reduced their enemy, not by felling them beyond the point of resistance, but by absorbing so many bullets that the Federal cartridge boxes were emptied. Sheridan found Thomas and told him that he had to withdraw, which would open a gap between Negley and Rousseau that the Confederates could exploit to cleave Rosecrans's army.

This was the crisis of the battle. When the Confederates saw Sheridan withdraw, they swarmed in for the kill. The combat became a running brawl. The Confederate troops slashed the Federal line into segments, like a raging river punching holes in a dike. The desperate Federal regiments remained intact, however, and fought their way clear when their flanks and rear were turned, holding again on successive lines set up by Thomas to buy time for Rosecrans to fortify a final position. Thomas simultaneously sent his artillery through the cedar corridors to high ground further in the rear, to the sites he had selected earlier, and from these elevations the cannon supported the beleaguered infantry.

The salvation of the center was an elite body of fighters, a "regular brigade" of academy officers and five battalions of soldiers of the regular army, which Thomas had organized in the weeks before the battle for just such an emergency. They were the last throw of the dice. Entering the maelstrom, the regulars absorbed the last frenzied thrust. The Confederate columns shuddered and slowed, providing time enough for Thomas's troops to clamber to high ground near the Nashville Pike and the adjacent railway and to reunite with the remainder of Rosecrans's army. As they climbed, the artillery roared over their heads and shells plummeted upon the Confederates. Hardee's drained brigades panted to a halt.

Bragg assessed his situation at midday. His soldiers had attacked with their typical fury and although they had hammered Rosecrans's army into a salient, it was still intact and dangerous. Hardee had nothing left to give, nor did Polk. Bragg's only uncommitted reserve was Breckinridge's division, which had been unengaged on the east bank of the Stones River. Bragg should have recalled it earlier, and perhaps he did, but Bragg's generals often found ways to disobey. It took until midafternoon for Bragg to get Breckinridge across the river, first two brigades and later the other two.

Rather than probing for weakness in the Federal line, Bragg directed his renewed attack against its strongest and most unyielding bastion. This would be remembered as the Round Forest, a high wooded ground on the extreme left of the Federal line near the convergence of the Nashville Pike and the railway. Colonel William B. Hazen and his brigade had defended the position throughout the day—the one body that had not changed position. "Upon this point," Hazen later wrote, "as a pivot, the entire army oscillated from front to rear the entire day."

Hazen was, recalled Bierce, "the best hated man that I ever knew, and his very memory is a terror for every unworthy soul in the service. His was a stormy life: he was in trouble all around. Grant, Sherman, Sheridan and a countless multitude of the less eminent luckless had the misfortune, at one time or another, to incur his disfavor, and he tried to punish them all. . . . He was aggressive, arrogant, tyrannical, honorable, truthful, courageous—a skillful soldier, a faithful friend and one of the most exasperating of men. Duty was his religion, and like the Moslem he proselyted with the sword."

Hazen had dug in behind the railroad embankment, artillery standing hub to hub in his rear. Before him lay a broad field, upon which the first two brigades of Breckinridge's division dressed their lines and marched forward with regimental colors snapping and drums rolling. An avalanche of Federal firepower blew them from the field. Two hours later, at four o'clock, the latter two brigades repeated the spectacle. "The battle had hushed," Hazen later reported, "and the dreadful splendor of this advance can only be conceived, as all description must fall vastly short. . . . The fire of the troops was held until the enemy's right flank came in close range, when a single fire from my men was sufficient to disperse this portion of his line. . . . This virtually ended the fight for the day."

The orders of Bragg and Polk for the ruinous employment of Breckinridge's division would be, in terms of poor judgment, the equivalent of Lee's orders at Malvern Hill and Gettysburg and of Hood's at Franklin.

At nightfall on New Year's Eve, the high commands on both sides assessed the damage. The Federal army was on different ground from whence the day had begun, but the battle was for survival, not real estate, and the army was intact. Bragg, on the other hand, was sure that he had won and that Rosecrans would retreat to Nashville during the night. Such was the tenor of the messages Bragg sent to Richmond and to Johnston.

Bragg's subsequent reports typified the wishful thinking of the Army of Tennessee throughout its disheartening campaigns under a succession of losing commanders. "Southern letters and diaries concentrate on this fact," wrote Larry J. Daniel in *Soldiering in the Army of Tennessee,* "detailing the large number of prisoners and cannon that were taken and the utter confusion that was inflicted on the enemy.

"Wrote Tennesseean Frank Carter after Murfreesboro: 'There is no doubt but that the Yankees were *badly whipped,* having lost in killed and wounded at least five to our one, also about 5,000 prisoners, while our loss in prisoners was comparatively nothing.' " In retrospect historians regard such western battles as Shiloh, Perryville, Murfreesboro, and Franklin as Confederate defeats. "The point is," wrote Daniel, "that many Southerners *believed* it to be otherwise."

Rosecrans called his wearied generals to a council of war and hashed over alternatives. Thomas already had made up his mind and slept. Rosecrans decided to withdraw. He awakened Thomas and asked him to command the rear guard.

"This army can't retreat," said Thomas. He closed his eyes and resumed sleeping.

The Army of the Cumberland was still in place when Bragg awoke on New Year's Day, which passed in lethargy and sporadic skirmishes. Bragg learned on January 2 that a Federal brigade had crossed the Stones River and occupied a ridge that would allow their fire to enfilade Polk's lines. Ignoring his two corps commanders entirely, Bragg ordered Breckinridge to attack that afternoon. Owing to Bragg's inability to coordinate any maneuver of consequence, the unfortunate soldiers of Breckinridge's already battered division had neither cavalry nor artillery support, nor did Bragg order diversionary attacks elsewhere. The outcome was predictable. Federal artillery pulverized the Confederate troops, and Federal infantry swept them away. Bragg could notch another ghastly failure to his credit.

The weather turned to sleet and snow that night, further sapping the strength and spirit of the tattered Army of Tennessee. Bragg's cavalry reported that Rosecrans was not retreating, was perhaps even being reinforced, and could attack at any time. It was too much for Bragg. He ordered a retreat south, abandoning Murfreesboro and his wounded to Rosecrans.

Rosecrans let him go.

Six months would elapse before the two armies met again.

PART IV

EASTERN
THEATER, 1863

18

CHANCELLORSVILLE

⟶•◆•⟵

Barlow's convalescence from his wounds at Antietam had extended into the spring of 1863. His appetite had not returned, and he needed extra sleep. "Frank Barlow is not fit but will return to active service," wrote Maria Daly, the New York socialite gossip, in her diary. "Arabella declares that he loves fighting for the sake of fighting, and is really bloodthirsty. . . . He looks very frail."

The Federal army changed as Barlow mended. Massachusetts, the seat of abolitionism, had raised its first black regiment in the spring of 1863, the Fifty-fourth Colored Infantry, under Robert G. Shaw, a scion of a wealthy Boston family with humanitarian convictions. Barlow had first known Shaw as a child in the days at Brook Farm. Barlow had tutored Shaw for Harvard in 1856, and they had stayed in touch. While recuperating in Boston, Barlow saw Shaw and the black soldiers he was recruiting.

At a time when many people in the North could not envision blacks bearing arms, and under no circumstances the equivalent of a white man as a soldier, Shaw's regiment impressed Barlow as potential fighters, as the kind of men he would like to lead in battle. Considering Barlow's standards of excellence and his caustic intolerance of imperfection, this was an extraordinary endorsement of their fitness as warriors. More regiments were sure to follow, and eventually they would become a brigade. Barlow let it be known that he would like to command the brigade. "I hope Frank Barlow can get the command," Shaw wrote his mother on March 17, 1863. "He is just the man for it, and I should like to be under him."

Although Barlow was not aware of it, influential intellectuals and abolitionists who had known him since his days as a student were advocating his name. They believed passionately in allowing blacks to fight, and they wanted Barlow to lead them. Such Boston powers as James Russell Lowell, the renowned New England man of letters, had pledged to recruit, train, and equip a black brigade, and they petitioned Stanton to assign Barlow as its commander. By the time Barlow learned about his nomination, he had returned to the Army of the Potomac, commanding a white brigade and wearing the single star of a brigadier general.

Barlow still wanted the black brigade. The only hitch was that he was expected to recruit it. That he did not want to do, for he was impatient to resume campaigning. He wrote to Lowell that if others would organize the brigade, he would welcome the command. "I am still anxious," he wrote to another influential abolitionist, "to take part in the black experiment. Will you state to Gov. [John A.] Andrew & to anyone else that is interested in this matter that my services are at their command whenever they can be used."

Barlow received a letter in early June from another source, Dr. Samuel Gridley Howe, a Boston reformer who had helped organize the American Freedman's Inquiry Commission, intended to train and educate emancipated African Americans. Its sweeping programs would require an organizational structure and someone to run them, and at this stage the position had been labeled Superintendent of the American Freedman's Bureau. The expectations of the post were ambiguous—the bureau still had to be created—but the concept was exciting. Howe offered the job to Barlow.

Commanding a black brigade was a military affair. The superintendent's position was civil. Still, it was attractive enough that Barlow wired Howe for details. "Politically it would be a great advantage to me," he wrote Almira, "but I doubt my ability to fill the place and I dislike the idea of leaving the active service for which I am well fitted."

We can never be certain as to Barlow's motives. Were they essentially political, as the letter to Almira implies? And to what extent was Barlow committed to furthering black freedom? While raised among abolitionists, there is no evidence that Barlow himself engaged in such activity, and when in 1863 he discussed the opportunities in family letters, he dismissively used the terms "darkey" and "nigger." In any event, chance and circumstances would prevent him from leading either black soldiers or freedmen.

Barlow may have been willing to try black troops because of his pessimism about his new brigade. A component of the Second Division in Oliver O. Howard's Eleventh Corps, it had in the course of the war attained a sorry reputation for bad luck and defeat. The brigade, indeed most of the Eleventh Corps, was comprised largely of men of German descent, many of whom had come to America to escape persecution during the revolution of 1848. They were among the North's most ardent abolitionists and, as a group, politically influential, the kind of people who would support the administration and volunteer to serve. "Dutchmen," its soldiers with broken English were called, and the anglicized soldiers of the Army of the Potomac held them in amused contempt. Consequently, Howard and Barlow had been assigned as brigade and corps commanders respectively in the expectation that they would whip them into shape.

The winter of 1863 was cruel to Lee's army. Heavy snow followed by thaws alternately froze and flooded the Confederate encampments. Lee's troops remained deployed along the Rappahannock, for he was certain that another Federal offensive was imminent. Supplies were delivered in pitiful quantities on the single rail line from Richmond to Fredericksburg, where Lee maintained his headquarters throughout the winter and early spring. Somehow his men survived, despite the austere rations and lack of clothing. Occasionally they left their encampments, straightened their ranks, and passed in review before Lee and his generals and their guests. Worship services were frequent and well attended.

The Federal armies had the weight of numbers on every front. Lee believed that if the Confederacy intended to survive, there was no alternative to total mobilization, which in his mind the people of the South had been shamefully avoiding. In a long, impassioned letter to James A. Seddon, the new secretary of war, Lee dispensed with his usual deferential style and spoke bluntly. "Let the State authorities take the matter in hand, and see that no man able to bear arms be allowed to evade his duty," Lee implored. "[L]et every effort be made, every means be employed, to fill and maintain the ranks of our armies, until God, in His mercy, shall bless us with the establishment of our independence."

The United States Congress, meanwhile, enacted legislation that mobilized the Union for total war. The first act was a conscription law that resembled the draft law enacted by the Confederacy. Other acts allowed the government sweeping authority to borrow money, to establish a national bank system and national currency, to prevent and punish frauds on revenue, and to turn over to the Treasury all captured and abandoned cotton, sugar, rice, and tobacco from states in the Confederacy. Still another act authorized the president to suspend the writ of habeas corpus at his discretion.

Lee's bitterness and frustration seethed in a letter of February 28 to his son Custis, a military aide to Davis and familiar with the supine, obstinate Confederate legislature. "You see the Federal Congress has put the whole power of their country onto the hands of their President," wrote Lee. "Nine hundred millions of dollars and three millions of men. Nothing can now arrest . . . the most desolating war that was ever practiced, except a revolution among their people. Nothing can produce a revolution except systematic success on our part." Southerners avoided combat, he complained, by applying to serve in the regiments of states removed from the war zones, and other laws allowed some to shirk service entirely.

Such outbursts were infrequent, and Lee, in spite of his frustration, stoically carried on using whatever he had been given to work with. His mood swings—anger, humor, teasing, resignation, optimism, self-deprecation—all were apparent in his family letters. Now and then he was sanctimonious, but not often. Nor did he succumb to despair, despite the circumstances. Like his army, Lee was tough, resilient, and scrappy. "Soldiers you know are born to suffer," he wrote Mary, "& they cannot escape it." He lived like his soldiers, in an austere tent that filled with snowmelt and provided only rudimentary shelter. "We are in a liquid state now," he wrote Mary on February 8. "Up to our knees in mud & what is worse on short rations for men & beasts. This keeps me miserable. I am willing to starve myself, but cannot bear my men or horses to be pinched. I fear many of the latter will die."

Although Lee missed his family and wrote them poignant letters, he remained at his headquarters. Mary wrote of her pains, but as Lee would not grant furloughs to his army, he remained in camp himself. In any case, he had no desire to go to Richmond under any circumstances, because unpleasant meetings with Davis and other politicians would be unavoidable. Nor did he encourage family visitors. Of one daughter he wrote, "Tell her . . . whenever she eats think of her papa & his military family . . . with their tin plates & cups freezing to their fingers out of doors enjoying their sup & tough biscuit." "The only place I am to be found is in camp," he wrote to another daughter, "& I am so cross now that I am not worth seeing anywhere."

Lee tried every possible expediency to feed his soldiers, except reforming the system itself. Raiding parties snagged every last cow on the hoof and every pound of bacon within reach. It was not enough. By late March, Lee reported to Seddon that each of his soldiers had a daily ration of "18 ounces of flour, 4 ounces of bacon of indifferent quality, with occasionally supplies of rice, sugar, or molasses." Scurvy had appeared, and Lee ordered daily details to find "sassafras buds, wild onions, lamb's quarters, and poke sprouts," but the quantities were inadequate. His soldiers did not complain and seemed cheerful, said Lee, but he doubted that they would have the health and vigor for an extended campaign.

Lee's clothing was as unpretentious as his headquarters. He sent away his ceremonial sash and kept but a single overcoat. When offered a new one, he told Custis that "my old Blue will serve me yet awhile." Mary, too, offered him another, permitting one for sleeping and one for wearing, an indulgence his frugality would not permit. His sole pair of pantaloons were so dilapidated, he wrote Custis, that he was "very sensitive, fearful of an accident," and he reluctantly ordered a replacement. ("I like the legs full, & so cut as to spring over the boot.")

When son Rob was short of socks, Lee sent some of his own. "I send [them]," he wrote Mary, "not on the grounds as you put it, 'if I wish to get rid of them,' but on the principle that ought to actuate me, a willingness to share any thing with a friend in distress."

Mary fretted about what he would wear in warm weather. "I do not know that anything can be done to my summer apparel," he responded. "You know it is very limited. Only a change of under garments. I dare say some of the socks are broken, but I have a good number of them & some are perfect. There are but two pairs left of my thinnest drawers, & I doubt whether anything can be done for them as far as I recollect their condition. My apparel gives me but little trouble. I may be so soon cast off."

Lee was fatalistic as to whether he would survive the war and saw little to look forward to in any event. "I have no time to think of my private affairs," he wrote Mary. "I expect to die a pauper, & I see no way of preventing it. So that I can get enough for you and the girls I am content."

Joseph Hooker relieved the hapless Ambrose Burnside on January 26 as commanding general of the Army of the Potomac, the fourth commander in seven months to confront Lee. By now Lee was indifferent. "Gen. Hooker is obliged to do something," he wrote a daughter. "I do not know what it will be. He is playing the Chinese game. Trying what frightening will do. He runs out his guns, starts his wagons & troops up & down the river, & creates an excitement generally. Our men look on in wonder, give a cheer, & all again subsides 'in statu quo ante bellum.' "

Nonetheless, Hooker kept Lee's army in the trenches and Lee guessing. In mid-February, Burnside, once again a corps commander, went by water transport to Newport News, raising fears of a Federal offensive in southeastern Virginia that would threaten either Richmond or the lines of communication passing through North Carolina, perhaps even the vital port city of Wilmington. Reacting to the threat, Lee sent two divisions to the region, commanded by Hood and George E. Pickett, and then sent Longstreet to command the entire district.

After a period Burnside reboarded his transports and went to the western theater in another Federal attempt to seize and hold East Tennessee, the recurring penalty for not having allowed Thomas to take the region earlier in the war. When Burnside left, the threat went with him, but Lee did not recall Longstreet. Instead, he changed Longstreet's mission to gathering provisions and forage, depriving Lee's forces on the Rappahannock of a fourth of the veterans of the Army of Northern Virginia.

The winter had been hard on Lee. Sickness sent him to bed in early April. Thought to be a bad cold, it more likely was pericarditis, the inflammation of the outer heart membrane. His pulse fluttered at ninety, and his doctors moved him from his tent to a house. In a way he enjoyed the change of scenery, the better food, and the attention of women spoiling him. Pretty women had been scarce, and he missed them. "I have only seen the ladies in this vicinity when flying from the enemy," he had written a daughter, "& it caused me acute grief to witness their exposure & suffering."

He hoped that he could get out of bed before it was time to fight again. Hooker would decide when and where, but Lee derided him. "I thought the late fine weather," he wrote Mary from his sickbed, "might bring Mr. Hooker over, as he has been so anxious, but he stands fast yet awhile. . . . The grass is springing. I suppose I shall hear soon from Genl Hooker." Just as Lee was nearly recovered, he received another mindless letter from Richmond, soliciting his cooperation in detaching some of his troops to reinforce Bragg in Tennessee. Lee grimly reminded the government on April 16 that he already was outnumbered two to one, worsened by the need to keep Longstreet further south to get supplies the government could not provide. "If it is determined to be best that the army here should remain inactive," he warned, "I doubt Genl Hooker will be quiescent."

Lee fashioned a plan to help Bragg without reinforcing him. The Army of Northern Virginia had enormous problems, to be sure, said Lee in a letter of April 16 to Davis. The condition of his horses had immobilized his army. "At present we are very much scattered and I am unable to bring the army together for want of proper subsistence & forage." Nonetheless, he would "assume the aggressive" by the first of May, he wrote Davis, because by then the enlistments of many of Hooker's soldiers would be expiring without immediate replacements (a mistaken assumption), compensating somewhat for the smaller number of Confederates. If he could somehow increase the readiness of his army in a period of two weeks—he did not say how—Lee intended to drive Hooker back across the Potomac and clear the Shenandoah Valley of Federal troops. Such a strategy, Lee asserted, more than any other, could bring relief to the other outnumbered Confederate armies.

Hooker beat Lee to the punch. The Army of the Potomac began crossing the Rappahannock on April 29.

Hooker's plan of attack against Lee was straightforward. He had to cross the Rappahannock to get at Lee on the opposite shore, and he wanted to cross without opposition. As Lee could not cover the entire river, Hooker feinted here and there. His right wing of three corps crossed well upriver at several undefended fords, while two others, comprising his left wing commanded by John Sedgwick, crossed just below Fredericksburg and pinned Lee in place. Hooker had trapped Lee between two powerful wings of his army.

At first Lee assumed that Hooker would advance once across the river. Within a day he sensed that Hooker had lost his nerve, because he was entrenching. The initiative belonged to Lee. He could maneuver as he pleased.

Lee wanted to strike at Hooker, but he was not ready to act. His span of control was restricted to the 60,000 men precariously stretched along the Rappahannock. His remaining troops, including those of Longstreet, Hood, and Pickett, were stationed helter-skelter in Virginia and North Carolina, all reporting to Davis. Lee had known that he would be outnumbered whenever the battle with Hooker began, yet he had not worked out a reinforcement plan with Davis beforehand. Which, if any, of these scattered troops would be made available in a crisis had never been determined. When Hooker crossed the river, Lee belatedly asked Davis for reinforcements. Davis was caught without warning. Lee would have to do the best he could with what he had.

Lee had likewise neglected the need for accurate maps. The Rappahannock was the principal line of defense, yet Lee was uninformed as to the road network that paralleled the river and led to and from the fords where the Federal army would cross. The terrain, known as the Wilderness, was largely dense woods. Everything would have to move on the roads. Yet these roads, which for four months had been within a day's ride of Fredericksburg, were a mystery to Lee, Jackson, and their staffs, who apparently had never ridden them in the idle days.

Lee had had at his disposal the best cartographer in the army, Jedediah Hotchkiss, whose maps of the Shenandoah Valley had contributed to Jackson's earlier successes there. Hotchkiss's best friend was an army topographer, Captain James K. Boswell, who kept a map sketchbook in his breast pocket. Lee wasted their skills. No one ordered them to make accurate maps of places where Lee intended to fight. Instead, Lee and Jackson told Hotchkiss and Boswell to make maps to accompany earlier reports of battles elsewhere.

In March, and then again in April, Lee asked Hotchkiss for a map of Spotsylvania County, the most likely battleground. It was for Lee's personal use, and no provisions were made for his generals to have maps. As Lee had not expressed any degree of urgency, Hotchkiss remained in camp and simply reproduced an existing map based on unreliable data, rather than surveying the countryside. Finally, on the eve of battle, Hotchkiss feverishly sketched maps for the senior generals, but they were as inaccurate as the earlier maps he had given Lee. Once the shooting started, the staffs would search frantically for local guides to lead troops down roads they had disregarded for four months.

Hooker had entrenched his right wing by May 1 into a fortified salient centered at a homestead called Chancellorsville, ten miles west of Fredericksburg. For the first of many times in the Wilderness, Lee split his army in the face of a superior enemy, as he had done so often before. It was a terrible risk if the enemy were aggressive, but there was no such risk with Hooker. Leaving Jubal A. Early's division (including Gordon, now fully recovered and commanding a brigade) at Fredericksburg to fend off Sedgwick's two corps, Lee hustled the bulk of his army to Chancellorsville. Civilian guides like Jackson's chaplain, Beverly T. Lacy, who once had had a church in the area, led the way. After some preliminary skirmishing, Hooker retracted his lines before Lee's lesser force, ending the day's fighting.

That night Lee and Jackson discussed how to flank the enemy, the tactic that had worked at Second Manassas. They decided to sweep far to the left, if roads permitted, and then descend upon Hooker's right flank. As they were without knowledge of the roads, they dispatched Hotchkiss to find a suitable route. When Hotchkiss returned with the information, the plan was confirmed. Lee would split his army once again. He would remain with two divisions at Chancellorsville. Jackson would march his entire corps around Hooker's army and attack its right wing from the flank and rear.

Jackson departed with clatter and commotion on the morning of May 2 with a full retinue of infantry, artillery, and wagons. In most circumstances it would have been a dangerous maneuver, for his entire corps of 26,000 men was strung out on a single road, his soldiers passing in front of the Federal lines a mile away. Hooker's bizarre mental paralysis guaranteed Jackson's security, however. By midafternoon Jackson was in position, and he began his preparations to attack. Before him lay Howard's Eleventh Corps, deployed along an east-west road with their guns pointing south. Jackson positioned his troops along a front a mile wide, perpendicular to the road. His plan was to sweep down the road, crushing everything before him.

For three hours, the German Americans of Charles Devens's First Division had listened to Jackson's troops floundering into position in the trees to their right, and their patrols had seen the gathering Confederates silhouetted in

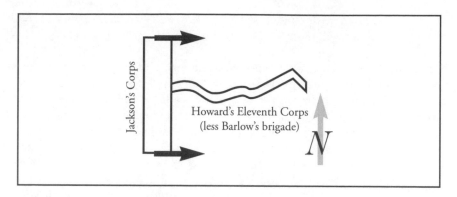

the setting sun. But Devens ignored the warnings. Howard had left with Barlow's brigade, his only reserve, which had been detached to go to the center of the line more than a mile away. Howard's staff disparaged the warnings. There was no danger to the Eleventh Corps. The Confederates were miles away, retreating, according to Hooker.

Jackson struck just before sunset. The shock of 26,000 shrieking, whooping Confederate soldiers overwhelmed the Federal troops, who fled in a rout of epic proportions. The runaway electrified Jackson's soldiers, and in a frenzy they surged ahead pell-mell. Pursuer and pursued became entangled, and Jackson's lines lost continuity against stiffening resistance in the thickets. At darkness the intensity of the battle gradually subsided, leaving the two sides scrambled across miles of terrain. Unable to see into the murk, jittery gunners fired at any noise or movement.

Jackson and his staff rode into the no-man's-land for a personal reconnaissance. Without a map, Jackson was a stranger to the terrain. His two cartographers, Hotchkiss and Boswell, accompanied him. They, too, were entering the countryside for the first time. Jackson and his cavalcade pushed into the darkness. Eventually they reversed course toward their own lines. Mistaking them for a Federal cavalry patrol, a North Carolina regiment fired at them, and the bullets shattered Jackson's arm. He fell from his saddle, and his staff bore him upon a litter. A firefight erupted; Jackson's litter crashed to the ground as his staff sought shelter. Another bullet wounded A. P. Hill, who was directing the return fire and trying to extricate Jackson.

Suddenly Lee was without his two best generals. Hill recovered. Jackson would soon die of his wounds. The next day Hotchkiss looked for Boswell. He found him dead at the scene. A bullet had pierced his map sketchbook and his heart.

The loss of Jackson was dire for the Army of Northern Virginia, already depleted of so many of its most experienced commanders. Jackson's corps at Chancellorsville, now under the temporary command of cavalryman J. E. B. Stuart, resumed its attack against the well-entrenched Federal army early on May 3. Without Jackson, a flank attack was too complex a maneuver to undertake; Stuart had no alternative to a conventional headlong assault, which was largely uncoordinated for want of competent leadership.

Once again the Confederates' aggressiveness caused the Federal command to flinch. Hooker withdrew from his salient around the Chancellorsville homestead, uncovering the road that allowed Lee to reunite both wings of his assault force. As a further gift to Lee, Hooker abandoned the high ground at Fairview Hill, which the Confederate artillery immediately occupied to bombard the contracting Federal lines.

Meanwhile, developments unfolded ten miles to the east at Fredericksburg. Lee had left a token force there under Early, with instructions to contain the larger Federal left wing under Sedgwick. May 1 had passed without incident. A great farce was enacted on May 2. Lee's chief of staff, Colonel R. H. Chilton, arrived late in the morning from Chancellorsville to relay oral orders from Lee: Early was to withdraw from Fredericksburg and join Lee at Chancellorsville. Early was astounded. Some 20,000 or more Federal soldiers threatened to cross the river. Was he to turn his back on them?

Yes, said Chilton. Those were Lee's orders.

But a withdrawal would be in full view of the enemy, said Early. If he withdrew, the enemy would pursue and reunite with Hooker at Chancellorsville. The order was madness.

Chilton insisted that Lee's order was rational and had to be obeyed. Racked with trepidation, Early started down the road to Chancellorsville. Another messenger arrived, bringing a written message from a horrified Lee rescinding Chilton's order. Chilton, wrote Lee, had misunderstood him. Early was to exercise his own discretion as to whether he could safely abandon Fredericksburg. Early countermarched and returned to Fredericksburg. Luckily for him, Sedgwick had not occupied the abandoned town.

Sedgwick brushed Early aside on May 3 and got underway to reinforce Hooker at Chancellorsville. Lee got word late in the morning, at a time when he wanted to believe that Hooker's force at Chancellorsville was on its last legs. It is a common belief that Lee had Hooker in his hand and would have destroyed him that day had not he been forced to detach a division to deal with Sedgwick, approaching from his rear. "Fredericksburg lost, the left of Early's line turned, the main army now between Sedgwick and Hooker," wrote Freeman, "this in the hour when one more blow, untroubled from the rear, had seemed to promise an overwhelming triumph!"

Such thinking is a fallacy. Lee thought himself successful because he had occupied the clearing at Chancellorsville. The house that had been Hooker's headquarters was in flames. If seizing that patch of tortured ground had been the objective of the battle, Lee was a winner. The Federal army, however, was unbeaten. It still outnumbered Lee, and it had contracted its lines into a horseshoe-shaped perimeter with extensive fortifications. Many of its brigades—including Barlow's—were still fresh, not having fired a shot. If Lee had continued his attack, he would have sustained yet more casualties without denting the Federal line.

As Lee could deal with only one Federal force at a time, he peeled away from Hooker and headed east toward Sedgwick. The Confederate forces tangled with Sedgwick at Salem Church late in the afternoon, midway between Chancellorsville and Fredericksburg. Darkness left both sides at a standoff. Feeling secure against any action from Hooker, Lee decided to muster three full divisions and attack Sedgwick on the morning of the fourth. As he was without either Longstreet or Jackson and doubted the ability of his division commanders to coordinate an attack, Lee decided to act as an impromptu corps commander, a role with which neither he nor his staff was accustomed.

There were two other difficulties. As we have seen, the generals and their staffs had neither accurate maps nor knowledge of the terrain. The only two experienced cartographers were gone: Hotchkiss was escorting the wounded Jackson to the rear, and Boswell was dead. Lafayette McLaws was fighting within a stone's throw from the site of his encampment of four months, yet he later wrote, "I knew nothing except by report." Second, the malnourished Confederate troops were physically drained, and their aching feet moved slowly and reluctantly. Adrenaline could not sustain them indefinitely.

Lee's exertions with his three divisions began in confusion at daybreak and concluded in frustration by nightfall. As McLaws and Richard Anderson straggled into place, Early independently started a morning attack to regain Marye's Heights. While Early brought up his two other brigades, Gordon advanced without orders. When Early returned, Gordon had disappeared. Early found him on the heights above Fredericksburg, which Gordon had easily occupied.

For the remainder of the day Early waited to hear the sounds of action from the other two divisions on his left. At six o'clock the attack began against the well-entrenched Sedgwick. It was predictably futile and desultory.

That night Sedgwick withdrew to the north bank of the Rappahannock. Lee ordered the exhausted divisions of McLaws and Anderson to return to Chancellorsville on May 5, and they limped back through a storm to arrive by evening. Lee planned to renew his assault against Hooker on the morning of the sixth, but Hooker, too, withdrew across the river.

The used-up men of Lee's army were fortunate. Lee had reverted to his practice of fighting for the sake of fighting, but there was little to fight with. Federal cavalry roamed freely in Lee's rear, severing his supplies. Lee's army was so battered by its ceaseless combat that it was inconceivable that he could have further damaged Hooker's entrenched forces. Perhaps even Lee experienced a sense of relief when he found the trenches empty.

Consistent with his practice of mapping where he had been rather than where he was going, Lee ordered Hotchkiss to survey the now abandoned battlefield and make a map. For the first time since reporting to Lee's headquarters, Hotchkiss left camp and went into the field with his surveying tools.

Lee was worse off than when he had begun. Combat attrition had reduced his army by 22 percent, irreplaceable losses. In fact, the only useful replacements were the unengaged veteran divisions of Hood and Pickett, which had languished in North Carolina with Longstreet and were slowly returning to

Virginia. The lack of supplies was beyond remedy. Although the Army of the Potomac had again been humiliated, it had suffered only 16 percent casualties. A manpower pool would make up the difference, and its material goods were available in growing abundance. While the Federal army could afford losses, Lee could not. So long as Lee continued in a war of attrition, his defeat was inevitable.

1 9

GETTYSBURG

General Scott on Southern soldiers. He says we have élan, courage, woodcraft, consumate horsemanship, endurance of pain equal to the Indians, but that we will not submit to discipline. We will not take care of things or husband our resources. Where we are, there is waste and destruction. If it could all be done by one wild desperate dash, we would do it.

Mary Chesnut

By May 1863, two years less a month had passed since Lee had first taken the Army of Northern Virginia into combat. After each battle a pattern of immediate tasks had taken his attention. One was to reorganize his army as a consequence of casualties and attrition. The other was to decide what to do next, for Lee had no long-range strategy beyond his most immediate campaign.

After Chancellorsville, Lee had to deal with another crisis in leadership. The flower of the officers' corps had again been spent. Generals killed, wounded, or found wanting created vacancies that had to be filled from a diminishing pool of talent. Jackson was the most prominent loss, and Lee's lamentations were profuse and heartfelt. Ironically, the superheated public tributes had elevated Jackson to Valhalla, and by inference Lee's stature was diminished. "Without disparagement to others," wrote Secretary of War James Seddon in his annual report, "it may be safely said [Jackson] has become, in the estimation of the Confederacy, emphatically 'the hero of the war.' Around him clustered with particular warmth their gratitude, their affections, and their hopes."

Public relations became paramount in replacing Jackson, for expectations were extravagant. "The leader who succeeds [Jackson]," wrote a Richmond newspaper, "be he who he may, will be impelled, as by supernatural impulse, to emulate his matchless deeds. Jackson's men will demand to be led in 'Stonewall Jackson's way.' The leader who will not or cannot comply with that demand, must drop the baton quickly. Jackson's corps will be led forever by the memory of its great chieftain." Rumors abounded as to who such a leader might be, and Lee heard from some who hoped that lightning would strike.

One of these was John Hood. He wrote Lee about his disappointment in missing the fight at Chancellorsville, especially as the Longstreet expedition had been barren of results. Lee responded warmly, explaining wistfully that God had prevented him from summoning Longstreet's two divisions (Hood and Pickett) from North Carolina. "Although separated from me," he wrote on May 21, "I have always had you in my eyes and thoughts. I wished for you much in the last battle, and believe had I the whole army with me, General Hooker would have been demolished. But God ordered otherwise."

Hood expressed his grief at the loss of Jackson and then introduced the issue of corps organization. They were too large, said Hood. Four divisions were too much for one general to control in the rugged countryside of Virginia. Lee agreed with him. As much as he would miss Jackson, the loss gave Lee the opportunity to create smaller, additional corps, which he would have done earlier but for lack of competent generals. Realizing that Hood was angling for a corps command, Lee let Hood know that although he was good, he still was not good enough. "I rely much upon you," wrote Lee. "You must so inspire and lead your brave division, as that it may accomplish the work of a corps."

That was not what Hood wanted to hear, but it was what he should have expected. He had not had the opportunity to prove himself as a division commander in combat, a prerequisite for a corps. Perhaps later. Lee already had written Davis that Hood was a "capital officer" who was improving and would make a good corps commander "if necessary," but the time had not come.

Lee concluded his letter to Hood with hope and hand-wringing. "I agree with you in believing that our army would be invincible," he wrote, "if it could be properly organized and officered. There never were such men in an army before. They will go anywhere and do anything if properly led. But there is the difficulty—proper commanders. Where can they be obtained?"

Such was Lee's dilemma. Most of his surviving senior officers were of rank either commensurate with or exceeding their level of competence. Few were ready for increased responsibility, fewer still for corps and division command. Disregarding qualified candidates elsewhere, Lee intended to promote from within to reward performance.

Just before receiving Hood's letter, Lee had made his recommendations to Davis for promotions and assignments. It was never easy. Regional rivalries bedeviled him. For example, a Virginian brigadier general had not done well at Chancellorsville, and Lee wanted him out. "The brigade is composed of 2 North Carolina and 3 Virginia regiments," wrote Lee. "The former have complained of being commanded by a Virginia brigadier, & I presume the latter would complain if commanded by a North Carolinian." Lee compromised by recommending Brigadier General George H. Steuart, a "neutral" Maryland native. As Steuart had been regular army, observed Lee, "no one has a right to complain."

Occasionally, decisions were easier. Gordon was one such example. His promotion to brigadier general was confirmed on May 6, immediately following his stint as an acting commander of Alexander R. Lawton's brigade at Chancellorsville. Lee planned to reassign Gordon permanently to command Rodes's brigade, where he first had begun his service. But Gordon had so inspired Lawton's brigade that its officers petitioned Lee to make him permanent. Gordon was delighted. He was from Georgia, and the brigade was entirely of Georgia regiments. It was a perfect fit: both the commander and the soldiers were happy, and Lawton was still disabled. Lee and Davis cheerfully assented.

Continuing his letter to Davis, Lee turned to corps reorganization. "Each corps contains when in fighting condition about 30,000 men," wrote Lee. "These are more than one man can properly handle & keep under his eye in battle in the country that we have to operate in. They are always beyond the range of his vision, & frequently beyond his reach. The loss of Jackson from the command of one half the army seems to me a good opportunity to remedy this evil."

Lee had illuminated the difficulty of commanding and controlling men and weapons in numbers that dwarfed earlier American wars. The remedy was not solely organizational. Take communications. As Lee was old school, he did not readily exploit technology to improve his span of control. His tactical messages went either orally or scribbled on scraps of paper and were delivered haphazardly by horse and foot. Delays and garbles were inevitable. Visual signaling was used sporadically with limited results.

The Federal armies, on the other hand, rapidly adapted technology to the battlefield. The telegraph had come of age for military purposes. Stanton, who had been a prewar director of the Atlantic and Ohio Telegraph Company, controlled the telegraph system from the War Department with absolute authority. Its lines and operators could be so rapidly deployed that generals maintained contact with their troops regardless of terrain, weather, and darkness. Lincoln conversed with his generals hundreds of miles away. The sophisticated Federal ciphers encrypted long, complex messages virtually impervious to compromise, and Stanton protected the codebooks with severe security and accountability procedures.*

The Confederate telegraph system, in contrast, was irreparably flawed. Like the railroads, the telegraphs remained under private ownership, with only a fraction of the capability of the Federal system. The South's scarce copper went for bullets and not telegraph wire. The Confederate codes were so inadequate

---

* Captain Samuel H. Beckwith was Grant's cipher operator during his final four campaigns and was expert with the pen. He transcribed the contents of each new edition of the cipher book into his own written copy, embellishing it with various colors of ink and different filler matter so as to make it "wholly unintelligible to any one but a shrewd cipher-operator. By the use of ink of various colors he combined two or three different codes in one book" (Bates, *Lincoln in the Telegraph Office*, pp. 56–58). When Grant once ordered Beckwith to give his cipher book to one of Grant's staff officers, Beckwith refused. Stanton berated Grant for disobeying his standing orders, and Grant never again attempted to bypass Stanton's rules. Beckwith was also the custodian of a special cipher book used exclusively between Grant and Stanton.

that whole phrases were transmitted in plain language. Only portions of classified messages could be encrypted, and often the people on the receiving end could not decrypt the coded portions. Intercepts of secret dispatches were routine. During the Wilderness campaign in May 1864, for example, Federal telegraphers intercepted a long, detailed status report from Lee to the Confederate secretary of war, which was promptly relayed to Stanton.

Lee, along with most of the Southern leadership, conceded the technological superiority of the North, and he relied upon the spirit of his soldiers and the leadership of his generals to compensate. Selecting the right generals was paramount. In his letter to Davis, Lee turned to recommending names to command his stripped-down corps. Longstreet would retain the First Corps. What then of Jackson's Second Corps? Lee wanted to promote from within, both to please the soldiers and to placate the press, which was demanding a replacement with a person of Jackson's stature. His choice was limited to the major generals who had been Jackson's division commanders: A. P. Hill, Jubal Early, and Richard Ewell.

Lee recommended Ewell, still recovering from a leg amputation suffered at Second Manassas eight months before, for the Second Corps, and Hill for a newly constituted Third Corps.

Ewell was a risky selection. Lee hardly knew him. In nominating him to Davis, Lee said only that Ewell was "an honest, brave soldier who has always done his duty well." His eccentricities were legion, however. A prewar cavalryman experienced in frontier combat, Ewell became frenzied in action. Gordon knew him well. "His written orders were full, accurate, and lucid," Gordon later wrote, "but his verbal orders or directions, especially when under intense excitement, no man could comprehend. [Moxley Sorrel remembered his lisp.] At such times his eyes would flash with a particular brilliancy, and his brain far outran his tongue. His thoughts would leap across great gaps which his words never touched, but which he expected his listener to fill up by intuition, and woe to the dull subordinate who failed to understand him!"

Why, then, did Lee choose this strange man? There are two probable reasons. One is that Lee did not realize that Ewell became irrational under stress. The other is that Jackson's old corps would accept him as their own, and popular sentiment would be appeased. In the estimation of such soldiers as Gordon, Ewell's idiosyncrasies were a source of affection and amusement.

Lee chose Hill for command of the Third Corps solely on competence. "I think upon the whole," he wrote Davis, "[Hill] is the best soldier of his grade with me." Jackson would have violently disagreed. Jackson and Hill had argued for months with vehemence. In exasperation, Jackson had resorted to arresting Hill and had tried to remove him from command. Without question, Hill had a chip on his shoulder and had provoked Jackson—and earlier Longstreet—into arresting him. Nonetheless, Lee liked him, and with Jackson gone Lee did as he pleased. Hill's fighting ability had never been questioned, although his health was often frail, and the army accepted his promotion with few complaints.

Longstreet, meanwhile, had his own ideas as to how the war should be fought. Having exercised independent command in North Carolina, Longstreet wanted more of it, and he was less willing to subordinate himself to Lee. For a time he advocated reinforcing Bragg and the armies in the west, a view which Lee found intolerable.

Longstreet's greatest difference with Lee was about tactics. Lee believed in attacking whenever possible. Longstreet had developed a different theory. As the Confederate army would always be outnumbered and outgunned, he believed that it should seek a strong defensive position and let the Federal army attack. A single, well-entrenched Confederate soldier could hold off two or three times the numbers of Federal soldiers. As Lee would never agree to such a fundamental change in Southern doctrine, Longstreet became a sullen and sulking lieutenant.

With his generals in place and his fingers crossed, Lee tried once again to get more soldiers and to retain what he had. One of his greatest problems was the wholesale desertion of North Carolina troops. A state judge had ruled that the militia could not arrest deserters, prompting North Carolina soldiers to head home in droves, taking their weapons with them. Lee pleaded with Seddon for help, sparking a bitter exchange of accusations and faultfinding between Seddon and Governor Zebulon Vance. None of this stemmed the flow of deserters. Lee tried ruthless measures of his own, which Sorrel later recalled.

"A whole [North Carolina] company had broken away," he wrote, "but were overtaken at a crossing of the James above Richmond. They showed fight and killed several of the pursuers, but were taken back and the leaders tried by court martial. Ten were convicted and sentenced to be shot. There had been too much leniency, and General Lee had the sentence executed. The unfortunates were tied to small sunken crosses in line about ten feet apart, with a firing party in front of each. Their division . . . was drawn up in three sides in a hollow square, the deserters being on the fourth. At the word the firing was accurately executed and the men sank dead or dying at their stakes. The division was then marched by, close to the bodies, and it was hoped the lesson would be salutary."

The other North Carolina headache was D. H. Hill, who commanded the troops assigned to the state, including some of those Lee had sent there temporarily. Hill would not return them, so angering Lee that finally he refused to deal with Hill and tossed the problem of troop assignments to Davis. The upshot was that Lee came out the loser by at least four brigades he had counted upon, for Davis was grudging in giving Lee what he needed.

Needed for what? We know now that Lee intended to invade Pennsylvania, but for reasons of security he wrote neither a plan nor orders beforehand. Secrecy was his chief concern. An invasion of Pennsylvania was an enormous risk, and in the past written intentions had been divulged in newspaper headlines and enemy headquarters. To prevent such leaks, all communications were by word of mouth to those who had a need to know.

Lee discussed the invasion on a visit to Richmond during three days in May. We know that he spoke with Davis and Seddon, and probably with other cabinet members, but minutes were not kept. From past experience, Lee knew that anything said in confidence in government chambers would be revealed afterward, so he would have withheld details and spoken of invasion in principle only. After guarded and confusing exchanges of subsequent correspondence, Davis gave conditional approval if Lee was still intent upon invasion. The decision was his. Lee decided to press on, regardless, and on June 3 he began the secret movement north that ended at Gettysburg.

It was an extraordinary gamble. The Army of Northern Virginia was shaky, at best, in its readiness to fight. Lee had completed reorganizing just four days earlier. He had no plan, no real objectives, other than to react fatalistically to developments as his scattered army meandered on country roads. Their march was leisurely, for they had no destination, no timetable. By marching slowly, wear and tear on man and beast was lessened, and time was given to forage. Having given up on the Confederate supply system, Lee counted on the Maryland and Pennsylvania countryside to feed his army. Eventually, of course, he knew that he would have to fight, for the Federal government would not allow him a free hand indefinitely.

Lee did not know where the Federal army was, for his chronically shaky intelligence system had fully collapsed. Stuart would misinterpret Lee's ambiguous orders, and the cavalry would raid wagon trains rather than report on enemy whereabouts. When the Army of the Potomac showed up, as it inevitably would, it would probably be a surprise, and then there would be a decisive battle against superior numbers of Federal troops fighting on their own soil. Where that battle would be was anyone's guess.

Given these terrible risks, why did Lee attempt the invasion? For want of documents written in his own hand, we must form conclusions about Lee's objectives from hearsay evidence. Here are some plausible possibilities: he no longer could feed his army in Virginia and sought provisions in the North; he wanted to fight outside his state to alleviate further devastation; he was overconfident that his army was unbeatable; he would impel the Federal armies to come after him and thereby relieve pressure on Confederate forces in other theaters.

Such explanations miss the point, however, because Lee held to a deeper, more profound view of the war. His only hope of winning was through propaganda and dramatic victories that would influence public opinion in the North. Such had been his consistent thinking. Revolution in the North also required a Confederate government willing to bend, but Davis had so far disdained compromise or negotiation. In Maryland, Lee had tried to treat the people gently to win their allegiance; Davis regarded the invasion as harsh retribution. Lee tried once again with Davis in Pennsylvania. If he could whip the Federal army on its own soil, argued Lee, the Northern peace party would demand a settlement. The problem, in Lee's view, was that Southern firebrands were so hostile to overtures that they were subverting any chance for peace on Southern terms.

With courtly phrases, Lee told Davis that military victory was impossible given the worsening disparity in resources. "Under these circumstances we should neglect no honorable means of dividing and weakening our enemies," Lee continued. Propaganda was the answer, "to give all the encouragement we can, consistently with truth, to the rising peace party of the North." The sticking point was that the peace party was divided between those willing to grant Southern independence and those who advocated restoration of the Union. For the moment, said Lee, the Confederacy should not make "nice distinctions." Lee had no scruples against deceiving the peace party into believing that the South would return to the Union.

Eventually the question of returning to the Union would have to be resolved, and Lee had no solutions. "When peace is proposed to us it will be time enough to discuss its terms," Lee concluded. "I think you will nevertheless agree with me that we should at least carefully abstain from measures or expressions that tend to discourage any party whose purpose is peace." To Lee's relief, Davis responded that he would cooperate.

It had been wrenching for Gordon to leave Fanny in Richmond when he had returned to duty for the Chancellorsville campaign. She had nursed him from near death with resolute devotion, and after months of intense intimacy the prospect of extended separations was unendurable. His letters in the following months would simmer with both passion and despair.

"I would like so much to have seen you once more before you left," Gordon had written in late April, "but these are times which try us in many respects. I had to leave you so hurriedly the other morning, that I did not give you the loving good bye, which would have made me happier now. But 'God bless you my dear dear wife' comes right from my heart. I am so glad I spent the last night with you. I was happy that night and the recollection of it is so sweet now, that I am constantly thinking of it. . . . My confidence, I think, that God will protect me, is pretty strong. I trust in Him. Pray that I may trust Him more & pray with faith."

Gordon and his brigade got underway from Fredericksburg with Ewell's Second Corps on June 3. Fanny remained in Richmond. "How far we will go, no one seems to know," Gordon wrote to Fanny on June 7. "I doubt Genl Lee himself knows. . . . Fan, your letters are the most beautiful evidences of a wife's devotion I have ever seen. Write them to me *dear dear* Fanny. They are so sweet to me, when I am so far away from you & on such a cheerless '*jaunt*' as this. . . . May God protect & bring us together again. Pray that I may have His spirit always in my heart. Good bye *darling, sweet* wife."

Throughout the campaign Ewell's corps would be in the van of Lee's army, with Gordon usually in the lead. Ewell's immediate task was to clear Federal forces from the Shenandoah Valley. The first contact came on June 13 at Winchester, the battered town on the north end of the valley, a place that changed hands repeatedly in the course of the war. As Early's division approached, an apprehensive Federal garrison guarded the turnpike south of the town. Gordon formed his brigade into line of battle, moved forward smartly, and drove the defenders into their main fortifications. Darkness ended the assault. Gordon and his men slept in the rain.

Gordon demonstrated the following day to allow Early to send three brigades around the village and to the foot of the Federal fort, north of the village. Gordon closed up in the afternoon. The fort surmounted a hill and seemed impregnable. "In the dim twilight," Gordon later wrote, "with the glimmer of [the Federal] bayonets and brass howitzers still discernible, I received an order to storm the fortress at daylight the next morning." Gordon was astounded. The order was madness. There was no need for such a direct assault, for the fort was isolated and could be cut off from its lines of communication. But orders were orders. Gordon assumed that he would be killed in the assault and wrote a final letter to Fanny. It was the only time during the war that Gordon had a presentiment of certain death.

He led his troops up the slope in the morning. "At every moment," he wrote, "I expected the storm of shell and ball that would end many a life, my own among them; but on we swept, and into the fort, to find not a soldier there! It had been evacuated during the night." A large United States flag still floated over the fort. Gordon had it hauled down. "I turned it over to the guard myself," he wrote Fanny. As a compliment to Gordon, Early wanted the flag to be returned to Richmond with an escort of Gordon's soldiers.

Gordon's brigade moved to Shepherdstown, just south of the Potomac, and waited for the remainder of the army to close up. His separation from Fanny became unbearable. He found lodgings for her and wrote her to join him. His "lovesick" letters were returned, undelivered, for Fanny had left Richmond to stay as close to Gordon as she could.

Not knowing where she was, Gordon became melancholy in the land of his enemies, and he so emptied himself in his letters that he became ashamed of his emotions.

> *Oh Fanny, what shall I say to you? How shall I tell you what I feel tonight? . . . If I could only lay my arms around my dear wife & press her close to this heart—how it would relieve me. If down my sunburnt cheeks a tear, which I can't control, steals when I write this, am I therefore unmanly & effeminate?*
>
> *Well then, be it so. But it is only when my heart is overwhelmed by such reflections as I have had tonight, that I am guilty of such unmanliness—and but for a moment then—I am almost sorry I confessed this to you. I shall control myself in the future. . . . Well rely on it, I shall shed no more tears soon.*

Ewell's corps had eaten its way through Maryland and into south central Pennsylvania by late June. Lee's orders to Ewell were discretionary, if not extemporaneous. "I think your best course will be towards the Susquehanna," Lee wrote on June 22. "It will depend upon the quantity of supplies obtained in that country whether the rest of the army can follow. . . . Your progress and direction will of course depend upon development of circumstances." Then, almost as an afterthought, he added, "If Harrisburg comes within our means, capture it."

Harrisburg it was then. Ewell dispatched two divisions toward the state capital, while Early and Gordon went to York. The farmers along the way seemed indifferent toward Gordon and his troops. "You can't imagine how singular one feels surrounded by Enemies," Gordon wrote to Fanny, "but they let us have milk and bread at low prices. . . . But before we occupy one position for two days, prices run up very high. Soldiers give any price you know." Gordon also shopped for material and clothing for Fanny, but the division ahead of him had taken most everything. Still, Pennsylvania was a land of abundance and prosperity, and Gordon acutely felt the contrast with the austerity of the South.

Dressed in Sabbath clothes, the Pennsylvania Dutch people of York were both fascinated and terrified when Gordon's gaunt and grotesque soldiers, like invaders from a strange planet, entered the town muttering Georgian dialect, their eyes gleaming behind masks of dust. The town fathers surrendered the town to Gordon, who assured them of its safety. "It would astonish you Darling," he wrote Fanny, "as it mortified me to see how much afraid of us these people were. I rode along at the head of my Brigade thru' the streets of York. [G]reat crowds of ladies & gents, boys & girls crowded the streets & side walks & houses. So dense was the crowd—so excited that I could scarcely get along the street."

Amid the hubbub a group of frightened women attracted Gordon's attention, and he turned his horse toward them. "[O]ne young lady, the nicest," he wrote Fanny, "ran from me as tho' I had been a demon." It was more than the Cavalier could endure. Gordon filled the air with Southern oratory, and to the extent that the people could understand his exotic tongue, their apprehensions were lessened.

"I assured these ladies that the troops behind me," he wrote in his memoirs, "though ill-clad and travel-stained, were good men and brave; that beneath their rough exteriors were hearts as loyal to women as ever beat in the breasts of honorable men; that their own experience and the experience of their mothers, wives, and sisters at home had taught them how painful must be the sight of a hostile army in their town; that under the orders of the Confederate commander-in-chief both private property and non-combatants were safe; that the spirit of vengeance and rapine had no place in the bosoms of these dust-covered but knightly men; and I closed by pledging to York the head of any soldier under my command who destroyed private property, disturbed the repose of a single home, or insulted a woman."

Gordon next marched to Wrightsville, where a bridge spanned the Susquehanna. It was a long and impressive structure, which Gordon tried to seize, thinking perhaps he could cross over and go on to Philadelphia. His brigade shooed away the militiamen defending it, but they ignited the bridge before Gordon's soldiers could occupy it. The flames swept into the town, and buildings caught fire. Gordon formed his soldiers into a bucket brigade. "[T]he people seemed utterly astounded," Gordon wrote Fanny, "for they expected us to destroy everything in our line of march. But little of the place was burnt."

As a campaign east of the Susquehanna was now impossible, Gordon waited for orders.

Francis Barlow, always irascible when soldiers failed to meet his standards, was blazing mad about Chancellorsville. "You can imagine my indignation & disgust at the miserable behavior of the 11th Corps," Barlow wrote to his mother and brothers on May 8. "You know how I have always been down on the 'Dutch' & I do not abate my contempt now, but it is not fair to charge it all on them. Some of the Yankee Regts behaved just as badly." Barlow fretted that his brigade, which had been detached before Howard's Eleventh Corps had collapsed under Jackson's attack, might mistakenly be censured in the papers. "The general impression," he wrote, "is that if my brigade had been there we could have done a good deal towards checking the rout."

Devens's division had taken the brunt of Jackson's onslaught, and Devens had been wounded. Barlow reluctantly took command of the shattered and demoralized division in the expectation that he could whip it into shape. "I was seduced," he later wrote bitterly. "The Corps is in a state of continual excitement & quarreling," he wrote Almira on May 29. "[O]ne Dutchman accuses another of misconduct in the late battles & the Dutch accuse the Americans and vice versa."

Barlow rolled up his sleeves. "I am too much occupied to go much of anywhere," he wrote Almira. "There is a terrible amount of work to do here." He was gratified when Adelbert Ames, a young West Pointer, was promoted to brigadier general and given command of one of the two brigades. The other brigade under Colonel Leopold von Gilsa, whom Barlow mistrusted, got most of Barlow's attention. His irritability recurred. "I am busily occupied with these miserable creatures," he wrote, "& get very little time to do anything. I am heartily tired of lying in this camp & wish for a fight or to go home. For a day or two past I have had a bad headache & been out of order in my bowels."

Barlow and Arabella visited the Second Corps on June 1 for a ceremony commemorating the first anniversary of the Battle of Fair Oaks. The practice of giving distinctive insignias to each corps had just been established for reasons of esprit and battlefield identification. A trefoil was now sewn on the caps of the Second Corps soldiers and on the headquarters pennants, red for the First Division, white for the Second, and blue for the Third. "The regiments are terribly small but brave looking," Barlow wrote Almira. "The 61st had hardly 75 men. . . . I went down into the camp and saw my old men who were very glad to see me."

After his defeat at Chancellorsville, Joseph Hooker had seemed unable to contend with Lee's invasion of Pennsylvania. Reports placed the Army of Northern Virginia in scattered locations, but its general movement was northward. "If the head of Lee's army is at Martinsburg," a frustrated Lincoln wired Hooker on June 15, "and the tail of it . . . between Fredericksburg and Chancellorsville, the animal must be very slim somewhere. Could you not break him?" As apprehension, and often panic, intensified in Maryland and Pennsylvania, Hooker told Lincoln that he could not prevent an invasion. Lincoln reacted to the threat by calling out 100,000 militia and exhorting the befuddled Hooker to act aggressively.

By June 27 the situation had become intolerable to Lincoln. Lee, by then actually north of Hooker, was exercising a free hand in Pennsylvania. At the eleventh hour Lincoln replaced Hooker with George G. Meade, a curmudgeonly, combative West Point graduate and corps commander, who accelerated the Army of the Potomac toward Lee while covering Washington and Baltimore. Barlow's division marched hard, as many as twenty-five miles in fifteen hours, and Barlow could sense that a decisive battle was imminent. The armies converged on Gettysburg on July 1 from unprecedented directions, Lee from the north and Meade from the south. The battlefield on the first day was a mile north of the village. The Federal cavalry arrived first, while the First and Eleventh corps hurriedly covered the ten miles from Emmitsburg to Gettysburg.

Barlow had arrested Gilsa for allowing more than one man at a time to fetch water, violating Barlow's policy to prevent straggling, and the colonel rode in disgrace at the rear of his brigade. Gilsa had a showy aide on his staff, Baron Frederick Otto von Fritsch, who had served three years in the Saxon cavalry. When Fritsch heard the roar of cannon late in the morning, the division broke into a trot. "I galloped forward to General Barlow, a very strict commander," he wrote afterward, "and praising the gallantry of my Colonel, asked him to allow me to return [Gilsa's] sword."

"You can do so," said Barlow, "but keep your men well together." As pitiless as Lee toward those who would not fight, Barlow added, "Staff officers may even shoot down stragglers, and I demand the strictest discipline." The sound of battle intensified when Barlow led his division through the streets of Gettysburg. The acting corps commander, Major General Carl Schurz, directed him to a knoll on the right wing of the developing defensive line. As Schurz was a Prussian émigré idolized by the German American soldiers, he believed in their merits, and he unwisely ordered Barlow to put Gilsa's brigade in the front line and Ames's brigade in reserve.

Barlow relished the prospect of battle. "I had an admirable position," Barlow wrote immediately afterward. "The country was open for a long distance around and could be swept by our artillery." To his left Barlow could see Confederate infantry assaulting the Federal First Corps, but the attack was confused and uncoordinated and was about to collapse. Knowing from experience, however, that the Confederates would escalate their momentum, Barlow was not surprised when Early's division, led by Gordon, came into view on the Heidlersburg Road, ahead and to his right. "We ought to have held the place easily," Barlow wrote Almira, "for I had my entire force at the very point where the attack was made."

"We charged the heavy lines of the Enemy & had a desperate fight," Gordon wrote to Fanny. "The Confederates approached slowly and in magnificent order," Fritsch remembered, "and after their first volley, our men sent a strong volley in return. Our men, now standing, fired twice more, then the Confederates charged across [Rock Creek], screaming savagely."

"Run for your lives, boys!" someone shouted, and Gilsa's brigade fled, chased by Gordon's howling soldiers. Ames's brigade was caught in the stampede and retreated. "[T]he enemies skirmishers had hardly attacked us before my men began to run," wrote an embittered Barlow. "No fight at all was made."

"I consider the action of the Brigade as brilliant as any charge of the war," wrote Gordon to Fanny. "You can't conceive of the destruction in their ranks. It surpassed anything I have seen during the war. . . . We drove them before us in perfect confusion." The effect was intoxicating. "Gordon was the most glorious and inspiring thing I ever looked upon," a Confederate officer later wrote.

> He was riding a beautiful coal-black stallion . . . a majestic animal, whose "neck was clothed with thunder." From his grand joy in battle, he must have been a direct descendant of Job's horse, or Bucephalus, or Black Auster. I never saw a horse's neck so arched, his eye so fierce, his nostril so dilated. He followed in a trot, close upon the heels of the battle line, his head right in among the slanting barrels and bayonets, the reins loose upon his neck, his rider standing in his stirrups, bareheaded, hat in hand, arms extended, and, in a voice like a trumpet, exhorting his men. It was superb; absolutely thrilling. . . .
>
> I distinctly remember, in a momentary pause, calling out to Gordon, "General, where are your dead men?" and his reply: "I haven't got any, sir; the Almighty had covered my men with His shield and buckler!"

Barlow was furious. Swinging his huge saber, he galloped among the stampede, yelling and cursing, trying to get the men to stop and fight. His efforts abruptly ended when a bullet tore into his side beneath his arm and lodged in his abdomen. Barlow tumbled from his horse and walked as far as he could, then collapsed, gushing blood, as his panicking troops fled around him. Bullets and shrapnel spattered him with dirt.

Helpless, Barlow could neither move nor hide, but he was still thinking clearly. He was carrying the letters from New York about mobilizing blacks. If he survived and was captured, his captors would find them. Considering the probable consequences ("[T]he enemy might not be inclined to parole so important a functionary as the 'Superintendent of the Freedman throughout the U.S.' "), he groped inside his blood-soaked jacket, crumpled the letters, and threw them away.

The kindness of Confederate officers saved Barlow's life. Early's chief of staff had Barlow moved to the woods and placed on a bed of leaves. Before nightfall, Federal prisoners carried him to the brick farmhouse of Josiah Benner, just below the knoll he had been defending. His pain was intense. Three Confederate surgeons administered chloroform and probed the wound. When Barlow regained consciousness, they told him that the bullet had punctured his peritoneum, had most likely severed his bowels, and was imbedded in his pelvic cavity. It could not be removed, said the surgeons; death was certain.

Convinced he would never die in battle, Barlow did not flinch. He understood anatomy and dispassionately discussed his wound with the doctors, who gave him morphine and left. During the night, other Confederate officers nursed him and bathed his wounds. It was then he learned that he had fought against Gordon's brigade.

Barlow asked that someone find Arabella, whom he had left in a carriage in the village. By dusk the Confederates had occupied Gettysburg, and a Confederate soldier walked the streets looking for her, but the people were too frightened to talk to him. No one knew of an Arabella.

Arabella was frantic. She knew her husband was wounded, but not where he was. That afternoon, oblivious to danger, she had ridden upon a horse through the Gettysburg streets swarming with Federal soldiers retreating to Cemetery Hill. By evening she had commandeered an ambulance and had found Ames and Fritsch on East Cemetery Hill. Together they told her where Barlow might be found. "The courageous lady, sitting next to the driver," Fritsch later wrote, "with a white flag in her hand, then drove quickly toward the town, although we could still hear firing."

Hood fretted about the omens at Gettysburg. Hitherto, the campaign had been characterized by optimism and high spirits. He remembered Stuart's cavalry review at Culpeper Court House in early June, where the invasion force had assembled. Eight thousand horsemen had displayed their style and panache, making a spectacle for the benefit of Lee and other people of rank with their ladies. Hood had unexpectedly brought his entire division to watch the show, and his dusty, ragged infantrymen had exchanged insults with the bespangled cavalrymen. Hood had roared with merriment, for the infantry despised the flamboyant cavalry whose flashing sabers rarely drew blood.

The insults of Hood's men had proved justified. Stuart had disappeared days before on frivolous raids, stripping Lee of his means for reconnaissance and mobile support. The two armies had converged at Gettysburg by accident, the battles had erupted spontaneously, and neither A. P. Hill nor Ewell had measured up on the first day. With Lee's army in such disarray, Longstreet believed that the Federal army was too powerful, too heavily entrenched, and that, unlike his predecessors, Meade meant to fight. The decisive battle should be another time, argued Longstreet, in another place more favorable to the Confederate army.

Lee dismissed Longstreet's objections. He was determined to fight at Gettysburg, but he would not lead with the resourcefulness of the past, for fatigue and inertia dulled his mind. It was in this context that Lee directed Longstreet on July 2 to move Hood and McLaws over strange roads into a position that would allow them to attack the extreme left flank of the Federal army on the south end of Cemetery Ridge. It was a place of boulders and steep hills that Lee had not seen for himself, so he could not envision the frightful conditions he was imposing on Hood and McLaws. Overruled and sullen, Longstreet went through the motions of moving to the jumping-off spot. Reflecting Longstreet's mood, the passage of Hood's division was slow and spiritless.

The most prominent landmarks were the hills of Little Round Top and, farther to the south, Round Top. As bold a warrior as he was, Hood knew it was madness to assault the hills frontally, as he had been ordered to do. Hood's scouts reported that the way was clear to circle around the south end of Round Top, providing the opportunity to fall upon the enemy from the rear.

Thrice Hood sent staff officers to Longstreet recommending that he bypass Round Top.

Thrice Longstreet replied that Lee had ordered a frontal assault. Finally a Longstreet staff officer came to Hood to confirm that a frontal attack was imperative.

Under protest ("[T]he first and only one I ever made in my military career," he later wrote), Hood ordered his four brigades to advance. Longstreet rode up, and Hood pleaded yet again. "We must obey the orders of General Lee," said Longstreet.

Hood rode off toward his division and into the firestorm. Within minutes Hood had entered the Peach Orchard. A bullet tore into his arm, and he was taken to the rear in a swoon. His soldiers proceeded without him, struggled up the boulder-strewn hills through Devil's Den, and almost seized Little Round Top. But they could not. Joshua Chamberlain and his Maine troopers, firing the last of their bullets, held. The Confederate survivors withdrew. Half of Hood's division had been lost.

Barlow was moved on the morning of July 2 to the John Crawford house on the north edge of the village, where the wounded were collected. Surgeons again confirmed that he would not live. Peritonitis—almost always fatal— was inevitable. Barlow remained imperturbable. Nursed by Crawford's mother-in-law and sister-in-law and by Federal prisoners, he read books, ate cherries and toast, and drank coffee. Morphine eased his pain. His sense of invincibility was reinforced.

Arabella resumed her search the same morning. She found General Howard, Barlow's corps commander, and expressed her determination to find her husband even though the two armies were engaged in massive battle. Howard provided an escort, Arabella dodged bullets, but again she was frustrated. Late in the day she heard that Barlow was in the McCreary home on Chambersburg Street. Two teenage boys were startled at dusk when two Confederate soldiers approached them in the town square, accompanied by Arabella on horseback. The soldiers asked for directions and took her to the house. For the second day, she still could not find her husband.

In the past, the Army of the Potomac had always cracked when Lee had applied unremitting pressure. His soldiers had pounded the Federal positions for two days, and to Lee it seemed worth the risk for a last throw of the dice on the third day, July 3. This was, after all, the same Federal army Lee had whipped only weeks earlier at Chancellorsville. The only question was the location of the final thrust. Round Top and Little Round Top, to his right, had proven unassailable the day before, and Ewell was stalled on the left. The objective thus came to be the Federal center at Cemetery Ridge, a grove of chestnut trees and a stone fence that Lee could clearly see. A field of wheat intervened between the Federal line and Seminary Ridge, where the last fresh troops of Lee's army lay poised.

Under Lee's orders, 12,000 Confederate soldiers marched in bannered ranks across the field onto the killing ground. Afterward the survivors straggled back. Lee rode among them. "It is all my fault," Lee said repeatedly. No one would have found reason to argue otherwise.

"I heard the battles of Thursday and Friday close to me," Barlow wrote Almira. "The enemy had no doubt of capturing or utterly destroying our army and I feared it would be so. Some of the staff officers of Ewell and Early came to see me and I talked very freely with them. They were pleasant fellows. They despised our army and meant to fight to the last. I saw a good many of their men also and was much pleased with them. They are more heroic, more modest and more in earnest than we are. Their whole tone is much finer than ours. Except among those on our side who are fighting this war upon anti-slavery grounds, there is not much earnestness nor are there many noble feelings and sentiments involved."

Lee began the long retreat to Virginia on Independence Day. As the Federal troops came down from Cemetery Hill to reoccupy Gettysburg, they met Arabella coming from the village in an ambulance. Barlow lay inside.

"God has spared my life," Gordon wrote to Fanny as the remnants of Lee's army passed through Maryland toward the Potomac. "I am yet alive. Thousands of as brave and good men as our country contains lie on the battle fields of Pennsylvania & yet I am spared. I, who so little appreciate God's peculiar favors to me, I who am so sinful, so thoughtless so *ungrateful* for God's goodness am spared. Oh Lord I pray to fill my heart and my dear wife's with gratitude & praise."

A week after the battle Gordon tried to sort out his feelings. He had been a spectator on July 2 and 3, his brigade so inactive that he had written in his battle report, "I do not consider it of sufficient importance to mention." Yet Gordon had been one of the few successes of the battle. "My Brigade has been greatly complimented," Gordon wrote Fanny during the retreat. "Genl Early & Ewell & others have paid me very high compliments; but Darling these things are worth very little to me.

> *I rarely give them a second thought. My soul is too much burdened*
> *with the terror of this war to think much of such stuff. My separation*
> *from you—the soul of my happiness on this Earth—the awful uncer-*
> *tainty as to the future—the seemingly endless blood shed that is to take*
> *place—the thousands of noble lives lost in the last horrid battle, all*

conspire to render every personal compliment and idle talk of glory *as exceedingly worthless to me.*

These times are too serious and my heart too deeply interested in the fate of our unhappy country and too burdened with the fact of my probable long separation from My Darling, *to think much of personal considerations. But I have been peculiarly fortunate & have made without an effort to do it, some reputation as a commander.*

My Dear girl, what shall I say to you, to give you an idea of my heart aching, when I think of our separation—I say when I think. Why Darling, except in the midst of battle, you are scarcely out of my thoughts. Indeed I am not at all sure that I do not think of you in battle. I am quite sure that the idea occurs to me, of the desolation which would reign in your heart if I should be killed. I think this occurred to me in the last battle at Gettysburg. . . .

Good bye. The Lord of Hosts bless you my dear dear wife & little boys. I am trying to rely upon the same protection I have felt in other battles. My Saviour I trust is my friend. If I am spared it is on His account.

Good bye again my sweet angel wife.

Beaten at Gettysburg and further demoralized by the want of food and necessities when it returned to Virginia, Lee's army hemorrhaged with desertions. Lee was in pain and, like his army, was wasting and debilitated.*

Lee offered to step down in a letter of August 8 that was distinguished by its equivocations. Lee considered himself and his officers above criticism from any source. "[A]s far as I am concerned the remarks fall harmless," he wrote to Davis on July 31. "I hope the official reports will protect the reputation of every officer." While not a victory, he had written, Gettysburg had not exactly been a defeat. As Lee saw it, God had guided his army to a "general success" at Gettysburg. Consistent with explanations of why he had fallen short in the past, he was sure that his Gettysburg plan had been good but, for reasons beyond his control, the execution poor. He would have won "if all things could have worked together."

What he did confess in his August letter was a feeling that he undeservedly had lost the confidence of the public and much of his army. "The general remedy," he wrote, "for the want of success in a military commander is his removal. This is natural, and in many instances proper." Expressing his recurring theme of pious self-deprecation, he continued, "[N]o one is more aware than myself of my inability for the duties of my position." Finally, he told Davis, he was old [fifty-six] and tired. "I sensibly feel," he wrote, "the growing failure of my bodily strength. . . . Everything, therefore, points to the advantages to be derived from a new commander, and I the more anxiously urge the matter upon Your Excellency from my belief that a younger

---

* Studies suggest that he was suffering from rheumatism, hypertension, and possibly heart disease.

and abler man than myself can readily be attained." Lee was mute as to who
that might be. Lee's letter was solely for the record, because he knew that
Davis would not possibly relieve him, not only because of Davis's demonstrated unwillingness to remove other generals, but also because of a letter
Lee had received from Davis a few days before his own.

"Misfortune often develops secret foes," Davis had written on July 28,
"and oftener still makes men complain. It is comfortable to hold some one
responsible for one's discomfort. In various quarters there are mutterings of
discontent, and threats of alienation are said to exist, with preparation for
organized opposition. There are others who, faithful but dissatisfied, find an
appropriate remedy in the removal of officers who have not succeeded. They
have not counted the cost of following their advice. Their remedy, to be
good, should furnish substitutes who would be better than the officers dis-
placed. If a victim would secure success of our cause I would freely offer
myself, and there are many of those most assailed who would, I am sure,
contend for the place, if their sacrifice could bring such reward."

Davis was not going to sacrifice Lee.

PART V

WESTERN

THEATER, 1863

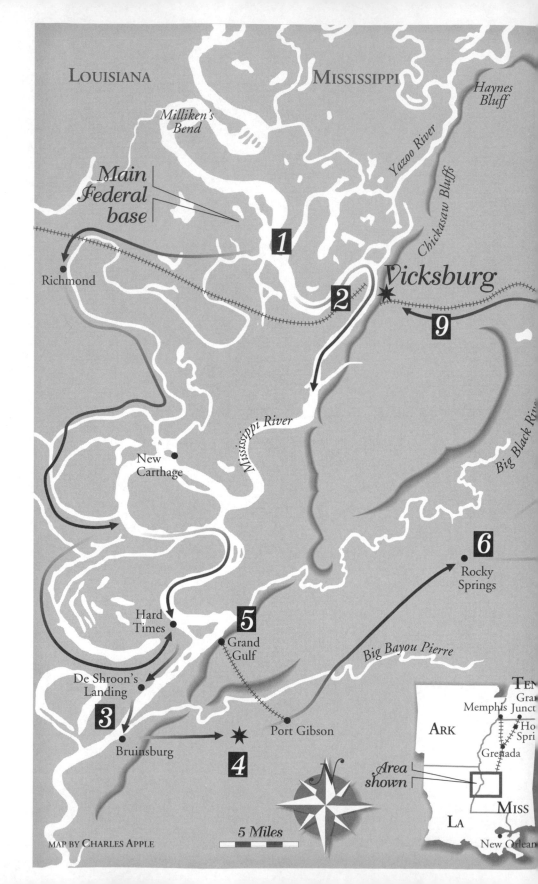

LOUISIANA

MISSISSIPPI

Haynes Bluff

Milliken's Bend

1

Main Federal base

Richmond

Yazoo River

Chickasaw Bluffs

2

Vicksburg

9

Mississippi River

New Carthage

Big Black River

6

Rocky Springs

Hard Times

5

Grand Gulf

Big Bayou Pierre

De Shroon's Landing

3

Port Gibson

Bruinsburg

4

N

5 Miles

MAP BY CHARLES APPLE

TEN

Gra Junct

Memphis

ARK

Ho Spri

Grenada

Area shown

MISS

LA

New Orlean

Grant Takes Vicksburg

1 **April 5:** Grant begins moving his army below Vicksburg by marching overland, west of Vicksburg.

2 **April 16:** Porter moves his fleet past the batteries at Vicksburg to rendezvous with Grant south of Vicksburg.

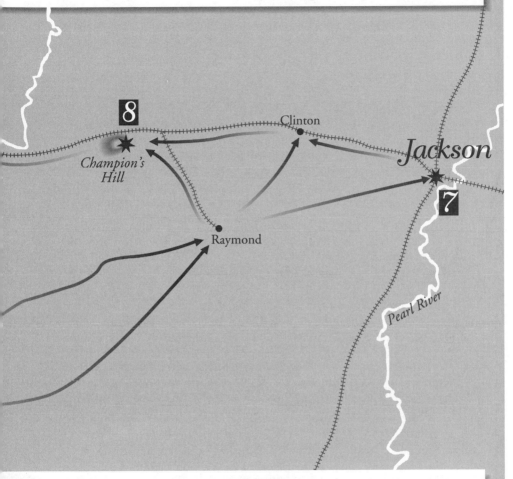

3 **April 30:** Porter transports Grant's army across the Mississippi.

4 **May 1:** Federal army wins battle of Port Gibson.

5 **May 2:** Confederates abandon Grand Gulf, allowing Federal army to use it as major river port to land troops and supplies. Pemberton remains near Vicksburg, Johnston near Jackson.

6 **May 11:** Grant advances to Rocky Springs. Decides to live off the country and first to attack Jackson and deal with Johnston.

7 **May 14:** Sherman and McPherson assault and occupy Jackson. Johnston withdraws to the north. McClernand at Raymond and Clinton protects against Pemberton attack from the west.

8 **May 16:** Grant defeats Pemberton at Champion's Hill. Pemberton retreats to Vicksburg. Grant follows.

9 **May 18:** Grant arrives at Vicksburg. Attack on May 19 unsuccessful. Invests the city. Pemberton surrenders on July 4.

2 0

VICKSBURG

If in the accounts given us by historians . . . we find that wars and battles appear to follow a definite plan laid down beforehand, the only deduction we can make . . . is that these accounts are not true.
                                                        Tolstoy, War and Peace

Halleck left a vacuum in organization and strategy when he went to Washington in July 1862, for the western theater was without a unified commander. Grant and his Army of the Tennessee remained in western Tennessee trying to pacify a hostile countryside. Confederate raiders and guerrillas roamed freely inside Grant's jurisdiction, making the summer and fall an anxious time of swatting at swarms of hornets. Halleck had given Grant no instructions before he departed, nor did he send any from Washington. Bragg's invasion of Kentucky (chapter 16) and Lee's maneuvers in the east (chapters 10 and 11) so absorbed the administration that offensive operations for Grant's army were considered neither in Washington nor in Grant's Memphis headquarters. Grant was forgotten.

Federal control of the Mississippi River had been a strategic goal from the beginning of the war. Once this was achieved, the Confederacy would be unable to communicate with the secessionist states on the west bank, and Southern commerce would be throttled. Northern commerce, on the other hand, could resume all the way to the Gulf of Mexico. Militarily, Federal forces could use the river to stage invasions into the Deep South. Part of that goal had been achieved in the lower river with the occupation of New Orleans, and in the upper river with the fall of Memphis.

The three hundred miles of river in between, primarily along Mississippi's western border, remained in contention. While the Confederacy had no navy, fortified strategic points on the river prevented the passage of Federal warships and waterborne transportation. The major fortification was the river town of Vicksburg. Cannon on high cliffs could fire down upon the river, but Federal gunboats could not return fire because of the elevation. Infantry could not assault from north of the city because of the rugged terrain or from the west because of the river. Hence the city had to be assaulted from the south or the east. The strategic challenge was to get troops into either of those two quadrants. If Vicksburg could be seized, the Mississippi River would pass to Federal control.

Neither Halleck nor Grant had developed any plan or concept for seizing Vicksburg by the fall of 1862. This was not the Grant of 1864, who would conceive a sweeping master plan for defeating the Confederacy. The Grant of this period had no grand vision, nor did he express any enlightened strategic thinking. Perhaps he had become so intimidated by Halleck's disdainful rejections of his recommendations that he was demoralized. The result was that for months to come Grant would wait for developments and then react to protect his self-interests.

It remained for a politician in uniform, John A. McClernand, to advance a proposal. A major general of volunteers, McClernand was on leave from Grant's army, where he had served competently in the early 1862 campaigns. An ambitious and influential Illinois politician, he was a Democratic member of the U.S. House of Representatives and corresponded directly with Lincoln. In late September he proposed to the president that he command an army which, in cooperation with the navy, would steam down the Mississippi and capture Vicksburg. McClernand personally would raise the regiments in the midwestern states, where he was assured of the cooperation of impatient governors anxious to open the Mississippi and resume commerce.

Lincoln approved the proposal for what seemed to him good reasons. Given the many midwestern Peace Democrats, or Copperheads, who opposed emancipation and wanted to end the war on Southern terms, McClernand was a welcome bipartisan supporter whom Lincoln wanted to accommodate in a tough election year. McClernand promised movement, which Lincoln wanted and could not get from his West Point generals, and opening the Mississippi would be widely popular in the midwest.

Lincoln told Halleck and Stanton of his decision on October 9, 1862. Halleck, of course, objected—he loathed political generals. Lincoln was insistent, but he did agree that McClernand would report to Halleck. With that concession, Stanton wrote a charter for McClernand to carry on with his proposal. Grant, meanwhile, remained uninformed of developments.

McClernand met with Rear Admiral David D. Porter, who would command the forces afloat. He and the Navy Department agreed to cooperate, and plans were made to procure the necessary river craft to support the expedition. With these arrangements in place, McClernand returned to the midwest to recruit his army. Still in the dark, Grant occupied himself with Confederate reinforcements threatening his depots and garrisons.

Halleck began almost immediately to sabotage McClernand's efforts. As fast as McClernand collected troops in the midwest, Halleck ordered them to report either to Grant or Sherman, who accepted them with delight while not knowing why they were coming. Without Lincoln's knowledge, Halleck expanded Grant's jurisdiction from a district to a department, which included the very areas where McClernand would have to operate. He would not tell Grant outright of McClernand's charter, but he suggested that Grant start thinking offensively about Mississippi.

Grant was perplexed as to what Halleck expected of him. "You have never suggested to me any plan of opperations in this [new] Department," he wrote to Halleck on October 26, "and . . . I do not know anything of those of commanders to my right or left." For the first time Grant suggested moving south by railroad to cause the *evacuation* of Vicksburg, among other tentative alternatives. "I am ready however," he concluded, "to do with all my might whatever you may direct, without criticism."

A week later Grant boarded five divisions on trains and headed south into Mississippi. There is no record as to why he decided to move. "I was prepared to take the initiative," he simply said in his memoirs. "The campaign against Vicksburg commenced on the 2d of November."

Grant actually had embarked on a campaign, not to take Vicksburg, but to try his luck. Vicksburg was over two hundred miles away at the end of a single rail line that passed through western Mississippi, as hostile and dangerous a territory to Northern invaders as could be imagined. In his status reports to Halleck, Grant did not even mention Vicksburg as an objective, but rather cited such intermediate way points as Holly Springs and Grenada and others as opportunity might offer, and he frequently asked Halleck how far south he should proceed.

However far south that circumstances allowed him to venture, Grant intended to maintain communications by rail, repairing the railway as he advanced and remaining wholly dependent on it for supplies. Such a self-defeating strategy had sunk the unfortunate Buell on his way to Chattanooga earlier in the year. It required that Grant guard an ever lengthening rail line and vulnerable depots, which he was not prepared to do, as each depot had but a corporal's guard commanded by officers unfit for frontline operations. Attacks on such irresistible targets by Confederate cavalry were foreordained. The farther south Grant went—whatever his ultimate destination—the more vulnerable his line of communications became.

Grant had come south to fight military battles. Concurrently he would shred the Southern infrastructure. As the army of Northerners marched into the bowels of the Deep South for the first time, they discovered the area's huge cotton plantations and the thousands of slaves who labored in their fields. No happy and contented blacks these, with benevolent masters. The scales fell from the soldiers' eyes at the stunning magnitude of the evil, the wretchedness, and the inhumanity of large-scale plantation slavery.

The owners and overseers fled, leaving the black families on their own. By default they became Grant's responsibility, something he had not sought but could not escape. The blacks greeted the Federal soldiers as saviors. Tens of thousands swarmed about Grant's army in anticipation of finding the gifts of freedom and kind treatment. "Humanity forbade allowing them to starve," Grant later wrote.

Grant's solutions were ingenious. He appointed a chaplain, John Eaton, to establish a refugee camp at Grand Junction, Tennessee, at the Mississippi border, where black families could be fed and protected. In some instances politics transcended charity. As early as September, Grant had sent freed women and children to Cairo, anticipating that they could find employment in Illinois. At first Stanton approved, but within a month he forbade any further transfer of blacks into the state. It was an election year.

Meanwhile, Grant put blacks to work picking cotton for sale by the Federal government. They also worked as laborers, cooks, and teamsters. Their wages were deferred, because, for want of appropriations, even the soldiers were not being paid. But the blacks were wage earners nonetheless. The organization expanded in scope and effectiveness, and Eaton got invited to the White House.

The former slaves became "freedmen" on January 1, 1863, and the idiom "contraband" was discontinued. During the Chattanooga campaign later in the year, Rosecrans used the term "American citizens of African descent," the antecedent of the expression used today.

Cotton speculators who wanted to buy the scarce commodity for resale in the North were another distraction. Despite Grant's efforts at regulation, the speculation got out of hand, and a flustered Grant blamed Jews for the most flagrant abuses. On December 17, he issued his infamous Exodus Order.

> I. *The Jews, as a class, violating every regulation of trade . . . are hereby expelled from the Department.*
> II. *Within twenty-four hours from the receipt of this order by Post Commanders, they will see that all of this class of people are furnished with passes and required to leave, and any one returning after such notification, will be arrested and held in confinement until an opportunity occurs of sending them out as prisoners. . . .*
> III. *No permits will be given these people to visit Head Quarters for the purpose of making personal applications for trade permits.*

Grant's order precipitated confusion and outrage. As it seemed to include all Jews, questions arose from his field commanders as to whether Grant intended to include officers and soldiers in his army, sutlers, officeholders, and local citizens. Soldiers evicted Jews from towns as far north as Paducah, Kentucky. Non-Jewish speculators were delighted to see their competitors expelled.

Protests engulfed the administration. Congressman Washburne called on Halleck, who told him there would have been no problem if Grant had confined his orders to Jewish "peddlars &c." But as it was, the expulsion order was too broad and had to be rescinded. Grant was under fire in any event, for by then both he and Sherman had failed in their first shot at taking Vicksburg, and the congressional Democrats were censuring Grant on the floor. Grant revoked the order three weeks after it had been issued, and the controversy subsided.

In the beginning, Grant had thought only of the strictly military considerations of invading Mississippi. Saying nothing about McClernand, Halleck wired his after-the-fact approval of Grant's vague plans on November 6.

Additional reinforcements were on the way, Halleck said a few days later, but he suggested they go to Memphis, where Sherman awaited orders.

Grant asked, Why Memphis?

"Memphis," wired Halleck a few days later, "will be made a depot of a joint military & naval expedition on Vicksburg." Grant became increasingly confused, and he asked Halleck about the "misterious rumors of McClernands command." He loathed McClernand and had pleaded beforehand with Halleck not to send him as he was "unmanageable and incompetant." "Am I to understand that I lay still here," Grant persisted, "while an Expedition is fitted out from Memphis or do you want me to push as far south as possible? Am I to have Sherman move subject to my order or is he & his forces reserved for some special service? Will not more forces be sent here?"

"You have command of all troops sent to your Dept," Halleck answered, "and have permission to fight the enemy when you please." This was nonsense: advice and admonitions from Washington would whiplash Grant incessantly. Moreover, Lincoln and Stanton expected Grant to share command authority with McClernand. But when McClernand got to Memphis after recruiting and personal business in the midwest, he found it deserted. Grant and Sherman had taken off with his soldiers.

Thus thwarting McClernand became the genesis of Grant's strategy in Mississippi. Grant first revealed his intentions by summoning Sherman (with McClernand's troops) from Memphis to join him on the overland approach. When Halleck persisted in demanding a river expedition, Grant ordered Sherman to go downriver before McClernand arrived. To further preempt McClernand, Sherman rashly attacked north of Vicksburg at Chickasaw Bluffs. The Confederates repulsed him. When Sherman withdrew to regroup, McClernand arrived and took command of the river expedition. Abandoning his plans to take Vicksburg, McClernand led a raid into Arkansas.

Meanwhile, Grant continued his tortured overland descent into Mississippi. Far to the rear, Confederate general Earl Van Dorn destroyed Grant's supply depot at Holly Springs, and Brigadier General Nathan Bedford Forrest ruptured his railway lines. Stranded in enemy territory, Grant swallowed hard and retreated through the Mississippi countryside swarming with guerrillas and jeering civilians.

When he got back to Memphis, Grant recalled McClernand from Arkansas. As much as Grant disliked McClernand, he had to admire his Vicksburg strategy, especially as it had Lincoln's blessing. McClernand's plan then became Grant's plan, and, with Halleck's concurrence, Grant assumed personal command of the river expedition. McClernand was included, but as an outraged subordinate.

Thus the grand strategy for seizing and opening the Mississippi River was born of deceit. With deceit as its foundation, the campaign was destined to be governed by audacity and expediency, with colossal wastage of time, matériel, and lives. The campaign consumed nine months of false starts and missed opportunities. It succeeded because the Yeoman was able to arouse and direct, however imperfectly, the enormous energy of the Federal forces on the Mississippi.

The campaign was ugly to watch. During the winter months of 1862–63, Grant's army floundered and flailed in the bayous west of Vicksburg, felling trees and dredging canals as they tried to construct a passage for boats to bypass the Vicksburg batteries. Grant cynically disguised the brutal physical activity as purposeful progress. Afterward he revealed that his intent was "to consume time, and to divert the attention of the enemy, of my troops, and of the public generally. . . . I let the work go on, believing employment was better than idleness for the men."

This was not conventional leadership by any means, but it worked for Grant. His men suffered terribly, hardly able to remain warm and dry as they labored in the bayous. Nonetheless, like their general they were yeomen, accustomed to exercising brute force, and they directed their anger at the obstacles before them. The Federal supply system kept them fed and clothed. The result was extraordinary individual effort. Suffused with the fervor of their general, the soldiers moved heaven and earth to give Grant what he wanted.

Grant would have us believe that, all the while, he had conceived a master plan which he kept to himself. "I had had in contemplation the whole winter," he wrote in his memoirs, "the movement by land to a point below Vicksburg from which to operate, subject only to the possible but not expected success of some one of the expedients resorted to for the purpose of giving us a different base." Grant said further that Rear Admiral Porter was the first person to whom he shared his vision, and that Porter immediately agreed to run his fleet past the Vicksburg batteries to support Grant's campaign south of Vicksburg. Many historians have cited this as a model of combined army-navy operations.

Historian Rowena Reed has a different judgment of events. "Much had been written about Grant's 'brilliant' strategic insight during the final Vicksburg campaign," she wrote in her book *Combined Operations in the Civil War*. The common view that Grant and Porter worked hand in glove to develop the "correct" strategy of attacking from below the city, said Reed, "is extravagant as well as factually wrong. Most of these claims are nonsense. Grant had no real strategic plan for the movement which led to the siege, let alone a combined plan. Nor did anyone in the Union Navy, including Admiral Porter, formulate such a plan."

Reed is correct. Grant's Vicksburg strategy actually evolved spasmodically. His thinking careened from one extreme to the other, from either no plan at all to spur-of-the-moment impulses, with no objective in mind other than somehow "opening the Mississippi." Porter did want to get below Vicksburg, but for different reasons. The navy had distractions and problems of its own; it had to get gunboats downstream to regain control of the river between Vicksburg and Port Hudson. Porter's and Grant's needs conveniently coincided.

That came later, however. For most of the winter and well into March, Grant's main effort was focused against Haynes Bluff on the Yazoo River, north of Vicksburg, where Sherman had failed the previous December. Porter's gunboats and transports tried to help, but they got stuck trying to squeeze through a narrow bayou canal to the Yazoo. Confederate troops nearly captured them, stopped only by Sherman's paddling a canoe leading boatloads of soldiers to the rescue.

Grant had relied upon Porter getting to the Yazoo. Failing that, he admitted to Sherman on March 22 that he had no alternative in mind. In a letter the same day to Major General Nathaniel P. Banks, commanding a Federal army downriver at Baton Rouge, he wrote, "[T]here is nothing left for me but to collect all my strength and attack Hains [Haynes] Bluff. This will necessarily be attended with much loss but I think it can be done."

Grant began considering alternatives the following day. He would carry on with his plan to attack Haynes Bluff but was willing to send a corps downriver to cooperate with Banks in taking control of the lower Mississippi. For the first time, he asked Porter if he would be willing to run the Vicksburg batteries with his fleet, *but only to support Banks downriver*. He still had not spoken to Porter about moving his entire army south to attack Vicksburg.

Five more days passed as Grant chewed over alternatives. The idea of running the batteries *to attack Vicksburg from below* was first expressed in a letter to Porter on March 29. Porter replied that he was willing to cooperate, but he warned Grant that, once his gunboats were below the Vicksburg batteries, they could not return upstream against the current. As Grant's request was on short notice, he would need time to get coal and supplies to support his fleet. Finally, he needed clarification: was Grant proposing to abandon his Haynes Bluff operation altogether?

Grant still was not sure. He, Porter, and Sherman steamed up the Yazoo on April 1 to Haynes Bluff to reconnoiter the Confederate fortifications. They were formidable. "I am satisfied that an attack upon Haines Bluff," he wrote Porter the next day, "would be attended with immense sacrifice of life, if not defeat. This then closes out the last hope of turning the enemy by the right [i.e., north of Vicksburg]."

Three days later, Grant had decided what to do, and he wrote his intentions to Halleck:

- The navy gunboats would run the Vicksburg batteries.
- His troops would march south through the bayous west of Vicksburg and cross the river to the east bank below the city.
- From the east bank he would have good roads to either Jackson or Vicksburg.

"This is the only move I see as practicable," he wrote, "and hope it meets your approval." Grant said nothing about cutting loose from his base of supplies; in fact he said the opposite. "I will keep my army together," he assured Halleck, "and see that I am not cut off from my supplies or beat in any other way than a fair fight."

Grant hated journalists for two reasons. One was that they vilified him. The other—with which Lee would have agreed—was that they published military secrets in their papers. Generals on both sides routinely scanned enemy papers as a prime source of information on movements and intentions. Now that he had his strategy in hand, Grant hoped to move stealthily to reduce the risks he was facing.

Hence he was outraged when Memphis newspapers announced details of his plans for Vicksburg within four days after he had sent them to Halleck by confidential letter. A seething Grant sent orders to the Federal general commanding the city. "Suppress the entire press of Memphis," he charged, "for giving aid and comfort to the enemy by publishing in their columns every move made here by troops and every work commenced. Arrest the Editor of the Bulliten and send him here a prisoner."

Such was Grant's frame of mind on the arrival of New York journalist Charles A. Dana, whom Stanton had sent to report on Grant and his activities. Dana's ostensible mission was to investigate the condition of soldiers' pay in the western army (which was terrible), but Grant and his advisers knew better. Rather than resenting his presence, Grant was smart enough to welcome Dana, to make him comfortable, and to confide in him.

Flattered at the attention at headquarters, Dana sent glowing reports to Washington, allowing Grant time to carry on his campaign with diminished interference and finally to win full support from Washington. Because Stanton increasingly relied upon Dana's reports as the most accurate source of information from the field, the journalist became a conduit between Grant and Washington.

After Grant had decided to bypass Vicksburg by river, no one could change his mind. Some tried. Sherman protested that the risk was too great and that Grant should consult his corps commanders for a consensus so that all would cooperate. Sherman himself wanted to pull out of the bayous of Vicksburg and urged a renewed operation from the north of the city, by the overland route.

Grant insisted on his river plan. McClernand would lead the attack, he said, despite protests from Sherman and Porter. Lincoln had wanted McClernand to command the campaign from the beginning, and McClernand certainly was motivated to make the plan successful (it had been his, after all). His troops had already worked their way through the bayous to a position where they could cross the river below Vicksburg. As much as Grant disliked McClernand, for the moment he was the best person to help Grant succeed.

Grant's span of control and tactical vision went far beyond the battlefield immediately before him. In order to cross the Mississippi below Grand Gulf and to establish a bridgehead on the eastern shore, he decoyed the Confederate troops elsewhere so they would not oppose him during the early, critical phase of the operation. Demonstrations north of Vicksburg, most prominently a cavalry expedition under Colonel Benjamin Grierson, thoroughly confused Lieutenant General John C. Pemberton, commanding at Vicksburg. When it was too late for the Confederates to oppose his landing, Pemberton finally realized what Grant had done.

Porter ran the batteries and ferried Grant's army to the eastern shore, some thirty miles south of Vicksburg. McClernand's corps and a division of James B. McPherson's corps were ready to move inland by April 30. At the moment Grant simply "felt a degree of relief scarcely ever equalled since." Even then he still was undecided on his ultimate objectives; earlier he had told Halleck and McClernand that he intended to seize Grand Gulf, proceed south to rendezvous with Banks and attack Port Hudson, then take the combined armies back north to capture Vicksburg.

VIPs gathered at Grant's headquarters, watching him at first hand: Governor Richard Yates of Illinois, his mentor Congressman Washburne, and of course Dana. Washington, too, was watching from the telegraph wire. Lincoln kept a map displayed on a tripod in his office to follow Grant's progress. McClernand captured Port Gibson on May 1, and the Confederates abandoned Grand Gulf. Grant now had his base of operations, and, contrary to his announced intentions, his momentum was decidedly northward, away from Banks.

As the whole of Grant's army arrived, Grand Gulf became clogged, a place of chaos, where each general engaged in a free-for-all to commandeer wagons and supplies for himself. All the while Grant was seething, straining to hit the Confederates before they hit him. "Rations now are the only delay," he telegraphed upriver, but it was an immobilizing delay.

Grant sent the least competent of his staff officers, Colonel William Hillyer, to unsnarl the waterfront and get supplies moving forward. A worse choice could not have been made. Hillyer was in intense pain from rheumatism, he already had submitted his resignation, and he wanted to go home. But not even a dynamo could have compensated for the lack of logistical planning. Sherman wrote from Grand Gulf on May 9 that it was futile to try to supply an army of 33,000 men over a single road. "Stop all troops," advised Sherman, until enough wagons had come across the river to haul the necessaries. Grant realized that he was immobilized, stuck in his tracks, not by Confederate troops, but by his lack of logistical support.

In his headquarters tent, Grant pulled thoughtfully on his cigar. The reports piled on his table led to an inescapable conclusion: days would be required before enough supplies would be available to allow him to resume his offensive. The longer he waited, the greater the probability that the Confederates would recover from their surprise and concentrate their scattered forces at his front. He remembered the richness of the Mississippi countryside during the overland campaign the summer before. Thinking with inspired clarity, Grant realized that the farms lying within his reach could feed his troops in lieu of the army provisions marooned on the river.

Grant's hunch, he discovered, was correct. His scouts reported that the region was abundant with beef, mutton, fowl, cornmeal, bacon, and vegetables.

Mississippi would feed his soldiers, allowing them to move out immediately. Sweeping his table clear, Grant put a fresh sheet of paper before him and began to write.

Orders issued from headquarters to seize every bit of rolling stock in the countryside, from hay wagons to ladies' carriages, and upon them to heap ammunition, hard bread, coffee, and salt. Nothing more. Mississippi mules would pull the wheels. "[T]he country is full of them ready to go to work for the Union," wrote Grant. "About the only loyalty in this region is possessed by mules and contrabands." Food would be forcefully requisitioned. "No formalities were to retard our progress," he later wrote, "until a position was secured when the time could be spared to observe them."

Still unannounced was Grant's ultimate objective. Where were his men to go, and whom were they to fight? Even at that late hour, Grant still had not confirmed his intentions. He had promised Banks earlier that he would head south to consolidate their forces before undertaking extended operations. That would take time, however, and time would allow the Confederates to reinforce Vicksburg still further. McClernand and McPherson had already made a preliminary move to the northeast. Should they now be recalled? At the moment the two main enemy components were still separated, the armies of Pemberton at Vicksburg and General Joseph Johnston, the ostensible unified commander in the west, at Jackson.

Grant now made the most brilliant decision of his career. He would attack first Johnston and then Pemberton before they could unite and thereby outnumber him, the classic example of defeating an enemy army in detail. Grant advised Banks on May 10 that he would not head south as promised, but intended instead to take Vicksburg immediately. Banks could join him if he wished. Banks declined.

The resulting campaign was the equivalent of a Second World War blitzkreig. Grant's span of control and command of his forces were exquisite. Moving swiftly and decisively, Grant first sent Sherman against Johnston, who, having failed to rendezvous with the Confederate forces at Vicksburg, was hovering near Jackson, the state capital. Sherman swept away Johnston, raised the United States flag over the Mississippi Capitol, then put the torch to the city so that it could not threaten the Federal rear when Grant turned toward Vicksburg. McClernand and McPherson stormed westward to meet and defeat Pemberton at Champion's Hill. There Grant's blitzkreig stalled, and Champion's Hill became his Dunkirk. Pemberton escaped into Vicksburg on a road that Grant had inadvertently left open, and Grant was forced to besiege the city.

Grant's capacity for supreme command came to fruition in the Vicksburg campaign, but in a singular way. His success had been due, not to planning and preparation, but to improvisation. "In war," as he had once remarked to a staff officer, "anything is better than indecision. We must decide. If I am wrong, we shall soon find it out, and can do the other thing. But not to decide wastes both time and money, and may ruin everything." After Vicksburg, Grant felt that his philosophy was vindicated.

What Grant had also done was to establish precedents. He had inaugurated unrestricted warfare in a coordinated theater campaign, the precursor to his grand strategy against the Confederacy when he became general in chief. By employing every means in his domain to bear on his enemy and—this was new—on his enemy's resources, Grant had developed a style of warfare that extended beyond forced requisitions for his main army. He had, for example, ordered Major General Steven A. Hurlbut, commanding divisions in northern Mississippi, to attack into the countryside to divert Confederate forces from Vicksburg and Jackson. Send your cavalry, said Grant. "They must live as far as possible off the country through which they pass and destroy corn, wheat crops and everything that can be made use of by the enemy in prolonging the war. Mules and horses can be taken to supply all our wants and where it does not cause too much delay agricultural implements may be destroyed. In other words cripple the rebellion in every way without insulting women and children or taking their clothing, jewelry &c."

By encouraging the destruction of the South's resources, Grant manifested the feasibility of mobilizing freedmen as combatants. He had given search-and-destroy instructions to Major General Frederick Steele, who commanded troops on the western side of the river in an area that had provided provisions for Pemberton's army. "Rebellion has assumed the shape now," Grant instructed, "that it can only terminate by the complete subjugation of the South or the overthrow of the Government. [I]t is our duty therefore to use every means to weaken the enemy by destroying their means of cultivating their fields, and in every other way possible. All the negroes you have you will provide for where they are issuing necessary rations, until other disposition is made of them. You will also encourage all negroes, particularly middle aged males to come within our lines."

"It is becoming a perfect mania with the colored population to become yankees," Steele responded, "and most of the men express their willingness to fight for their freedom." Such reports encouraged the administration. "[W]e must try to use [freedmen] with the best possible effect against the rebels," Halleck urged. "And it is the opinion of many who have examined the question without passion or prejudice, that they also can be used as a military force. It certainly is good policy to use them to the very best advantage we can."

Reports that some of Grant's generals balked at helping the freedmen disturbed Halleck. Not so, Grant assured him. "At least three of my Army Corps Commanders take hold of the new policy of arming the negroes and using them against the rebels with a will," wrote Grant. He was as good as his word. When Confederate guerrillas attacked the Milliken's Bend depot in particularly vicious fighting on June 7, the black and white Federal troops (known as the African Brigade) held. Federal officers who had doubted now believed.

White Southerners were horrified. For generations they had feared armed insurrection, and now their nightmare was upon them. Confederate soldiers, as a consequence, were merciless to black soldiers and their white officers, for the latter were considered, like John Brown, to be inciting insurrection, a capital offense. Davis announced in early 1863 that those captured would be executed, a policy confirmed by the Confederate Congress in May 1863. "The enlistment of our slaves is a barbarity," declared a ranking Confederate official.

When Grant received information that black soldiers and two white officers captured at Milliken's Bend had been hanged, he protested to Confederate General Richard Taylor, who allegedly had condoned the hangings. Taylor denied the charges. Nonetheless, he wrote Grant, captured black soldiers would not be treated as prisoners of war. The Confederate government had ordered that they be turned over "to the civil authorities to be dealt with according to the laws of the state wherein they were captured." Taylor left unsaid that those laws were at worst a death sentence, at best a return to slavery.

The Civil War had exploded into unrestrained violence against armies, civilians, and property. Halleck hated the South, and his ad hoc directives became harsher and more punitive. Lawyer that he was, Halleck wanted to anchor his edicts on legal and ethical footing. He engaged Francis Lieber, a renowned German American political philosopher at Columbia University, to prepare a paper that would codify the rules of war.

Lieber told Halleck that no work of the kind then existed. Starting from scratch, he described his guiding principles as "Usage, history, reason, and conscientiousness, [and] a sincere love of truth, justice, and civilization." To Halleck's delight he produced a paper entitled "Instructions for the Government of Armies of the United States in the Field." Lieber claimed that it conformed to two criteria: to prevent unnecessary injury and destruction to belligerents on both sides; and to exert the greatest energy in conducting the war so as to end it as soon as possible.* In April 1863, Halleck published Lieber's work as General Order No. 100.

Grant redeemed himself at Vicksburg. By surrendering on Independence Day, Pemberton gave Grant and the administration a stunning public relations bonanza. Grant was a winner when Lincoln and the United States desperately needed wins, and now Grant became a hero. Lincoln appointed him a major general in the regular army, which unlike volunteer commissions meant that he would retain the rank after the war. He had proven himself to be a bold, risk-taking combat general who could coordinate and maneuver a field army under fluid conditions. Thrashing Johnston and Pemberton in detail was the masterstroke, for had the two Confederate armies massed against Grant, he would have been outnumbered and possibly defeated. If he lacked a certain ability to plan and make long-term strategy, he compensated by improvising and infusing his army with an extraordinary energy to move

---

* These principles appear to clash, perhaps because German philosophical reasoning is sometimes obscure. Nonetheless, Lieber's work was the basis for later efforts to codify the international law of war.

and to strike and to carry on regardless of obstacles. Porter and the navy caught the spirit and became enthusiastic brothers in arms.

The bad news was that both Confederate armies managed to withdraw and survive. When Pemberton got back to Vicksburg, Grant had no room to maneuver and had to besiege the city. Grant had no special genius for taking down a fortified city, neither Vicksburg in 1863 nor Petersburg in 1864–65. In both instances he resorted to conventional, costly frontal assaults. Predictably, they failed. Had Pemberton the stamina and grit of a Lee, he could have held on longer, and Grant would have been forced into more futile assaults and casualties.

While besieging Vicksburg, Grant kept track of Johnston, who could have come to the rescue of the city at any time. Grant had Sherman face east should Johnston come, while the remainder of his army faced west against Vicksburg. When Vicksburg fell, Sherman lunged after Johnston and chased him away, again allowing a Confederate army to fight another day. Meanwhile, Grant sent reinforcements to Banks, and shortly the Mississippi was open from Minnesota to the Gulf.

And then nothing happened. After the victory celebrations, and when the cheering had stopped, Federal leaders again dithered. The thinking in Washington did not extend beyond the immediate objectives of the current campaign. Neither Lincoln, nor Stanton, nor Halleck, nor Grant yet understood the only way to defeat the Confederacy. Destroying cities and farms, blockading seaports and mobilizing freedmen, all such strategies did indeed reduce the Confederacy's ability to make war, but they would not win the war. So long as the Confederacy could put armies in the field, the war would go on. The Confederate armies had to be destroyed for the war to end.

The Federal government had not recognized that logic in 1863, for prisoners still were being exchanged. The men could fight again, prolonging the war. Grant captured over 20,000 soldiers when Vicksburg surrendered on Independence Day 1863. All were allowed to return to their lines under the terms of a cartel, and a like number of Federal prisoners returned to the North from other theaters. Neither side wanted to bother with prisoners, and each was happy to send them back. Upon their return many of the Confederate prisoners were hustled off to Bragg in Chattanooga, in violation of the cartel. When Grant realized the folly a year later, by his order all exchanges ended.

Grant proposed a drive against Mobile, Alabama. Although Halleck would not hear of it, he proposed no meaningful alternatives. Rosecrans and Thomas had begun the long-awaited Tennessee offensive against Bragg, but no suggestion was made to send any of Grant's troops in support. That would come later, and too late. Instead, Grant's splendid army was frittered away on garrison, a division here, a brigade there, with neither direction nor purpose, while Grant stewed on the great river, trying to regulate trade so that the Confederacy would not benefit.

Grant had anticipated the impasse during the siege. He realized that he had lost the initiative and shared his gloomy feelings with Julia. "If . . . I could have carried the place on the 22d of last month," he wrote, "I could have by this time made a campaign that would have made the state of Mississippi almost safe for a solitary horseman to ride over. As it is the enemy have a large Army in it and the season is so far advanced that water will be difficult for an Army marching besides the dust and heat that must be encountered. The fall of Vicksburg now will result in the opening of the Miss. River and demoralization of the enemy. I intended more from it. I did my best however and looking back can see no blunder committed."

Grant's drinking had not ended, especially when things were slack and he was bored. During the siege of Vicksburg he spent two days on a riverboat drinking himself insensible. During a trip to New Orleans in early September, Grant rode an unruly horse that unexpectedly threw him. He was terribly injured and remained bedridden for weeks, suffering an agony of pain. When Rosecrans and Bragg drew up before Chickamauga Creek later in the month, Halleck belatedly ordered reinforcements from Grant's district. Before Grant could act, Rosecrans had been devastated, and Bragg went on to besiege Chattanooga. Within weeks, Grant would follow his reinforcements there for his final campaign in the west, as we shall see in chapter 23.

2 1

THE APPROACH TO CHICKAMAUGA

For where jealousy and selfish ambition exist, there will be disorder and every vile practice.

The Letter of James 3:16

The war in central Tennessee became a stalemate in the winter months of 1863. The ferocity of the Confederate attacks at Murfreesboro had stunned Rosecrans. Bragg had nearly overwhelmed him. Rosecrans now had a more profound respect for his enemy, and he needed a whole new set of equations to determine how to achieve the combat superiority necessary to win the next battle.

Bragg had retreated but a short distance before establishing a new line on the Duck River, twenty-five miles to the southeast of Murfreesboro. There he was secure. Rosecrans would not undertake a winter campaign with his confidence shaken, his army bruised, and the roads a quagmire. Instead, he consolidated the region he had just seized and transformed Murfreesboro into a fortress depot.

An air of garrison routine pervaded the Army of the Cumberland. Absentees reduced the army to half the strength of its muster rolls. Although other officers and men took leave, especially to nearby Nashville, Thomas never did. He remained at headquarters, training the four divisions of his corps, which by mid-June had grown to a force of 32,000 soldiers. As spring arrived, Halleck beseeched Rosecrans to move against Bragg. The two generals burned the wires with discussions of strategic theory and principles of war, but Rosecrans stayed in place.

Halleck was free with advice, but he would not dictate. He goaded by turning the screw, sometimes with threats, at other times with such blandishments as promotion opportunities for those who followed his suggestions. But he never gave an order. "To order a general to give battle against his own wishes and judgment," said Halleck, "is to assume the responsibility of a probable defeat. If a general is unwilling to fight, he is not likely to gain a victory." (Jefferson Davis, incidentally, would have agreed, for he once observed that it was unwise to insist on fighting when the commander predicted failure.)

While Rosecrans used the first six months of 1863 to strengthen his army, Bragg absorbed himself in purges and vendettas against his generals, a spewing of mutual loathing and recrimination that cursed the Army of Tennessee. Debilitated by both sickness and insecurity, Bragg in blind and bitter tirades humiliated and insulted his proud and sensitive subordinates. They might have tolerated his behavior had he proven competent in combat, but his ineptness in the Kentucky and Murfreesboro campaigns had compromised his credibility as a soldier. While his generals could agree on little else, they were of one mind about Bragg. In a bizarre ploy he asked them for a vote of confidence, and they rejected him. No matter, they were stuck with Bragg, for Davis was incapable of dealing decisively with a bad choice.

One monumental defect of the Confederate command system was that if Davis fired someone of full rank, he had no suitable replacements. Samuel Cooper was an old man who remained in Richmond as adjutant general, and Lee was fixed in Virginia. Hence Davis continued to rotate the same tired, discredited trio of Johnson, Beauregard, and Bragg in and out of army commands throughout the war. None of the three could be forced into retirement to create vacancies for promising lieutenant generals. Hood and Kirby Smith were the only exceptions of later promotions to full rank.

When Rosecrans shaped up his army during the six-month stalemate, he hit on the idea of mobilizing a new kind of assault force that would counter the Confederate cavalry and provide mobile firepower. Spencer repeating rifles that could fire seven rounds in rapid succession were becoming available. Give these splendid weapons to his soldiers, Rosecrans argued, put them on horses, and call them mounted infantry, different from cavalry because they would be in the thick of battle and not on the periphery.

Halleck dismissed the idea, but the concept appealed to one of Thomas's infantry brigade commanders, Colonel John T. Wilder, an innovative, enterprising volunteer who scorned army conventions if they impeded combat readiness. With Thomas's permission and Rosecrans's blessing, Wilder obtained enough horses, mules, saddles, and bridles from the Murfreesboro region to mount his five regiments of Indiana and Illinois foot soldiers. He still needed firepower, however. Fortuitously, Christopher Spencer visited Murfreesboro in March to market his rifle, which the army's ordnance chief refused to purchase in quantity because he felt it wasted ammunition. Wilder and his men saw that it was a superb weapon, accurate, rugged, and dependable. They enthusiastically ordered enough to equip the brigade and paid for them out of their pockets. Rosecrans had his mounted infantry.

Rosecrans finally was ready to move by mid-June with an army of 65,000 to Bragg's 44,000. He had fortified Murfreesboro and stocked it with supplies to support the campaign. His plan was for Thomas's corps to maneuver to the rear of the Confederate army, turn its right flank, and prevent a retreat. Corps commanders McCook and Crittenden would join Thomas and seek a decisive battle in the open. Gordon Granger, commanding the Reserve Corps, would feint on the Confederate left.

Conceding the initiative to Rosecrans and consigned solely to reacting, Bragg by then had lost his will to fight and his grip on his army. His defensive position was superficially substantial. A range of rugged hills and the Duck River lay at his front as natural barriers, Tullahoma served as a depot fifteen miles to his rear, and a rail line connected him to his main base at Chattanooga. On his left, Polk's corps was entrenched near the river town of Shelbyville, twenty-five miles from Murfreesboro. Hardee on the right presumably guarded the passes through which Thomas had to transit to contact the right wing of the Confederate army. If properly fortified, the Confederates could have held the passes indefinitely.

Rosecrans correctly predicated his plans on the assumption that Hardee would not expect an attack, because Hardee's brigades were not in the passes, where they should have been. Instead they camped in the open countryside, believing that the Federal army, slow moving and burdened as always with trains, could not come their way. The roads were muddy ruts, the country barren, the gaps nearly impassable. Continual rain made an attack seem even less likely.

If, nevertheless, a Federal army did come his way, Hardee still expected that the Confederate cavalry would alert him as before. But Bragg had frittered away half of his cavalry arm in distant raids and reassignments. Brigadier General Joseph Wheeler commanded the remnants. When Rosecrans demonstrated on the Confederate left wing, Wheeler moved his cavalry there, uncovering the passes in front of Hardee.

The easternmost pass was called Hoover's Gap, several miles long and so narrow and precipitous that wagons and batteries could barely squeeze along the trail. Thomas's entire corps had to get through. To avoid detection, Thomas stopped the lead division, led by Joseph J. Reynolds, six miles short of the entrance to the gap, then released Wilder's mounted infantry brigade, which thundered off and disappeared into the rain. Reynolds resumed his march, stopping again some three miles from the gap to await developments.

Thomas joined Reynolds, spoke briefly, and then sat under a tree and whittled. He heard gunfire. Still he waited. A mud-covered officer from Wilder's staff rode up to report the gap had been so lightly defended that the enemy had fled when Wilder's troopers galloped through. From the summit Wilder had seen the Confederate encampment below, and he had decided to stay and hold on. The Spencers had demolished the Confederate counterattack. Wilder still held, Thomas ordered Reynolds to advance to reinforce Wilder, and the gap was breached. Rosecrans beamed at Wilder's achievement. The mounted midwesterners became known evermore as Wilder's Lightning Brigade.

When Bragg learned that Thomas's corps had turned the Confederate right flank and threatened the rear of his army, he decided to evacuate Tennessee. His army first retreated to Tullahoma, then took trains to Chattanooga. Thomas tried to get to Tullahoma first, but mud and incessant rain impeded him. When he got to Tullahoma, he heard the trains leaving.

Rosecrans's nine-day campaign had flushed the Confederate Army of Tennessee from the state with scarcely more than five hundred Federal casualties. Considering the ferocity of the Confederate soldiers at Murfreesboro six months before, Rosecrans undoubtedly was amazed that the enemy had fled this time around. He considered the outcome a triumph of strategy and execution, a near perfect application of power and maneuver that had won territory without a fight.

Territory, however, had become a secondary objective in the war. Rosecrans's original intention had been decisive battle with Bragg, and in that respect he had failed. As Bragg's army had escaped unbroken, Stanton and Halleck withheld congratulations. "I beg on behalf of this army," wired a miffed Rosecrans, "that the War Department may not overlook so great an event because it is not written in letters of blood."

On July 4, 1863, the day that Grant accepted the surrender at Vicksburg and Meade defeated Lee at Gettysburg, Rosecrans ended his pursuit of Bragg. Before him lay terrain so hostile to the passage of an army that it could have been conceived by the devil himself. Mountains covered his entire front, with river valleys that were narrow and steep. Trails and footpaths were barely wide enough for wagons or too fragile to withstand the pounding of a passing army. If it got through the mountains, the Federal army would have to cross the Tennessee, a river of sheer banks and swift currents, its bridges and ferries destroyed. And if Rosecrans got across the Tennessee, more mountains awaited him on the other side.

Foraging in such country was nearly out of the question. Subsistence farmers scratched out a living on tiny fields in the valleys. At best Rosecrans could anticipate a limited supply of corn for animal forage. The rest of his supplies had to come from his depots. Thomas was a master at logistical planning, and he knew that the daily needs of the Army of the Cumberland were measured in tons. Because of his splendid maps he was familiar with the roads, bridges, and fords in his theater and could calculate with precision what could be moved by wagons. The rudeness of the roads limited their capacity. Railroads would have to carry the load.

When we consider these circumstances, we begin to understand why railroads dominated military strategy in the west. Armies followed rail lines as surely as water follows a riverbed. Both the Federal and Confederate armies depended upon them, the Federal armies perhaps to a somewhat greater extent. A corollary to railroads was the need to accumulate supplies at depots on the rail lines, primarily at cities and towns. Every prudent army commander predicated his operations on having one or more depots in his rear and a rail line connecting his army to them. Thus we may state a military theorem of the war in the west: wherever a major battle was fought, there was either a railroad, or a river that served the same purpose, or both.

This fact was understood by the western generals. It was not understood by Lincoln or Stanton, who never visited the western theater and were conditioned by the likes of McClellan to regard logistical requirements as an excuse not to fight. Halleck was duplicitous. During the Corinth campaign, for example, he had been the slowest and most cautious of generals, but from his perch in Washington he was unrestrained in prodding the western commanders.

Rosecrans's situation in Tennessee during July and August was a case in point. After chasing Bragg from the state in late June, Rosecrans stopped and positioned his army across a sixty-mile front connected by rail lines, from Fayetteville in the west, through Decherd and Tullahoma, to McMinnville to the east. These would be the depots for his ultimate advance to the Tennessee River, Chattanooga, and beyond. To accumulate supplies at these places, Rosecrans had to mend bridges and restore the rail lines all the way to the river. A Michigan pioneer brigade of a thousand men labored mightily while Halleck and Rosecrans exchanged their customary angry messages about resuming the march to the Tennessee.

Halleck issued uncharacteristically unequivocal orders to Rosecrans on August 4 to move forward and do battle and to send daily progress reports. Rosecrans was nearly ready; most of the trains were running and making deliveries. Rosecrans polled his generals to confirm they had adequate supplies. Thomas replied he had five days of forage and eight days of provisions, and he gave Rosecrans a thumbs-up. Crittenden and McCook reported that they too were primed.

Thanks to the maps prepared by Thomas's topographical engineers, updated with last-minute information from cavalry patrols, Rosecrans and his generals had studied the roads leading to the river, knew their capacities and limitations, and knew where they could find water and forage. Rosecrans incorporated this comprehensive data into a detailed marching order, and his army confidently got underway for the distant river on August 16. Rosecrans assumed that Bragg had not stationed troops north of the Tennessee River, but crossing the river was inherently dangerous if Bragg had the prescience to oppose it from the opposite shore. The best way to keep Bragg away, reasoned Rosecrans, was to confuse him with diversions.

Again Rosecrans called upon Wilder's Lightning Brigade, which cantered to the western shore of the Tennessee River across from Chattanooga. It was August 21, a day that Davis had proclaimed be set aside for fasting and prayer. D. H. Hill took the proclamation seriously. When Lee had banished Hill to the backwaters of the war, his career seemed over. Then the July disasters at Gettysburg and Vicksburg, together with Bragg's abandonment of Tennessee, had rocked the Confederate government. With calamity came opportunity. A panicky Davis had suddenly offered Hill a corps command in Bragg's army, to replace Hardee, together with a promotion to lieutenant general. Hill was reborn.

Now Hill was in Chattanooga, trying to size up Bragg and to learn his way around the Army of Tennessee, so different from the Army of Northern Virginia. One of Hill's first orders was a call to prayer on the twenty-first:

> *Upon that solemn day which we are about to dedicate to God and our country, let each patriot mourn the sins which have brought disaster upon us. Let us renew the pure vows of constancy and devotion with which he drew his sword, and the issue may be safely confided to the trial of arms. With hearts thus chastened the defenders of Christian homes, of civil and religious liberty, of all that is beautiful and pure, and of good report, may fitly invoke the God of Battles, the God of Truth and Justice. . . .*
>
> *It is therefore ordered that all military exercises and all work not absolutely necessary be suspended on Friday, the 21st instant, and that every encouragement be offered to the troops to attend divine service, and to humble themselves in prayer and supplication to the almighty Ruler of the Universe, that He would succor our beloved country and defeat the machinations of our enemies.*

As Wilder's brigade unlimbered its artillery, Confederate generals and Chattanooga's civilians gathered in the local Presbyterian church to hear a visiting preacher equate God's will with Confederate aspirations. Exploding projectiles rapidly cleared the pews. Wilder and Hazen ranged along the riverbanks above Chattanooga for the next several days, demonstrating like an army corps about to assault. As the Confederates sent forces upriver, Rosecrans and his army crossed downriver, not without difficulty, but without one shot being fired at them. Undisturbed by Confederate resistance, the Army of the Cumberland took ten days to prepare and another week to cross the wide, swift Tennessee, using anything that would float.

Once across the river, Thomas's corps scaled Sand Mountain on narrow roads so steep that the teams were doubled and soldiers had to push. Then came Lookout Mountain, and again animals and men strained to get up and over it. At the summit Thomas could see Chattanooga twenty miles to the north, and twenty-five miles ahead of him lay the Western and Atlanta Railroad, Bragg's only line of escape to the south.

With Thomas nearly astride his line of communications, Bragg abandoned Chattanooga. Rosecrans and Thomas had cleared the entire rebel army from Tennessee by maneuver alone (albeit strenuous swimming and mountain climbing), with scarcely more than isolated skirmishes. The Army of Tennessee, however, was still intact and, with arriving reinforcements, was growing progressively more potent.

The loss of Chattanooga without a fight concluded a summer of horrors for Davis. July had been the worst month of the war: Confederate armies had fled from Tennessee and crumpled at Vicksburg and Gettysburg. Davis solicited Lee's counsel in a letter of July 28. "I have felt more than ever before," he wrote, "the want of your advice during the recent period of disaster." Chastened, perhaps, that he had contributed in large measure to the disaster, Lee had nothing to say. Then, on August 24, three days after

Wilder's bombardment of Chattanooga, Davis asked Lee to come to Richmond "to consult with you on military questions of a general nature."

When Lee met with Davis, the "general" questions quickly became specific, for events in Tennessee had taken precedence over the war in Virginia. Where and whether and when Bragg would fight was the issue. Davis wanted to send part of Lee's army to Chattanooga and Lee himself to relieve Bragg. But Lee's vision and span of interest did not extend beyond the borders of his own state. He resisted any reduction in his army and argued that resources—men, matériel, food, and forage—should be sent his way so that he could resume operations against the Army of the Potomac.

Lee wanted to return to his headquarters, but Davis, trying to wear him down, insisted that he remain in the capital. It was misery for Lee. "I have been suffering ever since my last visit to Richmond," he wrote Mary on September 4, "from a heavy cold taken in the hot & badly ventilated rooms in the various departments which resulted in an attack of rheumatism in my back, which has given me great pain & anxiety, for if I cannot get relief I do not see what is to become of me."

The unfolding crisis intensified as Rosecrans crossed the Tennessee and closed in on Chattanooga. The loss of Knoxville to Burnside on September 2 made it imperative that Davis act. Although Lee still objected, Davis decreed that a corps be shipped west. As Lee would not leave Virginia, command of the expedition fell to Longstreet.

Longstreet was delighted, because he had been lobbying for weeks to be sent west. His corps, Hood's division among them, withdrew from the front lines and assembled in Richmond. Hood had been recuperating in the city, and, as he welcomed his comrades, they saw that his arm was still in a sling, torn and useless from his wound at Gettysburg. Nonetheless Hood stood tall, talking with his officers and men about past battles and chuckling in remembrance of escapades. His soldiers realized how much they missed him and wanted him now. Hood's eyes glistened as they spoke excitedly about their mission to Tennessee. When the Knight-Errant impulsively said that he wanted to go with them, they cheered, and a delegation went to Longstreet and got his permission.

Hood packed his bag and climbed aboard one of the makeshift troop trains with its whooping soldiers. By the time the first train had gotten underway on September 9, Bragg had abandoned Chattanooga, but there was no change in plans. Longstreet, Hood, and their troops would join Bragg wherever he might be found.

When Bragg abandoned Chattanooga, Rosecrans assumed that the Confederates were retreating to points south. Twice before, at Murfreesboro and Tuscumbia, Bragg had left the field, and Rosecrans had let him go. This time Rosecrans decided to pursue, but he first wanted to talk to Thomas. Rosecrans summoned him to his headquarters before dawn on the ninth.

Rosecrans was an insomniac. Whether he thought clearly without sleep was questionable. What was unusual in this instance was that his decision had been impulsive. Normally he sought consensus by talking for hours at nighttime councils of war. Thomas often slept through the meetings. Now Rosecrans wanted to talk only to Thomas, not to ask advice but to announce his decision.

Rosecrans, smarting from complaints that he had dragged his feet, now wanted to demonstrate his aggressiveness. Lacking hard intelligence, he made himself believe that Bragg's forces were strung out for seventy miles on the railroad line to Rome, Georgia. His plan was to cut them off. Crittenden would push Bragg down the road from Chattanooga, while Thomas and McCook swooped down from Lookout Mountain and dashed eastward twenty or thirty miles across the flatlands to intercept Bragg's army on the railroad. Speed was essential, Rosecrans emphasized, in order to snag the bulk of Bragg's army before it got away.

Rosecrans's rashness appalled Thomas. Three Federal corps—those of Thomas, McCook, and Crittenden—were scattered along a forty-mile front, separated by miles of wilderness. If Bragg kept his army intact and was not retreating, he could pick off any one of them. Thomas implored Rosecrans not to assume that Bragg was hightailing it down the railroad. Be prudent, said Thomas, and consolidate in Chattanooga before resuming the offensive. But Rosecrans was adamant. He issued the marching orders that Thomas dreaded.

Thomas's apprehensions were well founded. Bragg had known Rosecrans's intentions since September 5, thanks to a copy of the *Chicago Times* that had come to Bragg's attention. The paper contained a revealing article written by a correspondent at Rosecrans's headquarters who was indifferent to security. Nonetheless, Bragg dithered for the next four days, marching his troops aimlessly to and fro. He finally felt certain on September 9 that he knew when and where Thomas's corps would debouch from the mountains, and he ordered an ambush for the next day. Thomas smelled a trap and withdrew his lead division, provoking a scolding from Rosecrans for delaying the "pursuit."

Thomas escaped the ambush because Bragg's generals would not obey his confounding orders. Taking advantage of the delay, Thomas's division commanders skillfully withdrew to the safety of the heights. Still striving to strike Rosecrans before he could reassemble his corps, Bragg ordered Polk to attack Crittenden, isolated and vulnerable near Chattanooga to the north. In keeping with the spirit of the campaign, Polk refused to obey Bragg's orders, and Crittenden was delivered from peril. The gift of Confederate bickering had spared Rosecrans from his folly.

Thomas's reports of foreboding developments staggered Rosecrans in his Chattanooga headquarters. The Confederate army was not retreating, but lurking, looking for a fight, somewhere near Thomas, and Rosecrans issued immediate rendezvous orders, praying that he could reassemble before Bragg jumped someone who was still isolated. Rosecrans wired Halleck on the twelfth that, while he felt he had enough troops to handle Bragg, he was worried about his communications in the rear. He requested that Burnside come down from Knoxville to cover his left flank, and that Grant send troops from Mississippi to protect his right.

Halleck, who had the responsibility to coordinate the strategic deployment of the Federal armies, suffered from the handicap that he could not plan ahead. Thus, once the action started in one theater, he would demand that other commanders send reinforcements at short notice. The other commanders, not knowing what was going on, were naturally reluctant to disperse their own forces, especially as they had such low regard for Halleck.

Such was the situation now. With a decisive battle imminent, Halleck's frantic efforts to move troops were too late. A message to Grant in Mississippi was delayed and not delivered until after the Battle of Chickamauga. And despite Halleck's emphatic orders to Burnside to unite with Rosecrans, he stayed in Knoxville. Rosecrans was on his own.

Bragg, on the other hand, had got reinforcements. Halleck was in the dark as to their origin. He had some indication that Buckner had reported in from East Tennessee and that two divisions had arrived from Mississippi. Later, he would discover that some of the Confederate prisoners paroled at Vicksburg had been sent to Bragg without being exchanged. But Halleck was ignorant of events a day's ride from Washington. He did not know that an entire corps of Lee's army had disappeared from the Virginia front and had gone to Chattanooga.

2 2

THE ROCK OF
CHICKAMAUGA

*He held his army in his hand, keeping it, with unmitigated labor,
always in a fit state to march or to fight. . . . Sometimes he was
indebted to fortune, sometimes to his natural genius, always to his
untiring industry; for he was emphatically a painstaking man.*
Sir William Napier on Wellington

The two armies groped and scrambled south of Chattanooga for nearly a week. The terrain so concealed large bodies of troops that the generals were blinded. Cavalry scouting on both sides was poorly handled and produced little hard intelligence. Anxious staffs were reduced to acting on the suspicious tales of deserters and civilians or to speculating on clouds of dust rising above the forest canopy. Eventually the armies would happen onto each other, but under conditions beyond the control of either Rosecrans or Bragg.

Confounded by the hostility and inertia of his generals, Bragg suspended his attempts to attack long enough for a shaken Rosecrans finally to pull his army together. By the evening of September 17 the army was in line on the west bank of Chickamauga Creek, Thomas Crittenden on the left wing nearest to Chattanooga, Thomas in the center, and Alexander McCook on the right.

The initiative belonged to Bragg, although he was unsure what to do with it. Eventually he settled on a concept that would thrust his army against the Federal left wing and isolate Rosecrans from his base in Chattanooga. His subsequent orders contradicted these intentions, however. Bragg made his right wing—the juggernaut of his plan—the weakest segment of his army.

On September 18, troops unfamiliar with the terrain and uncertain as to their purpose groped their way through dense woods. Bragg fumed at their flagging progress. When Hood arrived that afternoon from Virginia, Bragg told him to expedite matters. Aggressive as always, although entirely ignorant of the terrain and troop locations, Hood crossed Chickamauga Creek to

261

the west bank seeking contact with the enemy. Wilder's pickets reported a Confederate general with his arm in a sling leading a column of infantry down the road in their rear. Seizing the moment, Wilder galloped his brigade up the creek bank to get ahead. Hood blundered into Wilder's trap just at dusk. "They attacked us at dark with cheers," Wilder advised Rosecrans, "but were held in check."

For all intents lost in a wilderness, Hood ordered his troops to dig in for the night. Sounds of movement in the darkness were ominous, convincing the Confederate soldiers that they were alone on the west bank among the entire Federal army. Hood's troops discovered at sunrise on the nineteenth that they were surrounded by their brethren, who had crossed the creek during the night. The crossings had been haphazard, and no one from Bragg's staff had aligned the brigades for morning battle. The generals and their staffs and their soldiers brewed coffee and fried bacon, waiting for someone to tell them what to do.

A long column of Federal troops marched northward on a road that paralleled the creek a mile and a half to the west. It was Thomas's corps, closing up in response to Rosecrans's frantic summons. Thomas and his soldiers were exhausted, for they had been on the road for almost twenty-four hours. The forest between the creek and the road masked the columns from the Confederates fixing breakfast and awaiting orders. Thomas was left undisturbed to begin building the left wing and connecting with Crittenden to form an unbroken front.

A brigade commander reported to Thomas that a Confederate brigade (it was Hood) had crossed the Chickamauga the afternoon before and headed upstream. It was easy pickings, and he urged Thomas to bag it. Thomas peered toward the creek, saw nothing, and dispatched a division to reconnoiter. The soldiers disappeared into the trees.

Forrest and a single cavalry brigade had been bedded down near the creek. Shortly after sunrise, Forrest saddled up and plodded along a road to find the enemy. Sometime after seven o'clock he collided with a brigade commanded by Colonel John T. Croxton, one of those Thomas had sent forward.

Thomas had kicked off the Battle of Chickamauga.

The crackling of the guns of Croxton and Forrest created a spontaneous combustion, and the generals fed the fire. Thomas was at breakfast when he heard the gunfire. As he would need the food to sustain himself for the long day ahead, he finished eating before going forward to see what Croxton had gotten into. When he realized that the Confederates were ahead of him in force, Thomas ordered another division forward.

Hood and General William H. T. Walker, too, had been at breakfast, waiting for orders from Bragg. The sound of gunfire startled them. Walker hurried off to find his corps under heavy attack by Thomas's troops. Hood uncharacteristically stayed out of the action (perhaps because he was under Bragg for the first time and was unsure how to proceed), allowing Thomas to hammer Walker and Forrest a stone's throw away. As the day wore on,

Bragg bestirred himself to reinforce Walker with two more divisions, but he left the remainder of his army adrift. Unable to restrain his impatience further, Hood got underway on his own by midafternoon.

Thomas had meanwhile been reinforced. By midday he controlled five divisions on the left wing, fully half of Rosecrans's army on the Chickamauga, against some eight Confederate divisions. Thomas was at his best, confident that he could wear down the enemy and ultimately beat them. The line of battle had become a series of pulsating salients shaped by attacks and withdrawals. When Hood, now in action on his own initiative, threatened to exploit a break in the line on Thomas's right flank, Thomas shifted a division from the far left to his right to contain Hood's attack.

The fighting continued into the night. The groans and cries of the wounded resonated along the line. As Thomas worked with his generals to adjust their lines—for the battle was sure to resume in the morning—he received a summons from Rosecrans to another midnight council.

When Thomas got to Rosecrans's headquarters, he learned that the entire army had been engaged throughout the day. Wherever Bragg had thrown forces piecemeal into line, Rosecrans had countered. The telegraph system seemed to have worked well, allowing Rosecrans to stay in close touch with his generals and with his base in Chattanooga. Dana was there as well, reporting on events as he had earlier in the year with Grant in Mississippi. Thanks to the telegraph, Dana had sent reports directly to Washington throughout the day. Now he watched and listened as Rosecrans spoke with his generals, perhaps a dozen or more. Where were their lines, what was the condition of their troops, what did they think should be done in the morning?

Confederate soldiers taken prisoner, they had discovered, had come from Lee's army in Virginia, from Johnston's army in Mississippi, and from Buckner's forces in East Tennessee. Thus Bragg had been reinforced, while nothing had arrived either from Burnside or from Grant. Reasoning that he was outnumbered, Rosecrans intended to defend himself on the morrow and had no incentive to attack.

Thomas presumed that the main attack would come at his sector—the Federal left. That was the direction of Chattanooga, and Bragg surely would try to get between Rosecrans and his base. "I would strengthen the left," said Thomas, dozing in his chair, for he had been without sleep for more than thirty-six hours. When wakened by Rosecrans, he repeated his recommendation, then nodded and closed his eyes. "Where are we going to take them from?" Rosecrans asked lamely.

Ultimately Rosecrans decided that Thomas would hold what he had with the five divisions under his immediate command, McCook would close up on Thomas, and Crittenden, with two divisions, would stay in immediate reserve. Gordon Granger with the Reserve Corps would stay several miles to the north of Thomas, on the road from Chattanooga.

Before the meeting adjourned, Rosecrans eased the tension by ordering in food and coffee. Turning to McCook, Rosecrans asked him for a song. As McCook sang a familiar ballad, the others slumped in their chairs, alone with their thoughts. The weary generals stumbled back to their headquarters around midnight. Thomas ordered his division commanders to construct such breastworks as they could, then fell into a deep sleep.

Longstreet had arrived at the train station at Catoosa Platform on the afternoon of the nineteenth, some seven miles from the battlefield. He and his staff were miffed that Bragg had not sent a staff officer to meet them. Wandering along strange roads and the backwash of the rear of an army, Longstreet stumbled into Federal pickets and barely escaped. When he found Bragg sleeping in his tent, it was nearly midnight.

Longstreet and Bragg spoke for about an hour. Bragg had reorganized the army into two wings. Polk would command the right and Longstreet the left. At dawn they would attack en echelon, starting with the right wing at the north end and rippling southward down the line, the preferred Confederate tactic that so rarely could be executed. While Longstreet had been so baffled by the strange countryside that he had taken eight hours to find Bragg's headquarters, at daybreak nonetheless he was to command half of Bragg's army in a battle over terrain he had never seen. The subordinate generals and their staffs were largely strangers to Longstreet (Hood was an exception), and their locations were guesswork. Not one general that night could have described the chain of command that Bragg had cobbled together, nor explained his plan of attack for the morning.

Because Bragg had trusted Polk and Longstreet to explain the plan to the subordinate commanders, it remained a mystery. (Unlike Rosecrans, who had convened a well-attended council of war, Bragg had spoken solely to Longstreet and Polk individually.) Longstreet, however, went to sleep shortly after talking with Bragg. Not until well after daybreak did people finally discover that Longstreet was in command and what he expected of them. What Polk said and did that night is conjecture, but the upshot was that D. H. Hill, the right-wing corps commander, was unaware that Bragg expected him to attack at dawn.* When Polk castigated Hill for not attacking, Hill was outraged. After the rumpus subsided, Hill's assault against Thomas's left flank began, four hours late.

Events on the Federal side were somewhat more orderly. Thomas inspected his left flank at dawn and saw Confederate skirmishers extending beyond his picket line. Assuming that a battle force was behind them (actually Breckinridge's division, waiting for someone to send them forward), Thomas realized that he was about to be outflanked and got reinforcements. Ultimately Breckinridge's division attacked and went down under Thomas's firepower. A Federal counterattack flushed the survivors. Breckinridge's division had shot its bolt.

The remainder of the Confederate right wing threw itself against Thomas's defenders, who were concentrated in an area known as Kelly Field.

---

* Dawn was at 5:47 A.M.

Barraged with Thomas's repeated requests, Rosecrans sent reinforcements from right to left by dictating a welter of messages. Chief of staff James A. Garfield (a future president of the United States) normally transcribed them in a format beginning with the phrase "The commanding general directs. . . ." If Rosecrans's intentions were hazy in the heat of battle, Garfield clarified them as he wrote. And if Rosecrans was about to do something inadvisable, Garfield would speak up.

The quantity of messages had so saturated Garfield by midmorning that he pressed an aide-de-camp, Major Frank S. Bond, into service. Unaccustomed to interpreting Rosecrans's agitated instructions, Bond was too intimidated to challenge their wisdom. The period after 10:30 A.M. was particularly hectic. Rosecrans had set his right wing in motion to the north, toward Thomas, and Garfield was absorbed in writing the necessary orders. It was then that a disoriented Rosecrans committed the act of folly that nearly lost his army.

The catastrophe began with a garbled report. Rosecrans was given to believe that Brannan had pulled out of line to reinforce Thomas and had uncovered Reynolds's flank.* Brannan's division was actually where it belonged, alongside Reynolds, who was not endangered. Nonetheless, Rosecrans impulsively decided that Thomas J. Wood—commanding a division on Brannan's immediate right—had to close up on Reynolds.

Bond prepared the message at about 10:45 A.M. as Rosecrans dictated. "The commanding general directs," he scribbled, "that you close up on Reynolds as fast as possible, and support him." Rosecrans handed the written order to Crittenden's chief of staff, Lieutenant Colonel Lynn Starling, to deliver on the gallop to Wood. Starling was puzzled. "There was no firing," he later said, "and no evident need of support for any one, and I hesitated, not understanding the object of the order." Garfield explained that the object was for Wood to occupy the vacancy left when Brannan had withdrawn to reinforce Thomas.

Starling promptly delivered the order to Wood, some six hundred yards away. When Wood said that Brannan was still alongside Reynolds, Starling responded that Wood should properly disregard the order. Starling immediately returned to Rosecrans, told him what Wood had said, and added "that General Wood had a nice little breastwork in his front and ought not to be moved, as the enemy were in the very act of attacking him, and had driven in his pickets while I was there." Rosecrans could reasonably believe that Starling's initiative had saved him from a fatal error.

Wood, however, then betrayed Rosecrans in an act of insane vindictiveness. Hating Rosecrans because of earlier reprimands, he wanted revenge. Carefully retaining Rosecrans's message as evidence, Wood ordered his brigade commanders to withdraw from their fortifications, just as

---

* Generals James S. Negley, John M. Brannan, Absalom Baird, and John F. Reynolds commanded the divisions of Thomas's corps.

Longstreet's columns began their attack directly at Wood's abandoned position. If Wood had been wearing a Confederate uniform, he could not have brought a greater disaster upon the Army of the Cumberland.

Hood commanded 11,000 Confederate soldiers assembled six hundred yards south of the breastworks that Wood had constructed and now was leaving. They were in dense woods, some eight brigades—three divisions—in a deep, narrow column like a battering ram. As Bragg wanted the attack to kick off at dawn, Longstreet had left the frontline divisions where he found them. Having given Hood overall command of the strike force, Longstreet waited for something to happen on the right, unaware that Polk and Hill, arguing violently, had delayed opening the assault.

At about ten o'clock Hood and Longstreet finally heard the sound of battle to their right, under normal conditions the signal to join the assault en echelon. But as they were strangers to Bragg's idiosyncratic style of command, neither general was bold enough to begin his phase of the assault without confirmation from higher authority. Becoming increasingly nervous, Longstreet himself sent a message to Bragg urging him to release the left wing, unaware that Bragg expected him to do so independently. At about eleven o'clock Longstreet heard the sound of movement along his own front. Having finally gotten Hill in motion, Bragg had bypassed Longstreet and had sent a staff officer with attack orders to the individual left-wing division commanders. Longstreet was aghast. Bragg's flagrant violation of his own chain of command worsened the disorder along the Confederate front.

Hood's troops emerged from the darkened woods and into the Sunday morning sunlight of the fields. Expecting gunfire, they were amazed to see the disappearing backs of Wood's soldiers. Ambrose Bierce had gone to the rear to get ammunition for Hazen, whose brigade was near the point of attack. He climbed a ridge and looked back. "[T]o my astonishment," he later wrote, "I saw the entire country in front swarming with Confederates; the very earth seemed to be moving toward us! They came on in thousands, and so rapidly that we had barely time to turn tail and gallop down the hill and away, leaving them in possession of the train, many of the wagons being upset by frantic efforts to put them about."

Some of the Federal troops made a stand and took Confederate attackers with them. Most, like Bierce, fled the screaming onrush. Horrified, Rosecrans watched the tumult from a hill as bullets toppled his staff. Frightened soldiers trampled the more disciplined regiments trying to contain the rout. The irresistible flood swept the generals with it. Rosecrans, Crittenden, McCook, Negley, Jefferson C. Davis, and Philip Sheridan had but one thought, to get to the safety of Chattanooga. Dana was delirious, and his messages from Chattanooga to Washington reflected his hysteria.

Thomas's indomitable provost marshal, Colonel John Parkhurst, was as usual attending to the rear. "About 1 o'clock a large body of troops, several batteries, and transportation wagons came rushing through the woods and over the road in the utmost confusion," he later reported. "I formed a line of battle across the line with fixed bayonets, and with much difficulty succeeded in checking the stampede."

Parkhurst had collected enough men to make a stand when Crittenden and his staff came down the road. "I immediately rode up to him," Parkhurst reported, "and respectfully asked him to stop and take command of the forces I was collecting and had then collected, and place them in a position to resist an attack or take them back to the battle-field, which I then supposed and now believe could have been successfully accomplished." But Crittenden continued to the rear. Eventually the provost marshal found generals willing to take command of his regiment of refugees.

Entirely occupied in holding the left wing intact, Thomas was for a long period entirely unaware of the disaster on his right. Having succumbed to panic, the generals fleeing from Hood made little effort to join Thomas. "I met General Negley," wrote Bierce, who recovered from his fright, "and my duties as topographical engineer having given me some knowledge of the lay of the land offered to pilot him back to glory or the grave. I am sorry to say my good offices were rejected a little uncivilly, which I charitably attributed to the general's obvious absence of mind. His mind, I think, was in Nashville, behind a breastwork."

When Negley disappeared he took along Thomas's artillery corps, some forty-eight pieces, plus several brigades of infantry that had been guarding the Dry Valley Road, which led to the rear of Thomas's position and ultimately to Chattanooga. No one knew why Negley had left or where he was going. As Thomas confronted the entire Confederate force, he would be without the artillery he had used so well in earlier battles.

Thomas still did not know that Hood had crushed the Federal right, and he remained absorbed with the battle immediately before him. He still expected reinforcements, especially Negley and Sheridan, but none came. Thomas dispatched an aide, Captain Sanford C. Kellogg, to find Sheridan. To his surprise, Wood came to his command post at about 11:30 A.M.

Without asking why Wood was there, Thomas pointed north. Send a brigade to reinforce Baird, he said, who was still trying to hold the left flank. Gladly, replied Wood, except that Rosecrans had ordered him to reinforce Reynolds. Thomas stared at him uncomprehendingly. "General Thomas," said Wood, still punctilious to the point of absurdity, "if you will take responsibility for changing my orders, I will gladly obey whatever you ask of me." Consider them changed, Thomas replied. Wood hustled off to accelerate his division's movement away from Hood's murderous assault.

By noon the thunder on the right transcended even the clangor of his own battlefield. Thomas rode south to investigate and met Kellogg hustling back toward him. Instead of finding Sheridan, he reported, he had come upon a large force of soldiers in a cornfield to the rear of Reynolds. Skirmishers had fired on him, and Kellogg had turned tail to report back to Thomas. The skirmishers were wearing blue uniforms, said Kellogg. Perhaps they were Federal soldiers and had fired by mistake.

Thomas went to the nearest brigade, commanded by Colonel Charles G. Harker of Wood's division. Together they peered at advancing troops, trying to identify them. Thomas told Harker that he was expecting Sheridan's troops from that direction. Something was terribly wrong. "I don't know who they are, but if those troops fire at you after seeing your flag," Thomas told Harker, "you must return their fire and resist their advance."

Harker was in a quandary. He did not want to fire upon Federal troops, but if they were enemy, he was losing time by not shooting at them. Harker went forward for a closer look. The advancing troops fired at him; he could see their Confederate colors. As the guns roared, Harker returned to his command.

The strange soldiers in blue were the Texas Brigade of Hood's division, commanded by Brigadier General Jerome B. "Polly" Robertson. (After Gettysburg the Confederate government had issued Lee's army new blue uniforms, indistinguishable from Federal uniforms.) Hood had wheeled his three brigades toward Thomas, but his grip on them was shaky. Each brigade commander was on his own in the melee. Robertson was out of touch with the other brigades when Harker's soldiers opened fire. In the smoke and excitement Confederate troops mistook Robertson's blue uniforms and poured in fire from the flanks and rear. It was too much for the Texans, who broke and scrambled for cover.

When Hood saw the brigade—his first command—scatter, he tried to rally it. Robertson saw Hood and rode toward him. Just then a bullet—possibly from a Confederate rifle—struck Hood in the upper leg. As he toppled from his horse, soldiers caught him and eased him to the ground. At the field hospital a surgeon amputated the leg at the thigh.

Hood's division collapsed with him. Federal fire so ravaged his three brigades that they were out of the fight for the remainder of the day. Nonetheless, Longstreet had committed his entire wing. Where Hood's men faltered, fresh brigades irresistibly surged forward.

The impact of the impending catastrophe could have staggered Thomas. His mind had been focused on his left flank and center. He had once believed that to be the danger point. That was where he had sent every reinforcement he could find. He thought that the Federal right was secure.

Suddenly Thomas realized that he had been dreadfully wrong. The Confederate army had such numbers that it could assail the *entire* Federal line from north to south, left to right. His persistent calls for reinforcements had unintentionally weakened the Federal right. Instead of a Federal line of entrenchments with hospitals and ammunition trains and artillery limbers, he saw before him a huge, sprawling mass of Confederate soldiers that had come from God knew where. The two Federal corps under McCook and Crittenden had vanished. Rosecrans had disappeared. Only a few scratch brigades of Federal soldiers scrambling for position stood before the enemy host.

Thomas's fatigue-numbed mind confronted this frightening new reality. He would have to fight, to hold on until darkness, and then withdraw. He had to stay fixed as long as there was light to see. Thomas could not possibly retreat. The Confederates would smell blood if they saw the Federal soldiers backing away. Any attempt at an orderly daylight withdrawal would collapse into a rout and total destruction. Thomas and the remaining pieces of the Army of the Cumberland had to survive the afternoon. Survival would depend on some things that Thomas could control and on some that he could not.

Thomas could control his behavior. If he kept his head and remained collected, poised, he would steady his soldiers. His strength would be their strength, and his courage would reinforce their own. They would suppress their instinct to run from the terror that had carried away the rest of the army.

Thomas's military intuition was to hold the high ground. A series of hills and ridges near the Snodgrass farm seemed best for defense; that was where he would position such troops as he had. Some already were there, stout officers like Brannan, Hazen, and John Beatty. Harker fell back with them, as did his division commander Wood, who hoped to redeem himself. Thomas joined them and established his command post near the Snodgrass cabin. His presence was reassuring. He quietly spoke to his commanding officers. Here, he told them, they must hold.

Beyond that was the uncontrollable. Thomas could not dictate what the Confederate generals did. He had to hope they would make mistakes that would help him. And so they did.

Bragg removed himself from the picture altogether. An officer recalled his appearance as Longstreet's legions rolled forward. "Our division, in advancing," he wrote, "passes the spot where Gen. Bragg is seated upon his horse on the Chattanooga road. He looks pale and careworn, his features rendered more haggard by a white Havelock he wears over his cap and neck."

Polk helped Thomas to survive by omission. His right wing had so spent itself against Thomas in the morning that his divisions had retired. Instead of renewing their attacks to support Longstreet, they remained quiescent throughout most of the afternoon.

That left Longstreet, who had to sort out the strategic alternatives that would determine whether or not Thomas pulled through. The opportunity lay before Longstreet to bypass Snodgrass Ridge, drive up the roads behind Thomas, and sever his communications with Chattanooga. This would deprive Thomas both of ammunition (already critically short because the ammunition train had skedaddled) and of the means to escape and rejoin the troops that had fled to Chattanooga. Longstreet could then crush Thomas at his leisure.

Instead, Longstreet chose, almost by default, to attack frontally at Snodgrass Ridge. He had some seventeen brigades—20,000 or so men—under his immediate command to throw against Thomas's five thousand.

Longstreet fancied himself an army commander, and Bragg's passivity provided him the opportunity to function in that capacity. It was Thomas's luck that Longstreet on that afternoon failed to measure up. With Hood gone, the chain of command, tenuous in any event, approached anarchy.

Generals compared dates of rank to determine seniority and then negotiated whether to cooperate. Longstreet was not among them to sort things out. Wheeler's cavalry could have pursued the troops and trains streaming to the rear, and Forrest could have done the same from the north. Neither Longstreet nor Polk had the presence to issue such orders, and the cavalry were largely spectators. Wasted effort and lost opportunities were inevitable.

Longstreet remained serene, taking lunch with Buckner while the midafternoon fighting roared ahead of them. After asking for tobacco from a passing artillery officer and lighting his pipe, he seemed open to discussion. Was the enemy beaten? asked the officer. "Yes," Longstreet said, "all along his line; a few are holding out upon the ridge up yonder, not many though. If we had our Virginia army here, we would have whipped them in half the time." Longstreet offered the officer some of the captured artillery. "You can have as many as you want," he said. The officer said he would be happy to have them, but would Longstreet kindly put it in writing? Longstreet laughed.

When Thomas had not cracked by midafternoon, Longstreet asked Bragg to employ Polk's idle right wing. Polk's troops were useless, Bragg said bitterly, because Thomas had so thoroughly whipped them in the morning. Although he had unengaged reserves, Bragg would not release the remaining troops, or he forgot that he had them. Dejected, out of touch, and unable to grasp developments, Bragg withdrew himself from the battle as surely as had Rosecrans.

Still, it was a matter of time until the weight of numbers would favor Longstreet, who maintained sufficient control to send repeated waves of assault troops against the Federal bulwarks. Thomas grimaced through the smoke at the sun hovering in the afternoon sky, near despair at the odds of survival until nightfall. "The battle was fierce and continuous," wrote Bierce, who stood alongside Thomas, "the enemy extending his lines farther and farther around our right, toward our line of retreat. . . . Looking across the fields in our rear (rather longingly), I had the happy distinction of a discoverer. What I saw was the shimmer of sunlight on metal: lines of troops were coming in behind us! The distance was too great, the atmosphere too hazy to distinguish the color of their uniform, even with a glass."

If the troops were enemy, it was doom; if friendly, salvation. "Find out who they are," roared Thomas, and Bierce galloped off. Thomas waited, so nearly overcome with tension he could scarcely stand. Bierce returned, waving his cap. "Those boys are ours," he yelled. "They're wearing the blue!"

Thomas was ecstatic. "Bring them here, Bierce, bring them here," he thundered, and Bierce again left at the gallop.

The troops were the Reserve Corps commanded by Granger, who on his own initiative had sent them to the rescue, with division commander James B. Steedman in the van. Thomas greeted Steedman exuberantly, then ordered him to the hills of Snodgrass Ridge on the right, where the enemy was threatening the flank. Steedman deployed his two brigades of 3,900 men with parade ground precision and swept the Confederates from the summits. For the remainder of the day Steedman held the hills, helped by other reinforcements that providentially appeared. Steedman had also brought desperately needed ammunition, but still not enough. Thomas sent off aides to get ammunition wherever it might be found.

Garfield arrived at Thomas's command post at about 3:45 P.M. and explained the full extent of the disaster on the right. Not until then did Thomas understand what had caused the collapse. Garfield also told him to expect neither reinforcements nor ammunition. "A good deal of nonsense used to be talked about the heroism of General Garfield," wrote Bierce, "who, caught in the rout of the right, nevertheless went back and joined the undefeated left under General Thomas. There was no great heroism in it; that is what every man should have done, including the commander of the army. We could hear Thomas' guns going—those of us who had ears for them—and all that was needed was to make a sufficiently wide detour and then move toward the sound."

A message came from Rosecrans at Chattanooga. "Assume command of all the forces," he instructed, "and with Crittenden and McCook take a strong position and assume a threatening attitude at Rossville.* Send all the unorganized force to this place for re-organization. I will examine the ground here and make such dispositions for defense as the case may require and join you. Have sent out ammunition and rations."

The puzzling message reflected Rosecrans's blurred state of mind. The written time of its release was 12:15 P.M., although Rosecrans had dictated it four hours later upon his arrival in Chattanooga. And what was a "threatening attitude" supposed to mean? In any event, neither Rosecrans nor either of the corps commanders was coming to Thomas. He would have to go to them at Rossville, four miles distant. Deciding to withdraw just before nightfall, Thomas hoped that the Confederate attacks would have diminished by then.

The retrograde movement would be tricky and dangerous. The troops would have to disengage from the front line in stages. A rear guard would have to hold off the attacking Confederates, while their comrades made their way to the rear. Another line farther back would have to be established to cover the rear guard when it pulled out. Because a concerted Confederate attack could transform an orderly withdrawal into a catastrophic rout, Thomas's troops would be in jeopardy at every moment.

Thomas decided first to withdraw the divisions on Kelly Field, on the left, which had been unengaged most of the afternoon because of Polk's inertia. Thomas's staff apprised the division commanders of the order of withdrawal. The first would be Reynolds. Telling Granger to take command at Snodgrass Ridge, Thomas left to show Reynolds where he was to reposition himself to cover the other divisions. Both wings of the entire Confederate army kicked off one final attack against Thomas's contracting lines. Thomas continued to position his rear guards, allowing some of his brigades to

---

* Rossville, Georgia, lay astride a gap in Missionary Ridge leading into Chattanooga.

"come off in good style," he later reported, while others "were thrown into some confusion."

"At last it grew too dark to fight," wrote Bierce. "Then away to our left and rear some of Bragg's people set up 'the Rebel yell.' It was taken up successively and passed around to our front, along our right and in behind us again, until it seemed almost to have got to the point whence it started. It was the ugliest sound that any mortal ever heard—even a mortal exhausted and unnerved by two days of hard fighting, without sleep, without rest, without food and without hope. There was, however, a space somewhere at the back of us across which that horrible yell did not prolong itself; and through that we finally retired in profound silence and dejection, unmolested."

The yells that Bierce heard were cheers of relief and triumph from the Army of Tennessee, for Polk and Hill had stopped the pursuit. "At sunset," a Confederate soldier remembered, "everyone seemed wild with joy, from generals down to privates, all joined in the exultant cheer that rang over that blood-stained field, telling . . . that we were victorious. Wild shouts ran from one end of our lines to the other and even the poor wounded fellows lying about the woods joined in."

When the cheering stopped, a torpor enveloped the Confederate high command. Neither Longstreet nor Polk told Bragg what had happened, and Bragg made no effort to find out for himself. All slept. After awakening in the morning, the Confederate generals were unaware at first that Thomas had gone away. When they finally grasped that Thomas was no longer in front of them, some among them urged Bragg to pursue up to Rossville and into Chattanooga if necessary. But Bragg had no stomach for more fighting, and he refused to advance.

Thomas had to decide what to do with his strung-out, straggling troops. He could not remember when he had last slept. Nothing was heard from the demoralized Rosecrans, who remained in Chattanooga. Thomas continued to be on his own. Somehow he mustered his last reservoirs of energy to deploy a hasty defensive line around Rossville, but he could readily see that the location was untenable. Thomas recommended final withdrawal to Chattanooga, and in the early evening of the twenty-first Rosecrans sent a response concurring. Thomas again fashioned a withdrawal plan by stages and with rear guards. His army made its way to Chattanooga that night without opposition, as Bragg had not moved from his position. Once in Chattanooga, his divisions went to their assigned locations, dug in, and waited for the Confederate attack that never came.

The soldiers of the Army of Tennessee, together with their comrades from Virginia and Mississippi who had reinforced them, had fought with valor and enthusiasm. Their victory was all the more worthy because it was achieved despite the inertia and divisiveness of its senior generals. Yet after the soldiers had finally slept a full night, they awoke to the realization that their victory was transitory. Any private, however pleased with the prisoners and cannon and colors his regiment had seized, could wonder at just what had been won. The Confederate army stood in possession of several square miles of blood-soaked hills and woods and a meandering stream. These had no strategic value, and the privates knew it. The Federal army still occupied both Chattanooga and Knoxville, indeed the entire state, while the Army of Tennessee would have to recuperate in Georgia.

Thus Chickamauga had followed the familiar pattern: several days of brutal fighting, enormous casualties (16,000, or 28 percent, of the Federal troops; 18,000, or 27 percent, of Confederates), and then withdrawal with both armies still intact. Bragg's refusal to press on against the Army of the Cumberland was justified to the extent that his army had suffered terribly and was without the logistical means to undertake a conventional campaign. The welfare and readiness of his army was not his principal concern, however. Instead, Bragg focused his remaining energy on yet another purge of his internal enemies.

Bragg's campaign against the Army of the Cumberland went into abeyance. When word got back to Richmond, Mary Chesnut wrote sadly in her diary, "Bragg, thanks to Longstreet and Hood, had won Chickamauga; so we looked for results that would pay for our losses in battle. Surely they would capture Rosecrans. But no! There sat Bragg like a good dog, howling on his hind legs before Chattanooga, and some Yankee Holdfast grinning at him from his impregnable heights. He always stops to quarrel with his generals."

Had Bragg fought the Federal army with the same savagery that he fought his own generals, his record as a battlefield commander might well have included a number of successes. Bragg charged Polk with disobedience and banished him to Atlanta, but Polk retained his rank, swapped corps with Hardee in Mississippi, and ultimately returned to the Army of Tennessee after Bragg left. Hill was relieved for being obnoxious; Davis did not nominate him to the Confederate Congress for permanent promotion to lieutenant general, and his participation in the war was as much as over. Longstreet, the third lieutenant general, developed a loathing for Bragg. Eventually Longstreet took his Virginia corps to besiege Burnside in Knoxville and confirmed his incapacity for independent command.

The remaining generals petitioned Davis to remove Bragg, spurring Davis to come west to placate the rebellion. Davis brought along John Pemberton of Vicksburg notoriety, whom Bragg was willing to accept as Polk's replacement. The other generals were outraged and told Pemberton to go home, humiliating Davis and Bragg.

With Chickamauga officially declared a Confederate victory, Davis could scarcely relieve its winning commander. Hence Davis dithered while the generals bellyached, reinforcing Bragg's assertions to Davis that they were a disobedient cabal. Davis ultimately endorsed Bragg, who undertook to rid his army of his enemies. During the next several months he reorganized the Army of Tennessee solely on the basis of those he could tolerate and those who had to be humiliated and eliminated.

Lincoln and Stanton meanwhile purged the Army of the Cumberland. Dana had recovered his composure after his hysterics during the battle, and he now urged Stanton to fire the generals who had lost their heads under the stress of combat. Lincoln relieved McCook and Crittenden of their corps commands soon afterward. Courts of inquiry followed, and neither again held field commands. Rosecrans relieved Negley because of charges by Wood, who had precipitated the disaster in the first place. But Wood had stayed and fought alongside Thomas, while Negley had disappeared, and so Negley too left active service in shame.

Rosecrans was another matter. Dana argued strenuously for his relief, seconded by Garfield, who wrote secretly to influential people in Washington. Rosecrans had so alienated Dana that Dana's reports to Washington were uniformly hostile. Rosecrans hurt himself further with messages to Washington that manifested mood swings and emotional instability.

Lincoln decided by early October that Rosecrans had to go, but political considerations governed the timing. Ohio voters were going to the polls on October 9 in a gubernatorial election that was, in effect, a vote of confidence. The Republican candidate, John Brough, supported Lincoln's war program. The Democrat was Clement Vallandigham, a Copperhead who advocated Confederate independence and denounced emancipation. The Copperhead party inflamed the issue of race. "Let every vote count in favor of the *white* man," went their platform, "and against the Abolition hordes, who would place negro children in your schools, negro jurors in your jury boxes, and negro votes in your ballot boxes!"

Lincoln was anxious, for Pennsylvania too had a Copperhead gubernatorial candidate. The two elections were a plebiscite on Lincoln's conduct of the war, and he desperately wanted to win both by large margins. The victories at Vicksburg and Gettysburg would bring him votes, but he wanted everything in his favor. As Rosecrans was popular in Ohio and aligned with the Republicans, it would be impolitic to fire him before the election. If Brough won with a huge majority, Rosecrans would be expendable.

Without question Thomas was the best-qualified relief. The Rock of Chickamauga, the papers now called him. His stature was such that Lincoln, the cabinet, the Congress, and the public all together acclaimed him. But would Thomas willingly relieve Rosecrans? Perhaps not. Those in Washington could not understand Thomas, for he seemed guided by principles different from other generals. He had refused to relieve Buell and then had complained when he had been passed over by Rosecrans the second time around. Dana certainly liked him and said so in his messages to Stanton. "He refused before because a battle was imminent and he was unacquainted with the combinations," said Dana. "No such reasons now exists, and I presume that he would accept."

Stanton sent a reply to Dana on September 30, perhaps to test Thomas's willingness to succeed Rosecrans. "If Hooker's command can get safely through,"* said Stanton, "all the Army of the Cumberland can need will be

---

* Hooker was on his way west with belated reinforcements from the Army of the Potomac.

a competent commander. The merit of General Thomas and the debt of gratitude the nation owes to his valor and skill are fully appreciated here, and I
wish you to tell him so. It was not my fault that he was not in chief command
months ago."

Dana read the dispatch to Thomas, placing him in a predicament. He was
loyal to Rosecrans and had no wish to replace him under the circumstances;
even talking to Dana had the appearance of intrigue, which he abhorred.
Obviously Stanton—and presumably Lincoln—intended to replace Rosecrans with a "competent commander." It appeared that Stanton considered
him a candidate.

Thomas chose his words carefully. He was grateful, he replied, for the
expression of approval. As much as he would like to command an army—
and this he said emphatically—he would not consent to relieving Rosecrans.
Would Dana please convey his position to the secretary of war? Dana did not
do what Thomas had asked, for his report of Thomas's reaction was a
laconic, noncommittal postscript to a lengthy message to Stanton on October 4. "General Thomas desires me to say to you," he wrote, "that he is
deeply obliged to you for your good opinion."

Thomas may privately have expressed his feelings about the enemy, the
causes of the war, and why he fought—perhaps even about Rosecrans's
abandonment of the Chickamauga battlefield—but for the record he was
extraordinarily impersonal, circumspect, and discreet. Thomas B. Van
Horne, both confidant and biographer, probably knew Thomas's thinking as
well as anyone. In his judgment, Thomas did not want to mix military operations with political motives. "He entertained the opinion from the beginning to the close of the war," wrote Van Horne, "that military considerations
should alone rule in shaping military operations; and he desired no prefer-
ment for himself which could be gained by political influence, or would
entail political entanglements. . . . Thus anxious, as he frankly expressed
himself to be, to command an army, he was still unwilling to accept such
command unless it came to him without the menace of political complica-
tions, and without the humiliation of another general."

But Thomas could not have things his way when it came to assignments,
and he was naive to think so. A general in high command could not stay
aloof from politics, for a civil war is the most political of all wars, and surely
Thomas realized that. In any event, for whatever reasons—and several come
to mind—Dana apparently did not advise Stanton of Thomas's reservations,
and the Lincoln administration proceeded on the assumption that Thomas
would follow orders when the time came. Meanwhile, Bragg had besieged
Chattanooga, isolating the city from its sources of supply, and Rosecrans
verged on nervous collapse.

The frustrating inability to reinforce Rosecrans with other western forces
convinced Lincoln and Stanton that a unified commander was needed in the
western theater, someone who could see the situation firsthand and move
forces expeditiously and with unquestioned authority.

Lincoln and Stanton selected Grant as the man for the crisis. Since winning at Vicksburg on July 4, Grant had marked time on the Mississippi,

owing to the absence of any strategic guidance from Washington and the seriousness of his injury in New Orleans. In early October he received orders to go with his staff to Cairo, the prelude to a rendezvous with Stanton. Stanton and Grant met in Indianapolis on October 17 and spoke while their train proceeded to Louisville. Stanton gave Grant two sets of nearly identical orders, appointing him to command the entire western theater. Grant could choose which set to accept. One left the army commanders as they were. The other relieved Rosecrans and appointed Thomas in his place. The administration had passed the buck to Grant.

Grant chose Thomas, principally because Rosecrans had been insubordinate to Grant the year before, and he did not want to deal with Rosecrans again. That night Stanton and Grant arrived in Louisville. They talked the next day, the eighteenth, and then Grant and Julia went out for the evening. Grant returned later to find Stanton fretting about a telegram from Dana. Rosecrans was in a frenzy and about to abandon Chattanooga unless Stanton prevented him. Grant wrote two telegrams to Rosecrans, one assuming command of the western theater, the other relieving Rosecrans and assigning Thomas to command the Army of the Cumberland.

Rosecrans received the telegrams on October 19 and called Thomas to his headquarters. The change of command would be immediate, said Rosecrans. He knew and appreciated Thomas's feelings and his loyalty, but Thomas had no choice in the matter. Rosecrans dictated his final general orders to his army, a gracious farewell message in every respect, with praise for Thomas. He discussed matters with Thomas well into the night and left the following morning before sunrise.

Thomas received his first message from Grant during Rosecrans's last night in Chattanooga. "Hold Chattanooga at all hazards," Grant directed. "I will be there as soon as possible. Please inform me how long your present supplies will last and the prospects for keeping them up." Thomas replied with a typically detailed inventory: 204,462 rations in the storehouses, 90,000 to arrive shortly. Then he made an uncharacteristically melodramatic announcement: "I will hold the town till we Starve." Grant liked that. "I appreciated the force of this dispatch later," he wrote in his memoirs, "when I witnessed the condition of affairs which prompted it."

2 3

CHATTANOOGA

*The siege of Chattanooga was the only one which any one of the
Union armies suffered or sustained. It is a singular fact . . . that the
troops of the Union never abandoned a siege once begun, nor surrendered a position regularly besieged; and that, on the contrary, the
rebels never carried a position regularly invested, and were compelled to surrender all those fortresses in which they were besieged.*
W. F. G. *Shanks*, Chattanooga, and How We Held It

Grant sat alone in his railway coach taking him across Tennessee. Distracted by the noise of his boisterous staff, he had sought solitude to
gather his thoughts. Rain pelted the windows; when he wiped away
the condensation, he could see only forested hills and mountains extending
to the horizon. He lit a fresh cigar and grimaced from the pain in his leg
when the coach lurched, a throbbing reminder of his accident in New
Orleans. Still on crutches, he dreaded the prospect of riding a horse, but the
Confederates had closed the rail line into Chattanooga. There was no alternative to a long trail ride from the railhead at Bridgeport, Alabama, into the
besieged city.

How bad was it in Chattanooga? he wondered. His private train had to
labor to negotiate the steep grades, and he could feel the bridges wobble as
it crossed the chasms and gorges. It had to be grim there, Grant reckoned, if
this damned rail line was the only way to transport supplies to the Army of
the Cumberland. And could it even fight after being whipped at Chickamauga? Probably not, even with George Thomas now in command. That
was why he had summoned Sherman and his Army of the Tennessee from the
Mississippi Valley. They had won for him at Vicksburg; he could rely on
them at Chattanooga.

Other troops were also available, for the defeat at Chickamauga had ener-
gized the administration to send immediate reinforcements from the Army of
the Potomac. In an extraordinary logistical feat, the Northern railroads had
transported Hooker and two army corps of 23,000 men over a thousand miles
in fourteen days. Their support equipment quickly followed. But Hooker's
force was stuck in Bridgeport, because it could not be fed in Chattanooga.

Grant considered Hooker more of a liability than an asset. Blustering and pretentious, he had commanded the Army of the Potomac in early 1863 until Lee had trounced him at Chancellorsville. Like Burnside, Hooker had reverted to corps command, though he tried to pull rank when Grant arrived in Bridgeport. Grant ignored him and resolved to exclude Hooker from an active role in the Chattanooga operations.

After resting overnight in Bridgeport, Grant mounted a horse for the first time in weeks and set off with his staff on the hair-raising ride to Chattanooga. It was then that Grant realized why Thomas's army was short of supplies. "There had been much rain," he wrote in his memoirs, "and the roads were almost impassable from mud, knee-deep in places, and from wash-outs on the mountain sides. I . . . had to be carried over places where it was not safe to cross on horseback. The roads were strewn with the debris of broken wagons and the carcasses of thousands of starved mules and horses."

Grant arrived in Chattanooga around dark on October 23. The city reflected the misery of its outlands, ugly and battered, like Vicksburg when it had surrendered to Grant, perhaps worse. Cadaverous horses quivered in the pounding rain. The faces of the soldiers were gaunt with hunger, the city's civilians more so. "They were forced to huddle together in the centre of the town as best they could," wrote journalist Shanks, "and many of the houses occupied by them during the siege surpassed in filth, point of numbers of occupants, and general destitution, the worst tenement houses of New York city. If there was little of beauty or elegance in the place when our troops retreated into it from Chickamauga, there was a great deal less a fortnight subsequently. Like many another Southern town Chattanooga grew suddenly old; one might say it turned gray during the brief but dark night of the siege."

Thomas had been in command of the Army of the Cumberland for three days when Grant arrived. Grant went to Thomas's headquarters and remained there for several days until his own were established. He delivered a glowing letter from Stanton. "You stood like a rock," wrote Stanton, "and that stand gives you fame which will grow brighter as the ages go by. You will be rewarded by the country and by the Department." Four days later Stanton was as good as his word, and Grant was the messenger. "Allow me to congratulate you on your appointment as Brig. Gen. in the regular Army for the battle of Chickamauga," he wrote Thomas. "I have just received a dispatch announcing the fact."*

Grant and his rain-sodden retinue discovered that Thomas's headquarters contrasted with the despondency outside. The atmosphere was cool and efficient, almost intimidating, the staff officers well dressed and businesslike, the servants unobtrusive and attentive. Accustomed to a freewheeling, impulsive

_____

* An appointment in the regular army conveyed tenure and retention in that rank after the war. Thomas was already a major general of volunteers, but such rank was temporary for the duration of the war. Most regular officers held high ranks in the volunteers during the war but reverted to lesser ranks afterward.

style of administration, and to amusing themselves with drinking and raucous parties, Grant and his staff felt awkward and self-conscious in the presence of the magisterial Thomas.* "One of the visiting officers was a guest at the headquarters mess and was oppressed by its formality and solemnity," wrote McKinney. "Not a word, he said, was spoken during the meal. In this environment both servant and chief-of-staff seemed to acquire some of Thomas' basic characteristics. Even his horses, the mules around his headquarters and the sleek cat that rubbed against his legs or lay purring at his feet seemed to shape their temperaments in accordance with their master's influence."

The two chiefs of staff manifested the contrast. Rawlins was blunt and brawling. His simmering impatience came to a boil when he was provoked by Grant or anyone else. Recently promoted to brigadier general, he was nonetheless a civilian short on military foresight and intuition, such that the staff was usually a step or more behind unfolding developments. Thomas's temporary chief of staff was Major General Joseph J. Reynolds, a West Point graduate and regular army veteran who had commanded a division in Thomas's corps at Chickamauga and had stood by him on Snodgrass Ridge.

Brigadier General William D. Whipple, another West Pointer and a career staff officer, reported to Thomas as his adjutant general in early November and a month later became chief of staff. "Thomas and Whipple," wrote McKinney, "had many of the same characteristics. Both were studious, reserved, formal and meticulously observant of the punctilios of official relationships. They refused to tolerate the haphazardness which had become characteristic under Rosecrans. Order and punctuality now prevailed. Headquarters became quiet, dignified and solemn."

With other officers of his generation, Grant could unbend and revert to his normally gregarious personality. A Grant staff officer, James H. Wilson, recorded one such occasion in a November 6 letter to a friend. "Yesterday afternoon while it was raining," he wrote, "Generals Baldy Smith, John Reynolds, and Gordon Granger were in the General's room, chatting over cadet days. The scene was very amusing to me—Grant and Reynolds were classmates and the others not greatly different in age. Reynolds would call Grant 'Sam'—Grant called him 'Joe,' so it was 'Sam' and 'Joe' and 'Baldy' and 'Gordon'—speaking of Thomas it was 'old Tom'—of Sherman 'Cump'— and similarly with reference to all or nearly all of our leading men."

Wilson tried to promote a measure of amicability between Grant and Thomas and their staffs. The bull session was encouraging, even though Thomas was not part of it. Years later, Wilson admitted that his self-appointed efforts to facilitate goodwill had been largely futile. "[A]fter all," he wrote in retrospect, "they were both strong men with different points of view, habits of mind, and idiosyncrasies, and it is by no means strange that their prejudices and their preferences should have pushed them in different directions."

---

* Grant did finally fire C. B. Lagow, the staff alcoholic, for a drinking party at Chattanooga.

The Yeoman would work with the Roman at Chattanooga because Grant needed Thomas and respected his stature, irrespective of personal feelings. Thomas may have resented the inference that Grant had come to Chattanooga to "rescue" him, for Thomas already had plans to break the siege before Grant's arrival. Professional that he was, however, Thomas would suppress his animosity and support Grant as he had Grant's predecessors.

The resident generals introduced themselves during Grant's first evening in Chattanooga and started to take the measure of the man whom Lincoln had chosen to lead them. Supply was first on Grant's agenda, and Thomas explained the precarious situation. Bragg intended to starve the Federal army into submission by interdicting the principal lines of communication between Chattanooga and the river town of Bridgeport, on the west bank of the Tennessee twenty-five miles west of Chattanooga, where the railroad line from the north terminated. In peaceful times a bridge had spanned the river, and a rail line and a road went from there into Chattanooga. That was the shortest and most efficient way to bring supplies into the city. The Tennessee River was another.

The river, the road, and the rail line from Bridgeport to Chattanooga all passed below the towering north face of Lookout Mountain, about a mile west of Chattanooga. Rosecrans's final mistake in the campaign had been his failure to occupy Lookout Mountain, which Bragg took by default. From its commanding heights the Confederate troops could stop eastbound traffic into Chattanooga.

Under the circumstances, the only way to get supplies from Bridgeport into Chattanooga was via the brutal, roundabout mountain trails north of the city and thence across the river to the city on the southern bank. Grant had just taken the route and nodded in understanding. Food for the soldiers took priority. Even so, the men went on reduced rations. Animal food—forage like hay and corn—came in driblets, enough to keep only the most important horses alive. The artillery horses took lowest priority and had to die or pull wagons.

Before Grant's arrival, another newcomer, Brigadier General William F. "Baldy" Smith, had proposed a plan to restore the normal route between Bridgeport and Chattanooga. Smith had been sent west as chief engineer of the Army of the Cumberland. The assignment was a comedown. He had commanded a corps in the Army of the Potomac, but his unsparing criticism of Burnside's leadership had resulted in demotion and banishment. A West Point graduate and an engineer in the old army, in the course of the war he would be recognized as an engineering genius.

Smith's idea was to build pontoon bridges that bypassed Lookout Mountain. He proposed to build one such bridge at Brown's Ferry, about three miles downstream and beyond the range of guns on Lookout Mountain. Supplies from Bridgeport could be brought overland on the south bank and taken over the Brown's Ferry pontoon bridge. Other supplies could come by water and unload at Brown's Ferry. Wagons would haul the supplies a mile and a half to another pontoon bridge into Chattanooga.

The first step was a beachhead at Brown's Ferry. Smith proposed sending an elite assault force on pontoons downriver from Chattanooga under cover of darkness, seizing Brown's Ferry by surprise, and holding it while Hooker marched up the south bank of the river from Bridgeport. Once Hooker arrived the area could be held, the pontoon bridge constructed, and supplies brought in directly from Bridgeport. Thomas approved the plan on October 22. Smith would exercise command on the principle that the person who conceives an operation should execute it. The only action required of Grant was to approve what Thomas and Smith already intended to do.

Grant wanted to see things for himself, and in the morning he began his inspection tour with Thomas and Smith. The city, he soon discovered, was a fortress, thanks to the efforts of Smith's predecessor, Brigadier General James Saint Clair Morton. After graduating second in his class at West Point, Morton became one of the most brilliant and ingenious officers of the corps of army engineers. In his hands rested the construction of the city's fortifications. He practiced neither mercy nor economy. Shanks recalled that a fellow officer once said of him, "[I]f Morton needed a certain quantity of earth for a fort, the fact that it was a gold mine would make no difference to him; he would only say, 'Gold dust will resist artillery. It will do.' "*

"So laying out his line of works," wrote Shanks, "Morton budged from his course not an inch to spare the town. Residences were turned into block houses; black bastions sprang up in former vineyards; rifle-pits were run through grave yards; and soon a long line of works stretched from the river above to the river below the city, bending crescent-like around it, as if it were a huge bow of iron, and rendering it impregnable. For a fortnight the whole army worked on the fortifications, and it became literally a walled city."

Missionary Ridge overlooked the fortified wall. Bragg's headquarters and its Confederate flag were flaunted on its summit, where Bragg surveyed the city below him and its blue fields of Federal troops. They in turn looked upward and saw Bragg's aerie, the artillery along the crest, and infantry entrenchments from top to bottom and into the wide, two-mile plain that separated the base of the mountain from the Federal fortifications. From all appearances, Bragg's position was as impregnable as Chattanooga.

Grant saw where the bridge would be located at Brown's Ferry and approved the plan. The operation succeeded. Hazen's brigade charged from the pontoons and secured the beachhead from the startled Confederates. Longstreet, in command of the left wing, including Lookout Mountain, was by then scarcely on speaking terms with Bragg. The two generals conferred long enough to confirm that Hooker was coming and that Hazen occupied Brown's Ferry. Longstreet tried to attack Hooker at night and failed. Thus to Thomas's satisfaction and relief, the shorter route between Bridgeport and Chattanooga was restored and made secure. As backlogged supplies began

---

* Morton voluntarily (and inexplicably) reverted to his rank of major in the regular army and forfeited his commission as brigadier general of volunteers. He later became the chief engineer to Burnside in the east and was killed in action at Petersburg.

Pontoons like these helped to lift the siege of Chattanooga. Thomas's shock troops first used them as landing craft in their amphibious assault at Brown's Ferry; then his engineers lashed them together to bridge the Tennessee River, allowing supplies to enter the city out of range of the Confederate guns on Lookout Mountain. (Library of Congress)

to flow to Thomas's army, its morale immediately improved, the first phase of Thomas's restoration of its spirit and combat power.

Thus Thomas quietly and deliberately restored the élan and reputation of an army that had been disgraced in battle and mortified by siege. Getting them fed was a good start. Refusing to retreat was another. Screening the generals was next. Those who had stayed with Thomas at Chickamauga were the ones who remained closest to him. Two of his most important staff appointments had been division commanders at Chickamauga: Brannan became chief of artillery, and Reynolds served as interim chief of staff. The irrepressible Granger commanded the newly organized Fourth Corps, the combined corps of McCook and Crittenden that had been mauled at Chicka-mauga. As evidence of his faith in volunteer officers, Thomas assigned John M. Palmer to Thomas's former command, the Fourteenth Corps.*

Altogether the turnover of division and brigade commanders was substantial. Those with the right stuff were retained and sometimes rewarded with new capacities and higher rank—Thomas recommended nineteen senior officers for promotion. Some twenty-five general officers occupied the principal field commands and staff positions, half of them West Point graduates and career officers, the other half volunteers distinguished for their fighting and

---

* Commanding a division in Crittenden's corps, Palmer had stayed the course with Thomas at Chickamauga.

leadership skills, including a pair of eccentrics, Russian and German, who had been trained in Europe. For the remainder of the war, the core of the western armies would always be the Army of the Cumberland and the generals whom Thomas had selected in the first weeks of his command at Chattanooga.

The seizure of Brown's Ferry was the first indication that Bragg's siege was collapsing, in large measure because of self-inflicted hindrances. In the six weeks that Bragg had invested Chattanooga, he had again given his attention to eradicating officers he considered disloyal. To fragment blocs of imagined opposition, Bragg shifted brigades among divisions and eliminated other divisions altogether. The result was three reconstituted corps, commanded by Longstreet, Breckinridge, and Hardee. Morale predictably suffered owing to the continued dissension, disease, desertions and the customary lack of food and clothing.

Preoccupied with his purges, Bragg was unable to counter Federal initiatives. He had heard that Grant was in Chattanooga and that Thomas had replaced Rosecrans, and he had seen for himself that Hooker had arrived with more than 20,000 reinforcements from the east. He also knew that Sherman was coming with even more reinforcements from Mississippi. Supplies now were freely entering Chattanooga. Bragg's opportunities to retake Chattanooga were fast disappearing.

Davis had suggested to Bragg on October 29, almost as an afterthought, that he detach Longstreet from the Chattanooga siege to expel Burnside from East Tennessee. Anxious to get Longstreet out of his hair, Bragg agreed, even though the move would reduce his strength while the Federal army was daily increasing its combat power. Perhaps he hoped that Grant would chase the departing Longstreet and thus shift the locus of fighting away from Chattanooga.

When the pathetic Burnside retreated into Knoxville, Washington took Longstreet seriously, for he gave the appearance of once again taking control of East Tennessee for the Confederacy. "The situation turned desperate," Grant later wrote. "The authorities at Washington were now more than ever anxious for the safety of Burnside's army, and plied me with dispatches faster than ever, urging that something should be done for his relief."

Grant's solution was characteristically hasty, simple, and thoughtless: (1) Attack Bragg, who would then (2) recall Longstreet to Chattanooga and thus (3) make Burnside safe. Grant felt that it could be done because Baldy Smith had recommended an attack on the north end of Missionary Ridge, where Bragg's army had a precarious lodgment.

Without seriously considering the consequences, Grant ordered Thomas immediately to clear the Confederates from the north end of Missionary Ridge and then proceed some twenty miles east to attack the railway line carrying supplies north to Longstreet. "The movement should not be made one moment later than tomorrow morning," Grant concluded. "You having been over this country, and not having had a better opportunity of studying it myself the details are left to you."

Thomas received the written order and assessed it as so much arm waving. While there was no question that Bragg had to be cleared from Missionary Ridge, and that an attack on the north end was the best way to do it, Thomas had assumed that Sherman's army, still en route, would participate. If Thomas attempted it alone, he would have to pull out of Chattanooga and leave it open to enemy assault.

Thomas summoned Smith and told him that the order meant disaster. As its genesis was Smith's idea, Thomas wanted him to convince Grant to cancel the operation. After a protracted discussion, the two rode to the northern end of Missionary Ridge and surveyed the Confederate right flank. If Thomas were to turn that flank, it was self-evident that he would have to uncover Chattanooga and leave it unprotected. Smith was convinced. He saw Grant and told him the bad news. "The order was at once countermanded," Smith later wrote.

Grant was angered and embarrassed for at least two reasons. The first was personal. Thomas had exposed the deep flaws in Grant's thinking. Second, Grant impetuously had announced to Halleck, Sherman, and Burnside that the attack was his idea. Now he had to tell them it would not happen. Had Grant and Thomas been willing to talk frankly and informally and with mutual respect, they might well have agreed upon a less risky alternative, a demonstration that perhaps would have prompted Bragg to recall Longstreet. But both generals had become so distant within days of Grant's arrival that letters and emissaries were the preferred medium of communication. It was not a good working relationship.

Grant longed to have his comrade Sherman and his veteran army from the Vicksburg campaign with him in Chattanooga, for he would depend on them to whip Bragg and rescue Burnside. He disdained Thomas's Army of the Cumberland for its defeat at Chickamauga and its immobility for want of healthy animals. "I have never felt such restlessness before," he wired Halleck, "as I have at the fixed and immovable condition of the Army of the Cumberland. Genl Meigs states, that the loss of animals here will exceed ten thousand.* Those left are scarcely able to carry themselves."

In reality, Sherman's army was scarcely more mobile than Thomas's. Its movement from Vicksburg eastward had begun in late September, but when Grant arrived in Chattanooga on October 23, Sherman was still 160 miles away. Grant ordered Sherman to expedite his march, but swollen rivers and bad roads limited his advance to an average of six miles a day. "[Sherman] may have established the record for the slowest relief march in American history," wrote McKinney. "He was shamed and mortified by his failure. Grant was pressing him to get up and Sherman answered with awkward

---

* Stanton had the foresight to send his quartermaster general, Major General Montgomery Meigs, a man of exceptional talent and enterprise, to Chattanooga with carte blanche to cut red tape. A word from Meigs would speed quantities of critical matériel that heretofore had required months of haggling.

apologies." The advance guard of Sherman's army finally arrived in Bridgeport on November 15.

Grant and Sherman met and spoke privately. Grant confided that Thomas's army was demoralized, unwilling to move from its trenches. Sherman's army would have to lead the way. Aware of Grant's prejudiced opinion, Thomas seethed when he realized that he was expected to play second fiddle to Sherman. He had built the Army of the Cumberland into a crack war machine, and Chickamauga had been an aberration. His army fervently wanted to redeem its reputation, and Thomas intended to allow his soldiers to demonstrate their keenness at the first opportunity. Meanwhile he would clamp his jaw and try to keep Grant thinking straight.

With Sherman's arrival, Grant felt ready to attack. Thomas and Smith joined their party, and the four generals rode along the front to examine the possibilities. At Chickamauga the forests and undulating countryside had concealed the combatants. All was different at Chattanooga. Both armies were in full view in an amphitheater of war. The Confederates occupied the grandstands on Missionary Ridge and Lookout Mountain, the Federal army the stage on the plains between the city and the foothills. Every soldier was visible by day, and by night their campfires glowed. Colors and pennants fluttered along the miles of encampments. The generals could plan great things and watch them unfold in panorama.

As Smith had first reported, the northern end of Missionary Ridge seemed to be lightly fortified, and so it was chosen as the point of attack. Grant wrote his orders on November 18. Concealing his army by passing behind Chattanooga on the north bank of the river, Sherman would secretly move his army from Bridgeport and, under cover of darkness, cross opposite the north end of Missionary Ridge. Thomas would build the bridges, provide artillery support, and mass his army on Sherman's right, augmented with Oliver Howard's corps from Hooker's force. Reinforced with a division from Thomas, Sherman would attack the northern end of Missionary Ridge on the morning of November 21. Thomas would attack simultaneously and converge with Sherman. Together their combined armies would sweep the ridge. Hooker, left near Lookout Mountain with a single division, was to stay in the trenches.

Grant had been too optimistic. Despite Sherman's frantic efforts, his army could not reach its position on the left wing because the narrow roads, shaky pontoon bridges, and rain impeded progress. To his discomfiture, Grant had to postpone the attack date successively to the twenty-fourth.

Bragg reacted like a pendulum. On November 20 he informed Davis that Sherman had arrived and asked for reinforcements. "Our fate may be decided here," he wrote, "and the enemy is at least double our strength." Having asked for reinforcements, Bragg weakened himself further by dispatching two additional divisions (Patrick R. Cleburne and Buckner) in response to Longstreet's request for reinforcements at Knoxville. It seemed a characteristic of Bragg—and later Hood—to disperse rather than mass his army in the face of a superior enemy.*

The visibility of the opposing lines revealed the withdrawal of Cleburne and Buckner. "[M]uch movement, some of it singular and mysterious, was observed in the rebel army," wrote Wood, commanding his division in front of Chattanooga. Instructions were issued for vigilance. Two Confederate deserters in the early morning of the twenty-third reported that Bragg was withdrawing from his position. Deserters were a constant, but unreliable, source of information about enemy intentions. They were often planted and always suspect, especially so in Bragg's army. As his field commanders rarely understood Bragg's intentions, enlisted men knew even less. But as the Confederates had been conspicuously bustling the day before, Grant took the report seriously and wanted confirmation. In a single sentence he gave the task to Thomas. "The truth or falsity of the deserter," he wrote Thomas in the early morning, "who came in last night stating that Bragg had fallen back should be ascertained at once."

There were many ways to do this: further interrogation of the deserters; sending out spies and scouts; a cavalry patrol perhaps. Grant left it to Thomas's discretion. While Thomas was a stickler for authenticating intelligence, he now had bigger plans in mind than to find out if a deserter was truthful. He would manipulate Grant's terse discretionary order into a massive display of strength by the Army of the Cumberland. Once his design unfolded, it would be too late for Grant to interfere. Whatever Thomas's motives—perhaps to boost his soldiers' morale and intimidate the Confederates or to impress Grant with the power of his army—Thomas's employment of brute force was out of proportion to Grant's intentions.

By Thomas's orders, two divisions would take a rugged hill called Orchard Knob, midway on the two-mile plain separating the Chattanooga fortifications and Missionary Ridge. The Confederates had made Orchard Knob a fortified outpost, bolstered with outlying trenches and gun pits. It had become a familiar landmark for every Federal soldier in Chattanooga, symbolizing the Confederate's ascendancy over the Army of the Cumberland. Hence it was a natural objective for purposes of morale. It was also a sound military objective; its seizure would advance the Federal line a mile closer to Missionary Ridge. And when Sherman got into position, it would be a natural command post for Grant to coordinate the ultimate attack on Missionary Ridge.

The orders that day were a classic model of the delegation of authority—clear, concise, identifying the objective and assignment of forces, while allowing the exercise of initiative for those responsible for the execution. To demonstrate that his army had fully recovered, Thomas shrewdly gave the assignment to Granger, whose Fourth Corps contained the divisions that earlier had panicked and fled at Chickamauga. The two lead division com-

---

* The estimated strengths of both armies when they ultimately joined battle were Federal 56,000 and Confederate 46,000.

manders—Wood and Sheridan—were itching to restore their reputations. Granger told Wood to seize Orchard Knob; Sheridan would back him up and protect his flank.

By noon the two divisions were assembled in precise formations, with pageantry, drums, and airs. Tens of thousands watched the unfolding spectacle, the Confederates with idle interest, thinking perhaps it was a review for dignitaries. "Then, at the bugle signal," Wood later wrote, "the magnificent array, in exact lines and serried columns, moved forward. It scarcely ever falls to the lot of man to witness so grand a military display. . . . In front plainly to be seen was the enemy so soon to be encountered in deadly conflict. My division seemed to drink in the inspiration of the scene, and when the 'advance' was sounded moved forward in the perfect order of a holiday parade." Wood had seen military pageants in Europe before the war. "In none of these displays," he wrote, "did I ever see anything to exceed the soldierly bearing and the steadiness of my division."

The leading brigades of the indomitable Hazen and the Prussian drillmaster August Willich crunched the startled Confederates and occupied Orchard Knob. Thomas ordered Granger to dig in and advanced the remainder of the Chattanooga forces a mile closer to Missionary Ridge. Grant was amazed. "The troops moved under fire with all the precision of veterans on parade," he wired Halleck.

Because of Thomas's feat, Grant now faced entirely changed circumstances. Plans are based upon premises. When those premises change, as usually they do, the general must consider whether to press on with his original plan or to modify it in light of the new developments. His thinking must be flexible, his powers of reasoning adaptable. That predicament now lay before Grant. Five Federal divisions in his center had unexpectedly advanced to the proximity of Missionary Ridge. Paradoxically, the operation had not revealed whether Bragg was withdrawing from his front, the intent of Grant's original order.

Whatever Bragg's dispositions before Thomas's grand march, Grant should have surmised that Bragg certainly would react afterward by shuffling troops like musical chairs. Grant's plan was predicated on his inspection of Bragg's lines on November 15, which revealed the weakness of Bragg's right wing on the northern end of Missionary Ridge. Six days had passed. Was an attack there still prudent? Had Bragg reinforced his right wing? Scratching his head on Orchard Knob on the afternoon of the twenty-third, Grant did not know.

Regardless, Grant doggedly pressed on with his original plan. Sherman would attack on the Confederate right. Thomas would support the attack. Such was the inference of the message that Grant sent Halleck. "Thomas' troops will entrench themselves," he wrote, "and hold their position until daylight when Sherman will join the attack from the mouth of the Chickamauga & a decisive battle will be fought." It was a message of fantasy. Sherman was still stuck in the mud on the wrong side of the river. He would be in no position to attack at daylight. There would be no decisive battle, not that day.

Until then, Thomas had supported Grant's plan. His engineers were ready to throw bridges across the river near the north end of Missionary Ridge, and his artillery was sited to support Sherman's assault. But surely, reasoned Thomas, because of the delays in getting Sherman into position, Bragg must have gotten wind of Grant's intentions and very likely was reinforcing his right wing, Sherman's point of attack. Surprise, a vital element of Grant's plan, was probably compromised. Hence it made sense for Hooker to attack on Bragg's left, on Lookout Mountain, for two reasons. First, it would distract Bragg from Sherman's eventual assault. Second, it would clear the Confederates from Lookout Mountain, opening the principal lines of communication from Bridgeport and relieving the strain on the overburdened pontoon bridge at Brown's Ferry. Furious that Grant had disdained him, Hooker was ready to scale the mountain.

Thomas proposed this alternative to Grant, but Grant held to his original plan, and Hooker had no place in it. Thomas persisted. Sherman would never be ready in the morning. As night fell on the twenty-third, Sherman's rearmost division, commanded by Brigadier General Charles R. Woods, still had not crossed the river at Brown's Ferry, because the pontoon bridge had given way. If Woods's division remained marooned, recommended Thomas, why not have it report to Hooker, who was nearby, and allow Hooker to attack Lookout Mountain? Grant grudgingly agreed. When it was apparent that the bridge was hours away from repair, Woods reported to Hooker, who already had one of his own divisions and one from Thomas standing by.

Cold rain, clouds, and mist obscured the view of the amphitheater when, on the morning of the twenty-fourth, Hooker launched his assault on Lookout Mountain. At a distance the fighting could be heard but not seen. Fragmentary dispatches from Hooker during the morning indicated that he was making headway up the mountain. By early afternoon Hooker had made the most of his opportunity. His troops were near the summit but out of ammunition, the enemy lost in the overcast. He rested. Thomas sent a resupply on the backs of a reserve brigade, allowing the Federal troops to hold their gains. Exercising his artillery instincts, Thomas signaled distant batteries to shell a road from the summit, where Confederate troops scurried.*

Granger's chief of staff, Joseph S. Fullerton, later wrote about the battle above the clouds. "In the morning it had not been known in Chattanooga, in Sherman's army, or in Bragg's camp, that a battle was to be fought," he remembered. "Soon after breakfast, Sherman's men at the other end of the line, intent on the north end of Missionary Ridge, and Thomas' men in the center, fretting to be let loose from the entrenchments, were startled by the sound of artillery and musketry firing in Lookout Valley. Surprise pos-

---

* Thomas employed the modern technique of indirect fire control, that is, of directing artillery fire from a location distant from the firing batteries. The following day he used signalmen to direct artillery fire against Confederate emplacements near Sherman.

sessed the thousands who turned their anxious eyes toward the mountain. The hours slowly wore away; the roar of battle increased, as it came rolling around the point of the mountain, and the anxiety grew. . . . They could hear, but could not see how it was going.

"Finally, the wind, tossing about the clouds and mist, made a rift that for a few minutes opened a view of White House plateau. The enemy was seen to be in flight, and Hooker's men were in pursuit! Then went up a cheer from the thirty thousand in the valley that was heard above the battle by their comrades on the mountain."

In contrast, Sherman was floundering on the other end of the line. His operation had begun with promise. Baldy Smith's pontoon bridges and boats, having been concealed for several days, floated into place in the darkness, allowing two divisions to cross over to the Confederate side of the shore by daybreak. It was then that Grant had expected Sherman to attack, when the Confederates were unprepared and vulnerable. But Sherman delayed. He seemed lethargic, with no sense of urgency. His lead divisions remained idle while the remaining two crossed during the remainder of the morning. While Sherman dawdled, the alarm reached Bragg, who sent his finest division, Cleburne's, to the right wing. Sherman could have used his first two divisions at daybreak to capture the objective, a railroad tunnel about a mile down the ridge, because it was undefended. When Sherman finally got underway at one o'clock, Cleburne was already there, entrenching and prepared to fight.

Sherman finally assembled his three assault divisions and aligned them to his satisfaction.* There was little opposition to his initial advance, for Cleburne was still a mile away, digging in on what was later known as Tunnel Hill. Sherman's unfamiliarity with the terrain was a handicap. Although he had had the opportunity in previous days to scout his objective, it was as if he were seeing things for the first time. Sherman had thought that Missionary Ridge was continuous. Instead, as he discovered in the mist and rain, it was a baffling series of hills. Therefore the location of the tunnel was a puzzlement to him, and he slowly advanced in its approximate direction while engaging Cleburne's skirmishers. By late afternoon Sherman halted his divisions and ordered them to dig in, forfeiting his last opportunity for success.

Grant pondered how to support Sherman once he had gotten underway. He had a notion to have Thomas attack simultaneously, but nothing materialized because he was unsure what Sherman was doing. By nightfall Grant received Sherman's report that he had reached the tunnel. Actually Sherman had fallen short three-quarters of a mile, and Cleburne was waiting for him there from the commanding heights of Tunnel Hill. Grant was unsure of Hooker's status on Lookout Mountain; he believed that another day of fighting might be required there. He did not know that Bragg had ordered the

---

* Sherman apparently wanted to use his own troops, some three divisions, and he left Davis's division, borrowed from Thomas's army, to guard a bridge.

mountain to be abandoned and that the battered Confederate troops already were leaving and headed toward Missionary Ridge.

That evening Grant wrote his orders for the next day. Sherman would attack at dawn. Thomas would attack simultaneously, either taking the rifle pits at the base of Missionary Ridge or moving left to support Sherman. Hooker was to attack Missionary Ridge from the south if circumstances allowed him to withdraw from Lookout Mountain.

"As the sun went down," wrote an observer, "the clouds rolled away, and the night came on clear and cool. A grand sight was old Lookout that night. Not two miles apart were the parallel camp-fires of the two armies, extending from the summit of the mountain to its base, looking like streams of burning lava, while in between, the flashes from the skirmishers' muskets glowed like giant fire-flies."

The morning of November 25 was clear and bright. Sherman and Hooker were lodged at either end of the Confederate line, while Thomas's troops fidgeted in the central plain before the loom of Missionary Ridge. Such was the situation when Grant and Thomas went to Orchard Knob to view the decisive battle. The two men stood stoically, suppressing any display of emotion, while their staffs clustered in two separate groups apart from the generals. The flag of the United States flew from the summit of Lookout Mountain, confirming that the Confederates had conceded it to Hooker. Thomas immediately ordered Hooker to descend from his Mount Olympus and assault Bragg from the south end of Missionary Ridge.

Sherman kicked off from the north end of Missionary Ridge as ordered, puzzled at Thomas's lack of action in the center. When he had received Grant's orders about midnight, Sherman later wrote in his report, he "noticed that General Thomas would attack in force early in the day." Sherman had misinterpreted Grant's intentions. Grant actually expected Thomas to do one of two things: carry the rifle pits at the foot of Missionary Ridge, or "move to the left to [Sherman's] support as circumstances may determine best." What Grant had left unsaid was that he would not send Thomas forward unsupported. The Confederate defenses frowning down on Thomas from Missionary Ridge appeared insurmountable—Thomas's troops would be murdered if they tried independently to assault the summit. Thus Grant's intention was to send them to the *base* of the ridge *only if Sherman was near the summit*. Once at the base, Thomas's troops could then reassemble and ascend with less hazard, or so Grant believed.

Sherman got nowhere, for the Confederate positions on Tunnel Hill were nigh impregnable, and Sherman seemed unable to turn the flanks. When it was apparent that Sherman was stalled, Grant sent reinforcements, but Sherman did not know what to do with them and sent back one division. What Sherman wanted, but Grant would not deliver, was an attack by Thomas that would divert the Confederate forces opposing his own troops. "The day was bright and clear," Sherman wrote in his report, "and the amphitheater of Chattanooga lay in beauty at our feet. I had watched for the attack of

General Thomas early in the day." By midafternoon, it had not happened. For good reason. Grant would not sacrifice Thomas's troops.

Tunnel Hill had become a maelstrom, sucking in Bragg's mobile reserves. Grant could see them double-timing northward along the ridge. If they were coming from the Confederate left wing, it obviously was being progressively weakened. With this in view, Grant and Thomas agreed upon a new plan, changing Grant's earlier plan that had been predicated upon Sherman's sweeping the ridge from the north. The revised plan would be in two phases. Hooker would intensify his assault at the south end of Missionary Ridge. When Grant saw Hooker's troops on the crest of the ridge, he would release Thomas to advance no farther than the base of the ridge. That would complete phase one.

Having seized the rifle pits on the base, Thomas's troops would re-form. When Grant released them for phase two, they would drive up the face of the ridge to join Hooker's troops at the top. Thomas understood what Grant intended: the signal for Thomas to advance would depend upon Hooker, not Sherman. Thomas advised Hooker at noon of these expectations. Grant did not know that the destruction of a key bridge over Chattanooga Creek had delayed Hooker, and that a stubborn defense at the south end of Missionary Ridge would slow him still further.

By midafternoon the anxious scanning through long glasses revealed no sign of Hooker's troops. The November sun was descending; perhaps two hours of daylight remained. Grant's pacing betrayed his desperation to carry the ridge before sunset. Thomas and his generals remained immobile, their faces expressionless. All else having failed, an order for them to attack the ridge seemed inevitable, a prospect they dreaded. Their troops would be stuck on the foot of the towering ridge and subjected to a torrent of enemy fire from the crest. Nonetheless, Thomas had issued instructions beforehand so that his infantry and artillery would be poised and ready should Grant cut them loose.

Nervous and indecisive, Grant hinted that he wanted Thomas and his generals to volunteer to attack. Wood simply replied that he would obey orders when they were given. Thomas remained cold and silent. While Grant wavered, his staff fumed. Rawlins finally demanded that Grant act. Spurred by Rawlins's vehemence, Grant snapped an order to Thomas to take the rifle pits. His voice fatalistically calm, Thomas summoned his aides and told them to relay Grant's order to the commanding generals. The signal to advance would be six cannon shots.

"Orchard Knob was in view," wrote a lieutenant in Hazen's brigade, "and all eyes were leveled in that direction. Suddenly a commotion was discernible on Orchard Knob. Officers were seen mounting their horses and riding toward their several commands. Then every man in the line knew the crucial hour had come. Intense excitement seemed to stir every soldier and officer. Excitement is followed by nervous impatience.

> *Time moves slowly. Here and there a soldier readjusts his accouterments or relaces his shoes. . . . The delay is becoming unbearable.*

> *At last the first boom of the signal is heard. Men fall in and dress without command. Another gun, and nervous fingers play with gunlocks. . . . [A]s the report of the fifth gun breaks upon their ears, the line is moving without a word of command from anyone, and when the sixth gun is fired the troops are well on the way, with colors unfurled and guns at 'right shoulder shift.' All sensations have now given way to enthusiasm. It is a sight never to be forgotten. Fifteen to twenty thousand men in well-aligned formation, with colors waving in the breeze, almost shaking the earth with cadenced tread, involuntarily move to battle.*

The advance began at about half past three. As Thomas's four divisions—Wood, Sheridan, Baird, and Johnson—marched forward, a crescendo of artillery fire soared overhead into the Confederate lines. Because the outnumbered Confederate soldiers were under orders to fire for effect and then withdraw up to the summit, the Federal troops overwhelmed the first line of defense at the base of the ridge. The sight of the Confederates scrambling up the slopes inspired the Federal artillerymen to slam explosives into their backsides, hastening their ascent.

Thomas's soldiers at the base of the ridge took stock. They were entirely exposed to hostile fire from above and could not stay where they were. "To remain is to be annihilated," wrote Hazen's lieutenant. "To retreat is as dangerous as to advance. Here and there a man leaps the works and starts toward the hilltop; small squads follow. Then someone gave the command, 'Forward!' after a number of men began to advance. Officers catch the inspiration. . . . The cry, 'Forward!' is repeated along the line, and the apparent impossibility is undertaken." An irresistible impulse both to survive and conquer impelled the soldiers spontaneously to charge up the slopes of the ridge.

Grant was stunned and turned angrily to Thomas.

"Who ordered those men up the ridge?"

"I don't know," Thomas replied slowly and quietly. "I did not."

Grant turned to the excitable Granger, whose divisions under Wood and Sheridan were battling upward behind their colors. "Did you order them up, Granger?"

"No," replied Granger. "They started up without orders. When those fellows get started, all hell can't stop them!"

Grant muttered that someone would suffer if the attack failed and looked toward Missionary Ridge. He gave no more orders. The battle was beyond his control.

The disciplined formations that had marched across the plain erupted into jagged knots of soldiers, like triangular tongues of blue flame with the colors at the apex. "First one flag passes all others and then another leads," Hazen's lieutenant remembered. "One stand of colors, on our left, is particularly noticeable. The bearer is far ahead of his regiment and advances so rapidly that he draws the enemy's concentrated fire. Then another color-bearer dashes ahead of the line and falls. A comrade grasps the flag almost before it reaches the ground. He, too, falls. Then another picks it up, smeared with his comrade's blood, waves it defiantly, and, as if bearing a charmed life, he advances steadily towards the top. Up, up he goes, his hat pulled over his eyes, his head bent forward as if facing a storm of rain and wind. The bullets whistle about him, splintering his staff. Onward he goes, followed by the admiring cheers of his comrades, who press close behind."

Bragg watched in horror from his headquarters on the summit as the Federal colors surged toward him from below. His own soldiers were scrambling up the slopes, not in measured withdrawal but in fear of their lives, and they were unintentionally shielding the Federal soldiers. Some of his soldiers held fast. Those who had made it from the bottom lay gasping and unable to fight. Bragg's line on the summit began to disintegrate as the blue uniforms came nearer. The Federal colors made the top. Turning his horse toward the reverse slope, Bragg became a fragment carried along in the flood of human debris.

There was hot pursuit for a day, but, as in major battles of the Civil War heretofore, the losing army remained intact. Washington was somewhat to blame. The urgent summons to relieve Burnside detracted Grant; he decided to let Bragg escape and sent a relief force to Knoxville, where Sherman and Granger discovered Burnside comfortably fortified with ample stores. Longstreet had gone to a cozy valley in East Tennessee to pass the winter.

Missionary Ridge had been extraordinary. Other Civil War armies had tried similar frontal assaults on the grand scale and had failed. Lee at Malvern Hill and at Gettysburg and Burnside at Fredericksburg were three such examples. Grant would use such tactics the next summer against Lee, and many would miscarry, most notably at Cold Harbor.

Why, then, had Thomas and the Army of the Cumberland been successful when other armies, with soldiers equally capable and courageous, had not? Bragg's destructive leadership was one reason. He had demoralized his troops when they were not fighting, and he was indecisive when they were fighting. Nonetheless, the Army of Tennessee had been a dangerous opponent. At Chattanooga it went head-to-head with three distinct Federal armies with different results.

One separate battle was against Sherman's Army of the Tennessee at Tunnel Hill. Sherman stubbornly had used only his own soldiers. Davis's division, on loan from Thomas's army, remained in the rear; Baird's division was sent back, and Howard's corps was hardly used. Cleburne and William Walker fought Sherman to a standstill.

Hooker commanded elements of all three Federal armies in another series of separate battles. Because Bragg had stripped Lookout Mountain of most of its defenders, Hooker had the numbers in his favor and made the most of it. Alexander P. Stewart held off Hooker on the southern end of Missionary Ridge until sunset on the twenty-fifth, another example of the Confederate ability to fight against odds.

The final distinctive battle was in the center, a three-mile front, pitting four of Thomas's divisions—the core of the Army of the Cumberland—against Bragg's central divisions on Missionary Ridge. The Confederates had humiliated these men at Chickamauga and had taunted them from the heights of Missionary Ridge during the siege. Wood and Sheridan commanded the two leading divisions, and the Federal troops and their leaders had something to prove.

Thomas had been with the Army of the Cumberland since the beginning. Those elements of the army under his immediate command had always been the hard core, and the other corps had absorbed its example by osmosis. In command of the entire army but a month, Thomas had put a fire in its belly that won the most spectacular victory of the war.

It was an army transformed with the military virtues that Clausewitz described in this way:

> *An army that maintains its cohesion under the most murderous fire;*
> *that cannot be shaken by imaginary fears and resists well-founded ones*
>   *with all its might;*
> *that, proud of its victories, will not lose the strength to obey orders and*
>   *its respect for its officers even in defeat;*
> *whose physical power, like the muscles of an athlete, has been steeled*
>   *by training in privation and effort;*
> *a force that regards such efforts as a means to victory rather than a*
>   *curse on its cause;*
> *that is mindful of all these duties and qualities by virtue of the single*
>   *powerful idea of honor of its arms—*
> *such an army is imbued with the true military spirit.*

On the afternoon that his army took Missionary Ridge, Thomas had watched a brigade of Sheridan's men descend from a hill nearby. The Roman saw that the hill had beautiful, curving terrain over which the men flowed like a current of humanity. Many of them would soon die, and he thought of those who already had died in the campaign. The scene so moved him that he pointed to the hill and told his astonished staff that he would build a cemetery upon it.

After the battle, Thomas acted. On December 24, 1863, he appropriated the hill, some seventy-five acres, to be a shrine to the honored dead. Thomas wanted it to be a lasting memorial of beauty and grandeur, and only his soldiers of the Army of the Cumberland could do the work. The graves on its slopes overlooked the amphitheater of Missionary Ridge and Lookout Mountain. He frequently visited the site to watch its progress. His chaplain supervised the construction and asked Thomas if the graves should be grouped by state.

Thomas was at first silent. "No, no," he replied. "Mix them up. Mix them up. I am tired of states' rights."

The cemetery later received the remains of soldiers scattered from the road to Atlanta, from Chickamauga, from other regional battlefields, and from the hospitals in Chattanooga. Eventually 8,512 Federal soldiers were buried there, a quarter of them unknown. Others from later wars joined them. Some 13,000 graves now occupy the cemetery. Decades later the historian of the Office of the Quartermaster General wrote, "General Thomas took advantage of the pause at Chattanooga to put his impress on one of the most beautiful cemeteries in the national system."

Thomas always had been attentive to the proper burial of fallen warriors. At the start of the war the practice had been to send the bodies home or to bury them in makeshift graves where they fell. Given the numbers of casualties and the mortality from disease, Congress enacted legislation in July 1862 to establish national cemeteries, conferring the responsibility upon the commanding generals of the districts. At first they were located at large camps and hospital sites. Thomas had been the first to establish a national cemetery at a battlefield, Mill Springs, Kentucky. That cemetery had accommodated a relatively small number of fallen. Now he wanted to care for dead soldiers by the thousands. Chattanooga established the precedent. Later he established yet another national cemetery at Murfreesboro.

Thomas and his army were much in the news. Victory at Chattanooga had coincided with Lincoln's third national Thanksgiving holiday, "the greatest day of rejoicing the people had experienced since the war began," recalled Lincoln's telegrapher. Quartermaster General Meigs wrote to Stanton that the western armies deserved some recognition from Washington. "It would be well to visit us here," said Meigs, "and also for the President to review an army which has done so much for the country and which has not yet seen his face." It never would. Lincoln was tied to the White House, and his attention again turned to the Army of the Potomac. It looked bad by comparison, having made no headway since Gettysburg. Meade assumed that his relief was imminent. Rumors were that it would be Thomas. Garfield was in Washington, pushing his name.

Thomas was appalled. "You have disturbed me greatly," he wrote Garfield on December 17, "with the intimation that the command of the Army of the Potomac may be offered to me. It is a position to which I am not the least adapted, and putting my own reputation entirely aside I sincerely hope that I at least may not be victimized by being placed in a position where I would be utterly powerless to do good or contribute in the least toward the suppression of the Rebellion. The pressure always brought to bear against the commander of the Army of the Potomac would destroy me in a week without having advanced the cause in the least. Much against my wishes I was placed in command of this army—I have told you my reasons—now, however, I believe my efforts will be appreciated by the troops and I have reasonable hopes that we may continue to do good service."

The victories at Chattanooga and then Knoxville were a triumph for Grant. Congress gave him a vote of thanks and a gold medal. Lincoln called him to Washington in March 1864, promoted him to the newly established rank of lieutenant general, and appointed him general in chief of the Federal armies. Grant's position in the west became vacant. Sherman and Thomas were the only logical candidates. Sherman's selection was foreordained. Thomas retained command of the Army of the Cumberland.

PART VI

EASTERN

THEATER, 1864

24

VIRGINIA: THE
WILDERNESS

*He is their man, a bullheaded Suwarrow. He don't care a snap if
they fall like the leaves fall. He fights to win, that chap. He is not
distracted by a thousand side issues. He does not see them. He is
narrow and sure, sees only in a straight line. . . . He has the dis-
agreeable habit of not retreating before irresistible veterans.*

Mary Chesnut

The Yeoman came to Washington from the western theater in March
1864 to accept a promotion as the sole lieutenant general in the Federal army. With the promotion came the assignment as general in chief
of the Federal armies, the post held heretofore by Halleck. Grant then made
the principal decision that he believed would win the war: he would subordinate himself to the political leadership and give Lincoln what he wanted.
The war was being fought for political objectives. Grant had to understand
what they were and to conform his military strategy accordingly. He dis-
cerned that Lincoln had three fundamental concepts which he expected
Grant to support.

First, *the principal objective was to destroy the Confederate armies.* The
war had been prolonged because the Confederate armies had survived every
battle and every campaign and somehow had found ways to resurrect themselves to fight another day. Despite disasters on the battlefields, despite
desertions of enormous proportions, despite a logistical system that could
neither feed nor clothe nor equip its soldiers, despite a primitive grasp of military and industrial technology, and despite a political system that was fragmented and bankrupt, the Confederate armed forces continued to fight with
savage, fanatical resolve. So long as the Confederate armies remained intact,
however diminished, the war would continue.

"I have constantly desired the Army of the Potomac to make Lee's army
and not Richmond, its objective point," Lincoln had instructed Halleck in
October 1863. "If our army cannot fall upon the enemy and hurt him where

he is, it is plain to me it can gain nothing by attempting to follow him over a succession of entrenched lines into a fortified city."

Second, *politician-generals had to be allocated selected major commands to bolster Lincoln's political support in Congress and in the statehouses.* Inept as some might be, Grant would have to tolerate such generals because Lincoln needed their influence on his behalf. Halleck hated the political appointments. "It seems little better than murder," he wrote to Sherman, "to give important commands to such men as Banks, Butler, McClernand, Sigel, and Lew Wallace."

Third, *Washington had to be protected.* Any Confederate threat to the capital embarrassed Lincoln regardless of other developments, a condition of acute sensitivity that Grant could never disregard.

From these three principles Grant formed his way of war with the half million men under arms in the Federal armies.

Grant would execute a strategy of coordinated, unremitting pressure on all fronts and in all theaters to exploit the Federal preponderance in men and matériel. It was a strategic concept that Lincoln, Stanton, and Halleck applauded but had been unable to achieve. The Army of the Potomac would confront the Army of Northern Virginia. Sherman would operate in the western theater against the Army of Tennessee, now commanded by Joseph Johnston. Benjamin Butler would move up the Peninsula to threaten Richmond, Nathaniel Banks would operate against Mobile, and Franz Sigel would move down the Shenandoah Valley.

Grant's strategy had only a limited success, in part because of Lincoln's selection of the latter three as theater commanders. They were politicians whose appointments were based entirely on their clout with voters. "[Grant] makes quiet, sarcastic remarks," wrote an aide to George Meade, "without moving a line on his face. He said . . . that 'Banks' victories were of a kind that three or four would ruin anybody.'* He added that 'there were some Generals who had not enough patriotism to resign.' " Griping in private was the extent of Grant's objections, for he dared not cross the political heavyweights. Butler, for example, was a terrible military liability, yet face-to-face he easily intimidated Grant.

Thereupon arose the question of Grant's headquarters. Grant could have gone to Washington, for to exercise power one presumably must be at the seat of power. His predecessor Halleck had functioned in the offices of the War Department in close touch with the White House and Congress. Grant, however, chose to avoid Washington to escape interference and second-guessing. Although Halleck once had made Grant's life a misery, Grant kept him in Washington as his chief of staff and factotum.

Grant pitched his tent with the Army of the Potomac and left Meade in command. Meade was surprised, being certain that he would be relieved for his desultory campaigning following Gettysburg. The upshot was that the

---

* Banks had commanded a failed major expedition up the Red River into Louisiana, in which he had lost numbers of men and quantities of matériel, including ships and guns.

Army of the Potomac had two commanders. The consequences would be orders missed and misunderstood, imperfect liaison and faulty coordination, missed opportunities and near misses. Grant's attention would shift between the battle raging at close hand with Lee, developments in other theaters, and relations with Washington.

With Grant's attention so divided, his behavior became unpredictable. Meade tried to anticipate Grant's thinking. If Meade guessed wrong, the orders were countermanded; if he waited for an order from Grant, time was lost. All orders were subject to rescission on short notice, since Grant changed his mind unexpectedly. At times Grant issued exacting instructions, perhaps through Meade, perhaps not. At other times it might be a broad directive, permitting Meade to develop the details. The arrangement was cumbersome.

At least Grant was blunt in his expectations. Wherever Lee goes, he told Meade, there you will go also.

Theodore Lyman, a young Boston Brahmin, was among the aides on Meade's staff. A Harvard classmate of Barlow, he had stood fourth in his class and upon graduation had earned a reputation as a scholar in the natural sciences. While on a Florida research expedition he had met Meade, then an army engineer building lighthouses. The two had become friends despite thirteen years' difference in ages. When Meade became commanding general of the Army of the Potomac, he invited Lyman to join him. Lyman's letters and diaries became a rich store of information about the brutal year-long campaign in Virginia that ended at Appomattox.

Lyman was dining at Willard's Hotel in Washington when he first saw Grant in March 1864. "General Grant came in," he wrote his wife, "with his little boy, and was immediately bored by being cheered, and then shaken by the hand. . . . He is rather under middle height, has a spare, strong build; light-brown hair, and short, light-brown beard. His eyes of a clear blue; forehead high; nose aquiline; jaw squarely set, but not sensual. His face has three expressions: deep thought; extreme determination; and great simplicity and calmness."

Grant and Meade first met on April 5. "It was raining hard," Lyman wrote. "Gen. Meade, attired in the knit jacket of a common soldier, opened his tent door half way, put out his arm and said, 'Good morning, General Grant. Pray come in.' " A week later Meade and his staff rode to Culpeper to see Grant. "Grant is a man of a good deal of rough dignity; rather taciturn; quick and decided in speech," wrote Lyman. "He habitually wears an expression as if he had determined to drive his head through a brick wall and was about to do it. I have much confidence in him."

Contrasted to the punctilious eastern staffs, Grant's staff was an embarrassment. One of his aides, wrote Lyman, "was oblivious of straps [spats], and presented an expanse of rather ill-blacked, calfskin boots, that took away from his military ensemble a good deal. When a man *can* ride without straps, he may do so, if he chooses; but when he possesseth not the happy faculty of keeping down his trousers, he should make straps a part of his religion." Grant made a stab at discipline, as when two aides carelessly passed him by. "What is the new regulation," Grant barked, "by which aides ride before their general?"

Grant, too, committed a faux pas. When he reviewed the Sixth Corps on parade, he received John Sedgwick's salute with cigar in mouth, which, wrote Lyman, "gave some offence." Lyman held Meade partially to blame, for he had assured Grant there was no harm in it, "for the good [Meade] has the failing of nine tenths of our officers, a disregard of formal details that brings more trouble than one would think."

Meade prepared his army intensively for the 1864 campaign. Enormous quantities of supplies had been accumulated, recruits had bolstered shriveled regiments, and training had been intensive and realistic. Officers supervised firing practice two hours each day. A wholesale reorganization consolidated five corps into three, engendering bitterness among those whose corps were dissolved and brigades reassigned. Nonetheless the army was the better for it. Gouverneur Warren, whose prescience the year before had saved Little Round Top, commanded the Fifth Corps. Sedgwick, one of the most capable and admired of all Union generals, commanded the Sixth Corps. A sniper would kill Sedgwick at Spotsylvania, and Horatio G. Wright would replace him. The jewel in the crown was the Second Corps under Winfield Scott Hancock.

Hancock was a hero. "He is a tall, soldierly man," Lyman wrote in his diary, "with light brown hair and a heavy military jaw; and has the massive features and the heavy folds round the eye that often mark a man of ability." His sole indulgence was a freshly laundered shirt each day. He had been with the Second Corps since the beginning and had fought with gallantry, distinction, and success in every campaign. His finest hours had been at Gettysburg. On the first day he had restored the shattered First and Eleventh corps, anchored them on Cemetery Ridge, stymied Ewell, and advised Meade that there the army should stand and fight. On the second day he had commanded the line that broke Longstreet's attack with the divisions of Hood and McLaws. And on the third day Hancock threw back Pickett's charge, receiving a thigh wound from which he never fully recovered.

Hancock was exacting in selecting the commander of the First Division, his division the year before. He knew he had found the right man when he heard that Barlow wanted to serve with him. The Puritan was ready again for action after recuperating from his Gettysburg wounds. The healing had been long and painful. He had returned to Boston, Arabella had nursed him, and by early spring he considered himself fit. Nothing had come of the proposed superintendency of the freedman's bureau.* When Hancock asked

---

* The competition was intense and politicized, and Barlow was passed over. Eventually Major General Oliver O. Howard received the appointment, and from his efforts came the genesis of Howard University.

The leaders of the Second Corps helped make it the iron fist of the Army of the Potomac. Standing left to right are division commanders Francis Barlow, David Birney, and John Gibbon. Corps commander Winfield Scott Hancock is seated. All had been wounded at Gettysburg. The left side of Barlow's face is heavily scarred, and Hancock still carried bone fragments in his groin which often incapacitated him. Barlow used his huge saber to pummel laggards and shirkers. This photograph was taken on June 10, following thirty-seven days of continuous combat. (National Archives)

him to take command of the First Division, Barlow promptly accepted. After a recruiting stint in New England, he returned to the Army of the Potomac in mid-April and established his headquarters.

At age twenty-nine, Barlow commanded the largest division in the Army of the Potomac, some four brigades, numbering nearly 8,000 men at the start of the campaign, a third of them recruits. Nelson Miles, twenty-four, whom Barlow extolled, commanded the First Brigade; Thomas A. Smyth, thirty-two, an Irish immigrant, the Second; and John R. Brooke, twenty-five, the Fourth. All were combat veterans (Miles and Brooke had been wounded) and became general officers. Paul Frank commanded the Third Brigade, but Barlow soon jettisoned him for incompetence. None of the brigade commanders were West Point graduates.

The commanding generals of the Second and Third divisions, Brigadier General John Gibbon and Major General David B. Birney, were among the

finest in the army. Like Hancock and Barlow, they had been in the thick of
the fighting at Gettysburg. Gibbon, whose division also contained four
brigades, was a Military Academy graduate and an officer in the prewar
army. At dinner with Lyman, he recalled the story of his Gettysburg wound.
The surgeons had told him it would have been fatal had the bullet passed a
quarter inch further to the left. "Ah," said Gibbon dryly, "the quarter-inches
are in the hands of God."

Birney, a Philadelphia lawyer before the war, was the senior division
commander. His father was a famous antislavery leader, and his brother
William commanded a division of black troops. At Gettysburg, Birney had
temporarily commanded a corps, but he now commanded a smaller division of but two brigades from the disestablished Third Corps. He twice had
been charged with dereliction of duty but had been vindicated and restored
to duty.

The Fourth Division of two brigades, it too formerly of the Third Corps,
was commanded by Brigadier General Gershom Mott, who had performed
acceptably as a brigade commander. The responsibilities of division command, however, would prove too much.

Altogether, the Second Corps mustered some 30,000 soldiers ready for
combat. It would be the fist that hammered Lee.

Barlow was pleased with his division and said so in letters to Almira. He
would have a month to prepare it for combat.

> It has a spirit and tone to it and a pride in its past successes which
> will always make it fight well. It is rather loose in some matters of dis-
> cipline but it is improving every day and everyone is taking hold with
> the best spirit. It has the misfortune to having a very large number of
> new men but I hope the old ones will teach them how to fight and
> become good soldiers. . . .
>
> I am very well satisfied with what has been accomplished since I
> came here. I think I have been successful in making a good impression.
> I have not lost my temper or spoken or acted harshly to anyone and
> though I am thought strict I am well liked. . . .
>
> One of our men sentenced to be shot . . . has been pardoned by the
> Pres. and I dare say the other will be before the time comes though I
> think it is mistaken humanity to do so. 3 or 4 men per diem desert from
> the Division.

Barlow's old regiment, the Sixty-first New York, belonged to the First
Brigade. Together with Miles, he went for a nostalgic dinner. "It was very
pleasant to see them again and talk over old times," he wrote Almira. "There
are quite a number of the old officers remaining in the Reg't but very few of
the old men. Now and then I see one and I always shake him by the hand for
I have a real affection for the old fellows. . . . The 61st is almost entirely a
new Reg't. It now has some 250 men present for duty and some two hundred
recruits are yet to come."

April was a time of hope and optimism in the Army of the Potomac. Lyman, the naturalist, was lyrical in his diary descriptions of blossoms and rejuvenation. Parades and reviews were unceasing, the uniforms dazzling, thousands of soldiers faultlessly equipped. The effect was heart pounding. Lyman watched one such display, then wrote to his wife, "I beheld a distant figure, attired in a General's hat and approaching on horseback. Approaching nearer still I recognized the countenance of the commander of the 1st division, Gen. Barlow. With characteristic gravity he remarked 'What a symmetrical and elegant pair of boots you have on Col. Lyman; and I am glad to see that another officer has as ugly a horse as I have.' (I was on my new filly.) You will understand however that I was extremely elegant in sash & white gloves."

Barlow's turn to shine on parade came on April 19. "Well," wrote Lyman to his wife, "Barlow's review was a big affair. . . . The particular Barlow had caused them to wash their pantaloons, even, and their knapsacks were packed with the utmost precision.

"I thought it almost a dream to see the companion of my boyish evildoing, gravely riding past, and solemnly saluting Major General Hancock; and to think that he commanded such a long procession of regiments! Some of his battalions were more than half raw men, who hurt the marching, though it was excellent, considering; and all were admirably clean and orderly."

Barlow was ecstatic when he wrote Almira that evening. "In the cleanliness of the persons and clothes of the men and the perfection of their equipment and the soldierly way of wearing their knapsacks it was confessed by all to be superior to the others. We have more recruits than the rest of the corps and did not so excel in marching but we were equal to any of them."

Barlow was host to a champagne luncheon afterward. His band, considered the best in the army, serenaded the guests and included a new composition, "Gettysburg." One of his guests, Brigadier General Stewart Webb, had commanded a brigade by the grove of trees at Gettysburg, the focus of Lee's attack on the third day. He had been wounded and awarded the Congressional Medal of Honor. A precise, formal man, Webb was eating an apple when Barlow approached him. "General," said Barlow, "there is some punch, if you prefer to get drunk on *that*." Webb was horrified. "Barlow is the same as ever," Lyman remarked.

Grant reviewed the Second Corps on April 22, with Meade and Hancock standing on either side. "There seemed to be enough men to beat the whole world," wrote Lyman. Barlow led the parade. The Sixty-first New York occupied the traditional place of honor, at the extreme right of the entire Army of the Potomac, and was the first regiment to pass in review. "It was the best and most complete Review of such a body of men that I ever saw and is so considered here," wrote Barlow. "I was well satisfied which is a good deal for me."

Lyman watched Grant intently and later described his impressions:

> He is very fond . . . of horses, and was mounted on one of the handsomest I have seen in the army. He was neatly dressed in regulation uni-

form, with a handsome sash and sword, and the three stars of a lieu-
tenant general on his shoulder. He is a man of natural, severe simplic-
ity, in all things—the very way he wears his high-crowned hat shows
this: he neither puts it on behind his ears, nor draws it over his eyes;
much less does he cock it to one side, but sets it on straight and very
hard on his head. His riding is the same: without the slightest "air,"
and, per contra, *without affectation of homeliness; he sits firmly in the*
saddle and looks straight ahead, as if only intent on getting to some
particular point. . . .

In each direction there was nothing but a wide, moving hedge of
bright muskets; a very fine sight. . . . General Grant is much pleased
and says there is nothing of the sort out West, in the way of discipline
and organization.

Both Barlow and Lyman sensed an expectancy to move, but they knew
not when or where. Security was good.

The Aristocrat and the Army of Northern Virginia were near collapse when
the year 1863 came to a close. Meade had maintained continuous pressure
on the Confederates, and heavy marching and inconclusive battles had further eroded the readiness and morale of Lee's army. The two armies went
into winter quarters on the opposite banks of the Rapidan River.

Lee's personal life was miserable. Rheumatism immobilized Mary; Lee
himself suffered the painful spasms of heart disease. Son Rooney was a prisoner of war, and his wife, Charlotte, lay deathly ill. Custis, the eldest son,
remained unhappily stranded on Davis's staff, unable to arrange a field
assignment. Lee rented a small house in Richmond for Mary and two of their
daughters, and he went there in mid-December to see his family and confer
with Davis.

Davis had summoned him as a consequence of a letter Lee had written in
early December, following the Federal victory at Chattanooga. Worried that
the next most logical move was an invasion of the Deep South, Lee urged a
concentration of Confederate troops not otherwise engaged (none of his,
however) to reinforce the Army of Tennessee. Bragg had asked to be relieved,
and Lee recommended that Beauregard replace him. To Lee's chagrin, Davis
responded with a telegram asking Lee to go west. With his usual protesta-
tions of inadequacy for high office, Lee begged off by return letter, but Davis
was insistent and summoned Lee to Richmond. After long discussions, the
game of musical chairs resumed. Davis decided that Johnston would replace
Bragg. Having proven himself a dismal combat commander, Bragg would
return to Richmond as Davis's military advisor. Beauregard would remain
exiled in Charleston. Lee would stay in Virginia.

Lee returned to the doldrums of his headquarters just before Christmas.
The timing set an example for his army, since he tried by every means to discourage furloughs and leaves of absence. His personal staff had dwindled to
three officers, a few clerks, a cook, and a servant. Departing officers were

not replaced. Lee settled in for another winter of deprivation for himself, his soldiers, and his horses. The leadership of his army continued to deteriorate. Ewell was feeble but decided gamely to carry on with his corps command. Longstreet, for the moment stranded in East Tennessee, would return in the spring failed and fractious, threatening to resign, many of his generals under arrest.

Other generals in Lee's army, contentious about promotions and assignments, slights and wounded pride, bucked their grievances to Lee for adjudication. As unpleasantness and controversy were repugnant, Lee employed stratagems either of silence or diplomatic equivocation. His staff shielded him from aggrieved officers seeking an audience. When one such obnoxious individual blustered his way into Lee's tent, he berated the staff. "Why did you permit that man to come to my tent and make me show my temper?" said Lee, his face flushed.

Rarely would Lee act decisively or publicly. Tactful measures and guarded negotiations were his style. Never did he initiate courts-martial and rarely courts of inquiry, for they resolved nothing, satisfied no one, and required sitting officers who were needed at the front. Yet in one respect Lee was resolute: his generals were to convene courts-martial to punish and condemn deserters. Death sentences were final, and Lee would hear no appeals for clemency. Leniency encouraged more desertions, he believed, and he scolded Davis for issuing a general amnesty to entice men to return, for the good intentions had boomeranged. Only the swift and consistent use of the firing squad, Lee believed, could stanch the hemorrhaging from the Army of Northern Virginia. "[The number of desertions] is sufficiently great," he wrote to Davis on April 13, "to show the necessity of adhering to the only policy that will restrain the evil, and which I am sure will be found to be truly merciful in the end."

In other ways Lee exercised restraint. Southern generals hotly resented criticism as insulting their honor. If it came from Lee, it would be especially humiliating. Thus, for Lee's purposes, overt faultfinding was impractical, however egregious the circumstances. Lee's battle reports reflected his meticulous discretion. They were months in preparation, first being drafted by a staff officer who tried to reconcile delayed and conflicting information, and in the end they contained not a word of censure. Yet in extreme circumstances Lee would speak to offenders privately and tactfully. Other traits that were recognized as expressions of his displeasure were voice inflections, a flushed face, a glaring eye, and sometimes silence. But blunt words, never.

Lee was aware of Lincoln's call for more recruits, and he knew that Lincoln would get them by the scores of thousands. Peering across the river at the sea of tents, Lee could see fresh manpower swelling the Federal ranks. The anemic Confederate head count made Lee voracious for warm bodies. As Lee had urged, the conscription laws now included boys and old men, allowing him to scour the land to dragoon males of any age who could bear arms, regardless of occupation or possible contribution to the war effort. As farmers were not delivering food nor artificers manufactured goods to his army, Lee reasoned they might as well join the ranks. Gorgas alone retained most of his skilled craftsmen for the manufacture of armaments.

Lee employed draconian expediencies to try to feed his men and animals. His raiding parties scoured western and southwestern Virginia to collect cattle and swine. Cavalry and artillery horses were pastured across Virginia and North Carolina to consume forage that farmers had grown for their own livestock. Hesitant as Lee was to release soldiers from his span of control for fear of desertion, selected men were granted furloughs to ease the burden on the army's commissary. The mobilization for war was ruthless, indiscriminate, and total.

Confederate strategists and planners exchanged schemes for the campaigns of 1864, most of them madness. The perennial dream of invading Kentucky and driving to the Ohio River resurfaced. Indeed, in an exercise of fantasy Davis so instructed Johnston, as if oblivious to the mighty army that Sherman was assembling for the invasion of Georgia. Lee, too, proposed to attack the Army of the Potomac as a matter of principle, but he conceded that his thinking was entirely academic given the reduced condition of his army. In reality, the initiative belonged solely to Grant. The Confederate armies would react and strive to survive. The greatest Confederate hope lay in the very act of survival. If the armies still were intact and fighting come November, a peace candidate might defeat Lincoln for the White House and negotiate an end to the war on Confederate terms.

Gordon and his brigade had been inactive for ten months following its return to Virginia from the Gettysburg campaign. Camp life along the Rapidan had been austere and enervating, a struggle to survive for want of food, clothing, and blankets. The bleakness dispirited the suffering soldiers. They commonly believed that their misery was God's punishment, that somehow they had displeased God for things done and left undone, or for lack of faith and piety. Whatever the reasons for God's wrath, the pain and anguish were intense, and the soldiers sought His redemption. Crowds of penitents went to the many revivals, prayer meetings, and other religious functions. Inspired by his spiritual rebirth after recovering from his Antietam wounds, Gordon used his powers of oratory to preach and seek converts during the dark ages of the winter.

The Cavalier waited for the Army of the Potomac to begin the campaign.

"The leaves continue to open," Lyman wrote his wife on May 2, "among them the tulip trees with their green flower-buds. Lilacs are in full leaf and the flowers formed ready to open, in a few days. Strawberries are in full flower. But this country is terribly desolate looking, despite the struggling green; it is a worn brown with the passing of trains & horses; and the wood is so cut off; while, on every hand you see the rubbish of deserted camps. No moving orders yet, though one would say they must come soon."

Meade's headquarters was packing the following day. "We have much in our favor," wrote Lyman. "A large, well disciplined army, with most excellent corps commanders, and very few subordinate generals who are not just first rate. . . . Of course our success depends on a thousand pieces of good or bad fortune; and we have a man of the first ability opposed to us."

Grant ordered the army to cross the Rapidan that evening, hoping to clear the Wilderness and gain open ground before Lee reacted. Lee was free to maneuver because he had no fortifications, and for the last time in the war he was capable of attacking with his entire army. He chose the Wilderness as his battleground, where he had turned back Hooker a year earlier. Perhaps he could do it again; the narrow roads and dense forests restricted visibility and mobility and mitigated the Federal advantage of numbers and firepower.

Grant accommodated Lee by halting Meade's army in the midst of the Wilderness rather than pushing into the open. Francis A. Walker, a Second Corps staff officer and later its historian, believed that it was one of the blunders of the war, because in this terrain Grant squandered the training and organization, and with it the manpower, of the Army of the Potomac.

> All the peculiar advantages of the Army of the Potomac were sacrificed in the jungle-fighting into which they were thus called to engage. . . . How can a battle be fitly ordered in such a tangle of wood and brush, where troops can neither be sent straight to their destination nor seen and watched over, when, after repeatedly losing direction and becoming broken into fragments in their advance through thickets and jungles, they at last make their way up to the line of battle, perhaps at the point they were designated to reinforce, perhaps far from it?
>
> Here chance has heaped up regiments till the men are six or eight deep; there, a single thin line continues to the front, westward or eastward; here, again, a gap appears. Appears, did I say? No, it does not appear at a greater distance than fifty or a hundred yards; but it exists, nevertheless, and through this accidental breach may, at any moment, enter a hostile column which shall disrupt and throw back the whole line, so that the extremity of valor shall be useless; so that the highest soldiership shall be in vain; so that brigades shall not know whether the fire from which men are dropping by hundreds in their ranks comes from the foe or from their own comrades who have lost their way in the tangled forest. . . .
>
> As it was, of the one hundred and fifty guns accompanying the infantry corps into the Wilderness, there was not real use for one third in that battle; while the ablest general was able to control his men and influence their actions in only the faintest and remotest degree. *

As columns of Federal troops crossed on pontoon bridges and were swallowed in the Wilderness, Lee sent corps commanders Ewell and A. P. Hill

---

* "Our victory consisted in having successfully crossed a formidable stream, almost in the face of an enemy, and in getting the army together as a unit," Grant wrote in his memoirs. After two days of fighting Grant believed that the relative strengths were about the same "as when the river divided them. But the fact of having safely crossed was a victory."

eastward to intercept, followed far to the rear by Longstreet. The myopic armies groped toward one another, and the battle began with a chance encounter between Ewell and Warren on a road three miles west of Wilderness Tavern on the morning of May 5. As the Federal troops hammered Ewell's advance divisions, the advantage went to Warren in the beginning. Ewell galloped down the road looking for reinforcements and found Gordon hustling his brigade toward the sounds of the guns. Ewell urged him on to blunt the Federal advance.

Gordon was again in his glory. His voice and sword spurred his soldiers to plunge into the disoriented Federal lines. Their momentum carried them so deeply into the midst of the enemy that Gordon found himself nearly surrounded. Redeploying his regiments into a square, like Wellington at Waterloo, Gordon clung to his ground until other brigades had closed up by nightfall. That night Ewell ordered him to shift to his far left and anchor the left wing.

Once in position, Gordon dispatched scouts to locate the enemy. To his delight he discovered that by great good fortune his brigade overlapped the end of the Federal line. The opportunity was dazzling. With rising excitement he envisioned doing what Jackson had done at Chancellorsville, to maneuver shock troops behind the unsuspecting enemy and tear into the rear. The blow would so overwhelm the enemy, Gordon believed, that a victory as stunning as Chancellorsville surely would follow.

Gordon sought out Ewell and Early with his revelation, requesting additional troops and permission to attack. To Gordon's dismay, Early thought such an operation unsafe on the supposition that Burnside's corps was nearby. (As it happened, Burnside was far away, but perception governed thinking.) Ewell deferred to Early. Both had slapped Gordon across the face, giving more credence to unsubstantiated reports than to Gordon's personal reconnaissance.

Early reconsidered by late afternoon and reinforced Gordon with an additional brigade. Gordon kicked off his assault at sunset and was initially successful. Two Federal generals were captured with hundreds of other soldiers, but then darkness, confusion, and stiffening resistance ended Gordon's chances for glory. Afterward, Gordon wrote bitterly of what might have been. Having failed to replicate Jackson's success, Gordon very nearly got himself killed, as Jackson had, by wandering beyond the lines in the dark and blundering into a Federal patrol. Spurring his horse, he escaped as a fusillade whistled about him. What had been "a cautious ride to the front," Gordon later wrote, became "a madcap ride to the rear." The stallion he had commandeered a few hours before from a captured Federal general got him out safely.

Grant, too, would muff the first of several opportunities in the campaign to attack in flank, albeit on a grander scale. While Warren and Sedgwick faced westward to meet the advancing Hill and Ewell, Grant directed Hancock to swing southwest to get at Lee's lines of communication. A flanking attack requires both skill and daring, for the elements of the army are initially separated, as one force holds the enemy in check while the detached force maneuvers independently to the flank and rear of the enemy. When Lee had Jackson, such tactics were aggressively and successfully executed. Although Jackson was gone, Lee still tried flanking attacks when the opportunity arose, despite the limitations of his remaining corps commanders.

While Grant had employed strategic flanking operations, rarely had he attempted to outflank a fully engaged opponent. His one major endeavor had been at Chattanooga, with Sherman doing the flanking and failing. Hence Grant was hesitant to attempt to flank an enemy army at close quarters, preferring to mass his own army, which always had the greater manpower, and to rely on frontal assaults to grind it out by attrition. So it was in the Wilderness. Grant recalled Hancock from his turning movement and ordered him to rendezvous with Warren and Sedgwick.

Hancock collided head-on with Hill on the afternoon of May 5. "[A]mid those dense woods, where foemen could not see each other," wrote Walker, "where colonels could not see the whole of their regiments, where, often, captains could not see the left of their companies—these two armies, thus suddenly brought into collision, wrestled in desperate battle until night came to make the gloom complete. Thousands on either side had fallen. Of those that survived many had not beheld the enemy; yet the tangled forest had been alive with flying missiles; the whistling of the bullets through the air had been incessant; the very trees seemed peopled by spirits that shrieked and groaned through those hours of mortal combat."

The year before, Hooker had circled his wagons after Lee had struck. Things were entirely different with Grant and Meade, who issued orders to resume attacking at daybreak on the sixth. The Second Corps, comprising the left wing, would be reinforced and would constitute the principal assault against the Confederate right, the Third Corps commanded by Hill. Forewarned that Longstreet was fast approaching from the south and would try to turn the Federal left, Hancock prudently detached Barlow with artillery to guard in that direction. When it became apparent that Longstreet was coming in behind Hill, Barlow was not recalled and missed the ensuing action owing to misunderstandings between Hancock and Gibbon. As a consequence, a large gap opened between Barlow and Hancock, through which the Confederate force struck.

While Gordon fretted to the north over missed opportunities, Hill reeled from Hancock's pounding to the south. By Lee's orders Hill had not entrenched—entrenching would soon be routine, but not yet—and since Hill was a sick man, his corps had been wholly unprepared. Tradition has it that Lee lost his equilibrium and was about to lead the Texas Brigade himself; calmer heads restrained him until he recovered his poise, so it was said. By late morning the Federal attack lost momentum from the friction of the forest obstacles that scrambled the once orderly lines. When Longstreet arrived at about eight in the morning with fresh divisions, he shoved his way through the tangle of trees and retreating soldiers to stabilize a defensive line.

Barlow directs his troops in the Wilderness. An aide carries the red trefoil pennant that identifies Barlow as commander of the First Division, Second Corps. In this instance, Barlow moved his division to protect the army's flank and missed the main action. Combat artist Alfred Waud instructed the engravers to add "a good deal of smoke from burning brush." (Waud—Library of Congress)

Lee and Longstreet instinctively considered a flanking movement for the next phase of the battle, but as always their crude maps handicapped planning. The Wilderness maps were characteristically incomplete, showing only the main roads and none of the secondary roads. The staffs had again stayed in camp instead of surveying potential battlefields. Jedediah Hotchkiss had spent the winter in the Shenandoah Valley, working on maps of Pennsylvania and West Virginia. Joining Lee just before the start of the campaign, he would serve largely as a courier.

Thus ignorant of the Virginia terrain where he was fighting, Lee dispatched Brigadier General Martin L. Smith, his chief engineer, to reconnoiter and find a route. Smith returned and reported he had found an unfinished railway embankment nearby, which would allow a large body of troops to circle about the Federal left. Lee crudely traced the railway line on his map and authorized a flanking attack.

Moxley Sorrel scratched together four brigades, slipped between Barlow isolated to the south and Hancock's left flank, and attacked at about eleven o'clock. Longstreet simultaneously charged ahead with his main force, compelling Hancock to retreat on the same ground he had advanced upon but a few hours before. "A large part of the whole line came back," wrote Lyman, "slowly but mixed up—a hopeless sight! American soldiers, in this condition are enough to sink one's heart! They have no craven terror—they have their arms; but, for the moment, they will not fight, nor even rally. Drew my sword and tried to stop them, but with small success." Falling back to his entrenchments on the Brock Road, Hancock restored his line, and Longstreet went no further.

Lyman reported the developments to Meade. An attack by Burnside and his Ninth Corps, operating independently of the Army of the Potomac, had been part of Grant's plan.* Grant had sent him a staff officer as a guide, but true to form Burnside had failed to appear. "Grant, who was smoking stoically under a pine," wrote Lyman, "expressed himself annoyed and surprised that Burnside did not attack." Lyman returned to Hancock at Brock Road and found him fatigued and alone, inasmuch as all his staff had been dispatched to position the brigades. His troops were rallied, he told Lyman, but very tired and mixed up, in no condition to advance. They would wait for Longstreet to resume the action.

While Longstreet discussed a renewed assault with his officers, his own troops shot at him as he rode among them. A bullet to his chest knocked him to the ground. In light of the turbulence among the Confederate formations, Lee canceled any further attacks for the day. After Gordon's assault at the other end of the line fizzled with the darkness, the battle in the Wilderness was over. Both armies lay panting. The dry undercover caught fire, and flames consumed the dead and the screaming wounded.

---

* Burnside had such seniority in the Federal army that Grant thought it would be awkward to make him subordinate to Meade. Hence Burnside reported directly to Grant, an arrangement that produced confusion and misunderstandings.

25

VIRGINIA: SPOTSYLVANIA

I n the past, a battle such as the Wilderness would have ended the Federal offensive for the summer. The Army of the Potomac would have with-drawn, and the initiative would have passed to Lee. Grant was different. Grant was going to stay and fight it out, with the Army of Northern Virginia, and not Richmond, as his objective. Never before had Lee been confronted with a Federal general who intended to exert unremitting pressure with unlimited resources.

On May 7, Grant began the first of many strategic maneuvers to isolate Lee from the Confederate capital. The Overland Campaign would last for six weeks, a series of parallel races southward to strategic crossroads. The armies would pause to fight, then resume the race to the south. Grant would invariably swing to his left, eastward of Lee, in order to maintain his supply lines to the rivers on Chesapeake Bay.

The first objective was Spotsylvania Court House, twelve miles southeast of Wilderness Tavern. The intersection of roads there leading to Richmond made it a strategic location. If Grant got there first, Lee would be cut off from Richmond. After a running battle Lee finally got possession, then turned northward to receive the next blow.

For the first time in the war, Lee ordered his soldiers to entrench, for he rec-ognized the craving for self-preservation. By the third year of the war soldiers on both sides instinctively sought shelter from shot and shell. Once, the Army of Northern Virginia had considered it beneath contempt to fall prone, to dig pits, and to construct fortifications of trees and stone. Now the soldiers will-ingly consented with Lee and his generals to perfect the art of defense.

Theodore Lyman described the difficulty in taking an entrenched position, because Lee's soldiers had become expert in hiding and concealing themselves.

These were their first ideas at every halt, to protect their lives by a parapet . . . in the edge of a wood where it would be hidden and would

Grant orders the Army of the Potomac to press on into Virginia after the Battle of the Wilderness. In earlier campaigns the Federal army had withdrawn after costly battles with the Army of Northern Virginia. The soldiers cheered when they realized that they would never again retreat before Lee. "I shall take no step backward," Grant told Lincoln. "I propose to fight it out on this line if it takes all summer." (Forbes—Library of Congress)

yet command a wide field of fire. In front were the entrenched pickets, not as mere videttes, but strictly as a fighting line, with good supports and perhaps a grand guard in the rear. Behind the main line and concealed with equal ease were the field batteries.

In approaching [Lee's] army thus posted, what can be seen? The answer is in one word—nothing! Perhaps an active signal officer has climbed a tall tree and can thence descry a rod or two of fresh earth that indicates a breastwork, or a drooping battle flag, or some gray staff officer who gallops across an opening. Such are the meager signs that invite a reconnaissance.

As the infantry deploys and the skirmishers push out, the stillness is occasionally broken by the scream of a passing shell, followed immediately by the distant sullen report of the gun that threw it. A neighboring battery captain immediately trains a piece on the little puff of smoke and tries to silence his opponent. Presently in the dense woods, far in front, are heard two or three musket-shots, the signal for a violent spattering fire. The skirmishers have struck the entrenched picket line.

> *And now begins the serious and tedious task of getting back this force, and determining the position and nature of the main entrenchments. To effect this sometimes requires the advance of a line of battle; and even when a part of the pickets are forced back, a brigade may come out and recover the lost ground. Many weary hours are usually occupied in this desultory but destructive fighting; and, at the end of that time, the result along a front of several miles is in no sense uniform. In some places the hostile pickets may be well crowded back, while in others covered by natural obstacles and strongly defended, the attacking troops may be still far off.*
>
> *Meantime the enemy's general has had leisure to strengthen and reinforce the most exposed parts of his front. These parts, although best prepared to resist an assault, are precisely those most likely to be assaulted because they are the only ones which have been determined by reconnaissance. And now, even with the best haste much time must be occupied in bringing up the troops and forming them for attack; for the woods are imperfectly known, the roads mere cart paths, and the advancing columns are exposed to heavy artillery fire. Thus it happens that, when a charge is finally made, the enemy is found in two well manned lines of breastworks with entrenched batteries in the rear and perhaps a slashing in front.*
>
> *The whole of such a complex and protracted military operation is well summed up in a single phrase of Gen. Meade spoken after the fight at Cold Harbor: "In this country I must fight a battle to reconnoiter a position."*

As the Confederate army burrowed into the soil of Spotsylvania County, Lee had appointed two replacement corps commanders. Richard H. Anderson now commanded Longstreet's First Corps. A. P. Hill had been invalided with undiagnosed ailments, and so Early commanded the Third Corps. Lee wanted to promote and appoint Gordon to the vacancy in Early's division, but other brigadier generals were senior and by custom had precedence. A series of complicated shufflings removed them from contention, and Gordon would become a major general. "Old soldiers might have asked themselves," wrote Freeman, "whether so many changes ever had been made by Army Headquarters to give a Brigadier General a Division."

The Confederate army at Spotsylvania occupied an irregular salient some two miles in depth and two and a half miles wide at its base, with its right wing anchored at Spotsylvania Court House and its left at the Po River near Blockhouse Bridge. Trees and extended skirmish lines concealed the soldiers. Artillery covered their positions. The only weakness was the center, the apex of the salient, which was like an awkward finger jutting from a fist. The skinny, vulnerable extension reflected Ewell's bad judgment, but neither Lee nor his chief engineer altered its alignment. It pointed across vacant field and forest and was squeezed between the two converging Federal wings, Meade from the northwest toward the Confederate left and Burnside from the northeast toward the right and Spotsylvania Court House.

The Federal Second Corps paused on the north bank of the Po River on the afternoon of May 9, about a mile to the west of Lee's left wing. Lyman later remarked that Barlow was "a queer, lean figure, in a cap, checked shirt and blue pantaloons, mounted on a tall horse." As Grant, Meade, and Hancock met and talked, a Confederate wagon train passed on the opposite shore; it was within such tempting range that a battery fired upon it, and the teamsters fled.

What happened next has neither been explained nor understood. On the spur of the moment, Grant and Meade decided that a division should cross the river and chase the wagons. Barlow went across. When Birney and Gibbon followed, a whim had blossomed into a major turning movement against Lee's left flank.

It was an uncharacteristic maneuver for Grant to undertake, for, as we have seen, he had never commanded a successful envelopment on such a scale. (Meade was undoubtedly surprised. Before the campaign had begun, Grant had told him that, once across the Rapidan, "there is to be no maneuvering with this army for position.") In this case it meant that the Second Corps would operate independently with a river at its back. There were risks: the decision was impetuous, all was improvisation, and the terrain and the location of enemy forces were unknown. Yet the Second Corps troops did not deploy helter-skelter, for they were disciplined and well led. The rewards would be stupendous if they could get into the rear of Lee's army.

Grant already had reduced the probability of success by impulsively kicking off the maneuver in late afternoon, forfeiting surprise and preventing the Second Corps from closing with the enemy before nightfall. Lee was forewarned and had all night to shift troops toward the commotion on his far left. Had Grant waited until the next morning, allowing Hancock time to plan and coordinate a powerful turning movement, the chances of success would have been immeasurably greater, but Grant was not given to patience.

Barlow's First Division, together with the divisions of Birney and Gibbon, would twice have to cross the Po River. The first crossing, over pontoon bridges spanning the fifty-foot-wide turbulent river, went well; opposition was sporadic. The Federal soldiers went on through dense woods and veered in toward the second crossing, but owing to darkness they stopped short. When the Second Corps reconnoitered the Blockhouse Bridge over the Po the next morning, on May 10, they found it was fortified. One of Barlow's brigades went downstream, forded the river, and established a beachhead on the opposite bank. Now they were behind Lee's left flank. The Second Corps was poised to assault Lee's army from the rear, where there were no fortifications to protect the Confederates.

It was not to be. Grant lost his nerve, and he ordered Hancock to return forthwith with two of his divisions to join in a massed assault on Lee's left wing. Hancock headed back with Gibbon and Birney, leaving Barlow to remain in place "with a threatening attitude on the enemy's left." Grant had botched his one great opportunity to destroy Lee's army in the early stages of the campaign.

With the Po River on three sides, Barlow had been left isolated from the remainder of the Federal army. A Confederate division commanded by Henry Heth arrived to secure the left wing; when Meade heard that Barlow was tangling with Heth's skirmishers, he feared that Lee's army could pin Barlow against the bend in the river. Meade ordered Hancock to return to Barlow to help extricate his division, but Barlow was enjoying the action. No longer fighting from his stand-up mode of earlier years, Barlow had radically transformed his style and, remembered Francis Walker, now had "made skirmishing a profession.

> *It is a melancholy fact that three men out of four who entered the service of the United States left it, if alive, without ever having seen a really good piece of work of this character. Indeed, most regiments in the service had as little idea of skirmishing as an elephant. But to Barlow's brigades the very life of military service was in a widely extended formation, flexible yet firm, where the soldiers were thrown largely on their individual resources, but remained in a high degree under the control of the resolute, sagacious, keen-eyed officers, who urged them forward, or drew them back, as the exigency of the case required; where every advantage was taken of the nature of the ground, of fences, trees, stones, and prostrate logs; where manhood rose to its maximum and mechanism sank to its minimum, and where almost anything seemed possible to vigilance, audacity, and cool self-possession. . . .*
>
> *It seemed a pity to interrupt the fight that was imminent; and had it been left to the vote of Barlow and his brigadiers the duel would have come off. A prettier field for such a contest was rarely to be found in that land of tangles and swamps. The forces were far from being unequally matched. A Confederate division was, in general, much larger than a division of Union troops; but Heth's column had suffered heavily in the Wilderness; while Barlow's was at this time much the strongest division of the Army of the Potomac. Never, to the end of the war, did the officers of the First Division, there present, cease to speak with an affectionate sadness of the chance that was that day lost.*
>
> *In the situation existing, to fight seemed as easy as it was imminent; [but] to retreat with their backs to a river, the enemy in full advance, was a most critical matter.*

Critical indeed. The complex withdrawal began at two o'clock in three stages, the last being across the military bridges. Barlow and Hancock were everywhere, directing, leading, encouraging. Half the division at a time disengaged and leapfrogged to the rear to take up new positions, while the other half held off a full Confederate division building up a head of steam, encouraged by thinking that the Federal soldiers were on the run. Artillery from the Second Corps roared overhead to pummel the advancing Confederates. The woods caught fire, adding smoke and noise to the battlefield.

Barlow and his division made it across the river and tore up the bridges. The battle of the Po River ended for the day. Barlow had left behind a single artillery piece that had gotten stuck in the trees. "This was the first gun ever lost by the Second Corps," Hancock reported mournfully.

"I shall take no step backward," Grant had wired on May 10. "Send to Bell[e] Plain all the Infantry you can rake and scrape." Ten thousand men, declared Grant, could be spared from the Washington defenses. A day later he wired Washington that he had sustained heavy losses in the first six days of fighting, some 20,000 men and eleven general officers. Grant wanted speedy reinforcements. "I hope they will be sent as fast as possible," he wrote, "and in as great numbers. . . . I am satisfied the enemy are very shaky, and are only kept up to the mark by the greatest exertions on the part of their officers, and by keeping them entrenched in every position they take. . . . I propose to fight it out on this line if it takes all summer."

Lyman saw things entirely differently. "The newspapers would be comic in their comments," he mused, "were not the whole thing so tragic.

> More absurd statements could not be. Lee is not retreating: he is a brave and skilful soldier and he will fight while he has a division or a day's ration left. These Rebels are not half-starved and ready to give up—a more sinewy, tawny, formidable-looking set of men could not be . . . they know how to handle weapons with terrible effect. Their great characteristic is their stoical manliness; they never beg, or whimper, or complain; but look you straight in the face, with as little animosity as if they had never heard a gun.
>
> I will remark that I had taken part in two great battles, and heard the bullets whistle both days, and yet I had scarcely seen a Rebel save killed, wounded, or prisoners . . . the great art is to conceal men; for the moment they show, bang, bang, go a dozen cannon, the artillerists only too pleased to get a fair mark. . . . "Left face—prime—forward!" and then wrang, wr-r-ang, for three or four hours, or for all day, and the poor, bleeding wounded streaming to the rear. That is the great battle in America.

Grant was in a dilemma. Lee lurked menacingly in the woods north of Spotsylvania, Grant knew not where, as dangerous as a wounded lion. He knew vaguely that the Confederate line was a salient, with Meade's Army of the Potomac on the western flank and Burnside with his independent Ninth Corps on the eastern side. As neither was connected, the apex of the salient was interposed between the two forces. Whether Lee would strike, hold what he had, or withdraw was unpredictable.

Grant was determined to retain the initiative, to keep Lee off balance, and to make Lee react to him and not conversely. The apex intrigued him. Although no one at headquarters had seen it, in his mind's eye Grant reasoned that it had to be vulnerable. Surely the Second Corps, striking at dawn, could smash the center of Lee's salient and so too Lee's army. Grant convinced himself that the concept was brilliant. His blindness as to the conditions at the apex was no impediment. At three o'clock on May 11, Grant issued the assault order to Meade. It was sweeping in concept and barren of particulars. Meade and his subordinates could figure out the details.

Meade summoned his three corps commanders. Hancock was to withdraw his three divisions (Barlow, Gibbon, and Birney) from his lines on the right flank, pass to the rear of the Fifth and Sixth corps, assemble near the apex, and attack at dawn. Meade could tell Hancock nothing about the roads to get there or what they would find. Orders were orders.

Hancock met with his three division commanders at about seven o'clock. Barlow was stunned at the lack of foresight. The only certainty was that his division would lead the assault force of 20,000 Federal troops. A long march—at night—would get them into position. Staff officers Lieutenant Colonel Charles H. Morgan, Hancock's chief of staff, and Lieutenant Colonel G. H. Mendall, a Hancock aide, would show the way. Both were furious with the absurdity of the operation as Barlow and the legions got underway. Rain fell, fog moved in, and the black night became blacker. Soldiers floundered through the muck, guided by the profanity at the head of the column. "It was an exquisitely ludicrous scene," Barlow recalled, "and I could hardly sit on my horse for laughter."

When the exasperated guides seemed lost, Barlow was irrepressible. "For heaven's sake," he gibed, "at least face us in the right direction so that we shall not march away from the enemy and have to go round the world and come up in their rear." Riding nearby, Miles and Brooke were furious, "loud in their complaints in the madness of the whole undertaking," said Barlow. Telling everyone to shut up, Barlow pressed on. A mule loaded with cooking utensils broke loose and galloped toward Barlow's column. Thinking themselves under attack, soldiers stampeded. Officers restored order, and the march continued.

Barlow had gotten his division in position by early morning. Morgan and Mendall pointed into the darkness where the enemy presumably lay, but again they confessed their ignorance. Desperate for intelligence, Barlow groped from one encampment to another until he found a regimental commander, Lieutenant Colonel Waldo Merriman, who told Barlow of a field between the woods, which was a natural corridor leading to the Confederate lines, and other sketchy details of the terrain. Merriman's information was still not enough.

Morgan remembered Barlow's anxiety about the ground over which he had to move his division. Someone guessed the distance to the enemy line as less than a mile. Could there possibly be, asked Barlow sarcastically, a thousand-foot-deep chasm between him and the enemy? "When he could not be assured even on this point," recalled Morgan, "he seemed to think that he was called upon to lead a forlorn hope, and placed his valuables in the hands of a friend."*

---

* The phrase "forlorn hope" was commonly used in the mid–nineteenth century to express a terribly dangerous undertaking with but two possible outcomes, glory or death, the latter more likely. It will be recalled that Lee had used it to describe his operations in western Virginia.

Barlow announced that he intended to form his four brigades into a block formation, with Brooke and Miles in the lead, and Smyth and Hiram L. Brown (who had relieved the drunken Paul Frank) immediately behind. They would follow the course of the field wherever it might lead. Birney would form his division into two conventional lines and advance through the dense woods on Barlow's right. Mott and Gibbon would follow in reserve.

Barlow's aide-de-camp, Captain John D. Black, remembered Barlow's pessimism:

> *I never remember seeing General Barlow so depressed . . . he acted as if it was indeed a forlorn hope he was to lead. His voice was subdued and tender as he issued his orders to the staff, for the formation of the command; very different from the brusque and decided manner usual for him, accompanied by the remark we had heard so many times on similar occasions, "Make your peace with God and mount, gentleman; I have a hot place picked out for some of you today"; or the consoling remark that would sometimes follow, after hearing of some general officer who had particularly distinguished himself and had certain of his staff killed or wounded. "Well, gentlemen, it beats Hell that none of my staff get killed or wounded."*

Equivalent confusion permeated the Confederate high command. Lee had received reports on the eleventh of activity on all fronts. When Grant had sent his wagons back to Belle Plain for fresh supplies, there was speculation that it was a prelude to an imminent retreat. Miles and his brigade had reconnoitered on the far left on the Po; perhaps another flanking movement was imminent. Burnside had been stirring on the right. Something was up. Grant already had shown in the Wilderness that he would pick up and move fast on short notice. Lee mistakenly concluded that Grant was withdrawing, his destination speculative, and that he did not intend to attack Lee's current position.

Lee wanted to be ready to move promptly. He ordered Ewell to remove both the artillery and the infantry from the apex so they could be underway without delay when Grant's direction of movement became known. In the mix-up only the artillery was relocated. Major General Edward Johnson, commanding the division at the apex, was astonished when the twenty-two guns of the corps artillery were hitched up and taken to the rear at sunset. No one told him why they were being removed. He did not seek out Ewell for an explanation. The batteries passed through Gordon's division in the rear, at the base of the salient, where Gordon was posted in reserve.

Confederate pickets heard the sound of 20,000 men gathering in the darkness, and their alarm rippled up the chain of command. An agitated Johnson demanded the return of the artillery, and Ewell concurred. Far to the rear, Confederate artillerymen harnessed their horses and lashed them pell-mell through the rain and fog back toward the apex. Morning twilight was beginning, but as no one had alerted him, Lee slept.

The attack jumped off at 4:30 A.M. on May 12, through haze and first light. Barlow's advance guard was not yet able to see the Confederate fortifications a half mile ahead. The men marched silently, their ranks aligned, then merging as the pace accelerated. "The Confederate pickets were only a pistol's shot away," recalled aide-de-camp Black, "and, as they challenged, the low order was passed along our line, 'Double-quick,' replied to by a scattering volley from them, and then with a mad rush our boys were upon them and a dull thud here and there, as the butt of a musket compelled a more speedy surrender, told how well the order had been obeyed, and the way was open for the attack."

Birney's soldiers on the right had a harder time of it in the dense woods, but somehow they kept up. The inexorable mass of Federal soldiers flushed the Confederate pickets, who scampered ahead like heralds of the Last Judgment. When the Confederate line came in view a yell went up, unleashing the roar of a thousand voices, and the Federal troops broke into a run, as if releasing the frustration of past recalls and retreats and humiliations in one mad explosion of human energy. The last obstacle was an abatis of sharpened pine poles, demolished in moments with axes and hands. Then they were upon the Confederate soldiers.

Within minutes Barlow's and Birney's men had captured several thousand soldiers and two mortified general officers, Johnson and one of his brigade commanders, George H. Steuart. Confederate cannon returning belatedly to the front were seized before they could unlimber. As the supporting troops piled in behind Barlow's division, the battlefield became bedlam. Barlow's own men scuffled with prisoners, grabbed trophies, and banged away at desperate enemy soldiers emerging from the haze. Trying to exploit the breakthrough as integral units, Barlow and his commanders attempted to separate and coordinate the scrambling, brawling soldiers. But the Federal army was unaccustomed to cracking a Confederate line so rapidly, and the once disciplined ranks became uncontrollable. The flood of Federal reinforcements was unabated, piling men upon men into a struggling, flailing arena of pandemonium.

Because of the darkness and fog, Gordon, who was in reserve a quarter mile from the breakthrough, at first could rely only upon his hearing. He had heard a spatter of gunfire, then silence. Mustering his one immediately available brigade under Robert D. Johnson, Gordon led it forward, groping through the clinging mist, until it collided with the leading edge of Barlow's soldiers, who sent a volley into the Confederate ranks. Still uncertain as to the numbers of the enemy, Gordon deployed the brigade in line and charged into the vapor. Sheets of fire tore into his men. At that moment Gordon comprehended the extent of the crisis: the Federal army had split the salient in two and was in a position to annihilate Lee's army.

Gordon's second brigade, commanded by Clement A. Evans, now became available. Gordon went with three of its six regiments into the mist to distract and delay the enemy while his staff positioned the remainder and guided his third brigade, under J. William Hoffman, into line. Still he could

Barlow's troops storm the Confederate line at Spotsylvania on May 12, 1864. After a midnight march in a thunderstorm, his First Division attacked at dawn and overwhelmed the astonished defenders. Gordon led a counterattack, and the murderous battle seesawed for the remainder of the day. (Painting by Thure de Thulstrup, courtesy Massachusetts Commandery Military Order of the Loyal Legion and the U.S. Army Military History Institute)

not see the enemy, but by the sound of their gunfire they were moving to his right and advancing. When Gordon returned to the rear once again, he found his men in line of battle. Lee was in their midst, his eyes glazed, dumbfounded by the unfolding disaster.

Lee's presence made Gordon frantic. At any moment the Federal troopers would burst through the fog; instead of organizing his men, Gordon was forced to plead with Lee to find safety. He and others tried to break Lee's trance by shouting, but the old man could not hear them. In desperation Gordon seized Lee's bridle, and staff officers jostled their mounts to shield him from the approaching gunfire. An enlisted man grasped his reins and led Lee to the rear, still in shock and speechless. Gordon wheeled to the north, unsheathed his sword, and bellowed charge. His frenzied soldiers screamed their Rebel yell and tore into Barlow's approaching outliers.

Barlow no longer was in the salient. Agitated and frustrated at the fresh brigades barreling into his rear and disrupting his ranks, he had gone to the rear to seek out Hancock, whom he had not seen since the seven o'clock

the toughest fight yet -

After Gordon's counterattack the Spotsylvania line stabilized along the original fortifications, and the killing along the salient went on well into the night. Soldiers huddled on either side of the wooden fortifications and fired at point-blank range over and through the logs. When soldiers on both sides raised their hats to gauge the intensity of the enemy fire, the hats were instantly shredded. (Waud—Library of Congress)

meeting the night before. Barlow found Hancock at the Landrum farmhouse, a quarter mile north of the apex, and he spoke harshly, the only time in their association that Barlow did not address him as "general."

"For God's sake, Hancock, do not send any more troops in here," said Barlow, and he explained the chaos. But Hancock was not in control, and the division officers were on their own and had been from the beginning. Gibbon, for example, had been in reserve behind the First Division. His first indication that Barlow had begun the attack was the sound of gunfire. Having received no orders, he rode forward and saw that Barlow had broken through. Riding back to his own division, he found Hancock at the Landrum house. "I informed him of Barlow's success," he later wrote, then pushed his division forward.

As Gibbon had moved into the salient on his own initiative, so had other commanders, and the battle became a gruesome free-for-all. Hancock had ridden into the salient with his staff, seen the extent of the disorder, then helplessly returned to the Landrum house. Gordon's counterattack cleared Barlow's division from the eastern side on the salient and captured Hiram

May 12th 64

An artillery battery careens into action at Spotsylvania. As more artillery came on line, the fire against the Confederates intensified. (Forbes—Library of Congress)

Brown, commanding the Third Brigade. Robert Rodes pushed Birney and Mott from the western half. The battle line stabilized where it had begun, at the original parapets, with the Confederates inside and the Federal soldiers immediately outside, each within a stone's throw of the other, thrusting their weapons over and through the logs and barricades to fire.

Two divisions from Wright's Sixth Corps came on the field and closed up to the line, relieving the pressure on Barlow and Gibbon, who reassembled their divisions on the slopes. As his division was neither in the immediate battle nor in any shape for another attack, Barlow went to the Landrum house for the remainder of the day as a spectator. Rain fell without ceasing. Ten thousand guns roared throughout the day and well past midnight. The intensity of the firepower and the great weight of projectiles felled trees and reduced bodies to pulp. The carnage was indescribable.

Gordon kept two of his brigades at the barricades and gathered the remainder of his own and Johnson's division to construct a new line across the base of the salient. At about three in the morning on the thirteenth the Confederate survivors withdrew from the salient and staggered back to the fresh entrenchments. Lee knew that Gordon had saved the Army of Northern Virginia. To reward his heroics, Lee telegraphed Jefferson Davis to ask

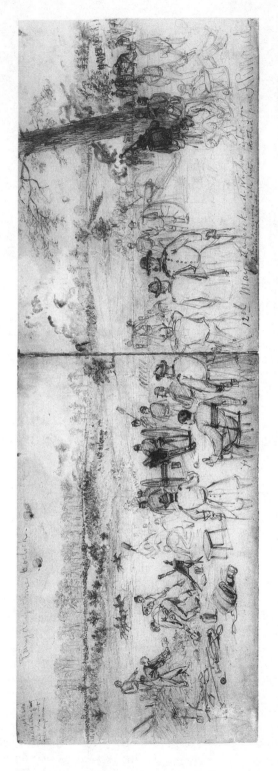

Hancock established his headquarters at the Landrum house, about a half mile distant from the outer line of the Spotsylvania salient. Here he confers with Horatio Wright, commanding the Sixth Corps, and they continue to pour in troops. Both Grant and Meade were absent throughout the battle, so the Federal assault lacked coordination. Barlow is seated in the center, taking a breather; his division had been withdrawn after the initial assault to regroup and was in reserve. (Waud—Library of Congress)

Barlow's soldiers captured several thousand prisoners and two generals in the initial assault against the Spotsylvania salient on May 12. Soldiers of the Second Corps hustled them to the rear. Artist Waud incorrectly identified the Sixth Corps as having captured the prisoners. (Waud—Library of Congress)

The Spotsylvania prisoners were transferred to the "Punch Bowl" at Belle Plain Landing. Eventually they went north to Federal prison camps for the duration of the war. Determined to reduce Lee's army by attrition, Grant no longer authorized prisoner exchanges. (Library of Congress)

that Gordon be promoted to major general. Gordon's promotion was approved on the fourteenth.

Afterward promotions also came in the Federal army. Barlow was not on the list, although Hancock recommended that Barlow be promoted to major general. Meade did not forward the recommendation for lack of vacancies. As Gibbon was senior, Meade felt he should get the preference. Barlow was furious. "[Barlow] to whom, of all others, the success of our assault was due," wrote Gibbon afterward, "received no promotion."

Until he received the news that he had been passed over, Barlow had been in a good mood, taking lunch with Lyman three days after the battle. "[Barlow] wrote a letter to his wife at Fredericksburg," Lyman recorded.

> *"Headquarters are a good place," said he. "You can get victuals and stationery there." He related many anecdotes of the "Salient." How he whacked one officer with his sabre, for being in a hole. How he had compelled two officers to resign and had endorsed that they were "cowards" on their applications &c &c. He believes greatly in the close column of attack.*

Shirkers in the Second Corps were treated unmercifully. "In their leisure," wrote Lyman on May 26, "the 2d Corps commanders had turned their attention to the prosecution of stragglers. Barlow, in particular, tied them up in strings and thrashed them, to the great benefit of the service."

Gibbon was among those infuriated by those who avoided combat. "Immense numbers of men," he wrote after the war, "would quit the ranks upon the slightest pretext or none at all, leaving the more faithful to do the fighting . . . the evil continued and even increased. . . . [I recommended] that these be collected by patrols and one out of every hundred of them be summarily shot and the men informed that in all subsequent battles the percentage of executions would be increased."

Shortly afterward, Meade authorized the trial by summary court-martial of all deliberately deserting the ranks in battle. Gibbon fumed that such a measure was halfhearted and time-consuming, but he enforced it immediately by ordering a court convened for a notorious offender. "The court was organized," wrote Gibbon, "the charges read to the accused, his plea taken, and witnesses called to testify under oath, but no evidence recorded. The case was reported as a flagrant one and the evidence showed that the man was *in the habit of running away* every time the regiment went into action. The court found him guilty and sentenced him to be shot at 7 o'clock the next morning.

"Late at night the case was acted upon by me, and during the night it was sent back from army Headquarters approved. At 7 o'clock, the prisoner was paraded in front of a firing party in the presence of the brigade to which he belonged and with an open grave behind him, he was shot and buried."

26

VIRGINIA: STALEMATE

T he two armies lay glowering and gasping on the Spotsylvania battlefield. As Gordon continued to improve the line at the base at the
salient, Grant lashed his exhausted soldiers into maneuvering through
trackless countryside by night, but the weather beat them. There were no
more miracles to be had. Grant ordered three corps to undertake another
assault against the Confederate center at dawn on May 18. Again Barlow's
division took the leading edge, but Gordon waited behind impenetrable
defenses and beat him back. Spotsylvania became a stalemate.

To end the impasse, Grant renewed the race to interpose his army
between Lee and Richmond. And, as before, Lee had the interior lines and
the shortest distance to travel. The two armies raced south, colliding at the
North Anna River, then moving south again ever closer to Richmond.
Marching and fighting were continuous, nearly a month without respite.
Exhausted Federal soldiers fell insensible in the heat and dust, so fatigued
that Gibbon once lost his trailing brigade after a rest break. Everyone had
fallen asleep and was unaware that the leading brigades had resumed the
march.

Barlow's division never lagged. Lyman once came upon it en route to
Petersburg. "We kept on," he wrote,

> admiring its excellent marching, a result partly due to the good spirits
> of the men, partly to the terror in which stragglers stand of Barlow.
> His provost guard is a study. They follow the column, with their bay-
> onets fixed, and drive up the loiterers, with small ceremony. Of course
> their tempers do not improve with heat and hard marching. There
> was one thin, hard-featured fellow who was a perfect scourge. "Blank
> you!———you———" (here insert any profane expression, varied to
> suit the peculiar case) "get up, will you? By blank, I'll kill you if you
> don't go on, double-quick!" And he looked so much like carrying out
> his threat that the hitherto utterly prostrate party would skip like a
> young lamb. . . .

As Grant endeavors to interpose the Army of the Potomac between Lee and Richmond, Barlow leads a skirmish line to reconnoiter the Confederate positions at Totopotomy Creek on May 29. No longer fighting from his stand-up mode of earlier years, Barlow had radically transformed his style and now had "made skirmishing a profession." (Waud—Library of Congress)

> *The column marched so fast that I was sent forward to tell General Barlow to go more gently. I found that eccentric officer divested of his coat and seated in a cherry tree. "By Jove!" said a voice from the branches, "I knew I should not be here long before Meade's staff would be up. How do you do, Theodore, won't you come up and take a few cherries?"*

A crossroads named Cold (Cool) Harbor, about twelve miles northeast of Richmond, became the next point of confluence for the two exhausted armies. Grant wanted to fasten again on Lee and try to subdue him with finality. Then Richmond would be defenseless, and the Confederacy would be finished. Grant again demanded an immediate assault, irrespective of conditions, for in his mind speed of execution always took precedence over readiness to execute. "All delays are dangerous in war," John Dryden once wrote, and Grant held dearly to the principle.

As Grant tried to hustle his divisions into place, Lee lashed out, trying to regain the initiative. On June 2, Early's corps struck against Grant's right wing, held by Burnside. Gordon found the extreme right flank, which the Federal commanders believed was protected by a swamp. Gordon moved three of his regiments to the far bank, then ordered them into the water up to their waists. Wading through the muck, the soldiers fell upon the startled Federal soldiers. "I struck them exactly in the flank," he wrote proudly to Fanny, "& routed them for a great distance—capturing 3 lines of breast works & several hundred prisoners & killing & wounding many, with very slight loss. . . . I am trying to thank God for my success and safety." Overall, however, Early's attack petered out, and the Confederate troops withdrew to their fortifications.

The Second Corps arrived at Cold Harbor early on the same morning after a ghastly forced march. Looking for a shortcut, one of Meade's staff officers had led it up a dead end at midnight. Reversing the order of march of a corps hemmed in by trees on a narrow road was a nightmare. When the corps finally arrived in the morning, the men were used up.

Meade and his staff arrived on the field two hours later. "Of all the wastes I have seen," wrote Lyman, "this first sight of Cool Harbor was the most dreary. Fancy a baking sun to begin with; then a foreground of breast-works . . . in the front, an open plain, trampled fetlock deep into fine, white dust, and dotted with caissons, regiments of weary soldiers, and dead horses killed in the previous cavalry fight. On the sides and in the distance were pine woods, some red with fires that had run through them, some white with the clouds of dust that rose high in the air. It was a Sahara intensified and was called Cool Arbor."

Meade postponed the attack until five o'clock. Given the piecemeal arrival of the remainder of the weary Federal army, it appeared that the forces would not be ready for a coordinated action before nightfall. Finally the order came to postpone action until morning, June 3. The delay gave the Confederates additional time to construct fortifications, and Lee struck at an open flank of Warren's corps in the late afternoon. Grant could not believe that the Confederates still had the will and combat power to hit back. "We ought to be able to eat them up," he told Meade. Grant thought aloud about a night attack, then confirmed he wanted an assault at 4:30 A.M. in the morning. A rain fell and was sucked into the dust. It was the last rain for forty-seven days.

There was little time to reconnoiter or to brief the troops, who flopped to the ground and slept. The attack orders had sent shudders through the men, from generals to privates. It was strange ground; again they would be attacking over terrain sight unseen, for Grant did not consider it necessary to reconnoiter beforehand. Such considerations were irrelevant in his reasoning as to whether to attack, for his assumptions—as always—were based upon what he wished things to be rather than what they were.

Miles and Brooke led the assault with their brigades, carried the first line, and seized several hundred prisoners, along with colors and cannon. Of the entire three corps, Barlow's division alone had advanced, leaving it exposed on three sides. Confederate firepower converged and slowly squeezed Barlow into a gradual withdrawal, until his soldiers dug trenches with bayonets and mess tins. Elsewhere along the line the attack was over before it had begun. In an hour the Federal army had suffered 7,000 casualties. Both sides dug in at close range, and a grinding trench warfare began, the prelude to Petersburg. Lyman passed by Barlow's headquarters several days later. "He was in a merry state," wrote Lyman, "for he had put some hundreds of his stragglers in an open field & left them there while the shells were flying, and one got hit."

The dead and wounded lay unattended for five days, as Lee and Grant could not agree on a truce. "It was understood at the time," staff officer John Morgan later wrote, "that the delay was caused by something akin to points of etiquette, General Grant proposing a flag as a mutual accommodation, and General Lee replying that he had no dead or wounded not attended to, but offering to grant a truce if General Grant desired it to attend to his own.

"[T]he wounded who had not been able to crawl into our lines at night were now past caring for, and the dead were in a horrible state of putrefaction. Better the consuming fires of the Wilderness and the Po than the lingering, agonizing death of these poor men, whose vain calls for relief smote upon the ears of their comrades at every lull in the firing."

Grant assessed the results of his campaign. After six weeks of continuous combat and 50,000 casualties, the Army of the Potomac was mired in stalemate at Cold Harbor. Grant had set out to destroy Lee's army and had found the task impossible. Lee too had suffered casualties, a number known only to God. Nonetheless Lee still fought, his army intact, dangerous, and seemingly indefatigable.

Breaking from past practices, Grant decided that he no longer would exchange prisoners. "We ought not to make a single exchange nor release a prisoner on any pretext whatever until the war closes" he wrote a government official in August. "We have got to fight until the military power of the South is exhausted, and if we release or exchange prisoners it simply becomes a war of extermination."

Barlow's division was the sole Federal force to penetrate the Confederate line at Cold Harbor on June 3. Fresh troops of the Seventh New York Heavy Artillery led the attack and seized several hundred prisoners. Because of the terrible losses in foot soldiers suffered by the Army of the Potomac, Grant sent cannon to the rear, saying that he had more than enough, freeing the artillerymen to charge Lee's trenches. (Waud—Library of Congress)

Confederate prisoners captured by Barlow at Cold Harbor await transportation to the rear. "He admired the rebels," a friend of Barlow's wrote, "what constancy, endurance, and discipline they showed, with what bravery they fought. Their long grey lines, he said, their shaved heads, their lank, emaciated forms and pale, cadaverous faces made them seem like an army of phantoms awaiting you. They were terrible, he said, and fearful from their fierce hate." (Library of Congress)

"It is hard on our men held in Southern prisons not to exchange them," Grant explained to one of his generals, "but it is humanity to those left in the ranks to fight our battles. Every man we hold, when released on parole or otherwise, becomes an active soldier against us at once either directly or indirectly. If we commence a system of exchange which liberates all prisoners taken, we will have to fight on until the whole South is exterminated. If we hold those caught they amount to no more than dead men."

Cold Harbor humiliated Grant, the culmination of failed battlefield tactics and a failed military campaign that he feared could drive Lincoln from office in the fall. Elsewhere, Butler, Banks, and Sigel had fallen short. Confederate troops from their theaters were free to reinforce Lee. Only Sherman in the west experienced success.

Grant and his generals finally conceded that frontal attacks were futile. "We had never succeeded in forcing Lee, by battle, from any position he assumed," wrote Gibbon afterward, "nor had he succeeded in forcing us from any. A few hours were all that was necessary to render any position so strong by breastworks that the opposite party was unable to carry it, and it became a recognized fact amongst the men themselves that when the enemy had occupied a position six or eight hours ahead of us, it was useless to attempt to take it. This feeling became so marked that when troops under these circumstances were ordered forward, they went a certain distance and then lay down and opened fire. It became a saying in the army that when the old troops got as far forward as they thought they ought to go 'they sat down and made coffee.' "

Reversing his instructions to Meade, Grant resorted to maneuvering for position, since movement conveyed the perception of energy and decisiveness, of great power aggressively deployed to batter the enemy. As he could not defeat Lee in his entrenchments, Grant's only alternative, as he saw it, was to try to sever Lee's communications with his sources of supply. All roads into southern Virginia led through Petersburg, twenty miles south of Richmond.

The race to Petersburg began on June 12, with the Second Corps in the van. Its energy was fast ebbing. Reinforcements had largely replaced the casualties, but the new men were markedly inferior. By the end of May, for example, Gibbon had lost half of his division. "The quality of the loss was what made it almost disastrous," he wrote, "for the very best officers, and the very bravest men were those who fell. These always remained in the ranks and did the fighting and by their example and spirit stimulated the rest. When they were gone the number who served as leaders was fearfully reduced and this, of course, immensely to the detriment of the fighting force of the division."

The loss of veterans was indeed irreplaceable. "Those who had fallen were men inured to camp life," wrote Walker,

> to hardship, exposure, and fatigue; in bivouac they knew how to make themselves almost comfortable with the narrowest means; how to cover themselves in rain and storm; how to make fires out of green wood, find water in dry ground, and cook their rations to the best advantage.

On the march they had learned to cover the greatest distance with the least wear and tear; on picket and skirmish they had learned a score of tricks by which they at once protected themselves and became more formidable to the enemy. In battle, officers and men had become veterans through a score of fierce encounters; no form of danger would be a surprise to them. With a high price bought they this knowledge! Thousands had died that these regiments might know how to advance and how to retire as occasion should demand; how to cover themselves most completely through long hours of waiting and how to throw themselves, body and soul, into one tremendous blow, on the vital spot, at the critical instant.

The leadership of the corps wavered. Hancock was in intense pain from his Gettysburg wound. Dislodged bone fragments inflamed his flesh, and he collapsed. Coordination was lost and orders became contradictory and confused. The Second Corps tried to take Petersburg on June 16 but lost the race. Another series of endless battles resumed, resulting in setbacks and worsening casualties. Hancock became so disabled on June 18 that he left the field, and Birney assumed temporary command of the corps until Hancock returned on the twenty-seventh.

The soldiers were zombielike, their assaults ever weakening, with none of the zeal and élan of the opening weeks. "The limit of human endurance had been reached," wrote Walker. Of Barlow's original brigade commanders, by July 1 only Miles remained. That summer the Second Corps ultimately lost 19 brigade commanders, about 100 regimental commanders, and 17,000 men. Many veterans had gone home with expired enlistments. The replacements were draftees and bounty jumpers, untrained, ill-disciplined cannon fodder who often either deserted or were quickly killed by their inexperience. "[R]eaching the regiments in the midst of a campaign when so many good men were gone," wrote Gibbon, "they but added to the existing evil. It was like deluging a drop of spirits with a bucket of water."

In the continuing battles around the city, Barlow alone seemed irrepressible. Lyman found him on June 21 returning from a raid on a railroad.

"Hullo! See here!" shouted he. "I've caught a Cambridge man." Sure enough, there was a stout, handsome man, mounted on a fine white horse, and daintily dressed, with the three stars of Colonel on his collar and a fanciful sort of helmet of grey felt. It was a certain Baker, in the law school in the time of Daves, &c. His effect was spoiled by Barlow's quaint device of mounting a most scaly looking Adjutant, en croupe, behind him.

Lyman visited his classmate at his headquarters on July 7. "Found him lying in his tent," wrote Lyman, "in his shirt and drawers, listening to his band which is reckoned the best in the army. He hospitably besought me to 'take off my trowsers and make myself comfortable.' Truly, as De Chanal [a French army observer] says: 'He has the look of a Parisian youth.' He discoursed on the loose discipline of the troops (and he has true ideas about this) & the advantage of the assault in column. He said he was ready for another assault and would lead the men himself, and have no more trifling."

While Lee and Grant fought their huge battles in southeastern Virginia, another campaign raged in the Shenandoah Valley as part of Grant's master plan. The fertile valley provided food for Lee's army and had served as a concealed highway for Lee to threaten Washington and to invade Maryland and Pennsylvania. In early May, Sigel moved down the valley to clear Confederate troops and to bring the area under Federal control. John C. Breckinridge commanded the few forces that Lee could assign to the region.

Breckinridge and Sigel came together at New Market on May 15. After an intense battle, Sigel withdrew and left the valley, and Breckinridge returned to Lee. Major General David Hunter replaced Sigel, returned to the valley, and scorched the earth from Winchester to Lexington, where he battered the Virginia Military Institute, the West Point of the South. Believing that he could hold Petersburg with reduced forces, Lee dispatched Early on June 9 with the Confederate Second Corps, along with Gordon, with orders to force Hunter from the valley, thereby saving what was left of homes and farms and protecting the crops for harvest.

Then Lee thought of opportunities beyond clearing the Shenandoah Valley. If the siege of Petersburg continued, Grant ultimately would wear him down and win the war. Lee's last desperate hope was a raid against the Federal capital, something so spectacular that the Lincoln administration would be voted out of office. If circumstances permitted, Lee instructed, Early was to continue north into Maryland and threaten Washington, with the minimum expectation that Grant would have to send reinforcements north and so ease the pressure on Petersburg.

Early was in Lynchburg by June 17, where he rendezvoused with Breckinridge. Together they chased Hunter into West Virginia; phase one of Lee's plan had been promptly accomplished. Phase two looked feasible since Early had an open road to Washington. Early and Gordon crossed the Potomac into Maryland on July 6. By then three weeks had elapsed since Early had pulled out of Petersburg, and Grant finally realized that he was gone. As Grant had stripped the Washington defenses of able bodies to replace his casualties, panic struck the Federal capital. The only Federal soldiers who could check Early near Washington were an irregular force commanded by Lew Wallace, augmented with another division Grant had belatedly dispatched. The troops dug in at Monocacy Junction, a river town forty miles from Washington, and awaited Early's advance.

At first Gordon remained in reserve, watching with detached interest as the Federal troops threw back the initial Confederate assault. When it was apparent that reinforcements were needed, Early ordered Gordon to send in his division. His breathing quickening, his eyes widening, Gordon tingled with the familiar, irresistible impulse to throw himself and his men against the enemy. His voice rose with his heartbeat, and, as they had countless times before, the soldiers of his command leaped into action.

At the river ford his men paused to remove their footwear, but Gordon hurried them on. "Plunge right in, boys," he roared, "no time for taking off shoes." As his dripping, muddy men assembled, Gordon surveyed the terrain between him and the Federal lines, and he saw fences and large grain stacks. Barlow had learned to use such means to conceal and protect an attacking skirmish line, but Gordon's style had remained unchanged since the start of the war. In his view they were barriers that impeded a well-aligned formation marching straight at the enemy.

"When the word was given," remembered one of Gordon's soldiers, "we moved forward according to instructions and, in spite of the rough ground, kept our alignment perfect. When we came within sight of the enemy's forces in the open field, we brought a yell and started toward them. They replied with a well-directed volley that seemed to kill or wound every officer in the brigade and very many men in the ranks."

Gordon lashed his men forward. The casualties were frightful, but they overwhelmed the first and then the second line of Federal defenders. Unable to reinforce his three battered brigades, Gordon gathered them for a final effort. "There was Gordon," recalled a soldier, "sitting on his horse as quietly as if nothing was going on, wearing his old red shirt, the sleeves pulled up a little, the only indication he was ready for a fight."

Gordon had routed the last of his enemy by the end of the day, and they fled toward Washington, heightening the growing terror in the city. In the past Gordon would have been exultant, but now, when the muskets were stilled, he was depressed and weary of leading men to their death. "I have been preserved through another severe battle," he wrote Fanny. "But my Darling my heart bleeds to tell of its cost." A third of his division were casualties. His senior brigade commander, Clement Evans, was wounded. Some of the losses were intensely personal. Gordon's brother Eugene had a shattered elbow and would lose his arm, perhaps his life.

One of Gordon's closest friends, Colonel J. H. Lamar, had been killed. "It is one of the saddest events to me of this war," he wrote to Fanny. "I feel as tho' I had lost a brother; but it is for his poor wife & mother & sisters that I feel most deeply . . . how that affectionate heart must be wrung with anguish. It will nearly kill her, Fanny—Oh I would to God I could do something for that crushed heart—*Dear, dear girl*—Oh Lord why am I spared & so many & so good men are taken around me? I cannot repay such mercy. . . ."

Gordon's spirits improved as he and Early's army marched to the outskirts of Washington, for he was convinced that the capital of the United States was for the taking. But the occupation would have to wait, for the Confederate soldiers were strung out for miles and too tired to walk farther. The sun set on the exhausted troops straggling to their evening encampments before the empty Federal fortifications. Gordon and Early talked through the night about plans for their triumphal entry.

"General, come look at what has happened!" A staff officer shook Gordon awake. In the morning sun he saw the glint of thousands of Federal bayonets and the banners of countless regiments. The Sixth Corps had arrived during the night from the Petersburg front, for Grant had finally recognized the threat to Washington. Gordon was devastated. Sustained only by his pride, Gordon mounted, squared his shoulders, and began the long retreat to the Shenandoah Valley.

Along the way Gordon wrote again to Fanny:

> *My sweet wife -*
> *I have just returned from the woods, where I had a most delightful*
>   *hour of prayer -*
> *I do love these hours -*
> *I can not always meet you at the appointed time, but can generally -*
> *I rarely fail to receive a blessing -*
> *Let us be better Christians my Darling*
> *& let us grow in grace -*
> *not be idlers in the vineyard -*

"Until the news came last night that the rebs were retreating," Barlow wrote to Almira on July 15, "we did not suppose indeed that we should ever see any of you again. We supposed that you would all be carried south with the rest of the plunder. Is not this last raid the most disgraceful thing that has happened in the war? Not a gun seems to have been fired until the 6th Corps reached Washington except for the disgraceful affair at the Monocacy. If the cowards of the North choose to let what now proves to have been a very small force march through their country at will I am only sorry that they did not destroy every man and thing in Maryland and Pennsylvania. . . .

"I am utterly disgusted with the craven spirit of our people. I wish the enemy had burned Baltimore and Washington and hope they will yet."

Infuriated by the debacle, Grant ordered Philip Sheridan to clear out the Shenandoah Valley and to raze it so that the Confederate army could never again eat its food or march on its roads. Early cooperated by impetuously confronting the Federal army at Winchester on September 19. After desperate fighting, Sheridan overwhelmed Early and Gordon.

Fanny had followed Gordon to Winchester, and she screamed at Gordon's troops, fleeing through the streets, to rally against the enemy. Gordon hustled her into a house for safety, then rushed off with his troops. Fanny would not stay behind. She left the house, found a carriage and driver, and one step ahead of Sheridan's troops sped after her husband.

The final battle came a month later at Cedar Creek. Sheridan's troops dozed in their tents while Gordon and Hotchkiss, the mapmaker, led three divisions over a mountain trail by night and attacked at dawn. The surprise was complete, the execution brilliant. Two Federal army corps collapsed under the shock of the assault and stampeded away from Gordon's exultant soldiers. But Early forbade Gordon to pursue, despite Gordon's livid protests, and the Confederate troops halted and stood in a thin gray line while Sheridan reorganized his army. Sheridan's afternoon attack demolished Early's corps, and its shattered fragments scattered before the firestorm.

Barely escaping capture in the darkness, Gordon spurred his horse down the steep banks of a creek, and both spun out of control into the water. Regaining consciousness, a bruised and sodden Gordon remounted his wobbly horse and got away. As he returned to the trenches of Petersburg, pillars of smoke rose above the Shenandoah Valley, monuments to Lee's utter failure to change the course of the war. Washington was secure, Grant's siege of Petersburg was intact, and Sheridan would devastate every field and farm in the valley.

After the distractions of Early's raid against Washington on July 26, Grant decided that he would strike against Richmond while maintaining pressure against Petersburg. His plan was made of fantasies. The Second Corps and Sheridan's cavalry would march north behind Butler's lines at Bermuda Hundred, cross the James at a bend in the river called Deep Bottom, midway between Petersburg and Richmond, and proceed to take the capital some ten miles away. Meanwhile, Burnside would detonate a huge mine, comprising tons of explosives that his Pennsylvania coal miners had placed beneath the Confederate fortifications at Petersburg, and then his troops would storm through the crater. Lee could not have his army everywhere. Either Hancock, Burnside, or both would outnumber the fragments of Lee's army at their front. Grant would beat Lee's trenches either by blowing them into oblivion or going around them.

Fearing that Hancock's turning movement was a major assault against Richmond, Lee indeed did send troops to counter the Second Corps, some 65 percent of his available forces. Once again, as he had done at the Po River, Grant suddenly changed his mind about a two-pronged attack, and he recalled Mott's division to participate in the crater assault, leaving Barlow and Gibbon to demonstrate against more than half of Lee's army. After convincing Lee that an assault against Richmond was imminent, Barlow and Gibbon returned to Petersburg after nightfall on the twenty-ninth.

Having successfully spread out Lee's army with deceptive maneuvering, Grant was poised to blast through the Petersburg fortifications with the buried mine. Foresight and initiative would be required to organize the assaulting force to exploit the rupture. Grant inexplicably entrusted the task to Burnside, whose reputation for immutable lethargy was unchallenged in the Federal army. Burnside, in turn, selected generals James H. Ledlie and Edward Ferrero to lead the assault. The lead Second Corps division arrived in Petersburg, recalled Walker, "in time to see the vast mass of earth . . . rise into the air, with guns and hundreds of human bodies." Ledlie and Ferrero occupied a shelter when the mine exploded, where they remained to share a bottle of rum. As Burnside's confused, awestricken soldiers jammed themselves into the huge crater, Confederate rifles blazed from the rim. The uncoordinated, haphazard assault failed with heavy casualties. Grant—finally—removed Burnside from command.

Arabella Barlow was dead. Since the campaign began, she had nursed soldiers in the fields and at the army hospitals at Belle Plain, Fredericksburg,

City Point, and White House, the huge river base of the Army of the Potomac. She had been a godsend of energy and ingenuity. "We called her 'the Raider,' " a colleague remembered. In Fredericksburg she had appropriated a cart and pony, which she drove about the village to scour materials for the makeshift hospitals. As if by a miracle, she had confiscated straw to fill empty bed sacks. "She then helped to fill and arrange the sacks," said the colleague, "and afterwards drove about the town in search of articles, which, by the time the ambulances brought in their freight of misery and pain, had served to furnish the place with some means of alleviation."

Arabella had so driven herself in the brutal heat that she no longer had resistance to disease. Finally she collapsed from typhus, a pestilence transmitted by the ticks and lice that afflicted everyone in the field. "Arabella is sick in Washington & I feel dangerously so," Barlow wrote Almira on July 2. "She is all run down from fever." He was hopeful on the fifteenth: "Arabella has been seriously ill but the fever is broken and in time she will be well again." Word of her death reached Barlow on July 28, as he was in combat at Deep Bottom.

"Barlow was entirely incapacitated by this sudden grief," wrote Lyman. Meade granted him leave when he learned that Arabella had died without friends about her, and Hancock arranged for a tug to take him from Deep Bottom. Barlow returned several days later, indefatigable no longer, for he was broken mentally and physically. Persistent diarrhea had ravaged his body for some six weeks, and the loss of Arabella so added to his burden that he could scarcely function. He carried on ("more like a dead man," wrote Walker) as Grant planned yet another expedition to Deep Bottom, this time by steamer up the James River.

As before, Grant based his thinking on the false assumption that Lee had weakened the defenses of Richmond. The Second Corps would debark over gangways onto piers on August 14 and once again attempt to seize the city. It was a typical Grant scheme, impulsive, haphazard, and uninformed, plausible in theory but corrupt in detail. Hancock discovered that the piers where the vessels were to unload were wrecked. Fortuitously, he dispatched a load of lumber and carpenters to precede the flotilla of elephantine deep-draft vessels. After loading their soldiers, the vessels proceeded upriver with flashing lights and screeching whistles, trying to avoid collision and grounding on the narrow, shallow river.

"The temperature of the day," wrote Walker, "was something dreadful. The columns, moving out from the landing, literally passed between men lying on both sides, dead from sunstroke. . . . The rays of the August sun smote the heads of the weary soldiers with blows as palpable as if they had been given with a club." Hancock gave Barlow temporary command of both the First and Second divisions, ostensibly to give him the experience of corps command and to secure his chances for promotion. But Barlow, like the soldiers, was prostrate, and the feeble attack fizzled. Two more days of desultory skirmishing accomplished nothing.

Barlow composed the most difficult letter of his army career on August 18, a formal request to Hancock that he be allowed to go to the hospital. To ask was humiliating, for he had not been wounded, and he had excoriated any-one with flesh intact who sought the rear in the face of the enemy. "I have been suffering from diarrhea for the last seven weeks," he wrote with tor-tured hand, "& have become much weakened thereby. I cannot have here the diet & [rest] emphatically prescribed by the surgeon as necessary for recov-ery. In my present condition I am unable to [function] & am becoming worse. By a few days of perfect quiet with proper food I shall probably become better & avoid the necessity of applying for a leave of absence."

Barlow appended the surgeon's diagnosis. As diarrhea was a common cause of death, hospitalization was imperative for Barlow's recovery.

Miles took temporary command. Barlow returned several days later. When he again collapsed, he was removed by stretcher. He remained in Boston, prostrate, his mind numbed, Arabella no longer there to nurse him. Barlow received a letter from Walker in October, asking him to write his report of the campaign for the record. Barlow could not. "I am still confined to my bed," he replied, "unable to write even a simple letter of any length without difficulty."

His gloom was briefly alleviated when he learned that his long absent father had been found living in Pennsylvania, and both men hoped for a reunion and reconciliation. His wishes were crushed when a classmate wrote that David Hatch Barlow had just been murdered. When he could again function, Barlow went to Europe to recuperate.

When Barlow returned in the spring of 1865, he called on Maria Daly, who had been Arabella's New York friend. "Had a visit a few days ago from General Barlow," she wrote in her diary. "He had poor Arabella's ring on his finger. He will now marry some young woman who will share his glory and prosperity. Poor Belle . . . so short a life for one so full of energy, so untiring."

PART VII

WESTERN
THEATER, 1864

27

MUSTER IN THE WEST

John Hood returned from Chickamauga a hero in the late fall of 1863. The first rumors in Richmond reported him dead on the battlefield. Great was the relief when the news came that he had survived after the surgeons had amputated his shattered right leg. Hood recuperated in Atlanta for two months and regained his strength, and the private car of a railroad president then took him north. He arrived in Richmond on November 17 to continue his convalescence.

Hood gradually regained the mobility of his crippled body. One-legged soldiers were a common sight, and physicians had devised ways to help them get around. Hood's condition was complicated by his paralyzed arm, but he learned to use a single crutch under his good arm to assist him in walking. Despite his herculean efforts, Hood's movements were excruciatingly slow and cumbersome. He knew that he had to return to the saddle to prove he could again command in the field; an aide boosted him up, and a false leg in the stirrup assisted his balance. Physicians prescribed potentially addictive drugs to mitigate the pain, but outwardly Hood seemed lively and alert. His will power and inherent robustness seemed to overcome what might have been debilitating wounds.

The capital was crowded with government officials, speculators, seekers of patronage, special pleaders, and generals wanting assignments. Gossip and rumors swirled in the parlors and anterooms. Parties and receptions, dinners and balls flourished, with enforced gaiety to erase temporarily the specter of an end to the Confederacy. Anxious people lived for the moment. The wealthier still somehow procured abundant food and wine for feasting. Romances were fevered and urgent, for young men came and went, and nothing seemed permanent but death.

Army officers, the sole hope of the Confederacy, became the focus of adoration and hero worship. Officers with scars and amputations were esteemed, and no social gathering was complete without them. Crippled soldiers scoffed at their own disfigurements. A guest arrived at a Christmas Eve dinner (Hood was there) with a throat wound that muffled his voice. "We have all kinds now," said an observer, "but a blind one." The dinner was sumptuous. "There is life in the old land yet," someone remarked.

The galas intensified in January, the most lavish hosted by the wife of the secretary of war. Hood went with Sally "Buck" Preston, with whom he revived his on-again, off-again courtship. Hood was but one of many suitors with whom she had dallied, and he had been ardently pursuing her before he left for Chickamauga. Jefferson Davis and his wife were there, with members of the cabinet and legislators, general officers and distinguished visitors, and beautiful women. Costumed guests entertained the others with elaborate charades. Mary Preston, Buck's sister, dressed in Grecian robes, chose a poem to represent knighthood. Hood sat in the front with Buck.

> Knight *is my first, the second is a name*
> *That's doubly linked unto enduring fame;*
> *The gentle poet of the Bridge of Sighs,*
> *The hero, cynosure of tenderest eyes.*
> Hood, *whose keen sword has never known a stain*
> *Whose valor brightened Chickamauga's plain*
> *Well might he stand in glory's blazing roll*
> *To represent to future times my whole;*
> *For goodlier knighthood surely never shone*
> *Round fair Queen Bess upon her stately throne*
> *Than his, whose lofty deeds we proudly call our own.*

The prolonged applause raised Hood from his chair. Buck steadied him, and he turned with crimson face to acknowledge the ovation.

Women had always been attracted by Hood's masculinity and physique and by his earnest striving for good manners. Now disfigured and uncoordinated, he needed reassurance that women still found him appealing. Buck's ambivalence frustrated and confused him, and the courtship became an amusing spectacle to the Richmond sophisticates. Hood pleaded with Mary Chesnut to be both surrogate and counsel, and Chesnut's diary recorded both her dialogues with the anguished "wounded knight" and Buck's complaints about Hood's rough and awkward behavior, exacerbated by his immobility.

Inflamed by her flirting and maddened by his clumsiness, Hood was reduced to lunging when once he would have been self-assured. "I think it began with those beautiful silk stockings that fit so nicely," Buck told Chesnut. "You ought to hear him rave about my foot and ankle. Then he seized me round the waist and kissed my throat—to my horror—and when he saw how shocked I was, he was frightened." Mumbling apologies, Hood told Buck that her throat was so soft and white that he had lost control. "I drew back and told him I would go away, that I was offended," Buck continued. "In a moment I felt a strong arm around my waist—I could not move. He said I should stay until I forgave his rash assumption, and he held me fast."

Buck's parents, people of wealth and status, had tolerated her romantic whimsies but would not consent to her marrying Hood. According to Chesnut, they believed that the provincial Kentuckian lacked the breeding and social graces necessary to merit their daughter's hand. Hood's love affair slowly dissolved.

His military reputation, however, prospered. The Confederate House of Representatives invited Hood to a seat on their floor, but his public association with Davis provided the most visible recognition of his favored status. Davis's carriage was at Hood's disposal, and Hood shared Davis's pew at his church. It was in their mutual interest to be seen together. Battered politically for his feuds with senior officers, Davis, for once, was arm in arm with a universally popular general. Hood, in return, was shameless in his ambition for promotion, and Davis alone could make that happen.

Common sentiment—in the army, the government, and the newspapers and among the public—favored Hood's promotion to lieutenant general, but the promotion could not be made solely as a reward for his past performance. Promotions to high rank were not conferred like brevets or medals, however popular the officer. Of greatest importance to the military and the government was whether Hood was capable of discharging the responsibilities of the second highest rank in the army. And if so, a vacancy at that rank had to be available, as well as a suitable command. When all these pieces were in place, Davis could legally nominate Hood for promotion, and the Senate could confirm his nomination.

Lieutenant generals commanded corps, and only two Confederate armies contained them, the Army of Northern Virginia, and the Army of Tennessee under Johnston. Lee already had Longstreet, A. P. Hill, and Ewell. Hood could go west where the second corps command was vacant, as Hardee was Johnston's sole corps commander. Davis also could vacate a lieutenant general position by withdrawing an earlier nomination (D. H. Hill, who had commanded a corps at Chickamauga and had again lost favor).

Whether Hood could command a corps was a question not easily answered. Successful division command did not guarantee that Hood could handle a field command three times larger. Age too posed problems. Not yet thirty-three, he would have to earn the respect and cooperation of older subordinates. The final question was whether the mutilated Hood was physically capable of commanding in the field. Still, he seemed ready, and Davis felt the risk worth taking. Davis made the nomination, and the Senate confirmed it on February 2, 1864, with date of rank from September 20, 1863, the day that Hood had fallen at Chickamauga.

At the end of February, Hood reported to Johnston's headquarters at Dalton, Georgia, thirty miles south of the Federal base at Chattanooga and a hundred miles north of Atlanta. The Army of Tennessee was trying to recover from its humiliating defeat at Missionary Ridge in the fall. Bragg had been in command then, and he had asked to be relieved. Davis accepted his request and had brought Bragg east with the nominal title of general in chief of the Confederate armies.

Johnston, who had assumed command in Dalton on December 12, 1863, would prove consistent in leading his army to the rear, as he had done during the Peninsular Campaign in early 1862 and in the Vicksburg campaign in 1863. He would be equally consistent in not revealing his plans and intentions either to Davis or to his subordinates, in large measure because he had no plans. His strategic thinking, such as it was, conflicted so profoundly with the expectations in Richmond that military failure was foreordained.

Such strategists as Davis, Lee, Bragg, and Secretary of War James A. Seddon expected Johnston to seize the initiative in the west by routing the Federal army at Chattanooga, reoccupying Tennessee, and sweeping through Kentucky to the Ohio River. Their thinking was not predicated on such practical considerations as military capabilities, relative combat power, logistical support, transportation, and the like, but rather by self-delusion. They were driven by the recurring, irrepressible dream of a crusade to cleanse the two states of their Northern occupiers and thereby restore them to the Confederacy. A Confederate army entering the two states would grow in strength, so they thought, reinforced with eager recruits and a bounty of food and supplies from loyal farmers. Although this had never happened in earlier campaigns, faith dictated that such rewards were awaiting.

Johnston did not share this dream. He could see that he did not have the resources to attack the more powerful Federal army. Instead he intended to concede the initiative to Grant (and by March to Grant's successor, Sherman), somehow defeat the Federal army by allowing it to attack him, and then pursue it into Tennessee. Beyond that, Johnston would reveal nothing more of his intentions.

Johnston and Richmond had vastly differing ideas of the combat readiness of the Army of Tennessee. Johnston lamented that he had neither the manpower, the firepower, nor the transportation to consider an offensive. Davis—accustomed to Lee's aggressiveness regardless of his army's handicaps—refused to believe Johnston. The Davis administration credited only what it wanted to hear. When Hardee, for example, relinquished command to Johnston, he had claimed that the army was in splendid condition. Hood, too, wrote optimistically to Davis, Bragg, and Seddon. Within a week after arriving he reported that the Army of Tennessee was ready and willing to do what Richmond wanted done.

The gist of Hood's letters was that the Army of Tennessee was in good shape but needed reinforcements before it could attack. If reinforcements were not forthcoming, the Federal army would grow in strength and seize the initiative. A Federal victory would then be inevitable. Thus Hood both supported and disputed Johnston's official assessments. While Hood's letters reinforced Davis's misgivings about Johnston, Johnston considered Hood his confidant and closest lieutenant.

Davis, meanwhile, sent other observers to Johnston's headquarters to evaluate his numbers. Although their reports confirmed Johnston's reasons for pessimism, Richmond still wanted something done. When Grant went east in March, Lee's demands for action by Johnston—any kind of action—intensified. Lee assumed that Grant would bring troops with him. Attacking in the west, Lee argued, would stop their flow eastward. On the other hand, if western troops already had transferred to Virginia, by simple arithmetic Sherman's army had lost numbers and had become more vulnerable to an attack from Johnston. What Lee did not realize was that the Federal army had enough manpower for both major theaters. In any event, Johnston would not budge.

Patrick Cleburne, the finest division commander in the Army of Tennessee, was so concerned about the manpower disparity that in December 1863 he had offered a startling proposal. Slaves should be enlisted as soldiers, he argued, with emancipation as a reward for service. He circulated his proposal among his officers; all four brigade commanders, some ten regimental commanders, and a cavalry general signed in agreement. The principal generals met with Cleburne on January 2 in Johnston's headquarters, and Cleburne read his paper. The arguments were heated, pro and con; slavery advocates called the others abolitionists and traitors. Cleburne was not considered a legitimate Southerner anyway—he had immigrated from Ireland but ten years before. He and those who agreed with him would have to be watched for their radical views. When an astonished Davis heard about Cleburne's paper—that it was even being seriously considered by some of his western generals—he ordered Seddon to suppress it entirely. Nothing more was heard.

Black soldiers meanwhile entered the Army of the Cumberland, some six regiments by the end of March. Sherman did not want them, but the Lincoln administration did, and more would follow. "I am honest in my belief," Sherman would write that fall to Halleck, "that it is not fair to our men to count negroes as equals. . . . I have had the question put to me often; 'Is not a negro as good as a white man to stop a bullet?' Yes, and a sand-bag is better; but can a negro do our skirmishing and picket duty? Can they improvise roads, bridges, sorties, flank movements, &c., like the white man? I say no. Soldiers must do many things without orders from their own sense, as in sentinels. Negroes are not equal to this."

George Thomas thought otherwise. The War Department had solicited his opinion in November 1863, and Thomas had responded as he prepared to break the siege at Chattanooga. "[T]he Government has a perfect right to employ negroes as soldiers," he wrote. "The Confederates regard them as property. Therefore the Government can with propriety seize them as property and use them to assist in putting down the Rebellion. But if we have the right to use the property of our enemies we have also the right to use them as we would all the individuals of any other civilized nation who may choose to volunteer as soldiers in our army.

"I moreover think in the sudden transition from slavery to freedom it perhaps is far better for the negro to become a soldier, and be generally taught to depend on himself for support, than to be thrown upon the cold charities of the world without sympathy or assistance."

Black troops would help open the campaign in May at Dalton, and some would be captured. The Confederate army, in line with government policy, would not treat them as prisoners of war, but rather as renegades deserving severe punishment. Some would still be alive that fall, but barely. "I saw a number of Negroes captured at Dalton," wrote a Confederate chaplain, "some in the most distressing condition—evidently dying." A pious man in most respects, he expressed no pity in this instance.

Hood energetically organized his corps for combat. Less than a week after reporting he had assembled a staff—some twenty-three officers, large by any standard—covering all of the functions necessary to sustain a campaign. Hood stirred his men for battle with Napoleon-like proclamations. "The lieutenant-general commanding desires to say," he wrote, "he has come to share their hardships and their dangers, their pleasures and their triumphs. The welfare of the command will be the object of his most anxious solicitude. To fight it successfully in the day of action is his highest ambition, but the history of war teaches that two-thirds of the elements of success in battle consist in preparation for it."

To build their self esteem, Hood assembled his soldiers as an impressive body, three divisions totaling 20,000 men and 1,600 officers. Soon he had them marching in review and maneuvering in mock battles, improving both readiness and morale.

Hood wanted them to fight by his standards, which embodied the most fundamental precepts of Southern military leadership. His tactics were entirely frontal. "[I]n attacking an enemy," he wrote in his fighting instructions, "it is all-important to break his front line promptly, as the confusion to which he is thereby subjected renders it comparatively easy to break his second and even third line, which should always be done by our first line if possible." Remembering that in earlier battles his soldiers, after smelling blood, had gone howling after a fleeing enemy, Hood admonished his brigade commanders to rein them in throughout the battle. Later, Hood would recognize that soldiers on both sides preferred to fight from behind fortifications, but that would not be his kind of war.

If a regiment or brigade were outflanked, he wrote, there was no reason to panic. The commander should change front and ask for reinforcements. Ground once taken should never be relinquished, nor should troops retire to replenish ammunition, "much of which," he wrote pragmatically, "can be obtained from our own and the enemy's dead and wounded."

Firing at long range wasted ammunition and was forbidden. "In receiving an attack," instructed Hood, "the enemy should be permitted to come close enough to enable our men to select the man they fire at, and in making an attack our fire should be held until it can be delivered with deadly effect, and, if practicable, should be followed by a determined charge, as it is all important to break the enemy's line, not merely for the encouragement it gives our men, but the demoralization and confusion it forces upon him. Every officer and man should understand that in long-range fighting the Yankees are our equals, but at close quarters we are vastly superior to them. The history of the war abundantly proves that they have never repulsed a determined and well-sustained charge."

Hood's rhetoric is puzzling in light of such repulses as Pickett's charge at Gettysburg, Thomas's repulse of the entire Army of Tennessee at Chickamauga, and the repulse of his own division at Little Round Top. Either Hood was unable to grasp their lessons, or else he was incapable of conceiving an alternative style of warfare. He was not alone in his thinking, of course. Lee and Gordon would keep on with their murderous assault tactics to the very end.

Each regiment was to fly only the Confederate battle flag and not its own personalized flags, which were difficult to distinguish from the Federal banners. Battle flags and cannon, Hood said, represented the soul of an army. They were the symbols of glory and the greatest prizes of warfare. The object of combat was to prevent their capture and to capture those of the enemy. The numbers of such trophies measured victory and defeat.

Johnston reviewed the entire army on April 19 and awaited Sherman's first move. At the end of the month the Confederates broke camp and prepared for battle.

Grant and Sherman went on leave after the Chattanooga campaign. Thomas remained in Chattanooga to feed three Federal armies and their starving draft animals, with the added burden of feeding the citizens of Chattanooga and Knoxville as well as Confederate prisoners and deserters. All supplies came by rail from Nashville and depended on 150 miles of vulnerable track through tunnels, across bridges, and over mountains. At first everyone was on short rations. Not until mid-January 1864 was the rail line continuous and capable of transporting supplies to Thomas's Chattanooga storage sheds.

Operations in the entire western theater depended on smooth and reliable connections with Thomas's huge depot at Nashville. His senior quartermaster was Colonel James L. Donaldson, who typified the competent professionals that Thomas recruited for his staff. Donaldson's assistant, James F. Rusling, once described the staggering magnitude of its operations. "We have over a dozen quartermasters on duty here in Nashville," he wrote his family. "We employ over twelve thousand laborers, mechanics, and clerks. Our disbursements alone amount to over five million dollars per month. We run over six hundred miles of railroad, providing rolling stock, employees, and everything. We supply over a hundred thousand men, scattered from Knoxville to Chattanooga, and thence to Memphis. This is the biggest army depot to-day on the face of the earth. We have an office with seven clerks and five detectives; and thus run the whole machine."

Thomas's logistical challenge was not only to provide daily rations, but to accumulate supplies for the 1864 spring offensive. These came on the railroads in and out of Nashville, but the man running them, John B. Anderson, was not up to the task. Originally with the Louisville and Nashville Railroad, Anderson had been recommended by Grant and Quartermaster General Meigs in the desperate days when Chattanooga was besieged. Stanton had appointed him as military director of railroads, with broad powers, but Thomas wanted him out. Thomas asked for and got Daniel C. McCallum, an architect, builder, and railroad engineer who had been appointed director of all the military railroads in early 1862. Stanton cooperated, and when McCallum came to Chattanooga, the delivery of supplies improved by orders of magnitude.

The railroad was the favorite target of the Confederate cavalry under Forrest, Morgan, and Wheeler. Federal cavalry had been unable to prevent their raids. Thomas devised a new tactic, however, using the talents of his chief engineer and chief topographer, William E. Merrill. He and Merrill decided to build stout blockhouses to defend the most vulnerable sections of the rail line. Some 169 were constructed by the spring of 1864, well stocked to withstand a siege from lightly armed Confederate cavalry. Thomas expected them to be held. When enemy cavalry ripped up rails and structures at undefended points, mobile repair teams with tools, heavy equipment, and prefabricated materials quickly restored the damage. The trains kept moving.

Grant meanwhile wanted to resume operations with an aggressive winter campaign. In late January Sherman volunteered to lead a raid in the Mississippi Valley. Grant immediately agreed. "I am preparing to take the offensive," Grant wired Thomas on January 31. Sherman's February raid burned the town of Meridian and nothing more, yet his reports were so glowing that a reader had to be reminded that Sherman had not accomplished what he had set out to do: seize Mobile and defeat Forrest's cavalry.

While Sherman was engaged in river raids, Grant at his Nashville headquarters received news that Longstreet, reinforced with forces from the east, was about to launch a major campaign in East Tennessee. And Johnston, he also believed, was dispatching reinforcements both to the Mississippi and to Longstreet. "This makes it evident," he wired Thomas on February 6, "that they intend to secure East Tennessee, if they can, and I intend to drive them out, or get whipped this month." None of this was true. Longstreet was immobilized, Johnston was inert, and Lee had sent not a single soldier to join Longstreet.

Grant was reacting to ghosts. Envisioning a decisive battle shaping up, he issued imperative orders to Thomas to mobilize his army to react to the phantom threat. Reasoning incorrectly that few Confederate soldiers remained at Thomas's front, south of Chattanooga, Grant dispatched a flurry of orders for Thomas immediately to send reinforcements to Knoxville, which would of course weaken Chattanooga, and to reconnoiter in force toward Johnston's headquarters in Dalton. Thomas soon confirmed that Johnston's army was intact and Grant's view of the situation a delusion.

While Grant seemed incapable of distinguishing fact and fiction, Thomas regarded rumors with skepticism. After this experience with Grant's imagination, Thomas released a general order trying to avoid recurrences. "All officers are cautioned," he wrote just before starting the Georgia campaign, "against the mischievous and criminal practice of reporting mere vague rumors, often sent into our lines by the enemy for his own purposes. Actual facts should be reported to the headquarters in the field, that they may be

Nashville, with its Capitol surmounting a hill, was the largest Federal supply base in any theater. Sherman's campaign into Georgia depended on these locomotives pulling trainloads of supplies across Tennessee and delivering them to his army. Thomas's quartermasters in the Army of the Cumberland managed this immense logistical operation. (Library of Congress)

judged in connection with other known facts. An army of a million men could not guard against the fabulous stories that are sent to headquarters. Officers must scrutinize and see with their own eyes, or those of some cool, experienced staff officer, before making reports that may call off troops from another quarter where there may be more need of them."

Grant expected Thomas to attack Johnston's mountain fortress in late February. "It is not possible to carry this place by assault," Thomas wired Grant on February 26. "I will wait the development of this day, and advise you further." Grant ranted from Nashville, insisting that Thomas launch an all-out assault against Johnston and offering improbable schemes to overcome obstacles. "It is of the utmost importance," he wired Thomas on the twenty-seventh, "that the enemy should be held in full belief that an advance into the heart of the South is intended, until the fate of General Sherman is fully known." Grant wired later in the day that information had reached

Confederate cavalry raiders were a constant threat to Federal rail lines in Tennessee. Knowing that he could never corner the elusive Confederate horsemen, Thomas constructed sturdy fortifications at his bridges and tunnels to protect them from the lightly armed raiders. This bridge across the Cumberland near Nashville is one such example. (Library of Congress)

Washington that Johnston had fallen back from Dalton, and he again urged
Thomas to advance. The fact that Thomas was at the front and had seen
Johnston's entire army, larger than his own, dug in and ready to fight, was
immaterial. Out of touch with conditions at the front, Grant was frantic for
Thomas to do something, anything.

Thomas met Grant halfway, responding that he was ready to march upon
Atlanta, not immediately as Grant wished, but once the Army of the Cumberland was consolidated. His recent skirmishing against Johnston had
revealed a flaw in the Confederate defenses: an undefended passage through
the mountains fifteen miles south of Dalton, called Snake Creek Gap, would
allow the Federal army to sever the railway line to Atlanta and attack Johnston from the rear.

Grant calmed down with the news that Longstreet was leaving East Tennessee and returning to Virginia. Realizing that he had been reacting to a
false alarm, Grant abandoned his idea of an imminent decisive battle, and
Thomas returned to Chattanooga. When Grant was ordered to Washington
on March 3, his plans for the western theater were forgotten.

The indecisive February operations compounded the worsening relations
between Grant and Thomas. Persistently uninformed, Grant had acted
impetuously, demanding movement for the sake of movement and unques-
tioning obedience without an appreciation of what he was asking his subordinates to do. Grant's ill-considered orders, like those he had issued at
Chattanooga, put Thomas in a difficult position. He tried to support his
commanders—whether Buell, Rosecrans, Grant, or Sherman—with loyalty
and cooperation, but only so far. Thomas would not waste lives. His tactful
demurs implied that Grant was often wrong. Grant rankled with resentment,
and it would explode months later.

When Grant went east, he selected Sherman to succeed him as supreme
commander in the western theater. Sherman's role would be part of Grant's
grand strategy to overwhelm the Confederate forces by simultaneous offensives in the principal theaters. His primary objective would be to seek out
and destroy Johnston's Army of Tennessee, exerting constant pressure to prevent Johnston from reinforcing the eastern theater. And, to the extent possible, Sherman was to tear at the guts of the Confederacy.

Three armies comprised Sherman's unified command. Thomas had the
Army of the Cumberland—the largest of the three—with 61,000 troops, 130
guns, and all the cavalry. (Howard commanded his Fourth Corps, Palmer the
Fourteenth, and Hooker the Twentieth, each with three divisions.) The next
largest was the Army of the Tennessee, once under Grant and then Sherman
and now commanded by James B. McPherson, first in his class at West Point
and groomed by Grant and Sherman for bigger things. The smallest, commanded by John M. Schofield, was actually a corps, but it was designated
the Army of the Ohio. (Coincidentally, McPherson, Schofield, and Hood
were classmates.) Altogether Sherman's army comprised 100,000 men and
254 guns. Johnston had three corps of 62,000 men, commanded respectively
by Hardee, Hood, and Polk.

Sherman came to Chattanooga to see Thomas and devise their campaign strategy. Remembering the open road to Johnston's rear at Snake Creek Gap, Thomas recommended (as he had to Grant) that his army swing wide to the west, pour through the gap, destroy the railroad, and then close on Johnston's rear. McPherson and Schofield could pin down Johnston at Dalton, and the two forces could then crush Johnston from the north and south.

Sherman rejected Thomas's plan, for he had a different role in mind for the Army of the Cumberland. Sherman's strategy was elementary. He would advance with a broad front against Johnston. Thomas and the massive Army of the Cumberland would occupy the center, acting as the fulcrum upon which McPherson and Schofield would pivot on the wings. While Thomas pinned down Johnston, McPherson and Schofield would sweep around the flanks and rear, threatening Johnston's lines of communication.

The Federal generals decided that the army would follow the railroad. Johnston would, of course, destroy the railroad as he retreated. Hence Thomas and McCallum would build—or rebuild—the railroad as the Federal forces advanced. To plan properly, Thomas needed to know about the existing rail system leading to Atlanta so he could use and adapt it to the extent possible. He had established an elaborate intelligence system for just such purposes, and his scouts and spies brought back detailed information. This allowed Thomas's engineers to prefabricate bridges and procure portable sawmills to cut lumber at the bridge sites. The Nashville shops were prepared to service thirty-four locomotives simultaneously and to maintain three thousand freight and baggage cars. The shops also built hospital cars, armored cars, and other special units. Thomas's specialized knowledge of military rail systems was paying off.

Meanwhile, Sherman was intent on accumulating the supplies in Chattanooga necessary to support his spring offensive. Thomas was his agent in making the railroads function, and complaints arose from Thomas's rules and priorities. The complaints provoked Sherman to assume control of the railroads and ruthlessly to enforce priorities and standing operating procedures. "As the accumulation of supplies at Chattanooga had hitherto been slight," wrote Van Horne, "General Sherman restricted railroad transportation to dead freight, and forbade passage to citizens or private property. He also forbade further issue of rations to the destitute citizens of the country. The people complained of these measures; but such was the necessity for the accumulation of supplies, that he persisted in their maintenance, against the protests of the citizens, remonstrances of Washington, and what under other circumstances would have been the demands of humanity. . . .

"During the month of April Chattanooga was the scene of the greatest activity. Troops were constantly coming up from the rear and moving to position in the front. The quartermaster and commissary departments were pressed to extreme exertion building steamboats, erecting and filling vast storehouses, bringing forward artillery and cavalry horses, mules, and cattle; while the railway was almost constantly trembling under the long trains heavily loaded with supplies and munitions."

The Federal army that assembled—and particularly the Army of the Cumberland—was the most modern of the Civil War, so advanced was it in technology and organization. Maps, as we have seen, were one example. Chief cartographer Merrill provided accurate, identical maps to all of the field commanders. Every unit down to brigade size had an officer or sergeant assigned to provide new data to Merrill's mapmakers, while Thomas's intelligence section interrogated deserters, prisoners, spies, and Georgia civilians for additional data. New information was rapidly incorporated into revised editions that were produced in the field and promptly distributed. Sherman demanded that all officers work off the same map. At first he used letters on place-names as coordinates; later, grid coordinates would be used. Made of linen, the maps could be folded, easily stored in a saddle bag, and washed without smearing the lines.

Thomas alone of the western generals was a champion of engineering in making war. Others never understood the role of engineers, and it will be recalled that Congress was slow to realize the need to augment and mobilize engineering manpower.* The regular army officers in the corps of engineers numbered but eighty-six in the summer of 1864, of which but nine were assigned to Sherman's western army. Hitherto Thomas had improvised with volunteer pioneer battalions, led by officers from the line with engineering experience, and they had performed with distinction. Nonetheless, Thomas wanted a permanent engineering organization in his army. So adamant was he that Thomas went directly to Congress and requested authorization to raise an additional ten-company volunteer regiment of engineers, which was approved on May 20.

The pioneers performed marvels, as, for example, in crossing rivers. Pontoons, made of canvas stretched across a wooden frame, had become standard in both the Federal and Confederate armies. Twenty-one feet long, they were difficult to transport by wagon, and Thomas asked Merrill to find a better way to move them. Merrill hinged the pontoons to fold in half. Standard quartermaster wagons then took them from river to river, where they could be quickly unfolded and launched, either to ferry troops or to support a floating bridge. Merrill provided these pontoons for each of the corps in Sherman's army and trained the pontoniers. As a consequence, Sherman crossed wherever he pleased, since Johnston was unable to defend every foot of riverbank.

Sherman's plans were predicated in large measure on information gathered by Thomas's intelligence service. His spies were everywhere, including Johnston's headquarters, giving Thomas access to Johnston's correspondence and message traffic. Observation stations covered all the roads far in advance of the Federal front lines, and telegraph, visual signal, and courier

---

* See chapter 8.

systems connected them to command posts. Thomas's staff evaluated the accumulated information as it poured into headquarters and sent digests to Sherman. So valuable and revealing were these digests that Grant continued to receive them after he had gone east.

Newsmen were the greatest threat to Federal security. Thomas's signal officers had broken the Confederate cipher and read intercepted secret telegrams. A reporter snooping around headquarters published this news in his paper, and the Confederates changed their code. Sherman, who despised the press, arrested the reporter and gave him to Thomas, who wanted a firing squad. (In the end he was banished.) Nonetheless, reporters had to be allowed to accompany the troops. Thomas protected his own material and warned his officers to guard their talk.

Care of the wounded in the past had often been primitive and haphazard. Thomas thoroughly reorganized his medical services. For the first time, cooks were detailed to prepare food as a measure of preventative medicine. Chloroform came into prescribed use as an anesthetic. Horse-drawn wagons with specially fitted bunks had been used as ambulances in past campaigns but too often had been commandeered for other purposes. Thomas wanted them solely for the wounded, so he grouped them by corps under the command of the medical directors, anticipating by ten weeks a similar War Department order for ambulance trains.

Once the ambulances delivered the wounded to the railroads, hospital trains took the casualties north. Rosecrans had organized the first such trains when he had commanded the Army of the Cumberland, and Thomas improved upon them by consigning dependable equipment operated by skillful crews. The hospital trains were identified with red paint and signs and with red lanterns for identification in the darkness, assuring them safe passage past guerrillas and raiders.

Thomas's preparations were extraordinarily thorough. His army would be the heart of the campaign in terms of size, logistical support, intelligence, and communications, providing for the needs of his own army and those of McPherson and Schofield as well. Sherman relied entirely upon Thomas, not only for the combat power of the Army of the Cumberland, but also for the staff work and coordination of the campaign.

Sherman intended to lead an army of 100,000 by traveling light with a staff of but twelve officers and a single wagon to transport his headquarters equipment. To set an example for the Federal army, he brought no tents. "Soldiering as we have been doing for the past two years, with such trains and impediments," he wrote to Quartermaster General Meigs, "has been a farce, and nothing but absolute poverty will cure it."

Thomas continued his practice of traveling comfortably with the amenities, and Sherman and his staff soon joined Thomas's mess.

2 8

ATLANTA

The Atlanta campaign began in early May and would have ended in a week if Sherman had listened to Thomas. The key to a prompt victory was getting a Federal army in Johnston's rear through Snake Creek Gap. Thomas knew the roads and the mountain passes in the Georgia country: Snake Creek Gap was an open door that he saw clearly and the Confederate generals saw not at all. Johnston had not posted so much as a corporal's guard there, as Thomas had known ever since February.

Like Lee in the east, the generals in the Army of Tennessee did not take the time to learn the terrain where they would be fighting. Johnston was a prime example. "For one who planned to dog Sherman at every step and strike north of the Etowah at the first available opportunity," wrote Thomas L. Connelly in *Autumn of Glory,* "Johnston was ill prepared. Seemingly, he knew little of the terrain, although he had been there five months. That his Dalton position turned out to be a defensive trap was proved by Sherman's flank move. If [Johnston] planned to make the fight at Dalton, as he sometimes claimed, why had he neglected to blockade both the passes in Rocky Face Mountain and Snake Creek Gap?"

Sherman forfeited his great chance to capitalize on Johnston's blunder. Half-listening to Thomas, Sherman decided to send McPherson through the gap. His orders to McPherson were discretionary, primarily to cut the rail line and then ambush Johnston if he retreated south. This was contrary to what Thomas had recommended—a powerful force with cavalry that would aggressively fall upon Johnston's unprotected rear and crush the Confederate army. McPherson's force was a third the size of Thomas's army and was without cavalry.

Uncertain as to his mission, McPherson got through the gap undetected on May 8, while Thomas dutifully demonstrated in front of Johnston's fortifications. The railroad town of Resaca lay five miles beyond Snake Creek Gap, and through it went the sole rail line leading from Atlanta to Johnston's army at Dalton. McPherson ventured cautiously toward Resaca on May 9, apprehensive that he was heading into a trap, although there was but one Confederate brigade opposing his army of 20,000 men; Johnston's army was fifteen miles to the north. Blinded without cavalry for reconnaissance, McPherson returned to Snake Creek Gap to await developments. Afterward he offered the excuse that dense woods had impeded his movement toward the railroad. "Where were their axes?" growled Thomas.

Johnston and Hood returned to Dalton on the evening of the ninth from the front lines, where Thomas had occupied their attention. When Johnston heard that Federal troops were at Resaca, he ordered Hood there with three divisions. Hood hurried down to Resaca during the night, looked about him at dawn, and could not see the army commanded by his classmate McPherson. Telegraphing Johnston that Resaca was not in danger, Hood returned to Dalton, telling Johnston that the main fight would be there.

Sherman was dismayed that McPherson had not cut the rail line and lay supine. But Thomas reckoned that there still was time to assault and hold Resaca, for Johnston had not withdrawn from the Dalton front. Detach Hooker's Twentieth Corps, urged Thomas, and send it south to reinforce McPherson. McPherson might then be emboldened to do what Sherman wanted done. Sherman concurred, Hooker was sent on his way, and other divisions followed. Thomas remained at Dalton with Howard and his Fourth Corps to try to distract Johnston from developments in Resaca.

Johnston could no longer ignore the reports of enemy columns moving south toward Snake Creek Gap. On the eleventh, he again sent Hood to Resaca to evaluate the situation. Once more Hood reported that Resaca was not in danger. In the evening he boarded the train to return to Dalton, accompanied by Leonidas Polk, whose corps of 18,000 troops was arriving from Mississippi to reinforce the Army of Tennessee. Johnston met with his corps commanders. Despite Hood's negative report, Johnston sensed that Resaca might be threatened, and he directed Polk to return there and defend the town with his arriving troops.

Before leaving, Polk went to Hood's headquarters, for Hood had asked to be baptized by the Episcopal bishop. Hood had been touched by the religious revivals sweeping the Confederate armies, and a soldier's relationship with God had become a matter of great individual importance. Sensing his own mortality and feeling the need for God's grace in undertaking his enormous responsibilities, Hood sought the comfort of the sacrament of baptism. Witnesses watched Polk open his *Book of Common Prayer,* and together he and Hood read the service by candlelight. Polk dipped a tin cup into a bucket. "I baptize thee John Bell Hood," said the bishop as he poured water over the long blond hair, "in the name of the Father, and of the Son, and of the Holy Ghost. Amen." The bishop made the sign of the Cross upon Hood's forehead and said a final blessing. Afterward Hood breathed deeply, and his soul felt repose. Alone in his tent, he fell into a deep sleep.*

---

* Later in the campaign Polk baptized Johnston. When Polk was killed by a Federal artillery shell, Alexander P. Stewart was promoted to lieutenant general and took command of his corps. During the siege of Atlanta, another bishop confirmed Hood into the Episcopal Church.

Reconnaissance on the morning of the twelfth confirmed that Thomas's army no longer was at Johnston's front. Johnston realized his mortal danger and withdrew his army on the rail line to Resaca. Sherman had not moved smartly, mistakenly assuming that he had time to get to Resaca before Johnston, confident that Johnston would not readily abandon his elaborate Dalton fortifications. By the time the Federal divisions debouched from Snake Creek Gap, however, Johnston had dug in around the town. Sherman's first opportunity to win an early, decisive victory had vanished.

One more chance remained for Sherman to defeat Johnston where he stood. Johnston placed his army north of the Oostanaula River, which flowed east-west just south of Resaca. Five miles down the rail line from Resaca lay the town of Calhoun. Sherman had at his disposal the pioneer brigade from the Army of the Cumberland and a train of the hinged pontoons that chief engineer Merrill had designed specifically to cross rivers in a hurry. Someone thought to order the pontoons to the river, and there they spanned the waters at a place called Lay's Ferry. Sherman was free to send a powerful force unopposed to Calhoun to slam shut the door on Johnston's line of withdrawal southward toward Atlanta.

Such a maneuver did not enter into Sherman's thinking. The pontoons across the river would provide a means to *pursue* Johnston once he began his retreat, but they would not be used as a means to *prevent* the retreat. Two brigades from Sherman's army of 100,000 crossed the river and established a beachhead, with no intention of interfering with Johnston's retreat when and if it came. Sherman reverted to two days of futile frontal assaults that shed blood but left Johnston's army intact.

In one of the ironies of the campaign, the two lonely brigades at Lay's Ferry compelled Johnston to abandon Resaca. When Johnston received reports that the river had been spanned, he assumed—incorrectly—that Sherman would seize Calhoun. In the face of Sherman's entire army, Johnston's troops and wagons withdrew, groped their way across the Oostanaula on their own shaky pontoon bridges, and chugged south on the railway while Sherman occupied the abandoned town.

Sherman's stop-and-go pursuit of Johnston lasted for eight weeks. Whenever Sherman turned his flank, Johnston bolted down the railroad toward Atlanta. When Johnston did stop to fight, his entrenchments held fast, and continual rain impeded Federal mobility. Grant's expectations hovered like a demon at Sherman's shoulder. Sherman neither understood, nor had he mastered, warfare of such complexity and scale. He was a raider accustomed to swift action, to movement. Thomas's deliberate way of war could not calm the churning that Sherman felt in his gut. Thomas measured the feasibility of Sherman's orders and circumvented those that bordered on the absurd, yet not to the extent of disobedience. His artillery continued to hammer the enemy, and his infantry developed the Confederate positions.

Sherman reported developments daily by wire to Halleck, who relayed them to the administration and to Grant. Sherman wrote privately to Grant to explain in carefully chosen words why he was stalled. Grant wanted him to succeed, and Sherman's reports were as upbeat and optimistic as events would allow, telling Grant what he believed Grant wanted to hear. If short-comings could not be concealed, Sherman held himself blameless, as he always would, lest anyone suspect that he had relapsed into the state of nervous collapse that had grounded him early in the war.

If Sherman held himself blameless, by implication his generals had to be at fault. It was convenient to blame Thomas, for Sherman knew that Grant would willingly believe whatever he might say in criticism. Framing one such letter was therefore straightforward. After a poke or two at McPherson and Schofield, Sherman got down to business. "My chief source of trouble," he wrote to Grant on June 18, "is with the Army of the Cumberland, which is dreadfully slow. A fresh furrow in a ploughed field will stop the whole column, and all will begin to entrench. I have again and again tried to impress on Thomas that we must assail and not defend; we are on the offensive, and yet it seems the whole Army of the Cumberland is so habituated to be on the defensive that, from its commander down to its lowest private, I cannot get it out of their heads. . . . This slowness has caused me the loss of two splendid opportunities which never recur in war." *

Johnston came again to bay at Kennesaw Mountain, twenty miles north of Atlanta, on June 27. Sherman unwisely ordered Thomas to make a frontal attack against earthworks, which Johnston repulsed. A dejected Sherman advised Washington that he was unable to whip Johnston and had run out of ideas. The Lincoln administration did not want to hear this kind of news. Grant had sustained horrendous casualties in Virginia and had begun the siege of Petersburg, where Lee and the Army of Northern Virginia remained intact. Sherman now seemed to be proposing a similar stalemate against Johnston in Georgia.

Grant's grand strategy had failed grandly, and Lincoln's chances for reelection in the fall seemed doomed. Consequently Grant could not allow Sherman to remain immobile on any pretext. Sherman had anticipated the slap on the wrist. He had to cut loose from the railroad and resume his flanking maneuvers, and he asked Thomas if he were willing to risk it.

"What force do you think of moving with?" Thomas asked. "If with the greater part of the army, I think it decidedly better than butting against breastworks twelve feet thick and strongly abatised."

That stung. "Go where we may," Sherman replied, "we will find the breast-works and abatis, unless we move more rapidly than we have heretofore."

---

* Sherman referred to Hooker's failed late afternoon attack, on May 25, at New Hope Church and to the failure of Thomas's army to break the Confederate line on June 17, the day before his letter, when Sherman had mistakenly thought that Johnston was retreating. Neither was an opportunity to the extent that Sherman implied, nor were they equivalent to the missed opportunities at Resaca in May, for which Sherman was responsible. See Albert Castel, *Decision in the West: The Atlanta Campaign of 1864*, pp. 284–85.

Sherman told Grant he would press on. Johnston again fell back, this time
to his fixed defenses encircling Atlanta, thereby allowing Sherman to cross
the Chattahoochee River without opposition, the last natural barrier
between the Federal army and the city.

The news of yet another retreat shook Davis. Throughout the campaign
he had not known what Johnston intended to do, for Johnston was characteristically mute. Davis knew only that Johnston was continually withdrawing into the interior of Georgia, and whether he intended to defend Atlanta
was unknown. Johnston might well abandon Atlanta without a fight, and
Davis would not know about it until after the fact.

Despite his misgivings, Davis hesitated to relieve Johnston, especially on
the eve of battle. Moreover, Davis would have to find someone who was
more qualified than the general he intended to relieve. Thus Davis was in the
same dilemma he had faced eight months before when he had to find a successor for Bragg. Looking for help, Davis asked for Lee's advice and his opinion of Hood as a successor. Lee's response was so equivocal and conditional
that it was, in effect, no advice at all.

Increasingly desperate, Davis sent Bragg to Atlanta in early July to assess
Johnston's intentions and to evaluate the situation. Having distinguished
himself for his ineptitude as commander of the Army of Tennessee, Bragg
arrived in Atlanta on July 13 to pass judgment on the man who had relieved
him. As Bragg claimed his visit was unofficial, people wondered why he was
there, although many must have suspected. After looking around and talking
with Johnston and with others, Bragg sent a series of damning telegrams that
convinced Davis that Johnston had no plans to defend Atlanta.

Bragg's presence crystallized Hood's feelings about the campaign thus far.
Clearly Davis was concerned about Johnston's leadership, or else Bragg
would not have been sent to Johnston's headquarters to snoop around. What
was it that Davis wanted? Sitting before the campfire and rubbing his temples, Hood tried to clear his head of the clouds that came after taking his
laudanum, and he wrestled with the misgivings gnawing at his gut. He
remembered the meetings in Richmond with the Confederate high command—Lee had been there—and the unanimous consensus that Johnston
should act aggressively. The thought, then, of a grand campaign on the scale
of Gettysburg had thrilled him as he listened to the hierarchy discuss western
strategy for 1864.

But the opposite was happening, retreat after retreat with very little fighting, and now they were in Atlanta, no one knew for how long. This was not
Hood's kind of war, for it was beyond any experience he had had when fighting as one of Lee's lieutenants. Lee would have attacked by now. He would
have found a way to outwit Sherman, maybe by attacking his lines of communication. This damned retreating by Johnston was preposterous.

Hood was not a deep thinker, and he saw things in simple terms. The
fighting instructions he issued when he first arrived had become a mockery.
Not once had he written about how to retreat, only attack. "Ground once
taken should never be relinquished," he had said, and he remembered the

magnificence of his corps assembled for parades and maneuvers. Now they were being ill used by Johnston, and their fighting spirit was ebbing. He owed loyalty to Johnston, certainly, but what about a greater loyalty to his soldiers and to the Confederacy? His head pounded with surging thoughts, and suddenly he was aware of the painful itching in his leg stump. Ferociously he dug at his skin and then lunged upright on his crutch. He had to see Bragg.

After talking privately with Bragg, Hood committed himself to writing. According to Hood, in the previous weeks Johnston had missed opportunities to "strike the enemy a decisive blow." Under no circumstances, argued Hood in his letter, should the Federal army be allowed to seize Atlanta. "I have so often urged," wrote Hood, "that we should force the enemy to give us battle as to be almost regarded reckless by the officers high in rank in this army, since their views have been so directly opposite. I regard it as a great misfortune to our country that we failed to give battle to the enemy many miles north of our present position [Atlanta]. Please say to the President that I shall continue to do my duty cheerfully and faithfully, and strive to do what I think is best for our country, as my constant prayer is for our success."

Hood's claims of frustrated chest thumping were largely fabricated, for while he truly believed what he said, on the whole he had gone along with Johnston's decisions. Regardless, Bragg predictably liked what he read and enclosed Hood's letter with a long letter of his own to Davis, urging that Hood replace Johnston. Before the two letters got to Richmond, however, Davis already had acted by wiring Johnston on July 16 with an ultimatum for a statement of his intentions. Johnston's terse reply that he intended to pull his army out of Atlanta destroyed Davis's last shred of confidence in him. The President of the Confederacy promoted Hood to the rank of full general and ordered him to relieve Johnston.

We cannot be entirely sure as to what Hood expected as a consequence of his communication with Bragg at Atlanta or of his earlier letters to Richmond. In any event, Johnston's fall from grace was largely self-inflicted. Hood was surprised, if not shaken, that, on the eve of a battle with the largest and most powerful army in the Union, Davis had abruptly given him command of an army equivalent in size to Lee's Army of Northern Virginia. As Hood tried to grasp the situation, he had two deep misgivings. One was that the other corps commanders, Hardee and Stewart, would believe that he had conspired with Bragg to disgrace Johnston and get the promotion. Literally, at least, his hands were clean, for Davis had acted before receiving Hood's letter. Hood quickly spoke with Hardee and Stewart to gauge their reactions. Neither wanted Johnston relieved, and Hood felt it expedient to join with them in asking Davis to rescind the order.

Davis responded that he would not undo what he had done. Anxious to leave, Johnston had written his farewell address the night of July 17, when he had received the telegraph orders, and he promptly departed after a perfunctory turnover. A young staff officer wrote home that Johnston seemed almost cheerful once he no longer had responsibility for the army: "No one could have told from his countenance or manner that anything unusual had occurred. Indeed he seemed in rather better spirits than usual though it must have been at the cost of much exertion."

Hood suddenly found himself in command, the last and, at age thirty-three, by far the youngest of the eight generals of the Confederacy. His second misgiving, more serious than the first, was that he might not be equal to the task. Hood's initial doubts were recorded by an aide on his staff, Second Lieutenant Halsey Wigfall, the son of Louis Trezevant Wigfall, who it will be recalled commanded the Texas Brigade before becoming a member of the Confederate Senate. Halsey was perceptive, intelligent, and sensitive. His letters to his family are especially revealing, for they mirror both the view of the war from Hood's headquarters, if not of Hood himself, and from the perspective of an ardent Southern advocate.

Wigfall told his family of the immediate reactions to Hood's ascension. At first, he wrote his mother, Hood "seemed to feel very fully the weight of responsibility thrown upon him." When Wigfall had congratulated him, Hood "spoke very sadly and said he hardly knew if it were a subject of congratulation."

Emotions in the army of 50,000 men were mixed. Many had liked and admired Johnston and had been content with his way of passive warfare. No one knew, based on his past reputation, what to expect from Hood other than immediate fighting. The staff officer that Hood needed the most left him immediately. Brigadier General William W. Mackall had been on the staff of the Army of Tennessee since the beginning of the war and had served as chief of staff both to his classmate Bragg and to his friend Johnston. An officer of the prewar regular army, Mackall had graduated from the Military Academy sixteen years before Hood. Believing that Bragg and Hood had betrayed Johnston, he bitterly refused to subordinate himself to the shavetail army commander.

As his new chief of staff, Hood chose an officer younger than himself, Brigadier General Francis A. Shoup, an Indiana native who had graduated from West Point two years after Hood. Shoup had practiced law in Florida, distinguished himself in western campaigns, and served most recently as Johnston's chief of artillery.

Hood also needed a replacement to command his own corps. He asked for and got Stephen D. Lee, another West Pointer younger than he, who had commanded cavalry, artillery, and infantry and was then in the Mississippi region. With the assignment came promotion; Lee became the youngest lieutenant general in the Confederate army. Until Lee arrived, Benjamin F. Cheatham, one of Hood's division commanders, acted as corps commander.

While Hood sorted out his staff, Sherman closed upon Atlanta. He and Thomas had first seen the spires of the city on July 5 from a bluff on the Chattahoochee River, the moat that guarded Atlanta and its rail lines radiating into the Deep South. "Mine eyes have beheld the promised land!" wrote a Federal officer to his wife.

[A] cheer went up as must have been heard even in the entrenchments of the doomed city itself. In a very few moments Generals Sherman and Thomas (who are always with the extreme front when a sudden movement is taking place) were with us on the hill top, and the two veterans, for a moment, stared at the glittering prize in silence. I watched the two noble soldiers—Sherman stepping nervously about, his eyes sparkling and his face aglow—casting a single glance at Atlanta, another at the River, and a dozen at the surrounding valley to see where he could best cross the River, how he could best flank them.

Thomas stood there like a noble old Roman, calm, soldierly, dignified; no trace of excitement about that grand old soldier who had ruled the storm at Chickamauga. Turning quietly to my General, he said, "[S]end up a couple of guns and we'll throw some shells over there," pointing to some heavy timber across the River.

In a moment I was off down the road, to the rear, to order up some artillery; the infantry column separated and opened the road, the artillery came thundering along through the long lines of men, and in fifteen minutes . . . a Parrott shell went screaming from the high point, and burst beautifully on the south side of the Chattahoochee—the first since the war began. That was a glorious moment, and I felt proud that I belong to this grand army, and that I was at the front instead of at the rear, doing "fancy duty."

Sherman shuddered when he saw the elaborate entrenchments surrounding the city. If Johnston decided to stay within them, the campaign would become a stalemate, which neither Lincoln nor Grant could tolerate as the fall elections approached. Sherman remembered the siege at Vicksburg a year earlier and shuddered again. Since confronting Johnston at Dalton, Sherman had come to respect his skillful maneuvering, and when Johnston had withdrawn, it had been in good order, with nothing left behind.

Sherman had no military solution for overcoming the entrenchments. With Kennesaw Mountain fresh in mind, he wanted to avoid frontal assaults. Following the war one of his soldiers wrote of the futility of assaulting the kind of entrenchments that Sherman faced at Atlanta. After charging through rifle and artillery fire that ripped their lines, he remembered, the attacking soldiers would come upon the man-made obstacles.

The abatis with its tangled intricacy of sharpened branches snares your line. Tripping, falling, rising again, the men struggle through this abatis. . . . You get through a part of [the men] and still rush on; the firing grows more fierce, the men grow more desperate. Your three lines have been almost reduced to one, and you strike another line of abatis.

In this abatis are the palisades, which must be uprooted by force before a man can pass. You stumble, fall, tear your flesh on these stakes, and must stop to pull them up—stop, when every instant is an hour—stop, when you are already gasping for breath; and here open

up the masked batteries, pouring the canister into that writhing, strug-
gling, bleeding mass—so close that the flame scorches, that the smoke
blinds from those guns.

Is it any wonder that your three lines are torn to pieces, and have to
give back before the redoubled fire of an enemy as yet uninjured com-
paratively? And then the slaughter of a retreat there! Oftentimes it is
preferable to lie down and take fire there until night rather than lose all
by falling back under such circumstances.

Such was the kind of fighting that Sherman had before him. Then he learned that Hood had replaced Johnston. "At this critical moment," Sherman wrote in his memoirs, "the Confederate Government rendered us most valuable service. . . . The character of a leader is a large factor in the game of war, and I confess I was pleased with this change, of which I had early notice." Sherman wrote this passage years after the fact, as if he had relished the opportunity to meet Hood in decisive battle, as if in all probability Hood would be true to character and emerge from behind those intimidating fortifications and attack in the open, where Sherman could maneuver and exploit his greater combat power.

The fact is, however, that Sherman did not want to confront Hood's army. He wanted to seize and occupy Atlanta. If Hood chose to abandon the city, Sherman would open the door and stand aside for him to leave.

When and how Hood would attack were unknown; meanwhile Sherman had to press on against Atlanta on "the principle that 'an army once on the offensive must maintain the offensive.' " A characteristically bogus warning from Grant impelled him to hustle. After Early had withdrawn from his raid against Washington, Grant hypothesized that he intended to go to Atlanta, since Lee presumably would not be able to feed Early's 25,000 soldiers if they returned to Petersburg. As he had to take Grant's assessment seriously, wrong as it was, Sherman told his army commanders that it was essential to seize Atlanta before Early arrived to reinforce its defenders. "It behooves us therefore to hurry," he told them, and he dispatched a division of cavalry far to the east to destroy the rail line over which reinforcements would have to arrive.

As Sherman outnumbered Hood two to one, Hood planned to attack a segment of Sherman's army when it was beyond supporting distance of the remainder of the Federal army. That time was now. Sherman had split his army into two wings as it approached Atlanta from the north and east, in the same way that Rosecrans had divided his army on the approach to Chattanooga the year before. Thomas commanded the right wing (his Army of the Cumberland), McPherson and Schofield constituted the left wing, and a gap of several miles separated them. Hood decided to attack Thomas on July 20, after he had crossed Peach Tree Creek, the last natural barrier north of Atlanta. He would use two-thirds of his army, the corps of Hardee and Stewart, which would corner Thomas into the apex of a triangle formed by the confluence of Peach Tree Creek and the Chattahoochee. Hood's own corps, now temporarily commanded by Cheatham, would block any reinforcement from the Federal left wing.

The plan was sound in concept. It held the prospect of repeating the success Lee had achieved at Chancellorsville, for the terrain and the numbers and the disposition of the forces were similar. (Hood would even be attacking the same general, Hooker, only this time in command of a corps and not an army.) Lee had smacked the Federal right wing while pinning the left in place. The bold plan had worked for Lee; perhaps it could work for Hood as well.

By coincidence, Sherman made a decision that helped Hood's chances for success, for Sherman was another general who made plans based on what he wanted the enemy to do, rather than on what the enemy was capable of doing. Expecting that Hood would attack the left wing and not Thomas on the right, Sherman transferred two of Thomas's divisions from Howard's corps to the left wing, so that it became the stronger of the two. "With McPherson, Howard, and Schofield," he wrote Thomas on the evening of July 19, "I would have ample to fight the whole of Hood's army, leaving you to walk into Atlanta, capturing guns and everything."

In the morning Sherman issued his field order for the converging attack on Atlanta. His movement instructions were detailed, as they had been since the start of the campaign. Thomas's superb maps allowed him to deploy his divisions with precision, and he was able to specify grid coordinates for rendezvous sites and for the routes each army was to follow.

Sherman also knew the details of the Atlanta approaches, which were terra incognita to the Confederate generals defending the city. Sherman designated an exact position two miles northeast of Atlanta where Thomas's left was to converge with Schofield's right, finally closing the gap that separated the two wings. Sherman's objective was the city and not the enemy army, and so his orders were cautious, predicated on reacting to what Hood might do. If the Federal troops got within artillery range of the spires of the city, they were to stop and await orders. Combat could not be avoided, of course, if Hood willed it so. "Each army commander will accept battle on anything like fair terms," read Sherman's order. "If fired on from the forts or buildings of Atlanta no consideration must be paid to the fact that they are occupied by families, but the place must be cannonaded without the formality of a demand."

Thomas's divisions crossed Peach Tree Creek against light opposition and moved cautiously into the thickets beyond. Hooker interrogated prisoners, who told him that Hardee and Stewart were immediately in front of him. Similar reports convinced Thomas by midnight that most of Hood's army was at his front. Nonetheless, Thomas intended to finish crossing Peach Tree Creek and press on toward Atlanta, as Sherman had ordered him to do. "If the prisoners' report be true," he notified Sherman, "his attention is fully occupied by us, and I am in hopes Generals McPherson, Schofield, and Howard will be able to fall upon his rear without any very great difficulty."

Hence, as the Federal armies maneuvered into position to close on Atlanta, Sherman and Thomas had entirely different estimates as to the whereabouts of Hood's army and what he intended to do with it. "In advancing this morning," Sherman wrote to Thomas in the predawn darkness of July 20, "of course we will bring on a heavy battle, and should be as fully prepared as possible." Sherman confirmed that Thomas was to send Howard's two divisions to the left wing, where Hood did not intend to attack. Sherman then went to Schofield's headquarters, where throughout the day he would be out of touch with the battles on either of his two wings and so lose the opportunity to destroy Hood's army in the first battle of Atlanta.

Meanwhile, that night Hood met with Stewart and Hardee to issue his orders to attack Thomas on July 20. It was the first time Hood would have to deal with corps commanders who were older and wiser. His debut as an army commander was incongruous. Hardee had graduated from West Point in 1838, when Hood was seven, and Stewart in 1842, eleven years ahead of Hood. Each had been fighting continuously as general officers since the beginning of the war. And now Hood presumed to tell them how to attack the Federal general who had been his instructor at West Point and had never been defeated in any battle. Perhaps Hood felt presumptuous, and perhaps he felt intimidated, with good reason. He told the two grizzled corps commanders what he wanted done, but not how to do it. Hardee would attack on the right, followed en echelon by Stewart on the left. Together they would drive Thomas until he was trapped by the river and the creek at his back, and then they would destroy his army.

Hood retired to his headquarters in the rear, deliberately removing himself from the operation on the assumption that Hardee and Stewart would cooperate to do what he wanted done. Hood interfered but once, by moving Cheatham's corps to the right to cover the threat from Sherman's left wing, requiring Hardee and Stewart to shift to the right before attacking. The clockwise shuffling delayed the assault for three hours. At four o'clock in the afternoon Hardee and Stewart were finally in position, and they attacked.

Thomas's generals were not surprised. They had smelled the enemy, had watched their flanks, and had erected hasty fortifications. Thomas ordered Brigadier General John Newton, one of his finest division commanders and a hero at Gettysburg, to feel out the front and find the enemy. Newton reported that the situation had an "ugly look," and he constructed log barricades. As Newton held the extreme left of Thomas's front, the Confederates hit his left flank and rear with the intention of rolling up the line. Two of Newton's batteries temporarily held them off.

Thomas saw the danger, galloped across the bridge where he knew two other batteries had just arrived, and ordered them forward, lashing the horses with his sword. With four batteries in hand, Thomas then sat quietly on his mount and directed their fire against the Confederates threatening the flank. The shot and canister were so deadly that the Confederate attack disintegrated. Thomas had saved his left flank and kept it intact.

The execution of the Confederate attack was badly managed, and by evening Thomas had them beaten. Removed as he was from the action,

Hood lost control of his army. Thomas, on the other hand, appeared every-where, deploying his forces, backing up his commanders, and sending rein-forcements where they were needed. When the day was over, Hood gathered his bloodied army and retreated behind the Atlanta fortifications.

Sherman, like Hood, was incommunicado and out of the picture. He did not know that Thomas was locked in battle with two-thirds of Hood's army and Schofield with the remaining third, or that a small force of Wheeler's cavalry and a few militia had flummoxed McPherson and prevented him from marching into Atlanta. Sherman's ears betrayed him: he could not hear the Peach Tree battle raging on his right. Hearing cannonades on his left, he assumed by midafternoon that McPherson was engaging the bulk of the Confederate army and Schofield the remainder. Then McPherson reported that the enemy was at such strength on the eastern road to the city that he could not advance. Reasoning that Thomas had no enemy in his front, Sher-man ordered him to push hard for Atlanta, sweeping everything before him.

At eight o'clock Sherman was still unaware of the developments of the day. He assumed that Thomas had simply been slow and had failed to march unopposed into Atlanta while Schofield and McPherson had pinned down all of Hood's army. "I think," he wrote to McPherson, "that our only chance of entering Atlanta by a quick move if possible is lost." At midnight Sherman finally received Thomas's 6:15 P.M. dispatch reporting his major battle of the afternoon.

Sherman was shocked. As Hood's army had been on the right, McPherson on the left should have been able to march easily into Atlanta. This unwel-come revelation was confirmed when he received a report from McPherson sent at 8:15 P.M. Sherman finally realized what had happened. McPherson had thought—as had Sherman—that he faced the bulk of Hood's army. As apprehensive as he had been at Resaca, McPherson had inched toward Atlanta wholly intimidated by a scratch force of cavalry and militia. He had stopped well short of the city and had surrendered his glorious opportunity.

Hood was determined to persist in his attacks against Sherman. Having failed against Thomas on the right, Hood decided to assault McPherson on the Federal left, and throughout the next day, July 21, he consulted with his corps commanders. Hood's plan was conceptually bold, and it represented the kind of Confederate assault that had broken Federal armies in the past. Hood operated on a fundamental assumption—which was correct—that Sherman, having been stung the day before, would stay in place, allowing Hood the freedom to maneuver on interior lines and to strike at places of his choosing. Accordingly, Hood ordered Hardee to withdraw his corps from the left, swing wide to the right, and in the early afternoon of the twenty-second to turn the Federal left held by McPherson's Army of the Tennessee. Cheatham would cooperate by hitting McPherson from the front. Stewart meanwhile would withdraw into the northern Atlanta defenses and divert Thomas. Historians later would call this the Battle of Atlanta.

Sherman altogether misjudged what Hood was doing. When the Confed-erate troops moved as Hood had ordered, Sherman assumed that Hood was abandoning Atlanta, since that was what he wished to believe. "I am satis-fied the enemy will not attempt to hold Atlanta," Sherman informed Thomas. "I do not believe the enemy will repeat his assaults, as he had in that of yesterday his best troops and failed signally." Sherman did not intend to prevent Hood from withdrawing, since he hoped that Hood would leave Atlanta without further fighting. At the most, Sherman would pursue for perhaps two days and then allow Hood to continue unmolested.

Thomas's generals did not share Sherman's wishful thinking. Throughout the day they moved forward, cautiously feeling for the enemy. By evening Thomas knew that Stewart was well entrenched in front of him, and he told Sherman so. Still, Sherman thought that Hood had left the city, and his orders for the twenty-second were a cautious approach toward Atlanta by all three armies. By eleven o'clock, when artillery fire from the city whistled over his head, Sherman finally realized that Hood intended to fight. "[W]e were mistaken in assuming the enemy gone," he wrote Thomas.

Hardee's soldiers meanwhile struggled through treacherous terrain south of McPherson's left flank, attempting to get into position to attack, and the ultimate assault was uncoordinated and piecemeal. Still, it sur-prised both Sherman and McPherson, for there was no cavalry guarding the flank—Sherman had ridden his cavalry out of the battle by sending it thirty miles to the east to destroy track in order to slow the phantom rein-forcements from the east.

Sherman allowed McPherson to slug it out alone. He later said that McPher-son's army needed to win by itself for its self-esteem and to redeem McPherson from missed opportunities in the past. "I purposely allowed the Army of the Tennessee to fight this battle almost unaided," Sherman wrote in his memoirs, "because I knew that . . . if any assistance were rendered by either of the other armies, the Army of the Tennessee would be jealous." McPherson went to the front to rally his soldiers, and Confederate skirmishers shot him dead. Sherman grieved, for he and Grant had been McPherson's friends and mentors, and Sherman had hoped that McPherson one day would be general in chief of the army.*

Hood could hear the clangor of battle, but he allowed Hardee to fight alone. He committed Cheatham at a late hour, but the Army of the Ten-nessee, temporarily commanded by John A. Logan, held on until nightfall. Hardee's corps limped back to Atlanta in the darkness.

The forty-day siege of Atlanta began. Hood sent his new corps commander, Stephen Lee, south of the city on July 28 to protect his sole remaining rail

---

* McPherson's death created a daisy chain of command changes in the Army of the Cumber-land. Howard (Fourth Corps) took command of the Army of the Tennessee, and David S. Stan-ley took command of the Fourth Corps. Miffed that he had been passed over for the vacant army command, Hooker (Twentieth Corps) asked to be relieved of duty, and Henry W. Slocum took his place. John Palmer (Fourteenth Corps) squabbled once too often with Sherman and asked to be relieved; Jefferson C. Davis assumed command. Hence, Thomas had three new corps commanders.

line into Atlanta, and he sent Stewart to follow. While Hood remained in the city, his two corps commanders did as they pleased. Impulsively and unwisely they attacked Federal lines at Ezra Church, while Hood remained unaware that two-thirds of his army was engaged. The outcome was a waste of Confederate lives and the continuation of the siege.

There had been three costly, losing battles in the two weeks since Hood had taken command. He had tried to do what Lee used to do—especially when Hood had been there: to fight aggressively, forcing the Army of the Potomac time and again to retreat and withdraw. Davis had banked on Hood doing the same in Georgia. Now he told Hood to refrain. "The loss consequent upon attacking [Sherman] in his entrenchments," wired Davis, "requires you to avoid that, if practicable." The only alternative was to raid Sherman's lines of communication, especially the railroads, a philosophy held dear by the Confederates when their armies were weak. In this instance Davis endorsed Hood's plan for cavalry raids, both men wistfully hoping that a severed rail line would make Sherman retreat when fighting could not.

Sherman, too, was an apostle of this indirect approach to warfare. He sought not to destroy Hood's army but to emasculate it, destroying its means of subsistence so that it would leave Atlanta. Rail lines and bridges, and not enemy soldiers, were his prime objective. He instructed his troops exactly how they were to proceed. "Be prepared with axes, hatchets, and bars to tear up sections of the track and make bonfires," he would typically say. "When the rails are red hot they must be twisted. Burning will do for bridges and culverts, but not for ordinary track. Let the work be well done."

And so it was that both Sherman and Hood adopted the same strategy. Like other Civil War generals before them, they failed to recognize that so long as opposing armies remained intact, the war would go on. Sherman sent his cavalry south of Atlanta to destroy the rail line coming north from Macon. The Confederate cavalry beat them off, and then Hood sent Wheeler north into Tennessee to attack the sole Federal rail line from Nashville to Chattanooga, upon which Sherman depended. Sherman considered the outcome a matter of endurance and patience. "If Wheeler interrupts our supplies," he told his army commanders on August 16, "we can surely cut off those against Hood, and see who can stand it the best." With Wheeler no longer a local threat, Sherman was ready to wage war against Hood's last uninterrupted line of communication. "I do think our cavalry should now break the Macon line real good," he wrote Thomas. "If we can . . . break the Macon road for many miles, we can wait as long as Hood."

Sherman issued his field order against the Macon railroad. His armies would disengage from their positions around Atlanta and move south by stages. When they encountered a section of the Macon railroad, they were to dig in while a third of the troops destroyed the rail line. As Sherman's army disappeared from their front, wishful thinkers in the Confederate army thought the Federal troops were retreating because Wheeler had cut off their supplies. Wheeler's raid had, in fact, been a joyride. He rarely attacked the rail facilities, and when he did, the blockhouses and repair crews minimized the damage. Wheeler's fiasco would not become known for weeks.

While Sherman moved to Hood's rear, Hood tried to administer an army and a city under siege. Atlanta was in pandemonium. Federal artillery shells thumped into buildings and streets, while maverick Confederate soldiers marauded the city and terrified the citizens. The fabric of the city seemed about to break. Never could Hood have imagined the weight of responsibility he now had to bear. A lesser man would have gone under by then, but, thanks to his resolution and stamina, Hood found that he was able to survive the chaos, if not to bring it under control.

The three July assaults had devastated Hood's officer corps. The scarcity of healthy division and brigade commanders impelled reorganizations and the shuffling of assignments. Hood began blaming his subordinates for the failure of his plans, in this instance Hardee, who begged Davis for relief and reassignment. While the generals bickered, sickness and desertion drained the combat readiness of the beleaguered army.

Some still hoped that Sherman would give out, would, by a miracle, go away. As Grant put it to Sherman on August 18, "[T]hey expect something to turn up." Hood remained indomitable, as he always would regardless of circumstances. "He is in excellent spirits," Wigfall wrote his mother on August 7, "and bears the burden as though he felt himself entirely equal to it." Wigfall mirrored the sense of unreality at Hood's headquarters. "All here," he wrote his father, "seem to be looking forward to starting before long in the direction of Tennessee. . . . I should like to get into Yankee-land once more before the war ends. One feels much more like a spectator and doesn't have any sense of regret at the unavoidable destruction in the line of march of an army. . . . When I crossed into Maryland last summer I felt almost as though I were at the theater."

Hood knew that Wigfall was writing to his influential father. "[Hood] begged to be remembered to you," the son wrote. "I don't think he is the most sincere person I ever saw."

By sweeping wide to the west, Sherman positioned his army along six miles of track on the Macon line between Rough and Ready and Jonesboro, fourteen miles south of Atlanta. As Sherman did not intend to carry the fight to Hood's army, he employed his soldiers in busting miles of rails. At least twice Sherman told his generals that he intended to destroy the enemy, yet in the end he could not bring himself to do more than harass and skirmish and order yet more rail busting. Hence, by the time Hood's army hurried out of the city to avoid being trapped, there was no trap. When Thomas proposed to intercept the Confederates, Sherman would not allow it. "I would rather," Sherman responded, "you should follow the enemy as he retreats." Sherman considered his operation a raid, a term he used repeatedly in his reports and orders, and as such he was unwilling to engage his full forces in decisive battle.

Still, Sherman's instincts told him that he should at least go through the motions of preventing Hood's escape, and he told Schofield and Howard on the evening of September 1 of his intention to fall upon the fleeing enemy. "Hardee cannot move south now without our seeing him," he advised Schofield, "and if all of our army is concentrated on him we should make quick work." During the night Hood decided to evacuate Atlanta, and his withdrawal was explosive. Eighty-one railway cars at the downtown terminal were put to the torch. Twenty-eight contained Hood's ammunition reserve, and their explosions were seen and heard at the Federal lines south of the city.

Sherman assumed that the fireworks announced that Hood was abandoning the city and heading his way. He told Thomas to hunker down and spoke no more of destroying or intercepting Hood's army. As evening came, Sherman ordered Thomas to send Slocum and his corps into the city to reconnoiter. "Until we hear from Atlanta the exact truth," he advised Thomas at eight o'clock, "I do not care about your pushing your men against breastworks." The same message went to Schofield. If Hood had abandoned Atlanta, said Sherman, "it is unnecessary for us to go farther at this stage." Again Sherman ordered more destruction of track, while Hood's soldiers hustled south on farm roads.

When Hood's army passed to the east of Jonesboro, Sherman waved him on by. "So Atlanta is ours, and fairly won," Sherman reported to Halleck in Washington. "I shall not push much farther on this raid, but in a day or two will move to Atlanta and give my men some rest." The jubilation in the North was so intense that few grasped—or even cared—that Sherman had not done what he had set out to do four months before. The destruction of an enemy army is difficult to visualize and quantify, and the public had been deceived by past claims that had proved false. But the seizure of a city the Confederacy held dear—that was understood by everyone, both North and South.

Lincoln would now be reelected, and the war would go on.

29

RETURN TO
TENNESSEE

———◆———

With Atlanta in his possession and Hood over the horizon, Sherman appraised what he had accomplished. He wanted it understood on his terms. On September 4, 1864, the day after he had decided to end the campaign, he addressed a long, self-serving letter to "My dear friend" Halleck, the conduit for all high-level communication in and out of Washington.

Anticipating questions as to why Hood had escaped, Sherman had ready answers. He had intended to crush Hood's army, he maintained, but his generals had failed to execute his plan. "I ought to have reaped larger fruits of victory," he wrote. "A part of my army is too slow, but I feel my part was skillful and well executed." Only his former command, the Army of the Tennessee, had moved "rapidly" enough to threaten Hood's army. If Thomas and Schofield had moved as swiftly, said Sherman, he would have bagged the entire enemy army. Sherman naturally excluded the fact that he had ordered them to undertake the time-consuming distraction of busting miles of track.

Sherman then assessed his own achievements in generous measure, and, less generously, those of his three army commanders. "[The soldiers] all seem to have implicit confidence in me," he wrote. "They observe success at points remote, as in this case of Atlanta, and they naturally say that the old man knows what he is about. They think I know where every road and by-path is in Georgia, and one soldier swore that I was born on Kennesaw Mountain. [A tribute to Thomas's maps, with no credit to Thomas.] George Thomas, you know, is slow, but as true as steel; Schofield is also slow and leaves too much to others; Howard is a Christian, elegant gentleman, and conscientious soldier. In him I made no mistake. Hooker was a fool. Had he staid a couple of weeks he could have marched into Atlanta and claimed all the honors."

Union leaders rarely had follow-on plans after seizing a major objective with a strenuous campaign. So it was with Sherman. His most immediate goal was to rest his army and to transform Atlanta into a citadel unencumbered with civilians. Disregarding pleas from city fathers, Sherman ordered the people of Atlanta to leave. The brutality of the war had intensified.

Hood too was corresponding with his superiors, for he, like Sherman, needed to put the best light on events without delay. When he received reports that Sherman's army was returning to Atlanta instead of pursuing, Hood could scarcely believe his good fortune. His own army was totally used up, his men battered and embittered. Nearly all his stores and quartermaster supplies had been abandoned in the city, where mobs had ransacked the warehouses even as they burned. Worst of all, his soldiers were down to their last rounds of ammunition, for the twenty-eight railway cars containing Hood's reserve had not been evacuated in time from the city and had been destroyed in thunderous explosions. It would be difficult to express anything positive to Richmond under the circumstances.

From his temporary headquarters in Lovejoy's Station, thirty-five miles down the track from Atlanta, Hood watched his groaning troops collapse into heaps of ragged clothing and bloodied dressings. With the cessation of combat, Hood finally had time to think without distraction. Why had Sherman withdrawn into Atlanta? he wondered. It could only be that Sherman must be worse off than Hood. Was Sherman hurting from his recent casualties around the city? Probably so, thought Hood. And Sherman had to be short of supplies—Wheeler and his cavalry must have succeeded in cutting Sherman's rail lines from Tennessee. That had to be it! Not until weeks later would Hood discover that Wheeler had done nothing of the sort.

From his association with Davis and the military authorities in Richmond, Hood knew that a Confederate general was expected to act aggressively. His experience with the Army of Northern Virginia after a costly campaign was that Lee immediately would ask for men to replace his losses while promising to resume offensive operations. In light of those precedents and Sherman's reluctance to fight, Hood felt it proper to follow Lee's example.

Shutting himself in his tent, Hood began to write a dispatch to Bragg in Richmond. Its deliberate tone of bravado was a facade to mask his desperation. Reinforcements were absolutely necessary, Hood wrote, but not because his back was against the wall. Quite the opposite. There must be a prompt and vigorous movement against Sherman before his divided forces could make a junction, or before reinforcements could be sent from Tennessee and Mississippi. Hood's telegram implied that Atlanta was no more than a temporary setback in the larger canvas of the western campaign.

A day after recommending an offensive movement, Hood's tone changed abruptly. Reports from his generals revealed the dimensions of the calamity. Now Hood beseeched Davis for reinforcements because he feared for the very survival of his army and the potential loss of the Deep South. Through no fault of his own, insisted Hood, his army was near mutiny, and his officers and men would no longer charge breastworks. In what would be a recurring theme during his tenure as commander of the Army of Tennessee, Hood blamed others for the failures of leadership, in this instance the old warrior Hardee.

Davis's chilling reply dashed Hood's expectations: the countryside had already been scoured, and all available troops had been sent. Hood could not possibly need reinforcements, said Davis, because he had been informed that Hood was sending home soldiers as no longer needed. Davis could not reconcile this with Hood's demand for more men. Hood was on his own, for Davis offered only platitudes. "It is now requisite that absentees be brought back," Davis wrote, ". . . and that the means in hand be used with energy proportionate to the country's need."

Hood's charges against Hardee intensified to the extent that he held Hardee responsible for the loss of Atlanta and demanded his relief. So severe was the destructive hostility within Hood's command that Davis visited Hood's headquarters in Palmetto, Georgia, in yet another of his periodic efforts to resuscitate the Army of Tennessee after a losing campaign. As before, his presence exacerbated the animosity among the generals, and their accusations poured freely into his ear. In the end, Davis sent Hardee away and appointed Cheatham to command the corps in his place. Stephen Lee and Stewart retained command of the two other corps. Hood was without a cavalry commander, since Wheeler was on his wasteful operation in Tennessee and Forrest was raiding in the Mississippi Valley.

Davis no longer was willing to allow Hood free rein in the west. He had hoped that Hardee, older and more seasoned than Hood, would act as a counselor and restrain Hood's impulses, but now Hardee was gone. Davis decided to restore Beauregard from his two-year exile in the east and bring him west as Hood's nominal superior.

Even though ostracized, Beauregard had irrepressibly bombarded the Confederate government with white papers on grand strategy, which Davis had ignored. Now Davis offered him the Military Division of the West. Consistent with Davis's past practices, Beauregard's pretentious new title was hollow, but Beauregard, desperate for redemption, accepted.

Meanwhile, Hood and Davis discussed their immediate strategy. They agreed that Hood, no longer constrained to defend Atlanta, was free to maneuver at will. The city—or what remained of it—was now Sherman's albatross. As Hood was outnumbered, he would avoid battle and attack Sherman's lines of communication, especially the rail line between Chattanooga and Atlanta. In the broadest sense, Hood's army would become hit-and-run raiders, roving just beyond the reach of Sherman, who might pursue but never sink his teeth into Hood. So long as Hood could keep Sherman distracted, he could not make mischief elsewhere in the South. Such a strategy could prolong the war indefinitely.

Hood's first series of raids north of Atlanta in early October got Sherman's attention. Still in Atlanta, Sherman had been uncharacteristically lethargic while mulling over plans to wedge more deeply into the South, burning bridges behind him and opening new lines of communication from Gulf and east coast ports. Now Hood burned the bridges for him. It was a tactic that Sherman readily understood. With Hood on the loose in northern Georgia, Sherman went back from where he had come, in fruitless pursuit and profound embarrassment. The situation had become ludicrous: Hood was farther north than Sherman. Sherman's earlier tactics of destroying Confederate rail lines had become irrelevant.*

Thomas had been in Nashville since October 3, when Sherman had sent him there to coordinate operations against the raids of Forrest and Wheeler. Afterward an embarrassed Sherman returned north in futile efforts to come to grips with Hood, who had raided the rail line between Atlanta and Chattanooga and was last seen headed southwest, toward Gadsden, Alabama. "To pursue Hood is folly," Sherman wrote to Thomas on October 20, "for he can twist and turn like a fox and wear out any army in pursuit."

To counteract Hood's elusiveness, Sherman had a plan that would radically change the intent of the campaign. He first broached the plan to Grant and Thomas on October 1, a month after he had seized Atlanta. *Hood's army would no longer be his objective.* Instead, Sherman proposed to take 60,000 picked men, abandon his supply lines, and march across Georgia, living off the land and devastating the countryside. "I can make the march and make Georgia howl," he wrote Grant on October 8. The war would be directed against civilians so as to break the Confederate will to resist. "By this," Sherman wrote Thomas, "I propose to demonstrate the vulnerability of the South, and make its inhabitants feel that war and individual ruin are synonymous terms." If Hood tried to stop him, Sherman would have his decisive battle. If Hood went north into Tennessee, then Thomas would deal with him.

Sherman intended to take the muscle of the Federal army, including two-thirds of the Army of the Cumberland, and leave Thomas but a single corps, the Fourth under Stanley, plus "all dismounted cavalry, all sick and wounded, and all encumbrances whatever. . . . Hood's army may be set down at 40,000 of all arms fit for duty [a good estimate]. He may follow me or turn against you. If you can defend the line of the Tennessee [i.e., the Tennessee River] in my absence for three months, is all I ask."

It was a defining moment for Thomas. If he felt that he was holding the bag, this was the time to say so; Sherman intended to allocate to him an inferior force less than half the strength of Hood's. Perhaps Thomas was too eager to have an independent command and promised too much with too little. Perhaps also he was supporting Sherman like a good soldier. In any event, Thomas miscalculated. "I feel confident," he assured Washington, "that I can defend the line of the Tennessee with the force General Sherman proposes to leave with me." Thomas dug himself into a deeper hole on the subject of mounted troops. "I shall be able to send General Sherman all the cavalry he needs," said Thomas, "and still have a good force left." When a

---

* Hood's raids were not uniformly successful. His army returned to Resaca on October 12 and demanded that the garrison commander surrender. "In reply," wrote the colonel in command, "I am somewhat surprised at the concluding paragraph to the effect that 'if the place is carried by assault no prisoners will be taken.' In my opinion I can hold this post. If you want it come and take it." The colonel's courage and the robustness of Merrill's fortress construction persuaded Hood to cancel his siege and move on.

month later Thomas told Washington that he could not attack Hood for lack of cavalry, the statement was regarded with disbelief.

After Sherman had lumbered north, Hood sidestepped to the west to contemplate his next move. Beauregard passed through headquarters for the first of several inconclusive conferences, for Hood's intentions were unclear and subject to revision. Had he chosen, Beauregard could have taken command of Hood's army then and there. Davis had given him discretion to do so, but as he was unfamiliar with conditions, he deferred to Hood and departed to inspect the remainder of his nebulous command.

Hood would tell Beauregard as little as possible and treat him with contempt for the remainder of the campaign. As Hood was careless and haphazard about logistical planning (indeed, in nearly all matters of administration), Beauregard would work in the rear to expedite supplies over dilapidated railroads and in creaking wagons to the places he thought Hood would be, although he often guessed wrong.

Both Davis and Beauregard expected Hood to stay in contact with Sherman, like a pit bull harassing a grizzly bear, slashing at its tendons but avoiding its blows. Such a prolonged and inconclusive strategy clashed with Hood's temperament, for he seethed to do something dramatic, something that would bring closure to the war.

Hood remembered how Lee had emphasized that the most promising strategy was to do something that would so shock and demoralize Northerners that they would turn Lincoln out of office and elect a president with a mandate to negotiate peace. Lee had had such an opportunity in his grasp when he invaded Pennsylvania the year before. By Hood's standards, Lee's concept had been good, his execution faulty. Hood still sighed and shook his head when he thought about it—as much as he admired the old man, his thinking had gone awry at Gettysburg, and Hood's withered arm was a recurring reminder of Hood's hopeless charge across Devil's Den and onto Little Round Top.

By mid-October 1864 Hood had gathered his thoughts and was ready to act with breathtaking boldness. His vision had two objectives. One was to retake Tennessee and Kentucky to compensate for his abandonment of Georgia—and indeed of the Deep South. The second objective, predicated on the Northern presidential elections in three weeks, was a throw of the dice with potentially great rewards. By taking his army through Tennessee and Kentucky to the shores of the Ohio River and humiliating the Federal government, Hood could precipitate Lincoln's defeat in the election and bring the appeaser McClellan into office. Reinforced with indigenous volunteers, Hood would then march to Virginia and join forces with Lee to lift the siege at Petersburg. If Sherman followed, Hood would turn upon him from a position of strength. From Hood's point of view, his plan, albeit grandiose, was pregnant with possibilities.

Although such a strategy had proven disastrous in earlier campaigns, its emotional appeal was undiminished. Hood knew that his resurrected plan, its ideas borrowed from those in the past, would be endorsed in Richmond and executed with fervor by his army. "Everybody expects to start for Tennessee," Halsey Wigfall wrote his sister on October 20, "as soon as men and horses are shod." Hood notified Richmond on October 19 and began his movement before anyone could demur.

Beauregard was in the dark until he caught up with Hood, already on the march, at Gadsden on October 21. Beauregard readily endorsed Hood's plan. It was understood that Hood would cross the Tennessee River at Guntersville, thirty miles north of Gadsden, and continue north into central Tennessee. Beauregard would adjust Hood's supply routes and transfer Forrest from Mississippi to rejoin Hood.

Once underway from Gadsden, however, Hood bypassed Guntersville and continued westward, ostensibly looking for a better place to cross the Tennessee River. He finally settled at Tuscumbia, a hundred miles west of Guntersville. Beauregard tagged along, fussing at Hood's ambivalence but deferring to his whims. Hood stayed in Tuscumbia for three weeks to accumulate supplies from his patchwork logistical system and to wait for Forrest. Storms eroded the roads and rail lines, reducing Hood's flow of supplies to a trickle. Meanwhile his soaked and shivering troops slowly crossed the churning, rising river on a pontoon bridge at nearby Florence.

Beauregard persistently asked Hood to report his movements and intentions, but Hood responded with excuses, including his poor health. "It is not possible for me to furnish any plan of my operations for the future," he wrote Beauregard, "as so much must depend upon the movements of the enemy." Thus neither Beauregard nor Richmond knew when the northward march would begin or where it would go. Because of the delay in crossing the river, Hood forfeited the opportunity to influence the election. Lincoln was returned to office.

Hood's reticence was the consequence not of secrecy, but of fluster. The responsibilities of commanding an army on campaign had confounded him and his staff. A month's hard marching from Palmetto to Tuscumbia had crippled man and beast. Draft animals staggered in their harness, unable to move. Short both of rolling stock and teams, Hood ordered all baggage wagons converted for hauling ordnance and commissary supplies. Clothing and tents would be left behind despite the impending winter weather.

The inspector of field transportation described the ensuing chaos in a report to Richmond. "It will take a first rate Philadelphia lawyer to sift out this conglomeration of trains," he wrote, "and tell what transfers have been made. Everything is in greater confusion than I have ever seen it. . . . I think we may safely say that 1,500 animals have been utterly used up on this march, and the number will be doubled if we make as hurried a trip into Tennessee as it is expected we will. . . . We have gotten no benefit from any of the many horses and mules captured since the campaign commenced. . . . Many of the horses are being constantly sold and traded off by parties capturing them. . . . General Hood steadily refuses to let us have anything to do with them, and nobody else takes any interest in it."

By November 13 the relationship between Hood and Beauregard had become ludicrous. Beauregard renounced any ownership of the pending operations and was reduced to asking for permission to visit. Colonel George Brent, Beauregard's adjutant, went to deliver the message and discovered that Hood had crossed the river to Florence to escape Beauregard's nagging. Brent "went in pursuit," as he later reported to Beauregard, but Hood would not agree to a meeting. His head hurt, his mangled arm ached, and his stump throbbed. The generals remained on opposite shores.

It became obvious in Washington, and to Sherman, that Thomas needed more troops. Grant and Halleck summoned reinforcements from many corners, including Schofield's Twenty-third Corps, dismounted cavalry under Brevet Major General James H. Wilson, and miscellaneous garrisons. As further insurance, Sherman ordered Major General Andrew J. Smith to come from Missouri with some three divisions that had fought throughout the western theater.

The impression that Thomas was thereby strengthened was illusory. Although by mid-October reinforcements arrived at the rate of a regiment a day, veterans left at the same rate, some because their enlistments were expiring, others because the War Department wanted them home to vote in the presidential elections. Ordered to furlough all Illinois troops for voting at the time of greatest crisis, Thomas refused, sending only those unfit for combat. In all the coming and going, his net gain, Thomas reported, was about 12,000 "perfectly raw troops."

Thomas found it impossible to assess the numbers of troops he would have in hand at a given time. They were scattered over five states, some on the way, others awaiting orders. Tennessee and Kentucky, although under nominal Federal control, were ridden with guerrillas and a rebellious civil population. Under these circumstances, Federal garrisons had to protect rail lines and hold towns and crossroads. Hence Thomas could not prematurely strip troops from the turbulent countryside to concentrate them against Hood.

Hood's army was intact and could act on short notice, while Thomas had to coordinate his mishmash of forces, some here, some there, to react to whatever it was Hood decided to do. The danger was that Hood's army would smother each outpost one by one, progressively seizing the countryside teeming with Confederate sympathizers. While earlier Confederate invasions had not attracted them to the extent that they actually volunteered to join the army, at the least they had the capability to aid and comfort Hood's forces. As the vast area had to be kept pacified for political reasons, Lincoln and Grant would get progressively more agitated and apprehensive as Hood penetrated the region.

Such was the challenge before Thomas, to sort and to move thousands of troops and their equipment by rail, water, and road so that their combat power would coalesce at the right place and the right time to meet and defeat Hood's army in decisive battle. It was the great good fortune of the Federal army that Thomas had mastered the science of military transportation. He knew every road and river crossing in Tennessee, and he could calculate time, distance, and capacity with unerring precision.

As Thomas remained optimistic into early November, Sherman urged Grant to approve his plan, emphasizing that Thomas had not objected to his role as defender of Tennessee. Grant approved the operation on November 7. When Sherman moved into deepest Georgia, Thomas sent him an upbeat farewell message. Sherman's telegraph ticked an acknowledgment, and then there was silence.

Davis had proclaimed November 16 as a day of prayer and fasting. An Episcopal bishop offered "A Prayer for Our Country" in a church filled with uniforms: "Thou seest the many evils we suffer from this cruel and unrightous war. And although we acknowledge the just of all that has come upon us, yet we beseech Thee to hear our supplication and bring to an end our present calamities. . . ."

As the Army of Tennessee worshiped and listened to sermons, a message from Wheeler to Beauregard reported that Sherman, with three corps, was moving out of Atlanta into central Georgia. Beauregard was stunned, for Georgia had nothing but makeshift forces. Messages streamed from Beauregard's pen, alerting commanders and governors in Sherman's path and urging them to lay mines on the roads, or to "cut up and block all dirt roads in advance of him; remove or destroy supplies of all kinds in his front." Beauregard was using spit to stop a conflagration.

The Army of Tennessee—the sole army capable of stopping Sherman—was three hundred miles to the west in Tuscumbia. With each passing hour the distance increased. As Sherman's intentions were now manifest, Beauregard released himself from any obligation to influence how Hood's army should respond. The decision was entirely Hood's.

A letter of instruction from Davis, dated November 12, would in large measure condition Hood's thinking as he contemplated what he would do. The letter contained several assumptions. First, Grant would be unable to send any reinforcements west from the Virginia theater. Second, Sherman's army was scattered across Tennessee and Georgia. "The policy of taking advantage of the reported division of [Sherman's] forces, when he cannot reunite his army, is too obvious to have been overlooked by you. I therefore take it for granted that you have not been able to avail yourself of that advantage, during his march northward from Atlanta. Hope the opportunity will be offered before he is [Davis had written and then crossed out "reinforced"] extensively recruited."

Chagrined that Davis had rebuked him for a lack of initiative, Hood read on as to Davis's expectations. "If you keep [Sherman's] communications destroyed, he will most probably seek to concentrate for an attack on you. But if, as reported to you, he has sent a large part of his force southward, you may first [Davis had written and then crossed out "retreat"] beat him in detail and subsequently, without serious obstruction, or danger to country in your rear, advance to the Ohio River."

Davis clearly had pointed Hood northward and did not expect him to follow Sherman into Georgia. Thus Hood's decision was straightforward. On
November 19 he advised Davis that he would move into Tennessee within
two days. By inference he would not oppose Sherman's march through Georgia, which Hood persisted in regarding as nothing more serious than a raid.
While Hood's "expedition" (as he called it) could be construed as a quid pro
quo, few could hope that even a single soldier marching with Sherman would
turn back when Hood entered Tennessee.

The four weeks in Tuscumbia and Florence had been agreeable for Hood
and his staff. The young officers were attractive to the women, who had
been, Wigfall rhapsodized, at their flirtatious best. Hood would always
occupy the best home in the community, and his staff pitched tents on the
grounds.

Wigfall captured the mood of Hood and his headquarters. "We shall
probably march tomorrow morning," Wigfall wrote to his family on
November 20, "and there seems to be quite a probability of our having a
winter campaign." The thinking was that, even without interference from
Hood's army, Sherman would self-destruct for lack of supplies. What was
needed, said Wigfall, was the will to scorch the earth in advance of Sherman's march, as the Russians had done against Napoleon. What the people
of Georgia did not destroy, the Confederate cavalry should put to the torch.
"If all this were to be done," wrote Wigfall, "I think Gen. Sherman will
reach the end of his march with his army demoralized and its organization
destroyed.

"He has left Gen. Thomas in our front in command of the 4th and 23d
Army Corps of his army and perhaps some other troops which have been
brought in as re-inforcements. The opportunity seems to me the most brilliant that the war has yet given for striking a decisive blow and I trust and
believe it will be struck. . . . Though if it be necessary that we continue our
active movements for the next four years I know that you would consider the
reason and not murmur of the deprivation."

The Roman was on his own, responsible for the entire western theater. Not
only was he expected to deal with the Knight-Errant, but he also had to deal
with the political turmoil in Kentucky and Tennessee, the two states which
Hood most threatened. The Lincoln administration had appointed military
governors whom the people loathed. Brigadier General Stephen G. Burbridge, the incumbent in Kentucky, had treated the state as occupied enemy
territory, invoking martial law and outraging the elected civil authorities. His
most recent mischief had been to arrest people as traitors if they campaigned
for McClellan in the fall presidential campaign. (Kentucky was one of three
states that voted against Lincoln in the November 8 presidential elections.)
The governor demanded Burbridge's relief.

With Kentucky in such an uproar, Thomas was understandably apprehensive about his lines of communication passing through the state from the
Ohio River into Tennessee. If Hood came north, there was every reason to
fear that his presence would incite Kentucky to erupt into a fresh rebellion.

Central and western Tennessee were even more volatile. Its people were largely allied with the Confederacy and presumably would help Hood in every possible way, with the exception of actually joining the ranks; they had not done so in the past, but Thomas could not discount the possibility. Emotions were intense. Regardless of shortages in clothing and shoes and food, the Tennessee soldiers were coming home on a crusade of redemption, willing to endure hell to see their families again and drive away the Northern invaders. Their zealous spirit swept along their comrades from other states. The Army of Tennessee had suffered defeats and indignities throughout the war, in large measure through the ineptness of its leaders, but under Hood it had one last opportunity for atonement, and in that spirit it would carry on.

Thus the possibility of Hood entering Tennessee and then Kentucky horrified Lincoln, Stanton, and Grant. Their concern went beyond the potential of local political havoc. When the Lincoln administration, on Grant's endorsement, had permitted Sherman to march through Georgia, Lincoln had also repudiated his most fundamental wartime policy: the destruction of the Confederate army was the first priority and the only way to end the war on Union terms. Grant had attempted to carry out that policy in the 1864 campaign but had failed. He personally had commanded the Army of the Potomac, which sustained appalling casualties against Lee, yet the Army of Northern Virginia remained intact behind the Petersburg trenches and would remain so for months to come.

Sherman, too, had failed to destroy the Army of Tennessee and eventually said it couldn't be done. While the seizure of Atlanta had reelected the Lincoln administration, Hood's army remained dangerous and unpredictable. Now Sherman had come up with the unprecedented idea that the wholesale, systematic punishment of Georgia civilians would end the war, when fighting the Confederate armies had not. Sherman had taken the cream of his army—of Thomas's army—even though Sherman would face only token opposition, the equivalent of using a sledgehammer to smash a bug. Thomas had been left with fragments of several armies, scattered garrisons, and green replacements to fight the most dangerous army in the Confederacy, for unlike the Army of Northern Virginia, the Army of Tennessee was free to maneuver and to strike where it chose.

Lincoln and Grant had to make a story that this absurdity somehow made military and strategic sense. Their predicament was the genesis of the onerous interference that Washington and Grant would exert on Thomas. Despite his record, Thomas was an unknown quantity as an independent army commander. Hitherto he had been under the thumb of others: Buell and Rosecrans, Grant and Sherman. The latter two said that Thomas was slow, in defense indomitable but in offense conservative and cautious, a general who had to be prodded into risk taking. This kind of disparagement conditioned the thinking and perceptions of Lincoln, Stanton, and Halleck and intensified their apprehensions as Hood marched into Tennessee.

Lincoln and Stanton were accustomed to receiving timely field reports from the War Department telegraph office adjacent to the White House. When a battle was imminent or in progress, Lincoln customarily sat in the office, a shawl over his shoulders, chatting with the operators during a lull, then waiting expectantly when he heard the chatter of the key. Not all messages came from his generals, for the operators often sent their own informal versions of unfolding developments, which Lincoln compared to what the generals told him. Thomas's situation reports would be carefully examined and read between the lines for every nuance. Second-guessing would be rampant.

Thus Washington took immediate notice when Thomas began to qualify his estimates of what he could do. On November 8 (coincidentally election day), Thomas slipped in a single cautionary sentence in messages to Halleck and Sherman. "As soon as General Smith's troops arrive, and General Wilson has the balance of his cavalry mounted, I will be prepared to commence a movement on the enemy."

This was the first of a series of conditional messages involving Smith's infantry and Wilson's cavalry. Both would be late owing to circumstances beyond Thomas's control. The need for the infantry was self-evident and uncontested. Grant would send Rawlins to St. Louis to expedite both Smith and the miscellaneous replacements coming from the midwest. Smith, nonetheless, would be delayed until the eleventh hour.

The cavalry was another matter. It was a combat arm dear to the heart of the old cavalryman Thomas. At the last moment Sherman had assigned Wilson, a rising, ambitious young general of twenty-seven, as Thomas's chief of cavalry. But Sherman had stripped his troopers of horses and equipment, and Wilson was trying desperately to remount and rearm them in Louisville.

Thomas believed that Wilson's newly designated Corps of Cavalry was essential to smiting Hood, for two reasons. The first was Thomas's respect for Forrest. Second, Thomas intended to use cavalry in an unprecedented fashion. While Wilder's Lightning Brigade had proven the effectiveness of mounted firepower, the concept had not been exploited on a larger scale. Cavalry was still largely employed for raids and reconnaissance, screening and skirmishing, and rarely, if ever, as a massed, mobile strike force against entrenched infantry and artillery. Thomas envisioned a decisive new role: dismounted troopers with rapid-fire carbines that would overpower the muzzle-loaded rifles of the Confederate infantry. Once Hood cracked, the troopers would mount and pursue relentlessly, as no other army had done in the war.

Thomas intended to destroy Hood's army, but his vision was entirely misunderstood in Washington and by Grant. Sherman had led them to believe that cavalry was useless. Grant had used his cavalry in the Virginia campaign almost entirely for raids, and it had rarely influenced the outcome of battles. In Halleck's mind, the lack of cavalry was an excuse for inaction. He remembered that Rosecrans had refused to move without it the year before and had delayed his campaign seemingly indefinitely for want of horses. Hence, when Thomas insisted upon mounting his cavalry before attacking Hood, Halleck was dismissive and contemptuous. Grant would demand that Thomas attack Hood regardless of the condition of Wilson's cavalry.

As Hood came north, Thomas coolly shifted forces like chessmen on a massive game board. The telegraph was his lever. It served many purposes, intelligence for one example. While Grant read Southern newspapers and was deceived, Thomas ordered his field complex to be alert and to send him facts and not rumors. Thomas's way of deriving information foreshadowed twentieth-century intelligence methods: his messages to subordinates cited the source of his data, evaluated its reliability, and then explained the reasoning behind his conclusions. The benefits were twofold: his generals understood his way of thinking and gained confidence in his intelligence reports, and they could follow his example in the reports they sent him.

Thomas's messages crackled from the nerve center at Nashville through a network of hundreds of miles of wire. Like a maestro conducting a symphony, Thomas expressed his self-control, his resolution and expectations, and his grip on the coordination of his forces. He was determined to prevent the kinds of communication errors that created self-defeating misunderstandings and snafus as deadly as enemy bullets. Messages to him were immediately acknowledged and acted upon. His own messages were clear and concise, his intentions unmistakable. Their tone and content rallied, reassured, and steadied. At times he permitted latitude; at other times he issued precise, mandatory, detailed orders. Above all, Thomas wanted certainty that his messages had been received, read, and obeyed. A critical message would conclude, "Acknowledge receipt." If there was no response, another message would demand, "Answer at once."

When the Tennessee campaign ended, Thomas had performed the unsurpassed masterpiece of theater command and control of the Civil War. So modern in concept, so sweeping in scope, it would become a model for strategic maneuver in twentieth-century warfare.

3 o

FRANKLIN AND
NASHVILLE

*"I am not going to be taught my duty by anybody, but I can face
death with my men as well as any one," he said, and he marched
forward with one division. The valiant Bagovut, not considering in
his excitement whether his advance into action now with a single
division was likely to be of use or not, marched his men straight forward into the enemy's fire. Danger, shells, and bullets were just what
he wanted in his fury. One of the first bullets killed him, the other
bullets killed many of his men. And his division remained for some
time under fire for no object whatever.*

Tolstoy, War and Peace

Chaplain Charles Todd Quintard of the First Tennessee Infantry hurriedly traveled north "over indescribable roads" to rejoin Hood's
army. He was a pious Episcopal priest who prayed constantly for the
deliverance of the Confederacy. Quintard kept a diary, recording what he
had seen and heard and thought.

The priest stayed overnight with a man and his family north of Florence.
"The enemy has taken all his negroes and other property," he wrote, "even
his provisions, and he is compelled to move to Mississippi to feed his house-
hold. He told me of his trials with a stout, brave heart. He has lost two sons
in the war." Quintard said good-bye and followed Hood's trail. "The ground
is frozen hard and a sharp, cold wind is blowing, but as my face is towards
Tennessee, I heed none of these things. God in mercy, grant us a successful
campaign. . . . Crossed the line into Tennessee at 4½ P.M. Bless the Lord O
my soul and all that is within me bless His Holy Name."

Quintard reached the rear elements of the army on November 23, 1864, and
was welcomed by his friends among the generals and other officers. The army
marched rapidly, on November 24 alone making some twenty-two miles. The
next day Quintard found Hood in his headquarters at Mount Pleasant, Tennessee, in good health and high spirits. Quintard pressed on to the Polk plantation, five miles south of Columbia, and to the family compound of four homes

389

and a Gothic chapel. The grandeur and serenity of the grounds hushed the passing troops. Hood and his generals called to pay their respects to Lucius J. Polk, the patriarch and the brother of the late bishop-general. They spoke in reverent voices as musicians from a Louisiana regiment serenaded the gathering; one of them remarked that all Louisiana soldiers had idolized Leonidas Polk as their father. "This has indeed been a day of great enjoyment," wrote Quintard. "I realized I was once more in Tennessee."

Quintard led Morning Prayer in the Lucius Polk home on Advent Sunday, November 27. "This was my first full service in Tennessee since entering the state," he wrote in his diary, "and my heart went up in gratitude to God for all his great goodness in delivering us from the snare of the fowles." Afterward he visited Hood in his headquarters at a home three miles south of Columbia. "During the evening," wrote Quintard, "had much pleasant conversation with him in which he expressed such an earnest trust in God and such deep religious feelings that I could plainly discern the Holy Spirit's work upon his heart."

Tennessee governor Isham G. Harris had accompanied Hood from the beginning of the campaign, and when Hood reached the state line, Harris ceremoniously welcomed him. Once in Tennessee, Hood's army moved on three parallel routes, which accelerated their rate of advance. The Federal cavalry had been in contact from the beginning, but Forrest had brushed them aside, and they had not impeded Hood's progress. So confident was Hood that he assumed Thomas was already abandoning Nashville, and he ordered Forrest to cut the lines of communication north of the city to prevent Thomas from taking supplies with him. Hood wanted them for himself.

Hood had known from the beginning that Schofield's Twenty-third Corps and Stanley's Fourth Corps were ahead. He had hoped to outrace them to Nashville, but they had gotten to Columbia before him and had dug in facing south, the Federal flanks touching the Duck River, which ran east-west through the town. Hood's troops took up position nearby, catching their breath after marching the seventy-five miles from Florence in a week. Nashville lay but forty miles to the north—a three-day march.

Hood's swift advance jolted Thomas into the realization that he was unprepared to fight the Confederate army. He had counted on Andrew Smith reinforcing him from Missouri, but now Hood was closer to Nashville than the slow-moving Smith, stuck somewhere far to the north. Neither horses nor equipment had arrived in Louisville to remount Wilson's cavalry. A staff major struggled desperately to expedite matters by himself, as Wilson had gone afield with the few mounted troops he had, trying to deal with Forrest, who outnumbered him at least two to one.

Thomas needed time to get Smith, the cavalry, and his garrisons into Nashville. He put Schofield in command of the only two corps that were immediately available and ordered him to delay his classmate Hood to the extent possible. Outnumbered and in double jeopardy, Schofield had to check Hood, yet pull back in time to prevent the Confederates from getting behind him and cutting off his escape route to Nashville. Schofield would have to employ extraordinary judgment to know when to fight and when to withdraw.

Although Thomas exercised independent command in the developing crisis, he did not have freedom of action. The telegraph delivered a stream of intrusive advice and admonishments from Grant, and sometimes Halleck, that Thomas could not disregard. Although Grant was conducting a siege five hundred miles away at Petersburg, he presumed to have a better grasp of the Tennessee situation than Thomas. Grant's source of information was largely propaganda and rumor planted in the Southern newspapers to deceive the Federal high command.

Grant fell for it. He worried about the security of Sherman's expedition, whose progress he could follow only by Southern newspaper accounts. As Beauregard had no forces of consequence in Georgia, he fabricated threats against Sherman, which Grant took seriously. His consistent, half-cocked remedy was to demand that Thomas instantly attack Hood to relieve the imagined danger to Sherman's safety. Thus when Grant read a bombastic Beauregard proclamation to Georgians in a Savannah newspaper, he relayed it to Thomas on November 24 with the ambiguous admonition, "Do not let Hood's forces get off without punishment."

It was time for Thomas to tell Grant of developments. "Hood's entire army is in front of Columbia and so greatly outnumbers mine at this time that I am compelled to act on the defensive," wired Thomas, and he enumerated his problems with Smith and the cavalry. "The moment I can get my Cavalry I will march against Hood." It was a theme upon which Thomas would stubbornly persist and one that the government and Grant would misunderstand and angrily decry.

Grant again reacted to the Savannah papers on November 27 when they reported (falsely) that Forrest was after Sherman and that Breckinridge was coming from East Tennessee. "If this proves true," wired Grant, "it will give you the chance to take the offensive against Hood and cut the rail-roads up to Virginia with a small cavalry force." Thomas responded that there was no evidence that Forrest had left Tennessee (he was beating up Wilson), but that he was about to move against Hood regardless. Thomas's spurt of optimism sprang from hopes that Schofield would prevent Hood from crossing the Duck River, that Smith soon would arrive in Nashville, and that Wilson's cavalry would soon be ready. He was wrong on all counts.

While Grant goaded Thomas to assault Hood, Beauregard entreated Hood to relieve the pressure of Sherman's raid. Hood showed Beauregard's telegram to Quintard. He would, of course, comply, said Hood. He would press on with all possible speed to Nashville, convinced that the city would be easy pickings once he got there. Schofield might get there first in a dead run, but at the moment he was in Columbia. Hood would skirt him by crossing upriver and then going "through the woods."

"God speed us on our way," wrote Quintard. On Thursday, the twenty-ninth, Hood arose at 3 A.M. When he said good-bye to Quintard, the priest offered prayers and blessings. "Thank you, Doctor," said Hood. "That is my hope and trust." He paused. "The enemy must give me fight, or I will be in Nashville before tomorrow night."

Hood hobbled out the door to his mount. Staff officer Joseph B. Cummings remembered the ritual. "General Hood was physically handicapped," he wrote, "if not wholly disqualified from active service in the field. . . . He wore a wooden leg, but except when in the saddle, moved only on crutches. . . . [L]eaving in the morning his quarters of the night before, he would go on crutches to the side of his horse, pass the crutches over to an orderly, and while another orderly would support him from behind, he would himself raise his left foot into the stirrup, and then an orderly would pass the right wooden leg over the horse's back, and place the right wooden foot in the stirrup. Thus mounted the General would ride long distances at a slow pace."

While Stephen Lee demonstrated at Columbia to hold Schofield's attention, Forrest, Cheatham, and Stewart crossed upriver, bypassed Columbia, and chased away Wilson's cavalry. By midafternoon they had converged at Spring Hill, a village ten miles north of Columbia. Hood was now nearly astride Columbia Pike, Schofield's escape route to Nashville. A single Federal division opposed Cheatham's corps at Spring Hill, and Stewart's corps would arrive momentarily. Schofield was in extremis, his troops, trains, and artillery strung out and utterly exposed on the pike between Columbia and Spring Hill.

Hood was baffled. His mind had been set upon a dash to Nashville, a race against Schofield that Hood intended to win. He would fight only if Schofield got in his way, but Schofield was lagging behind him. Hood was about to win the race, but what was he to do with Schofield? It was all so complicated: the terrain was strange, and his crude map blurred in front of his swimming eyes. His body sagged. After twelve hours in the saddle he craved respite and laudanum. His vague and contradictory orders befuddled his commanders. Were they to block the pike, and if so, with whom? Were they to attack the Federal columns, and if so, when and where? But Hood could do no more. In the late afternoon he went to his overnight headquarters at the Absalom Thompson House, a plantation home three miles east of Columbia Pike.

At the house Hood dismounted and found a place of repose. As dusk settled, generals and staff officers came to the house, puzzled by what was happening in the places Hood could not see. Now composed, Hood confirmed what they were to do and then went to dinner. His host served a banquet to celebrate the liberation of Tennessee, and toasts were freely offered.

When Hood's orders reached the field commanders, some roused their troops and marched away from the pike. Others could not do what they had been ordered to do and in weariness bivouacked where they had stacked arms. Meanwhile 20,000 Federal troops and 800 wagons escaped northward on the pike during the night, their route illuminated by Confederate campfires. They passed unchallenged.

Hood's quickness to censure any departure from his orders had intimidated his generals not to act independently. If orders seemed confusing, they went back to Hood for clarification. From time to time his generals, and once a private, awakened Hood to report that Federal columns were hastening by the slumbering encampments. Numbed by laudanum and wine, Hood mumbled dismissals and fell back asleep.

Hood's head throbbed when he awoke on the morning of November 30. Everyone near him was quiet, their faces impassive. What was it that he had intended that day? he wondered. Yes, that was it, he had isolated Schofield from Nashville, and now he could finish him off. He rode toward the pike, puzzled that his soldiers were at breakfast instead of forming battle lines. At the pike he looked with disbelief at the debris left by the retreating army. Involuntarily he felt his gorge rising. "Where are they?" he asked. The staff milled at a distance. His voice rose to a bellow. "Where is Schofield's army? Is everyone struck dumb?" A ragged private ventured toward him. "General, the whole dang Yankee army passed by here last night, and we just let 'em go."

Hood was enraged. His staff was shocked; never had they seen him so angry. "Why wasn't I informed?" he demanded. "General, I believe you were," responded a shaken staff officer. Hood struggled for self-control. "Send for my generals," he said, and then he went inside the nearby Rippavilla mansion for breakfast.

Everyone present at Rippavilla would always remember the cursing, as Hood lashed at his corps and division commanders standing rigidly about him. "You disobeyed my orders, damn you," he shouted. When his wrath finally subsided, he glared into their bulging eyes and flushed faces. "Go after Schofield," he breathed. "Get him."

Hood's generals found Schofield late in the day entrenched in a pretty town named Franklin on the south bank of the Harpeth River, fifteen miles south of Nashville. Schofield could go no farther because the bridges across the Harpeth had been too damaged to cross. While engineers were repairing the bridges, the infantry had manned the fortifications south of the village.* By midday the bridges were ready, permitting the wagons and artillery batteries to trundle across to the north bank. The infantry dozed and ate in the afternoon sun.

Schofield was nervous from his close call at Spring Hill. He distrusted Wilson and the Federal cavalry, for they had not prevented Hood from fording the Duck River and turning his flank. It could happen again at Franklin. Hood would have to try a flanking maneuver, thought Schofield. Not for a moment did he expect Hood to assault the Federal lines at Franklin.

Schofield needed advice from Thomas and asked by wire at 9:50 A.M., "Do you desire me to hold on here until compelled to fall back?" Thomas

---

* The extensive fortifications had been constructed some time before, as part of the outlying Nashville defense system.

weighed his answer. So much depended on Smith, whose delays were mad-dening. Thomas had sent fusillades of telegrams trying to expedite his arrival. How and when Thomas would be able to consolidate Schofield and Smith was still impossible to determine. Perhaps Schofield could continue to parry Hood. It was up to Schofield. "If you can prevent Hood from turning your position at Franklin, it should be held," replied Thomas, "but I do not wish you to risk too much." More telegrams revealed that Schofield did not want to stay in Franklin. Thomas gave him permission to evacuate the town and withdraw to Nashville at his discretion.

Meanwhile, Hood's generals stopped their columns where the road descended into Franklin and surveyed the scene below them. A broad plain two miles in depth gave them a clear view of the formidable lines of earth-works in front of the town, and of the artillery at Fort Granger on the heights across the river. They thought of ways to bypass Schofield as before, to probe for weaknesses. Waiting for Hood to arrive, they anticipated that he would discuss their options before taking action.

Hood's mind had been churning as he rode in the midst of his army. He had looked searchingly at the soldiers about him, ragged and footsore, good men certainly, but something was missing. That fiasco at Spring Hill. To have allowed Schofield to escape, his officers and soldiers must obviously have lost their fighting spirit and their discipline. All those excuses. There could be no more excuses. His generals had to be punished for letting him down the night before, and he knew that he had humiliated them by questioning their courage during the stormy meeting at Rappavilla. Their pride would take over now; they would want to show him that they would obey even in the face of certain death.

Hood joined his generals and peered toward the Federal lines. Then, without discussion, he ordered an immediate attack, frontal, straight ahead. His abruptness staggered the commanders. An attack was out of the ques-tion, they protested. Stephen Lee's corps and the artillery marching "leisurely" (at Hood's orders) from Columbia had not arrived. An assault would be suicidal.

Hood would not yield. It had come to this: commanding an army had been too much. His attempts to delegate authority had failed, and he had been unable to coordinate flanking movements and other complex maneu-vers. His logistics and staff work had been shameful. At Franklin he finally had a situation he could understand. He could revert to the maneuver he had used in the glory days under Lee: the straightforward head-on assault.

Hood's orders were explicit and conformed to the fighting instructions he gave when he had taken command that spring at Dalton. No firing at long range. Close the enemy line in a compact formation to point-blank range, then fire and charge with bayonet. The Federal line would break, because in hand-to-hand combat the Confederate soldier was superior.

His army obediently formed into orderly ranks and unfurled their battle flags, and the bands played "Dixie." They began their march forward at about four o'clock, a half hour before sunset, massed on a battlefield where it seemed that one could see forever. They were a stunning spectacle. The astounded Federal troops took arms and hurried to their parapets.

Brigadier General George D. Wagner had unwisely stationed two of his Federal brigades in an open field a half mile ahead of the main Federal line. The brigade commanders pleaded for permission to withdraw to the main line, but Wagner ordered them to stand fast. Under pressure, the brigades broke and ran, the screaming Confederate soldiers in pursuit. The impact of friend and foe alike broke the center of the Federal line. The frenzied Confederates and desperate defenders merged into a gigantic melee, and the Federal center was near collapse. Poised in reserve, gritty Emerson Opdycke and his Federal brigade plunged into the chaos, dislodged the Confederate soldiers, and sealed the gap. Successive waves of Southern soldiers plunged into the great clouds of gun smoke that enveloped the killing ground.

Hood had gone to the rear, out of touch with the battlefield. He reclined on the ground, an aide made a fire, and Hood stared into the flames, now and then lifting his head to receive reports. Stephen Lee arrived with the vanguard of his corps, surprised to find a battle in progress. Hood seemed serene and casually ordered Lee to go forward and support Cheatham. Obediently, Lee ordered Edward Johnson to attack with his division at about nine o'clock, and the Federal troops leveled his men in the darkness. The firing finally subsided around midnight.

Hood lost 6,300 men, nearly a quarter of the attacking force. Thirteen of the twenty-eight general officers who had been in the combat were killed, wounded, or captured. Patrick Cleburne fell among the dead—he had been seen riding pell-mell before going down at the barricades. Some sixty-five division, brigade, and regimental commanders became casualties in the firestorm that swept away the leaders of the Army of Tennessee and shattered its soul. Its remnants were a shell. Franklin was the last Confederate attack of any consequence in the war.

Hood assembled his three corps commanders in the pitch of night. They could not assess the losses—darkness compounded the confusion—but knew they had been severe. Nonetheless, Lee had two divisions that had not been chewed to pieces, and the Confederate artillery had finally arrived. Hood ordered his corps commanders to resume their attack in the morning. The artillery would be put in place to bombard the Federal lines beforehand.

At daybreak it was discovered that the Federal troops had withdrawn from Franklin. Even the toughest veterans of the Army of Tennessee shuddered, for bodies lay in heaps as far as could be seen. As Hood rode among them, the stunned survivors stared at the man who had ordered the carnage.

Hood issued a general order to be read that day before the remnants of each regiment: "The commanding general congratulates the army," he wrote, "upon the success achieved yesterday over our enemy by their heroic and determined courage. The enemy have been sent in disorder and confusion to Nashville, and while we lament the fall of many gallant officers and brave men, we have shown to our countrymen that we can carry any position occupied by our enemy."

Hood's reports to his government were a sham, deliberately concealing that he had ruined his army. He sent a five-sentence letter to Richmond on December 3 (received on December 14) and to Beauregard. Franklin had been a victory, Hood asserted, although he had suffered "many" losses, naming the generals who had been casualties. A follow-up letter on December 5 was similarly vague and misleading. Hood submitted a detailed report in mid-February 1865, the first of many documents in which he would attempt to achieve with his pen what he had failed to do on the field.

Here are two examples of his deceit:

Hood's decision to attack had been insane. His generals had begged him to outflank Schofield by crossing upriver as he had at Columbia. Hood explained away his madness in his report to Seddon. "The nature of the position was such," he wrote, "as to render it inexpedient to attempt any further flank movement, and I therefore determined to attack him in front and without delay."

Hood also had to explain why artillery had not supported his infantry. The Federal artillery on the hills above and beyond the town had been unchallenged, and its unobstructed field of fire had devastated the Confederate formations. The Confederate artillery had not fired, of course, because it had been miles away, en route from Columbia, its weakened horses unable to pull the heavy guns and caissons at more than a crawl. Hood's boldness in lying on the matter is breathtaking. "During the day," wrote Hood in his version of events, "I was restrained from using my artillery on account of the women and children remaining in the town."

Hood had proclaimed victory at Franklin. A victor could not turn back when Nashville was but twelve miles farther up the road, for that would have admitted failure. The city had been his goal since entering Tennessee. Hood had to go on, even to ultimate self-destruction. The remnants of the Army of Tennessee therefore marched out of Franklin and stopped at Nashville's fortified gates, placing itself within easy reach of Thomas when he decided to attack.

Hood had no plan other than to get to Nashville and await developments. The city being too strong to assault, his soldiers dug trenches, though limited manpower left the army's flanks in the air. Cavalry normally protected the flanks, but in an act of folly Hood further attenuated his forces, for he sent Forrest, his cavalry, and several brigades of infantry thirty miles to the southeast to besiege Murfreesboro. Unable to man a continuous line, Hood compensated by constructing redoubts, small elevated forts with interlocking fields of fire, like a primitive Maginot Line.

The rigors of campaigning had debilitated Hood's soldiers, who were increasingly ill nourished and poorly clothed. Moderate weather and the excitement of seeing Nashville within their grasp provided a temporary amelioration, but a winter storm aggravated their suffering. Hood tried in his way to improve his flow of supplies—predictably without success—and he resorted to such expedients as fashioning shoes from raw cowhide. He had wired a pathetic requisition to Beauregard for fifty bales of blankets and ten thousand suits of clothing, but no such supplies were available in the whole of the Confederacy. Troops adjusted defensive lines to get nearer to firewood, and civilians mourned as campfires consumed their cherished trees.

In contrast to the harsh conditions imposed on his soldiers, Hood established luxurious headquarters at Traveler's Rest, the home of John Overton six miles south of Nashville. It was a place of warmth and hospitality and of the pleasure of women. Hood's staff pitched tents in the yard. "We had an abundance of good food: beef, mutton, pork, flour, and potatoes," remembered staff officer Cummings. "At the door of our tent stood a barrel of Robinson County whiskey, for the solace and inspiration of our mess."

Halsey Wigfall was pleased with the accommodations. "There are several young ladies from Nashville here," he wrote his sister, "who are very pretty and agreeable and the most intense Southerners." Privy as he was to Hood's thinking, Wigfall tried to explain why Hood had placed his spent, shivering army beneath the guns of Nashville. He recalled the sign at the border that had read, "Tennessee. A grave, or a free home." "A good many graves have already been filled," he wrote his sister on December 8, "but better we should all meet that fate than fail to gain the prize we struggle for. . . .

"If we can gain Nashville what a glorious termination it will be for the campaign. Even if we fail in this, for I fear the fortifications are too strong, and hold the enemy within his lines round the city, and hold Tennessee in our lines, it will be one of the grandest achievements an army had ever performed. Think of it. Starting from Lovejoy's thirty miles beyond Atlanta on the 18th Sept., here we are on the 8th Decbr. in front of Nashville with the enemy cooped up in his works and the fruits of two years hard marching and fighting lost to him."

Thomas met the frazzled Schofield when he arrived in Nashville the day after the battle of Franklin. Thomas J. Wood* limped in from Franklin and joined them, and they were still talking at midnight. Thomas was worried, for he was unaware of the extent of the damage done to Hood's army, which still loomed large and dangerous in his mind. Smith still had not arrived by riverboat from Missouri. Where is Smith? asked Thomas repeatedly of his staff. "If Smith does not get here tonight," said Thomas, "he will not get here at all; for tomorrow Hood will strike the Cumberland and close it against all transports." Quartermaster James Rusling assured Thomas that Smith's steamers were approaching the levee.

"And, even as I spake," remembered Rusling, "the door opened, and in strode General A. J. Smith, a grizzled old veteran but a soldier all through. They all four greeted each other eagerly; but Thomas (undemonstrative as he

---

* Still on crutches from a shattered leg at Atlanta, Wood temporarily commanded Stanley's Fourth Corps at Franklin after Stanley was wounded. It will be remembered that Wood had precipitated the disaster at Chickamauga when he foolishly withdrew his division as Hood attacked (see chapter 22). Since then he had redeemed himself many times over.

was) literally took Smith in his arms and hugged him; for he now felt absolutely sure of coping with Hood, and defeating him duly. They first discussed Franklin, and rejoiced over it, and then Thomas spread his maps on the floor and pointed out his Nashville lines, explaining their bearing and significance. I left them at 1 a.m., all four down on their knees and examining attentively the positions to be assumed next morning."

Thomas finally had assembled his full measure of infantry. Together with Smith's three veteran divisions, Thomas had summoned James Steedman from Chattanooga with a provisional division that included regiments of black troops. Schofield reverted to commanding solely the Twenty-third Corps, and Wood took permanent command of the Fourth Corps. Thomas conscripted civilians to enlarge and improve the city's fortifications, and they ruthlessly leveled homes, buildings, and shade trees to make way for trenches and fields of fire.

Wilson returned to Nashville with 6,500 worn-out troopers, claiming that Forrest had four times his numbers. Schofield complained that Wilson had abandoned him at Spring Hill and had exposed him to near disaster; clearly Forrest had outridden and outfought the young cavalry general. Thomas sent Wilson north of the city to rest and refit. He still intended to use the Federal cavalry as a strike force and to deal with Forrest, but that would now take time. Thomas would wait until Wilson was ready. Meanwhile he counted on Hood's staying put. Should Hood again become irrational and attack, Thomas was confident that he could hold Nashville.

When Thomas informed Halleck of his intentions, he unwittingly used the words "retire" and "wait," which rang alarm bells in Washington. Lincoln spoke to Stanton, who sent a wire to Grant at City Point. "The President feels solicitous," wrote Stanton, "about the disposition of Thomas to lay in fortifications for an indefinite period 'until Wilson gets equipments.' This looks like the McClellan & Rosecranz strategy of do nothing and let the rebels raid the country. The President wishes you to consider the matter."

Why, it may be asked, did Lincoln feel that Thomas intended an "indefinite" cessation of fighting? Thomas had not used such a phrase. In fact, the suggestion came from Halleck, for in his opinion Wilson had enough horses. Rosecrans had stalled for months the year before on this same "pretext." Hence Thomas's calls for cavalry mounts as a condition for offensive operations were treated with scorn; the inference was that Thomas too was stalling. No one in the east understood that Thomas intended to use his cavalry, not for scouting and raids, but as a hammer to demolish Hood. Thomas had himself to blame for this dire misunderstanding, for he failed to explain his intentions either to Washington or to Grant.

Stanton's message fueled Grant's smoldering enmity for Thomas. The first of Grant's ultimatums "to attack immediately" sped westward by telegraph. Subsequent telegrams suffocated Thomas with condescending lectures implying that he was unable to think for himself. Thomas stifled his outrage, patiently explained to Grant why he could not attack immediately, and promised to act within a few days.

Stanton seemed to sense the situation and gave Thomas carte blanche to get horses and equipment. Wilson was ruthless, and outraged Louisville officials complained to Stanton. "The general impressment of horses by the military is so oppressive here," they fumed, "that we cannot think it meets your approbation. All horses are taken without regard to the occupation of the owner or his loyalty. Loaded country wagons with produce for market are left in the road; milk carts, drays, and butcher's wagons are left in the street, their horses seized. We know not the immediate necessities of the service, but we are certain that great wrong is being done in carrying out the order."

Such measures were not enough. Grant had lost all patience by December 6, a week after Franklin. "Hood has Thomas close in Nashville," Grant wrote to Sherman. "I have said all I could to force him to attack without giving the positive order until to-day. To-day however I can stand it no longer and gave the order without any reserve. I think the battle will take place tomorrow."

Grant sent his ultimatum: "Attack at once and wait no longer for a remount of your Cavalry. There is great danger of delay resulting in a campaign back to the Ohio River." An aide brought the telegram to Thomas as he sat in his room at the St. Cloud Hotel. As he read the chilling words "Attack at once," Thomas bowed his face into his hands. His fingers slowly rubbed his temples, and he felt his body sag from the accumulated weight of the cascading telegrams. How typical of Grant, he mused, and he remembered the first of the many times that Grant had done this to him. It was at Chattanooga, a foolish order to attack immediately outside the city; in that instance Thomas had used Baldy Smith as his emissary to get the order canceled.

Now he had to deal with Grant at a distance, and the difficulties were proving immeasurable. How ironic that three words on a scrap of paper had the power to move an army and precipitate thousands of deaths and wounds. And to what purpose? Thomas leaned back in his chair and unconsciously stroked his beard. The outcome would undoubtedly be a Federal victory, but at what price? Would Hood again withdraw and regroup as he had done at Atlanta, allowing the war to go on as before? Couldn't Grant and the people in Washington understand that he needed Wilson's cavalry to overpower Hood and destroy his army with crushing finality?

Thomas read Grant's telegram again. Grant seemed to be concerned with Hood casting loose and heading toward the Ohio unless Thomas attacked immediately. Wrong, all wrong. Hood was staying put. Thomas rose from his chair and stretched to ease the pain in his chronically sore back. There was simply no reason to attack him before Wilson's cavalry was ready. He returned to his desk and pulled a blank telegram from the drawer.

As he had done so often in the past with irrational orders (not only from Grant, but also from Sherman and others), Thomas would *conditionally* obey, but he would warn Grant of his reservations and the consequences. Thus Thomas responded that he would comply, but he cautioned Grant of the hazard of attacking without adequate cavalry. Again Thomas's choice of words worked against him. While he portrayed Hood's army as dangerous, he inexplicably failed to say that there was no possibility of its marching unopposed to the Ohio. Nor did he explain his sweeping concept of employing the cavalry as his principal striking force. To Grant and those in Washington, his telegrams confirmed their notion of Thomas as a conservative, slow-moving plodder.

Watching the exchange of messages, Stanton needled Grant for his inability to get Thomas to move. "Thomas seems unwilling to attack because it is hazardous," Stanton wrote on December 7, "as if all war was anything but hazardous. If he waits for Wilson to get ready, Gabriel will be blowing his last horn."

Grant protested that he had ordered Thomas to attack immediately. If he did not, said Grant, Schofield should take his place. A day later Grant repeated his recommendation. This was not a solution that pleased Washington. Hood had pummeled Schofield from Columbia to Nashville. The great political risk in having *anyone* relieve Thomas was that the new man might utterly fail, and neither Lincoln nor Stanton wanted to pick a loser. Hence they tossed the ball to Grant. "If you wish Genl Thomas relieved from command, give the order," wired Halleck on December 8. "No one here will, I think, interfere. The responsibility, however, will be yours, as no one here, so far as I am informed, wishes Genl Thomas' removal." Grant chose to withdraw his recommendation temporarily.

With Wilson's cavalry nearly ready, Thomas told his commanders to plan to begin the attack against Hood on December 10. Weather intervened. On the morning of the ninth, Thomas was awakened by the moaning of the wind and the rattle of sleet on his hotel window. Pulling on his boots, he walked through the lobby into the street. A sheet of ice covered the ground.

The telegraph keys continued to clatter. Grant finally instructed Halleck to send a relieving order. As Halleck sat with a draft in hand, he received Thomas's wire that a winter storm had immobilized the army. "I have nearly completed my preparations to attack the enemy tomorrow morning [December 10]," Thomas wired, "but a terrible storm of freezing rain has come on to-day, which will make it impossible for our men to fight to any advantage. I am, therefore, compelled to wait for the storm to break and make the attack immediately after."

By then Thomas seemed to have sensed that Grant was trying to remove him from command. So be it. Thomas shrugged his shoulders and added a final note to Halleck. "I have done all in my power to prepare," he wrote, "and if you should deem it necessary to relieve me I shall submit without a murmur." With the storm, however, came a temporary reprieve: Grant told Halleck to cancel the relieving order.

Nonetheless, the tormenting threats from Grant and Halleck continued undiminished. Grant finally sent a savage ultimatum on December 11 to attack regardless of the weather. Thomas could no longer delay. Clearing the bile from his throat, he spoke to his chief of staff. Orders left his headquarters on December 12 to move the army into position. For the remainder of

the day Thomas watched helplessly as both men and mounts slithered and
tumbled upon the ice covering the countryside.

This could not go on, and Thomas summoned his corps commanders.
One by one they entered his room, stomping their feet and rubbing their
hands to restore circulation. When all were assembled, their conversations
stopped, and they directed their attention to the somber Thomas. "I have
advised General Grant of the circumstances of this ice storm," said Thomas.
"As anxious as we all are to get on with this war, I have recommended that
the attack be deferred until the ice melts. General Grant, in turn, has ordered
this army to attack the enemy and to disregard the weather. You have been
in the field today and have seen things for yourself. I would be grateful for
your counsel."

"The men cannot walk, sir. If they cannot walk, they cannot advance
upon the enemy," said one corps commander. "And it might be added," said
another, "that we can be assured that Hood shall neither attack us nor part
our company to go to the Ohio, as General Grant seems to fear he might. He
will stay where he is, as we must. This fight must wait until the ice thaws."
The consensus was unanimous.

"Thank you, gentlemen," said Thomas. Those in the east had no need to
know what his generals had said, for suspicious minds might construe the
meeting as a conspiracy to disobey Grant. Retaliation, should it come, would
be borne by him alone. In a telegram to Halleck, Thomas described how the
weather had frozen his army in place. "Under these circumstances," Thomas
concluded, "I believe that an attack at this time would only result in a useless sacrifice of life." A day later the weather had not improved. When it did,
Thomas wired, he would attack.

Grant had stopped sending messages to Thomas.

On the evening of December 13 Grant conferred with Major General
John A. Logan, a corps commander in Sherman's army who had just
returned form leave and was paying his respects. Logan was an Illinois congressman and a Lincoln ally, and he had taken leave to help Lincoln's reelection campaign. He once had served under Grant, who admired him both as
a fighter and for his support of the administration's war policies. Logan had
temporarily commanded the Army of the Tennessee when McPherson fell at
Atlanta. But Sherman gave Howard the permanent command, and Logan
was embittered, believing that he had been passed over because he was not a
member of the West Point fraternity.

Grant gave Logan conditional orders that evening. He was to proceed to
Nashville. If on arrival Thomas had not attacked, Logan was to relieve him
of command. Grant left for Washington in the morning, and after a day's
travel arrived there on December 15. He met with Lincoln, Stanton, and
Halleck that evening to discuss developments in Nashville. The storm had
taken down the lines. Major Thomas T. Eckert, the chief of Stanton's telegraph office, confirmed that nothing had been received from Thomas for the
past twenty-four hours.

Wholly in the dark as to what Thomas was doing even as they spoke, Grant argued forcefully that Thomas had to be relieved immediately. Lincoln and Stanton reluctantly acquiesced. Having won his case, Grant told Lincoln that he intended to continue to Nashville and take command when he got there. He would place Schofield in temporary command until his own arrival.

Grant wrote the relieving order and gave it to Eckert for transmission. Then he went to the Willard Hotel to prepare for his departure in the morning. He may not have told Lincoln and Stanton of his orders to Logan, for if he had, they might well have questioned the wisdom of redundant orders to Schofield. And when Grant left to go to Nashville, he became the third of three officers simultaneously set in motion to replace Thomas.

Eckert knew from months of handling high-level message traffic that Grant "was not favorably disposed toward Thomas." With Grant's relieving order in hand, he returned to the telegraph office where he had been working ceaselessly for a week. He learned that the lines were now open to Nashville. Remembering the reluctance of Lincoln and Stanton to fire Thomas, and exercising a degree of common sense that had been absent in the White House, Eckert decided to do nothing until he heard from Major John C. Van Duzer, the chief telegrapher in Nashville. The two of them had exchanged informal, as well as official, messages for months. Eckert waited for more than an hour, and then at about eleven o'clock encrypted messages began to arrive.

One was from Thomas, sent at eight o'clock the night before, so it had been delayed more than a day. The weather had improved, Thomas had said. He would attack in the morning. The next was from Van Duzer, sent from Nashville in the past hour. It was long, some three hundred words.

Eckert laid his cipher book alongside Van Duzer's telegram and began his decryption. His hand began to tremble as he transcribed the emerging plaintext. Thomas had attacked at nine o'clock that morning. His right wing had smashed Hood's line and had driven it back some five miles, and the center had advanced from one to three miles. "From our new line General Thomas expects to be able to drive the enemy at daylight," Van Duzer reported. "The whole action of today was splendidly successful. . . . I have never seen better work."

Eckert let out an exuberant cry and ran to the ambulance always in readiness at the door. Arriving at Stanton's residence on K Street, he pounded at the door. Stanton appeared at the window, as if he had been expecting Eckert's arrival.

"What news?"

"Good news!" yelled Eckert.

"Hurrah!" shouted Stanton. Eckert heard Stanton's wife and children cheering.

They boarded the ambulance and went to the White House. On the way Eckert silently handed Grant's order to Stanton. Has it been sent? asked Stanton. Eckert said that it had not and explained why. Stanton said he had done the right thing. Eckert was overjoyed that he would not be court-martialed.

At the White House Eckert never forgot "the tall, ghostly form of Lincoln in his night-dress, with a lighted candle in his hand, as he appeared at the head of the second story landing when the two callers were ushered upstairs by the doorkeeper." An elated Lincoln, too, approved his not having sent the message.

A copy of Van Duzer's telegram went to Grant at his hotel. "I guess we will not go to Nashville," Grant remarked to his cipher operator.

Twenty-four hours later Thomas reported that he had routed Hood's army, and he was generous in his praise of his commanders. Van Duzer again sent his own report to Washington. "Everybody, white and black, did splendidly."

"Sunday again and with it peace and quiet," wrote Maggie Lindsey in her diary at her home south of Nashville. "The battle is over. Confederates have retreated, General Thomas pursuing. Last night our army was at Franklin. Glorious Thomas! (I cannot speak his name without tears, and from that I know I am pretty well shattered by all the recent excitement.) Countless blessings on his noble head!"

31

AN ARMY DESTROYED

⸻◆⸻

Having believed since their arrival that Thomas would never attack, Hood and his staff had lulled themselves into a torpor. The parties and festivities had been unabated in Hood's headquarters mansion. While Thomas's thousands moved into position on the eve of the attack, Chief of Staff Francis Shoup made a terse diary entry, "No change in the line." With such a state of mind, Hood and his staff were jarred by the assault.

Thomas attacked Hood on December 15 with a well-defined plan. The Federal right wing, 80 percent of the Federal army, would crush the Confederate left, while the Federal left wing made a diversionary attack to occupy the enemy in its front. Wood, Smith, and Wilson comprised the right wing, and Steedman the left. Schofield was in reserve, but when he protested, Thomas added his corps to the right wing. When the infantry moved out of the city's inner trenches, Colonel Donaldson's quartermaster force took their places.

Fog delayed the attack and confused the coordination between the corps, whose soldiers still were largely strangers to each other. Nonetheless, by midafternoon the Federal right wing enveloped the Confederate left and pounded it back some five miles. It was the first time in the war that massed, dismounted cavalry had worked alongside infantry in the main point of attack, and their rapid-fire carbines added enormous firepower. On the other end of the Federal line, Steedman's black soldiers attacked valiantly. They suffered immense casualties but nonetheless diverted reinforcements from moving to the collapsing Confederate left wing.

Darkness ended the first day of operations. Hood's army was battered and shaky but still intact. Hood contracted his lines, erected such fortifications as were possible during the night, and decided to stand a second day. Inexplicably, he failed to recall Forrest, still away with the bulk of the Confederate cavalry at Murfreesboro.

Thomas did not know whether Hood intended to fight or to flee; cornered and unpredictable, he might lash out at any moment. Wary of ambushes, the Federal divisions advanced cautiously on the second day, the sixteenth, to develop the Confederate positions. By noon they regained contact with Hood's front lines.

Wilson, on the extreme right, got his cavalry behind the Confederate left wing by midday and was ready to attack Hood's rear. Schofield was adjacent to Wilson and was expected to attack simultaneously, with the Federal corps to Schofield's left to follow. But Schofield had been snakebit at Spring Hill and Franklin. Hesitant to again tangle with Hood, Schofield was immovable.

A drizzle began in the afternoon, hastening early darkness. Schofield's procrastination maddened the other generals. Steedman and Wood on the left went forward, but without success. Still Schofield delayed, on the pretext of needing reinforcements. Thomas provided them, but Schofield asked for even more and still would not act. A Smith division commander, John McArthur, was bursting to go forward, but Thomas restrained him, holding to the plan that Schofield and Wilson would attack first. McArthur went forward nonetheless.

Thomas rode to Schofield's headquarters to impel the apprehensive general to attack—the general whom Grant had twice advocated to lead the Nashville army in lieu of Thomas. Schofield trembled. Look to your left, said Thomas, and see that Smith has gone forward without waiting for you. Go forward, sir, go forward. Wilson arrived and pointed to his cavalry troopers attacking the rear of Hood's lines. Go forward, *now*, said Thomas.

By then what Schofield did or did not do was immaterial. McArthur and Wilson went on without Schofield to crush Hood's left wing between them. The Confederate troops fled in terror. With a yell the remainder of the Federal army surged ahead, scattering Hood's army into the storm of the night.

The pursuit phase of Thomas's master plan began. Wilson's cavalry mounted and charged into the darkness, with Wood's infantry close behind. The pursuit would continue for twelve days and a hundred miles. Only weather and Forrest prevented the annihilation of Hood's army. The winter storms so inundated the fields that horses sank in mud to their bellies. The Federal cavalry had to remain on the roads, unable to outflank and overtake the fleeing Confederate infantry. Whenever the Federal cavalry closed up, Forrest met them. As Hood crossed the swollen rivers he destroyed the bridges behind him, and the rivers stopped the pursuing Federal soldiers.

The Duck River at Columbia, thirty-five miles below Nashville, was at high flood, too deep and swift for the pursuing Federal troops to ford. Pontoons would have gotten the soldiers, their mounts, and their trains across, but Thomas misdirected his pontoon train, and Wilson and Wood stared glumly at the impassable torrent. Still they roused their soldiers into the sleet and rain. With hands frozen and uniforms sodden, the men cobbled together makeshift bridges, but they collapsed under the weight of horses and wagons. Eventually the pontoons arrived, the Duck was crossed, and the pursuit resumed. The final race was for the Tennessee River, the last obstacle between the remnants of Hood's army and the Deep South.

Thomas's army in the lines around Nashville awaits orders to attack Hood's Army of Tennessee. The countryside had been shorn of its trees, which were used for firewood and fortifications. Fighting was delayed by a fierce ice storm, but when the weather warmed, the Federal army demolished its Confederate enemy in the most decisive battle of the Civil War. (Library of Congress)

Thomas tried other means to trap Hood on his flight from Tennessee. He sent Steedman by train to Decatur, Alabama, with orders to proceed downriver and prevent Hood from crossing at Florence. Thomas also asked the navy to send gunboats. Neither gambit worked, and Hood crossed over into safety.

Meanwhile, hundred-gun salvos in the east saluted Thomas's victory. Jubilation swept the North, for Thomas had done in two weeks what Grant had failed to do in six months: he had destroyed a Confederate army. Congratulations from the government and fellow generals followed Thomas as he went with his pursuing army. Then the patronizing telegrams resumed, drafted with soft hands in the warmth and comfort of Washington offices.

"Permit me, general," oozed Halleck on December 21, acting as Grant's mouthpiece, "to urge the vast importance of a hot pursuit of Hood's army. Every possible sacrifice must be made, and your men for a few days will submit to any hardship and privation to accomplish the great result. If you can capture or destroy Hood's army Sherman can entirely crush out the rebel military force in all the Southern States. He begins a new campaign about the

1st of January, which will have the most important results, if Hood's army can now be used up. A most vigorous pursuit on your part is therefore of vital importance to Sherman's plans. No sacrifice must be spared to attain so important an objective."

Thomas lashed back with scarcely restrained fury. "General Hood's army is being pursued as rapidly and as vigorously as it is possible for one army to pursue another. We cannot control the elements . . . I am doing all in my power to crush Hood's army, and, if it be possible, to destroy it; but pursuing an enemy through an exhausted country, over mud roads, completely sogged with heavy rains, is no child's play, and cannot be accomplished as quickly as thought of."

Sherman's operations were a burr under Thomas's saddle, and as Halleck had opened the subject, Thomas unburdened himself. Sherman had taken the cream of the army and its equipment, Thomas reminded Halleck, and had left Thomas a scratch force to deal with a Confederate army that Sherman had been unable to defeat. Thomas had defeated Hood and had done what Sherman with twice the force could not do. "Although my progress may appear slow, I feel assured that Hood's army can be driven from Tennessee, and eventually driven to the wall, by the force under my command. . . . I can safely state that this army is willing to submit to any sacrifice to oust Hood's army, or to strike any other blow which would contribute to the destruction of the rebellion."

Stanton scrambled to soothe the infuriated Thomas. "[T]his department has the most unbounded confidence," he wired immediately, "in your skill, vigor, and determination to employ to the best advantage all the means in your power to pursue and destroy the enemy. No Department could be inspired with more profound admiration and thankfulness for the great deeds you have already performed, or more confiding faith that human effort could accomplish no more than will be done by you and the gallant officers and soldiers of your command."

On Christmas Day, Thomas received a telegram from Stanton saying that Lincoln had nominated him for promotion to the permanent rank of major general in the regular army. "No official duty has been performed by me with more satisfaction," said Stanton, "and no commander has more justly earned promotion by devoted, disinterested, and valuable service to his country."

His forbearance finally at an end, Thomas could no longer contain his bitterness. He glanced at the message and tossed it away. "I earned that a year ago at Chattanooga."

Two weeks later Thomas returned to Nashville. He was about to leave again, however, for Grant had ordered Thomas to undertake a winter offensive, and he was taking a train south to concentrate his scattered forces. It was against Thomas's better judgment. "[T]o continue the campaign without any rest," he wrote to Halleck, "I fear, will cost us very heavy losses from disease and exhaustion." He recommended taking time to refit the army. Grant and Halleck again called Thomas slow. Grant had found his excuse to remove Thomas from active operations for the remainder of the war.

As Thomas gloomily went to the train, he spoke confidentially with his chief quartermaster, James Donaldson. He thanked Donaldson for the magnificent support from the quartermaster's department. "He said it was the most thorough and complete thing he had ever seen," Donaldson wrote to Quartermaster General Montgomery Meigs, "that it had done everything he could desire for his army."

By then Thomas had heard the story about Logan. "[Thomas] opened his heart to me," wrote Donaldson. "He feels very sore at the rumored intentions to relieve him, and the major-generalcy does not heal the wound. You know Thomas is morbidly sensitive, and it cut him to the heart to think that it was contemplated to remove him. He does not blame the Secretary, for he said Mr. Stanton was a fair and just man."

Thomas learned about Grant's order to Schofield much later, when he called on Stanton in his Washington office in the summer of 1865. Eckert came into the office with Grant's message, and Stanton handed it to Thomas. Thomas read it, then raised his head. Stanton turned to Eckert. "This is the man who withheld that order and saved you from the mortification of a summary removal."

The question that tormented the Confederate officers was *Why?* Their soldiers had been courageous beyond measure at Franklin. Why had they broken and fled two weeks later at Nashville?

The campaign was exposed as an illusion. Common, dearly held beliefs about Southern patriotism and loyalty were shattered. Hood had come to liberate the people of Tennessee, but they turned their backs, especially after his troops plundered Columbia in the run-up to Franklin. "The people have hidden away their goods," wrote Quintard in disbelief, "and seem unwilling to dispose of them for Confederate money." Federal greenbacks, he discovered, were the coin of the realm.

Because Hood's army held no attractions, the expected number of Tennessee volunteers had never materialized. In fact, so hostile were the Tennessee natives that they attacked his wagons and destroyed the mills that were making flour for his soldiers. Hood was mortified and ordered Forrest to suppress the home guards and to conscript men forcibly into the ranks. Stephen Lee estimated that six to seven thousand local men had fled into Nashville ahead of the army to escape conscription. Hood's provost marshal reported that only 164 recruits had been received since the army had entered the state on its crusade.

Hood also had inexplicably weakened his forces at Nashville by sending Forrest and several infantry brigades to invest Murfreesboro, thirty miles to the southeast. Murfreesboro obsessed Hood, and he continued to fritter away his dwindling forces there and elsewhere, as if he expected Thomas to remain inside the Nashville fortifications indefinitely. Hence he and his generals were stunned when Thomas attacked, and Forrest and other dislocated forces were too distant to support the troops remaining at Nashville.

When Wilson's cavalry and McArthur's infantry crunched the Confederate left flank on the second afternoon, Hood's army collapsed like a house of cards. "Hood was swept off the field with the mass of fugitives," said Cummings. "As he rode off he directed me to go back to General Cheatham, and direct him to rally as many men as he could on a hill which General Hood pointed out, and hold it all hazards and cover the retreat." Hood galloped off and disappeared among the human avalanche.

Hood fashioned his explanation of the debacle within forty-eight hours, and Quintard was among the first to hear it. The priest met with Hood and his staff near the Polk homestead south of Columbia. "The General bears up with wonderful faith," Quintard wrote in his diary. "He gave me the following letter which explains the disasters." The letter was from Colonel Andrew J. Kellar, commanding a regiment near the point of collapse on the left wing. He had seen a brigade in William B. Bate's division surrender a hill without a struggle. When the Federal troops had occupied the hill, it triggered a chain reaction.

To Kellar's shame and mortification, his troops had fled with the others. "It was not fighting—nor the force of arms—nor even numbers which drove us from the field. . . . For the first time in this war, we lost our cannon. Give us the first chance and we will retake them."

Hood tried for the remainder of his life to divert the blame from himself onto others. He would argue with heat and passion that the Army of Tennessee had not broken for any fault of his, if indeed it had broken at all, for he maintained that the Battle of Franklin had restored its élan. To divert attention from what he had done and left undone, Hood needed a scapegoat. Kellar's letter provided it: Bate was the culprit. Hood waved an earlier letter from Forrest reporting that Bate's division had been shameful at Murfreesboro. Ergo, the fault lay not with the Army of Tennessee and Hood its commander, but with Bate. Hood's litany of deceit had begun. In time it would expand to include free-swinging accusations against Johnston, Hardee, and Cheatham.

The groping for rationalizations continued into the late hours. Quintard urged Hood to make his stand at the Duck River, for if that line could be held, the campaign would still be a splendid success. The discussion drifted into matters of theology. "God is on our side," said a staff officer, "so manifestly that no man can question it, yet it is apparent that our people have not yet passed through all their disappointments and sufferings." Hood agreed that God's plans did not at the moment seem to include a Confederate triumph. At Spring Hill, said Hood, the enemy had been in his grasp. Despite his best efforts to strike a blow (Hood forgot that he had slept the night away) the enemy had escaped. Proclaiming his faith in God undiminished, Hood retired to his room still undecided as to plans.

The next morning Forrest advised Hood to quit Tennessee, and Hood assented. The retreat resumed. Quintard increasingly became Hood's confessor. "The General says he is afraid he had been more wicked since he began this retreat than for a long time past," wrote Quintard.

[H]e had so set his heart upon success—had prayed so earnestly for it— had such a firm trust that he should succeed—that his heart has been

very rebellious—but said he "let us go out of Tennessee singing hymns of praise."

This has been a terrible day, and exceedingly cold rain in the morning and snow in the evening. So many of our poor boys are bare footed that there is great suffering and my heart bleeds for them. . . .

Dined with Major Jones, and for wonder as to time and place, had oyster soup. General Hood and myself enjoyed the rarity.

The last of the tattered Army of Tennessee straggled into Tupelo, Mississippi, on January 12. Two hundred miles of retreating in winter weather had taken its remaining energy. Perhaps one-third of the original army remained—the numbers will never be known—and it was wrecked. Hood continued to maintain that its spirit and morale were excellent, but the disaster could not be concealed from inspectors and visitors, and word got back to Richmond.

Although he was still hoping that Davis would retain him, Hood asked to be relieved of command. Davis approved the request, and Hood was out.* The Army of Tennessee was dispersed. Two skeleton corps went east to help Johnston fight Sherman in the Carolinas. The third corps, perhaps 2,000 men, remained in the west, the last fragment of an army once among the two most powerful in the Confederacy.

Hood sulked in his tent waiting for Beauregard officially to relieve him. The Louisiana band that had serenaded Hood at the Polk plantation came by and played for him again. The musicians urged him to speak. Hood came out and swayed before them on his crutches. He spoke bitterly of betrayal, his voice angry and rambling. Then he returned to his tent. He had said nothing about the Tennessee campaign.

Hood boarded a train and returned to Richmond on Monday morning, January 23, 1865.

Lincoln sat in relaxation among his cabinet. It was obvious that he would tell a story, a parable, as he often did, and the officials settled in to listen.

> *Out in Illinois, in my country, there was a certain rough, rude, and bullying man, who had a bulldog, which was as rough, rude, and bullying as his master. Dog and man were the terror of the neighborhood. Nobody dared to touch one for fear of the other. But a crafty neighbor laid a plan to dispose of the dog.*
>
> *Seeing Slocum plodding along the road one day, his dog a little ahead, this neighbor took from his pocket a chunk of meat, in which he had concealed a big charge of powder, to which he had fastened a Deadwood slow-match. This he lighted, and then threw all on the road. The dog gave one gulp at it, and the whole thing disappeared*

---

* Davis afterward wrote in his memoirs that he had acted solely at Hood's request, not because of his performance of duty in Tennessee.

down his throat. He trotted on a few steps, when there was a sort of smothered roar, and the dog blew up in fragments—a forequarter lodging in a neighboring tree, a hindquarter on the roof of a cabin, his head in one place, his tail in another, and the rest scattered along the dusty road.

Slocum came up and viewed the remains. Then, more in sorrow than in anger, he said, "Bill was a good dog, but, as a dog, I reckon his usefulness is over."

Hood's army was a good army. We have been very much afraid of it. But, as an army, I reckon its usefulness is over.

PART VIII

FINIS

32

APPOMATTOX

⸺◦◦⸺

Th e Army of Northern Virginia crouched in agony behind its Petersburg ramparts. During the winter of 1864–65 the siege had degenerated into trench warfare of the most desolate kind. The Confederate
soldiers lived in squalor and misery, neither fed nor clothed nor sheltered,
while Federal artillery and sharpshooters fired at anyone who moved.

The army's leadership had collapsed. Generals contrived excuses to abandon their commands. Captains neglected their men. Lee with dismay read
the December inspection report for Longstreet's corps, a doleful indictment
of the apathy of its officers. Lee angrily scratched out a letter to Longstreet
demanding that he remedy the evils, but spilling ink on paper could not
impede the disintegration. In the absence of leadership, the sick, starving,
dispirited enlisted men had incentive neither to drill nor to fight. Thousands
deserted.

Bad news came from every quarter. Wilmington, North Carolina, the only
seaport still able to receive blockade runners, was the Confederacy's last link
with the outside world. Davis sent Bragg there in January to command the
defenses at Fort Fisher and so hastened its collapse and the Federal occupation of the city. Johnston's cobbled-together army unsuccessfully attempted
to protect the Carolinas. He glumly reported to Lee that he could "do no
more than annoy" Sherman, who was driving north to rendezvous with
Grant.

A negotiated peace remained impossible because the objectives of the
United States government and the Confederacy—emancipation and reunion,
slavery and Southern independence—were irreconcilable. Hence, there was
no possibility of Union concessions to the Confederacy. Had Lee been a
statesman, he would have had the wisdom to ask for peace; instead, he gave
himself wholly to prolonging the war indefinitely. "[T]rusting in a Merciful
God," he wrote Mary on February 21, "who does not always give the battle
to the strong, I pray we may not be overwhelmed. I shall however endeavour
to do my duty & fight to the last." To what and to whom Lee's sense of duty
applied is unclear, but it was neither to his soldiers nor to the people of Vir-

ginia. In his "fight to the last" he would protract a devastating war for no purpose whatever.

Within the Confederate high command, no one dared whisper "Shall we surrender?" While generals had surrendered brigades and divisions under honorable conditions in the past, it had not meant that the war was over. Now the word "surrender" had become synonymous with a humiliating conclusion to the war. Continuing to pursue the illusion of negotiation, Longstreet met under a flag of truce with the Federal general Edward O. C. Ord, a prewar comrade who had relieved Butler of command of the Army of the James. From their amiable meeting came a proposition from Longstreet that Lee try to meet with Grant. Lee gamely composed a letter to Grant on March 2. Avoiding even the hint of a surrender, he suggested they explore "the possibility of arriving at a satisfactory adjustment of the present unhappy difficulties by means of a military convention." His choice of words was preposterous. Grant's dismissal of Lee's proposal was foreordained.

The extent of the South's desperation was revealed by a newfound willingness to use soldier-slaves in the Confederate army. Cleburne, it will be recalled, had advanced such a proposal in January 1864. The idea came into the open again as the war went against the Confederacy, and the press and government bodies fiercely debated the pros and cons of arming slaves. Davis submitted legislation and asked for its approval.

The votes in the Confederate Congress were nearly evenly divided, and Lee's recommendation was expected to determine the outcome. His prestige had been bolstered by his appointment as general in chief of the Confederate armies in late January 1865.* Lee endorsed the concept and it passed in the House, but the two Virginia senators voted no and so the measure failed. After more logrolling, Congress enacted the law in mid-March, but by then the war had almost ended and nothing came of it.

When Gordon returned from the Shenandoah Valley debacle in December 1864, he took command of the 8,000 members of Early's corps that had made it back with him.† (Early remained in the valley with a corporal's guard, consigned by Lee to oppose Sheridan's legions.) Gordon soon became Lee's confidant, becoming closer to him than perhaps any other of Lee's lieutenants throughout the war. Together they reasoned that Grant ultimately would grind them to oblivion if they remained in Petersburg. Unlikely as it was that Lee's starving men and horses could outrun Grant's powerful army, Lee and Gordon searched for ways to escape encirclement and to unite with Johnston.

---

* It was an empty title, conferred by the Confederate Congress primarily as a vote of no confidence in Davis as commander in chief. Lee continued to focus his entire attention on his own theater of operations.

† Gordon technically became a corps commander and was nominated for promotion to lieutenant general. Because of the confusion of the last months of the Confederacy, the Confederate Senate did not act on his nomination, and he ended the war as a major general.

In the history of warfare, armies in extremis have often made one final, frenzied counterattack when least expected, attempting to postpone an otherwise looming defeat. The Battle of the Bulge and the Tet Offensive are two well-known examples. So too with the Army of Northern Virginia at Petersburg, for Gordon proposed a risky breakout scheme that he felt could conceivably allow an ultimate rendezvous with Johnston.

Gordon's plan was ingenious, for it contained measures of stealth and deception not unlike a commando raid of the Second World War. Picked troops in a surprise predawn attack would rush the Federal lines at a redoubt called Fort Stedman. After the initial breakthrough, crack teams would infiltrate to three redoubts farther to the rear that were believed to contain artillery. The teams would seize the artillery and bombard the adjacent Federal lines while follow-up infantry consolidated the breakthrough. Gordon theorized that the bulk of Lee's army could escape through the gap and rendezvous with Johnston.

Gordon's plan was patterned after his surprise attack at Cedar Creek the year before, which initially had been hugely successful. In Gordon's mind it ultimately had failed only because Early had not exploited the advantage. Conditions, however, were entirely different at Petersburg. As a consequence, Gordon's meticulous Fort Stedman plan was solely an infantry operation with inadequate forces and scant knowledge of the terrain, and it was based on the assumption that the Federal forces would not counterattack. Nevertheless, Lee approved it for the morning of March 25. Predictably, it failed absolutely.

Gordon's shock troops got their first objective, Fort Stedman and its adjacent trenches. The infiltrating teams could not, however, locate the redoubts in the rear; Gordon had guessed at their location based on faulty intelligence, and he had guessed wrong. Nor had Gordon provided for artillery support; thus at daylight the Federal artillery pounded Gordon's soldiers trapped in their small, vulnerable salient. The Federal cross fire slew soldiers attempting to retreat, so they huddled within any shelter they could find until they could surrender.

Lee canceled the attack at 8 A.M., three hours after it had begun. The Federal commanders, who reckoned that Lee had pulled troops from other locations, commenced a general assault against the weakened Confederate lines, which managed to hold despite punishing casualties. The debacle ended at sunset. Lee's loss in prisoners was greater than at any time since Spotsylvania. The loss of life was correspondingly severe. Lee promptly reported the results of the attack to Davis. It had not been successful, said Lee, because the rear redoubts (which had not been found) "were found enclosed and strongly manned."

Lee abandoned Petersburg and Richmond on April 2. He had to move because Grant had knocked off half of Lee's remaining forces at Five Forks and was about to sever Lee's last supply line from the west. When Davis and his government officials fled the Confederate capital, the last trace of authority disappeared; straightaway a mob pillaged and burned the city. Gordon kissed Fanny good-bye and left her in Petersburg, for she had just given birth to their third son.

Lee's most pressing need was to feed his men, so he hugged the westward rail line that paralleled the Appomattox River, where he expected to find freight cars with food. The mirage of provisions waiting just over the hill was the soldiers' prime incentive to move, for they were scarcely able to place one foot in front of the other. Gordon commanded the rear guard fighting desperately to protect hundreds of wagons loaded with paraphernalia, their burdens a sea anchor to Lee's once mobile army. The pursuing Army of the Potomac and Army of the James swallowed chunks of Lee's dwindling ranks, and in the developing calamity Lee calmly dictated orders to regiments and brigades that no longer existed.

The two Federal generals commanding the pursuit were sick men. Meade was prostrate and moved by ambulance. Grant was in agony from migraines. Seeking relief, he bathed his feet in hot water and mustard, and mustard plasters were applied to his wrists and the back of his neck, but nothing alleviated the searing pain. His dread that Lee might escape was greater torture, and Grant thundered at his generals to be relentless; lagging was unforgivable. Grant dismissed Gouverneur Warren, a hero of Gettysburg, for moving too slowly with the Fifth Corps at Five Forks.

Andrew Humphreys led his Second Corps like a wolfhound. Nelson Miles—now commanding Barlow's First Division—had the same killer instinct, but William Hays of the Second Division had no fire in his belly. When Humphreys found Hays and his staff sleeping at his headquarters on the morning of April 6, he banished him on the spot. Humphreys had an immediate replacement looking for a fight: the Puritan had returned from his extended convalescence.

Barlow went to war within the hour. He and Miles led the van of the onrushing Federal army that pursued Gordon in a running battle over a fourteen-mile stretch of road from Amelia Springs to Sayler's Creek. Gordon tried desperately to protect the encumbering train, fighting and then falling back to fight again. The horses and mules straining in harness were skeletons, unable to move the wagons that sank to their axles in the bog of the creek. Gordon's soldiers bent their backs to the wheels and then again fired their weapons. As Barlow and Miles closed down upon them, Gordon's soldiers finally fled into the night.

Most of their wagons were left behind. The Federal soldiers tore into their cargoes and gorged on the great quantities of food they discovered—boiled ham, beef, bacon, onions, pickles, and toasted hardtack, which unaccountably had been denied the Confederate soldiers. Barrels of applejack were cracked open and drunk, and the whooping soldiers put on new Confederate uniforms to replace their worn clothing and rummaged among officers' trunks for souvenirs like dress swords and luxury goods. One wagon had a litter of puppies, another bundles of Confederate currency, which the Federal troops freely distributed to their prisoners. Lee's soldiers threw them contemptuously aside, where they intermingled with the thousands of sheets of army records littering the hillsides.

Theodore Lyman, still a member of Meade's staff, came upon the battlefield on the morning of April 7. "The way was completely strewed," he wrote, "with tents, ammunition, officers' baggage, and, above all, little Dutch ovens—such a riches of little Dutch ovens I have never seen! I suppose they bake hoe-cakes in them. You saw them lying about, with their little legs kicked up in the air, in a piteous manner."

Gordon's survivors stumbled across the Appomattox River at High Bridge in the morning light of April 7, hoping that the river would delay their pursuers long enough to allow them rest and time to eat. It was a tremendous bridge that spanned the entire river valley, an engineering marvel arising unexpectedly from the desolate countryside. The Federal pursuers could hardly believe that Southerners had been able to construct a bridge so massive, so high, and so broad. Roads descending into the valley led to a smaller adjacent wagon bridge, crossing only the river.

Lee had expected Major General William Mahone, an engineer and a prewar railroad president, to destroy the bridges after the last Confederate soldiers had cleared to the north shore. Mahone's engineers started late; when Barlow arrived at 7 A.M., he overwhelmed the rear guard and rushed the bridges to extinguish the burning timbers. Other of his soldiers got a beachhead on the opposite shore and held off frenzied counterattacks. Spans on the High Bridge blazed and disintegrated, but the wagon bridge was saved intact. Humphreys arrived with the remainder of the Second Corps and thundered to the opposite shore to resume the pursuit.

Humphreys split his corps into two columns. Two divisions went northwesterly with Humphreys to follow Mahone toward Cumberland Church, three miles north of Farmville. Barlow followed Gordon's footsteps to the southwest, down the track to Farmville. Lee and Longstreet were there with the remainder of the army, feeling secure on the north side of the Appomattox, for they thought that they had bought time to recuperate by burning the bridges at Farmville and High Bridge. They were astonished when, as the whole of Lee's army was cooking breakfast with food from the waiting railroad cars, Barlow with his lone division attacked Gordon's rear guard. Lee was seized with rage when he learned that the bridge had not been burned, for he knew then that his army was doomed.

Barlow flushed Lee from Farmville, sending the Confederate soldiers wearily north toward Cumberland Church while Barlow followed. Humphreys and Miles assaulted the gathering Confederates until darkness. The battle was all but over. Grant and Lee began to exchange messages that evening.

When the Aristocrat arose on Palm Sunday, April 9, he dressed himself faultlessly in a formal uniform with sash and sword, an ensemble that he had brought with him from Petersburg in anticipation of the end. Gordon made one final lunge at the encircling lines west of Appomattox Court House and reported that the situation was hopeless. That was it. Lee mounted and went looking for Grant, while impromptu truces stilled the guns. Another exchange of messages arranged a meeting at the McLean house in Appomattox Court House. Lee got there first and waited, attended by a lone aide.

Wearing mud-spattered field dress, the Yeoman arrived with his retinue. He had begun the day with his mind still focused on maneuvering his army. When he received Lee's message that he wanted to discuss surrender, Grant later wrote, "I was still suffering with the sick headache; but the instant I saw the contents of the note I was cured."

The two generals exchanged greetings, shook hands, and took seats at separate tables. The staffs pressed against the walls of the small parlor. "What General Lee's feelings were I do not know," Grant later wrote. "As he was a man of much dignity, with an impassible face, it was impossible to say whether he felt inwardly glad that the end had finally come, or felt sad over the result, and was too manly to show it. . . . [M]y own feelings, which had been quite jubilant on the receipt of his letter, were sad and depressed. I felt like anything rather than rejoicing at the downfall of a foe who had fought so long and valiantly, and had suffered so much for a cause, though that cause was, I believe, one of the worst for which a people ever fought, and one for which there was the least excuse."

Grant fully understood the scope and limitations of his authority in dealing with Lee. Political discussions were forbidden; how the Federal government ultimately would treat the high Confederate officials was not his concern. His primary objective was to disarm and disperse the Army of Northern Virginia. Lee had expected the worst, surely his arrest and court-martial for treason and perhaps the same for Gordon and Longstreet, his two remaining senior generals.

Lee could scarcely suppress his anxiety as he was forced to make small talk with Grant about the old army they had known before the war. Finally Lee interrupted Grant and asked for terms. "General Lee, your army must lay down its arms." said Grant. "It must not take them up again unless your officers and men are duly exchanged." It was a clever, foolproof way to disarm Lee's army forever, for there would never again be an exchange of parolees.

Again the conversation drifted while Lee fidgeted. Once more Lee interrupted Grant and asked that the terms be written out. Paper and pen appeared before Grant, and he wrote for several minutes. He passed the document to Lee. To his relief, he found that Grant was not vindictive. Arms, cartridge cases, and colors had to be surrendered and parolees signed promising not to take up arms against the United States government. Officers could keep their horses and swords.

Lee signed the document surrendering his army.

Humphreys's finger was on the trigger, ready to unleash Barlow and Miles for the coup de grâce if he heard nothing by two o'clock. He waited as rumors of surrender reached him. Presently Humphreys looked at his watch.

"Two o'clock. No answer," he growled. "Go forward." At that moment, two officers—one Federal, one Confederate—came into view bearing an order from Grant to halt the troops. "Major Wingate, of General Lee's Staff," wrote Lyman, "was a military-looking man, dressed in a handsome grey suit with gold lace, and a gold star upon his collar. He was courageous, but plainly mortified to the 'heart.'

> *"We had done better to have burnt our whole train three days ago," he said bitterly. "In trying to save a train, we have lost an army." And there he struck the pith of the thing.*
>
> *And so we continued to wait till about five, during which time General Humphreys amused us with presents of Confederate notes, of which we found a barrel full in the Rebel waggons. It was a strange spectacle, to see the officers laughing and giving each other $500 notes of a government that had been considered as firmly established by our English friends.*
>
> *About five came Major Pease. "The Army of Northern Virginia has surrendered!" Such a scene followed as I can never see again. The soldiers rushed, perfectly crazy, to the roadside, and there crowding in dense masses, shouted, screamed, yelled, threw up their hats and hopped madly up and down. The batteries were run out and began firing, the bands played, the flags waved. The noise of the cheering was such that my very ears rang. And there was General Meade galloping about and waving his hat with the best of them. Poor old Robert Lee. His punishment is too heavy—to hear those cheers, and to remember what he once was.*

The Army of Northern Virginia as it existed on that Palm Sunday was a tattered fragment of its former incarnation. Grant could have crushed it in an hour between thumb and forefinger. The final roll call listed 7,892 organized infantry with arms and a guess of not more than 2,000 cavalry. One hundred thousand Federal soldiers surrounded them.

Meade went to visit Lee the next day, accompanied by Lyman. Lee rode out to meet the small Federal entourage. Meade removed his hat. "Good morning, General," said Meade. Moments passed before Lee recognized the commander of the Army of the Potomac.

"But what are you doing with all the grey in your beard?" asked Lee.

"You have to answer for most of it," said Meade.

Lyman recorded his impression of the Aristocrat. "Lee is . . . a stately-looking man," he wrote, "tall, erect and strongly built, with a full chest. His hair and closely trimmed beard, though thick, are now nearly white. He has a large and well-shaped head, with a brown, clear eye, of unusual depth. His face is sunburnt and rather florid. . . . [H]e is exceedingly grave and dignified . . . but there was evidently added an extreme depression, which gave him the air of a man who kept up his pride to the last, but who was entirely overwhelmed. From his speech I judge he was inclined to wander in his thoughts. You would not have recognized a Confederate officer from his dress, which was a blue military overcoat, a high grey hat, and well-brushed riding boots.

"As General Meade introduced his two aides, Lee put out his hand and saluted us with all the air of the oldest blood in the world. I did not think . . . that I should ever shake the hand of Robert E. Lee, prisoner of war."

Gordon, Longstreet, and William Pendleton worked out the details of the surrender with three Federal generals. The Confederate soldiers would march in formation before a line of Federal troops and formally stack arms and colors.

The Cavalier led the Army of Northern Virginia to the surrender ceremony on the morning of April 12. Joshua Chamberlain of Gettysburg commanded the soldiers of the Army of the Potomac who would receive the surrender. As Gordon approached with the procession, Chamberlain ordered his men to present arms. He remembered afterward how Gordon had looked up and recognized the salute of respect.

> *Gordon instantly assumed the finest attitude of a soldier. He wheeled his horse, touching him gently with the spur, so that the animal slightly reared, and as he wheeled, horse and rider made one motion, the horse's head swung down with a graceful bow, and General Gordon dropped his sword point to his toe in salutation.*

Gordon spoke to the troops behind him, and they too saluted in their own way. One by one the tiny regiments stacked their arms and furled their colors. Then they went home.

EPILOGUE

He that outlives this day and comes safe home,
Will stand a tip-toe when this day is nam'd,
And rouse him at the name of Crispian.
He that shall live this day, and see old age,
Will yearly on the vigil feast his neighbours,
And say, To-morrow is Saint Crispian:
Then he will strip his sleeves and show his scars,
And say, These wounds I had on Crispin's day.
Old men forget; yet all shall be forgot,
But he'll remember with advantages
What feats he did that day. . . .

                                        Shakespeare, Henry V

Lincoln was assassinated on the evening of April 14, two days after Gordon had surrendered the Army of Northern Virginia at Appomattox. When he died the next morning, Andrew Johnson of Tennessee became president. Jefferson Davis was on the run, as Confederate commanders everywhere surrendered to Federal armies. Johnston and Sherman negotiated a sweeping, liberal peace protocol near Durham, North Carolina, on April 18, which President Johnson rejected because Sherman had exceeded his authority. The two generals resumed negotiations, and Johnston surrendered his 30,000-man army on April 26 under terms similar to those of Appomattox. Surrenders at Confederate outposts in Alabama and Mississippi followed. James Wilson, commanding a cavalry corps that had swept the South, coordinated the pursuit of Davis, and Federal cavalry captured the Confederate president and his party near Irwinville, Georgia, on May 10. With that, President Johnson proclaimed armed resistance to have ended. The war was over.

Grant received the rank of full general a year after the war. He engaged in politics and allied himself with Stanton and the Radical Republicans against President Johnson. The resultant visibility made Grant the Republican presidential candidate in 1868, and he was easily elected. Grant continued to be a poor judge of character. Graft and cronyism corrupted his administration, but the electorate nonetheless returned him to office for a second term.

After his presidency he and Julia traveled abroad. Upon his return Grant tried to get the nomination for a third term, but a coalition of enemies chose James A. Garfield, who had been army chief of staff at Chickamauga. Because Grant depended on the generosity of others for his income, it was difficult for him to live in dignity. He eventually went bankrupt by investing in a fraudulent scheme. Friends then restored his rank on the retired list, which brought in a modest pension. In his last years, while dying of throat cancer, Grant wrote his memoirs, which were a great publishing success and made almost half a million dollars for his family. Grant died on July 23, 1885, and his body lies within a Federal monument in New York City.

The status of high officials in the former Confederate government provoked controversy immediately after the war. President Johnson proclaimed a general amnesty and pardon on May 29, 1865, to those who would take a specified oath to support the Constitution and the laws of the United States. The proclamation excluded fourteen designated classes of Confederates, including Lee, who were required to apply individually to the president for pardon. Meanwhile, the Federal government indicted Lee and other generals for treason. The trial date hinged on proceedings against Davis, then imprisoned at Fort Monroe, and those would take time.

Lee decided to apply for a pardon and await developments on his indictment. He sent his request via Grant to the president on June 13, 1865. On a technicality, Lee did not subscribe to the oath to support the Constitution and the laws of the United States, but he simply applied "for the benefits and full restoration of all rights and privileges" offered by the May 29 proclamation. "No single act of his career aroused so much antagonism," wrote Freeman. "Twenty years after his death some of the 'unreconstructed' Southerners were still insistent that Lee had erred, and, by asking for a pardon, had admitted a fault."

Had Lee's application been made public, his Southern critics would have realized that Lee had neither asked for a pardon per se nor sworn an oath of loyalty to the government in Washington. He had admitted no fault. Lee belatedly submitted an oath of allegiance on October 2, 1865, but it got buried in government files and was only accidentally discovered in 1970.

Thus Lee did not receive a pardon during his lifetime. On August 5, 1975, President Gerald R. Ford restored Lee's citizenship, making it retroactive to June 13, 1865.

In 1869, after the decision was made not to prosecute Davis, Lee's indictment was dropped, as were those of the other generals. Meanwhile, Lee served quietly as president of Washington College, now Washington and Lee University, in Lexington, Virginia. He died there on October 12, 1870, and his remains are in the chapel crypt. He wrote no memoirs.

After the war Thomas carried on as a major general in the regular army. He remained in the western theater as an enlightened military governor of several former Confederate states, dealing with the political, social, and economic turmoil of reconstruction. Thanks to his sagacity, civil government was restored to Tennessee and the state itself back to the Union. An appreciative Tennessee legislature made him a resident (Virginia no longer claimed him) and awarded him a gold medal on the anniversary of the Battle of Nashville.

Meanwhile, President Johnson, facing possible impeachment, wanted to remove Grant as general in chief because of his affiliation with the Radical Republicans in Congress. Without consulting Thomas, Johnson nominated him as Grant's successor on February 21, 1867. When Thomas read the newspapers, he declined by telegram, offering the explanation that he had done nothing since the Civil War to merit the compliment and that it was too late to consider the appointment as a reward for wartime services.

In those days generals were prime candidates for office. For years, Virginian John Tyler, Jr., a distant relative and son of the former president, had been urging Thomas to run for president. Each time Thomas refused to enter politics. "My only desire," he wrote Tyler in December 1867, "is to serve my country in my present capacity and to preserve untarnished my individual integrity."

Three weeks before his death at age fifty-three, Thomas said no for the last time in a letter to the persistent Tyler:

> *My life for the last thirty years has been passed in the Military Service. . . . My services are now, as they have always been, subject to the call of the Government in whatever military capacity I may be considered competent and worthy to fill, and will be cordially undertaken whenever called upon to render. All civil honors and duties I shall continue to decline.*

Thomas destroyed all of his personal papers and wrote no memoirs. He died of a stroke while on active duty in San Francisco on March 28, 1870. His death evoked countrywide mourning. A special train brought his body east, and silent crowds at every station gathered in respect as the entourage passed through. President Grant and General in Chief Sherman were among the thousands that attended his military funeral in Troy, New York, the home of his wife.

An equestrian statue of Thomas stands in the nation's capital. While his name remained unspoken for generations of Southampton County residents, today the county displays its pride as the home of George Thomas. Signs everywhere commemorate his name and reputation.

Hood moved to New Orleans after the war, married Anna Marie Hennen, who was from a prominent family, and had eleven children (including three sets of twins) in eleven years of marriage. His life there is largely unrecorded; we know, however, that he had an unsuccessful cotton business and then went into insurance. Hood devoted the remainder of his life to blaming others for the disastrous Tennessee campaign and to refuting Johnston's version of the Atlanta campaign. His memoirs, *Advance and Retreat,* are largely a compendium of apologias for his decisions and ripostes against his enemies.

Hood went to Washington in 1879 to try to sell his papers to the War Department for ready cash; despite Sherman's help, nothing came of it. Hood left the papers with Sherman and returned to New Orleans. Yellow fever attacked the city that summer. Hood's wife went first, the eldest child next, and then Hood himself. When he died on August 30, 1879, he left his children destitute. To raise money, Beauregard and other former Confederate officers sold postcards with the family's photograph.

In time of plague the dead are quickly buried. Trinity Episcopal Church was nearly empty for Hood's funeral the afternoon after his death. A few comrades accompanied the casket to the cemetery, where a scratch honor guard fired a salute.

The United States Army established Camp Hood, Texas, in September 1941. It comprised over 158,000 acres during the Second World War for tank destroyer training, with a peak wartime population of 81,000 men. After the war it became the army's primary armored training base and was redesignated Fort Hood in 1950. Today its 340 square miles are home to two heavy divisions, a combat air brigade, and a military population of 45,000.

Gordon engaged in a tumultuous life of politics and business speculation that lasted forty years. His flamboyant oratory and shady practices aroused strong feelings of both admiration and hatred. He served as governor of Georgia and was three times elected to the United States Senate. His passion was to restore home rule to Georgia by returning whites to power and subjugating blacks, often through his leadership positions within the Ku Klux Klan.

As a national figure Gordon represented the reconstructed South in action and spirit, making no apologies for the righteousness of the Southern cause but striving for reconciliation with the North. His crusades to defend and promote Southern interests were unceasing and often successful. He wheeled and dealed and compromised both as a politician and as a businessman, one step ahead of bankruptcy, scandal, and charges of corruption. Gordon's enterprises rarely prospered and usually failed.

Gordon was a fervid champion of the idea of the Lost Cause and a founder of the United Confederate Veterans, serving as its commander in chief from 1890 until his death. His lecture tours in the last decade of his life were popular from Vermont to Alabama. Entitled "The Last Days of the Confederacy," they glorified the myth of the Old South. His memoirs, *Reminiscences of the Civil War,* which were derived from his lectures, relived the war as he wished to remember it. They reflect his spirit and élan, as well as a selective memory.

Gordon died on January 10, 1904, a day of grief for Georgia and the South. Eulogies and memorials came from all parts of the country and political spectrums. The funeral service was ornate and impressive.

An equestrian statue of Gordon stands on the Capitol grounds in Atlanta.

Soon after the war the Republicans nominated Barlow for the office of secretary of state, and he easily won the election. His party soon realized to its

Gordon engaged in postwar politics and business speculation with energy and zest. Often on the verge of bankruptcy, he nonetheless symbolized the reconstructed South. The Cavalier helped set the course that resurrected the shattered states of the former Confederacy and brought them into the twentieth century. (Author's Collection)

After the war Barlow engaged in New York politics, but his efforts at reform made him unpopular with his party. He returned to his private law practice and withdrew from the corruption he could not tolerate. The new age had passed him by. He was the Last Puritan. (National Archives)

dismay, however, that Barlow was a zealous, uncompromising reformer. He was not renominated. Barlow married Ellen Shaw, a sister of Robert Gould Shaw, and returned to the practice of law in New York City.

President Grant appointed him United States marshal for the Southern District of New York in 1869, an office noted for graft and dishonesty. Barlow fired everyone and replaced them with honest people. While in office he mobilized and coordinated Federal forces on the east coast to defeat attempts to gather arms and supplies for a Cuban insurrection. Bodyguards protected his home because of threats. After capturing a ship in New York Harbor that was headed for Cuba, Barlow considered his job done, and he quit after six months.

Barlow helped to found the New York City Bar Association in the early 1870s and became one of the Committee of Seventy, a private reform group that assailed corruption in the judiciary, eventually leading to the impeachment of crooked judges in high places. His prominence led to his election to the office of New York State attorney general, where he served from 1872 to 1873. Barlow's greatest achievement in that capacity was the prosecution and conviction of William M. "Boss" Tweed of Tammany Hall.

From time to time Barlow resumed his involvement in public affairs, but gradually he withdrew from view. He died on January 11, 1896, at age sixty-two, in New York City. He is buried in Brookline, Massachusetts, near Boston.

Barlow's classmate Edwin H. Abbot wrote a tribute in memoriam that was published in the *Harvard Graduates' Magazine*. He concluded his piece with an observation about Harvard's Memorial Hall. It was a huge brick building, built to honor the university's Civil War veterans, and its windows contained stained glass portraits of distinguished alumni. Only two vacant windows remained, and they were reserved for the class of 1855. By the rules a person must have been dead at least a century before he could be portrayed. Abbot advocated that the rule be waived, however, allowing the windows to depict Barlow and the late Phillips Brooks, who had been the Episcopal bishop of Massachusetts.

The rule was not waived, but it was bent to honor Abbot's classmates. In 1902 the window was completed with the portraits of two medieval heroes who would have been quite recognizable to the Harvard men who passed beneath them. For the figure labeled Saint Bernard of Clairvaux, the Middle Ages' greatest cleric, is a portrait of Phillips Brooks, and that labeled Godfrey of Bouillon, the era's greatest soldier, has the face of Francis Channing Barlow.

ACKNOWLEDGMENTS

The foundation of this book is its research. Thanks to my appointment as a writer-in-residence, it was my great good fortune to enjoy faculty privileges at the Davis Library at the University of North Carolina at Chapel Hill. It is without question one of the finest research libraries in the United States in terms of resources, facilities, and staff. It was here that I conducted the greatest portion of my research, and my gratitude to the university and its magnificent library is beyond expression.

I wish to thank other research institutions, as well, where I was pleased and gratified to receive uniformly considerate attention and prompt assistance. These include the Southern Manuscript Collection at the University of North Carolina, the Perkins Library and Manuscript Collection at Duke University, the Library of Congress, the National Archives, the Massachusetts Historical Society, the Virginia Historical Society, the U.S. Army Military History Institute at Carlisle Barracks, Pennsylvania, Harvard University, the University of Georgia, the University of the South, the Boston Athenaeum, the Walter Cecil Rawls Library & Museum in Courtland, Virginia, the Southampton County (Virginia) Historical Society, and the Somerset County (New Jersey) Historical Society.

My thanks also to those who gave generously of their time to read my manuscript and offer invaluable insight and recommendations: Jim Abrahamson, Don Higginbotham, Louie Howland, and Herman Wouk.

I am especially fortunate that Peter Ginna was my editor, and I am grateful for his wisdom, empathy, encouragement, and sound judgment. I also want to express my gratitude to my agent, Suzanne Stein, for her steadfast support and her advocacy in my behalf.

Finally, I reserve my most profound thanks for my wife Marilyn, who is my best friend, severest critic, and most trusted adviser. This book came to be written because of her unselfish, loving commitment to helping me realize my dreams.

APPENDIX A: CHRONOLOGIES

GRANT CHRONOLOGY

April 17, 1822	Born at Point Pleasant, Clermont County, Ohio, to Jesse R. and Hannah (Simpson) Grant.
May 29, 1839	Reports to United States Military Academy, West Point.
June 1843	Graduates from Military Academy, commissioned second lieutenant of infantry.
March 28, 1846	Grant's regiment arrives at Rio Grande to provoke war with Mexico.
April 24, 1846	Mexico declares war against the United States. Grant serves during war as a quartermaster.
July 1848	Returns to United States after Mexican War.
August 22, 1848	Marries Julia Dent. Resumes peacetime duty at various garrisons.
April 11, 1854	Submits resignation. Returns to civilian life as farmer and store clerk.
April 12, 1861	Confederates fire upon Fort Sumter.
April 29, 1861	Military aide to Governor Richard Yates during mobilization of Illinois regiments.
June 15, 1861	Yates appoints Grant a colonel and gives him command of Twenty-first Illinois Volunteers.
August 5, 1861	Promoted to brigadier general, United States Volunteers.
September 1, 1861	Establishes district headquarters at Cairo, Illinois. Takes command of Army of the Tennessee.
February 19, 1862	Promoted to major general, United States Volunteers, after victories at Forts Henry and Donelson.
April 30, 1862	Halleck demotes Grant to second in command for Corinth campaign.
June 10, 1862	Restored to command of Army of the Tennessee.
July 16, 1862	Appointed to command all troops between Tennessee and Mississippi Rivers.
January 1, 1863	Lincoln issues final Emancipation Proclamation.
July 7, 1863	Promoted to major general, United States Army, after victory at Vicksburg.

March 2, 1864	Promoted to lieutenant general, United States Army, and general in chief of the army.
March 8, 1864	Arrives in Washington and meets Lincoln. Decides to keep headquarters in the eastern field.
April 9, 1865	Receives Lee's surrender of the Army of Northern Virginia at Appomattox.
April 14, 1865	Lincoln assassinated. Andrew Johnson becomes president.
May 10, 1865	Jefferson Davis captured. President Johnson declares end of Civil War.
July 23, 1866	Promoted to general of full rank, United States Army, previously held only by George Washington.
May 21, 1868	Republicans nominate Grant for the presidency. Grant accepts but does not overtly campaign.
November 3, 1868	Elected president of the United States with 52.7 percent of the popular vote.
November 5, 1872	Reelected president of the United States with 55 percent of the popular vote.
May 17, 1877	Begins well-publicized world tour after finishing presidency.
September 20, 1879	Arrives in San Francisco after touring the world.
June 7–8, 1880	Loses Republican presidential nomination on thirty-sixth ballot to James Garfield.
1881	Invests $100,000, his entire liquid capital, in banking firm headed by his son and Ferdinand Ward.
May 1884	Firm collapses. Ward revealed to have been defrauding investors. Grant financially ruined.
June 1884	Begins writing articles about the Civil War to earn money.
August 1884	Begins writing memoirs for publication.
February 19, 1885	Diagnosed as having fatal throat cancer. Continues writing memoirs despite worsening health.
July 23, 1885	Dies at summer resort in the Adirondacks.

Lee Chronology

January 19, 1807	Born at Stratford Plantation, Virginia, to Harry and Ann Hill (Carter) Lee.
June 1825	Reports to United States Military Academy, West Point.
June 1829	Graduates from Military Academy, commissioned second lieutenant of engineers.
June 30, 1831	Marries Mary Anne Randolph Custis at Arlington, Virginia.

September 21, 1846	Reports to San Antonio for engineering duty in the Mexican War.
June 28, 1848	Returns to Arlington after Mexican War. Resumes peacetime engineering duty assignments.
September 1, 1852	Reports as superintendent, United States Military Academy.
April 1855	Promoted to lieutenant colonel. Transfers to infantry. Ordered to Second Cavalry Regiment in Texas.
July 1857	Assumes command of the regiment.
October 1857	Father-in-law dies. Takes extended leave to manage Arlington Plantation.
October 1859	Commands troops that seize John Brown at Harper's Ferry.
February 1860	Returns to Texas and resumes command of Second Cavalry.
February 13, 1861	Relinquishes command of Second Cavalry and returns to Washington.
March 30, 1861	Accepts promotion to colonel, United States Army, and command of First Cavalry Regiment.
April 12, 1861	Confederates fire upon Fort Sumter.
April 20, 1861	Tenders resignation to the secretary of war in Washington.
April 23, 1861	Travels to Richmond. Accepts commission as major general in Virginia army.
April 25, 1861	Resignation approved by secretary of war in Washington.
May 10, 1861	Takes command of all Confederate armed forces in Virginia.
May 14, 1861	Commissioned brigadier general in Confederate regular army.
June 10, 1861	Jefferson Davis takes command of all Confederate forces in Virginia.
August 31, 1861	Promoted to general of full rank in Confederate regular army.
September 12, 1861	Commands Confederate forces in western Virginia.
October 31, 1861	Having lost campaign in western Virginia, returns to Richmond.
November 6, 1861	Assigned to Charleston, South Carolina, to construct coastal defenses.
March 14, 1862	Assigned duties as military aide to Davis in Richmond.
June 1, 1862	Assigned command of Army of Northern Virginia, replacing the wounded Joseph E. Johnston.
April 9, 1865	Surrenders Army of Northern Virginia to Grant at Appomattox.
June 13, 1865	Applies to President Andrew Johnson for full pardon.

October 2, 1865	Submits oath of allegiance to the United States.
October 2, 1865	Inaugurated president of Washington College in Lexington, Virginia.
October 12, 1870	Dies at Lexington, Virginia.

THOMAS CHRONOLOGY

July 31, 1816	Born in Southampton County, Virginia, to John and Elizabeth (Rochelle) Thomas.
August 22, 1831	Nat Turner rebellion.
July 1, 1836	Enters United States Military Academy, West Point.
July 1840	Graduates from Military Academy, commissioned second lieutenant of artillery.
April 30, 1844	Promoted to first lieutenant after duty in Seminole Wars.
January 1846	Arrives at Rio Grande, Republic of Texas, for Mexican War.
February 1849	Returns to United States after end of Mexican War. Resumes peacetime duty at various garrisons.
April 3, 1851	Reports to Military Academy as instructor of cavalry and artillery.
November 17, 1852	Marries Frances Lucretia Kellogg in Troy, New York.
December 24, 1853	Promoted to captain.
May 1854	Leaves Military Academy. Takes command of artillery battalion en route to California.
July 1854	Commands garrison at Fort Yuma, Arizona Territory.
May 12, 1855	Promoted to major. Ordered to Second Cavalry Regiment, Jefferson Barracks, Missouri.
September 1855	Reports to Jefferson Barracks; Grant farming at nearby Hardscrabble.
May 1, 1856	Joins regiment in Texas.
August 26, 1860	Wounded in action in skirmish with Indians. Only wound of his military career.
November 1860	Takes leave of absence and departs for New York. Injures back severely en route.
April 12, 1861	Confederates fire upon Fort Sumter.
April 14, 1861	Returns to active duty and refurbishes Second Cavalry at Carlisle Barracks, Pennsylvania.
April 25, 1861	Promoted to lieutenant colonel.
May 3, 1861	Promoted to colonel and assigned command of Second Cavalry.
July 1861	Commands a brigade in limited action in western Virginia.
August 1861	Promoted to brigadier general, United States Volunteers. Reports to western theater.

December 2, 1861	Assigned division command in Army of the Ohio under Buell.
April 9, 1862	Assigned command of right wing in Halleck's army group, replacing Grant.
April 25, 1862	Promoted to major general, United States Volunteers.
June 10, 1862	Relinquishes command of Grant's Army of the Tennessee and resumes command of division.
September 29, 1862	Refuses order from Halleck to relieve Buell in command of the Department of Tennessee.
October 27, 1862	Rosecrans given command of the Department of Tennessee, and Thomas objects strenuously.
January 9, 1863	Assigned command of Fourteenth Corps, Rosecrans's Army of the Cumberland.
October 19, 1863	Grant orders Thomas to relieve Rosecrans. Assumes command of the Army of the Cumberland.
October 27, 1863	Promoted to brigadier general, United States Army.
December 1, 1863	Reorganizes Army of the Cumberland into three corps and three cavalry divisions.
October 3, 1864	Takes command of western department as Sherman prepares to march through Georgia.
December 19, 1864	Promoted to major general, United States Army.
May 1865	Military governor of Tennessee, Kentucky, Georgia, Alabama, and Mississippi, among others.
May 30, 1869	Takes command of the Military Division of the Pacific in San Francisco.
March 28, 1870	Dies of a stroke in his headquarters.

HOOD CHRONOLOGY

June 29, 1831	Born in Owingsville, Kentucky, to John W. and Theodosia (French) Hood.
July 1, 1849	Enters United States Military Academy, West Point.
July 1853	Graduates from Military Academy, commissioned second lieutenant of infantry.
July 1853	Assigned to Fourth Infantry Regiment in California.
1855	Assigned to Second Cavalry Regiment in Texas.
September 1860	Begins eight-month leave of absence. Refuses orders to West Point.
January 1861	Returns to Second Cavalry Regiment in Texas while still on leave of absence.
February 1861	Second Cavalry Regiment betrayed into surrender. Hood leaves regiment.
April 12, 1861	Confederates fire upon Fort Sumter.

April 16, 1861	Tenders one-sentence resignation to the secretary of war.
April 20, 1861	Commissioned first lieutenant of cavalry, Confederate regular army.
April 25, 1861	Resignation approved by secretary of war in Washington.
May 1861	Reports to Lee in Virginia. Receives field promotion to major of cavalry.
October 1, 1861	Promoted to colonel and given command of the Fourth Texas Regiment, Army of Northern Virginia.
March 1862	Promoted to brigadier general and given command of the Texas Brigade.
October 1862	Promoted to major general and given division command in Longstreet's Corps.
July 2, 1863	Wounded in the arm at Gettysburg. Goes on extended convalescence leave.
September 5, 1863	Rejoins his division in Richmond, en route to Chattanooga as reinforcements.
September 20, 1863	Wounded in leg at Chickamauga and leg amputated. Goes on extended convalescence leave.
February 2, 1864	Promoted to lieutenant general, with date of rank September 20, 1863.
February 28, 1864	Takes command of Second Corps, Army of Tennessee.
July 18, 1864	Takes command of Army of Tennessee at Atlanta. Promoted to general of full rank.
January 23, 1865	Relieved of command of remnants of army following disastrous Tennessee campaign.
May 31, 1865	Surrenders at Natchez, Mississippi, and is paroled.
1866	Takes up residence in New Orleans. Undertakes enterprises in cotton trading and insurance.
April 13, 1868	Marries Anna Marie Hennen.
August 30, 1879	Dies in New Orleans of yellow fever.

Barlow Chronology

October 19, 1834	Born in Brooklyn to David Hatch and Almira (Penniman) Barlow.
July 1855	Graduates from Harvard as first scholar. Moves to New York City.
May 1858	Admitted to the New York bar.
April 12, 1861	Confederates fire upon Fort Sumter.
April 19, 1861	Enlists as a private in the Twelfth Regiment, New York State Militia Volunteers.
April 20, 1861	Marries Arabella Wharton Griffith.
April 21, 1861	Marches to Washington with his regiment.

May 1861	Promoted to first lieutenant.
August 5, 1861	Mustered out of service.
November 9, 1861	Appointed lieutenant colonel of Sixty-first New York Infantry Regiment.
April 14, 1862	Promoted to colonel and given command of Sixty-first New York Infantry Regiment.
September 17, 1862	Wounded at Antietam. Goes on extended convalescence leave.
September 19, 1862	Promoted to brigadier general, United States Volunteers.
April 17, 1863	Commands Second Brigade, Second Division, Eleventh Corps, Army of the Potomac.
May 23, 1863	Commands First Division, Eleventh Corps, Army of the Potomac.
July 1, 1863	Wounded at Gettysburg. Goes on extended convalescence leave.
January 26, 1864	Recruiting duty for Second Corps in New York and New England.
April 1, 1864	Commands First Division, Second Corps, Army of the Potomac.
July 27, 1864	Arabella Barlow dies of typhus contracted while serving as nurse.
August 17, 1864	Sent to hospital for acute diarrhea.
August 24, 1864	Goes on extended convalescent leave. Visits Europe.
April 6, 1865	Commands Second Division, Second Corps, Army of the Potomac.
May 25, 1865	Promoted to major general, United States Volunteers.
September 1865	Elected to office of New York secretary of state.
November 26, 1865	Honorably discharged from the service.
1867	Marries Ellen Shaw.
May 1869	Appointed U.S. marshal, Southern District of New York.
1871	Cofounder of the New York City Bar Association.
1872	Elected attorney general of New York.
1874	Withdraws from public life. Continues law practice.
January 11, 1896	Dies at home in New York City.

GORDON CHRONOLOGY

February 6, 1832	Born in Upson County, Georgia, to Zachariah H. and Malinda (Cox) Gordon.
January 1851	Enrolls in Franklin College (later the University of Georgia).
October 14, 1852	Withdraws from school without explanation.
April 1854	Moves to Atlanta. Reads law with firm of Overby and Bleckley.

September 18, 1854   Marries Fanny Rebecca Haralson.

September 1855   Journalist for the 1855–56 session of the Georgia legislature.

March 1856   Enters partnership with his father in the coal-mining industry.

April 12, 1861   Confederates fire upon Fort Sumter.

April 1861   Raises volunteer company. Enters Confederate service in Sixth Alabama Regiment.

May 14, 1861   Elected and commissioned major in Sixth Alabama Regiment.

July 1861   Regiment joins Army of Northern Virginia.

December 26, 1861   Elected and commissioned lieutenant colonel of regiment.

April 28, 1862   Elected and commissioned colonel of regiment.

September 17, 1862   Wounded at Antietam. Goes on extended convalescence leave.

April 15, 1863   Returns to duty in Army of Northern Virginia.

May 6, 1863   Promoted to brigadier general.

May 15, 1863   Temporary brigade command in Early's Division, Jackson's Corps.

May 7, 1864   Temporary division command in Ewell's Corps.

May 14, 1864   Promoted to major general.

May 21, 1864   Permanent command of new division in Ewell's Corps.

January 1865   Command of Second Corps, Army of Northern Virginia.

April 12, 1865   Leads Army of Northern Virginia to surrender ceremony at Appomattox.

September 15, 1865   Restored to full citizenship.

November 1865   Begins developing lumber business in Georgia, first of many enterprises.

1866   Begins organizing Ku Klux Klan in Georgia.

April 20, 1868   Runs for governor of Georgia and loses.

June 21, 1873   Elected as United States senator from Georgia.

November 19, 1878   Reelected as United States senator from Georgia.

May 15, 1880   Resigns from the Senate, saying that he wants to retire from public life.

May 1886   Resumes public life. Barnstorms Georgia with Jefferson Davis.

November 9, 1886   Inaugurated governor of Georgia after winning Democratic nomination in July.

November 1888   Inaugurated governor of Georgia for second term.

November 18, 1891   Elected for third term as United States senator from Georgia.

June 1895   Announces that he will not seek reelection.

January 10, 1904   Dies at winter home in Biscayne Bay, Florida.

ENGAGEMENT SUMMARY

Battle	Dates	Chapter	Grant	Lee	Thomas	Hood	Barlow	Gordon
Belmont	11/7/61	13	x					
Mill Springs	1/19/62	14			x			
Forts Henry and Donelson	2/4–16/62	14	x					
Shiloh	4/6–7/62	15	x		x			
Fair Oaks/Seven Pines	5/31–6/1/62	7					x	x
Seven Days	6/25–7/1/62	8–9		x		x	x	x
Second Manassas	8/27–9/2/62	10		x				
South Mountain	9/14/62	11						x
Antietam	9/16–17/62	11		x		x	x	x
Perryville	10/8/62	16			x			
Fredericksburg	12/19/62	12		x		x		
Murfreesboro	12/31/62–1/2/63	17			x			
Chancellorsville	5/1–5/63	18		x			x	x
Champion's Hill	5/16/63	20	x					
Vicksburg	5/18/63	20	x					
Tullahoma	6/24–30/63	21			x			
Gettysburg	7/1–3/63	19		x		x	x	x
Chickamauga	9/19–20/63	22			x	x		

Engagement	Date	Page						
Chattanooga	11/23–25/63	23	x		x			
Wilderness	5/5–7/64	24	x	x			x	x
Spotsylvania	5/12/64	25	x	x			x	x
Cold Harbor	6/1–3/64	26	x	x			x	x
Petersburg	6/15–18/64	26	x	x			x	x
Monocacy Junction	7/9/64	26						x
Peach Tree Creek	7/20/64	28			x	x		
Atlanta (Hood's attack)	7/22/64	28			x	x		
Deep Bottom	8/14–19/64	26	x	x			x	
Winchester	9/19/64	26						x
Cedar Creek	10/19/64	26						x
Franklin	11/30/64	30				x		
Nashville	12/15–16/64	30–31			x	x		
Fort Stedman	3/25/65	32	x	x				x
Sayler's Creek	4/6/65	32	x	x			x	x
High Bridge	4/7/65	32	x	x			x	x
Farmville	4/7/65	32	x	x			x	x
Cumberland Church	4/7/65	32	x	x			x	x
Appomattox Court House	4/9/65	32	x	x			x	x

FEDERAL STATISTICS

Battle	Dates	Chapter	Commanding General	Strength	Casualties	Percent Casualties
Mill Springs	1/19/62	14	Thomas	4,000	262	7
Fort Donelson	2/12–16/62	14	Grant	27,000	2,832	10
Shiloh	4/6–7/62	15	Grant	63,000	13,047	21
Fair Oaks/Seven Pines	5/31–6/1/62	7	McClellan	42,000	5,031	12
Seven Days	6/25–7/1/62	8–9	McClellan	91,000	15,849	17
Second Manassas	8/27–9/2/62	15	Pope	76,000	16,054	21
South Mountain	9/14/62	11	McClellan	28,000	1,813	6
Antietam	9/16–17/62	11	McClellan	75,000	12,410	17
Perryville	10/8/62	16	Rosecrans	37,000	4,211	11
Fredericksburg	12/19/62	12	Burnside	114,000	12,653	11
Murfreesboro	12/31/62–1/2/63	17	Rosecrans	43,000	11,577	27
Chancellorsville	5/1–5/63	18	Hooker	105,000	16,792	16
Champion's Hill	5/16/63	20	Grant	29,000	2,441	8
Vicksburg	5/18/63	20	Grant	46,000	3,199	7
Tullahoma	6/24–30/63	21	Rosecrans	65,000	560	1
Gettysburg	7/1–3/63	19	Meade	83,000	23,049	28
Chickamauga	9/19–20/63	22	Rosecrans	58,000	16,179	28

Chattanooga	11/23–25/63	23	Grant	56,000	5,824	10
Wilderness	5/5–7/64	24	Grant	102,000	17,666	17
Spotsylvania	5/12/64	25	Hancock	66,000	6,820	10
Cold Harbor	6/1–3/64	26	Grant	108,000	12,000	11
Petersburg	6/15–18/64	26	Grant	64,000	8,150	13
Peach Tree Creek	7/20/64	28	Thomas	20,000	1,600	8
Atlanta (Hood's attack)	7/22/64	28	Sherman	30,000	3,722	12
Deep Bottom	8/14–19/64	26	Hancock	28,000	2,901	10
Cedar Creek	10/19/64	26	Sheridan	31,000	5,665	18
Franklin	11/30/64	30	Schofield	28,000	2,326	8
Nashville	12/15–16/64	31	Thomas	50,000	3,061	6
Appomattox campaign	3/29–4/9/65	32	Grant	113,000	10,780	10

CONFEDERATE STATISTICS

Battle	Dates	Chapter	Commanding General	Strength	Casualties	Percent Casualties
Mill Springs	1/19/62	14	Crittenden	6,000	533	9
Fort Donelson	2/12–16/62	14	Floyd	21,000	no data	no data
Shiloh	4/6–7/62	15	A. S. Johnston	40,000	10,694	27
Fair Oaks/Seven Pines	5/31–6/1/62	7	Joseph Johnston	42,000	6,134	15
Seven Days	6/25–7/1/62	8–9	Lee	95,000	20,614	22
Second Manassas	8/27–9/2/62	15	Lee	49,000	9,197	19
South Mountain	9/14/62	11	D. H. Hill	18,000	2,685	15
Antietam	9/16–17/62	11	Lee	52,000	13,724	26
Perryville	10/8/62	16	Bragg	16,000	3,396	21
Fredericksburg	12/19/62	12	Lee	72,000	5,309	7
Murfreesboro	12/31/62–1/2/63	17	Bragg	37,000	9,865	27
Chancellorsville	5/1–5/63	18	Lee	57,000	12,764	22
Champion's Hill	5/16/63	20	Pemberton	20,000	3,851	19
Vicksburg	5/18/63	20	Pemberton	22,000	no data	no data
Tullahoma	6/24–30/63	21	Bragg	34,000	1,634	5
Gettysburg	7/1–3/63	19	Lee	75,000	28,063	37
Chickamauga	9/19–20/63	22	Bragg	68,000	18,454	27

Chattanooga	11/23–25/63	23	Bragg	46,000	6,667	14
Wilderness	5/5–7/64	24	Lee	61,000	doubtful data	doubtful data
Spotsylvania	5/12/64	25	Lee	no data	no data	no data
Cold Harbor	6/1–3/64	26	Lee	no data	no data	no data
Petersburg	6/15–18/64	26	Beauregard	42,000	2,970	7
Peach Tree Creek	7/20/64	28	Hood	19,000	2,500	13
Atlanta (Hood's attack)	7/22/64	28	Hood	37,000	8,000	22
Deep Bottom	8/14–19/64	26	Lee	20,000	no data	no data
Cedar Creek	10/19/64	26	Early	18,000	2,910	16
Franklin	11/30/64	30	Hood	27,000	6,252	23
Nashville	12/15–16/64	31	Hood	23,000	no data	no data
Appomattox campaign	3/29–4/9/65	32	Lee	50,000	no data	no data

APPENDIX E: CONFEDERATE RANKS AND ORGANIZATION

Rank and precedence were all-consuming to the general officers of the Confederacy (and in the Federal army, as well). In organizing its armed forces, the Confederate government tried to duplicate the structure of the prewar Federal army. It envisioned a small, permanent, elite regular army (CSA, the Confederate States Army), augmented in time of war with a large army of temporary volunteers (PACS, Provisional Army, Confederate States). The regular army never materialized except for a select number of officers and a handful of enlisted units. The great majority of officers and men of the Confederate armed forces were members of the PACS. Nevertheless, it has become customary in the postwar literature, almost without exception, to insert CSA after the rank of nearly all Confederate officers and soldiers. PACS, while more correct in nearly all instances, is never seen.

There is yet more confusion and ambiguity in terms of insignias. In the haste of enacting early legislation, the Confederate government established but one rank of general, that of brigadier. The authorized insignia of the brigadier general was a wreath enclosing three stars. When the government soon after established the next three senior ranks—major general, lieutenant general, and full general—it failed to authorize corresponding insignias. As a consequence, all four grades of general officers wore the identical three stars and wreath.

While the original Confederate regulations attempted to prescribe a standard uniform, general officers wore what they pleased. Following the custom of the Federal army, some Virginia generals wore different button arrangements to designate their rank. None of this made any difference to Lee. Throughout the war he wore the insignia of a Confederate colonel—three stars without wreath—and a general's button arrangement.

It was a young man's war, although the full beards give a misleading impression of age. Hood may look mature to us, but he was only thirty-three years old when promoted to full general.

Of the 8 generals of full rank in the Confederate army, the average age was forty-eight.

Of the 17 lieutenant generals, the average age was forty-one.

Of the 72 major generals, the average age was thirty-seven.

Of the 328 brigadier generals, the average age was thirty-six.

The great preponderance of Confederate generals were professionals, either graduates of the Military Academy or experienced in army service.

BIBLIOGRAPHY

The tens of thousands of books written about the Civil War can daunt the researcher. One wades into them and discovers both wheat and chaff. In some instances the scholarship is sound, the data authentic, and the writing lucid. Such works were vital to my research, and I freely and gratefully acknowledge them herein.

On the other hand, as I observed in the introduction, much of the war's written history is warped. Those things about which we think we are well informed often are discovered to be cliché, legend, and folklore. This is particularly true with the larger-than-life generals.

My approach to the research for this book was to use primary sources to the extent possible, augmented by selected secondary published sources. I am profoundly grateful to the University of North Carolina at Chapel Hill for allowing me unrestricted access to the splendid resources of the Walter Royal Davis Library, where I did the majority of my research. I also enjoyed access to the Southern Manuscript Collection at the University of North Carolina and to the Perkins Library and Manuscript Collection at Duke University. Other important archives that contributed to my research were the Library of Congress, the National Archives, the Massachusetts Historical Society, the Virginia Historical Society, the U.S. Army Military History Institute at Carlisle Barracks, Pennsylvania, Harvard University, the University of Georgia, the University of the South, the Boston Athenaeum, the Walter Cecil Rawls Library & Museum in Courtland, Virginia, the Southampton County (Virginia) Historical Society, and the Somerset County (New Jersey) Historical Society.

Altogether I studied innumerable books, records, manuscripts, and papers over a period of years; some I used extensively, some to an extent, and others not at all. As it would be impractical to cite everything I consulted, I shall discuss herein solely those that I found most useful for this book in the largest sense. Those that were applicable to individual chapters are cited in the bibliographical notes for each respective chapter.

My approach to research on a given topic is to identify the valid sources of information, examine all of those I can readily access, and then draw reasoned inferences and conclusions from the data. My research on a topic ends under one or more of the following conditions: (1) when creditable multiple sources repeat themselves; (2) when my intuition tells me what to believe if sources are contradictory; (3) when I have a source which I have come to consider as so consistently reliable that I can use it repeatedly to the exclusion of others. I do not consult additional references ad infinitum simply because they exist, especially if I feel that I have learned what I need to know. I say this because some scholars find fulfillment in the act of research alone, and seem always in search of yet one more reference before they feel their study to be complete. In such cases nothing gets written.

THE BEST UNIVERSAL CIVIL WAR REFERENCE

The single most important reference on the Civil War is the series *War of the Rebellion: A Compilation of the Official Records of the Union and Confederate Armies,* more commonly known as the *Official Records,* or simply *ORs.* The records represent an extraordinary feat: immediately after the war, a handful of army officers in the War Department compiled, collated, and edited thousands of wartime documents, primarily letters, reports, telegrams, and orders. The results of their labors were published in the last two decades of the nineteenth century in 128 books organized into 70 volumes of 138,579 pages.

Because Federal material was readily available, having been systematically collected and filed in Washington during the war, it predominates. For a number of reasons, Confederate records are often scanty. As an institution the Confederate army was often careless in its administration and indifferent to record keeping; other records were lost or abandoned as the army disintegrated, especially in the latter part of the war. Fearing postwar trials for conspiracy and treason, Confederate officers and government officials destroyed documents to remove evidence. At the close of the war, General Halleck confiscated the Confederate War Department records in Richmond, which he bundled up and sent to Washington as evidence in contemplated courts-martial of the Confederate high command for treason. The records never were used for that purpose, but they did comprise a major part of the record of the Confederacy. Other Confederate material trickled in over time from various sources.

By no means do the *Official Records* contain every surviving official record of the war, for many were located elsewhere, unknown to the War Department. In their discretion the editors may have chosen not to reproduce others in their possession. Those that were published were edited for grammar, spelling, punctuation, and usage such that the texts have a uniformity that often disguises individuality. In any event, the *ORs* remain the most important published record of the Civil War. I used them above all other references for every aspect of this book, especially for biographical and operational data.

As I examined the papers of the six protagonists in the National Archives, the added value of seeing original documents, in contrast to the edited *Official Records* versions, was reinforced. Encryption techniques are one example, for they can be appreciated only by examining the actual telegrams. The telegrams in Thomas's files are fully encrypted, representative of the more sophisticated Federal system. Because of the Confederacy's technical limitations, Hood's telegrams are only partially encrypted, and many phrases are in plain text. Hence when the Federal forces intercepted them, decryption was easier. Another violation of cryptographic security was the Confederate practice of superimposing the decrypted text over the coded portion of the telegram, thus compromising the codebook itself if the telegram fell into Federal hands.

In another example of different practices, the Federal army normally used regularized stationery and forms for its orders, messages, and correspondence. Thomas's records were especially thorough, complete, and systematic, reflecting his sense of order and disciplined administration. In contrast, the Confederate army usually used whatever miscellaneous paper was handy—some of Lee's orders, for example, were written on scraps of notebook paper. In light of these and many other instances, original documents with their smudges and stains give the researcher the smell and the feel of the battlefields and the headquarters which are simply unobtainable in edited, published versions printed on crisp, neutral paper. To an extent, even microfilm loses the sense of connection with the past.

OTHER USEFUL UNIVERSAL REFERENCES

Ezra J. Warner wrote the classic references summarizing every general of the war—*Generals in Gray: Lives of the Confederate Generals* (Baton Rouge, 1959) and *Generals in Blue: Lives of the Union Commanders* (Baton Rouge, 1964). *The Civil War Dictionary,* by Mark Mayo Boatner III (reprinted New York, 1991), is another classic reference that summarizes people, battles, and every other conceivable topic of the war. *The Civil War Day by Day: An Almanac, 1861–1865,* by E. B. Long and Barbara Long (New York, 1971), is a splendid compendium of what happened on every day of the war.

Yet another all-around reference set is the three-volume Time-Life series *Echoes of Glory* (New York, 1991). Its *Illustrated Atlas of the Civil War* supplements *The West Point Atlas of American Wars, 1689–1900* (see below), and its orders of battle and narrative summaries are a bonus. The other two volumes, *Arms and Equipment of the Confederacy* and *Arms and Equipment of the Union,* are comprehensive and inclusive, with brilliant color photographs so clear and distinct that they are like the real thing. Another excellent guide is *Arms and Equipment of the Civil War,* by Jack Coggins (reprinted Wilmington, North Carolina, 1990). Line drawings illustrate both the matériel of war and the tactics of using them. As cited in the front of this book, casualty data are largely from *Numbers & Losses in the Civil War in America: 1861–65,* by Thomas L. Livermore (Boston, 1901).

BIOGRAPHIES

As I stated above, the *Official Records* were a prime source for wartime biographical data on all six protagonists. Other sources are discussed below.

GRANT

Grant: A Biography, by William S. McFeely (New York, 1981), which won
the 1982 Pulitzer Prize for biography, serves as an introductory reference.
Ulysses S. Grant: Memoirs and Selected Letters, edited by William S.
McFeely and Mary D. McFeely (New York, 1990), is one of the more recent
editions of his memoirs (hereafter cited as *Grant Memoirs*). Written in the
last years of his life, when Grant was broke and dying of cancer, the memoirs
were a desperate attempt to provide a future income for his family. They
became a best-seller and yielded handsome royalties for Julia's well-being. As
a source of historical data, however, I used them with care, for—as with
most memoirs—they are self-serving and often inaccurate or misleading.

As to primary source material, Grant's military files in the National
Archives are largely on microfilm in a random format that is cumbersome to
examine. Fortunately, there is a godsend for researchers, the magnificent
eighteen-volume series *The Papers of Ulysses S. Grant,* edited by John Y.
Simon and published by the Southern Illinois University Press (hereafter
cited as *Grant Papers*). Begun as a Civil War centennial project, it obviously
was well funded, for the scholarship and thoroughness are exhaustive.
Grant's letters, orders, messages, and reports are meticulously reproduced,
exactly as written. Extensive footnotes and cross-references put each letter in
perspective and context; at times up to a dozen pages of commentary follow
a single letter. The synopses are thorough and account for nearly every day
of Grant's life. It is a jewel for any scholar conducting research on Grant and
the Civil War.

LEE

When stacked together, the biographies and studies of Lee would reach a
high ceiling. With the exception of *The Marble Man: Robert E. Lee and His
Image in American Society,* by Thomas L. Connelly (New York, 1977), and
Lee Considered: General Robert E. Lee and Civil War History, by Alan T.
Nolan (Chapel Hill, 1991), most are hagiographies. The most revered is
R. E. Lee: A Biography, the four-volume work by Douglas Southall Freeman
that won the Pulitzer Prize for biography in the mid-1930s. The author was
a Virginian and the son of a Confederate veteran, and his work popularized
Lee more than anything else ever written. Freeman was a historian by education and a journalist by profession, and his research was often exacting
and discriminating, although in other instances his citations are so nebulous
that they provide shaky foundations for some of his more earnest assertions.
For example, time and again Freeman insists that Lee was popular with his
men, but his footnotes do not support such a claim.

"Freeman portrayed a Lee almost without blemishes or warts," wrote
James M. McPherson, another winner of the Pulitzer Prize with his *Battle
Cry of Freedom: The Civil War Era* (New York, 1988). McPherson cited
some thirty-five virtues, ranging from "abstemiousness" to "wisdom," in
Freeman's index under the entry "personal characteristics," with nary a fault
or frailty among them.

While Freeman adored Lee, at times, however, he was surprisingly critical of Lee's performance in the early part of the war, either directly or by inference. Hence, I felt more comfortable in using his earlier material. Freeman passes over to hagiography by the time of Antietam and thereafter—he construes the debacle in Maryland as a triumph of generalship for Lee. Although Freeman does not quibble as to the extent of the disasters, Lee is rarely held accountable. Rationalizations become manifold. Thus, while *R. E. Lee* cannot be swallowed whole, the four volumes are nonetheless usable in those instances when legitimate references support the data, and I used the work throughout this book.

Another of Freeman's contributions to Civil War literature is his three-volume work *Lee's Lieutenants,* published in the mid-1940s. By design, it focuses more on his generals than on Lee himself, and it contains some helpful information on Hood and Gordon, as well as narratives on the battles and campaigns of the Army of Northern Virginia. When used with discretion, it is the source of worthwhile information, as its data often is valid.

Lee's papers are scattered among many repositories and collections and have never been gathered within one publication. The most ambitious attempt is the one-volume *The Wartime Papers of R. E. Lee* (Boston, 1961), edited by Clifford Dowdey and Louis H. Manarin. It has none of the explanatory footnotes, commentary, or cross-references of the eighteen-volume *Grant Papers.* Furthermore, it is heavily edited for spelling, grammar, and punctuation. It does contain "connective narratives" that introduce chronological sections, adding some perspective to the letters. There are gaping omissions, however, like the exclusion of Lee's letters to Davis reporting the outcome of Antietam and the subsequent disintegration of the Army of Northern Virginia.

Two other published works supplement Dowdey and Manarin to an extent. *Lee's Dispatches* (New York, 1915), edited by Freeman, contains a limited number of verbatim reports from Lee to Davis, together with extensive, but partisan, commentary. *Recollections and Letters of Robert E. Lee,* by Robert E. Lee, Jr. (Westminster, 1904), are largely edited letters from Lee to his family, embellished by his son's remembrances.

THOMAS
Letters between George and Frances Thomas are not to be found; the Thomases presumably destroyed them to preserve the sanctity of their private lives. The only personal letters I found consisted of some early family correspondence at the Virginia Historical Society (which also has custody of Thomas's beautiful ceremonial sword). Thomas's official papers are contained in eighteen boxes at the National Archives. The papers reflect his splendid professionalism, his span of control over vast theaters, and his clear thinking and writing. The documents are largely orders, reports, letters and letter books, telegrams and telegram registers, and his singular map journals. The bulk of this material is reproduced in the *Official Records.*

There are a number of biographies. *Education in Violence: The Life of George H. Thomas and the History of the Army of the Cumberland,* by

Francis F. McKinney (Chicago, 1991, a reprint of the original 1961 edition), is unquestionably the definitive study of Thomas and his army. It is particularly revealing as to Thomas's mastery of logistics and technology and his development of modern practices that became standard in twentieth-century warfare. *History of the Army of the Cumberland,* by Thomas B. Van Horne (Cincinnati, 1875), was written by a chaplain and confidant of Thomas who knew his thinking and had an intimate knowledge of the operations of the army. Van Horne published a sequel, *The Life of Major-General George H. Thomas* (New York, 1882), which is largely biographical but also provides additional details of army operations. Both are partisan, in large measure because Van Horne felt obliged to protect Thomas's reputation from the sniping of naysayers after his death in 1870. I occasionally used a half-dozen lesser biographies, which are cited in the relevant biographical notes by chapter.

HOOD

Hood's papers were loaned to the War Department in 1883 by one R. L. Gibson on behalf of Hood's heirs and have remained in government custody ever since. I found them in the National Archives, jammed into a single record box (with the papers of two other Confederate generals) and in a state of crumbling deterioration (Box #9, RG 109, War Department Collection of Confederate Records). They apparently had not been touched by an archivist since they were received over a century ago, and researchers using the collection had simply crammed them back into the box. I alerted the reading room supervisor, and he and his staff promptly made the first steps at preservation. After an exchange of letters with National Archives authorities, the Hood papers now have a box of their own in proper folders and envelopes. (Other priceless Civil War collections will continue to suffer from neglect unless National Archives practices change.)

Published works provide additional information. *John Bell Hood and the War for Southern Independence,* by Richard M. McMurry (Lexington, 1982), is a slim volume that nonetheless has important data. Oftentimes bibliographies led me to other useful sources, and McMurry was one such example. Thanks to him I discovered the diary of chaplain Charles Todd Quintard at the University of the South, and the memoirs of Joseph B. Cummings at the Southern Historical Collection in Chapel Hill. *The Gallant Hood,* by John P. Dyer (Indianapolis, 1950), is a lesser work which now and then supplements McMurry. *Advance and Retreat* (reprinted Bloomington, 1959) comprises Hood's memoirs. When not blatantly self-serving, the memoirs are occasionally helpful. *Lee's Lieutenants* provides limited information on Hood's performance when he served heroically in the Army of Northern Virginia. Thomas L. Connelly's *Autumn of Glory: The Army of Tennessee, 1862–1865* (Baton Rouge, 1971) is thorough, critical, scholarly, and comprehensive. His analysis of the leadership characteristics of the western generals—especially Hood—is particularly impressive.

BARLOW

Residing in the Massachusetts Historical Society, Barlow's wartime letters to his mother and brothers are a splendid source of information as to his activities and thinking. He was very close to his family and freely expressed himself when writing to them. Nearly all of his letters were written when he was in the field, with only a very few written when he was convalescing from his wounds and illnesses. His letters during the 1864 Virginia campaign are fewer than in the earlier war years. Fortunately, the letters and diaries of his friend and classmate Theodore Lyman supplement the period when Barlow's letters dwindle. An observant, intelligent, and articulate staff officer on Meade's staff in the Army of the Potomac, Lyman frequently saw Barlow and recorded what he said and did. Some of Lyman's remembrances are contained in *Meade's Headquarters, 1863–1865,* edited by George Agassiz (Salem, New Hampshire, 1987, is a recent edition). Additional Lyman letters and diary entries at the Massachusetts Historical Society further illuminate Barlow's activities.

Personal Recollections of the War of 1861, by Charles A. Fuller (reprinted Hamilton, New York, 1990), is a treasury of information on Barlow and the early operations of the Sixty-first New York Volunteers, his first and favorite command. Fuller was a survivor with the gift of narrative, and his memoirs are the best description of Barlow's leadership as a regimental commander. *History of the Second Army Corps in the Army of the Potomac,* by Francis A. Walker (New York, 1887), while essentially an operational history of the splendid corps in which Barlow served throughout the war, provides plentiful biographical data as well. Walker was the adjutant general of the corps and so had firsthand knowledge of its roles and players. When I examined Walker's papers at the National Archives, I found that he had corresponded extensively with veterans and seemed to have been painstaking in his research. While he naturally had the point of view of the Second Corps and was justly proud of its accomplishments, I found no discrepancies in his narrative and so consider it authoritative.

GORDON

Most of the Gordon family papers perished in a fire, but I found a few jewels—the touching love letters from Gordon to Fanny—in the Hargrett Library at the University of Georgia. The most substantive reference is *John Brown Gordon: Soldier, Southerner, American,* by Ralph Lowell Eckert (Baton Rouge, 1989). It is scholarly, objective, comprehensive, and balanced, and among the published works I used it almost exclusively. Toward the end of his life Gordon published his memoirs, *Reminiscences of the Civil War* (New York, 1904), which expressed his romanticized view of the war. In some instances his stories are fantasy, particularly his tale of succoring Barlow on the Gettysburg battlefield. Gordon also credited himself with enlightened strategic thinking that would have won battles had his superiors listened to him, but historians have largely discounted his claims. Now and then, however, portions of his narrative seem authentic, and I have used them appropriately. Freeman's *Lee's Lieutenants* is another source for selected information.

OPERATIONAL HISTORIES

This book focuses primarily on five armies in two theaters: (1) the Army of the Cumberland, the Army of the Tennessee (Federal), and the Army of Tennessee (Confederate) in the west; and (2) the Army of the Potomac and the Army of Northern Virginia in the east. Hundreds of books cover these five armies. To supplement the *Official Records,* the principal operational reference, I relied upon a few selected works for operational histories, several of which are also biographical.

WESTERN THEATER

Thomas L. Connelly wrote the authoritative works on the Army of Tennessee—*Army of the Heartland: The Army of Tennessee, 1861–1862* (Baton Rouge, 1967), and *Autumn of Glory: The Army of Tennessee, 1862–1865* (cited above). The lives of the common soldiers are contained in *Soldiering in the Army of Tennessee* by Larry J. Daniel (Chapel Hill, 1991). The operations of the Army of the Tennessee under Grant's command are best covered in *Grant Papers. Combined Operations in the Civil War,* by Rowena Reed (Annapolis, 1978), is an excellent reference on the joint army-navy operations that distinguished Grant's style of warfare in the west, with the author being critical of the want of planning in the major campaigns, especially Vicksburg. McKinney's *Education in Violence,* together with Van Horne's *History of the Army of the Cumberland* and *The Life of Major-General George H. Thomas* (all cited above), comprise the principal references for the Army of the Cumberland. Peter Cozzens has contributed three important books on the western theater: *No Better Place to Die: The Battle of Stones River* (Urbana, 1990); *This Terrible Sound: The Battle of Chickamauga* (Urbana, 1992); and *The Shipwreck of Their Hopes: The Battles for Chattanooga* (Urbana, 1994). Albert Castel's *Decision in the West: The Atlanta Campaign of 1864* (Lawrence, Kansas, 1992) is informative. Riley Sword's *Embrace an Angry Wind* (New York, 1992) is an excellent reference on Hood's 1864 Tennessee campaign. Henry Steele Commanger's *The Blue and the Gray: Two Volumes in One* (New York, 1991) contains excerpts from books and memoirs from participants that add color and additional information to the narrative.

EASTERN THEATER

Unlike my experience with the excellent references for the western theater, I did not rely extensively upon any one work (other than, as always, the *Official Records*) for the operational history of either army in the east, but rather I used an assortment of sources cited in the biographical essays for each chapter. Having said this, I will add that I did lean upon Walker's *His-*

tory of the Second Army Corps in the Army of the Potomac (cited above) as an important Federal operational history, given its focus on the Second Corps. Walker was contemptuous of Adam Badeau, a Grant staff officer who wrote the three-volume *Military History of Ulysses S. Grant* (New York, 1897), feeling that Badeau was an apologist for Grant, distorted the record, and explained away some of Grant's most grievous errors in both theaters. As Grant's memoirs endorse Badeau's version of events, by association Walker dismisses Grant's view of the war. To a large extent I agree with Walker.

Freeman's *R. E. Lee* and *Lee's Lieutenants*, together with *The Wartime Papers of R. E. Lee* (all cited above), in some instances are generally reliable in telling what happened, if not always why. (Antietam is one of the glaring exceptions.) One of the most useful books for enlightenment on Confederate attitudes is *Recollections of a Confederate Staff Officer,* by G. Moxley Sorrel (reprinted Jackson, Tennessee, 1958). Sorrel was an intelligent, optimistic, young chief of staff to Longstreet, with access to the inner circle. While an enthusiastic Confederate, he nonetheless expressed his criticism and dismay with the high command when things went wrong. Sorrel was made of tough stock and embodied the spirit and temperament that permitted the Army of Northern Virginia to survive. Through him the reader can begin to understand the durability and resiliency of the Confederate warrior.

TECHNOLOGY

A principal theme of this book is the incorporation of technology into the art of making war. Thomas mastered technology and developed techniques and practices that became standards for twentieth-century warfare. In contrast, Hood relied upon the warrior spirit to win battles. Here are my principal references.

LOGISTICS

Richard D. Goff's *Confederate Supply* (Durham, 1969), the published version of his dissertation, is a masterpiece of scholarship. The inability of the Confederate government to feed, clothe, and supply its armies is common knowledge, but the reasons have been largely speculative. Records are sparse and data scarce, but Goff dug the facts out and wrote his findings and analyses such that we can now understand why Confederate soldiers starved in an agrarian society. *The Railroads of the Confederacy,* by Robert C. Black III (Chapel Hill, 1952), complements Goff and explains why the Southern railroad system failed to support the Confederate war effort. *Quartermaster General of the Union Army: A Biography of M. C. Meigs,* by Russell F. Weigley (New York, 1959), is the standard reference on the hugely successful Federal logistical system and the general who made it work. *The Sinews of War: Army Logistics, 1775–1953,* by James A. Huston (Washington, 1966), is another useful reference work from the Office of Military History.

Two references cover the Federal railroad system. The best is *Civil War Railroads,* by George B. Abdill (New York, 1961), which is particularly thorough and comprehensive. The other is *The Northern Railroads in the Civil War, 1861–1865,* by Thomas Weber (New York, 1952), which is more elementary and does not address the role of the Federal generals in mobilizing the railroads.

COMMUNICATIONS SYSTEMS

Telegrams by the tens of thousands were dispatched during the war. Their impact on communications, command, and control was enormous. *Lincoln in the Telegraph Office,* by David Homer Bates (New York, 1907), describes how Stanton and the War Department controlled and exploited the telegraph, and how the system was managed and operated; the book also describes Lincoln's dependence upon its resources. Bates is especially valuable for intimate details on the exchange of telegrams between Washington and Thomas during the Battle of Nashville. *The Military Telegraph During the Civil War in the United States,* by William P. Plum (Chicago, 1882), is a two-volume operational history complete with war stories as well as nuts-and-bolts explanations of equipment and practices.

MAPS AND MAPPING

Maps and atlases of the Civil War abound, but in large measure they are notoriously inaccurate, misleading, contradictory, and difficult to interpret. As I wanted only the best, without hesitation I made my principal reference *The West Point Atlas of American Wars, 1689–1900* (New York, 1959), which for decades has been used by the Military Academy as a text and is the most accurate and authoritative Civil War atlas of which I am aware. Edward J. Krasnaborski, who is the legendary academy cartographer of the atlas, has been on duty for more than half a century, refining his maps with the help of generations of army instructors. Thanks to the cooperation of the academy's Department of History, I was permitted to use negatives of his base maps to construct the major maps for this book.

Mapping the Civil War: Featuring Rare Maps from the Library of Congress, by Christopher Nelson (Washington, 1992), contains data on how maps were made and a synopsis of the major battles. It confirms that the Army of the Cumberland—and thus Thomas—led the way in making and using maps, and that the Confederate army was largely deficient in cartography and knowledge of the terrain. Its color photographs of representative maps are excellent. *Make Me a Map of the Valley,* edited by Archie P. McDonald (Dallas, 1973), is the diary of Jedediah Hotchkiss, the premier cartographer of the Army of Northern Virginia. The title expresses the way in which Lee, Jackson, and other Confederate generals wasted his talents. Hotchkiss's maps of the Shenandoah Valley helped Jackson immeasurably in the spring campaign of 1862, but no one told Hotchkiss to make a map of any other Virginia battlefield. Denied a commission in the Army of Northern Virginia, Hotchkiss was a freelancer who came and went as he pleased.

CONCLUSION

This concludes my discussion of the sources used to write this book. My formal bibliography contains some 170 published references that I felt were important enough to read, if not always to cite. Hundreds more were scanned but deemed not of sufficient relevance to record in the bibliography. The numbers of original documents that I examined in various archives and repositories are beyond measure. I trust that this bibliographical essay, together with the bibliographical notes that follow, will inform readers as to the rigor of my research—the foundation for the thirty-two chapters of *The Warrior Generals*.

BIBLIOGRAPHICAL NOTES

CHAPTER 1—ORIGINS OF THE WARRIORS
Many books have been written about Brook Farm. The work I found most useful on Barlow's experiences there was Edith Roelker Curtis, *A Season in Utopia: The Story of Brook Farm* (New York, 1961). Two classmates wrote about Barlow's Harvard student days: James K. Hosmer in an essay in *The Last Leaf,* and Edwin H. Abbot in a eulogy in the *Harvard Graduates' Magazine* in June 1896. New York diarist George Templeton Strong knew both Barlow and Arabella Griffith and wrote about them frequently; see Allan Nevins and Milton Halsey Thomas, eds., *The Diary of George Templeton Strong v2, The Turbulent Fifties, 1850–1859* (New York, 1952). Information on Gordon's early days is largely from Eckert, *John Brown Gordon: Soldier • Southerner • American.* Gordon's anniversary poem is contained in Allen P. Tankersley, *John B. Gordon: A Study in Gallantry* (Atlanta, 1955). Hood's background is from McMurry, *John Bell Hood and the War for Southern Independence.* Three books were consulted for Thomas: McKinney, *Education in Violence*; Henry Coppée, *General Thomas* (New York, 1893); and Freeman Cleaves, *Rock of Chickamauga: The Life of George H. Thomas* (Norman, Oklahoma, 1948). Some of Thomas's very rare personal letters are in the Thomas Papers at the Virginia Historical Society. Lee's story is largely from volume 1 of *R. E. Lee.* Grant's first years are from *Grant Papers v1* and from *Grant Memoirs.*

Heretofore the woman in Winslow Homer's sketch has never been identified, but I am certain that it is Arabella Griffith Barlow. The sketch is included in the portfolio rendered by Homer in 1862 when he accompanied the Army of the Potomac as a combat artist in the Peninsular Campaign, so that the woman also had to be accompanying the Federal troops. Arabella was with her husband, and Homer stayed with his relative Barlow and the Sixty-first New York (Barlow wrote his mother how much he enjoyed Homer's company). Homer's portfolio also includes various sketches of a couple (an officer and woman), very likely Barlow and Arabella. There are also a number of fragments of sketches of a woman in various aspects. Hence, it is reasonable to conclude that the woman in the sketch is indeed Arabella Griffith Barlow.

CHAPTER 2—MEXICO: LEARNING THE PROFESSION
The references for this chapter are largely *Grant Papers v1* and *Grant Memoirs;* Freeman *Lee v1;* and McKinney *Education in Violence,* Cleaves *Rock of Chickamauga,* and Thomas's letters at the Virginia Historical Society.

456

CHAPTER 3—INTERLUDE: BETWEEN WARS
Data on the period between the Mexican War and the Civil War are contained in *Grant Papers v1* and in *Grant Memoirs; Lee v1;* and in McKinney.

CHAPTER 4—TAKING SIDES: THE WAR BEGINS
The officers of the Second Cavalry Regiment in Texas would emerge among the foremost leaders in the Civil War. Of its thirty-six officers on the 1860 roster, thirteen became Confederate generals and six others served in lesser ranks. Four would become full generals (half the total number): the commanding officer, Colonel A. S. Johnston; his second in command, Lieutenant Colonel Robert E. Lee; Captain E. Kirby Smith; and Lieutenant John B. Hood. Major William J. Hardee and Captain Earl Van Dorn became Confederate lieutenant generals. George Thomas and one other would be the only Southerners who did not resign from the Federal army.

Within the roster were four future Union major generals: Thomas, Captains George Stoneman and Richard W. Johnson, and Lieutenant Kenner Garrard. Thomas would fight Johnston, Smith, Hood, Van Dorn, and Hardee in the first half of the war. Later, with Johnson and Garrard among his subordinates, Thomas would face Hood and his Army of Tennessee.

Grant's entry into the war is contained in *Grant Papers v2* and in *Grant Memoirs.* James Harrison Wilson, *The Life of John A. Rawlins* (New York, 1916), describes Grant's indispensable chief of staff. Information on Thomas is primarily from the biographies by Van Horne, McKinney, and Frank A. Palumbo, *The Dependable General* (Dayton, 1983). After the war James A. Garfield often spoke on behalf of Thomas's reputation, and I used one such instance to illustrate the intensity of feeling in the North both about Thomas's loyalty and, concurrently, the belief that Lee had betrayed his country. Garfield spoke on these matters in an oration delivered to the Society of the Army of the Cumberland at its Fourth Annual Reunion in Cleveland on November 25, 1870, some eight months after Thomas's death. The speech was later published as *The Life and Character of Gen. George H. Thomas* (Cleveland, 1871).

Freeman treated Lee's decision to join the Confederacy at length and with great sympathy (*Lee v1*); his view that Lee was reluctant to draw his sword has since been the version generally repeated by other writers. The undisputed dates on which Lee acted and the disingenuous letters he wrote, however, support the contention that Lee conspired beforehand with the Richmond authorities to accept a commission in the Virginia armed forces, and that he did so without hesitation or moral reservation.

Hood's decision to resign and join the Confederacy is from his memoirs, *Advance and Retreat,* and from McMurry. Gordon's activities are described in Eckert and Tankersley. Barlow's marriage and immediate enlistment are discussed in *The Diary of George Templeton Strong v3* and 4. Barlow's feelings on patriotism and slavery are contained in a letter to E. L. Godkin, dated August 8, 1890, published in the *New York Evening Post,* and found in the collection of the Boston Athenaeum.

CHAPTER 5—CONFEDERATE FIRST ENCOUNTERS
Material on Lee is principally from *Lee v1*, augmented by *Recollections and Letters of Robert E. Lee,* by his son Robert E. Lee, Jr. Gordon's first days as a soldier are from his *Reminiscences of the Civil War* and from Tankersley. Hood is covered in McMurry. *Lee's Lieutenants v1* provides supplementary information on Hood and Gordon. Sorrel's *Recollections of a Confederate Staff Officer* describes the colors ceremony and the singing of *I Puritani* that evening. While teaching a Civil War class at Duke University, I played the rousing music and powerful singing to re-create the atmosphere of the time for my students. Afterward a student raised his hand. "Where do I sign up?" he asked.

CHAPTER 6—BARLOW BECOMES A SOLDIER
The sources for this chapter are Barlow's letters to his family in the Massachusetts Historical Society and Fuller *Personal Recollections of the War of 1861.*

CHAPTER 7—LAUNCHING THE PENINSULAR CAMPAIGN
OR v11 is the primary source for information on the battles of the Peninsular Campaign and on the roles of the participants. Barlow's letters to his family are particularly descriptive of the Federal role, augmented by Fuller and by Walker, *History of the Second Army Corps in the Army of the Potomac.* Secondary sources on Lee and the Confederate view of the battle include *Lee v2* and *Lee's Lieutenants v1*. Gordon is covered in Eckert, and Hood in *Advance and Retreat* and McMurry; additional information on both is found in *Lee's Lieutenants v1*.

CHAPTER 8—THE SEVEN DAYS
This chapter relies on essentially the same references as chapter 7, augmented by *OR v6* and by Gordon *Reminiscences of the Civil War. OR v11* contains a wealth of detail on the modern tactics and technology used by the Army of the Potomac. One such example is by Major Albert J. Myer, its chief signal officer, who submitted a masterpiece of reporting on visual signal methods and procedures (see Part 1, pp. 221–64). The deadly Federal artillery tactics are described by the chief of artillery, Henry Hunt, in Part 2, pp. 236–41. Barnard reports on the role of the engineers in Part 1, pp. 117–27. It is evident that McClellan had created a superbly equipped and trained army. Had he the requisite combat leadership skills, McClellan should have decisively defeated the Confederate army, but instead he squandered the splendid resources of the Army of the Potomac.

CHAPTER 9—THE SEVEN DAYS IN RETROSPECT
This chapter is based on essentially the same references as chapter 7, augmented by certain of Lee's letters in *The Wartime Papers of R. E. Lee,* and *Lee's Dispatches.*

CHAPTER 10—SECOND MANASSAS
Principal references are *The Wartime Papers of R. E. Lee*; *Lee's Dispatches*; *Lee v2*; and *Lee's Lieutenants v1*. The section on the shortcomings of Confederate logistics is from Goff's *Confederate Supply*.

CHAPTER 11—ANTIETAM
OR 19 is the principal reference, and its data reveals the misinformation and bias contained in *Lee v2* and *Lee's Lieutenants v1*, discussed at length in the introduction. It was at this point that Freeman changed from a reasonably balanced view of Lee into hagiography and apologia. For example, Lincoln issued the Emancipation Proclamation shortly after the battle, an unintended and unanticipated consequence of Lee's poor judgment in invading Maryland. The proclamation foreshadowed the end of the institution of slavery and made a negotiated settlement of the war an impossibility.

Freeman, however, considered the proclamation as fortuitous for the Army of Northern Virginia. He explained his astounding conclusion thusly: "This confirmed the belief of Southerners that the election of Lincoln was a conspiracy against the Constitution. A new sense of justification showed itself in the resistance of the South. A little later there began in the army a 'revival of religion' that spread from division to division for more than a year. This improved discipline and helped to give the army the quality that Cromwell desired when he said he wanted only such men as 'made some conscience' of what they did."

It is preposterous to rationalize that the Army of Northern Virginia (and by inference the Confederacy) was better off because Lincoln issued the Emancipation Proclamation. The fallacious suggestion that the Army of Northern Virginia was analogous to Cromwell's army reflects confused thinking about the aims of the Confederacy. The Confederate soldiers were fighting to *preserve* a status quo that favored a reactionary oligarchy whose time had passed, and they sought to *weaken* the powers of Congress. Cromwell's Puritans were fighting to *change* a status quo that favored a reactionary monarchy whose time had passed, and they sought to *strengthen* the powers of Parliament.

In addition to *OR 19*, the role of Hood is contained in his *Advance and Retreat*, in McMurry, and in Dyer *The Gallant Hood*; that of Gordon in his *Reminiscences* and in Eckert. For some reason, *Reminiscences* does not mention the battle on South Mountain, where Gordon's regiment fought so courageously and bought time for Lee to assemble his scattered forces at Sharpsburg. Sorrel's *Recollections* adds valuable information to the narrative. Barlow's activities are in Walker, *History of the Second Army Corps*, Fuller *Personal Recollections*; and the Issac Plumb Compilation of Letters, 1862–1864, in the U.S. Army Military History Institute.

CHAPTER 12—FREDERICKSBURG
OR 19 is the principal source for this chapter. *The Wartime Papers of R. E. Lee* provides additional primary source material. Sorrel, Walker, and *Lee's Lieutenants v2* were also used to an extent.

CHAPTER 13—GROPING IN THE HEARTLAND
This chapter introduces the western theater, and particularly Tennessee, a
region that hitherto has not been well represented in Civil War literature. I
selected the sources carefully to provide an authoritative overview. Reed
Combined Operations in the Civil War provides penetrating analyses of the
strategy and tactics centered on the rivers that dominated the western warfare. Goff *Confederate Supply* analyzes the economic importance of Tennessee to the Confederate war effort. Grant's leadership and operations are
exceptionally well covered in *Grant Papers v2–4*. Full documentation on the
allegations of Grant's drinking are contained in *Grant Papers v4*, pp.
110–19. Thomas's activities are covered largely in Van Horne *The Life of
Major-General George H. Thomas* and *History of the Army of the Cumberland*, as well as in McKinney. Scully's descriptive and revealing letters are in
the John W. Scully Papers in the Duke University Manuscript Collection. The
Confederate side of the early western campaigns is contained in Connelly
Army of the Heartland: The Army of Tennessee, 1861–1862.

CHAPTER 14—KENTUCKY AND THE FORTS
Thomas's operations at Mill Springs are covered in *OR 7*, Palumbo *The
Dependable General*, Cleaves *Rock of Chickamauga*, McKinney, Van
Horne, and Scully. Grant's campaign against Forts Henry and Donelson are
discussed in *Grant Papers v4* and in volume 7 of *OR 7*.

CHAPTER 15—SHILOH
The primary references for Grant are *OR 10*, *Grant Papers v5*, and, to a
lesser extent, *Grant Memoirs*. Thomas is covered in Van Horne, McKinney,
and Scully. Connelly *Army of the Heartland* covers Confederate operations
and is augmented with Joseph B. Cummings *Memoirs*, Southern Historical
Collection, University of North Carolina at Chapel Hill.

CHAPTER 16—THE KENTUCKY CRUSADE
The primary references *OR 16* and *30*. McKinney provides additional information on Thomas. Connelly *Army of the Heartland* again covers Confederate operations.

CHAPTER 17—MURFREESBORO
The Federal side of the battle is in *OR 20*, McKinney, and Van Horne.
Ambrose Bierce, a Federal staff officer, was a journalist by profession.
Ambrose Bierce's Civil War, edited by William McCann (New York, 1956),
is a compilation of Bierce's memoirs published after the war that rings with
authenticity, especially as Bierce was later known for the honesty and inci-
siveness of his editorials and columns. In my judgment, his descriptions of
what he saw and experienced in the Army of the Cumberland are accurate,
and I used them frequently.
    The Confederate data is from *OR 20* and from Connelly *Autumn of
Glory.*

CHAPTER 18—CHANCELLORSVILLE
The Wartime Papers of R. E. Lee was my primary source for this chapter, selectively augmented by *Lee's Lieutenants v2*. The diary of mapmaker Jedediah Hotchkiss, *Make Me a Map of the Valley*, edited by Archie P. McDonald, is very useful in reconstructing the flow of events. It reveals that Hotchkiss spent his entire time in camp prior to the battle of Chancellorsville and was not engaged in mapping the area south of the Rappahannock, where Lee intended to fight Hooker. *Lee's Lieutenants v2*, chapter 32, and *Lee v2*, pp. 519–24, are explicit about the fact that neither Lee nor Jackson had knowledge of the roads. For a discussion of Jackson's decisive flanking attack, see "Who Devised the Left Flank Movement at Chancellorsville?" appendix II-5, *Lee v2*, and *Make Me a Map of the Valley*, p. 137.

CHAPTER 19—GETTYSBURG
The primary references on the planning and development of the campaign are *ORs 25, 27, 36*, and *51*, and *The Wartime Papers of R. E. Lee*. The principal references for Hood's activity are *Advance and Retreat*, pp. 55–59, and *Lee's Lieutenants v3*, pp. 106–24. Gordon's letters to Fanny are from their rare surviving correspondence, located in the Gordon Family Collection at Hargrett Library, University of Georgia. Other data on Gordon is from Eckert and from Gordon *Reminiscences*.

The Robert L. Brake Collection in the U.S. Army Military History Institute is an extraordinary body of data compiled over some thirty years. Fascinated with Gettysburg, Brake gathered and collated thousands of references, never used them in a book of his own, and donated them to the institute. The collection is particularly valuable in reconstructing Arabella's attempts to find Barlow after he was wounded and Barlow's location while a prisoner during the battle. Barlow's letters before and after the battle are from the Massachusetts Historical Society.

Gordon concocted a fable about the battle that is still mistakenly believed by many today. It came into being on February 7, 1901, when he delivered a lecture in New York entitled "The Last Days of the Confederacy." He claimed that he had found Barlow mortally wounded on the battlefield, and that Barlow, as he lay dying, had asked Gordon to relay a melodramatic farewell to Arabella. Gordon also claimed that he found Arabella and gave her Barlow's message, but that he assumed Barlow had died by then. Gordon went on to say that Barlow also thought Gordon had been killed in the war. Finally, said Gordon, they met by chance some fifteen years after the war, discovered that the other was still alive, and had an emotional reunion as former enemies now comrades in arms.

Other than the fact that Barlow was indeed wounded while fighting Gordon's brigade, nothing else in Gordon's story corresponds to the evidence or to reason. For example, Barlow's letter to his mother, while describing his wounding and subsequent capture, makes no mention of talking with Gordon. There is no evidence that Arabella ever talked to Gordon. In his after-action report, Gordon wrote that Barlow had been taken prisoner, so he knew that

Barlow was alive. And Gordon had to have known that Barlow commanded a division that fought him time and again in the 1864 Virginia campaign.

Gordon got away with his popular speech because Barlow had died five years before and was not alive to contradict it. Because of its appeal, the speech drew considerable applause from Gordon's New York audience. Gordon included his fable in his *Reminiscences of the Civil War.* Contrived as it was, it was nonetheless well intentioned, for Gordon was continually trying to reconcile North and South by his generous praise of the bravery and dedication of the Federal officers and soldiers.

A final comment. Barlow's son Charles wrote in a letter, "The spring before his death I went with my father to Thomasville, Georgia. One night there was a knock on his door & a man came in who said, 'Gen. Barlow, I am the night watchman & was the Confederate soldier who picked you up at Gettysburg.' "

CHAPTER 20—VICKSBURG
Grant Papers v6–9 were my principal reference. Reed *Combined Operations in the Civil War* provides an excellent analysis of Grant's haphazard planning. *Halleck: Lincoln's Chief of Staff* by Stephen E. Ambrose (Baton Rouge, 1962) is a good reference on the view from Washington, and I used it in this and other chapters in which Halleck is involved in the narrative. I occasionally used *Grant Memoirs.* Charles Dana was managing editor of the *New York Tribune* until Greeley fired him in April 1862 for his militant views. He became an assistant secretary of war under Stanton and spent much time in the field reporting on Grant. Grant and his staff manipulated Dana shamelessly; see James Harrison Wilson, *Under the Old Flag* (New York, 1912). Nonetheless, his observations of Grant, contained in Dana, *Recollections of the Civil War* (New York, 1898), provide several useful details.

CHAPTER 21—THE APPROACH TO CHICKAMAUGA
ORs 20, 30, and *51* were my primary references. Secondary works include McKinney, Van Horne, and Ambrose. Connelly *Autumn of Glory* again covers the Confederate story. Cozzens *This Terrible Sound: The Battle of Chickamauga* is a useful comparison to these references for both the Federal and Confederate operations, although it has to be used carefully as it is prone to mistakes.

CHAPTER 22—THE ROCK OF CHICKAMAUGA
OR 30 was my primary reference. Others I used used included McKinney, Van Horne, Cozzens, Connelly, Bierce, and, to a much lesser extent, *Grant Papers v9, Grant Memoirs,* and Dana. McMurry and Hood *Advance and Retreat* add information on Hood's attack and his subsequent wounding. Cozzens *This Terrible Sound,* pp. 411–13, is very confused as to the circumstances of Hood's activities and the subsequent disintegration of his division.

Cozzens also is inconsistent as to the deployment of the Federal divisions on the day of the battle. He insists that Thomas thought that Brannan was in reserve and available as a mobile reinforcement, that he twice sent Kellogg to order Brannan to the left, and that in each instance Reynolds told Brannan to stay where he was. Most of this story was based on Reynolds's postwar writing. In reading *OR 30, Part 1,* however, it seems evident that initially Rosecrans and Thomas considered Brannan as a reserve, but that sometime after midnight Brannan received orders to go into line between Reynolds on his left and Wood on his right. Brannan did not say who ordered him to do so, but it must have been Thomas. Thomas must have known where Brannan was; indeed, he and Rosecrans rode down the line in the morning to inspect the positions, and it would have been apparent that Brannan was no longer in reserve but was in line. Rosecrans surely thought that Brannan was in line when he ordered Wood to close up. Hence there is nothing in *OR 30* to support Cozzens's assertions.

The approach of the troops of the Reserve Corps commanded by Gordon Granger, with division commander James Steedman in the van, was one of the most dramatic episodes of the battle. There are several versions as to whom Thomas sent to identify them. Cozzens (p. 443) cited the journalist W. F. G. Shanks (*Chattanooga, and How We Held It*), who claimed that Thomas sent a Negley staff officer named Gilbert Johnson to identify the approaching infantry. Bierce (p. 36) claimed that it was he who rode out at Thomas's order to see who was coming. Perhaps Thomas sent both Johnson and Bierce. As Bierce seems to be an accurate source of information in other instances, I chose his version for my narrative.

CHAPTER 23—CHATTANOOGA

OR 31 and *Grant Papers v9* were my principal references. Other important sources are McKinney, Van Horne, and Connelly. Commanger *The Blue and the Gray* includes excerpts of works from several participants that add color and drama to the narrative.

There is contradictory evidence as to the way that Thomas received Grant when he arrived in Chattanooga. In *Under the Old Flag v2,* pp. 273–74, Wilson wrote that Thomas was inhospitable and did not offer Grant dry clothing or food. Others since have repeated Wilson as an example of the ill will between the two generals. No one else who had knowledge of the meeting confirmed this, however. In *Military History of Ulysses S. Grant v1,* p. 443, Badeau, who otherwise deprecated Thomas in favor of Grant, wrote that "Thomas behaved with great magnanimity" when Grant arrived. Grant said nothing unusual about the initial meeting in his memoirs or in any letter to Julia, nor did Van Horne in his biography of Thomas. Grant's surgeon, who wrote to his own wife shortly after arriving at Thomas's headquarters, said nothing about any initial tension between the generals or their staffs (*Grant Papers v9,* pp. 317–18). It was some forty-nine years after the fact that Wilson stated he had had to urge Thomas to make Grant comfortable, and his memory may well have been faulty. There is no other evidence that Thomas was discourteous to Grant.

The first major disagreement between Grant and Thomas concerned Grant's preemptory order to pull out of Chattanooga and launch an immediate diversionary attack to assist Burnside in Knoxville. Thomas considered

Grant's plan as verging on madness. Grant's subsequent explanations for calling off the attack came later and changed with time. "After a thorough reconnaissance of the ground," said Grant in his official report (*OR 31, Part 2,* p. 29), "it was deemed utterly impracticable to make our move until Sherman should get up, because of the inadequacy of our forces and the condition of the animals then at Chattanooga, and I was forced to leave Burnside for the present to contend against superior forces of the enemy until the arrival of Sherman with his men and means of transportation."

When Grant wrote his memoirs twenty years later, the explanation had changed dramatically (*Grant Memoirs,* p. 425). The story became embellished to the effect that Thomas and his sick artillery horses had scotched a perfectly good idea. "On the 7th [November], before Longstreet could possibly have reached Knoxville," wrote Grant, "I ordered Thomas peremptorily to attack the enemy's right, so as to force the return of the troops that had gone up the valley. I directed him to take mules, officers' horses, or animals wherever he could get them, to move the necessary artillery. But he persisted in the declaration that he could not move a single piece of artillery, and could not see how he could possibly comply with the order. Nothing was left to be done but to answer Washington dispatches as best I could; urge Sherman forward, and encourage Burnside to hold on, assuring him that in a short time he should be relieved."

The sequence of Grant's plans and the roles given to Sherman and Thomas have frequently been misunderstood. McKinney states that Grant convened a meeting the night of November 15 and announced his plan. That is not so, for Grant and the others surveyed Bragg's line before making their final plans (*OR 31, Part 2,* p. 31). The orders were dated November 18 and gave equal weight to Sherman and Thomas (*Grant Papers v9,* pp. 410–12). This refutes most theories that Thomas was given a minor role because Grant did not trust the Army of the Cumberland (for example, McKinney, p. 284). Van Horne *Thomas* gives the best analysis as to how Grant's master plan kept changing because of developments on November 23 and 24. The cancellations of the plans for earlier attacks are in *Grant Papers.*

One of the more fascinating aspects of Chattanooga was Thomas's "reconnaissance in force" that became the spectacular advance to Orchard Knob. Thomas got Grant's order early in the morning of the 23rd (*OR 31, Part 2,* p. 94). The purpose of the operation was expressed in a single sentence: "The truth or falsity of the deserter who came in last night stating that Bragg had fallen back should be ascertained at once." (*Grant Papers v9,* p. 435).

What then was Grant's version? *Grant Memoirs,* pp. 433–35, wrongly asserts that he had ordered not a reconnaissance but a full-scale attack to relieve pressure on Burnside at Knoxville and that it was a substitute for Sherman's planned attack on the twenty-fourth. Thus, for whatever motives, Grant evades the real reason he ordered Thomas to undertake a reconnaissance in force. Altogether Grant's version of the battle is at variance with the messages and reports he sent at the time, and his self-serving memoirs distort the facts and mislead the reader. Grant wrote his memoirs as he wished the battle to have been, not as it actually was—that is, that the events unfolded as he had planned, not that he had been overtaken by events.

There is no question but that Grant wanted Thomas and his generals voluntarily to attack Missionary Ridge, which they would not do. In *Grant Memoirs*, p. 445, Grant recalled that he had ordered Wood to attack and was surprised to find an hour later that he had not done so. When writing his memoirs years later (and, we must remember, suffering intense pain from cancer), Grant may have been confused as to what he had suggested and what he had ordered. Once he *ordered* the assault, of course, Thomas and his generals immediately obeyed.

CHAPTER 24—VIRGINIA: THE WILDERNESS
Theodore Lyman's diary and letters are a wonderful source of information both on Barlow and Grant and about the operations of the Army of the Potomac. Many of his diary entries were published as *Meade's Headquarters, 1863–1865*, edited by George Agassiz. His diary in its entirety and his letters are in the Massachusetts Historical Society. Walker *History of the Second Army Corps* is a critical source for Federal operations. I again used Barlow's letters to his mother and brothers. Confederate operations are from *Lee v3* and *Lee's Lieutenants v3*. Gordon's activities are from Eckert and Gordon *Reminiscences*.

CHAPTER 25—VIRGINIA: SPOTSYLVANIA
Because of conflicting accounts, the sequence of events just before the Spotsylvania assault is difficult to establish. Hancock's role is hazy and his whereabouts difficult to ascertain. Barlow spoke about Spotsylvania in a blunt, descriptive paper read before the Military Historical Society of Massachusetts on January 13, 1879, and published as "Capture of the Salient May 12 1864," *Papers of the Military Historical Society of Massachusetts, vol. IV, 1905*. (This is one of the few times Barlow ever officially spoke or wrote about his Civil War experiences.) Another source is Lieutenant John D. Black, an aide to Barlow, who presented a paper that was published in *Glimpses of the Nation's Struggle: Fourth Series* (St. Paul, 1898). Black claimed that Barlow met late at night with Hancock and discussed the mode of attack. Black specifically talked about the remark on the thousand-foot chasm (p. 423). Walker *History of the Second Army Corps*, p. 469, quotes Morgan recounting the remark on the chasm but does not state that Hancock was present when it was made. In his 1879 paper (p. 257), Barlow said he was "absolutely certain" he did not communicate with Hancock from the time of the 7:00 P.M. meeting until well after the attack had begun, when he went to the rear to seek Hancock out. Hancock most likely was on the field, but for whatever reason he was not in contact with Barlow. Nor was Hancock in contact with Gibbon until Gibbon sought him out (John Gibbon, *Personal Recollections of the Civil War* [New York, 1928], p. 220). At 3:45 A.M., Hancock wired Humphreys that his troops were nearly formed but that, as it was misty, he would wait until it was a lit-

tle more clear (*OR 36, Part 2,* p. 656). Hence, Hancock might have delayed the kickoff until 4:30 A.M., as he said in his report, even though Barlow did not remember it that way.

Meade was in a quandary as to whom to recommend for promotion, for there was at most one vacancy for major general at the time. He decided to recommend Gibbon because he was senior to Barlow (*Lyman Diary v 13A,* 5/15/64, p. 36). Stanton wrote Grant that he would "Muster out some one for Gibbon," and Gibbon got his promotion (*Grant Papers v 10,* p. 435). Barlow fussed mightily (*Lyman Diary v 13A,* 6/11/64, p. 78), but the situation was beyond the control of either Hancock or Meade. Meade could have recommended Barlow for the record, to acknowledge his heroic performance, but he chose not to.

Gordon's dramatic role in the battle is contained in Eckert. There are many versions of "Lee to the rear," but I have synthesized Eckert, pp. 76–77; *Lee v3,* pp. 318–20; and William D. Matter, *If It Takes All Summer: The Battle of Spotsylvania* (Chapel Hill, 1988), pp. 200–202, the last a useful secondary source. The evidence is conflicting as to whether Lee had ordered Ewell to withdraw Johnson's infantry from the salient simultaneously with the artillery, although it does seem likely that he did. But, as it had begun to rain, Ewell probably convinced Lee that the infantry should be allowed to stay put in their shelters. (*Lee's Lieutenants v3,* p. 399, and Matter, pp. 175–78).

CHAPTER 26—VIRGINIA: STALEMATE
The principal Federal references are Walker, Lyman, and Gibbon, along with Barlow's letters in the Massachusetts Historical Society. Barlow's letters relating to his debilitating illness are in Folder #1, General's Papers Box 2, Records of the AG Office 1780–1917, RG 94, National Archives. The death of his father must have crushed Barlow's spirits even more, for he had hoped for a reconciliation. His classmate Phillips Brooks, an Episcopal priest and later a famous bishop, was in contact with David Barlow on behalf of Francis, and he sent Francis two long letters, one of hope, the other of his father's murder ("David Barlow" folder, Robert Gould Shaw Papers, Massachusetts Historical Society).

Eckert and Gordon *Reminiscences* told Gordon's story in this chapter.

CHAPTER 27—MUSTER IN THE WEST
OR 32 was my primary reference. Connelly *Autumn of Glory* describes the Confederate operations, and McMurry covers Hood's activities. McKinney and Van Horne cover Thomas and the Federal operations.

CHAPTER 28—ATLANTA
OR 38 was my primary reference, with secondary references the same as in chapter 27. The letters of Halsey Wigfall are in the Louis Trezevant Wigfall Family Papers at the Library of Congress. Castel *Decision in the West: The Atlanta Campaign of 1864* is an informative secondary reference.

CHAPTER 29—RETURN TO TENNESSEE

ORs 38, 39, and *45* were my primary references, with secondary references largely the same as in chapter 27. Bates *Lincoln in the Telegraph Office* and Ambrose *Halleck* describe the exchange of telegrams between Thomas and the Washington authorities.

The exchange of letters between Hood and Davis that led to Hood's invasion of Tennessee include some badly deteriorated Davis letters in the Hood Papers (National Archives), as well as letters contained in *Jefferson Davis: Constitutionalist: His Letters, Papers, and Speeches v6,* edited by Dunbar Rowland (Jackson, 1923). These critical letters are not in the *ORs.*

Beauregard's relationship with Hood was ambiguous, in large measure because of Davis's practice of limiting the authority of his senior generals. On October 31, 1864, when he was with Hood, Beauregard asked Davis to clarify his position, indicating that he did not want to relieve Hood but rather pass orders through him (*OR 39, Part 3,* p. 870). Davis responded on November 1 that Beauregard could tell Hood what to do but was not to relieve him of his army command. Beauregard chose to negotiate with Hood rather than command him (*OR 39, Part 3,* p. 874). Having received Davis's response, Beauregard told him on November 3 that he would not assume immediate command at that time (*OR 39, Part 3,* p. 879). In the end Beauregard exerted neither authority nor restraint over Hood.

CHAPTER 30—FRANKLIN AND NASHVILLE

Grant Papers v13 and *OR 45* served as my primary references, especially in describing the exchange of telegrams between Thomas, Grant, and the Washington authorities. The narrative of receiving the report of Thomas's assault at Nashville and of the Washington reaction is from Bates *Lincoln in the Telegraph Office.* After getting the news (presumably from Van Duzer), Grant's first message to Thomas, sent at 11:30 P.M. on December 15, said, "I was just on my way to Nashville, but receiving a dispatch from Van Duzer, detailing your splendid success of to-day, I shall go no farther. . . ." (*OR 45, Part 2,* p. 195). Grant did not mention his order for Schofield to relieve Thomas, so Van Duzer must have told Grant that it had not been sent. Thomas must have been puzzled by Grant's message, as he had received no indication that Grant was planning to go to Nashville.

Much of Hood's thoughts and activities are from Quintard's diary; a typescript copy is at the University of the South. Other sources include messages, reports, and the diary of Chief of Staff Francis Shoup, all in the Hood Papers in the National Archives. Sword *Embrace an Angry Wind* was my principal secondary source on the battles at Franklin and Nashville.

CHAPTER 31—AN ARMY DESTROYED

OR 45, the Shoup diary and Hood's dispatch book #4 in the National Archives, the Quintard diary, Sword, and Joseph B. Cummings *Memoirs* (Southern Historical Collection) were my principal sources. James F. Rusling was the assistant chief quartermaster of Army of the Cumberland, and his

Men and Things I Saw in Civil War Days (Cincinnati, 1899) provides several dramatic vignettes on Thomas's behavior under stress.

CHAPTER 32—APPOMATTOX

My principal references were *Lee's Lieutenants v3, The Wartime Papers of R. E. Lee, Grant Memoirs,* and *Meade's Headquarters.* I also used Eckert and Walker. Chris M. Calkins, *Thirty-six Hours Before Appomattox* (Farmville, Virginia, 1980), an excellent monograph by the park historian at Petersburg, provides detailed information not available elsewhere.

INDEX

NOTE: Italicized page numbers refer to picture captions.